WITHDRAWN

Augsburg College
George Sverdrup Library
Minneapolis, Minnesota 55404

D1314664

WITHDRAWN

Community Politics:

A Behavioral Approach

COMMUNITY POLITICS

A Behavioral Approach

Edited by

Charles M. Bonjean

Terry N. Clark

Robert L. Lineberry

The Free Press, New York

Collier-Macmillan Limited, London

Copyright © 1971 by The Free Press
A DIVISION OF THE MACMILLAN COMPANY

Printed in the United States of America

All rights reserved. No part of this book may be reproduced or transmitted in any form or by any means, electronic or mechanical, including photocopying, recording, or by any information storage and retrieval system, without permission in writing from the Publisher.

The Free Press, A Division of The Macmillan Company
866 Third Avenue, New York, New York 10022

Collier-Macmillan Canada Ltd., Toronto, Ontario

Library of Congress Catalog Card Number: 72-136273

printing number
1 2 3 4 5 6 7 8 9 10

Preface

HN
90
C6
B65

AMONG the numerous topics of sustained concern to social scientists, few have attracted more attention and few have more rapidly undergone the transition from an exploratory to an analytical level than the area of community politics.

Studies of urban government were traditionally in the domain of public administration, but Floyd Hunter's *Community Power Structure*, published in 1953, challenged long-standing assumptions concerning local government and opened the door to social scientists having divergent theoretical orientations and different methods of investigation. Theoretical and methodological traditions from both political science and sociology have been instrumental in the development of the basic themes in the community politics literature. Not infrequently major advances have been accomplished by a synthesis of overlapping contributions from both disciplines. Thus, this anthology was planned at the outset with an interdisciplinary orientation. In fact approximately half of its contents are reprinted from the "Community Politics" topical issue of an interdisciplinary journal, the *Social Science Quarterly*.[1] Additional articles were added to this core group because: (1) they introduced significant ideas and/or data about community politics which predated the *Quarterly* contributions; (2) they further developed the basic themes suggested by clusters of core articles; or (3) they were concerned with a basic community politics theme not included among the core articles.

The final selection of articles grouped themselves nicely about five community politics problem areas: the multiplicity of local governments, mass participation in community politics, elites and power structures, attitudes and values of local political leaders, and urban public policy. Within each of these topical divisions are contributions by both political scientists and sociologists.

110559 Note to the preface will be found on page 327.

As most of the contributions to this anthology were originally written for professional social scientists, we have found it necessary and desirable to introduce the student to these selections in two ways. An introductory section consists of discussions of basic concepts and approaches. Included here are an original chapter on the nature of community and differences among communities, an original chapter on approaches to the study of local politics, and a reprinted article (with comments by a political scientist and a sociologist) on the concept of power. Introductions to each of the five substantive sections of the book relate the concepts and ideas in the introductory section to the various articles in each subsequent part of the book. These introductions also highlight the basic themes of each of the contributions.

Finally two bibliographies are appended to lead the student and the instructor to significant related publications.

We are hopeful that the product of our efforts is an integrated anthology based on the three major themes set forth in our introduction as they apply to the five problem areas around which the anthology is organized; that the volume includes a representative sample of research contributions employing a variety of research designs and data-gathering techniques; and that it provides an orientation based upon current perspectives in both political science and sociology. We are hopeful that our readers will agree with us that, from the standpoint of theoretical orientations and research procedures, it has become pleasantly difficult to seek out the disciplinary boundaries among the endeavors which follow.

In addition to the authors and publishers who graciously consented to the republication of their works, we are indebted to many. In addition to our own original contributions, articles by Philip E. Jacob and Clifton McCleskey and Dan D. Nimmo appear for the first time in this volume. We are especially appreciative of their efforts to fill what would otherwise have been several important gaps in this collection. Especially helpful to the editors in handling many of the administrative tasks associated with a volume such as this one was Michael D. Grimes of the University of Houston. We are also highly indebted to the office and editorial staffs of the *Social Science Quarterly*, without whose efforts this volume would have been impossible. Among these individuals, special gratitude is due Harold Osborne, Dan D. Nimmo, Keith Petersen, Mrs. Ann C. Hardy, and Mrs. Jean Plummer Baker. Terry Clark is grateful to the Urban Institute, where he was a consultant during the preparation of this volume.

Any errors or shortcomings are exclusively our own.

Charles M. Bonjean, Terry N. Clark, and Robert L. Lineberry

Austin, Texas

Chicago, Illinois

Contributors

Robert Agger is professor of political science at McMaster University.
Robert R. Alford is professor of sociology at the University of Wisconsin, Madison.
Edward C. Banfield is professor of urban government at Harvard University.
Warner Bloomberg, Jr., is chairman of the department of urban affairs at the University of Wisconsin, Milwaukee.
Charles M. Bonjean is professor of sociology at the University of Texas at Austin.
Don R. Bowen is associate professor of political science at Case-Western Reserve University.
Terry N. Clark is assistant professor of sociology at the University of Chicago.
Frank C. Colcord, Jr., is chairman of the department of political science at Tufts University.
Robert M. Fogelson is professor of history and urban planning at Massachusetts Institute of Technology.
Edmund P. Fowler is assistant professor of political science at York University.
Claire W. Gilbert is assistant professor of sociology at Hunter College.
Daniel Goldrich is associate professor of political science at the University of Oregon.
Fred I. Greenstein is professor of political science at Wesleyan University.
Michael E. Grimes is assistant professor of sociology at the University of Houston.
Brett W. Hawkins is associate professor of political science at the University of Georgia.
Amos H. Hawley is professor of sociology at the University of North Carolina at Chapel Hill.
Robert B. Hill is research associate, Bureau of Applied Social Research, Columbia University.
Philip E. Jacob is senior specialist, Center for Cultural and Technical Interchange between East and West, University of Hawaii.
Yasumasa Kuroda is associate professor of political science at the University of Hawaii.
Eugene C. Lee is professor of political science at the University of California at Berkeley.
Robert L. Lineberry is assistant professor of government at the University of Texas at Austin.
Louis H. Masotti is professor of political science at Northwestern University.
Clifton McCleskey is professor of government at the University of Texas at Austin.

Dan D. Nimmo is professor of political science at the University of Missouri at Columbia.

David M. Olson is associate professor of political science at the University of Georgia.

Roland J. Pellegrin is professor of sociology at the University of Oregon.

Phillip Edward Present is assistant professor of political science at San Fernando Valley State College.

Florence W. Rosenstock is research associate at Albert Einstein College of Medicine, Yeshiva University.

Richard L. Simpson is professor of sociology at the University of North Carolina at Chapel Hill.

Bert E. Swanson is professor of political sociology and director of the Institute for Community Studies, Sarah Lawrence College.

John Walton is assistant professor of sociology at Northwestern University.

Roland L. Warren is professor of community theory at Brandeis University.

Lloyd M. Wells is professor of political science at the University of Missouri at Columbia.

Oliver P. Williams is professor of political science at the University of Pennsylvania.

James Q. Wilson is professor of government at Harvard University.

Basil G. Zimmer is professor of sociology at Brown University.

Contents

Community, Politics, and Power: An Overview

Introduction

COINCIDENT with the existence of any incorporated community in the United States are formal and informal arrangements for the resolution of conflict and distribution of resources. The number of formal governmental structures alone, over 81,000 in 1967, greatly exceeds the number of American communities. It is this multiplicity of local governments and effects and processes associated with their integration and fragmentation that will be our major concern in Section II of this anthology. From this we move in Section III to a concern with participation in local politics. Who participates in what ways, as well as the individual and structural facilitations and constraints to participation, are the major foci in that section. The degree to which participation is elitist, as opposed to pluralist or mass in nature, is the major concern in Section IV. Concern there is also with the nature of elites and the conditions that lead to or inhibit the development of elitist types of political structures. Even where democratic norms are effective, there are political leaders who are more active and more influential than other community residents. The attitudes and values of both formal and informal leaders is the topic integrating the contributions in Section V. Finally the outputs of political systems—public policies and their correlates—are of central concern in Section VI.

While the organization of this anthology is substantive in nature, several basic concepts and perspectives serve to further integrate the selections making up the basic parts which have been described above. The purposes of the five selections which follow are to identify and explain these integrative themes and thus to provide a general point of departure for the interdisciplinary approach to community politics which follows.

Selection 1 provides an introduction to the concept *community*. Traditional definitions are reviewed, and community is identified as a number of individuals more or less territorially rooted and interdependent as a point of departure. Traditional efforts to describe community variation—the use of size, location, historical development, and functional specialization as classification systems—are also reviewed and criticized from a number of standpoints. Then, recent empirical studies employing factor analysis are described in an attempt to locate relevant dimensions along which communities vary. Bonjean concludes his discussion by indicating that the variation in community characteristics is one set of variables associated with the differences in local political behavior and structure.

Lineberry, in Selection 2 notes that there have been two dominant perspectives in the study of local political phenomena. Some investigators have been concerned primarily with the community as their unit of analysis, and they deal primarily with community differences and their interactions. This *macro* approach is then contrasted with the *micro* approach, concerned primarily with subcommunity units including, for example, individual voters, city managers, power holders, or interest groups. Variations on each approach are explained and the reader is informed where, in this volume and elsewhere, he will encounter them. It is also suggested that the use of either of these approaches *in vacuo* is associated with certain sets of biases and is likely to yield an incomplete description and explanation of local politics. The simultaneous use of the perspectives and a focus upon those processes linking macro and micro phenomena is described as the perspective most likely to further contribute to our knowledge of local political structure and behavior.

As one would expect, almost every contribution in this volume is concerned directly or indirectly with the concept *power*. Clark, in Selection 3, notes the umbrella nature of the concept and isolates fifteen dimensions of it for analysis. Drawing from cognate works in both sociology and political science, he suggests that any analysis of power should include at least the following as a checklist: interpersonal influence, anticipated reactions, direct and indirect influence, reciprocity, action–inaction, patterns of value distribution, legitimation, number of participants, scope, visibility, bases, application, efficiency, and the allocation of resources and stratification. The alert reader will conclude from this listing that indeed both the macro and micro perspectives described in Selection 2 are necessary for the identification of the various dimensions of power outlined by Clark.

Using Clark's discussion as his point of departure, Simpson in Selection 4 suggests that the concept of power itself directs our attention to significant questions about politics. He then discusses four such questions which he believes have been relatively neglected: (1) What does the government do? Who benefits from it? and who does not? (2) Who decides what the government will do? (3) Through what processes do the decision-makers decide? (4) What are the causes of variation in the answers to the first three questions?

Olson, in Selection 5, combines some of the characteristics outlined by Clark and suggests additional questions. His concern is with external linkages, the nondecision, stage of issue development, measurement of the latent issue, and issue selection.

The general concepts and perspectives outlined in the five chapters which follow should help the reader place the more specific contributions in Sections II–VI in a meaningful frame of reference. These introductory statements may also provide the reader with bases for the evaluation of specific studies, as well as the general state of knowledge in each of the five substantive areas covered in this volume.

WHILE THE CONCEPT *community* has been more central in the history and development of the fields of sociology and anthropology than in political science, it has come to occupy a more important place in the latter discipline with the advent of behavioralism and the increasing number of empirical studies of political structure and behavior at the local level. The purposes of this chapter are: (1) to review some of the ways in which social scientists have used and defined the concept *community* and (2) to explore some of the ways in which communities have been found to vary. While the focus in this chapter will be explicitly on *community* and only incidentally on politics, it should be emphasized at this introductory juncture that one of the basic themes of this anthology is the *relationship* between the nature of the local political system and other local phenomena, the totality of which is subsumed under the general concept *community*. Thus, a review of some of the major contributions of community sociology is a logical antecedent to our review of approaches to the study of local politics (Selection 2) and our discussion of aspects of the concept of power (Selection 3). These three chapters provide the framework for the remainder of this book.

Toward a Definition of Community

The study of communities was a major, if not the central feature of American sociology during the early part of the twentieth century. For example, the first introductory sociology textbook devoted more space to community than to any other concept.[1] The approach there was primarily ecological—an approach that was the hallmark of the first, and for many years *the* leading department of sociology in the country— the department at the University of Chicago. From this department and this orientation came such community-related classics as Park, Burgess and McKenzie's *The City*,[2] Wirth's *The Ghetto*,[3] Zorbaugh's *The Gold Coast and Slum*,[4] Thrasher's *The Gang*,[5] Shaw's *Delinquency Areas*,[6] Frazier's *The Negro Family in Chicago*,[7] McKenzie's

The Community as Research Site and Object of Inquiry*

Charles M. Bonjean

The University of Texas at Austin

The Metropolitan Community,[8] and numerous other works that today are considered representative of "The Chicago School"[9] and the golden age of community studies. More or less central in each of these works was a conception of the community involving: (1) a territorially organized population, (2) a population more or less completely rooted in the soil it occupied, and (3) individual units living in a relationship of mutual interdependence.[10] The concept *community* and community studies was a central and distinctive feature of American sociology until World War II. But by that time, community sociology had lost its primacy and in 1942 the American Sociological Association, which until then included one or more sections on community at its annual meetings, combined the community and ecology sections. In 1957 community sections were dropped altogether.[11] The relative decline of community sociology during the postwar period was a consequence of many complex professional and academic trends including: (1) the development of research technology and large social science research organizations which made it more possible and practical for social scientists to study universes larger than the local community; (2) a decline in the pathological or applied orientation which characterized much of early sociology;[12] and (3) the belief among some sociologists that mass communication, rapid transportation, bureaucratization,

*Written for this volume. The author acknowledges with gratitude the suggestions made by Michael D. Grimes and Bobby Gierisch.

5

and urbanization minimized local differences and consequently increased the importance of societal characteristics in the description, explanation and prediction of social behavior.

Very recently, however, there has been a resurgence of interest in the community, due in part to a change (if not, in some cases, a reversal) of those trends which led scholars away from community study.

While quite popular just a few years ago, the mass society orientation, although by no means completely rejected, has been subjected to severe criticism based upon empirical findings.[13] That important local differences *have* persisted is perhaps best illustrated by comparing the findings of two of the most important contemporary studies of community politics—Hunter's *Community Power Structure*,[14] which suggests local decisions in Atlanta are made by an economic elite, and Dahl's *Who Governs*[15] which suggests that local government in New Haven is pluralistic in nature. These studies have not only induced skepticism in regard to the mass society perspective, but in themselves have been also at least partly responsible for the resurgence of interest in community studies. Indeed, although the field seemed to be withering 15 years ago, the number of community studies undertaken since (most with an emphasis on power and politics) has been overwhelming.[16]

Similarly, the self-conscious quest to become a "pure science" and corresponding disdain for "applied" research has been modified in recent years. The urban violence of recent summers and a new public awareness of poverty are probably responsible for increasing numbers of social scientists giving their attention to those settings where these problems are manifest —the community. Certainly reinforcing this orientation have been federal programs, such as the Community Action Program (CAP), which are based on the assumption that local participation is essential for amelioration. An indication of the relevance of the community orientation to current

problems is the fact that after a twelve-year absence, the 1969 American Sociological Association meetings included a special session on the community because of "... the rapid changes in community structures taking place in the context of recent urban programs and ... an increasing professional interest in the systematics of 'community theory' which not only provide some meaning to these changes in locality orientation but which clarify the fundamental directions of future change."[17]

Finally, the rise of the research institute has made a new type of community study possible—the simultaneous comparison of similar phenomena in a large number of communities to, in fact, assess the significance of community differences. Perhaps the most ambitious effort to date along these lines has been the establishment of a Permanent Community Sample by the National Opinion Research Center:

> The Permanent Community Sample consists of a data collection apparatus and data archives for conducting comparative community researches within a probability sample of 200 American cities with 50,000 or more population . . . . This investment will make it possible for social scientists, wherever they may be located, to collect comparative data at a reasonable cost and with considerably less effort than if a separate data collection operation were mounted for each research project. We believe that the PCS will make it possible to raise the level of community studies to the same degree that the development of national sample surveys raised the level of social psychological research.[18]

Thus it is interesting to note that one of the organizational advances in the social sciences which initially contributed to a decline in community research activity is now responsible for giving it a new emphasis. One of the first published reports of PCS data is included in this volume as Selection 28. That chapter and all of the other contributions to this anthology illustrate the social scientists' renewed interest in community.

As is the case in many substantive areas in the social sciences, community scholars have defined their object of inquiry in many different ways. A review of the community sociology literature by Hillery located 94 definitions of *community*.[19] While considerable disagreement in regard to content was found, it was also noted that 69 of the definitions suggested that community consisted, at least, of social interaction, area, and a common tie or ties—elements quite similar to those cited above which were set forth by Park years ago. Apparently, few investigators would object to the inclusion of these general attributes as part of a definition for the concept *community*, but finding agreement in regard to the *nature* of the interaction, common ties or bonds, and locality would be considerably more difficult. For example, there is little agreement in regard to how community boundaries—and thus the space or locality involved—should be determined. Looking at the same locality group as a trade unit, a governmental unit, a psychological entity and as a network of interaction would, in most cases, yield four different sets of boundaries. In most of the selections in this anthology, community area is identified by corporate boundaries. The use of such boundaries is not only appropriate for our purposes (because, in most cases, they are also the "political" boundaries), but it is also expedient since not only are census data reported in this manner, but so are the data compiled by and available from most other public and private agencies.

Attempts to Classify Communities

It is likely that one reason for the relative disagreement in regard to the nature of the concept *community* stems from the variability of communities themselves. A wide spectrum of attributes and variables have been used to differentiate between communities or to classify them. Among those which have been used most extensively are:

1. *Size*. This is such an obvious and pervasive criterion that it calls for little discussion. Since 1950 the U.S. Bureau of the Census has used a rather extensive size-of-place classification scheme which, as one would expect, is also used in a considerable amount of social science research. Two classes of villages—those of 1,000 to 2,500

The Community as Research Site   **7**
and Object of Inquiry
Charles M. Bonjean

inhabitants and those with fewer than 1,000 inhabitants—are distinguished, while all communities with a population of 2,500 or more are designated as urban. *Urbanized Areas* are made up of at least one city (or contiguous twin cities) with a population of 50,000 or more and the surrounding densely settled fringe areas. *Standard Metropolitan Statistical Areas* consist of one or more contiguous nonagricultural counties containing at least one city of 50,000 or more and which are integrated socially and economically. In 1960 the *Standard Consolidated Area* was identified. This is the megalopolis, of which there are two: The New York–Northeastern New Jersey SCA and the Chicago–Northwestern Indiana SCA.[20]

2. *Historical Development*. By far the best known attempt to classify cities by stage of historical development is that set forth by Lewis Mumford in *The Culture of Cities*.[21] The cycle of growth and decay of cities set forth there includes six stages and the following corresponding city types:

a. The *Eopolis*, or village community, is characterized by permanent dwelling places and important technological advances. The bases of association are kinship and neighborhood and thus primary groups predominate. Its major functions are protection, storage, and life maintenance.

b. The *Polis* is an association of villages or blood-groups having a common site that lends itself to defense. Other characteristics include civic unity, manufacturing and trade, and the development of the school, health sciences, and leisure time. More differentiated than the eopolis, the polis is still basically a collection of families and the way of life is homogeneous.

c. The *Metropolis* is a regional trade, transportation, and cultural center. It is characterized by even more specialization and differentiation than the polis and a "new individualism" develops which, according to Mumford, undermines traditional social bonds.

d. The *Megalopolis* is characterized by an emphasis on power, bigness, domination, and the subordination of everything to the acquisition and display of wealth. Standardization and mechanization prevail, even in the arts and sciences. According to Mumford, this stage represents the beginning of the decline of the city.

e. The *Tyrannopolis* represents the next stage of decline. Parasitism and exploitation pervade all areas of social, economic, and political life. Civic responsibility disappears; looting and blackmail are normal practices of business and government; the class schism widens; wars produce starvation, disease and demoralization; and the primordial functions of city life—security and protection—are undermined.

f. The *Nekropolis* is a picture of total ruin due to war, famine, and disease. There is a relapse to the primitive, rural occupations, and the physical city is an empty shell.

Mumford's classification scheme, especially the first three stages, has much in common with the sociological literature dealing with the folk-urban continuum. The folk community has been described as small, isolated, nonliterate, and homogeneous with a strong sense of group solidarity; behavior is traditional, spontaneous, uncritical, and personal, and the sacred prevails over the secular.[22] As a society matures, the dominant communal organization becomes urban; the large size of the city makes for a preponderance of secondary relations, anonymity, transitory social relationships and anomie; high density promotes division of labor and makes for high physical, but low social contact, while heterogeneity is a consequence of high mobility and accompanies depersonalization and mass production.[23] Sjoberg has postulated an intermediate type between the folk community and the city—

the preindustrial (or feudal) city.[24] While the classification of communities as folk, feudal, or urban is based, as suggested above, on numerous criteria, there has been a tendency to treat the classification scheme as a unidimensional one.

3. *Location.* The location of communities, particularly in reference to other communities, has long been used as a criterion for classifying communities, especially by ecologists. Bogue, for example, has used this traditional approach in his classification of cities by the amount of influence they exercise over their hinterlands (tributary adjacent territories, which include outlying communities).[25] While dominance is treated as a variable, rather than an attribute, communities may be divided into four major groupings:

a. *Dominant Metropolitan Centers*, which control many of the conditions of all communities lying within a broad area surrounding it;

b. *Subdominant Hinterland Cities*, which adapt to the conditions of general dependence upon a dominant and which function through specialization in one or more of the sustenance activities, as an intermediary between the metropolis and the outlying areas;

c. *Influent Communities*, which consist of the rural nonfarm communities;

d. *Subinfluents*, the rural farm communities, which have the smallest hinterlands and control the least number of functions.

It should be obvious that one of the criteria discussed above, size, is closely related to dominance, but its effect *is* modified considerably by location. For example, Long Beach, California and Birmingham, Alabama are approximately the same size. Yet because of their locations relative to other cities, Birmingham has a much larger hinterland and controls more of the conditions of communities surrounding it than does Long Beach.

4. *Economic Activity or Function.* Classification schemes based upon the premise that specialization is characteristic of cities are fairly common. Among the best known is one set forth by Ogburn in 1937,[26] where

the characteristics of seven types of specialized cities are described: trading centers, factory towns, transportation centers, mining towns, pleasure resorts, health resorts, and college towns.

While the four criteria discussed above have been used widely in the classification of communities, they hardly comprise an exhaustive list. There have been attempts to classify and compare cities on numerous other dimensions—even according to the "goodness of life" in them.[27]

Most of the single-criterion classification schemes, such as those briefly described above, may be criticized for one or more of the following reasons:

1. Differentiating between communities on the basis of a single criterion—size, location, historical stage, or economic function—may greatly oversimplify reality. It is likely that communities differ from one another on all of these dimensions as well as others which have not yet been discussed.

2. Some of the schemes currently in use tend to be arbitrary *ad hoc* classifications. The rationale for using the scheme is seldom given, nor are the criteria one should use for classifying. This criticism is especially valid in regard to the Ogburn-type categories.[28]

3. Sometimes the categories presented are not mutually exclusive. For example, a single community might logically be classified under more than one of Ogburn's categories.[29]

4. Related to the second criticism above is the observation that it has seldom been empirically demonstrated that the criterion for classification bears an important relationship with other significant features of community.[30] Thus, the theoretical importance of some of these schemes may be limited.

Although such classification schemes are still widely used, they provide a somewhat less than satisfactory means for describing community variation in most theoretical or research contexts.

Data Sources

Looking elsewhere to see how communities vary leads us away from the oversimplified single-dimension schemes into the jungle of data archives.

The single most comprehensive published source noting variations in demographic characteristics of American communities (and one of the most important data sources for the student of community) is the *County and City Data Book*.[31] In a single volume are relevant data from the most recent (at the time of publication) census of agriculture, business, government, housing, manufacturing, mineral industries, and population. Also included are recent data gathered by other governmental and private agencies including the Department of Agriculture, Federal Reserve System, Federal Home Loan Bank Board, Federal Power Commission, Public Health Service, Weather Bureau, American Hospital Association, and Governmental Affairs Institute. Data on 148 variables are presented for the 3,109 counties and county equivalents in the United States, for the 563 cities in the United States having a 1960 population of 25,000 or more, and for regions, divisions, and states. Data on 113 items are presented for the 224 Standard Metropolitan Statistical Areas.

Another rich data source, showing other ways in which communities differ, is *The Municipal Year Book* published by the International City Managers' Association. Data are of four general types: (1) governmental units (including such items as number, population, and type of units), (2) municipal personnel (including data on salaries of chief municipal officials, number of full-time employees, monthly payrolls and other such information), (3) municipal finance (including such data as revenue, expenditure and debt), and (4) municipal activities (including health statistics, housing data, educational data, etc.). The data have been gathered from published sources as well as from nearly 5,000 municipal officers and 50 state correspondents. In some instances, information is provided for all cities over 5,000, while in others it is presented only for cities over 10,000 or over 25,000.

If one of the major problems associated with the single-criterion classification schemes is that they tend to oversimplify community differences, the opposite problem manifests itself from even a cursory review of the *County and City Data Book* or the *Municipal Year Book*. The number of variables listed in either or both of these sources is overwhelming. In most research operations, it would be impractical to describe the communities studied in this much detail. If the problem is one of community comparison, the use of such a large number of variables becomes even less feasible. Thus, one problem associated with the use of such data sources involves the selection of a few community relevant variables from among many.

Factor Analysis Studies

A number of recent studies have sought to bring some order out of the mass of data available on local communities. Specifically, they have attempted to answer questions such as:

1. Can a small number of independent dimensions be found that will explain all of these variables? In other words, do a large number of variables cluster together and indicate the existence of more general community traits?

2. Given an affirmative answer to the first question, what are the best indexes or units of observation for collecting and analyzing data for each of these dimensions? Or, are some of the variables presented in the data books more closely related to the underlying dimension than others?

A statistical technique especially suited to research problems of this nature is factor analysis. The purpose of this technique

... is to determine from the interrelationships of a large number of variables the smallest number of factors (or underlying dimensions) whose association with the original variables will account for all of the observed interrelationships.[32]

A technical explanation of factor analysis is beyond the scope of this chapter. Briefly, this statistical technique involves correlating a large number of variables on an even larger number of units, identifying clusters of variables which are treated as indicators of underlying dimensions or factors, rotating the factors to see if more variation can be explained, and then identifying and naming the factors by examining those variables having the highest loadings on (i.e., most closely related to) each factor and relating them to theory and previous research.[33]

The identification of community dimensions (or factors) in this manner appears to meet some of the criticisms of other classification schemes discussed above:

1. Since such analyses usually yield from four to fifteen dimensions, the resulting description is not an oversimplified one. On the other hand, knowing that sixty to ninety or more variables represent many fewer dimensions and that some variables are more closely related to the dimensions than others, provides one with a rationale for the selection of a manageable number of items by which communities and their variation may be described.

2. The use of factor analysis does not impose an *ad hoc* conceptualization on the data. Rather, it yields a classification system that *minimizes* the importance that any preconceived order may have.

3. The problem of mutually exclusive categories is irrelevant. In the first place, the use of factor analysis (unless its results indicate otherwise) involves accepting the notion that the units of observation vary along more than one dimension. Secondly, the concern is with dimensions that vary, rather than with attributes.

4. The criteria for classification are explicit and are shown to be related to or independent of other criteria by the nature of the technique itself (factors are usually

independent of one another, while indicators are related, of course, to some factors, but not to others).

Several investigators have employed factor analysis to attempt to identify dimensions of community.[34] Three studies will be summarized here: (1) Jonassen and Peres' factor analysis of Ohio counties because it was the first published study of this nature to attract much attention;[35] (2) Hadden and Borgatta's factor analysis of all American cities having a population of 25,000 or more because of the scope of the investigation;[36] and (3) Bonjean, Browning, and Carter's factor analysis of all contiguous United States counties, because the universe includes units smaller than 25,000 and because the findings are compared with those of the two previous studies mentioned.[37]

Noting that the ambiguity of the concept *community* motivated their research, Jonassen and Peres gathered data (much from the *County and City Data Book*) on 82 variables for the 88 counties of Ohio. The county was selected as the unit of analysis because counties

> . . . constitute a type of community within which one might expect to find, to a measurable degree, all essential factors of the community phenomenon. The use, for example, of cities alone would immediately eliminate the rural factor and prohibit the measurement of the effect of the urban-rural determinants within the community system. Furthermore, the county is the formal unit for which the greatest amount of comparable data is available.[38]

Their analysis yielded seven factors which explained roughly 75 per cent of the total variance:

1. *Urbanism* was the name given to their first factor which had significant loadings on 51 of the 82 measures. Indicators of this factor were variables such as the proportion of clerical and sales workers, socioeconomic status, dwelling modernity, per cent population urban, and per cent with college education. The investigators note that the nature of these variables shows the urban community

> . . . to be one possessing wealth, power, education, professional abilities, vitality,

productiveness, and commercialism—qualities that make it the dominant type of community in our era.[39]

Although termed urbanism, it should be obvious to the reader that most of the socioeconomic status variables also had high loadings on this factor.

2. *Welfare* is a factor associated with such indicators as a health index, child neglect (negative association), unemployment (negative association), and other such items. This factor is bipolar with atony suggested as the opposite to welfare.

3. *Influx* is indicated by negative relationships with population stability, commercial activity, and wholesale trade and positive relationships with such items as migration population change, dwelling newness, and retail sales gain.

4. *Poverty* is characteristic of communities with a relatively high proportion of families having annual incomes of less than $2,000, a large dependent population, and a relatively high natural increase.

5. *Magnicomplexity* was named such because the magnitude and direction of the items with high loadings on this factor were associated with large size and complex social and economic organization (variables such as population size, educational plant size, governmental complexity, etc.).

6. *Educational Effort* is indicative of a community that ". . . puts a lot of effort into education, would sacrifice for it, spend more per capita on it and achieve, through its efforts a relatively high educational status."[40]

7. *Proletarianism* is used in the classical Marxian sense to identify the seventh factor. It indicates the presence of a large proportion of propertyless, relatively poor, low-skilled and poorly paid workers.

While Jonassen and Peres suggest that their factors may have high generality, a number of cautions should be introduced at this point, including the fact that they limited their investigation to Ohio counties rather than all or a sample of United States counties. The latter universe *may* be better described by a different set of dimensions. A related problem is whether or not the same factors would be identified using different community boundaries—cities, for example, instead of counties. Finally, in any factor analysis, there is the problem associated with the selection of input variables. Obviously, the factors identified will be determined, in no small part, by the indicators analyzed.

Problems such as those listed above can be assessed to some extent by looking at the results of similar analyses which have used different units, variables and universes. Hadden and Borgatta, in asking "What constitutes a meaningful set of variables that describe the characteristics of cities?"[41] employ the same general technique used by Jonassen and Peres, but select some different indicators, different units—cities rather than counties, and a different universe—the United States. Rather than conducting a single factor analysis, these investigators performed ten in order to:

1. Control for size. Thus they did an analysis of the 344 cities with populations of 25,000 to 49,999 (termed *town cities*), of the 150 *small cities* ranging in size from 50,000 to 74,999, of 106 *intermediate cities* ranging in size from 75,000 to 149,999, and of the 79 *large cities* of 150,000 or more.

2. Control for functional relationship. Thus separate analyses were done of the 246 *central cities* (defined as such in Standard Metropolitan Statistical Areas or Urbanized Areas), the 227 *suburbs* (those cities of 25,000 or more within Standard Metropolitan Statistical Areas), and the *independent cities* (those 171 cities of 25,000 or more outside of Standard Metropolitan Statistical Areas).

3. Control for the arbitrariness of boundaries. In addition to the analyses of cities listed above and the pivotal

analysis of all 644 cities, an analysis of the 212 Standard Metropolitan Statistical Areas and one of the 212 Urbanized Areas were also conducted.

The authors selected 65 variables, most of which came from the *County and City Data Book*, for their first eight analyses. Somewhat less data were available for the SMSA and Urbanized Areas analyses so 59 variables were used in the former and 47 in the latter. In selecting variables, Hadden and Borgatta attempted to avoid duplication and, with the exception of total population size, converted data to percentages, per capita or ratios to avoid the influence of size itself.

The authors found 13 more or less *parallel* factors—that is factors which emerged in a number of their separate analyses:

1. *Socioeconomic Status Level* emerged in all ten analyses. This dimension had significant loadings on 34 variables, almost all of which were stratification indicators such as median income of families, median monthly rent, per cent of college graduates, and per cent in white-collar occupations. The variables associated with this factor were similar to those having high loadings on Jonassen and Peres' *Urbanism* factor.

2. A *Nonwhite* factor emerged in six of the ten analyses. It was absent in the large city analysis, the SMSA analysis, the Urbanized Area analysis and the independent city analysis. The variables associated with this factor are those generally thought to be associated with nonwhite populations of low income, low education and crowded and poor housing. Obviously, per cent nonwhite itself had a high loading on this factor. The factor content is similar to the *Poverty* factor identified by Jonassen and Peres.

3. An *Age Composition* factor was found in all ten analyses. Positive loadings on such items as median age and per cent of population 65 years and older together with negative loadings on items such as per cent under five years, and per cent live births indicate clearly the nature of this factor.

4. *Educational Center* was identified as such because of high loadings on such indicators as the per cent living in group quarters and the per cent employed in education. It was found in all ten analyses.

5. *Residential Mobility* was found in all ten analyses and included indicators similar to those associated with Jonassen and Peres' *Influx* factor.

6. *Population Density* also emerged in all ten analyses, although the variance was more substantial and more clearly defined in the larger units of analysis, indicating, according to the authors, a size-density complex. The indicators of the factor bear some resemblance to those associated with Jonassen and Peres' *Magnicomplexity* factor.

7. A *Foreign-Born Concentration* factor was found in all but the analyses of large, intermediate and central cities. Items with high factor loadings included per cent foreign born, per cent with foreign or mixed parentage, and per cent single dwelling units (with a negative loading).

8. *Total Population* indicated by population size, age of city, density and per cent using public transportation was identified in nine of the analyses. The only set of data for which this factor did not arise was the all cities, or pivotal, analysis. This factor is related, also, to some extent to Jonassen and Peres' *Magnicomplexity* factor.

9. Five *Specialization* factors were also identified. *Wholesale Concentration*, *Retail Concentration*, *Manufacturing Concentration*, *Durables Manufacturing Concentration*, and *Communication Center* accounted for a relatively small proportion of the total variance explained. This, according to Hadden and Borgatta, raises even more doubt concerning the economic or functional typologies, especially since the number of variables associated with economic classification were purposely overemphasized in this study.

Because of the parallel structures observed in the ten analyses, Hadden and Borgatta criticize the use of single-dimension classification schemes and suggest that

the classification of cities might well proceed along the lines of the dimensions that they suggest. In fact, they present decile scores on twelve indicators or indexes for all cities in the United States of 25,000 or larger. This feature gives to *American Cities: Their Social Characteristics* the status of a source book as well as that of a soundly conceived study.

Some of the differences in the factors identified by Hadden and Borgatta and by Jonassen and Peres may be attributed to the fact that there was little overlap in the input variables. The two studies have only twelve variables in common, while only fourteen others are conceptually similar. To overcome this and some of the limitations previously cited (e.g., a one state universe), Bonjean, Browning and Carter used the county as the unit of analysis, all such units in the 48 adjacent states as the universe and 79 variables, 46 of which were the same or similar to those used in the American cities study. Eighteen factors, explaining almost 79 per cent of the total variation, were extracted from the correlation matrix. Eight of the factors explained considerably more variation than the others. These were discussed and compared with the factors identified in the other two studies.

Table 1 summarizes the similarities and differences of the three investigations and suggests the following tentative conclusions.

No matter what the unit of analysis, universe or (within limits) variables used, factor analysis indicates "communities" vary along the following dimensions:

1. *Socioeconomic Status.* The degree to which communities vary along this dimension is considerable. For example, in 1959, median family income in the United States was $5,560, yet in Nassau County, N.Y., the median income was $8,505, while in Tunica County, Mississippi it was $1,260. Family income and the cluster of socioeconomic status variables associated with it have been found to be related to many

aspects of community politics. The number of studies included in this volume using such variables at the macro or micro level (a distinction to be discussed in the following chapter) will soon become apparent to the reader. The political systems of rich and poor communities may vary as greatly as the political behavior of the well-to-do and poverty stricken members of these communities.

2. *Residential Mobility.* The United States has frequently been characterized as a nation of movers. That a number of demographic variables cluster together and indicate this fact is not surprising. For example, in 1960, the average United States county population included 17.4 per cent who had moved to that county within the past five years. But again this is a condition more or less characteristic of American communities. For example, in 1960, 55.9 per cent of the residents of Adams County, Colorado (which includes Denver) had migrated from a different county since 1955.

In Oliver County, North Dakota this was true for only 5.5 per cent of the residents. While this community characteristic has not been studied to the degree that socio-economic status has, its explanatory power may be great. Alford and Lee (Selection 10 in this volume) suggest, for example, that this dimension (which they term "community continuity") may be related to voting turnout. Masotti and Bowen (in Selection 29) note that it is related to municipal expenditures. Other studies in this volume deal only indirectly with residential mobility (e.g., Present in Selection 20), but implications of its relationship to political structure and behavior may be found throughout the volume.

3. *Urbanism.* As has been suggested at several points in this chapter, size and its correlates, density and heterogeneity, may be perhaps the most obvious and pervasive criterion used in distinguishing between communities. In 1960 the mean for county population in the United States was 57,828, but Cook County, Illinois had 5,129,725 residents while Arthur County, Nebraska counted 680. The influence of urbanism

TABLE 1. *Parallel Factors Found in Three Independent Investigations*

All U.S. Counties (1967)	Ohio Counties (1960)	All U.S. Cities (1965)
1. Socioeconomic Status	A. Urbanism	I. Socioeconomic Status
2. Family Life Cycle		III. Age Composition
3. Governmental Revenue and Expenditures		
4. Residential Mobility	C. Influx	V. Residential Mobility
5. Urbanism	E. Magnicomplexity	VI. Population Density
6. Manufacturing Concentration		XI. Manufacturing Concentration and
		XII. Durables Manufacturing Concentration
7. Commercial Center		IX. Wholesale Concentration and
		X. Retail Concentration
8. Unemployment		
10. ⎫	B. Welfare	II. Nonwhite
Unnamed Parallel	and	
⎬ Factors Explaining	D. Poverty	
11. Little Variation		IV. Educational Center
12. ⎭		VII. Foreign-Born Concentration
		XIII. Communication Center
	F. Educational Effort	
	G. Proletarianism	

on the nature of political structure and behavior is at the same level as the influence of socioeconomic status. Throughout this volume, the concept (or its equivalent) is used, in both theoretical and empirical contexts (see, for example, Selections 9 and 17).

4. *Nonwhite.* In 1968, 11 per cent (or 22 million) of the United States population was Negro. Community variation in per cent nonwhite varies from 100 per cent (for example, Boley, Oklahoma and Mound Bayou, Mississippi) to zero in numerous communities. In the past three decades many Negroes moved to the larger cities in our society. Thus, in 1965, the nonwhites in Washington, D.C. were estimated as 66 per cent of the city's population. Percentages for other cities include New Orleans, 41; Baltimore, 38; St. Louis, 36 and Detroit and Cleveland, 34. The importance of this community characteristic is obvious not only because of the recent civil disturbances and the Kerner Commission report, but the relationship of race to other social phenomena has long been of concern to social scientists. Race as a community and individual trait is explored in a number of the contributions to this volume and especially in Section III dealing with mass participation in urban politics.

The factor analysis studies also indicate that it is likely that communities vary also

along dimensions that may be termed *Family Life Cycle, Manufacturing Concentration, Commercial Center,* and (less surely) *Educational Center* and *Foreign-Born Concentration.* Reference to variables indicative of these dimensions may be noticed throughout this volume. In fact, no small number of the research findings to be presented could be inventoried by using these nine dimensions as the bases for a classification system. Three of them are discussed explicitly by Masotti and Bowen (Selection 29), who demonstrate the utility of factor analysis in a different problem area.

While factor analytic studies have contributed to some degree to our identification of dimensions along which communities vary, the conclusions summarized here should be regarded as tentative for the reasons suggested above and also because most of the studies which have been conducted to date used to a great extent only available *demographic* data. Undoubtedly communities also vary along other dimensions—perhaps on social control, moral integration, the nature and vitality of voluntary associations, and numerous other nondemographic dimensions such as that which is the focus of this volume—the nature and distribution of power.

Approaches to the Study of Community Politics*

Robert L. Lineberry

The University of Texas at Austin

EXECUTIVE ORDER 11365, issued by President Lyndon B. Johnson on July 29, 1967, following successive waves of violence in American cities, established the National Advisory Commission on Civil Disorders.[1] The primary charge by the President to the Commission was to explain one of the most important, yet seemingly inexplicable, events in contemporary urban life, racial violence. We shall attempt to explain some of the causes of rioting in cities as a first example to highlight two general approaches to community politics. Another example will be derived from the fact of differential participation in urban political life. Some individuals and groups take an active, intense interest in community life, participating in local elections, joining political groups, running for political offices, and campaigning for their favorite candidate. Others find community political life uninteresting, unimportant, or unworthy of attention.

How shall we seek explanations for either of these two features of urban life? This chapter will identify two general approaches to community politics, micro and macro approaches, patterned after the familiar distinction in economics. We will argue that neither of these approaches is satisfying *in vacuo*, that the use of one, uninformed by the perspectives from the other, leads to dubious and contradictory research conclusions, and that efforts to identify the relevant linkages between the two levels of analysis should be a major concern of students of community politics.

Written for this volume.

The distinction between macro- and micro-level analysis, especially familiar to economists and biologists, has only recently begun to penetrate the filmy curtains of disciplinary boundaries into sociology and political science. But, in viewing developments in political science over the past few years, Richard Snyder remarked that

> It may very well be that when future commentators look back on the history of our discipline during the twenty years after World War II, the significant differences among us will not necessarily best be described by "traditional" versus "behavioral" or the new political science versus the old. Rather, the spectrum of empirical inquiry will be seen as representing a division of labor as between *micro* and *macro* analysis. ... If we do look at our past twenty years through the framework of this dichotomy an interesting point emerges: and that basically, the conflict has been about the objects of inquiry and the level or source of explanations.[2]

For our purposes, we shall define macro-analysis as dealing with the behaviors or properties of *communities*, explaining either (1) their differences, taking them as units, or (2) their interactions, taking them as sets. Research, for example, into the spending patterns of American metropolitan areas involves the comparison among macro-units which are not interacting, while an exploration of factors producing cooperation of cities within a metropolitan area would investigate their interactions. Conversely, micro-analysis involves some *subcommunity units*, including political parties, individual voters, city managers, power holders, or politically relevant groups. Since the two perspectives can be viewed from a relative standpoint, however, we might, for some purpose, want to define the American social system as a macro-unit and examine communities as micro-units in relation to it. Or for some other purpose we may take a political party organization as a macro-unit, identifying individual party members or voters as micro-units. In this chapter, we shall view the urban community as the macro-unit and subcommunity actors (voters, power holders, interest groups, parties, and so on) as micro-units.

Notes to this selection will be found on pages 328–329.

The first, and perhaps the most important, perspective derived from the macro–micro approach to community politics is that micro-level phenomena cannot be explained solely by macro-level data, nor vice versa.[3] One reason for this rule is what W. S. Robinson, in a classic paper, called the "ecological fallacy."[4] Robinson argues that one cannot ordinarily utilize data about ecological aggregates, e.g., precincts, counties, states, and communities, to explain variations in individual attitudes or behavior. Finding that riot cities are characterized by recent heavy influxes of Southern Negroes says nothing one way or another about the participation of these migrants in riots, as we shall see. Blalock has, in generalizing and restating Robinson's position, argued that

> In shifting from one unit of analysis to another we are very likely to affect the manner in which outside and possibly disturbing influences are operating on the dependent and independent variables under consideration.[5]

Both Robinson's early position and Blalock's restatement explain our general rule, but they do so primarily in statistical and mechanical terms. According to Etzioni, there are important logical and empirical reasons why the behavior of one unit-type cannot be explained adequately by introducing properties of the other. In his words,

> It is productive for socio-political analysis to treat data about societies, their components and their combinations as distinct phenomena whose variance cannot be explained satisfactorily on the basis of the properties and relationships of lower level units such as small groups and individual roles.[6]

Etzioni argues further that

> Some social scientists still do not face the question of the units of analysis and, by discussing "man," shift back and forth between statements whose only referent can be a personality system or a small group and statements about nations and societies; often one statement implies an independent variable which is microscopic and a dependent variable which is macroscopic, without any hint as to what the inter-level mechanism may be.[7]

In considerably oversimplified language, the gist of Etzioni's position is that in the analysis of social units, the whole is greater than the sum of its parts. This antireductionist position holds that macro-variables are a function of, first, the additive sum of micro-variables, and second, properties characterizing relationships among micro-units.

An excellent illustration of these two kinds of macro-properties (the additive and the relational) concerns the income of a community. The simple addition of all individual incomes will produce the *aggregate* income of a city, state, or nation. But the *distribution* of income in a community may also be relevant to politics in a community. One might speculate, for example, that a city characterized by wide extremes in income distribution might contain more class conflict than a community with a very even income distribution, even if the aggregate income of each community were identical.

Thus far, we have identified two broad approaches to the study of community politics, the first of which (the macro approach) deals with the community itself as the object of concern, the second of which (the micro approach) deals with subcommunity units as its central interest. This, of course, parallels the distinction between the community as a research site (micro) and the community as an object of inquiry (macro) made in the previous selection. In the following section, we shall (1) discuss the use of each approach in attempting to explain our two illustrative problems —civil disorders and political participation— and (2) identify some of the problems in the use of one approach without the perspective of the other. Following that, (3) several micro and macro approaches to community politics will be briefly discussed. Finally, (4) we shall introduce the notion of "linkages" between micro and macro phenomena, illustrating that concept with each of our research problems.

The Two Approaches Illustrated

Ignoring the explanatory dualism implied by macro–micro distinction leads to confusion in the interpretation of findings, or, worse, to the puzzlement over seemingly contradictory findings. The civil disorder and political participation examples may suffice to illustrate in concrete form our theoretical arguments. Suppose, first of all, that we are interested in accounting for the phenomenon of urban racial disorders. Like the members of the Kerner Commission, we will inevitably approach the problem of riots with a variety of "hunches" about the causes of riots: they reflect hostility and frustration stemming from unemployment, low income and squalid housing; they are caused by "outside agitators" or by "police brutality"; or they result from sustained anger at a white power structure. It would be useful to begin with a cataloging of riots, both by their severity (using, perhaps, indicators of deaths, arrests, or property damages) and by their precipitating incidents. The Kerner Commission measured the severity of riots on what amounted to a 25-point scale.[8] Lieberson and Silverman, and, later, Downes classified riots in terms of their precipitating incidents.[9] Once such spadework had been accomplished, it would then be necessary to find some indicators of the "causes of riots."

Let us, for purposes of illustration, counterpose two studies of riot behavior, a macro-approach studying riot cities and a micro-approach studying riot participants. Bryan Downes, drawing upon a variety of data sources, identified 129 cities with populations greater than 25,000 in which "hostile outbursts" had occurred between January 1, 1964, and May 31, 1968. He then compared these cities to all other cities in the same population class (N = 547) which had experienced no riots. The riot cities differed from the nonriot cities on several dimensions. In particular:

a. Riot cities were those which experienced the heaviest influx of nonwhite population from the South;

b. Riot cities had more poorly educated populations than did nonriot cities;

c. Riot cities had lower income levels than did nonriot cities;

d. And, unemployment levels were higher in riot cities than in nonriot cities.[10]

Given these findings from a macro-level study, we could develop a very plausible theory about the causes of riots, concluding that deprivations like unemployment, low income, poor educational attainment, and disorientation of recently migrant ghetto residents accounted for, explained, or "caused" the riots.[11]

Micro-analysis, however, leads us to doubt the credibility of such a theory. A report prepared for the Kerner Commission (a part of that report, by Fogelson and Hill, is reprinted in Selection 14 of this volume) examined the characteristics of rioters, concluding that

a. Rioters are not only more likely than the noninvolved to have been born in the region in which the riot occurred, but also are more likely to have been long-term residents of the city in which the disturbance took place.

b. Level of schooling is strongly related to participation. Those with some high school education were *more likely* to riot than those who had only finished grade school.

c. In the Detroit and Newark survey data, income level alone does not seem to correlate with self-reported riot participation, and

d. . . . there are no substantial differences in unemployment between the rioters and the noninvolved.[12]

Interestingly, then, the implications of micro- and macro-analyses lead to diametrically opposed conclusions.

A second example of divergent micro–macro findings can be derived from individual and community data on electoral participation. One of the strongest and most revered correlations in all of social science research is the positive correlation between social class position (as measured by income, occupational status, or educational attainment), and political participation.[13] Milbrath found evidence confirming this relationship in at least six different countries.[14]

Nonetheless, one of the most remarkable relationships uncovered by Alford and Lee's study of community voting turnout (see Selection 10 in this volume) was the *negative* correlation between voting turnout and community educational level:

> Although not high, the ecological or aggregate [macro] correlation of registrants voting with education is the opposite of the well-known individual [micro] correlations.

Interestingly, too, John C. Bollens and his associates found in the St. Louis metropolitan area study that suburbanites participated in politics at about the same level as central city residents, even though the social rank of the former was higher than that of the latter.[15] Once again, that which seems to be true at the individual (micro) level of analysis is opposite to the findings at the community (macro) level.

How then shall we reconcile the "contradictions" which appear from the use of two different approaches to community politics? There are four possible ways to do so. First, we may introduce the "ecological fallacy," and argue that community-level data are a poor substitute for individual-level data. But the ecological fallacy tells us only that we cannot make assertions about individuals from aggregate data. It suggests no reason to explain why an explanation which is adequate at one level becomes inappropriate at the other level.

Secondly, we can claim that the relationships identified in one or both the analyses are spurious, reflecting the coincidental association of the test variables to some other factor which is the "real" cause of civil disorders or electoral participation. Certainly, the charge of spuriousness should always be entertained, since it can lead to the identification of other relevant variables. On the other hand, most of the studies reported here, both the macro- and micro-analyses, introduced several control variables, and the additional variables which

might be introduced to justify the charge of spuriousness are by no means obvious.

A third way out of our difficulty is by redefining our concepts. We might argue, for example, that unemployment at the macro or community level is functionally not the equivalent of unemployment at the micro or individual level. Although unemployment both at the community and the individual level reduces income, the secondary consequences for the individual are largely psychological (loss of esteem, frustration, or alienation) while for the community the effects remain almost wholly economic. Thus, even though we apply identical terminology to macro and micro properties, they are functionally different, and the contradictions become linguistic accidents rather than empirical divergences. There is some truth in this third approach to reconciling contradictory data, but it purports to explain the contradiction largely by sidestepping it.

The fourth and most productive approach, in our judgment, is to search for the relevant *linkages* between micro and macro phenomena. Linkages, in our argument, are similar to, although not identical with, what Etzioni calls "emergent properties."[16] According to his definition, emergent properties are "properties which appear on one level of analysis and are not present on another level."[17]

They are thus a function not only of the existence of interunit properties but also of the *relationship* between those properties. Our conception of linkages will be developed more fully below, when we return to our examples and attempt to account for the apparent contradictions.

THE CONSEQUENCES OF MICRO-ANALYSIS *IN VACUO*

The utilization of micro-analysis, without taking account of macro properties, is likely to lead to serious research distortions by confusing the discrete with the contextual factors of a behavior. In the first place, micro-analysis *in vacuo* is likely to

integration may be an effective way to promote efficiency, equality, and adequate political representation.

THE STRUCTURAL APPROACH

Municipal corporations which we ordinarily call "city governments" contain governmental institutions which are important determinants of group access and decisional style. Table 1 depicts the distribution of six particular institutional forms in American cities having a population of fifty thousand or more in 1960. Within each of the three institutional categories—form of government, type of elections, and type of constituencies—particular variations are identified as "reformed" or "unreformed." Council-manager governments (as well as the less popular commission form of government), nonpartisan elections, and at-large constituencies were each preferred by the "good-government" forces in American communities. These reformers sought to replace the older institutions of mayor-council government, partisan elections, and ward constituencies with new, efficiency-oriented, economical, and "nonpolitical" administrations.

The political institutions of a city, a part of its macro-structure, are crucial to a behavioral approach to community politics. First, the type of political institutions is related to (and, presumably, partially determinative of) patterns of participation in community politics (see

Selection 10 in this volume). Second, institutional structures may be influential in determining which groups will be advantaged and disadvantaged. And third, they will have some influence upon the degree to which community decisions are a product of intergroup conflict or of the decisions of professional administrators (see Selection 27 in this volume).

THE MACRO-POWER APPROACH

Hawley has argued that

> every social group or system is an organization of power. . . . The community, for example, may be conceived as an energy system. That is, as a system of relationships among functionally differentiated units, the community constitutes a mobilization of power—the capacity to produce results—for dealing with the environment, whether physical or social.[28]

Thus power, as a macro-level concept, refers to the capacity of a system to generate change in its environment. The macro-power approach directs our attention to questions like (a) How does the community manipulate resources to meet community goals? (b) How successful are communities, or certain types of communities, in producing environmental change? and (c) What factors affect the capacity of communities to alter their economic and social environments?

Ordinarily, communities manipulate their environment through the use of public policies. Wood's penetrating analysis of the political economy of the New York metropolitan region explains how, through

TABLE 1. Distribution of Political Institutions in American Cities with 1960 Populations of 50,000 or More (N = 308)*

	Reformed Institution		Unreformed Institution	
Form of Government	Council–Manager	45%	Mayor–Council	43%
	Commission	12%		
Type of Constituency	At-Large	63%	Ward	37%
Type of Election	Nonpartisan	67%	Partisan	33%

* The percentages are computed from data provided in Orin F. Nolting and David S. Arnold (eds.), *The Municipal Year Book 1963* (Chicago: International City Managers Association, 1963). A few cities (12 per cent of those over 50,000) use a combination of the ward and at-large plans. Cities using at-large elections for half or more of their council seats were coded "at-large"; those with less than half at-large seats were coded "ward." Washington, D.C., is excluded from the calculations.

a variety of policy mechanisms, including zoning and land use policies, fiscal patterns (i.e., spending and taxing), and the use of "appeal upstairs" (the community's effort to mobilize supracommunity actors like the federal government or the state), the community can attempt to induce environmental change (or to stave off change).[29]

The issues raised below in John Walton's treatment of vertical axis and power structure (see Selection 18 in this volume) concern the ability of the community to develop autonomy and change-generating capacity in the face of disproportionately powerful extracommunity forces. He notes, however, that as the capacity of urban systems to produce environmental alterations increases, the ability to maximize other values, especially that of democratic participation, may decline.

Some Micro Approaches

THE PARTICIPATION APPROACH

Men in American cities are not very good examples of Aristotle's dictum that "man is a political animal." Rather, for most, "politics is but a sideshow on the great circus of life."[30] Alford and Lee found that the mean turnout of adults in noncurrent city elections was 31.2 per cent (see Selection 10), hardly an indication of unrestrained revelry about local politics.

People participate, of course, for a variety of reasons—economic, social, psychological, and political.[31] But the decision to participate is not merely a function of micro-level factors, psychological, and sociological variables, but also of systemic, macro-level factors. System rules, particularly the method of registration, as Nimmo and McCleskey show (see Selection 11), may be an important factor. Structural variables like form of government also tend to produce differential participation. Alford and Lee found political structures, especially forms of government, to be among the most important correlates of electoral turnout (see Selection 10).

In communities where there is great homogeneity, there is likely to be less political and social conflict. And, where

there is less conflict, there is less incentive for participation. Conflict turns a languishing public into an aroused electorate; opposition breeds organization; antagonism yields activism. In the American states, for example, there is a clear correlation between interparty competition and higher participation rates.[32] In the local community, a competitive power structure generates more mass participation than does a consensual one.[33] Knowledge of the developmental sequence of these three variables—homogeneity, conflict, and participation—may help us reconcile the seemingly divergent relationships between macro-level and micro-level studies of participation which we explored above. Communities where the population is uniformly highly educated and, by implication, shares a considerable homogeneity of interest, contain less cleavage and political conflict to arouse participation. Conversely, the less well educated, heterogeneous community contains more sources of conflict (between classes, between ethnic groups, between occupational groups) and, therefore, more active participation. Thus by searching for a linkage—in this case, the degree of homogeneity—between micro and macro phenomena, we have offered an explanation for the apparent contradiction between macro and micro studies of electoral participation.

THE INTEREST-BROKERAGE APPROACH

Political parties, informal and associational groups, elected and unofficial decision-makers all provide for the brokerage of interests in a city's political system.[34] The political party has never been as cohesively organized in the United States as in other political systems. For a variety of reasons, described by Greenstein (see Selection 12 in this volume), the urban party organization is much weaker today than in the heyday of the party machine. Where parties do thrive (and sometimes they thrive even under the rubric of nonpartisanship, as in Chicago), they are dominant agencies for the aggregation of interests and the selection of community leaders. In the nonpartisan city, where parties tend to be either attenuated or hopelessly crippled, politics are more likely to consist of an interplay of group forces, a competition among the business–civic group faction, ethnic groups, liberals, the municipal bureaucracy, and, perhaps, the remnants of a decaying machine.

Again, however, the level and style of group activity are a function of macro- as well as micro-factors. In the prototypical dormitory suburb, homogeneous in its class structure, conflict is ordinarily minimal, with relatively few groups, other than the main street merchants, being mobilized. Despite the mythology of suburban participativeness, in the absence of tight linkages between cleavage, conflict, and mobilization, suburbia remains the place where "few rule . . . but many believe they could."[35]

THE MICRO-POWER APPROACH

The power approach has a micro as well as a macro version. While the macro-power theory emphasizes the capability of a system to generate resources to attain goals, the micro-power approach explores the ability of micro-actors to influence the behavior of other micro-actors. A classic treatment of power, by Max Weber, defined it as "the probability that one actor within a social relationship will be in a position to carry out his will despite resistance."[36] Since this concept is examined at length by Clark in the following selection, we shall not review it here, except to reiterate our argument that micro-power capability is partly a function of macro-level phenomena, particularly the distribution of community resources.

Linkages between Macro and Micro Phenomena

Two principal themes have dominated the argument in this chapter. First, we have argued that efforts to explain community politics which do not take account of the macro–micro distinction run the risk of logical and empirical difficulties. Second, however, a given phenomenon—rioting or participation, for example—may fruitfully be viewed as a function of *both* micro- and macro-level variables. The notion of "linkages" between micro and macro phenomena will be useful in describing the ways in which a particular behavior, taken as a dependent variable, may be a product of both kinds of variables. Research which specifies and measures linkages may be costly, both in terms of time and money, but it is likely to be quite productive. It involves the availability of both ecological and individual data and sometimes demands the development of ingenious indicators.

One excellent example of research concerning linkages is Putnam's effort[37] to test three theories, each of which purports to explain the impact of the community on political attitudes of individuals. The *party activity* theory hypothesizes that campaign activity is disproportionately concentrated in the majority party and that party activities, particularly of the major party, constitute the primary linkage of the community with individual attitudes. The *community identification* theory posits that individual adherence to perceived community norms constitutes the basic linkage, while the *social interaction* theory attributes community influence to primary and secondary associational networks. Although Putnam is careful to note both the temporal and spatial limitations of his research, his imaginative effort to relate macro to micro variables tends to confirm the social interaction hypothesis.

A second example, equally relevant to research in community politics, is Eyestone and Eulau's study of "policy maps" and council policy outcomes, an exploration of (1) community variables, including resource capacity, growth rate, and size; (2) councilmanic attitudes toward public policies; and (3) public policies, utilizing data derived from ninety Bay Area cities. Their model postulates that

city size, density and growth as well as resources are antecedent variables; that individual or group demands and decision-makers' policy orientations are intervening variables; and that policy outcomes and resultant stages of policy development are consequent variables.[38]

Their research also indicates the utility of efforts which combine the macro and micro perspectives, since both macro-variables such as size, and mediating, micro-level variables such as elite attitudes and group vitality had independent impacts upon policy outputs.

In line with both the Putnam and Eyestone–Eulau studies, then, linkages may be conceptualized as *intervening variables* between community phenomena and sub-community phenomena. Let us then return to our two examples on electoral participation and rioting and see what intervening linkages can be identified. For the former, we hypothesized above a developmental sequence, beginning with the macro-variable of community homogeneity, which in turn may cause variation in the politicization of conflict, which in turn may cause variations in the probability of individual participation. Clearly, of course, there are sublinkages between each of these, which would have to be established by careful research. Unless attention is given, however, to the interactions between community-level and individual-level properties, we shall continue to uncover perplexing "contradictions" in our data about community politics.

Explaining the linkages between macro-factors and the individual characteristics of rioters is a good deal more complex, depending upon the availability of socio-psychological data for identifiable groups of rioters and potential rioters. One fruitful line of inquiry, however, might proceed from the proposition that civil violence "presupposes the likelihood of relative deprivation among substantial numbers of individuals in a society."[39] The concept of relative deprivation emphasizes individuals' "perception of a discrepancy between their *value expectations* and their environments' apparent *value capacities*."[40] At the micro

or individual level, we thus have what is primarily a psychological explanation for civil violence.

The relevance of community (macro) factors, however, is seen in the individuals' perceptions of the environment's capacity to produce satisfying opportunities. Such perceptions will surely vary with objective conditions from city to city. Presumably, in cities characterized by high unemployment, low incomes, low educational attainment, and a heavy influx of recent migrants, the opportunities for social advancement would appear grim indeed. Macro-variables will thus, through a kind of sociopsychological filtration process, produce variation in the perceptions of environmental capacities by potential rioters.[41]

Micro-level variables, particularly the individual's level of educational attainment, will be related to both his aspiration level and his sheer capacity to perceive environmental constraints upon his aspirations. The higher his aspiration level, the more keenly he is apt to sense relative deprivation; the greater his educational accomplishments, the more knowledgeable he will be about the opportunities he is denied.

The foregoing is not intended as a "theory" of urban racial disorder. The effort is rather to portray, in a rather brief and simplified fashion, some possible linkages between macro and micro phenomena. That has been the major concern of this selection. We conclude by reiterating the argument that maximum explanatory capacity can be obtained only when that dichotomy is made a fulcrum for urban research. Although not all of the contributions included in this volume are explicitly concerned with those approaches, most are implicitly cognizant of it and the reader should have little difficulty using the macro–micro distinction as an organizing principle as well as a guide to evaluation.

The Concept of Power: Some Overemphasized and Underrecognized Dimensions—An Examination with Special Reference to the Local Community[*][1]

Terry N. Clark

University of Chicago

To say that much has been written on the concept of power would border on egregious understatement. The problem, however, is that many of the innumerable writers on this subject have chosen for investigation facets of the concept which overlap but little, if at all. Given such a division of labor, it has been generally true that any single author deals only with those aspects of power which are of particular importance in clarifying a specific theoretical problem. In this paper the most abstract as well as the most applied aspects of the concept are eschewed in order to formulate what might be called, following Merton, a middle-range conceptualization of power, with special reference to the local community.

Fifteen dimensions of the concept of power are isolated for analysis. It is doubtless true that a different approach would enable one to subsume two or more of the fifteen specific dimensions considered in this paper under a single more general heading (or, conversely, that one of the

fifteen could be broken down further); and such partial consolidation of the fifteen dimensions might be a valuable exercise from the standpoint of developing greater conceptual elegance. Nevertheless, it is still important to attempt to bridge the gulf (sometimes seemingly gigantic!) between the highly abstract formulations of the concept of power on the one hand, and the quasi-operational difficulties confronted by the community researcher on the other. This paper represents an effort to fill what at present remains an unfortunately deep chasm separating the most theoretical and the most applied discussions of the concept of power.[2]

The fifteen dimensions treated represent a diversity of approaches to the examination of power, for each singles out somewhat different theoretical questions or empirical problems of theoretical relevance. It is unquestionably true that the dimensions differ in their levels of generality—some are more abstract, some more concrete than others. The dimensions also vary greatly in their popularity: while none are entirely original to this paper, some have been widely accepted in both conceptual and empirical work, while others have been either frequently unrecognized, or, one occasionally feels, gently swept under the proverbial rug.

The order of presentation is not crucial, but the fifteen dimensions may be viewed as a checklist for any analysis of power (and not just in local communities) that seeks to be reasonably complete.

1. Interpersonal influence. The most general idea concerning power is that it involves an interpersonal relationship whereby one actor (A), an individual or a collectivity, is influenced to alter his attitudes or behavior as a consequence of some behavior on the part of a second actor (B), either an individual or a collectivity.[3]

2. Anticipated reactions. The alteration in A's attitudes or behavior need not, however, be the consequence of any direct action on the part of B. A may anticipate B's probable reactions to a possible future action on his part and modify his initial reaction accordingly. Friedrich has baptized

[*]Reprinted with permission of the author and publisher, from Terry N. Clark, "The Concept of Power: Some Overemphasized and Underrecognized Dimensions—An Examination with Special Reference to the Local Community," (Southwestern) Social Science Quarterly, 48 (December 1967), pp. 271–286.

26

Notes to this selection will be found on pages 329–332.

this phenomenon the "law of anticipated reactions."[4] The problems posed by anticipated alterations in behavior for the study of community influence are thorny from both conceptual and methodological standpoints. Failure to cope adequately with this aspect of power on a methodological level is perhaps one of the most critical weaknesses of the decision-making method.[5]

3. Direct and indirect influence. In one sense, the phenomenon of anticipated reactions might be considered a type of indirect influence. However, for present purposes, the term "indirect influence" will be strictly reserved for the situation where B influences A through an intermediary (C). Thus, as reported by a number of community power studies, the highest ranking executives of a large community corporation often do not *personally* serve on councils and boards of influential community organizations, but a middle-level executive from the corporation frequently does.[6] The implication is, of course, that in one way or another the middle-level executive *represents* the corporation.

4. Reciprocity. Power has been described as an asymmetrical interpersonal relationship.[7] This formulation is useful in that it calls attention to the important fact that while A influences B in many decisions, it is also true that B influences A, although less than vice versa. Hence the relationship is designated asymmetrical. The cliché that power corrupts refers to this reciprocal aspect of power. In many concrete situations it is difficult to state exactly who influences whom through what methods and to what effect because of the multitude of complicated reciprocal influences.

5. Action–inaction. However inapparent the manifestation, power may indeed be exerted—and quite forcefully—despite the absence of any overt action. Simply to maintain the *status quo* through inaction, or as a slight variation, to limit action within fixed boundaries (remember the policy of "containment"), may constitute a "mobilization of bias,"[8] which can result in significant advantages for one group over others, whether these advantages be material, religious, aesthetic, or whatever.

The Concept of Power: Some   **27**
Overemphasized and
Underrecognized Dimensions—An
Examination with Special Reference
to the Local Community
Terry N. Clark

One limitation of the decisional approach to the study of power (when not used in combination with other methods) is precisely its inability to cope adequately with this facet of power.

The concept of inaction can be further broken down into two types which have been termed "negative decisions" and "non-decisions."[9] A negative decision implies an actual decision situation where alternate courses of action are explicitly considered and where the outcome is negative, that is, not in favor of the proposed course of action. A non-decision, on the other hand, implies only a "latent issue," an aspect of the *status quo* that could be altered in some manner so as to reallocate community resources, but where no specific demands have been sufficiently articulated to produce any overt negative decision.

At least two difficulties are involved in the application of these concepts. First, in an empirical situation, a researcher may have trouble in distinguishing between negative decisions and non-decisions. For example, as will be discussed in the section on visibility (p. 31) a negative decision is often made by a small group within the community which is not visible to the community at large and may not even be uncovered by the researcher. Another possibility, even further removed from this situation, is that where a relatively invisible decision is made to attempt to suppress a latent issue from ever developing into an openly discussed community issue.

A second difficulty involved in the concept of "non-decision" concerns the *criteria* for identification of "latent issues" or the "mobilization of bias." As Dahl and Polsby have pointed out time and again, the values or theoretical orientation of the individual researcher may intrude into his analysis (and more than some writers have implied) when he declares that in a community there exists a mobilization of bias on a certain latent issue. If no organized group within the community has articulated demands which have actually been rejected by others (that is, an actual negative decision has not occurred), but the researcher still declares that the *status quo* involves a mobilization of bias, the burden of proof falls on him to make as explicit as possible the criteria by which he posits the presence of a latent issue. Only in this way can he avoid the accusation of imputing "false consciousness."

It is doubtless true that labeling a nondecision area a latent issue is an operation fraught with intellectual dangers. Still, it must be recognized that adopting a purely behavioristic position—refusing to acknowledge the existence of an issue until some group attempts to implement a decision—involves a strong conservative bias in favor of the *status quo*. If an effort is made to investigate the degree to which the (leading) decision-making organs of the community actually represent the values and interests of various community subsectors and the degree to which maintenance of the *status quo* favors certain of these values and interests, a more complete description of the community will result than if the researcher simply reports the absence of any important decisions in x, y, and z areas of potential conflict, or, as is more likely, if he simply neglects altogether to discuss these areas.

6. Patterns of value distribution. Power may be seen as the realization of values or the attainment of goals.[10] In addition to calling attention to the value element in power implementation, such a formulation of the concept also suggests certain conceptions of pluralism and democracy. Thus, pluralism based on patterns of value distribution could be defined as follows: to the extent that leaders in a social system differ from one another in their values, pluralism can be said to exist. To be sure, complete consensus (concerning values) is never attained in any group of leaders. Yet some sets of leaders' values are more similar

than others, and the more similar the values within a given group, the less pluralistic (according to this conception) is the system of government.

In order to state how divergent the leaders' values should be in order to posit the presence of democracy in any given situation, an additional criterion must be introduced: the values of the constituents. The more similar a leader's values are to those of his constituents, the more democratic the system of government (from this one point of view).

In analyzing the distribution of power, a frequent index for characterizing the degree of openness of an elite, and by implication the degree of democratization, is the social background of a social system's leadership. The rationale for this procedure is that the social background of an individual has an important influence on his values and behavior patterns.

In community analyses, the diversity in social background of key position occupants in the governmental or general community leadership structure has been used to measure the degree of pluralism. Analyzing the values of the leaders separately from their social backgrounds yields four possible types of leadership structures if the two variables, social background and value system of the leadership, are dichotomized as "unified" and "diversified."[11] Hunter argued that a monolithic elite controlled Regional City.[12] Rossi[13] has described leaders with similar backgrounds who act on the basis of different values. Agger, Goldrich, and Swanson describe a community, Metropolis, where leadership is diversified with respect to social background, and yet is relatively unified by a common ideology so that the power structure functions as a monolithic entity.[14] Dahl's description of New Haven's power distribution shows a leadership with members of different social backgrounds— Old Yankees, Italians, Negroes, and so on —all represented in institutions important for governing the city. In addition, Dahl shows that these leaders actually bargain for their constituents.[15]

A similar typology for democratic representation based on patterns of value

distribution can be constructed by dichotomizing the values of various groups within
a social system as similar or divergent and
leaders' values as similar to those of their
constituents or divergent from them.

It would be possible to introduce the
additional variable of the degree of homogeneity of values among leaders themselves,
as analyzed in the last substruction. This
would generate four types of oligarchy,
but only the same two types of democracy
as there would be two empty cells in the
eightfold table.

To date, remarkably few studies of community power have systematically investigated the patterns of value distribution
either within the community elite or
between the elite and broader sectors of the
community population. Of course, it can
be argued that community power is manifested in behavior, and that, therefore, the
actual decision process itself should be the
focus of research attention, values being
important for this problem only insofar as
they influence actual behavior. It is unquestionably important to measure actual
behavior. Nevertheless, the fact that,
whichever of the present community research methodologies is adopted, several
complex dimensions of the power structure
seem to be missed may be taken as support

The Concept of Power: Some **29**
Overemphasized and
Underrecognized Dimensions—An
Examination with Special Reference
to the Local Community
Terry N. Clark

for the thesis that a more careful and systematic analysis of the value patterns within
various elites and within the general
population of the community could serve to
add more depth and understanding to our
present ideas about the structuring of
community power.

One very important aspect of value distribution patterns is the *range* and *extent*
of activities considered appropriate for
various community institutions, both by the
elite and by the broader population. Careful
analysis of such patterns would help define
more clearly the structural context within
which the decision process takes place. If,
for example, the community elite feels that
the community's government should provide no more than the minimum of "care-
taker" services for the community, while
several subgroups of the population feel
that the government should extend its
range of services to serve the community
population over a broader range of activities, the differential distribution of values
could have important consequences for the

TABLE 1. *Typology of Value Systems and Social Backgrounds of Community Leaders*

| | | Social Background | |
		Unified	Diversified
Value System	Unified	Hunter	Agger, et al.
	Diversified	Rossi	Dahl

TABLE 2. *Typology of Leaders-Constituents Relationships*

| | | Group's Values | |
		Similar	Divergent
Leaders' Values	Similar	Homogeneous Democracy	Conflicting Democracy
	Divergent	Oligarchy	

flow of community influence. Ideally, the researcher should attempt to define the values of community members on issues relating to important community activities, specifying the areas of value consensus and dissensus, and pointing out the possible present and future implications for the distribution of community influence.

Closely related to this type of value pattern analysis is that associated with the concept of legitimation.

7. Legitimation. Since Weber, it is generally accepted that no discussion of the concept of power is complete without reference to the dimension of legitimacy. The Weberian typology of traditional, charismatic and legal-rational authority can be fruitfully applied to modes of legitimation for dominant individuals or collectivities within the community.[16] In addition, it is frequently useful to determine the type of legitimation characterizing the authority relationships between the leadership and specific subgroups within the general dominated population.

It is highly probable that all political regimes invoke all three types of authority patterns at one time or another. The structure of a regime's authority relationships can be delineated more precisely by indicating (for various subgroups within the general population)[17] the degree to which the regime is legitimated, as well as which mode of legitimation is most important.

8. Number of participants in decision. The primary variable determining the number of persons participating actively in any decision is the institutionalization of the means for continual decision-making, one extreme case being routine administrative decisions involving only a small number of administrators. At the other extreme is the situation where an entire community is mobilized on one side or the other of an issue which may only be resolved by a community-wide referendum or, in the limiting case, by the intervention of extra-community forces.[18]

The question of the number of participants is to be distinguished from the identity of the participants. The identity of the participants has been used as an indication of the representativeness of different decision-making institutions. The purely quantitative number of participants actively involved in a decision may be used to characterize community decision-making processes in various issue-areas, as well as the community as a whole. A community where a large number of persons are involved in almost every important community decision differs significantly from others where only a small number of persons take part in most decisions.

The number of participants involved in a decision is also intimately related to the importance of an issue.

9. Scope of power: issue importance. In his theoretical discussions of power, Dahl has repeatedly emphasized the necessity of specifying the scope of an actor's influence in altering the outcome of decisions.[19] This same orientation lies behind the decision in the New Haven study to undertake a detailed investigation of the decision-making processes in specific "issue-areas."[20] The importance of specifying the actual scope of an actor's influence as precisely as possible is irrefragable. There are difficulties, however, in translating this general principle into workable empirical procedures, most particularly in the process of selecting specific issues for study.

Whether the researcher employs the reputational or decision-making approach or some hybrid combination, insofar as specific issues are to be examined, he must consciously or unconsciously apply some criteria for the selection of these issues. Implicit in most community power studies is the assumption that the decision-making processes representative of the *most important* community issues are those being portrayed. But what is "important?" A number of criteria may be applied to facilitate the resolution of this problem.

First, an issue's importance may be measured by the number of persons directly participating in the decision-making process. This, however, if taken alone, is a rather crude and generally insufficient indicator, although helpful in conjunction with others.

A second criterion is the amount of importance accorded by members of the community to selected issues. Although in order to provide definitive results about community opinion on the relative importance of different issues it would be necessary to survey a random sample of community members, a less complicated and more frequently employed technique is to interview a sample of community knowledgeables as informants for the community at large.[21]

A third criterion is the amount of money allocated to a specific issue area. Education was the most expensive single item in the annual budget of New Haven, and this issue area was studied in detail to determine who governed in the educational sphere.[22]

For the selection of important issues, Polsby has listed four criteria which, it should be noted, omit the subjective evaluation of issue importance by members of the community:

a. How many people are affected by outcome,

b. How many different kinds of community resources are distributed by outcomes,

c. How much in amount of resources is distributed by outcomes,

d. How drastically present community resource distributions are altered by outcomes.[23]

A group of social scientists studying Syracuse, New York, investigated 39 separate issues resolved over a five-year period. To select issues, they interviewed a panel of informants to develop a pool of issues. An initial list of about 250 was then reduced to 34 separate issues by application of the following eight criteria.

a. Each issue must have been at least temporarily resolved by a decision.

b. The decisions must be perceived as important by informants representing diverse segments of the community.

The Concept of Power: Some   31
Overemphasized and
Underrecognized Dimensions—An
Examination with Special Reference
to the Local Community
Terry N. Clark

c. The decisions must pertain to the development, distribution, and utilization of resources and facilities which have an impact on a large segment of the metropolitan population.

d. The decision must involve alternative lines of action. The decisions must entail a certain degree of choice on the part of participants; the outcome must not be predetermined.

e. The decision must be administered rather than "market type"—one made by individuals holding top positions in organizational structures which empower them to make decisions affecting many people.

f. The decision must involve individuals and groups resident in the Syracuse metropolitan area.

g. The decision must fall within the time period 1955–1960.

h. The set of decisions as a whole must reflect the entire range of important institutional sectors, such as governmental, economic, political, educational, religious, etc.[24]

In point *b* the Syracuse group has not only included the attitudes of some community members but has stressed that "diverse segments" of the community must see the issue as important. Strict application of this criterion, however, could lead to the neglect of issues important by other criteria but relatively "invisible" as far as most citizens of the community are concerned.

10. Visibility. Closely related to the problems of indirect influence, the patterns of value distribution, the number of persons involved in a decision, and the importance of an issue, is an issue's visibility.

If the problem of issue selection appears rather elementary and seems to be a comparatively insignificant research operation, introduction of the dimension of visibility brings to the fore the degree to which a researcher can predetermine the outcome of his study in the initial selection of issue areas. It is also at this point more than at any other that, explicitly or implicitly, the personal values and theoretical orientation of the researcher are most likely to bias his scientific analysis.

There is probably no completely "satisfactory" solution to the problem of the differential visibility of issues (nor to the closely related questions of value patterns, indirect influence, and issue importance). One relatively safe conclusion, however, is that the investigator should not be content that he has adequately uncovered the community power system after investigating only a few issues, even if they are the most highly *visible* problems facing the community at one point in time. It is insufficient to describe a community power structure as pluralistic or monolithic on the basis of investigating solely the processes involved in a handful of decisions. As with any scientific finding, the investigator should attempt to fix limits to the generalizations he makes about a given phenomenon. He should attempt to describe some of the more implicit and less visible values as well as other constraining factors that provide the relatively constant structural context within which the system operates. As comparative anthropological studies have repeatedly demonstrated, the most deeply rooted value patterns of a society are those almost never overtly questioned or even explicitly stated.

11. Power bases. Another problem that must be dealt with concerns the bases of power, the social analogy of potential energy in physics. A number of writers on community power have compiled lists of important bases of power,[25] but the main variables are included in Dahl's list of nine, each of which will be discussed below at greater length.

a. Money and credit

b. Control over jobs

c. Control over the information of others

d. Social standing

e. Knowledge and Expertness

f. Popularity, Esteem, Charisma

g. Legality, Constitutionality, Officiality

h. Ethnic solidarity

i. The right to vote.[26]

12. Application of power. If power bases are analogous to potential energy, the application of power is analogous to kinetic energy. Following the physical analogy one step further, there is also a certain "loss" or "cost" involved in the process of applying power. Models for analyzing the application of power using the economic concept of opportunity cost will be discussed shortly.[27]

13. Efficiency of power application. Another important factor intervening between bases of power and application of power is the *efficiency* with which an individual is capable of exploiting his potential power bases. A skillful individual may be capable of combining a number of his bases so as to "coordinate and restructure," or "pyramid" his power resources.[28] One way of thus exploiting one's power bases more efficiently is to coordinate with other individuals for the pursuit of a common goal. Resources per individual in a power situation may be modest, but when mobilized with many others for collective action, the aggregate influence as a unified collectivity can be impressive.[29] Thus, the efficiency of collective action can lower the costs per individual below those for individual action toward the same end.

14. The zero-sum problem and the allocation of resources. In the process of coordinating and restructuring resources, a given actor (A) (individual or collectivity) may increase his power at the expense of other actors in the system (B, C, D, . . .). Or again, he (A) may simply coordinate and restructure resources to achieve goals without altering what the behavior of other actors would be in the absence of his activities. In other words, the quantity of power in a system may be conceived of as fixed, so that an increase of power on the part of one actor invokes a proportionate

loss on the part of other actors in the system, as in a zero-sum game; this is the case when a vote cast for one candidate is a vote lost for other candidates.

On the other hand, there are many situations where the application of power does not involve a restriction in the freedom of action of others; the structure of the system itself generates an increase in the total amount of power. Parsons, who has called attention to the zero-sum problem, offers the example of credit expansion through the banking system as a case in the economic system where the zero-sum situation does not obtain.[30]

Parsons has criticized Lasswell and Mills for analyzing political power as if it were a zero-sum phenomenon, and has himself argued that it generally is not. Dahl, treating the same general phenomenon somewhat differently, has pointed out that at any point in time a fairly large amount of "slack" may exist in a given system, and that it may be possible for an individual to pyramid his resources and increase his influence inside the system without significant resistance.[31] If many individuals begin to pyramid their resources, however, the amount of "slack" in the system will begin to decrease, and the zero-sum situation will be more closely approximated. In terms of Parsons' monetary analogy, the "easiness" of credit in the system will decrease, and the metallic bases of credit will be more and more frequently demanded in exchange situations. In terms of the "opportunity costs" model, as the cost of exerting influence in the political system increases, the marginal utility of political investments decreases, and it becomes proportionally more rewarding to reallocate one's resources to other spheres of activity outside the political system.

The most satisfactory answer to the zero-sum problem, it thus appears, is not one of either-or. In relatively democratic societies, there are probably very few empirical power situations even close to realizing the pure zero-sum situation where one player's gain precisely equals other players' losses. The contrary situation, which might be labelled a power-vacuum—where one

The Concept of Power: Some
Overemphasized and
Underrecognized Dimensions—An
Examination with Special Reference
to the Local Community
Terry N. Clark

33

player's gain implies absolutely *no* loss of any sort to any other player—may be, however, just as infrequently found. Most empirical power situations in democratic political arenas seem to fall somewhere between these two extremes. In such cases, the "opportunity costs" model can perhaps serve as a more useful analytical tool than the zero-sum model (or its converse), because the former brings intermediary (that is, the vast majority of empirical) cases into clearer focus.

15. Stratification of power. Is power stratified at all? If it is stratified, how unequally is it distributed? If it is not stratified, why is this the case? It has been in answering these three questions more than any others that students of community power have most frequently gone to war.[32] Initially the question was posed in terms of whether a power elite does or does not rule. Increasingly, though, this extremely broad question has been broken down into smaller conceptual elements which can be more clearly formulated and tested with existing methodological machinery.

The distinction between power bases and the application of power is a helpful one, for as the first step in investigation of the stratification of power one can examine whether or not the bases for power are stratified. Considering the bases listed in section 11, it would seem that in most American communities, (a) *money and credit* are unquestionably stratified, and to a large degree so are (b) *control over jobs*, (c) *control over information of others*, (d) *social standing*, (e) *knowledge and expertness*, (f) *popularity, esteem, and charisma*, and (g) *legality, constitutionality, officiality* (at least in gaining access to them through legal counsel, controlled in turn by money). (h) *Ethnic solidarity* (at least for elections) varies in proportion to the number of members of an ethnic group residing in a given community. Whether or not it is a stratified value depends on the specific empirical make-up of the individual community and cannot be answered for the general case. (i) *The right to vote*, with a few exceptions such as parts of the American South, in modern democracies is primarily unstratified.

Thus, of nine power bases, seven are definitely stratified to some degree and two probably unstratified in most cases. Still, the bases for power may not be activated by those who control them, and they may be inefficiently exploited even if efforts are made to influence the political system. In addition, different power bases imply different means of exerting varying *amounts* of influence in differing *scopes*. In some instances, the control of the ballot box may outweigh all other bases; in others, control of money and credit may have the final word. Any *a priori* answer to the question of whether power is stratified in communities *in general* seems doomed to failure or at least exception.

Dahl has argued that political inequalities in the past were often cumulative, but today tend to be noncumulative or dispersed.[33] In another context, distinguishing between direct and indirect influence, he has presented schematic diagrams of the distribution of influence suggesting that direct influence is largely stratified, but indirect influence is dispersed.[34]

Although the level of certainty with which it is possible to make such generalizations about a single city—such as New Haven—may be rather high, it would appear somewhat premature to generalize about the stratification of power. Even if power is rather widely dispersed in most American communities, systematic investigation of possible reasons for differing power structures in different communities remains a hitherto almost completely neglected enterprise.

Conclusion

On the basis of present knowledge, it seems judicious to conclude that different types of power structure arrangements have certainly existed in American communities in the past, and that several types of power structure are to be found in American communities today. Conceived thus, the problem of power stratification can be treated as a question that must be investigated empirically in test cases before broad generalizations are drawn. As a first step in this process, it is helpful to identify a number of different ways in which, at least theoretically, power can be stratified. A foundation for the next step—ascertainment of the conditions under which different types of power structure arrangements are likely to occur—will then be laid.

A number of typologies for power structure have been presented in the literature,[35] and in another paper the author has developed a series of thirty-four propositions relating demographic, economic, political, and cultural structural characteristics of communities to a general tendency toward a more monolithic or more pluralistic type of community power structure.[36] Work along similar lines is also being undertaken by several other persons. Indeed, a reorientation of the entire community power field toward the comparative study of community structural characteristics which predispose communities toward different types of decision-making processes is becoming increasingly apparent.[37] It would seem that if the question dominating the writings of students of community power from Floyd Hunter to Robert Dahl was "Who Governs?" then in the next years a number of researchers will be largely preoccupied with answering the fourfold question of *Who Governs?*—what is the structure of the decision-making process; *Where?*—in what kinds of communities; *When?*—under what conditions?; and *With What Effects?*—what is the impact on community outputs?[38]

The theoretical questions to be asked have been reformulated, and empirical work is presently underway that will provide a basis for quantitative testing of comparative hypotheses.[39] One important problem for the immediate future, however, is the standardization of at least certain core sections of comparative studies, so that in future years the various investigations presently underway will be more comparable with one another than were the many case studies conducted during the 1950's and early 1960's.[40] Several committees now exist to coordinate work among researchers, and important progress in the direction of creating a fund of comparable information on several hundred communities in numerous countries has already been made.[41] Steps have also been taken toward the creation of a data archive which would make information collected in several different studies broadly available to the scholarly community.[42] As the

The Concept of Power: Some   **35**
Overemphasized and
Underrecognized Dimensions—An
Examination with Special Reference
to the Local Community
Terry N. Clark

community power field comes to absorb the impact of these large-scale comparative studies, many of the questions that had to be left unresolved in the present paper will be answered more conclusively. And several of the heretofore underrecognized dimensions of power may become more clearly apparent.

The Concept of Power: A Sociologist's Perspective*[1]

Richard L. Simpson

University of North Carolina at Chapel Hill

THE CONCEPT of power should direct our attention to the significant questions about politics. If politics is a process by which values are allocated to groups and individuals whose interests differ, the thing to ask about the power arrangements of a community is, how adequately and in what ways do varying group interests find representation in them? Keeping this basic question in mind and assuming that Professor Clark's thorough survey indicates the range of topics which students have addressed, I will suggest some subsidiary questions the concept of power should help us answer, I will assess the extent to which the dimensions Clark discusses relate to these questions, and I will, in this way, identify what seems to be some relatively neglected aspects of community power.

Four Questions about Community Power

1. What does the government do? who benefits from it? and who does not? What actions does the government engage in? What program does it carry out? Only when we know this can we know in whose interests it is acting. When the government embarks on an activity at the behest of some group, we may usually assume that this group benefits; but it is also important to ask who *would* benefit from programs

*Reprinted with permission of the author and publisher, from Richard L. Simpson, "Comment by a Sociologist," (Southwestern) Social Science Quarterly, 48 (December 1967), pp. 287–291.

the government does *not* undertake. If a community operates ten programs in behalf of business groups but none in behalf of the poor, this fact indicates who has power whether or not a conscious decision against the poor has ever been made. Indeed, if the poor have lost a fight, this means they are strong enough to have started one, and it probably means they are more powerful than if they had not even tried—than if no "issue" had ever been joined.

For these reasons, community analysts must look behind overt decisions and ask how it is that certain issues are never brought up. This requires going beyond observed behavior to inquire about unrepresented latent or potential interests. Behavioral scientists may object that this gets us into metaphysics and risks erecting imaginary "objective interests" on the foundations of the investigator's biases. Perhaps so, but on balance this risk seems smaller than that of ignoring the realities of power which make it possible for some groups but not others to fight for their interests.

Marx's notions of objectively given interests and false consciousness seem closer to the mark than Bentley's assertion that an interest is nothing more than a group engaged in behavior to realize it.[2] The elitists perceive this while the pluralists, with their stress on overt decisions, sometimes miss it. Floyd Hunter feels, for example, that the trouble with Regional City is not so much that the business elite makes bad decisions, as that the system provides no way for other groups to be heard, or even—lacking organizations to inform them—to know their own interests.[3] People have objective interests if there are activities which, if carried out, would benefit them, whether or not they know this or do anything about it. Social scientists should recognize this and ask, not just who makes decisions or wins arguments, but who benefits from the actions of government.

2. Who decides what the government will do? This is the main question posed in the elitist vs. pluralist controversy over community power. Are decisions made by a

36

Notes to this selection will be found on page 333.

small unified clique, a small clique within which there are disagreements, or a broad aggregation of contending interest groups? Is the decision-making group the same for all major issues or do different people decide different issues? Answers to this question tend to take the form of "shape models," some of which Clark identifies in a footnote: Rossi's pyramidal vs. caucus vs. polylithic vs. amorphous structures, Dahl's parallel hierarchies vs. dual leadership vs. overlapping leadership vs. strictly nonoverlapping leadership vs. weak hierarchies, and similar typologies proposed by other authors.

These power shape typologies do not always go as far as they should. To say that a structure as a whole is polylithic does not tell us whether the substructures within it are of the same or different shapes. Neither does it tell us who is included in the structure, to whom else its members are responsive, and who is entirely outside the picture. The elite theorists have answers to these questions, but the pluralists who emphasize the variety of organized interest and decision groups often pay little attention to the many citizens who are not represented by any such group. Interests may go unrepresented for want of organization and leadership, even in pluralist structures.

3. Through what process do the decision-makers decide? Do they hatch plans behind closed doors or fight things out in the public arena? What techniques of influence do they use? How do representatives of different interests interact? This question is closely related to question No. 2, the "who decides" question. Elitists usually favor the invisible-government or smoke-filled-room hypothesis. Pluralists tend to see a variety of processes at work, and when they do speak of covert decision processes, they regard the decision-makers as arbitrating among a wider array of interests than are represented around the table. Pluralists are more inclined than elitists to analyze indirect influence, anticipated reactions of those not present, and the like.

4. What are the causes of variation in No. 1, No. 2, and No. 3? Not until the

end of his paper does Clark discuss this question, and he is forced to conclude that the study of it is in its infancy. Much of the work thus far consists of proposed frameworks of analysis and hortatory discussions of the need for comparative study, rather than of actual research. Those authors who have put forth hypotheses have tended to focus on nonpolitical attributes of community social structure as determinants of the shape of the power structure. These are good beginnings, but small ones when weighed against the range of questions I have noted and the variety of dimensions of community power which Clark has identified.

State of the Literature: The Four Questions and the Fifteen Dimensions

It is around questions No. 2 and No. 3 that the Hunter vs. Dahl controversy has raged, and it has been assumed implicitly—and wrongly, I think—that to answer these questions constitutes a full answer to the *cui bono* part of question No. 1. Clark surveys a fairly representative selection of the literature in presenting his fifteen dimensions of the concept of power, and when we relate his discussion to my four questions, a heavy concentration of the literature on questions No. 2 and No. 3 is apparent.

Five of Clark's dimensions, and the literature about them, concern mainly the process question, No. 3. These are dimensions 1 (interpersonal influence), 2 (anticipated reactions), 7 (legitimation), 12 (application of power), and 13 (efficiency of power-application). In addition, while dimension 10 (visibility) is chiefly a methodological matter as Clark discusses it, its substantive element concerns question No. 3. Dimensions 9 (scope of power), 14 (the zero-sum problem and allocation of resources), and 15 (stratification of power) are aspects of question No. 2, that of who has the power. Four dimensions overlap questions No. 2 and No. 3. These are dimensions 3 (direct and indirect influence), 4 (reciprocity), 8 (number of participants in decisions), and 11 (power bases).

This leaves only two dimensions which deal with question No. 1, other than by assuming that we know who benefits from the actions of government once we have named the people directly involved in making decisions. Dimension 6 (patterns of value distribution) raises the sort of question about the decision-makers which could lead to an analysis of whom, in addition to the constituencies they visibly represent, their actions are likely to help or harm. Dimension 5 (action-inaction) gets directly at question No. 1 by pointing to the fact that power is manifested, and values are allocated, in ways other than through overt decisions. As Clark's discussion makes clear, the literature on dimensions 5 and 6 is sparse.

What Is to be Done?

I am led to several conclusions about needed work on community power. First, we should pay more attention to question No. 1, the scope of government activity and who benefits from it. Elitists like Hunter have assumed that once we know who the main decision-makers are, the other significant facts follow from this. His pluralist critics made a step forward by examining closely the processes of decision-making, and they showed that an understanding of these can give a more accurate answer to Hunter's question as well. We will take a further step forward if we inquire into the distribution of benefits, not just of government actions or of overt decisions, but also of inaction; this may tell us more than we know about who has the power and how it is won and used. Vidich and Bensman did this in their analysis of systematic inaction and its benefits for certain groups in a small town.[4] Their example would be a good one to follow. It will help toward this

kind of analysis if we look systematically at who is outside as well as inside the power structure, and the reasons for the difference.

Second, we need to devote more attention to the causes of variation in community power arrangements, using the structure and dynamics of power as dependent variables in comparative research. The power bases discussed by Clark (dimension 11) could be one springboard for such research, in which community variations in power structure are examined against the background of community variations in the distribution of these resources. It is also probable that these power resources are differentially applicable to different kinds of issues and decisions. This likelihood leads me to my third suggestion.

Finally, we should ask not only how communities differ in their distributions and processes of power, but how issues and groups differ. Just as some kinds of communities may tend to be more monolithic in power than others, there may be identifiable kinds of issues that are determined by small elites in all types of communities, and interests that are typically unrepresented. The research problem is to find out, issue by issue as well as town by town and with potential interest groupings always kept in mind, what sorts of activities the government undertakes, for whose benefit, by whose decision, arrived at through what processes, and why.

Let me illustrate what I mean with some examples. We might hypothesize that if an interest in some issue is represented by a preexisting group, it will more likely be strongly represented in the political arena than if its expression would require that a brand new group be organized out of heterogeneous elements of the population. The political superiority of business producers over household consumers illustrates this principle. A second hypothesis is that some kinds of issues are those of superimposed or multibonded groups, other issues are those of nonsuperimposed or cross-pressured groups, and the former are more apt to be powerfully represented. A current manifestation of this concerns race and class politics in American cities. The two kinds of interests are converging, with the lower class composed increasingly of Negroes, so that less and less stands in the way of lower-class unity. These simple hypotheses are not new, but I am not aware that they have been tested through comparative community research. Doing this, and putting together hypotheses like these with the typical concerns of community power analysts, would be a fruitful departure.

Another kind of hypothesis would take characteristics of an issue or possible government activity, rather than of the groups interested in it, as the independent variable. The figure below illustrates this approach, predicting power outcomes with respect to potential government actions (shown in the cells) on the basis of two independent variables: salience of the issue

or activity to the ordinary citizen, and whether the action would affect different segments of the population differently or alike. (An example of an action that affects everyone almost alike is garbage collection, assuming that the system is fairly administered. Left out of the scheme are struggles of entire communities against outside enemies.)

If we start exploring hypotheses of the general kind I am suggesting, we will move toward answers to the basic question: how, and to what extent, differing interests find representation in community power structures.

TABLE 1

Extent to Which Action Affects Groups Alike or Differently	Salience of Activity or Issue	
	Not Salient	*Salient*
Affects All Alike	Inaction	Overt elite dominance (routine administration)
Affects Groups Differently	Covert elite dominance	Public controversy

The Concept of Power: A Political Scientist's Perspective*

David M. Olson

University of Georgia

THE ANALYSIS OF community power focuses on the interactions of those possessing decisive influence over community-wide issues. This definition is broad enough to include issues resolved through governmental as well as private means. The concepts themselves of power and of power structure are not limited to the community. They are generic concepts, possessing equal validity at the national as well as local levels,[1] and within private entities such as a corporation or interest group as well as within a public community.

The generic and versatile character of the concept of power has attracted interdisciplinary attention.[2] The Clark article relies upon and cites an extensive literature in sociology, political science and economics. This interdisciplinary attention indicates that the concept of power structure has the potential to contribute to a generalized theory, integrating many other concepts and models, including decision-making, role theory, interest group, social background analysis and ecology. It employs not only survey data, but also aggregate and documentary data. It probes not only contemporary events but also those in the past. Its concepts and methods invite research not only in the scholar's own home community, but also in foreign lands. In short, community power structure analysis is a prime example of a multi-discipline, multifaceted generalized field of study applicable in a wide variety of specific settings and at many levels of abstractness. So far, at least, community power structure analysis has demonstrated these attributes far more than some other interdisciplinary undertakings: for example, voter studies.

Given the generic nature of concepts of power and the many specific components subsumed under these concepts, any listing of dimensions, as Clark recognizes, is open to the twin observation that it is neither succinct nor complete. Several relatively neglected dimensions will be commented upon here, some of which are combinations of those in the Clark article while others are additions; together they provide more questions in the study of community leadership.

More Questions

Additional or restated questions in the analysis of community power include, (1) external linkages, (2) the nondecision, (3) stage of issue development, (4) measurement of the latent issue, and (5) issue selection.

1. External linkages. Communities do not exist in a vacuum. They are contained within counties, states and nations, possessing political, social and economic attributes. These attributes condition the character of the community while the community itself or subgroups within it may be active participants in the economic and political processes of the wider jurisdictions. The differences between New Haven and Atlanta are also the differences between Connecticut and Georgia. The differences between Syracuse and New Haven are in part the differences not only in their states but also in their respective metropolitan areas.

Localities not only are influenced by, but also participate in, wider political and governmental affairs. Some studies show that community leaders specialize by governmental level,[3] while other studies show that access to political power at higher levels is an important source of power in local affairs.[4]

*Reprinted with permission of the author and publisher, from David M. Olson, "Comment by a Political Scientist," (Southwestern) Social Science Quarterly, 48 (December 1967), pp. 292–296.

Notes to this selection will be found on page 333.

As a consequence, a concentration of research upon purely local events may very well ignore substantial but external influences upon the locality and would thus not necessarily reveal leaders within the community who act upon such issues. This neglect would also leave uncovered possible sources of value bias affecting the community and subgroups within it.

Studies touching upon external linkages have indicated the dependence of municipalities upon the state. The development of federal programs will shift that dependence, with the effect of also shifting the bases of local power, and hence the identity of local influentials. The relative dependence of the large city upon federal aid contrasted with the reliance of small localities upon the state, at least in the recent past, may be associated with power structure differences between New Haven, and say, the small cities of New York State.[5]

2. The nondecision. The extent and criteria of latency are ambiguous, for the studies classify an issue as latent if an issue has been suppressed, even though someone *does* attempt to articulate an issue and make it visible.[6] The *effort* to articulate and the *effort* to suppress are overt actions, about which evidence has been gathered and reported in the studies. This action itself may be covert from the broad public, but that action indicates that the issue is not latent. Someone in the community has recognized the issue and someone has attempted to initiate consideration. The issue and action may be private and may be nonvisible to the public, but that is a different matter than latency. Latency perhaps should be better designated as

"mobilization of bias,"[7] in which the status quo, perhaps unrecognized and probably unquestioned, distributes values within a community.

We are confronted with three categories of events:

1. The negative decision is overt and perhaps publicly visible.

2. The covert-negative decision is publicly invisible, but at least one or some individuals have engaged in efforts to raise and suppress an issue.

3. The latent issue is both unrecognized and unquestioned, leading to or resulting from such things as false consciousness or alienation.

To mix the second and third distinctions results in ironic descriptions like "the highly visible 'invisible' government."[8]

3. Stage of issue development. The above discussion assumes that decision-making develops through a cycle in which issues are initiated, actively considered, resolved and implemented.[9] Each stage involves different power acts and varies in its potential for visibility, controversy and for large numbers of diverse participants. The negative decision has proceded through the stages of initiation, active consideration and resolution. The covert-negative decision has at least reached the initial stage. The latent issue does not appear at any stage of

TABLE 1. *Negative, Covert-Negative, and Latent Issues by Stage of Issue Cycle*

Issue Types	Initiation	Consideration	Resolution	Implementation
Negative-	Yes	Yes	Negative Decision	—
Covert- Negative	Yes, Though Rebuffed	—	—	—
Latent	—	—	—	—

issue development. Table 1 illustrates these relationships.

4. Measurement of the latent issue. Granted the many problems inherent in the judgment that latent issues exist in a community, experiments are needed to develop measures of this phenomenon. Clark suggests the need for surveys among the general population. Another approach might be directed to panels of knowledgeables.

To test the latter approach, fifty participants in community affairs were asked "Are there any issues or problems facing the community which have not come up for some kind of discussion or action?" This question, inserted in a broader interview, drew two types of response. Some respondents did not grasp the meaning of the question and gave no answer, while others said there were such issues. The latter type named the very issues on which they themselves were actively—but to that point unsuccessfully—engaged. The few respondents who commented at length on this question felt themselves in the minority, not a part of the established community leadership, and held a conspiracy view of politics.[10] No direct interview method has yet been reported in the literature successfully measuring the latent issue.

5. Issue selection. Issues are usually categorized on the basis of manifest content[11] and importance. The criteria of importance, in turn are usually stated in terms of cost, multiple subgroups and perception.[12]

More analytic categories of issues are needed. What differentiates issues from one another, regardless of manifest content and of specific community sectors? Urban renewal, for example, may or may not be the same *type* of issue across a spectrum of communities. Although too many power structure studies have been financed by entities with an interest in a single substantive issue, the single-issue, multicommunity study may examine systematic variations in the issue importance, sector involvement and leadership patterns within those communities.

The most complete set of analytic categories of issues yet offered in the literature utilizes five dimensions: unique–recurrent, salient-nonsalient to leadership, salient–nonsalient to the public, options for action, and local–cosmopolitan.[13] Whatever the categories, issue sampling should help us understand why one issue is present in some but not other communities, or involves a single sector as opposed to multiple sectors, or is resolved through private rather than governmental means, or is initiated or resolved at one governmental and societal level rather than another.

Case Studies and the Comparative Method

The trend toward comparative studies in this and other countries are the preferable, though expensive, way to attack the many variables, methodological controversies and possible theories in the study of community power.[14] In the very short time of a decade and a half, this field has progressed from single case studies employing single methods to samples of hundreds of communities. The difficulty with case studies—however innovative and necessary they have been and remain—is that they cannot indicate either the range or the frequency of the phenomena they report. Are polar types of power structure really indicated by the Atlanta and New Haven studies? With what frequency are these types found? For the same reasons, case studies cannot indicate the range or frequency of associated variables.

Consequently, the major operational need is to develop collections of documentary, statistical and interview data from a large number of communities in this and other countries. The interview data may largely be reputational from panels of knowledgeables, and hence be open to considerable criticism.[15] The fact that these data will be comparative, however, and amenable to statistical analysis, makes them exceedingly useful. These data will increase the utility and power of the case study as well, for they will permit the case study to be used as a sample of some known category of community. Four case studies, for example, conducted in cities selected as a sample of four types of phenomena indicated by the comparative and extensive data, should be far more productive of

David M. Olson

insight and hypotheses than four cities selected in part for their accessibility to the researcher.

The Multiplicity of Local Governments

Introduction

> To an observer from the air, a metropolitan area looks like a single city or municipality. It is not governed as one, however. Hence, "the problem of metropolitan organization."[1]

Although it is convenient to think of Chicago, Atlanta, Denver, New York, or other urban areas as "cities," each is actually composed of scores (sometimes hundreds) of governments. Table 1 depicts the staggering number of local government units in the United States at three points in time. While the total number of units has declined (primarily because of the decrease in school districts through consolidation), the number of special districts has increased considerably. These special districts are usually single-purpose governments, given taxing power to perform some specific task, such as pollution control, sanitation, drainage, or water provision. Among the 227 Standard Metropolitan Statistical Areas,[2] Chicago holds whatever distinction goes with having the most governmental units, a total of 1,113, composed of 327 school districts, 6 counties, 250 municipalities, 113 townships, and 417 special districts.

Governmental fragmentation is normally associated with the largest metropolitan areas, but it exists throughout all size classes of communities. Vidich and Bensman, in their insightful study of a community of 2,500 persons in upstate New York, observed that

> There are three major areas of politics in Springdale: village government, town government and school government. However they do not involve the same constituencies or the same political interests. The village government is excluded from jurisdiction over those who live in the country so that farmers do not participate in its affairs. The town government and the school district potentially include all residents of the township but because each encompasses different interests and purposes—road issues in one and school issues in the other—quite different groups, especially leadership groups, are involved in the political process of each.[3]

Notes to this introduction will be found on page 333.

TABLE 1.   Number and Type of Local Governments, 1957–1967*

Type	1957	1962	1967	1962–1967 Percentage Change
All Local Governments	102,341	91,186	81,248	−10.9
School Districts	50,454	34,678	21,482	−37.2
Other	51,887	56,508	59,466	5.2
Counties	3,050	3,043	3,049	0.2
Municipalities	17,215	18,000	18,948	0.3
Townships	17,189	17,142	17,105	−0.2
Special Districts	14,424	18,323	21,264	16.1

* Source: U.S. Bureau of the Census, Census of Governments 1967, Vol. 1, Governmental Organization, Washington, D.C.: U.S. Government Printing Office, 1968, Table 1.

Some scholars and reformers have written for many years about the allegedly dire consequences of a multiplicity of local governments. An excellent summary of some of the fiscal and economic disparities among metropolitan governments is provided by the Advisory Commission on Intergovernmental Relations (see Selection 6). A dominant theme of much of this literature is an exhortation to metropolitan areas to eliminate separate jurisdictions and create a single area-wide government. A trilogy of problems is alleged to arise from the decentralized character of present governmental arrangements:

1. The fragmentation of governmental power means that no effective local agency exists to manage, to service, or to resolve conflict in the community socioeconomic system. Or, in Bernard Brown's words, it is the "non-coincidence of political and economic boundaries that is referred to as the 'metropolitan problem.' "[4]

Even though the metropolitan area is a functionally differentiated and interdependent whole, there is no vehicle for coordination of public policy-making. This is not to say that there is no coordination at all in the metropolis. But the regulation that does occur is a product of the private market mechanism. Some activities such as banking or commodity distribution, which Williams (see Selection 7) would call system-maintenance activities, may be quite efficiently coordinated. Other metropolitan functions, particularly life-style activities (again, see Selection 7), like land-use planning, schooling, or pollution control, are badly planned, poorly coordinated, and differentially administered by the multiplicity of local governments. If, for example, one municipality permits its factories to pollute the air, other communities can do little to exert control over either the pollutors or the municipality.

2. An uneven distribution of resources and a corresponding uneven distribution of "problems" follows from governmental fragmentation. It is surely common knowledge that the suburbs tend to be havens of the wealthy (Whitney Young calls suburbs "gilded ghettos") and the central cities the location of the poor, the blacks, and the working class.

Table 2 indicates that, for SMSA's as a whole, there is truth in this "affluent suburbia–poor central city" image. The ratio of rich to poor families is much higher in "outside central city" areas than it is in central cities for the United States as a whole. Generally, then, this means that central cities are likely to have more than their share of problems requiring governmental attention (unemployment, squalid housing, racial conflict) and less than their share of tax resources to finance governmental action.

TABLE 2. *The Ratio of Number of Families with Incomes over $10,000 to Those Families under $3,000 per 100 Families, by SMSA Size, 1959**

Population of SMSA	Entire SMSA	Central City (CC)	Outside Central City (OCC)	Difference in Ratio (OCC–CC)
United States	124.2%	93.9%	169.4%	75.5
Over 3,000,000	183.0	126.7	311.5	184.8
1,000,000 to 3,000,000	160.5	97.3	238.9	141.6
500,000 to 1,000,000	95.6	73.8	129.3	55.5
250,000 to 500,000	82.8	78.6	87.4	8.8
100,000 to 250,000	70.3	73.1	66.6	−6.5
Less than 100,000	67.0	76.3	44.0	−32.3

* Source: Alan K. Campbell and Seymour Sacks, *Metropolitan America: Fiscal Patterns and Governmental Systems* (New York: The Free Press, 1967), Table I-18, p. 237. The data are derived from U.S. Bureau of the Census, *U.S. Census of Population, 1960. Selected Area Reports: Standard Metropolitan Statistical Areas.* Fund Report PC(3)-ID.

But, like all generalizations, the "affluence gap" between central cities and fringe areas must be carefully qualified. In the larger metropolitan areas, particularly those over half a million, the conventional wisdom seems to fit the facts. In the smaller SMSA's, however, the pattern reverses itself, with central city populations having the higher incomes, as well as higher occupational statuses and educational attainments. But whichever pattern prevails, not all governments in the urban community share equally in either problems or resources.

3. *Patterns of social, economic, and racial segregation* dominate the metropolis, since sociospatial units struggle to preserve their life-style values. Zoning and land-use regulation are the primary instruments for maintaining socially supportive environments. A wealthy, well educated, white-collar suburb will permit neither industry, nor multiple-housing units, nor low-valuation housing units, in order to secure and maintain a "quality" neighborhood. Increasingly, Negro ghetto dwellers are urging the preservation of the "integrity of the black community," rather than joining the drive for "salt-and-pepper" neighborhoods. But the consequences of racial, social, and economic segregation include variations in the calibre of schooling, in political power relationships, and in employment opportunities.

According to the critics of governmental fragmentation, the results of these "metropolitan problems" are seen in slapdash, ill-coordinated efforts to grapple with fundamental economic and social ills and in a virtual absence of efficient, rational management of public affairs in the metropolis.

A variety of reforms have been urged by these critics of metropolitan fragmentation, including city–county consolidation, metropolitan-wide supergovernments, annexations, special districts to handle area-wide problems, and metropolitan federations. The special district approach has often been utilized to perform specific functions, but it purports to solve the problem of fragmentation by adding still another unit. For some cities, including Houston, Phoenix, and Oklahoma City, the annexation approach to governmental fragmentation has worked quite well, but it is difficult to replicate that experience in older central cities already ringed by suburbs or by cities in states with restrictive annexation procedures.

The fragmented metropolis has its defenders, however, particularly on two counts. First, the defenders argue that the present decentralized structure permits the operation of a free market mechanism in location choices. If a rational citizen–consumer in a metropolitan area prefers a low-taxing, low-spending community, he can choose accordingly; if he wants a high level of public services, which will cost him higher taxes, he can opt for an amenities-oriented municipality. Other defenders of the present structure argue that the creation of metropolitan supergovern-ments would dilute the political power of disadvantaged groups, par-ticularly blacks and the poor. Three big cities (Gary, Newark, and Cleveland) have elected Negro mayors, and more will probably follow. Including all metropolitan residents in a single political community might effectively eliminate whatever political advantages the black community now possesses, making governments more responsive to a new constituency of tax-conscious urban fringe dwellers.

Whatever the merits of either side, there are a variety of explanations for this decentralized governing pattern in the community. From a historical perspective, it may be argued that the American penchant for dispersing power and the Jacksonian emphasis on governments which were "close to the people" have led to this abundance of governments, each of which is rather severely constrained both by its limited formal powers and by the existence of other local governments. From a legal perspective, the ease with which smaller communities can incorporate and the difficulty which larger cities confront in annexing unincor-porated areas in most states are additional reasons.

The approach in this section to the multiplicity of local governments is primarily derived from political sociology. Oliver Williams in Selection 7 takes a very general, but very insightful, theoretical perspective. He begins with the argument that *sociospatial units*, which include house-holds, factories, stores, offices, and the like, desire to maintain "strategic locations which afford [a] favorable message-exchange arrangement." A cacophony of lower class voices may be a most unpleasant message to a middle-income home owner; location in the midst of a residential area would deprive a factory of needed messages and message-exchange routes. Sociospatial units thus pursue the strategy of locating themselves in (and attempting to preserve) homogeneous and/or complementary areas, in order to maintain life-style preferences. Where the ease of incorporation is facilitated by state law, certain sociospatial units can even claim the sanctity of their own municipality. While it is relatively easy to integrate system-maintenance functions, integration of life-style functions will be difficult because of the desire to maintain homogeneous and complementary groupings of sociospatial units.

Most of the research undertaken by sociologists and political scientists into metropolitan reorganization clearly supports the doubts raised by Williams' theoretical perspective about the political prospects for change. Hawkins (see Selection 8) utilized a comparative, macro-level research design in comparing fifteen referenda attempts to forge a consolidated city–county government. Only three such efforts in recent years (Nashville–Davidson County, Tennessee; Miami–Dade County, Florida; and Jacksonville–Duval County, Florida) have cleared the legal and political hurdles involved in city–county consolidation. Hawkins' study indicates not only why so few efforts have succeeded but also why so few efforts have ever reached the referenda stage. He broke down each referenda into the central city and the fringe-area components, with results which indicate considerable support for Williams' thesis that life-style variations are important determinants of attitudes toward metropolitan reorganization. Life-style indicators were considerably more important than social class indicators in explaining the voting patterns. Zimmer and Hawley's research (see Selection 9), a survey of six metropolitan areas, combines the macro and micro perspectives by comparing not only variations in individual and group attitudes, but also variations in attitudes toward school district reorganization in three size classes of cities. They found sharp contrasts between attitudes of central city residents and suburban residents on reorganization proposals, contrasts which were even more acute in the larger SMSA's of Buffalo and Milwaukee. They conclude that "resistance to change is such in the larger metropolitan areas that any proposal for reorganization would be faced with overwhelming odds." The evidence from the studies by both Hawkins and Zimmer and Hawley highlights the validity of Williams' observation that the second quarter of the twentieth century was marked by political scientists' urging of reforms upon the cities, while, "in the third quarter, a major theme has been documentation of how thoroughly this advice is rejected by the American people."

METROPOLITAN GROWTH in the United States is producing patterns of racial and economic segregation, with severe consequences for disadvantaged groups, for the communities where they are concentrated, and ultimately for the entire urban society. While large numbers of people have been moving from the older central cities to the suburbs, others have been moving from rural areas into the central cities. Since World War II, there have been vast migrations of southern Negroes, Puerto Ricans, and people from Appalachia to the great cities. And while more prosperous groups were moving to the suburbs to find better housing, many earlier residents of the cities remained—some because they preferred to live in the central cities, many because they could not afford the cost of a suburban house. Within the suburbs, there has been further segregation as different builders produced new one-class communities with housing entirely in a particular price range. Local government policies have had a hand in limiting the range of families who can afford to live within their borders. Because of the high cost of providing public services for new residents, many communities have made use of zoning and other land development controls to hold down population growth and to exclude middle and lower income families whose modest houses would not yield enough in property taxes to cover their service costs. In addition, racial discrimination on the part of builders, real estate brokers, and mortgage institutions has reinforced economic segregation with direct policies of racial exclusion.

As a result of this combination of forces, low-income families, broken families, the elderly, the unemployed, and Negroes are concentrated in the central cities of most large metropolitan areas. This segregation can lead to cultural isolation of disadvantaged groups from the rest of society. Current interpretations of urban poverty stress the self-reinforcing character of the culture of poverty in which economic

*Reprinted from Advisory Commission on Intergovernmental Relations, Metropolitan America: Challenge to Federalism (Washington, D.C.: Advisory Commission on Intergovernmental Relations, 1966), pp. 3–8 and 27–28.

Metropolitan America: Some Consequences of Fragmentation*

The Advisory Commission on Intergovernmental Relations

Washington, D.C.

deprivation leads to low levels of aspiration and destroys incentives for self-improvement. Concentrations of poor people lead also to impoverished governments, unable to supply services to people who are particularly dependent on government help. People in the central cities need many kinds of government services: welfare, education, health, police, and fire protection. Yet the tax resources of these cities are limited by the very nature of their population. With the loss of middle and upper income families, as well as industries and retail firms, the central cities have been increasingly unable to raise sufficient tax revenue for their mounting service needs.

Thus the social disparities between suburban and central city communities give rise to economic and fiscal disparities as well. Tax-poor governments provide inferior services for their citizens and deny them significant opportunities to participate in the benefits of metropolitan life. As James B. Conant has noted, the great disparities between public education in the slums and in the suburbs are incompatible with the American ideal of equal opportunity for all. Educating slum children is far more difficult than educating middle-class children; yet many schools in wealthy suburbs spend $1,000 per pupil annually and provide a staff of 70 professionals per 1,000 students, while slum schools are likely to spend only half as much and to provide 40 or fewer professionals per 1,000 pupils.[1] The low level of education and other public services that the poor receive

Notes to this selection will be found on pages 333–334.

is closely related to the pattern of urban development and to its impact upon government finances.

Other detrimental consequences result from suburban growth that serves privileged groups and excludes the poor. Where residential choices available to the poor are sharply restricted, public programs that involve relocation of low-income families create severe hardship for them and retard progress toward national housing goals. Relocation for urban renewal and highway construction is one of the most troublesome elements of these programs. The disappointing results of much relocation, occasioned by the shortage of housing that low-income families can afford, have created increasing opposition to the rebuilding of central cities and the construction of needed public works.

Metropolitan Interdependence

Underlying many metropolitan problems is the failure of governmental institutions to come to grips with the growing interdependence of people and communities within metropolitan areas. As urban settlement spreads across lines of local jurisdiction, the cities and suburbs together come to comprise a single integrated area for living and working. People look for housing and employment within a broad region circumscribed more by the convenience of commuting and by personal preferences than by local government boundaries. The existence of a metropolitanwide housing and job market is, in fact, the basis for defining metropolitan areas. In the definition of the U.S. Bureau of the Budget and the Bureau of the Census, "the general concept of a metropolitan area is one of an integrated economic and social unit with a recognized large population nucleus."

The detailed criteria used in defining "standard metropolitan statistical areas" (SMSA's) provide further insight into the integrated character of these areas. Each area must contain at least one city of 50,000 inhabitants or more, or "twin cities" with a combined population of at least 50,000. The metropolitan character of the county containing the central city or cities is established by determining that the county is a place of work or residence for a concentration of nonagricultural workers. The specific conditions that must be met include a requirement that at least 75 per cent of the labor force must have nonagricultural occupations, and other tests concerning population density and job concentrations. In New England, the components of metropolitan areas are cities and towns rather than counties. Outlying counties (cities and towns in New England) are considered part of the metropolitan area if they meet either of the following tests:

1. If 15 per cent of the workers living in the county work in the county where the central city is located; or

2. If 25 per cent of those working in the outlying county live in the county where the central city is located.

If the information concerning these two requirements is not conclusive, other kinds of information are considered: reports of newspaper circulation, the extent to which residents of outlying areas maintain charge accounts in central city retail stores, official traffic counts, and other indicators of central city–suburban interaction.[2]

Metropolitan areas are integrated in other ways, as well. Local communities share many kinds of natural resources used for urban living: water supplies, drainage basins, recreation areas. They also share many manmade facilities that cut across local boundaries, such as highway and utility systems, and many other facilities that serve large segments of the metropolitan population, such as airports and commercial centers. These forms of interaction, together with the metropolitan character of housing and employment markets, create a broad area of common interest. The optimum use of shared facilities and resources calls for a high level of cooperation and for coordinated action by interdependent communities.

The policies of any one community typically have considerable impact in other parts of the metropolitan area. If one locality fails to control air or water pollution, its neighbors suffer. This principle was illustrated recently when Nassau County, which borders New York City, demanded that New York put its mosquitoes under surveillance. The public works commissioner of Nassau County charged that swarms of mosquitoes from the city had been invading Nassau territory: "Mosquitoes have no respect for boundary lines or home rule," he complained.[3]

The effects of local action (or inaction) that spread into other communities have come to be known as "spillovers." They are very common in metropolitan affairs and often consist of indirect effects. Thus, suburban communities that succeed in excluding the poor impose considerable burdens on other communities where the poor are concentrated. Spillovers can also be beneficial to neighboring localities. Effective traffic control or public health measures benefit people outside a city or town as well as local residents. Spillovers usually imply disparities between tax and service boundaries. Thus the residents of central cities may be taxed to provide services that are important to the suburbs as well as to themselves. Or suburbanites may be taxed to clean up polluted streams that flow into neighboring territory. In all these cases, people who do not live in a particular jurisdiction nevertheless have a strong interest in its performance of government functions.

The prevalence of spillovers constitutes a strong case for cooperation in metropolitan areas. Metropolitan service needs also provide compelling arguments for joint action. In such fields as water supply and sewage disposal, the cost of service per household can be reduced dramatically in large-scale operations by joint agreement of local governments. Similarly, areawide transportation systems—highways, public transit—require joint planning if they are to provide needed service at reasonable cost.

Despite the evident and important benefits of cooperative action in metropolitan areas, many local governments continue to go it alone. The realities of functional interdependence in metropolitan areas are in conflict with concepts of home rule that predate the age of metropolitan growth. Home rule in the contemporary metropolitan setting has often led to local isolation and conflict, to the detriment of the metropolitan population at large. Each community, in pursuing its own interests, may have an adverse effect on the interests of its neighbors. A major task for government in metropolitan areas is to develop policies consistent with the integrated character of the modern metropolitan community. Federal policies are guided increasingly by an awareness of this need, as President Johnson emphasized in his message on the cities:

> The interests and needs of many of the communities which make up the modern city often seem to be in conflict. But they all have an overriding interest in improving the quality of life of their people. And they have an overriding interest in enriching the quality of American civilization. These interests will only be served by looking at the metropolitan area as a whole, and planning and working for its development.

Governmental Obstacles

The fundamental metropolitan problem is not that there are difficulties in supplying public services or ameliorating social and economic disparities. It is that governments in metropolitan areas are often unable to cope with these issues. The system of local government in the United States has many achievements to its credit, but, like any social system, it also has its disadvantages. Within metropolitan areas, many important issues of public policy can no longer be handled by local communities acting alone; their small areas of jurisdiction are inadequate for either administering areawide services or resolving areawide problems.

The close ties of people and businesses to one another in metropolitan areas have no parallel in government. While social and economic relationships have shifted to an enlarged metropolitan scale, governments and the loyalties they inspire have remained local. As Roscoe Martin has put it:

> The metropolitan area has no capital, courthouse, or city hall, no corporate existence, no body, no soul, no sense of being, indeed no being in any concrete meaning of the term. Al Smith was from the sidewalks of New York, not from the sidewalks of the New York-Northeastern New Jersey standard consolidated area.[4]

Metropolitan areas are governed not only by traditional cities, towns, and counties, but also by a wide variety of special districts that overlap other boundaries. The complexity of local government can be illustrated by listing the array of local jurisdictions responsible for Park Forest, a suburb of Chicago, as of 1956: Cook County, Will County, Cook County Forest Preserve District, village of Park Forest, Rich Township, Bloom Township, Monee Township, Suburban Tuberculosis Sanitarium District, Bloom Township Sanitary District, Non-High School District 216, Non-High School District 213, Rich Township High School District 227, Elementary School District 163, South Cook County Mosquito Abatement District.[5]

Fragmentation of this kind may appear to bring government "closer to the people," but it compounds the difficulties of achieving coordination within metropolitan areas. Political responsibility for government performance is divided to the point of obscurity. Public control of government policies tends to break down when citizens have to deal with a network of independent governments, each responsible for highly specialized activities. Even where good channels are developed for registering public concern, each government is so circumscribed in its powers and in the area of its jurisdiction that important metropolitan action is virtually impossible for local governments to undertake. If a few governments are prepared to agree on joint measures or coordinated programs, their efforts can be blocked by others that are unwilling to cooperate.

Local governments, fragmented as they are, nevertheless keep the metropolis running. They operate the schools, maintain the streets, take care of police and fire protection. But when issues of metropolitanwide importance arise—such as commuter transportation, water supply, or racial and economic segregation—people must turn to other channels for action. As Robert Wood has pointed out, an "embryonic coalition" of metropolitan leaders tends to emerge to tackle areawide problems. These leaders—politicians, editors, businessmen, labor leaders—operate informally and outside the regular structure of government, as they attempt to prod government into action. They lack the requirements for effective policymaking: an adequate institutional base, legal authority, direct relationships with the metropolitan constituency, and established processes for considering and resolving issues as they emerge.[6]

When important public issues can only be handled informally and outside government channels, it is time to review the system of government in metropolitan areas and to regard the shortcomings of this system as major problems in themselves. Norton Long has set the problems of metropolitan areas in this political context:

> The problems of the metropolis are important, but not because of flooded cellars or frustrated motorists, nor because they seriously threaten the viability of the metropolitan economy. They are important because they are symptomatic of the erosion of the competence of local government.... The threat of the eroded central city and the crazy-quilt triviality of suburbia is the threat to destroy the potential of our maintaining and reconstructing meaningful political communities at the local level. What has been treated as a threat to our physical well-being is in reality a threat to our capacity to sustain an active local civic life.[7]

Disparities and Fragmented Government

It is clear from this review that the metropolis occupies a key position in the social and economic life of the United

States. Most of the people and wealth of the country are now found in metropolitan areas, and virtually all future growth is expected to take place in a metropolitan setting. Metropolitan areas have many assets that help explain their prosperity and continued expansion. This survey is not concerned solely with metropolitan resources, however, but with several factors of prime importance for government performance in metropolitan areas: the distribution of people, economic resources, and the pattern of local government.

Two major themes emerge from this overview: the existence of social and economic disparities which tend to divide metropolitan areas into distinct groupings of people; and the complexity of government structure which also tends to divide the metropolis into diverse local units.

Analysis of data from the 1960 census confirms the prevalence of significant social, economic, and racial disparities which vary in degree and direction between central cities and suburbs according to the characteristics and location of metropolitan areas, The popular stereotype of central cities populated largely by the poor and surrounded by high-status, wealthy suburbs is subject to several important qualifications. There is much truth in this image in the large metropolitan areas and in those of the Northeast, but elsewhere the situation is different. Nevertheless, the disparities found within metropolitan areas indicate a number of gaps between human needs and economic resources in different parts of these areas.

Further constraints on governmental activity are to be found in the pattern of local government. The number of governmental units in metropolitan areas is large and still growing. The organization of government is extremely complex, with

considerable diffusion of responsibility and overlapping of jurisdictions. Complexity of the governmental pattern is not a problem in itself, but it may retard the coordination of public services in urban areas and the fixing of clear lines of responsibility for policy.

Information on local government revenues and expenditures provides some insight into the impact of local problems and public efforts to deal with them. Local governments within metropolitan areas receive more revenue per capita than those in the rest of the country, but they depend more heavily on property taxes and other local sources and less on State aid. They also spend more per capita overall, mainly because of a greater need for services that are basically urban, such as police and fire protection and urban renewal and housing. Within metropolitan areas, total central city expenditures per capita are higher than those in the suburbs: Expenditures for education and highways tend to be higher in the suburbs, but most other outlays, particularly for police and welfare, are higher in the core cities. . . .

The facts of population disparities, government structure, and expenditure patterns in themselves, however, go a long way toward explaining the conflicts of interest between local governments with different needs and varying resources. At the same time, they suggest the need for measures to overcome the frequency gaps between local needs and resources, such as government reorganizations within metropolitan areas and assistance from the States and the Federal Government.

Life-Style Values and Political Decentralization in Metropolitan Areas*

Oliver P. Williams[1]

University of Pennsylvania

THROUGH the second quarter of this century many political scientists were writing on why metropolitan areas needed to be politically integrated through local government consolidation. Thus far, in the third quarter, a major theme has been documentation of how thoroughly this advice is rejected by the American people. Assuming that the present, decentralized, metropolitan political structures are rather durable, instead of transitory, phenomena, it behooves us to develop models which enable us to understand them as well as to evaluate their social consequences. A substantial beginning has been made with respect to both of these concerns. This paper seeks to improve on existing analytical models of metropolitan politics as a step toward guiding empirical research and sharpening our perceptions of the social values served by the new metropolitan urban form.

Existing Models and Their Shortcomings

Essentially, three models have been developed to explain the proliferation of

*Reprinted with permission of the author and publisher, from Oliver P. Williams, "Life Style Values and Political Decentralization in Metropolitan Areas," (Southwestern) Social Science Quarterly, 48 (December 1967), pp. 299–310, and from Terry N. Clark (ed.), Community Structure and Decision Making: Comparative Analyses (San Francisco: Chandler Publishing Co., 1968), pp. 427–440.

governments and the relationships among them in metropolitan areas. These three—international relations, the market place and power structure—will be briefly reviewed, and then an alternative will be suggested. We will ignore here the eclectic approaches which list separate sets of "political" considerations to explain events in each metropolitan area. It is assumed that theories which promise a higher level of generality should be explored before we resign ourselves to *ad hoc* explanations.

The international-relations model was probably first suggested by Victor Jones,[2] then restated by Matthew Holden[3] and given an operational test by James V. Toscano.[4] The model relies primarily upon analogies between the relationships among nation states and those among municipalities in a metropolitan area. Parallels are seen between alliances and special districts, international organizations and councils of governmental officials (such as the Association of Bay Area Governments), and imperialism and annexation. The problem of any analogy is that it glosses over dissimilarities. For example, one of the old saws of international relations is that economic integration precedes political integration among nations. But metropolitan areas are economically integrated; that is what gives them their identity. Furthermore, most metropolitan areas were once more fully politically integrated than they are now. Despite economic integration, metropolitan areas have become politically decentralized.

The real test of the usefulness of international-relations analogies lies, however, in attempts at concrete analysis. One such attempt was made by Toscano,[5] who employed several transaction flow theories, taken from the literature on integration among nations. One hypothesis he tested was derived from spill-over theory. According to this theory, if municipalities learn to agree in one area, they are likely to agree in others. Thus, the experience of successful cooperation will have cumulative effect, and the areas of cooperation will be extended. Toscano's findings did not substantiate this hypothesis, for the substantive content of the service in question, rather than the

Notes to this selection will be found on page 334.

experience of interacting, appeared to be the controlling variable.[6] Communication, as such, was not the key.

The market-place model treats each municipality as an enterprise in the business of supplying services.[7] The core city, suburbs and satellite cities each offer a different bundle of services which attract a different type of customer. Thus, families seeking good schools for their children go to suburbs that offer quality school services. Resistance to consolidations is an expression of a desire to preserve a particular service mix. However, all services cannot be provided on a small-area basis. This problem is covered by the concept of "packageability" of Ostrom, *et al.*[8] Special districts emerge when the municipalities prove too small to comprehend a problem. Air pollution control needs a different size "package" from police service.

The market-place model does have certain attractive features which will be developed later. The fact remains, however, that there is a surprising incongruity between actual service areas and the technically required service area, such as, for example, in controlling pollution in most metropolitan areas. In addition there is some question as to whether the model conceives the time sequence properly. Which comes first, the specialized suburb or its specialized services?

The third model, power structure, raises the question of whether services, which are integrated on an area-wide basis, coincide with the interest of a metropolitan-wide political elite. Is there an elite which integrates those functions in which it has a particular stake and then ignores all others, which remain decentralized? The power-structure approach was first suggested by Floyd Hunter,[9] who defined the Regional City political community in metropolitan dimensions. A specific effort was made to verify this model in the Syracuse study,[10] which concluded that no overall elite existed and that political leadership varied from one functional service area to another. A more extreme statement rejecting the power-structure model was made by Norton Long,[11] who saw the relationships among the metropolitan political structures as

ecological in nature. He viewed the metropolitan governmental service pattern as resulting from unplanned and uncoordinated actions.

The shortcoming of all three models, as valuable as some of their insights are, is the failure to perceive the characteristic differences between the services which are centralized and those which are decentralized, or the misconstruction of the basis of the distinction where it is perceived. It is the thesis of this paper that a distinction does exist and that it can be identified in terms of values. Models which restrict their attention to economics, technology or communications will fail to be sufficiently comprehensive, despite the relevance of each of these variables to a theory of metropolitan politics.

The Development of Municipal Life Styles

While the service–market-place theory represents a sound observation, it starts too late in the process of metropolitan development. It is necessary to begin earlier and ask about the way the new metropolitan form emerged. This subject must be dealt with in a brief and suggestive manner here. Economic location theory and cultural ecology will be used as points of departure.

Locational theory endeavors to explain the urban land-use pattern in terms of space-friction costs and rent.[12] Every economic unit seeks that place in the urban environment where the cost of overcoming space friction is minimized. Space friction exists because of each unit's need of other units to carry out its own purposes. For example, a firm must assemble a labor force, obtain supplies and deliver its product to customers. As more than one economic unit attempts to occupy the same site in an effort to minimize the cost of overcoming space friction, rent becomes the determining factor in deciding site occupation. The unit which can exploit a given location most profitably will occupy it through paying higher rent. As similar units seek similar locations, certain homogeneous groupings emerge (*e.g.* industrial areas; CBD).

If we attempt to explain the location of homesites in the same fashion, after scant analysis, it becomes abundantly clear that the family is not simply an economic unit. Urban ecologists discovered years ago that social values contribute to homesite selection.[13] More recent surveys find families moving to suburbs for a syndrome of child-rearing reasons. Despite the influence of social values, rent also acts as a constraining factor. Thus both the theories of land economics and cultural ecology must be used in explaining urban location decisions.

By employing a slightly different perspective we can bring together the statements of the economic location theorists and the cultural ecologists, enabling us to talk of all locational decisions with one set of references, minimizing confusion in our discussion. Lewis Mumford has characterized a city as a "special receptacle for storing and transmitting messages."[14] This is to say that a city is a device for overcoming space friction for a social purpose. The content of these messages and the relative importance of particular types of messages vary over time and from city to city. Economic message exchanges are very important in our contemporary cities, but they are not the only ones. Middle-class families choose suburban locations with lots of grass, but more important, these are locations where the variety of home-related message exchanges are compatible with middle-class values. These are usually more social and educational than economic. Locational choices are made not only to increase the ease of exchanging rewarding messages, but also to minimize unrewarding and unwanted messages. This is particularly true of our homesite selection illustration. A middle-class family chooses a suburb which will also reduce unpleasant message exchanges from lower-class persons in the form of muggings, fistfights and uncouth syntax.

Strategic locations, which afford the favorable message exchange arrangement, once acquired, must be safeguarded. The location requires protection, for the curse of urbanism is the instability of site advantages. A variety of social institutions, of which the municipality is one, help to protect the place of advantage for its constituents and to slow down the forces of change. Strategic locations can be maintained, in part, by policies which regulate who will occupy adjacent locations. The values of one household are affected by the values of adjacent ones, particularly if there are children, for modes of child rearing become an issue. Viewed in these terms, zoning is a device for maximizing rewarding message exchanges and minimizing unpleasant ones, through assuring the spatial contiguity of compatible message generating units. This language may be a bit overwhelming for describing "neighboring," but it permits us to refer to such different social institutions as factories and homes with a common set of concepts.

The political unit in metropolitan analysis is a social unit which has a spatially definable domicile. These units (which we shall call *sociospatial* units) include households, factories, stores, churches, clubs, offices, etc. Each one of these sociospatial units possesses a hierarchy of values. For example, businesses generally wish to maximize profits, but the profit value subsumes intermediate values, such as a desire for expansion room, accessibility to a high-class labor force, protection from pilfering, etc. Households may seek quality education, convenient shopping, pleasant neighbors and a short trip to work. These sets of values may be called the unit's *life-style values*. The realization of some of these life-style values is enhanced by the locational choices of the unit; some require the support of local services for their realization. Those life-style values which depend upon location for their realization are the major sources of metropolitan politics. Local government, in its various manifestations, is the governmental level which has primary control over the immediate physical and social environment of any given sociospatial unit. The physical environment includes such factors as highway access patterns, parks, the location of facilities and other mapable and physically describable appurtenances. The social environment includes the proximate social processes and institutions.

One of the important strategies commonly pursued by sociospatial units in maximizing their possibilities for realizing life-style values is homogeneous and complementary groupings. Jane Jacobs' importations to the contrary notwithstanding, this remains a cardinal principle of most city planning.[15] Subdivisions, industrial parks and shopping centers are the norm. Following the logic of this strategy, a decentralized (suburbanized) metropolitan governmental pattern appears to be a superior mode to a centralized (consolidation) one for the enhancement of life-style values. Under the former arrangement, diverse groups need not constantly compete in the same political arena, a situation characteristic of heterogeneous units, such as the core city (particularly as it has existed traditionally). The more nearly the suburb specializes, the easier it is, politically, to maintain the primacy of the values prized by the dominant type of sociospatial unit. This point brings up the question of why any specialized suburb would ever voluntarily consent to amalgamate with another whose life style was different.

The above analysis is not incompatible with the market-place model; it is simply more inclusive. Location choices are made in relationship to many factors, of which municipal services is one—how important a one, we do not know. It is certainly the case that once established, suburbs offer specialized service packages. Some offer good schools, large lot zoning and a country squire physical setting. Some may be more predisposed to fitting parochial schools into the service set. A list of a few of the exotic types might include the suburb that caters to industries only, where night watchmen supply the required population to establish a voting citizenry; the vice suburb that services a metropolitan area in illicit entertainment by selective police-enforcement policies. California even has its dairy-

farm suburbs, sort of anti-urban islands in an urban sea. These places all have their specialized service packages, which do act as advertisements saying, in effect, "all those who like the kind of life symbolized by these services come and join us, if you can afford it."

THE INTERDEPENDENCE OF SPECIALIZED MUNICIPALITIES

What has been said up until now will enable one to understand much of metropolitan politics, but it only covers half of the situation. It is the other half that leads to many of the intense political battles. The municipalities of the metropolitan area are specialized and, consequently, interdependent. One specialized area can only exist if its complement in specialization exists elsewhere. If there is an industrial suburb, there must also be a residential one; if there is a rich man's suburb, there must also be one for the poor. The fact of inter-relatedness is dramatized twice daily by glutted commuter arteries, leading not only to the core city, but criss-crossing in every direction, through any major metropolitan area.

If it were not for this interdependence, each little specialized suburb could have its political cake and eat it too. All local policies could be conceived in terms of self images. But the dynamics of the metropolis will not let that occur. These dynamics are expressed through the need to create integrating mechanisms which, though they maintain the overall system of specialized areas, often transform the nature and character of individual municipalities in the process.

The *system-maintenance* mechanisms of the metropolis may be classified into two principal categories, the communications and utility systems. Here, "communication system" is intended to include what is traditionally called "transportation," as well as "communications." Mumford's messages, so to speak, take physical as well as symbolic forms. Highways, airports, mass transit, telephone, telegraph, radio, television, delivery services, mail and water transport facilities comprise the principal communications system. Each of these systems must have a jurisdiction larger than any single municipality, for it is their function to integrate the specialized municipalities into an operating whole.

The utility networks supply power, water and waste-disposal services which enable the technological appurtenances of each sociospatial unit to carry on. For technological and financial, rather than functional, reasons, the utilities are usually operated as large area networks, which supply services to more than one municipality. But strictly speaking, none of the utilities have to be larger than a given municipality in order to be functionally operative. Miniaturization of these services can take place in the form of on-site facilities and small package plants.

There is, in addition, a third set which might be considered system-maintenance mechanisms—the central facilities. These are the major service facilities in urban areas which sustain and support urban life. These exist in both the private and public sectors. In the more public sector, every metropolitan area requires the presence of one or more university, museum, stadium, arena, library, hospital, etc. These are most often handled through *ad hoc* and semipublic arrangements which infrequently demand intergovernmental cooperation for their creation. For those that are revenue producing, a single government, often the core city, will act as an entrepreneur in providing the service. Generally, central facilities are not major sources of political friction.

The system-maintenance functions do just what those words imply: they maintain the over-all system, and in the process, assure that particular life-style values are preserved or enhanced. In this sense, they are instrumental services. However, these services not only bind the specialized areas into an overall social and economic system; they also profoundly affect the spatial distribution of specialized areas. Strategic

locations are, in large part, defined in relationship to the system-maintenance functions. This is particularly the case with the communications systems, of which the ground transportation arteries are the most important. Utility networks play a similar role, but to a much lesser extent, and their role varies more radically from place to place. The existence of central facilities makes the truncated service complements of small suburbs possible.

It is the central argument of this paper that the sociospatial units resist integration of what I have called life-style services, but accept, and at times encourage, integration of system-maintenance services. More accurately, this is the response when the issues are perceived correctly. The consequences of structural changes in service arrangements are subject to numerous interpretations. Campaigns can be obfuscating, and adroit publicity in the context of a metropolitan referendum can at times place issues in a light which does not foretell their likely consequences. However, only occasionally will the campaign techniques by themselves control outcomes. The proposition about decentralized life-style services and centralized system-maintenance services generally holds true.

Metropolitan politics may be further understood by the realization that various systems-maintenance services have quite different impacts in the course of their creation or expansion. The most essential difference lies in their feedback effect on locational advantages. Several illustrations will help in clarifying this point.

Let us consider the differential effects stemming from the expansion of an intra-urban expressway and a telephone system in a metropolitan area. When a new highway is built, it alters the whole pattern of accessibility among points within the metropolis. Areas which were previously too remote for commuter homes suddenly become accessible in a time-of-travel sense. New interchanges in places which previously had no attractions for these uses, become desirable locations for shopping centers and warehouses. A new expressway causes many incongruities between social and economic values attached to locations and the existing zoning ordinances. The established life style of communities becomes threatened by the invasion of sociospatial units whose values are at variance with those already existing in the community.

Contrast this situation with the impact of the extension of a telephone system. Within certain limits, there are no spatially strategic access points in a telephone system. Aside from a few esthetic objections to new utility poles, telephone system expansion does not disturb the ecological balance of areal specialization. This, indeed, may explain why highways are publicly owned and telephones are not.

Let us look at the highway problem more closely. If highways do not comprise some semblance of a network, they are not even highways, because they are supposed to go to places where travelers want to go. To be integrated, they must be planned, not simply added to by each suburban increment to the metropolis. Therefore, there is a tacit consent that area-wide governmental agencies have control of highways (usually the state, and now, more and more, the federal government). At the same time, highway construction is the most volatile metropolitan policy area. Every new expressway is fought vehemently; yet it is built! The reason the battle is so intense and bitter is that the life style of some areas must be sacrificed to maintain the life styles of most other areas. There is a wrenching conflict between the benefited and the disrupted. Frequently, the problem is solved by building highways through areas with the fewest political resources for obstructionism, or through areas that may acquire actual benefits, such as an industrial or a commercial area. Highway politics cannot be explained in any economic gains and losses fashion. Communities in which land values will be enhanced by highway construction often still oppose it.

Thus it can be seen that the integration and centralization of system-maintenance functions does not always proceed with ease or without conflict. But the process does continue, though interrupted by occasional reversals. Strategies may have to be changed, but in the long run, the pattern does not.

While it is possible conceptually to classify municipal services into life-style and system-maintenance policies, it is more likely that we are dealing with a continuous, rather than a dichotomous, variable. The scale on the life-style side refers to the importance of the service in maintaining preferred values. Probably the most critical policy is land use regulation, with education a close second. Both of these policy areas have great potential for affecting the rate of rewarding or disruptive message exchanges. Following along the continuum, such policies as housing, urban renewal, recreation, libraries, police and parks follow in approximately that order of importance. Certain health and welfare functions may be affectively neutral, along with such minor administrative matters as joint purchasing and police radio networks.

A similar continuum exists on the system-maintenance side, which is related to the importance of the service to the continued existence of specialized areas. Here, central facilities are least important, utilities next, with the communication services most vital. In addition, different sociospatial units have different value hierarchies. It follows, therefore, that one suburb might bitterly oppose the integration of a certain service, while another would remain neutral on the issue.

INTERVENING VARIABLES

This life-style theory describes an ideal type; no metropolitan area behaves exactly as the theory predicts. However, if it is correct, deviations must be explained in terms of intervening variables. Alternatively, to the extent that actual metropolitan areas approach the ideal type, its politics will conform to that predicted. This can be stated in the form of propositions: for example, the more specialized the political sub-units of a metropolitan area, the more political behavior in the area will conform to that predicted. This means the factors which influence the development of municipal specialization are key areas for investigation.

Specialization should be considered an indicator, for it is only the precondition for a set of social actions. Specialization is the basis for a sense of community solidarity and identity which in turn leads to a protective posture. What can match tl.e political fervor of a Grosse Point on a zoning issue or a Cicero on civil rights.

The identification of the politically relevant kinds of specialization has not been developed. Some preliminary investigations have been performed by the author and associates[16] in relating demographic characteristics and policy variations among suburbs. This analysis was based largely on census and fiscal data, both of which are rather blunt instruments. However, positive relationships were established. Work needs to proceed, both in developing indicators of specialization and in establishing the critical breaking points.

Specialization has been chosen as the appropriate descriptive term over homogeneity because even the most suburban municipal units embrace a certain variety and range of sociospatial units. There are some extremely homogeneous suburbs, but they remain as examples of specialization fully developed. Normally, municipal boundaries do not operate as sharp demographic breakpoints. Any municipality can absorb a certain degree of internal diversity and still maintain a dominant style. In fact, a certain degree of internal diversity is often required for the maintenance of daily activities. However, a scanning of the range of mean values describing any municipal characteristic in a metropolitan area will quickly establish that real diversity (specialization) exists.

If the degree of specialization is a key to the decisions made in a metropolitan area, those factors which influence the degree of specialization become relevant intervening variables. Three conditions are likely to influence the degree of specialization.

1. *The larger the metropolitan area, the more specialized are the municipal units.*

Suburban specialization in a small metropolitan area is likely to be confined to the "good" and the "other" side of town, in a rudimentary Hoyt-sector fashion. Larger metropolitan areas are likely to contain the many gradations of status-class residential suburbs, as well as highly specialized industrial, commercial and other types of suburbs. It is probably also the case that specialization is somewhat related to the size of the municipality, with smaller places being more specialized.

2. *The older the metropolitan area, the more specialized its municipal units.* The assumption here is that place identities become crystallized over time. Moves are made with a greater awareness of the life style of each place. In the burgeoning, newer metropolitan areas, growth may take place so rapidly that the visibility of the life style remains low and the local political structures are not sufficiently stable to employ effective screening policies for entering sociospatial units.

3. *The more permissive state incorporation laws are for local self determination, the more specialized the municipal units.* The postulated metropolitan behavior should be most fully realized when the metropolitan citizens have free choice in drawing their municipal boundaries. In fact, the opportunities for doing so vary greatly from state to state. Some states, such as Michigan and California, for years gave suburban residents wide latitude in fringe incorporation decisions. In the East, suburban boundaries are largely predetermined by traditional town and township lines. In still other states, such as Texas, the core city has had the initiative with respect to annexing fringe areas. However, even under this circumstance a vigorous outcropping of fringe area incorporations has taken place.[17]

Metropolitan area politics is a function not only of internal circumstances, but also of outside influences emanating from state and federal governments. The theory is formulated with reference to indigenous forces. There remains the possibility that accommodations within the metropolitan areas can be amended by higher levels of government. This appears not to be the case to any great extent, because higher levels seem to respect, rather than disrupt, the metropolitan settlement. Interventions from the federal government are most forceful in the system-maintenance areas. The only substantial area in which the federal government is willing to require authoritative metropolitan-wide planning as a condition for receiving grants-in-aid is in the interstate highway program. Contrast its policies here with those in housing and urban renewal, where federal policy operates fully within the metropolitan framework of decentralizing decisions on life-style policies.

The policies of state governments do not vary radically from those of the federal government. Mandatory county assumption of services is likely to be confined to the more neutral or low-conflict service areas such as the distribution of categorical welfare payments or health benefits. In both of these areas, benefits are distributed to individuals and the policies have little affect on the life style of any community. (The county services which antedate metropolitan development may be exceptions to these observations.) In fact, state grant-in-aid programs financially underwrite the whole decentralized pattern of metropolitan areas. Particularly school aid provides a fiscal flow enabling poor suburbs to maintain autonomous school districts. This takes some of the pressure off the consolidation movement. Although there may be some states which are exceptions to the above generalizations, with reapportionment placing more power in the hands of the suburbs, future development is likely to follow the predicted course.

SOCIAL CONSEQUENCES OF SPECIALIZATION

At the outset, it was stated that we have, at present, neither an adequate analytical model of metropolitan area politics nor a proper appreciation of the social significance of what is occurring. If the life-style theory presented here describes the present state, but, more important, the future course of metropolitan development, its probable social consequences are worthy of serious consideration.

Metropolitan areas, as presently constituted, will eventually find solutions for

system-maintenance services. Many writers point to this trend as a proof of the ability to muddle through using present governmental structures. In the short run, it is often more of a muddle than muddling through, as some of the system-maintenance services are expanded only after protracted and costly delays. A twenty-year gap between need and construction of a given facility is not uncommon. Even if we accept this course of decision making as normal, the decentralization of life-style policies promises to remain a durable arrangement. It is easy to dismiss this as no problem. People are happier living where they have compatible neighbors; certain forms of specialization are highly efficient. But, is the new metropolitan form the best of all possible urban political structures? There remain a number of concerns.

Little research has been done in the United States on life in a specialized community. The English sociologists have shown greater interest in this subject partly because of the new towns policies. Peter Willmott reports on life in a large, homogeneous and mature working-class suburb of London.[18] Homogeneity has removed much conflict from the lives of its inhabitants and contentment is the norm. But there were other consequences of this specialized life style. The school system was miserable. Upward mobility was positively discouraged by the culture of the community. We are now developing our working class suburbs, and the school situations are similar. What does the new metropolitan form mean for the future of social mobility?

The metropolitan form, as it is now emerging, is an ecological heaven for whites only. The most disturbing incidences of racial violence in the North are not in the core cities, but in the suburbs. In the core cities, the police force must maintain some semblance of neutrality; at least there is political recourse when it does not. In the specialized suburbs, the whole power of law, police, and social institutions is likely to be arrayed on one side of the conflict, and this assures that the possibility for racial residental mobility will be narrowly circumscribed.

In every major metropolitan area, there are developing obsolete suburbs and satellite cities that are as dysfunctional, in terms of locational and physical requirements for contemporary urban life, as are the old prairie, wheat-belt service towns. As the suburbs spiral down, they have an accumulation of tax, service and leadership woes. Unlike the heterogeneous and diversely composed core cities, which mobilize strengths and resources from viable areas in order to cope with problem areas, the deteriorating suburb cannot employ this urban renewal strategy. When a suburb goes down, people just move away and normally there is no unit of local government that can or will assume responsibility for what happens.

There are other possible consequences of the new metropolitan form. Are we creating unemployment by decentralizing manufacturing, yet excluding low-wage persons from access to jobs because of the absence of suitable housing? Few suburbs will permit public or low-cost housing to be built near the very factories they seek to alleviate property-tax problems. Public health departments tend to exist more in the high-status suburbs than in the low-status ones. Libraries, recreational programs and government financed social services exhibit a similar pattern.

In brief, while our national attention is focused on the problems of our core cities as dumping grounds for the unfortunate metropolitan citizens, we may be creating a new system, which, in the long run, will have even more unfortunate consequences for the distribution of opportunities. At least the core city has high visibility; consequently, its problems are politically salient at the state and national levels. What is emerging in the new metropolitan form may be more easily overlooked. Thus, even if the study of municipal specialization falls short of explicating metropolitan intergovernmental relations, though this author believes this will not be the case, it is a subject worthy of our attention for other reasons.

OUR MAIN INTEREST in this study is an exploratory one of finding variables that are associated with voter support of city–county consolidation. Reformers who champion governmental integration often ignore the question of the political feasibility of their reforms. The necessary voter support has not usually been forthcoming. The present analysis of voter support focuses on the impact of different "ways of life" and thus connects this exploration with those theories of political integration that stress the relevance of life styles and demographic distance.[2] Several social scientists suggest that divergent life styles are an obstacle to the integration of political communities. Philip E. Jacob and James V. Toscano have said, for example, that "communities whose members are very different from one another will have a very hard time achieving or maintaining political integration."[3]

Life styles are thus considered to be one determinant of political integration. Proposed research strategies in this field have stressed the importance of understanding environmental correlates of the integrative behavior of areas and voters, the distribution of shared values within and among political communities, and the nature of various interactions or exchanges between communities.

This paper deals with environmental correlates of the YES vote of cities and fringes on proposals to consolidate American cities and counties. City–county consolidation was chosen for several reasons. The special interest of administrative reformers was one reason; another was the literature suggesting that central cities and fringes typically display divergent life styles. To the degree that cities and fringes do in fact display generic life-style differences, efforts to consolidate cities and counties seemed to be good places to explore the impact of different styles of life on the integration of political communities. A final reason for choosing this focus was

*Reprinted with permission of the author and publisher, from Brett W. Hawkins, "Life Style, Demographic Distance and Voter Support of City–County Consolidation," (Southwestern) Social Science Quarterly, 48 (December 1967), pp. 325–337.

Life Style, Demographic Distance, and Voter Support of City–County Consolidation*

Brett W. Hawkins[1]

University of Wisconsin, Milwaukee

that it offered a theoretically meaningful operationalization of the term "political integration."

The term is here operationalized as the attempted consolidation of a city and a county, the success of which is determined by local referendum. The latter seems important in an exploration of the relationship between locally divergent life styles and support of integration. The requirement of local approval would seem to arouse different emotions than referenda not requiring local approval. The referenda covered in this analysis are, as far as the author can determine, the universe of such city–county consolidation referenda since 1945:[4]

Baton Rouge–East Baton Rouge Parish[5]	1949
Hampton–Elizabeth City County	1952
Newport News–Warwick[6]	1958
Nashville–Davidson County	1958
Albuquerque–Bernalillo County	1959
Knoxville–Knox County	1959
Macon–Bibb County	1960
Durham–Durham County[7]	1961
Richmond–Henrico County	1961
Columbus–Muscogee County	1962
Memphis–Shelby County	1962
Nashville–Davidson County	1962
Virginia Beach–Princess Anne County	1963
South Norfolk–Norfolk County	1963
Chattanooga–Hamilton County	1964

65

Notes to this selection will be found on pages 334–336.

Hypotheses

The authors of one study using life-style
concepts suggest that the family-centered
style of life involves a commitment to the
local area; while the "urban" style of life,
with its non-familistic character, involves
little commitment to the local area. As a
result of this line of thinking, Kaufman and
Greer hypothesized that urbanism would be
positively related to voter support of an
area-wide special district (in St. Louis).
They also suggested that in low urbanism
areas an area-wide government proposal
would look like a threat to the local community, and might also raise the specter of
higher taxes. Based on this view of the
impact of low urbanism, the present author
expected that familism would be negatively
associated with voter support of city–
county consolidation.[8]

Kaufman and Greer also hypothesized
that social rank (social status) would be
positively related to the vote for an area-
wide government. Their reasoning was that
higher status voters would be more likely
to understand a complex governmental
reorganization proposal and more likely to
be swayed by its good government aspects.[9]
Dye, in addition, has tested and found
support for a similar hypothesis that city
social rank is positively related to city
annexation activities.[10]

Another way to analyze the impact of
locally divergent ways of life is to look at
demographic distance, or indicators of the
status and life-style differences between
communities or people. In his study of
conditions associated with annexation by
American cities, Dye examined the relationship between city annexation activity and
the status differential between city and
suburb.[11] An independent negative relationship was found between annexation activity
and demographic distance favoring the
suburbs. (By speaking of demographic
distance in "favor" of the fringe we refer to
conditions in which the fringe has a higher
per cent of high school graduates, more

single family dwelling units, more children
per 100 women, and so on.)

Still another variable of possible importance in life-style terms is the proportion of
typically segregated populations—foreign-
born and nonwhite, for example—in
different polities or communities. Such
segregated populations are likely to represent different ways of life. From the case
study literature on city–county consolidation, however, one is unsure about what
hypothesis to examine. In several of the
campaigns white voters, in both city and
fringe, allegedly supported consolidation
in order to dilute the growing power of
central city Negroes. On the other hand, it
has also been suggested that white fringe
dwellers oppose consolidation to avoid
governmental union with central city
Negroes. Given these contending propositions, both of them plausible, the author
decided to explore the relationship between
segregation and support of consolidation
without stating a hypothesis.

The hypotheses examined here are (1)
that social rank is positively related to
support of consolidation in both cities and
fringes (2) that familism is negatively
related to support of consolidation in both
cities and fringes and (3) that demographic
distance increasingly in favor of the fringe,
along both social rank and familism
dimensions, is negatively related to fringe
support of consolidation. Also, we expected
a strong positive correlation between social
rank and the YES vote of cities and fringes,
and a strong negative correlation between
familism and the YES vote of cities and
fringes.

Methods

The statistics used as measures of social
rank, familism, segregation, and demographic distance are suggested by the work
of Shevky and Bell.[12] Shevky and Bell,
however, made use of composite indices to
measure social rank, urbanism (the obverse
of familism), and segregation, while this
author used statistics similar to theirs as
separate indicators. Social rank is measured
here by per cent of high school graduates

and per cent of white-collar employees. Familism is measured by four statistics:

1. Per cent children under five years of age per 100 women age 15–44. This is an adaptation of the fertility ratio suggested by Shevky and Bell—number of children under five years per 1,000 females age 15–44.

2. Per cent females not in the labor force.

3. Per cent detached single-family dwelling units.

4. Per cent 14–17-year olds enrolled in school. This statistic is not the Shevky-Bell methodology but has been used elsewhere.[13]

A large number of children per 100 women, a large proportion of women at home, a large proportion of single-family dwelling units and teenage children in school suggest a family-centered way of life.

Segregation is measured here by per cent non-white.

The votes of cities and counties were gathered from a variety of sources, including local election commissions, the Advisory Commission on Intergovernmental Relations, and the *National Civic Review*. In most of the areas analyzed here the relevant social statistics were collected for the entire county and the central city; and a subtraction was made to get the fringe statistics.[14]

The demographic distance hypothesis was approached in the following manner. New percentages, made up of a fringe social statistic over the same statistic for the city, were computed. For example, per cent non-white in the fringe was put over per cent non-white in the city—resulting in a fringe-city ratio and a new percentage. The higher the resulting fringe–city ratio the greater the demographic distance in favor of the fringe.

Simple, partial, and multiple correlation coefficients were used to determine which variables are related to the YES vote on consolidation and to what degree.[15]

Findings

CENTRAL CITIES

The observed relationships between the measures of familism and the positive vote of cities (Table 1) generally support the relevant hypotheses. However, not all measures of familism are associated with voter support in the expected (negative) direction. The exception is "female domesticity," a measure of women not in the labor

TABLE 1. *City Life-Style Measures Correlated with City Vote for Consolidation*

	Social Rank			Familism			Segregation
Coefficients of Correlation	High School Graduates	White-Collar Workers	Children under 5 per 100 women age 15–44	Female Domesticity	Single-Family Dwelling Units	Children 14–17 in School	Non-white
A. Simple	.12	.31	−.41	.19	−.46	−.05	.15
B. Partial†	−.20	.35	−.47	.47	−.52	−.04	
C. Multiple		.37			.68		
D. Partial†	.39	−.19	−.51	.51	−.61	−.37	
E. Multiple				.75			
F. Multiple-Partial		.43		.70*			

* Statistically significant at the .05 level.
† Note: Row B shows partials when other measures within each category (social rank or familism) are controlled. For example, the partial −.52, between per cent single-family dwelling units and the yes vote, represents a control of the other measures of familism. Row D shows the relationship between the yes vote and each measure controlling for all other measures in both the social rank and familism categories.

force. It is positively related to support; and this relationship persists when the other three measures of familism are controlled (row B) and when all other measures of familism and social rank are controlled (row D).

Even so, a negative association between the measures of familism and the positive vote is the regular relationship.

The direction of the relationship between the vote and social rank is rather irregular but predominantly positive. Both simple correlations are positive, and weak, but when the per cent of white-collar workers is controlled the relationship between the per cent of high school graduates and the YES vote is negative. On the other hand, when all other measures of social rank and familism are controlled the relationship between the per cent of high school graduates and the YES vote is positive and higher than any of the other simple or partial coefficients. The latter result may be due to the indirect influence of the more powerful familism variables.

The coefficients of multiple correlation, in any case, show a greater degree of association between familism and the YES vote than between that vote and social rank. This finding persists when the effect of the two social rank variables is measured while controlling for the four familism variables, and the effect of the familism variables is measured while controlling for social rank.

In sum, in the central cities familism is more strongly related than social rank to support of consolidation, and predominantly in the direction predicted in the literature—i.e. negatively. Social rank also seems importantly related to the vote, but not entirely in the predicted (positive) direction. Segregation is positively related to the YES vote, but the coefficient of simple correlation is very low.

FRINGES

Correlating the positive vote of fringes with fringe social rank, familism, and segregation produces mostly weak coefficients; and the relationship between the measures of familism and support is irregular in direction. See Table 2. Fringe social rank, however, correlates positively with the fringe vote, as expected. But after the measures of fringe social rank, familism, and segregation have explained all of the fringe vote they can, there remains a great deal of variance—about 75 per cent—to be accounted for. In other words, the fringes' own life-style characteristics are not strongly related to the YES vote of fringes. But fringe–city "demographic distance" is related, and in a way that conflicts with the hypothesized relationship.

The almost uniformly positive correlations in Table 3 suggest that as social

TABLE 2. Fringe Life-Style Measures Correlated with Fringe Vote for Consolidation

| Coefficients of Correlation | Social Rank | | | Familism | | | Segregation |
	High School Graduates	White-Collar Workers	Children under 5 per 100 women age 15–44	Female Domesticity	Single-Family Dwelling Units	Children 14–17 in School	Non-White
A. Simple	.18	.25	−.07	.14	−.27	.06	.04
B. Partial*	.26	.31	−.08	.01	−.30	.11	
C. Multiple		.36			.33		
D. Partial*	.26	.33	−.01	.07	−.28	.04	
E. Multiple					.49		
F. Multiple-Partial		.38			.36		

* Note: Row B shows partials when other measures within each category (social rank or familism) are controlled. For example, the partial −.30, between per cent single-family dwelling units and the yes vote, represents a control of the other measures of familism. Row D shows the relationship between the yes vote and each measure controlling for all other measures in both the social rank and familism categories.

differences increasingly favor the fringe there is an increasing tendency for the fringe to vote *for* city–county consolidation. This finding is a deviant one and therefore raises numerous important questions. These are considered below.

Fringe–city familism is more strongly associated with the fringe YES vote than fringe–city social rank. (The fertility ratio is noteworthy for its independently strong relationship with the YES vote.) Both are strongly related to the YES vote, however. In fact, when familism is controlled the multiple partial correlation between the two social-rank variables and the YES vote is still .64.

Another way to bring data to bear on the question of the impact of demographic distance is to calculate the average vote of fringes when demographic distance is in the fringe's favor as compared with when it is in the city's favor. From much of the literature one would assume that when demographic distance favors the fringe the positive vote of the fringe would be well under 50 per cent. One would also assume that when demographic distance favors the city the positive vote of the fringe would be much higher, perhaps even over 50 per cent. The reasoning behind these assumptions is that fringe dwellers feel threatened by central city dwellers of lower status and non-familistic ways of life; but fringe dwellers do

not feel threatened by city dwellers of higher status and familistic ways of life.

The literature is less clear about the presumed behavior of central cities when demographic distance favors the fringe as compared with when it favors the city. This author, however, expected very little difference in the mean YES vote of central cities under the two conditions.

Computing the mean YES vote of the fringes when demographic distance favored the fringe and when it favored the city shows no difference, 38.7 per cent and 39.7 per cent respectively. This finding too suggests that in the population being studied, family-centered, higher status fringes felt less threatened by lower status cities than one would have expected. The mean YES vote of the central cities was higher than that of the fringes—55.1 per cent when demographic distance favored the fringe and 55.5 per cent when it favored the city. No one will be surprised, of course, by the finding that the fringes were less favorably disposed toward consolidation than the cities. But life-style differences do not appear to be a major factor in this differential voting pattern.

TABLE 3. Fringe–City "Demographic Distance" Correlated with Fringe Vote for City–County Consolidation

	Social Rank			Familism			Segregation
Coefficients of Correlation	High School Graduates	White-Collar Workers	Children under 5 per 100 women age 15–44	Female Domesticity	Single-Family Dwelling Units	Children 14–17 in School	Non-White
A. Simple	.17	.05	.44	−.08	.09	.07	
B. Partial‡	.16	.05	.64*	−.32	.46	.14	
C. Multiple		.17			.65		
D. Partial‡	.60	.48	.80†	−.57	.39	.09	
E. Multiple					.81		
F. Multiple-Partial		.64*			.80†		

* Statistically significant at the .05 level.
† Statistically significant at the .01 level.
‡ Note: Row B shows partials when other measures within each category (social rank or familism) are controlled. For example, the partial .46, between per cent single-family dwelling units and the yes vote, represents a control of the other measures of familism. Row D shows the relationship between the yes vote and each measure controlling for all other measures in both the social rank and familism categories.

The author also explored the possibility that a comparison of successful and unsuccessful referenda in terms of the direction of demographic distance would shed a little more light on the question of the impact of demographic distance. From the literature we would expect most of the failures to fall in the category "demographic distance favored fringe." And in fact the author found a pattern showing that when demographic distance favored the fringe a majority of the referenda were unsuccessful. However, this finding showed nothing about *whether fringes voted consistently unlike cities* on the unsuccessful referenda. If in unsuccessful referenda the cities and fringes behaved alike (both voting NO) there would be no grounds for assuming that demographic distance was an explanation of the failure.

Analysis of the votes of fringes and cities in the nine unsuccessful referenda shows that the two areas voted alike more often than they voted differently.[16] Although there were few instances in which demographic distance favored the city, a check on these referenda showed that fringes and cities voted alike in almost every case.[17]

All in all, our examination of the YES vote of fringes when demographic distance favored the fringe and when it did not suggests that social distance in favor of the fringe does not contribute much in explaining the success or failure of consolidation proposals, or in explaining fringe opposition.

Conclusions

The main findings of this paper are (1) that familism is strongly and independently related to the YES vote on consolidation; (2) that fringe–city demographic distance is more strongly related to the fringe's YES vote than the fringe's own life-style characteristics (see Table 4); and (3) that demographic distance increasingly in favor of the fringe is not associated with fringe opposition to consolidation.

The fact that the measures of familism are as good or even better than social rank in explaining the YES vote suggests that familism as a way of life is indeed relevant to the explanation of attempts to integrate American local governments. The work of Kaufman and Greer, and Dye suggests the same. However, the present data also suggest the need for more research into the exact nature of the relationship between familism and voter support of governmental integration. Here city familism was found to be negatively related to the city

TABLE 4. Summary Relationships between Measures of Social Rank, Familism, and Votes for Consolidation

	Multiple Correlation Coefficient	Multiple Correlation Coefficient	Multiple Correlation Coefficient	Multiple-Partial Correlation Coefficient	Multiple-Partial Correlation Coefficient
	$R1.23$	$R1.4567$	$R1.234567$	$R1.(23)4567$	$R1.(4567)23$
			Social Rank plus Familism	Social Rank Controlling for Familism	Familism Controlling for Social Rank
	Social Rank	Familism			
City Measures and City Vote	.37	.68	.75	.43	.70*
Fringe Measures and Fringe Vote	.36	.33	.49	.38	.36
Fringe–City Social Distance and Fringe Vote	.17	.65	.81	.64*	.80†

* Statistically significant at the .05 level.
† Statistically significant at the .01 level.

vote, as expected; fringe familism was irregular as to direction in its relationship with the fringe YES vote; and fringe–city demographic distance on the familism dimension was found to be positively related to the fringe YES vote. The data do not suggest, of course, that social rank variables are insignificant in explaining the YES vote (see footnote 20). As predicted, the direction of this relationship is predominantly positive in both cities and fringes. As for our measure of segregation, the weak simple correlation coefficients and other explorations indicate that it is not a strong explanatory variable in the present universe.

Finding number three is deviant and probably most important. Much in the literature leads one to expect the opposite. Why should demographic distance increasingly in the fringe's favor be associated with fringe support of consolidation? Why should demographic distance not be as important in explaining opposition as one would expect?

It seems likely that these relationships are a function of the particular universe analyzed here, and that they should be considered within this universe. In our view, useful theory,[18] systematic research,[19] and common sense all militate against generalizing beyond the present universe to statements about the unimportance of life style differences generally. A negative conclusion seems more appropriate—demographic distance was no real obstacle within the present universe.[20] It is possible, however, that the good-government, public-regarding ethos is stronger than supposed in the nation's suburbs. It may well have been the predominant factor in the unexpected phenomena discovered here. Only survey data can put such speculation to rest.

These cities are rather small on the whole, and they are entirely in the South and Southwest. What is there about smallness and "Southernness" that might diminish the impact of life-style differences? Two things come to mind. The first is that small urban areas display less intense life-style differences, less diversity and heterogeneity, than larger and more densely populated urban areas. Life-style differences in urban

Life Style, Demographic Distance,   71
and Voter Support of City–County
Consolidation
Brett W. Hawkins

subareas are generally thought to increase with increasing urban density and scale. Up to some unknown point, perhaps, life-style differences are not matched by separatist values among the voters; but beyond that point life-style differences are of such magnitude that separatist aspirations result. It is possible, in other words, that this relationship is curvilinear—with the breaking point coinciding with some unknown degree of urbanization.

The question of the impact of Southernness is also food for speculation. Perhaps in small and medium-sized urban areas in the South local elites have more influence over governmental structure than in other parts of the country. There are no data on elite influence here, of course, but some observers have suggested that in at least one Southern state, Virginia, the notion of value-sharing elites getting together on local government structure is not so far fetched. In the 1963 mergers in the Tidewater area of Virginia, agreement to support consolidation between city and county Democratic leaders was reportedly a major factor of those successes.[21] In spite of residential separation (which in Virginia means governmental separation also), political elites in the Tidewater area apparently shared many values about government and politics. Thus they were associated with the Byrd Democratic Party and seemed to accept a Virginia tradition of loose attachment to the structural status quo at the local level. City-suburban partisan similarities of course, are more generally characteristic of Southern urban areas than non-Southern areas.

The most general conclusion to be drawn from the data on demographic distance is perhaps a suggestive one. They seem to suggest a search for more carefully conditional statements about the impact of life-style differences on the integration of American local governments. Such differences appear to have been no real obstacle to the complete consolidation of American cities and counties.

Opinions on School District Reorganization in Metropolitan Areas: A Comparative Analysis of the Views of Citizens and Officials in Central City and Suburban Areas[*1]

Basil G. Zimmer

Brown University

Amos H. Hawley

University of North Carolina at Chapel Hill

ONE OF THE major trends of the present century has been the rise and development of the metropolitan community. Moreover, within the metropolitan community in recent years suburban areas have been growing at a much more rapid rate than central cities.[2]

As the population in the suburbs continues to grow at increasingly rapid rates, and as young families with children become more and more concentrated in these areas, there is an expanding need for school facilities and programs. But the needs cannot be met in many school districts, because of the lack of an adequate tax base; while in other adjacent districts the

Reprinted with permission of the authors and publisher, from Basil G. Zimmer and Amos H. Hawley, "Opinions on School District Reorganization in Metropolitan Areas: A Comparative Analysis of the Views of Citizens and Officials in Central City and Suburban Areas," (Southwestern) Social Science Quarterly, 48 (December 1967), pp. 311–324.

resources for school financing may be abundant, a circumstance preserved by the obsolete and inefficient type of school organization found in most areas.[3] In suburban areas throughout the country, demands for school facilities to keep pace with population growth have raised local taxes for school purposes to burdensome levels, especially where the district contains no industrial or commercial property. And only in rare instances is it possible to support an adequate school system through local resources where the tax base is limited to residential property.[4]

Despite the limitations of financial support at the local level, most districts attempt to provide full kindergarten through the twelfth-grade programs. The problem is most acute at the high school level, for there the burden on fiscal resources is heaviest. Thus James B. Conant argues, in his report on "The American High School Today," that "in many states the number one problem is the elimination of the small high school by district reorganization."[5]

Theoretically, the unification of administrative units would be a necessary step in the natural development of metropolitan areas.[6] However, even though in other stages of development many metropolitan centers in the United States have attained maturity, this last stage has yet to develop either in respect to the education or municipal functions.[7]

The segmentation of school districts in metropolitan areas is extensive. According to the last Census of Government, the 212 Standard Metropolitan Statistical Areas in 1962 included some 6,600 separate school systems.[8] The number of school systems outnumber the separate municipalities by more than 50 per cent. The nation's metropolitan areas, on the average, have some thirty-one school districts in each. It is noteworthy that in the largest metropolitan areas, only half of the systems had 96 per cent of enrollments and in the smallest metropolitan areas 13 per cent of the districts contained more than 90 per cent of the pupils enrolled in public schools in those areas.[9]

Of all the functions of government in metropolitan areas, education is clearly

Notes to this selection will be found on pages 336–337.

the major activity. The education function accounts for nearly half the total number of people employed by local governments,[10] and 42 per cent of the general expenditures.[11] Thus on both dimensions it is evident that the schools place a heavy economic burden on the residents of the area. Yet they tend to be organized on a basis which is inconsistent with the pattern of settlement. Rather, the new population aggregate in metropolitan areas has been largely superimposed on a structure of local school districts created for an earlier time when conditions of life were much different, and we find that little effective progress has been made toward the establishment of a more efficient type of system.[12] Small districts persist. The multiplicity of separate districts continues.

In a democratic society where change can come about only through popular support and where change in administrative structure is urgently needed, as in our metropolitan areas, the factors involved in resistance become of paramount importance.[13] For this reason, the present study attempts to determine how residents and officials compare in their views regarding a reorganization of the territorial basis of school administration, which would be more consistent with the social and economic structure of the larger community.[14]

Method

This study is based on data obtained in three different sized metropolitan areas which vary in their organizational complexity. The largest metropolitan areas such as New York, Chicago, and Detroit were excluded from the study on the assumption that the resolutions of local government problems in such areas were of a dimension so complex in scope, and were limited to so few areas, that it would be more beneficial to concentrate attention on the smaller, more representative metropolitan areas. The cities selected were: Large—Buffalo and Milwaukee; Medium—Dayton and Rochester; and Small—Rockford and Saginaw, all located in states with similar provisions for local governments.[15]

Opinions on School District   73
Reorganization in Metropolitan
Areas: A Comparative Analysis of
the Views of Citizens and Officials
in Central City and Suburban Areas
Basil G. Zimmer
Amos H. Hawley

The metropolitan area populations for these areas range from 1,300,000 to slightly less than 200,000, a range sufficient to permit a test of the significance of size of area in resistance to change. The study is based on a random sample of nearly 3,000 residents and 630 public officials in central city and suburban areas in the six different metropolitan areas in the three different population-size classes. The sample was designed so as to have an approximately equal number of residents and officials in each city and suburban area regardless of the size of the population.

The data for the present sample indicate that the centrifugal movement of population within metropolitan areas results in the effective sorting of populations between city and suburban areas so as to lead to marked differences in population composition. Not only are the families in the early stages of the family life cycle moving away from the city, but there is also a substantial withdrawal of the upper occupational, educational, and income levels. This pattern of movement has produced a school district and governmental segregation by social class,[16] and attempts at integration at the administrative level, as noted, continue to meet with strong and persistent opposition. Although it is a stage felt to be necessary by many, it has failed to develop. The present structure of the suburb in relationship to the city in metropolitan areas has been appraised by one observer thus, "there is no economic reason for its existence and there is no technological basis for its support. There is only the stubborn conviction of the majority of suburbanites that it ought to exist, even though it plays havoc with both the life and government of our urban age."[17] And since the reorganization of school districts is a crucial dimension in the more general problem, this provides sufficient justification for focusing on this issue.

Findings

We turn now to a discussion of how central city and suburban residents and officials compare in their views of the present organizational structure of education in metropolitan areas, and how they would respond to a proposal to establish a single area-wide school system. The first question pertains to an evaluation of the segmentation of school districts from the point of view of economy and efficiency. According to the data presented in Table 1, central city school and governmental officials are generally agreed that the present system of multiple school districts is wasteful, whereas suburban officials, except in the small metropolitan areas, are nearly equally in agreement that such is not the case.

In both large and small area central cities officials are nearly twice as likely as residents to view the present system as wasteful, whereas in the suburban areas the official–resident differences largely disappear. In the latter areas the responses of the school officials and residents are nearly identical; only three out of ten held the view that the present system is wasteful. Thus central city and suburban officials hold markedly different views on this issue; while much smaller differences are found among the residents of the two zones in

each size class, the direction of difference is the same.

A point to be stressed, with reference to the potential for reform in metropolitan areas, is not only that central city officials tend to view the present system as wasteful but that a substantial number of the school officials and residents in the small area suburbs share that view. Only half of the residents and slightly more than half of the school officials in the small area suburbs took the position that multiple districts are not wasteful. However, in the larger areas, more than half of the residents and nearly three-fourths of the officials expressed this view. Thus it would seem that the setting for change is much more promising in the small than in the larger metropolitan areas.

We turn now to the major point of the study which is the extent to which public officials and residents are opposed to change in the organization of school districts in the metropolitan community context. It is evident that there is rather widespread opposition among suburban residents while central city residents tend to favor reorganization. At this point, the issue is how these positions of residents compare with the views expressed by the public officials in each area. An inspection of the data presented in Table 2 would easily discourage anyone who was interested in bringing about a reorganization of school districts in metropolitan areas. For while central city officials tend to favor such a

TABLE 1. Per Cent Reporting that Separate School Districts Are and Are Not Wasteful, by Type of Respondent and by Residential Zone and Size of Metropolitan Area

Type of Respondent and Attitude toward Multiple Districts	Large City	Large Suburb	Medium City	Medium Suburb	Small City	Small Suburb
1. Percentage Reporting That Separate Districts Are Wasteful:						
School officials	86.7	28.3	42.9	22.6	75.0	44.3
Government officials	70.0	23.7	70.1	36.5	84.8	26.9
Survey population	37.1	30.3	42.0	35.7	43.9	40.0
2. Percentage Reporting That Separate Districts Are Not Wasteful:						
School officials	13.3	71.7	42.9	77.4	18.8	54.1
Government officials	20.0	69.5	20.8	58.7	9.1	71.6
Survey population	41.9	56.6	38.9	52.9	41.2	49.0

proposal, there is widespread opposition among suburban officials. And the opposition is particularly marked in the larger area suburbs. Three-fourths of the city school officials in the large metropolitan areas indicate that they would vote in favor of reorganization, but the proportion of school officials in the neighboring suburbs who would do so is a mere 10 per cent. Even less support for change is found among the suburban government officials. While residents in the larger area suburbs are more than twice as likely as public officials to favor change, the number who would do so is only slightly more than one in five. On the other hand, 88 per cent of the suburban school officials would oppose change as would 70 per cent of the residents.

Yet it is noteworthy that opposition, not only among residents, but school officials as well, tends to decline as size of area decreases. Thus in the small area suburbs more than one-third of the school officials and the residents would vote in favor of a reorganizational proposal. As we move from the large to the small area suburbs support for change increases more than threefold among school officials and nearly

Basil G. Zimmer
Amos H. Hawley

doubles among the residents. But opposition continues at the same high level among government officials. Even in the suburban zones of small areas, where opposition is least, approximately two-thirds of the school officials, and half of the residents, claim that they would vote against such a proposal. Thus even here opposition is still substantial, but it has reduced to a level where a reorganizational proposal has a much greater chance for acceptance than in the larger areas.

A very similar pattern of responses is also found in respect to administering high schools on an area-wide basis. Only a minority of either the central city officials or the residents would oppose such a proposal. In other words, such an issue would find ready support in the central cities. But this is not the case in the suburban zones. In the latter only a very small

TABLE 2. Per Cent in Favor or Opposed to a Single District or Area-Wide High School, by Type of Respondent and by Residential Zone and Size of Metropolitan Area

Type of Resident and Selected Attitudes	Large		Medium		Small	
	City	Suburb	City	Suburb	City	Suburb
1. Percentage Favoring Single District for Area:						
School officials	73.0	10.0	35.7	12.9	68.8	34.4
Government officials	51.4	8.5	59.7	28.6	54.5	10.4
Survey population	46.5	22.0	44.4	29.0	44.9	35.8
2. Percentage Opposed to a Single District for Area:						
School officials	26.7	88.3	50.0	79.0	25.0	63.9
Government officials	30.0	86.4	28.6	69.8	39.0	88.1
Survey population	36.3	68.9	34.8	60.6	37.5	49.8
3. Percentage Favoring Area-Wide High School:						
School officials	80.0	11.7	35.7	9.7	87.5	54.1
Government officials	74.3	8.5	62.3	26.9	66.7	19.4
Survey population	53.2	23.2	45.3	30.6	56.4	51.8
4. Percentage Opposed to Area-Wide High School:						
School officials	6.7	88.3	50.0	88.7	12.5	39.3
Government officials	17.1	91.5	27.3	73.0	30.3	77.6
Survey population	32.5	70.3	36.1	59.6	28.3	37.0

proportion of the school officials would
favor an area-wide high school. The only
exception occurs in the small area suburbs
where a majority of the residents report
that they would favor handling high schools
on an area-wide basis. In the small area
suburbs both school officials and residents
are much more likely to approve an area-
wide high school than a single overall
school district for the area. Apparently in
the small area suburbs the need at least
for a consolidated high school is evident,
and there is a willingness to move in the
direction of an area-wide school but they
want to do so without any sacrifice of their
independent school district status. In the
other suburban areas, handling the high
school on an area-wide basis is opposed
just as much as setting up a single school
district for the whole area.

Even in respect to a consolidated high
school, however, opposition is more frequently expressed by suburban officials
than by the residents of those zones, whereas, in the central cities, the opposite is
found; that is, officials tend to favor change
more than the residents. However, part of
this difference may be due to the larger
proportion of residents who have not yet
taken a position on this issue. (That is,
they have not yet decided how they would
respond to such a proposal.)

In short, while opposition to change is
widespread in the suburbs, it is more
frequent among officials than among the
residents whom they represent. The opposite pattern is found in the central cities
where officials are even more ready for
change than the residents. It is quite likely
that reorganization would be approved in

the central cities, regardless of size of area.

What officials and residents would expect
of others in their area is of more than
incidental interest, particularly because of
the sharp differences that are observed in
the suburbs and more specifically in the
large area suburbs, as is shown in Table 3.
In the latter, almost without exception
suburban school officials and to a slightly
lesser extent governmental officials, hold
the view that the residents in these areas
would be opposed to a reorganizational
proposal. By way of contrast, only seven
out of ten residents would expect others to
be opposed to such a plan. The proportion
of officials sharing this view is somewhat
lower in the medium-sized areas and substantially lower among school officials in
the small areas. In the latter only two-thirds
of the school officials feel that the residents
would be opposed to change, a view that is
shared by slightly more than half of the
residents. It is thus evident that suburban
officials are more likely to expect opposition
than are the residents in these areas. Turning to the central cities, we find that,
except in the medium-sized areas, there is
general agreement among officials and
residents in the proportion who would
expect others to be opposed to change.
And in none of these areas does the proportion deviate markedly from the proportion
of residents who reported that they would
vote in opposition. Why there is such a
wide discrepancy between what school
officials and residents would expect in the
medium-sized cities is not readily apparent.

In short, central city officials in both
large and small metropolitan areas display
a real capacity to correctly appraise how
their own constituents would respond to
change, while suburban officials consistently
overstate the amount of opposition that

TABLE 3.   Per Cent Reporting that Residents in Their Area Would be Opposed to Reorganization, by Type
of Respondent and by Residential Zone and Size of Metropolitan Area

Type of Respondent	Large		Medium		Small	
	City	Suburb	City	Suburb	City	Suburb
School officials	40.0	98.3	85.7	87.1	37.5	67.2
Government officials	38.6	88.1	51.9	71.4	50.0	85.1
Survey population	35.0	68.9	33.3	58.4	42.2	54.5

exists in the suburbs. However, the size of the gap between officials and residents declines in the small areas. On the other hand, residents in all segments of the metropolitan area seem to be quite capable of accurately assessing the views of their neighbors. At least there is little, if any, difference between what residents expect others to do and what the residents report they would do.

Apart from vested interests, these data suggest that one of the factors which may account for the high proportion of officials who oppose setting up a single district, particularly in the larger suburban areas, is the notion that this view is generally shared by the residents. In their interpretation of the issue they may feel that they are expressing the will of the people. Similarly, suburban residents may oppose reorganization of school districts, in part at least, because they think that the other people in their area share this view. That is, to oppose change is to share what is thought to be the view of others. It is quite likely that in responding to a proposal for change suburban residents, as well as suburban officials, would react on the assumption that other people in their area would vote in opposition. No doubt this factor plays an important role in resistance to change (not only among officials but the general population as well). One must interpret these data with particular caution, however, since it is not possible to determine whether the officials actually think that the people in the area would be opposed to change or

Opinions on School District 77
Reorganization in Metropolitan
Areas: A Comparative Analysis of
the Views of Citizens and Officials
in Central City and Suburban Areas
Basil G. Zimmer
Amos H. Hawley

whether they attribute this view to the residents so as to justify their own opposition.

Pursuing the issue further, there appears to be much more of a willingness on the part of public officials in the suburbs than among the residents in these zones to prefer the present school district even with higher taxes, over a single district with lower taxes. On the other hand, a substantial majority of the central city officials as well as the residents, state a preference for a single district with lower taxes. Although the proportion making such a choice increases as size of central city declines in all areas, officials are even more likely than central city residents to select this alternative. Quite the opposite is found in the suburban areas where a clear majority of the officials in each of the suburban zones state a preference for the present district with higher taxes. This type of choice, however, declines as size of area decreases. On the other hand, this view is not shared by a majority of the residents in any of the suburban zones. When the question is stated in these terms opposition to a single district for the whole area declines appreciably. These data are shown in Table 4.

It will be recalled that approximately two-thirds of the residents in the large area

TABLE 4. Per Cent Stating Preference for Present District with Higher Taxes or Single District with Lower Taxes, by Type of Respondent and by Residential Zone and Size of Metropolitan Area

Preference and Type of Respondent	Large		Medium		Small	
	City	Suburb	City	Suburb	City	Suburb
1. Percentage Stating Preference for Present District with Higher Taxes:						
School officials	26.7	71.7	35.7	74.2	6.3	55.7
Government officials	15.7	79.6	15.6	53.9	19.7	68.7
Survey population	23.1	47.9	23.4	39.1	22.5	28.7
2. Percentage Stating Preference for Single District with Lower Taxes:						
School officials	73.3	21.7	64.3	19.3	93.8	37.7
Government officials	74.3	15.3	75.3	38.1	71.2	25.4
Survey population	62.1	41.0	60.4	46.9	63.5	57.3

suburbs reported that they would vote against a single district; however, when the issue is stated in more specific terms and related to a differential tax burden, fewer than half would prefer the present district with higher taxes over a single district with lower taxes. Concern with costs is clearly evident. On the other hand, while only 22 per cent earlier stated that they would vote in favor of a single district we find that double this proportion (41 per cent) state a preference for a single district with lower taxes over the present district with higher taxes. Much the same kind of change in responses is found in the other suburban areas also. But it is only in the small area suburbs that a clear majority of the residents state a preference for a single district with lower taxes. This view is shared by fewer than two-fifths of the school officials and by only one-fourth of the municipal officials.

Although this question involves two different dimensions—that is, school district reorganization and a differential tax burden—the responses differ so markedly from those noted earlier in reference to the more general question of how people would vote on setting up a single district, that it would seem safe to infer that the economic dimension is of crucial concern in such an issue. At least this is suggested by the marked changes in the responses reported by residents in all zones. The economic influence is also evident among officials in both central city and suburban areas. In the central cities the tax dimension has the effect of increasing the size of the majority that supports change. But support for a single district, even given these conditions, falls short of a majority in both the large and medium-sized area suburbs. By the same token less than a majority indicate support for the status quo. Among suburban officials support for change increases when lower taxes are made a part of the proposal but even under these conditions a sizable majority of the suburban officials state a preference for the status quo. Although the tax burden does have some influence upon the thinking of suburban officials, it is not of sufficient importance to win their support for setting up a single district for the whole area. The highly significant role that taxes play in how residents view the issue of reorganization of school districts in the metropolitan context is noteworthy. Certainly any reform movement would have to come to grips with this issue. It is clear, however, that the promise of lower taxes would not successfully overcome the resistance of the suburban officials, though it might contribute substantially to the outcome of a popular referendum.[18]

According to the data presented in Table 5, there are marked central city and suburban differences as to perceived consequences following reorganization regarding the quality of schools and the tax burden. Moreover, the responses show the same pattern of difference by residential zones and size of area that was observed earlier concerning resistance to change. Turning first to what would happen to the quality of the schools, it is noted that central city officials are much more likely than those in the suburbs, or even the residents of the central city, to feel that the quality of the schools would improve. It is particularly noteworthy that this view is shared by a majority of the school officials only in the large cities. As the size of the metropolitan area declines there is a consistent decrease in the proportion of central city officials, as well as residents, who feel that the schools would improve in quality under a single system. But as already noted, officials are more likely to expect the schools to become better. This type of variation does not obtain in the suburbs. In general, there are no differences between officials and residents in the proportion who feel that the schools would improve. And in both the large and medium-sized area suburbs this view is shared by less than 15 per cent of either the officials or the general population. However, in the small area suburbs slightly more than one-fourth of the school officials and more than one-fifth of the residents would expect an improvement in quality.

Much more substantial differences are found in respect to the negative aspect of reorganization. Again we find that suburban officials are most critical, particularly in the large metropolitan areas, where they are nearly ten times as likely, as city officials, to report that the schools would not be as good after reorganization. This view is held equally by government and school officials. By way of comparison, among residents, the central city–suburban difference is slightly less than threefold. However, as the size of area declines we find a lower proportion who feel that the school would not be as good under a single system. Residents are much less likely to hold this view than the officials. In the small area suburbs, where we generally find most support for reorganization, only slightly more than one-third of the officials and fewer than one-fourth of the residents report that the quality of schools would decrease, if organized in a single system. This is by far the least amount of criticism expressed in any of the suburban zones.

**Opinions on School District 79
Reorganization in Metropolitan
Areas: A Comparative Analysis of
the Views of Citizens and Officials
in Central City and Suburban Areas**
Basil G. Zimmer
Amos H. Hawley

Discussion

It would seem that the judgment concerning what effect change would have on the quality of the schools is largely a function of whether or not officials or residents are opposed to or in favor of change. If they resist change, there is a marked tendency to report that reorganization would lower the quality of the schools. Whether this response is a defense of their position, or one of the reasons for their position regarding reorganization, is not at all evident. The original source of this attitude is unimportant, however, for the mere fact that suburban officials in particular can

TABLE 5. Per Cent Reporting Effect of Single District on Quality of Schools and Taxes, by Type of Respondent and by Residential Zone and Size of Metropolitan Area

Type of Respondent and Changes in Quality and Taxes	Large City	Large Suburb	Medium City	Medium Suburb	Small City	Small Suburb
Quality of Schools						
1. Percentage Reporting School Would Become Better:						
School officials	53.3	11.7	42.9	12.9	43.8	26.2
Government officials	41.4	10.2	32.5	14.3	34.8	16.4
Survey population	31.2	11.9	28.4	14.4	22.5	21.5
2. Percentage Reporting School Would Not Be as Good:						
School officials	6.7	60.0	14.3	58.1	12.5	39.3
Government officials	7.1	64.4	9.1	44.4	10.6	32.8
Survey population	17.4	48.5	19.3	39.6	18.9	22.8
Taxation						
3. Percentage Reporting That Taxes Would Increase:						
School officials	53.3	38.3	42.9	46.8	75.0	34.4
Government officials	41.4	45.8	45.5	34.9	47.0	55.2
Survey population	39.2	50.5	36.8	35.9	41.4	43.9
4. Percentage Reporting That Taxes Would Decrease:						
School officials	20.0	30.0	7.1	19.4	12.5	21.3
Government officials	24.3	13.9	13.0	15.9	12.1	13.4
Survey population	20.1	17.8	18.2	17.8	12.7	18.5

claim this as a consequence provides them ready support, as well as a justification for being opposed to reorganization. To oppose change for such a noble reason is to increase the influence and perhaps even the popularity of the officials among the residents of the zone.

The tax issue is much less clear. In all zones, in each class, there is a very substantial proportion of the officials who feel that taxes would increase under a single system. This view is held about as frequently by officials in both zones, and there is little consistent difference between officials and residents in either the central city or the suburban areas. On the other hand, only a small minority of the officials or the residents would expect a tax decrease. Again we find little or no difference between residents and officials. Even the usual central city and suburban differences are largely lacking. In short, there is a frequently expressed opinion that a reorganization of school districts would result in a tax increase. Since this view is shared as frequently by central city officials as by those in the suburbs, it is not possible to argue here as we did earlier, that this is merely a defense for the status quo, for as already noted, central city officials generally favor change while a majority of the suburban officials are opposed to it. Of course, it should be noted that each is using a different point of reference. Since the view is quite widespread that change would cause a tax increase, it seems reasonable to conclude that the cost factor is an important one in resistance to change. This takes on added significance when we recall the large proportion, even in the suburbs, who would prefer a single district with lower taxes over the present district with higher taxes. And although suburban officials are less sensitive to the tax dimension than either central city officials or the residents in either area, resistance to change decreases even among suburban officials when lower taxes are incorporated into the reorganizational proposal. Still a majority supports the present system even with higher taxes.

Thus, it would seem from these data that public officials in the suburbs provide one of the major obstacles to change.

Summary and Conclusions

In summary, three distinct patterns of difference are noted. First of all, suburban residents are much more opposed to change than city residents. Secondly, when residents and officials are compared, the opposite pattern of difference is found in the suburbs and in the central cities. For example, in the central cities school officials are less likely than residents to oppose change, whereas, in the suburbs, much more opposition is expressed by the officials. Thirdly, opposition among officials as well as residents, although always higher in the suburbs, nonetheless declines by size of metropolitan area. Even in the suburban zones of small areas, however, where suburban opposition is least, approximately two-thirds of the school officials and half of the residents reported that they would vote against the establishment of a single district for the whole area.

An overall appraisal of the data indicates that while central city officials tend to favor change, there is widespread opposition to reorganization among suburban officials.[19] And opposition is particularly marked in the large area suburbs. Rarely do the officials in these areas favor change. Although we consistently find size of metropolitan area differences, particularly in the suburbs within each area, support for change is most frequent among central city school officials and is least frequently reported by the officials in the suburbs.[20] For example, in the large metropolitan areas the proportion in favor of change ranges from only 10 per cent of the suburban school officials to 73 per cent of the city school officials. In the small metropolitan areas, where support for change is more frequent in the suburbs, the comparable proportions are 34 per cent and 69 per cent. The rank order of the proportions in favor of change follows the same pattern in each size class, that is, support for reorganization declines among each type of respondent in the following order: city school officials, city residents, suburban residents, and, lastly, suburban school officials. Conversely, opposition varies in the opposite direction, ranging from a high of 88 per cent among suburban school officials in the large metropolitan areas to only 27 per cent of the city school officials. Even though opposition is less frequent in the small areas the pattern is identical. Very similar patterns were also found in the responses to an area-wide high school, support for a single district with lower taxes, or the present district with higher taxes.

As we move from the large to the small area suburbs, support for change increases more than threefold among school officials and nearly doubles among the residents. Although support for change is substantially higher in the smaller suburban areas, it is still expressed by only a minority. Still, the important point to note is that opposition declines to a level where a reorganizational proposal has a much greater chance for acceptance even in the suburban areas.

Resistance to change is such in the larger metropolitan areas that any proposal for reorganization would be faced with overwhelming odds. In the smaller metropolitan areas, however, it would appear that residents, and to a lesser extent officials,

Opinions on School District   **81**
Reorganization in Metropolitan
Areas: A Comparative Analysis of
the Views of Citizens and Officials
in Central City and Suburban Areas
Basil G. Zimmer
Amos H. Hawley

would be quite receptive to a proposal to reorganize the schools on an area-wide basis. It is in such areas that we have consistently found the least amount of resistance to change. However, the longer efforts to bring about change are put off, the more difficult the task becomes. Already the larger metropolitan areas have reached the stage of development where a reorganization proposal would likely not survive a referendum. It would be approved in the cities but not in the suburban areas. Many future problems of segmented districts could be avoided, if reform were initiated in the hundreds of smaller communities before they emerged as larger metropolitan-like areas highly crystallized into a number of autonomous units. Clearly, efforts to be effective should be "preventive"; for as long as change is to be decided, either by public officials or by a referendum, the chances for success decline sharply as size of area increases. The relationship between size of area and resistance to change has been very evident throughout the study.

The Structure of Mass Participation in Community Politics

Introduction

THOSE ACTIVITIES by which people express their opinions about the scope of government[1] are many and varied. They include voting, plotting insurrections, discussing politics, joining political interest groups, running for political office, and civil disobedience. Despite the attention given to participation by political theorists and commentators, the most important feature of participation in community politics is how little there is of it. Although voting is only one way of participating, scholars have probably studied electoral turnout with greatest frequency. The turnout for an average Presidential election is a little less than two-thirds of the eligible adult population, while the average "off-year" state election (i.e., one held in a year in which the Presidency is not at stake) brings out about half the eligibles. Turnout in local elections is even lower. Alford and Lee, for example, note in Selection 10 that less than a third of the potential electorate went to the polls for non-concurrent local elections in 676 United States cities. McCleskey and Nimmo note in Selection 11 the marked dropoff in turnout from national to state to local elections on one city, Houston, Texas. As with other concerns in the study of community politics, participation may be approached from either a macro or a micro perspective. The former approach is adopted in the Alford and Lee study, where community turnout levels are related to other community characteristics, while the latter approach is utilized by McCleskey and Nimmo, who derive their data from the characteristics of registered voters.

This widespread apathy toward local politics may appear surprising in a nation still rhetorically euphoric about government "close to the people." Several explanations, however, can be found for such inattentiveness. Certainly the complexity of the American registration system which

Notes to this introduction will be found on page 337.

operates to reduce participation differentially among particular groups (see Selection 11) is one major factor. In their extensive study of the effects of one city's registration system, McCleskey and Nimmo identified three different electorates, which they called *potential, qualified,* and *actual.* They traced the filtration effect of the registration system and demonstrated that the participation of some groups is more significantly reduced than others by the operation of the registration process. However, the registration system alone does not account for the differences between national and local political attentiveness. The rise of a mass society, a centralized economic system, and large secondary organizations has produced a political culture in which national issues, symbols, and leaders are paramount. National issues of war and peace, poverty, and race relations seem more important than debate over traditional urban services. Moreover, the coverage of the mass media centers largely about national affairs and leaders, with a dull President obtaining better press coverage than a charismatic mayor. Finally, the sheer complexity of local government (already described in Section II of this volume) increases the urban electorate's information costs and operates to fragment its attentiveness.

At the community level itself, there are two important sets of variables, described by Alford and Lee, associated with participation. These are the community's political structure and its social structure. They found that manager governments and nonpartisan elections were associated with significantly lower turnouts in local politics, a finding which suggests that the "good government" reform movement (discussed in Selection 2 here) has weakened the structural incentives for participation. The reformed institutions like the manager plan may promote bureaucratic efficiency in municipal government, but they also replace the visible and politically conscious mayor with a more pristine, invisible, and politically "neutral" city manager. The nonpartisan election removes party labels from the ballot, thereby denying the voter the valuable cue of party identification to use in sorting out candidates. The social structure variables examined by Alford and Lee are quite similar to some of the dimensions of community discussed in Selection 1 of this volume. Education (measured by the percentage of persons 25 years old and over who completed four years of high school or more) is a *socioeconomic status* indicator. Ethnicity (percentage of the native population of foreign or mixed parentage) is an aspect of heterogeneity which, in turn, is an indicator of the factor (or dimension) *urbanism.* Finally, at least one of Alford and Lee's community continuity variables (percentage of migrants from a different county, 1955–1960) is also clearly an indicator of *residential mobility.* All of these variables were also found to be important predictors of voter turnout. Here and elsewhere in this volume the student will find it insightful to look for the relationship between community variables as described by different investigators and the description of more general community dimensions presented in Selection 1.

It is still impressive, however, that the most important single variable separating high- from low-turnout cities is form of government— a nondemographic community characteristic. Governmental reforms, which are characteristic of some cities but not others (see Selection 2), were a product of several generations of upper-middle-class civic activists, motivated by what Wilson and Banfield in Selection 13 describe as a "public-regarding" ethos. In large measure these reformers were reacting to machine politics which existed in a number of cities in the late nineteenth and early twentieth centuries. Few institutions have been as maligned as the machine, and few so little understood. As Greenstein suggests in Selection 12, the machine was surely not so corrupt, nor so universal, nor so hierarchical as its critics painted it. The good that the machine did was ordinarily buried with it, while the image of its evils lingers on. Whatever else may be said of the machine, it did activate participation by lower status groups, especially the immigrants, but also native, working-class whites and even Negroes. After describing the characteristics of the old-style machine, Greenstein sketches some explanations for its decline and fall. Perhaps most important were the development of a publicly funded welfare system, the decline in patronage resources available to machine leaders, and the decline in the value of material inducements. Today a great many, possibly a majority, of American communities are governed by public-regarding elements—upper-middle-status, white Anglo-Saxon Protestants. The public-regarding attitude syndrome is characterized by values of efficiency, rationality, centralized planning, by a concern for what is taken to be "the good of the community as a whole," and by an aversion to "politics." These public-regarding concerns, however much they are consistent with dominant value orientations in American society, may also have dysfunctional consequences at the lower levels of the community's status hierarchy. For while the machine may have taken advantage of the "private-regarding" elements of the community, it also, as Greenstein notes, "plied voters, who might otherwise have organized more aggressively" and "by siphoning off discontent and softening the law," it may have contributed to less violence than has been characteristic of our cities in more recent years.[2]

Partly because of the recent violence in American cities, the subject of political participation, which ordinarily has merely a hortatory ring to it, has become much disputed by political scientists and politicians alike. The characteristics of participants in civil disorders are discussed by Fogelson and Hill (see Selection 14), who test the adequacy of one explanation of the riots, which they call the "riffraff theory." That theory rests upon three tenets, each of which is, as they note, most comfortable to the white, middle-class community. First, that theory assumes that rioters constitute only a tiny fraction (one or two per cent) of the ghetto community. Second, rioters are portrayed as a part of a "criminal element," particularly unattached youths who are jobless and possess criminal records. And third, rioters and rioting engender little sympathy from the bulk of the Negro community. A thorough analysis by Fogelson and Hill of data from several riot cities, particularly Newark and Detroit, demonstrates how inadequately the riffraff theory corresponds to the evidence. While participation in the disorders fell short of a majority of the potential riot population, a significant minority of ghetto dwellers were participants. Nor were the rioters on the whole a part of the "criminal element," but they were rather remarkably representative of the ghetto community. They also found that support for the rioters, while not unanimous among residents of the riot area, was widespread. Such data cast serious doubt upon the viability of the riffraff theory as an explanation of rioting, as well as offering evidence of the profound dissatisfaction of ghetto residents with the shape of American institutions.

Another reason for the political debate over participation stems from the concern of some to arouse participation by the poor, especially through the Community Action Programs of the "war on poverty." Vice-President Spiro T. Agnew, before his inauguration, took pains to criticize programs which encouraged participation in community decision-making by those who were not "experts" in solving social problems. A similar criticism was made more recently by Daniel Patrick Moynihan, a founding father of the poverty program and now the urban affairs advisor to President Nixon, who attacked the legislative provision in the Economic Opportunity Act which required "maximum feasible participation" by the poor in policy formulation.[3] The research reported below (see Selection 15) by Bloomberg and Rosenstock details the social and political problems in stimulating participation of the poor. The report of their Milwaukee study begins with a statement of three theories of activation of the poor: a social-class theory, a social-activism model, and a community-development theory. Utilizing variables derived from each of these theories, they attempt to identify the most important predictors of participation of the poor. Their analysis suggests some critical questions regarding the macro and micro levels of analysis, since they raise the complex issue of whether the activation of the poor can be accomplished by changing individuals or only by systemic reconstruction.

Although each of the following selections represents a unique perspective on community politics, all of them focus upon the levels, types, directions, and structure of mass participation. The matter of elite participation will be considered in Sections IV and V.

WRITING ABOUT local elections in 1968, Charles R. Adrian and Charles Press report that, "It is not known whether . . . state and national voting-population characteristics fit municipal voting, too."[1] Although a number of important studies of politics and elections in individual communities have emerged in recent years, the data are far from sufficient to permit more than the most speculative generalizations about the nature of the local electorate.[2] This study draws back the curtain, albeit only a bit, on one aspect of local political participation— voting turnout. The data presented constitute, so far as we know, the first attempt at a comprehensive comparison among American cities with respect to turnout. As will be suggested and become obvious, the breadth of the data is not matched by their depth; data were received from only 80 per cent of the 729 cities above 25,000 population in 1962, and we were able to utilize comparative turnout figures from only 282 of these. While relationships are suggested between turnout, political and governmental structure, and characteristics of the population, these relationships must be regarded more as leads to future research, than as clear and unambiguous findings.

Previous work by the present authors has pointed to the importance of the political and social variables included in this analysis of American cities. Lee suggested in a study of nonpartisan elections and politics in California cities that nonpartisanship might tend to reduce voter participation.[3] In a study of American cities, this hypothesis was confirmed in a preliminary analysis of the same data used in this article.[4] The median turnout in partisan elections was 50 per cent, compared to 30 per cent in nonpartisan cities; in addition,

Voting Turnout in American Cities*

Robert R. Alford

University of Wisconsin, Madison

Eugene C. Lee

University of California, Berkeley

the related characteristics of council-manager government and the appointed mayor were also seen to have a negative relationship to voter participation. It was not possible, however, to determine whether these relationships were independently associated or, rather, merely reflected underlying characteristics of the cities themselves.

Parallel work on form of government by Alford and others posited the existence of a relationship between form of government and socioeconomic characteristics. For example, "white, Anglo-Saxon, Protestant, growing, and mobile cities are highly likely to be manager cities; ethnically and religiously diverse but nonmobile industrial cities are highly likely to be mayor-council cities." Other features of so-called "reform" type local government—nonpartisan elections, at-large elections, small city councils, local elections which are not concurrent with state or national elections— have a similar social base.[5] In this paper, the data and theoretical notions derived from these previous works are combined. The paper also draws upon two as yet unpublished studies, one of which included a factor analysis and multiple regression of these data.[6]

I. Concepts and Data

THE MEANING OF VOTING TURNOUT

Voting turnout in local elections is the most direct measure of participation in the electoral process, and possibly an indicator of other forms of political participation. We

Reprinted by permission from The American Political Science Review, 62 (September 1968), pp. 796–813. The authors are indebted to Michael T. Aiken, Ruth B. Dixon, Daniel N. Gordon, Willis D. Hawley, Robert L. Lineberry, Donald B. Rosenthal, Peter W. Sperlich, Frederick M. Wirt, and Raymond E. Wolfinger for comments and suggestions above and beyond the normal call of collegial duty. Their willingness to be of assistance in no way renders them responsible for the results. The senior author wishes to thank the Institute for Research on Poverty, University of Wisconsin, for research assistance.

Notes to this selection will be found on pages 337–339.

assume that a high level of voting turnout implies several things about the characteristics of the local electorate, although we do not have the data directly to test these assumptions.

For example, where there is a high level of voting turnout, one might assume there has been communication of political information to voters both about the particular election and about the political system of which elections form a part. This political information might be conveyed through a variety of reference groups—neighborhood groups, ethnic groups, political parties, voluntary associations—or through mass media such as television, radio, and the press. Whether such political communication exists or not, either the community as a whole or particular groups within it possess norms which define voting as appropriate and proper behavior. Voting turnout is defined thus as the dependent variable, although it would be just as legitimate to turn the question around and attempt to determine the consequences of higher versus lower levels of voting turnout. A few studies have dealt with this question, particularly with reference to referenda, finding that higher turnout is associated with negative voting.[7] There is no necessary connection between the causes and the consequences of different levels of voting turnout, however.

Varying levels of voting turnout in American cities may also be a consequence of political organization at the local level. For example, the more activity there is of groups interested in electoral outcomes, the more activity of party or other organizations seeking to get out the vote or to mobilize support behind slates of candidates, the higher voting turnout may be. On the other hand, high turnout may occur because of norms encouraging vote turnout held by members of other groups in the community with very little activity of political organizations *per se*.

As the above assumptions indicate, we see voting turnout as linked to the political and social structure of the local community.

It seems possible, however, that relationships of characteristics of a community with voting turnout may be cancelled out by idiosyncracies of a particular election: the personality of the mayor, the issues which happen to be salient at the moment, the accident of having a controversial referendum or bond issue on the ballot, whether or not the local election happens to be held at the same time as a particularly important state or national election. Unfortunately, comparative data are not available to test such "situational" factors influencing voting turnout, and we shall assume that the correlations that we discuss are only reduced by the operations of these situational factors, and not reversed.[8] It seems plausible to infer that if unique electoral issues and personalities account for most of the variation between cities in voting turnout, there should not be consistent associations between turnout and structural features of the local government and community. As will be indicated, however, this is not the case, and relationships do exist. Given the nature of the data in the study, particularly the fact that they relate to only one election for each city, the fact that even modest relationships can be discovered on a national basis is significant.

Our perspective here is one which looks at a "population of elections," not a "population of individual voters," as V. O. Key put it. Correlatively, electorates are not merely "arithmetic sums of individuals," but rather "units playing special and significant roles in the political process and therefore worthy of analysis in their own right," in Austin Ranney's words.[9] We are thus not inferring from our data on voting turnout anything about the characteristics of individual voters, nor do we invoke any social-psychological properties of individuals to explain our ecological correlations between characteristics of cities and the level of voting turnout. It would certainly be possible to develop propositions about the intervening processes of communication, definition of the political situation, and the formation of political identities in individuals and groups which connect structural features of American cities to the probability of high or low voting turnout, but these tasks are beyond our scope. We attempt, therefore, to avoid the pitfalls of "the ecological fallacy" (the generalization from group data to individuals) and "the contextual fallacy" (the prediction of group action from the characteristics of individuals).[10]

THE DATA

It is essential to an understanding of the data reported below that the nature of the original turnout figures and the ambiguity of certain of the variables be clearly understood.

1. No national source either collects or reports local voting statistics; few states do so. The data utilized here were collected by the International City Managers' Association in late 1962 from approximately 80 per cent of the nation's 729 cities above 25,000 population.[11] The missing cities tended disproportionately to be partisan, mayor-council and Eastern, all characteristics noted below as being associated with high voting turnout.

Robert R. Alford
Eugene C. Lee

2. For the bulk of the report, data are utilized only for those cities whose local election was *not* held concurrently with a state or national election, for we do not know for concurrent elections whether the turnout figures represent only the local increment—for example, the vote for mayor—or the vote in the larger race— for example, a vote for governor in 1962. Thus, a valid comparison of concurrent and nonconcurrent elections is impossible, and it is essential to use the narrower base, even though it reduces the number of cities to be analyzed by one-third.

3. An understatement of the mayor-council vote may result from the fact that in an undetermined (but quite small) number of such cities, only ward elections were held in 1961–62, which—in an unspecified (but even smaller) number of cities—involved only a portion of the city.

Characteristics	Cities in 1960		Cities Reporting Turnout		Cities with Noncurrent Elections Used in this Study	
	No.	Per cent	No.	Per cent	No.	Per cent
Form of Government:						
Mayor-Council	259	38%	130	30%	73	26%
Commission	77	11	37	9	30	11
Council-Manager	330	50	261	61	179	63
		100%		100%		100%
Form of Election:						
Partisan	193	29%	99	23%	50	18%
Nonpartisan	479	71	329	77	232	82
		100%		100%		100%
Region:						
East:	164	24%	84	20%	43	15%
Midwest	190	28	122	29	67	24
South	191	28	118	28	95	34
Far West	131	19	104	24	77	27
		100%		100%		100%
Total	(676)	100%	(428)	100%	(282)	100%

See Table 1 for the states comprising each region. By 1962, when the voting data were obtained, there were 729 cities over 25,000 population.

4. The data do not distinguish, either in mayor-council or manager cities, those elections in which a mayor appeared separately on the ballot from those in which he did not. The presence of the mayor on the ballot tends to increase voter turnout,[12] and the separately elected mayor is more likely to be found in mayor-council cities than in council-manager cities. Thus, the fact that in a small number of the mayor-council cities the mayor was not on the ballot in the election here reported tends to understate voter turnout in mayor-council cities, insofar as the impact of the mayor is concerned.

5. The data do not indicate whether the election here was a run-off or a primary. (Approximately 20 per cent of the nation's cities employ a run-off if no candidate receives a majority in the initial general election.) The consequences of this fact for turnout are not known. The local elections reported were held in 1961 and 1962, while the demographic data derive from the 1960 Census. Thus, as much as two years may have elapsed from the census to the election, so that changes in population characteristics in the intervening period are not reflected. Inasmuch as the voter-registration ratio is used as a measure of turnout, rather than the voter–adult population ratio, the impact of such changes is minimized insofar as the turnout percentages themselves are concerned. However, similar flaws exist with reference to the registration figures. States employ different laws, and cities and counties often administer the laws quite independently. Thus, the registration base in one city may be full of deadwood, another up-to-date, and the resulting percentage turnout figures be incomparable.

6. Finally, the use of "partisan" and "nonpartisan" as terms to describe the form of elections is a measure, not of the reality of political party activity, but merely of the form of ballot. While we assume that the existence of the party label on the ballot —the definition of a partisan election generally employed—is associated with a higher degree of party activity than is the case in which the nonpartisan ballot is employed, we have no evidence to support the assumption. "As some formally partisan cities are nonpartisan in fact, so some formally nonpartisan cities are *de facto* partisan in varying degrees."[13] Party activity may have a closer relationship to voter participation than the ballot form, but we have no way of assessing this on a comparative basis. Thus, we are forced to utilize a legal definition of partisan and nonpartisan elections, rather than an actual measure of partisan involvement. Similarly, the mayor-council form of government, associated with a separately elected mayor, includes mayors with widely varying powers and, theoretically, a wide range of impact upon the electorate and, indirectly, upon voter turnout. Again, however, we must employ a legal definition rather than a test of actual mayoral influence which might, in fact be more significant.

While none of these shortcomings appears crucial to us, they do suggest the tentative nature of both the data and the findings themselves, as well as the need for additional controls in subsequent studies.

CORRELATES OF VOTING TURNOUT

We shall consider three general categories of factors which may be related to the level of voting turnout in American cities: *political structure, social structure,* and *community continuity.* In addition, we shall include region as a separate category, although one of a totally different theoretical nature. The first two categories encompass a variety of possible specific factors related either to the institutions of government, party, and elections or to the demographic and group composition of the community. The third category is of a different order, referring to the development over time of interrelationships, contacts, or communications between different elements of political or social structure.

First, *political structure.* Institutions which allow greater access to political leaders and, theoretically, greater responsiveness to political demands should encourage higher levels of voting turnout. So, too, should the existence of institutions explicitly designed to mobilize the electorate. We shall follow the assumptions of the recent literature in taking the existence of *mayor-council form* of government[14] and *partisan elections* as indicating a greater probability of responsiveness "to class, racial, and religious cleavages . . . the enduring conflicts of political life."[15] We have already noted that earlier analysis of some of the data presented in this paper showed that the presence of the "reformist" institutions—council-manager government and nonpartisan elections—was associated with lower voting turnout.[16] The causal direction of the relationship is difficult to infer, however, since the activity of groups which favor certain political forms may influence both political structures themselves and also the level of turnout, or, on the other hand, once in existence, a political structure may be sufficiently inaccessible and unresponsive to discourage electoral participation.

Second, *social structure*. The existence in a community of groups which provide a social base for political organization would seem to be an important element of social structure which might be associated with voting turnout. Which elements or characteristics of population heterogeneity have an impact on turnout is an important theoretical question; we can only suggest a few possibilities, not all of which are testable with the data available. Religion, ethnicity, education, occupation, neighborhood, and race are obvious and standard bases of social differentiation in American communities. Yet it is not self-evident that variations in any or all of them should be systematically related to levels of voting turnout, at least as measured by aggregate and crude indicators such as those available for comparative studies. It may be, too, that variations in religious or ethnic composition expressed as a percentage of the total population are inadequate measures to relate to voting turnout. Very low or very high ethnicity, for example, may suggest little social cleavage and low turnout; figures between these two extremes, however, might reveal a divided community,

high cleavage, and high turnout. Only limited data exist on the numbers and social organization of religious or ethnic groups, or on the voluntary associations based on persons with similar occupation or education vis-a-vis aggregate data on their proportion in the electorate. We must, therefore, infer something about social structure from census data on the socioeconomic and ethnic composition of the communities.

We shall use the *ethnic* composition of a city, as measured by the proportion of foreign-born persons and persons of foreign or mixed parentage, and the educational composition of the city as our two indicators of social structure.

Arguments and some data on the persistence of ethnic voting are provided in several recent articles; the point is made that the political system is not merely a dependent variable, but that parties and candidates may continue to serve as a "mediator and mobilizer of minority symbols and interests."[17] Although admittedly a very inadequate measure, the proportion of persons of foreign stock is closely related ($r = .62$) to the only indicator of religious composition of a city which is available from the census (the proportion of children in private schools), and we shall use the former as a more direct measure of the religious-ethnic characteristics of a city.

Education would seem to be associated with voting turnout, if the logic of the oft-reported individual correlation of education with political participation can be extended to the ecological or aggregate level.[18] We might expect higher voting turnout in cities with a higher proportion of better-educated persons. Yet, such persons are often in a minority in a city, and therefore their behavior alone may not be able markedly to determine the absolute level of voting turnout. The opposite hypothesis also seems plausible: the higher the proportion of *less* well-educated persons and workers in a community, the higher the voting turnout, for these groups could form the social base for political movements likely to have a stake in influencing local leaders through elections. Here is a case which provides a direct test of alternative hypotheses suggested by an analytical framework which includes both individual level data and ecological level data.

Third, *community continuity*. The longer a community has existed, the more likely it is that there are groups, institutions and individuals with a stake in the city's political and governmental structures. Similarly, regardless of the age of the community, the more stable the population within the city, the greater the likelihood that such political attachments will exist. Thus, both the age of a city and the stability of its population would seem to have a probable relationship to voting turnout. We shall use two indicators to measure the continuity of the local social and political systems of American communities: *the age of the city* and *the geographic mobility* of its population. The age of the city, as measured by the decade in which the city reached 25,000 population, is a direct measure of the length of time that a social and political organization has existed on a given territorial site. City age does not measure, however, the age of either form of government or form of elections, both of which may have been altered one or more times during the life of the city. Thus, only indirect statements may be made about the continuity of *particular* political institutions. Geographic mobility—as measured by the proportion of the population who moved to their present home from a different county between 1955 and 1960—is an indirect indication of the continuity of a given set of families and households in a community. Where such mobility is low, a high level of out-migration may or may not have taken place, and thus geographic mobility may not be a good measure of population change. However, for that very reason it is appropriate for our purposes. The "residue" of families left behind is the appropriate

population which is attached or unattached to the electoral system. Conversely, a city which has experienced a high level of movement of its population from one county to another probably contains many residents who have lost their ties to social groups and political networks which have been their channels of communication of political stimuli.

Finally, *region*. It is difficult both conceptually and analytically to suggest or to test the notion that "region" has an independent relationship to voting turnout. As Lineberry and Fowler suggest, "region as a variable is an undifferentiated potpourri of socioeconomic, attitudinal, historical and cultural variations."[19] Nevertheless, while not capable of adequate analysis in this study, the possibility remains that such factors as political tradition or culture —the previous existence of particular institutions, the impact of previous events, or the existence of particular value systems —may have a relationship to the character of the community and, thus, to voter participation.[20] For example, our data do not permit us to measure the existence— past or present—of leaders or bosses, of citizen organizations and community controversies that may have an enduring impact upon patterns of community politics, including voting turnout. Such characteristics may not be randomly distributed throughout the country and may not be adequately "explained" by normal demographic data. Thus, the oft-asserted likelihood that working-class Eastern and Midwestern cities are more likely to have political machines with a stake in controlling local elections and getting out the vote is not revealed by the data available in this broad national survey.[21] Similarly, we cannot assess the possible impact, suggested by David Rogers, that many Southern communities have an authoritarian and conservative value system, reflected in a rigid class structure and one-party politics, all of which would be likely to have an effect on voter participation.[22] Nor are our data adequate for us to have confidence that the "independent effect" of region can be isolated. Nevertheless, the regional differences to be suggested may well hide more important variables than those which are available from census data.

II. Findings

Table 1 displays the correlations of the various indicators of social and political structure and community continuity with four different measures of voting turnout in American cities. In order to avoid the problem of variations in registration from city to city, both the proportion of registrants voting and of adults voting are shown. Also, because cities with elections which are concurrent with state or nation elections have higher turnout than those with nonconcurrent elections, cities are divided into those two categories. Thus, we have two independent replications based on two populations of cities.

All four general factors are associated with the level of voting turnout regardless of whether the proportion of adults or registrants voting is considered, and regardless of whether the local election was concurrent or nonconcurrent. With regard to political structure, cities without the council-manager form and with partisan elections have higher voting turnout than cities with other forms. With respect to social structure, cities with highly ethnic populations and *less* well-educated populations have higher voting turnout. With respect to community continuity and region, cities with stable populations, which are older, and which are located in the East have higher voting turnout than cities with a high level of in-migration, which are younger, and which are located in the Far West or South.

The same general patterns are found if other related indicators are used, such as the per cent of foreign born, the per cent of persons with five years of education or less, the per cent of college graduates, the per cent of children in private school, or the decade in which the city reached 10,000 population. Nor do other dividing lines for regions alter the general relationships.

We shall present only the proportion of *registrants voting* in subsequent tables, because we are concerned with the factors which bring eligible voters to the polls, not with the factors which influence the possibility of registration. Analytically, the two bases are distinct in terms of their relevance for political processes, since it is possible for a city to have an extremely high proportion of registrants voting but a very low proportion of adults voting (particularly in the South), although not vice versa. The act of registration is of course, an important aspect of political participation.[23] In any event, the correlation between adults and registrants voting in this study is high (.81), and separate analysis of the data shows that the relationships described here would not be altered by the use of the "adult" base.

As noted above, we shall report further data only for those cities whose local election was not held concurrently with a state or national election. The correlation of concurrence with the proportions of registrants voting was .30, with adults voting .35. The mean voting turnout of adults in cities with concurrent elections was 43.5 per cent, for nonconcurrent elections 31.2 per cent, and the "advantage" of concurrent elections is maintained in every subgroup we examined. Concurrent elections are slightly more likely in the East, in cities with partisan elections and a mayor-council form of government, and in older cities, all characteristics themselves linked to higher voter turnout. But, as Table 1 shows, the association does not account for the correlations of these other characteristics with voter turnout. While not included here, all subsequent tables shown were also separately computed for cities with concurrent elections, and the same patterns of relationships hold.

POLITICAL STRUCTURES AND VOTING TURNOUT

Table 2 attempts to assess the *independent* influence of political structural characteristics upon the level of voting turnout. The table shows that the over-all correlations of political structure and voting turnout remain while controlling for each demographic characteristic and the four

regions, although the magnitudes change. (The single disappearance of the association occurs for form of election in the Far West; in that region only 6 or the 77 cities with nonconcurrent elections also had

TABLE 1.   Correlates of Local Voting Turnout in American Cities, 1961–1962*
(Cities over 25,000 population in 1960)

| | | Correlation with: | | | |
| | | Registrants Voting | | Adults Voting | |
Characteristic	Cities With:	Nonconcurrent Elections	Concurrent Elections	Nonconcurrent Elections	Concurrent Elections
Political Structure					
Non-council-manager vs.					
council-manager		.43	.34	.50	.35
Partisan vs. nonpartisan		.28	.43	.29	.38
elections					
Social Structure					
Ethnicity: Per cent of the					
population native of foreign					
or mixed parentage, 1960		.32	.36	.51	.49
Education: Per cent of					
persons 25 years old and					
over who completed four					
years of high school or					
more, 1960		−.28	−.16	−.15	−.22
Community					
Mobility: Per cent migrant					
from a different county,					
1955–60		−.32	−.32	−.40	−.49
Age of City: Decade in					
which the city reached					
25,000 population		.27	.27	.28	.23
Regional Location					
East		.39	.58	.45	.51
Midwest		.04	−.13	.21	.02
South		−.15	−.29	−.44	−.45
Far West		−.19	−.25	−.10	−.20
Mean Registrants Voting		46.9%	59.0%		
Mean Adults Voting				31.2%	43.5%
N =		(282)	(142)	(294)	(146)

* Entries are product-moment correlations of the actual percentages of registrants voting or adults voting in the last local election held in the given city. Cities in which the local election was held concurrently with a state or national election are separated from those in which it was not concurrent. The N's shown are approximate for a few correlations, since not all data were available on political structure. The direction of the correlation is indicated by the italicized word. The two political structure variables and regional location were treated as dummy variables (presence or absence of the attribute named) for the correlations. All other correlations were computed from the actual percentages. Data on political structure were obtained from the *Municipal Year Book*, 1963, and all other data are from the 1960 U.S. Census of Population. The correlations are not significantly altered if commision cities are grouped with manager cities for the purpose of constructing a mayor-council/nonmayor-council dummy variable.

States comprising the indicated regions are as follows:
East: Maine, New Hampshire, Vermont, Massachusetts, Connecticut, Rhode Island, New York, New Jersey, Pennsylvania, Maryland, Delaware, District of Columbia.
Midwest: Ohio, Indiana, Illinois, Michigan, Wisconsin, Minnesota, Iowa, North Dakota, South Dakota, Nebraska.
Far West: California, Oregon, Washington, Nevada, Alaska, Hawaii, Montana, Idaho, Colorado, Utah, Wyoming, Arizona, New Mexico.
South (and Border): Texas, Oklahoma, Kansas, Missouri, Arkansas, Louisiana, Alabama, Mississippi, Florida, Georgia, North Carolina, South Carolina, Virginia, West Virginia, Kentucky, Tennessee.

partisan elections.) We may summarize Table 2 simply by noting that both aspects of political structure—the form of government and the form of elections—are related to the proportions of registrants voting, even when important characteristics of social structure and region are held constant.

The correlations suggest that form of government has a stronger relationship to turnout than form of elections. In an attempt to assess this more adequately, Table 3 examines each structural variable, holding the other constant. Form of government does have a more significant relationship to turnout than form of election. The election of a mayor (which occurred in 77 per cent of the mayor-council cities in the nonconcurrent elections covered by this study) may be a stronger motivating

force in relation to turnout than the existence of the partisan ballot. The latter is much more ambiguous in terms of its practical meaning; a partisan ballot, as we have noted, may mask a wide range of party activity, ranging from the total absence of political party organization to total mobilization. Thus, it is not surprising that the more clear-cut variable demonstrates a clearer relationship.

These findings are consistent with those reported by Ruth Dixon, utilizing the same base data as in this study. Analyzing all cities, regardless of the concurrency of the election, she reported a correlation of −.48 between council-manager form of

TABLE 2. *Correlates of Registrants Voting with Political Structures Controlling for Social Structure, Community Continuity, and Region**
(Cities with Nonconcurrent Local Elections)

Characteristic	Controlling for Social Structure and Community Continuity				Correlation within Region				All Cities
	Ethnicity	Education	Mobility	Age of City	East	Midwest	South	Far West	
Nonmanager vs. council-manager form of government	.38	.37	.34	.38	.40	.38	.28	.30	.43
Partisan vs. non-partisan elections	.27	.25	.23	.25	.14	.40	.27	−.01	.28
N =	(279)	(279)	(279)	(279)	(43)	(67)	(95)	(77)	(282)

* See Table 1 for the states comprising each region and the measures of each variable. Entries are product-moment correlates of the percentage of registrants voting with the two characteristics of political structure indicated. Entries under "Social Structure and Community Continuity" are partial correlations, controlling for each of the variables indicated. The direction of the correlation is indicated by the italicized word.

TABLE 3. *The Correlation of Registrants Voting with Each Element of Political Structure**
(Cities with Nonconcurrent Elections)

Characteristic	Correlation within Form of Election		Correlation within Form of Government	
	Partisan	Nonpartisan	Nonmanager	Manager
Nonmanager vs. manager form of government	.45	.36	—	—
Partisan vs. non-partisan elections	—	—	.24	.11
N =	(50)	(232)	(103)	(179)

* Entries are product-moment correlates of the percentage of registrants voting with each aspect of political structure, controlling for the other. The direction of the correlation is indicated by the italicized word.

government and per cent of adults voting and − .38 between adult turnout and the nonpartisan ballot. Furthermore, in a multiple-correlation regression including eight political variables, form of government accounted for 22 per cent of the variance in turnout, concurrency of election for an additional 11 per cent, type of election for 3 per cent and form of registration for 2 per cent. The author notes Lord Bryce's suggestion that "the most important single factor in affecting turnout is the color and appeal of the candidates," and goes on to state that "the predictive power of these governmental variables is considerable in view of the multitude of factors that are brought into play in influencing citizens to vote."[24]

SOCIAL STRUCTURES AND VOTING
TURNOUT

Table 4 shows the correlates of measures of ethnicity and of educational level with the voting turnout of registered persons in cities with nonconcurrent elections. Although several of the correlations are very weak, cities with more highly ethnic or less well-educated populations generally have higher levels of voting turnout, regardless of form of government and elections and in each of the four regions. (Again, the Far West does not have many cities with a highly "ethnic" population.)

In noting the relationship between ethnic

populations and the existence of mayor-council form of government, Kessel had suggested that the foreign-born "would be especially dependent on political activity because of its exclusion from alternative agencies of community integration."[25] Although our data are not strictly comparable, the parallel existence of a relationship between ethnicity and turnout would seem to support Kessel's assumptions.

However, the findings relating education to turnout appear to fly in the face of accepted conventional wisdom. If voting turnout reflects an "adding up" of the predispositions of individuals in cities to participate in politics, then we would expect that education would be closely correlated with voting turnout. This is not the case. Although not high, the ecological or aggregate correlation of registrants voting with education is the opposite of the well-known individual correlation.[26] (Use of other measures of education does not alter this generalization.)

Voting turnout (registrants voting) is thus *inversely* correlated with the educational level of a city. We conclude that high educational level of the city as a whole either has no effect or reduces the level of voting turnout. Although better-educated individuals may indeed vote more frequently than less-educated individuals, less well-educated communities vote more (or at least not less) than well-educated communities. We leave for further study the question of whether the relationship

TABLE 4. *Correlates of Registrants Voting and Social Structure, Controlling for Political Structure and Region**
(Cities with Nonconcurrent Local Elections)

	Correlation within								
	Form of Government		Form of Election		Correlation within Region				All Cities
Characteristic	Non-manager	Manager	Partisan	Non-partisan	East	Midwest	South	Far West	
Ethnicity	.38	.15	.26	.33	.29	.09	.21	−.06	.32
Education	−.23	−.15	−.43	−.20	−.32	−.33	−.19	−.03	−.28
N =	(103)	(179)	(50)	(232)	(43)	(67)	(95)	(77)	(282)

* Entries are product-moment correlations of the actual percentages for each city. States comprising the regions are given in Table 1 with the measures of ethnicity and education.

between education and voter turnout is curvilinear, a question unanswered by the existence of the single correlation. It may well be that turnout is lowest at either end of the aggregate educational scale but proportionally higher in communities falling between these two extremes.

COMMUNITY CONTINUITY AND VOTING TURNOUT

Table 5 shows the correlates of the age of the city and the geographic mobility of its population with voting turnout, holding form of political structure and region constant. The older the city and the less mobile its population, the lower the voting turnout, regardless of either form of government or form of election.

Mobility remains highly correlated with voting turnout in the East and Midwest, but drops to nothing in the South and Far West. The age of the city, however, is not correlated with voting turnout in any region except the Far West.

Such findings do not necessarily mean that these factors have no influence in those regions, but rather that we must reconceptualize their relationships to each other and to voting turnout. Community continuity does not appear to be a "factor" influencing voting turnout in the same way as contemporary features of the social and political structure of the city, but rather— we suggest—indicates a greater probability that stable communication networks linking

social and political groups to political leaders in a community may have developed. Also, sets of norms encouraging political participation may have developed as a consequence of the existence of networks of access to and influence upon political leaders. These, in turn, may bear some relationship to voting turnout, but a relationship too complex to be revealed by the gross data here employed.

The above findings concerning the positive relationship of mobility and ethnicity and the negative relationship of education to voter turnout are corroborated in a separate study by Dixon. Using multiple-correlation regression involving clusters of related demographic factors, she concluded that "the single most important factor to be considered in predicting the voter turnout of a city is the residential mobility pattern of its inhabitants, which alone can account for 31 per cent of the variability in turnout. Knowing the ethnic composition of the city increases the power of prediction an additional 19 per cent . . . [while] the factors 'age composition,' 'social status' [which included education as a variable], 'employment stability' and 'city size' contribute little or no information about whether a city has high or low turnout in local election."[27]

TABLE 5. Correlates of Registrants Voting and Indicators of Community Continuity, Controlling for Political Structure and Regions*
(Cities with Nonconcurrent Elections)

Characteristic	Correlation within Political Structure				Correlation within Region				All Cities
	Form of Government		Form of Elections						
	Non-manager	Manager	Partisan	Non-partisan	East	Midwest	South	Far West	
Mobility	−.23	−.16	−.41	−.26	−.49	−.47	−.03	−.06	−.32
Age of City	.11	.24	.22	.24	.15	.18	.03	.34	.26
N =	(103)	(179)	(50)	(232)	(43)	(67)	(95)	(77)	(282)

* Entries are product-moment correlations of the actual percentages for each city. States comprising the regions are given in Table 1 with the measurements of mobility and city age. The direction of the correlation is in terms of the *age* of the city; thus, the earlier the city reached 25,000 population, the higher the turnout.

REGION

The regional location of a city is associated with a wide variety of political and social characteristics, as Table 6 shows, and many of these characteristics are also associated with voting turnout. Eastern cities are older, have more out-migration and little in-migration, and have more persons native of foreign-born parentage. In addition, they are more likely to have partisan elections and less likely to have the council-manager form of government. Western cities are at the other extreme in all of these characteristics. Thus, it is no surprise to find that important differences exist among regions with respect to voter turnout, as has been suggested in tables presented above. The distinction is most apparent in a comparison of Eastern and Far Western cities. Eastern location is positively correlated with all the variables associated with high turnout. Eastern cities have a mean turnout figure of 64.0 per cent, compared to but 41.2 per cent in the Far West. Nevertheless, the table also reveals once again the difficulty of dealing theoretically and analytically with region as an independent variable. Since we are able to control for other than a very limited number of these variations, we only note the regional characteristics but offer little by way of explanation other than our previous reference to the possible existence of such factors as political tradition and culture.

SOCIO-POLITICAL STRUCTURES,
HISTORICAL CONTINUITY, REGION AND
VOTING TURNOUT

In the past few pages, relationships of varying strength have been noted between form of government, form of elections, ethnicity, education, and mobility and voting turnout. Age of city was seen to have little relationship independent of other characteristics, while region did seem associated with turnout but presented both theoretical and analytical problems which could not be resolved by the data here available. In the tables to follow, we review some of the previous findings by use of other data, in this case the mean turnout in various categories and sub-categories of cities. (The substitution of median for mean does not alter the results; the two

TABLE 6. *Correlations of Regional Location of a City and Selected Characteristics Related to Voting Turnout**
(Cities with Nonconcurrent Elections)

Characteristic	Region			
	East	Midwest	South	Far West
Political Structure				
Council-*manager* form vs. non-council-manager form	−.29	−.33	.23	.32
Nonpartisan vs. partisan	−.13	−.20	.13	.18
Social Structure				
Ethnicity	.56	.14	−.60	.06
Education	−.23	.03	−.21	.41
Community Continuity				
Mobility	−.34	−.22	.17	.32
Age of City	.29	.12	−.10	−.26
Mean registrants voting	64%	48%	43%	41%
Mean adults voting	49%	37%	23%	30%
N =	(43)	(67)	(95)	(77)

* Note that the table does *not* present correlates relating the characteristics to turnout, but shows the relationship of the characteristics to region. Entries are product-moment correlations of each variable listed with the regional location of a city, treated for computation purposes as four different dummy variables. Thus, "East"-"Not East" is a "variable" for purposes of computation of the correlations. See Table 1 for the states comprising the regions and the measures. The total number of cases is 282.

have a correlation of .97.) The demographic variables previously utilized are dichotomized above and below the median value for all cities in the United States, in order to develop a primitive typology of cities along the dimensions we have distinguished.

In Table 7, the average voting turnout is shown for cities classified simultaneously by form of government, form of elections, and the four demographic variables. In every comparison, the relationships appear as predicted. Holding all other variables constant, both partisan elections and non-manager (typically mayor-council) government show a higher turnout than nonpartisan elections and manager government. Similarly, again paralleling the results indicated above, the average turnout among cities with high ethnicity, low education, and low mobility is higher (with one minor exception) than among cities with reverse characteristics. Older cities, regardless of their form of government or election, are more likely to have higher voting turnout than younger cities, although the mean

differences are not as great as for the political structural characteristics.

Table 8 presents average turnout data by form of government and form of elections, classified according to region. As indicated above, region is itself related to various demographic characteristics themselves associated with turnout; multivariate analysis is thus handicapped by the small size of the frequencies in many of the sub-categories. Again, partisan non-manager cities tend to command a larger turnout than nonpartisan and manager cities. However, the impact of other variables hidden under the "region" label is similarly indicated. In the East, for example, the average turnout in nonpartisan non-manager cities is higher than in partisan mayor-council cities. Whether this reflects the impact of form of government—for example, the possiblity that the office of mayor "means" more in

TABLE 7. Mean Per Cent of Registrants Voting, by Social Structure and Political Structure*
(Cities with Nonconcurrent Local Elections) % and (N)

Characteristic	Partisan			Nonpartisan			All Cities		
	Non-manager	Manager	All	Non-manager	Manager	All	Non-manager	Manager	All
Ethnicity									
High	65 (19)	45 (9)	58 (28)	58 (44)	42 (57)	49 (101)	60 (63)	42 (66)	51 (129)
Low	62 (15)	49 (7)	58 (22)	48 (25)	40 (106)	41 (131)	53 (40)	40 (113)	44 (153)
Education									
High	59 (10)	45 (10)	52 (20)	53 (42)	39 (110)	43 (152)	54 (52)	39 (120)	44 (172)
Low	66 (24)	50 (6)	62 (30)	57 (27)	44 (53)	48 (80)	61 (51)	44 (59)	52 (110)
Mobility									
High	60 (10)	40 (10)	50 (20)	52 (26)	39 (122)	41 (148)	54 (36)	39 (132)	42 (168)
Low	65 (24)	58 (6)	64 (30)	56 (43)	44 (41)	50 (84)	59 (67)	46 (47)	54 (114)
Age of City									
Old	66 (21)	47 (10)	60 (31)	57 (41)	43 (63)	49 (104)	60 (62)	44 (73)	51 (135)
Young	60 (13)	45 (6)	55 (19)	51 (28)	38 (100)	41 (128)	54 (41)	39 (106)	43 (147)
All Cities	64 (34)	47 (16)	58 (50)	55 (69)	40 (163)	44 (232)	57 (103)	41 (179)	282

* 1. "Low ethnicity" means that there were less than 15 per cent of persons in the city native of foreign-born or mixed parentage in 1960. "High ethnicity" more than 15 per cent. This figure is the median for all 676 cities in the United States over 25,000 population in 1960.
2. Educational level was dichotomized, with "Low education" comprising cities which had 43 per cent or less persons 25 years or more who had completed high school in 1960.
3. Mobility was dichotomized with "Low mobility" comprising cities which had 15 per cent or less persons 5 years and over who were migrant from a different county between 1955 and 1960, "high mobility" those cities with more than 15 per cent migration.
4. Cities which reached 25,000 population by the census of 1930 are classified as "Older," those in the censuses of 1940 to 1960 as "Younger."

the East than in other parts of the country—or the association of these cities with demographic variables associated with turnout, or a number of other possibilities, cannot be determined with any degree of confidence from these data. Similarly, in the Far West, average turnout in nonpartisan-manager cities is the same as that in the very small number of partisan-manager cities, in contrast to the general pattern. Here, the ambiguous nature of "partisan" as well as "region" is evidenced, as well as the difficulty of generalizing from the very small number of deviant cases. It may well be that partisanship is lacking in those few Western cities, ballot form notwithstanding, that there is a "spill-over" effect from the prevailing nonpartisan policy of the area. Again, the data utilized here do not permit an evaluation of these important distinctions.

In Table 9, demographic and regional variables are examined simultaneously. Again, the mean turnout figures reported for the nation as a whole are consistent with the findings already noted: older cities with high ethnicity, low education, and low mobility show higher turnout than cities with the opposite characteristics. However, the relationships are reduced sharply and sometimes reversed when region is controlled. The tendency of Eastern cities to have a higher turnout, even when demographic characteristics are held constant, suggests again that the history and traditions of a region, its political culture, in short, may be as important variables as those which we have been able to utilize in this exercise. Our gross data do not allow a more extensive exploration of the links between the political and social structure of cities and their origins and development within a particular region.

In sum, the tables utilizing mean turnout data are generally consistent with the

TABLE 8. *Mean Per Cent of Registrants Voting, by Region and Political Structure**
(Cities with Nonconcurrent Elections) % and (N)

Region	Partisan			Nonpartisan			All Cities		
	Non-manager	Manager	All	Non-manager	Manager	All	Non-manager	Manager	All
East	66 (11)	— (1)	67 (12)	69 (19)	54 (12)	63 (31)	68 (30)	56 (13)	64 (43)
Midwest	61 (16)	53 (5)	59 (21)	49 (28)	35 (18)	43 (46)	53 (44)	39 (23)	48 (67)
Far West	— (1)	39 (5)	40 (6)	56 (7)	40 (64)	41 (71)	55 (8)	40 (69)	41 (77)
South	69 (6)	43 (5)	57 (11)	47 (15)	40 (69)	41 (84)	53 (21)	40 (74)	43 (95)
Total	64 (34)	47 (16)	58 (50)	55 (69)	40 (163)	44 (232)	57 (103)	41 (179)	47 (282)

* See Table 1 for states comprising the regions.

TABLE 9. *Mean Per Cent of Registrants Voting, by Region and Social Structure**
(Cities with Nonconcurrent Elections) % and (N)

Region	Ethnicity		Education		Mobility		Age of City		All Cities
	High	Low	High	Low	High	Low	Old	Young	
East	64 (41)	— (2)	56 (17)	69 (26)	52 (9)	67 (34)	66 (31)	60 (12)	64 (43)
Midwest	48 (40)	49 (27)	45 (41)	53 (26)	41 (25)	53 (42)	52 (39)	43 (28)	48 (67)
South	53 (10)	42 (85)	41 (45)	45 (50)	43 (70)	43 (25)	42 (45)	43 (50)	43 (95)
West	40 (38)	43 (39)	41 (69)	39 (8)	41 (64)	41 (13)	48 (20)	39 (57)	41 (77)
Total	51 (129)	44 (153)	44 (172)	52 (110)	42 (168)	54 (114)	51 (135)	43 (147)	47 (282)

* See Table 7 for explanation of demographic categories, Table 1 for states comprising the regions and the other measures.

findings based on correlations. The fact that these two approaches yield much the same results gives confidence in our conclusion that, regardless of the vulnerability of the data and the generally modest nature of the relationships, there is an association between voter turnout and the variables utilized. Cities with partisan elections, mayor-council (or nonmanager) government, high ethnicity, low education, low mobility, and Eastern location tend to have a higher voting turnout than cities with nonpartisan elections, council-manager government, low ethnicity, high education, high mobility, and Far Western location.

III. *Conclusions*

Voting turnout is generally higher in cities with either or both "unreformed" political structures and more explicit class or ethnic cleavages. Voting turnout is higher, not lower, in cities with less well-educated populations, perhaps because in those cities political cleavages based on economic interests are more explicit and visible than in middle-class suburbs or other communities likely to have high proportions of college-educated persons. Cities with more stable populations also have higher levels of voting turnout, possibly because of the greater likelihood of integration of the different elements of social and political structure. Whether or not there are direct links of community continuity—as represented by population stability—and stages of development to accessible and responsive political structures and to the existence and organization of social cleavages is a question we cannot answer from our own data. However, some evidence on the matter of integration can be inferred from a recent study.

Lineberry and Fowler found that cities with "reformed" political structures were less likely to be responsive to cleavages in their population than unreformed cities. Specifically, they found that there were higher correlations of ethnicity and religion (as measured indirectly by private school attendance) with taxation and expenditures in cities with the mayor-council

form of government and partisan or ward elections. They suggest that reformed cities have "removed" the influence of party as a mechanism for aggregating interests, and therefore they expected that the "effects" of social composition would be seen more clearly in unreformed cities. In brief, they suggest that the *political* structures of unreformed cities are likely to be more integrated with their *social* structures than those of reformed cities and that "the electoral institutions of reformed governments make public policy less responsive to the demands arising out of social conflicts in the population."[28] The fact that voting turnout tends to relate independently and positively both to "unreformed" political institutions and to characteristics of community cleavage is consistent with Lineberry and Fowler's conclusions.

With respect to partisanship, it comes as no surprise to find that in the absence of the political party label on the ballot and the assumed reduced likelihood of party organization and activity, voter turnout is generally less. Although there are many advocates of nonpartisanship who would espouse the thesis that local citizen participation should be just as great without the "artificial" injection of partisan politics, the fact remains that the party remains an agent of political mobilization, both symbolically and practically. To some, this is unfortunate. Richard Childs, perhaps the leading exponent of nonpartisanship and one of its "founding fathers" takes the view that "In partisan local elections, two prominent national party organizations consider it their noble duty to combat the other organization, disparage its achievements, advance rival candidates, and the 'outs' consider it necessary to oust the 'ins,' no matter how good a record the 'ins' may have been making. No matter how meaningless the contest for office may be in a given year, both forces must be marshalled for a fight. But what good is that, even if it does bring out a high percentage of the adult population to the polls?"[29]

Regardless of the various merits of non-partisan elections, and there are many,[30] Childs' view overlooks the fact that elections and participation in the electoral process are not just a means to an end— the election of qualified citizens to public office—but an end in themselves. In fact, one may well ask in 1968 whether a high rate of participation in local elections and the possible reduction of a sense of alienation of many citizens from their community would not more than offset the possible loss of an outstanding candidate.

Insofar as relatively greater turnout in nonmanager cities is concerned, both the theoretical and analytical questions are more elusive. The separate election of the mayor would seem to be the prime factor distinguishing manager and mayor-council cities (although there are some manager cities with a separately elected mayor and some mayor-council cities with an appointed mayor). Yet mayors have a wide range of roles in American cities, ranging from figure-head to strong executive; it would seem that these varying roles and the public's response to them would bear a direct relation to voter interest and turnout, but our data provide no assistance to assess such relationships. Nor do we have data, other than these gross turnout figures, to assess the importance of a separately elected chief executive to the community. Does the existence of an election for mayor serve to increase a citizen's attachment to and interest in the political life of the community? Does the personalization of politics around a contest between two individuals, so familiar at the state and national levels, serve in some sense as a bridge between the citizen and his government? We can only hint at the host of the social-psychological questions which the existence or non-existence of a contest for mayor may suggest.

An alternative, but not mutually exclusive, explanation is that electoral politics is simply regarded as less important in council-manager cities than in nonmanager communities. Council-manager theory notwithstanding, it may well be that the citizen feels that the manager has, in fact, reduced the scope of authority and responsibility of the city's elected officials. The manager hires and fires the department heads; the manager submits the budget and, in so doing, resolves many of the basic resource allocation policies before the council ever sees the document. Such matters may well fall on the administration side of the ancient administration–policy dichotomy, but they represent in many citizens' minds the stuff of city government and politics. Their removal, rightly or wrongly, from the overt political scene may be one explanation of the apparent relationship of the council-manager form to lower voter turnout. In a similar fashion, it could well be that the result of the manager plan and an effective manager is to so "manage" conflict and issues that they do not become political and, eventually, electoral issues. A resulting depressant effect on voter attention and participation would be a likely by-product.

In general, relatively high levels of voting turnout are probably the result of the combined influences of sustained and continuous political organization of parties, wards, neighborhoods, voluntary associations with local political concerns, and simply traditional behavior by social groups which does not require the mobilizing influence of political organization. Where there is high turnout without high activity of parties and interest groups, votes may be "available" for manipulation by political elites, because in such cities individuals vote because of their party identification and not their involvement in political organizations. Where there is a high level of activity of political organizations *without* high turnout, on the other hand, we might expect that the lack of electoral sanctions would result in a high level of competition and conflict between the relatively better-educated leaders of the active organizations.

Paradoxically, voting turnout may *not* necessarily be a good index of the politicization of the electorate. Voting may be a form of traditional behavior produced by membership in ethnic and other groups which have a certain party identification as part of their group identity. In such cases, a high vote turnout need not mean high issue consciousness or a high level of political conflict. Conversely, voting turnout may be low without denying the possibility of a high level of conflict and concern with issues among the minority of voters who have a high level of political interest.

Thus, it is possible that a high level of action on such policies as urban renewal and poverty programs may be found in cities with low conflict and issue-concern but high voting turnout, precisely because votes can be delivered by political leaders, and bargains and negotiations between local leaders and state and national leaders are possible. A highly active community may have so much conflict that activity leads to stalemate, because leaders are not able to mobilize clear majorities or count on the passive acquiescence of majorities. This argument is consistent with that of Crain and Rosenthal concerning the impact of high levels of education upon participation, conflict, and stalemate in fluoridation and other decisions. Although they noted exceptions at the highest educational level, they argued that high-status cities, precisely because they have citizens ready and able to participate in politics, will be less likely to be able to innovate new community programs and less able to make decisions because of higher levels of conflict which lead to stalemate.[31] The authors examined data on various types of community decisions—urban renewal, fluoridation, school desegregation, and others—which are related to the educational level of the population in the cities, and found that by and large the cities with better-educated populations have been *less* likely to undertake such programs.

Unfortunately, they did not have data on the key intervening variable in their theoretical proposition: political participation. Our data indicate that, in fact, cities with higher levels of education among the population are *less* likely to have high voting turnout than cities with low levels of education. This finding casts doubt upon the plausible assumption that political participation at the level of the city as a whole has the same relationship to education that it does at the individual level.

But if, in fact, there is *less* political participation in cities with high levels of education, this explanation of differences in decision-making processes cannot rest upon a presumed correlation between education and participation.

As suggested, the answer may partly rest on the possibility that voting turnout may be a poor indicator of other forms of the political activity of groups in cities. Groups composed of better-educated persons may have other channels through which to influence policy than mere voting turnout. Effective political participation by such groups might tend to resolve issues before they become relevant to a campaign and election. In any event, our findings about relatively low turnout in better-educated cities do at least raise questions about the assumption that correlations at the individual level can be casually extended to the level of community social organization. Crain and Rosenthal make the same methodological point in a different substantive context, suggesting that the greater likelihood of better-educated persons to accept innovation may not be true when the same factors are measured at the community "ecological" level.[32]

An investigation of the individual correlations of education and political participation in cities with different demographic and economic characteristics is clearly called for. It may well be true—and we suspect—that in *all* cities, the better educated are more likely to vote than the less well-educated, despite the higher overall levels of voting turnout in less well-educated cities. In high turnout cities, for example, the better-educated stratum in those cities may respond to the political mobilization of the ethnic less-educated majorities by even higher political participation than the majority social groups themselves exhibit. Nor would one expect that in middle-class, better-educated, Far West cities with low vote turnout, there would necessarily be any counter-response by the less well-educated elements in those cities to participate at higher levels. The very fact of the recent migration of less well-educated persons to Western cities should serve to break their ties to the local ethnic neighborhood organizations or other community groups which sustained high voting participation in the Eastern cities from which they came. Thus, a plausible case can be made for expecting the "normal' pattern of individual correlation between education and political participation in both types of cities. It would be possible to compute possible ranges of variations of the individual-level correlations, given certain marginal distributions of educational composition and voting turnout levels in cities, but that problem is beyond our present scope.

A final word on the implications of our data for the controversy over local political sub-cultures. The operations and functions of a political "ethos" or political culture at the local level may be best understood through a historical perspective of the continuity of social and political structures and the norms of behavior which they enforce, rather than through the current attitudes of social groups in a community. We have noted the difference in direction of the correlation between education and voting turnout at the city and individual levels. This may indicate that the consequences of structural features of a political system, derived in turn from its history, may be visible in collective patterns of political behavior, such as partisan strength, levels of voting turnout, or referenda outcomes, but not at all visible in correlations of political attitudes with individual characteristics.

Banfield and Wilson's original article[33] used ecological data on ethnic and class composition of tracts, in relation to referenda voting, which we would regard as appropriate kinds of data for inferences to collective processes, but their theoretical framework was based upon assumptions about *individual* behavior, not necessary to and even possibly misleading about the actual causal processes involved. Wolfinger

and Field questioned that certain ethnic groups hold "private-regarding" or "public-regarding" values, and therefore favor certain political structures in their community. They noted that when region was controlled, the correlations between ethnicity and various aspects of political structure and governmental functions presumed to be predicted by the "ethos" hypothesis vanished. And they suggested that regional variations in the age of cities may explain more than the "ethos" of groups residing in cities. As they put it, "regional variations may reflect to some extent interaction between cities' natural histories and prevailing political enthusiasms at crucial periods in those histories."[34] Our data indicating significant regional differences, particularly the tendency of Eastern cities to have relatively high voting turnout regardless of form of government, method of balloting and social characteristics is consistent with this view. Whereas region may not be a useful analytical tool, *as such*, the variations among regions suggest the need to introduce into the conceptual framework and research design a recognition of such phenomena as Wolfinger and Field describe.

The regional or even the state location of a city may not be sufficient to identify its political culture accurately. Samuel C. Patterson has recently suggested that while there may be interstate variations in basic political orientations, there are also important variations within states. A few studies have analyzed this topic.[35]

We have suggested that there is likely to be variation in community political systems linked to the regional location of the city, its age, and the extent of out-migration or in-migration. Sheer length of existence, as well as the proportion of the population which has lived in the city for a long or a short time, would seem to be plausibly related to the degree to which there is historical continuity of leadership patterns and policy-making patterns in a city. Again, these are indirect indicators, because, for example, some cities may have experienced what amounts to a revolution in leadership continuity in certain periods of their history. But we hypothesize that our indicators would correlate with more direct measures of continuity of leadership and policy-making.

Over a period of years, we suggest, communication networks between social groups and political leaders develop which have some continuity, although incumbents may change. Political roles and institutionalized locations for those roles develop which are linked to the historical success of

certain groups in winning electoral victories or exerting informal influence over policy-making processes. High voting turnout may be one consequence of the development over time of these links of social groups to political organization.

Voter Qualification and Participation in National, State, and Municipal Elections: The Case of Houston, Texas*

Dan Nimmo

University of Missouri at Columbia

Clifton McCleskey

University of Texas at Austin

A PLETHORA of voting behavior studies exist describing the factors underlying both varied levels of electoral turnout and the direction of voting decisions. It is interesting to note, however, that in the growing body of literature we find relatively few analyses devoted to examining the behavior of more than a single type of electorate in more than one election. The most prestigious of the voting studies, for example, have employed survey techniques designed to investigate the partisan leanings and voting preferences of a national electorate in presidential contests. Sophisticated as these inquiries are in developing models of voting in national elections, they prove less valuable in helping us to understand the voting act in state and local elections.[1] Studies at these subnational levels—frequently using aggregate techniques matching the socio-demographic characteristics of various areas with county and precinct returns[2]—tell us something about the types of people who vote in particular contests, but provide little data for comparing voter types at state and local levels with participants in presidential elections.[3] Finally, with rare exceptions,[4] few studies using either survey or aggregate

Written especially for this volume.

techniques explore voter registration,despite the fact that it is a prerequisite to voting in most regions of the country.

Within this context of previous examinations of voter turnout in national, state, and local elections the intent of this inquiry is limited, but nonetheless significant. Our purpose is to examine the characteristics and turnout of qualified voters in a single metropolitan setting—Houston (and Harris County), Texas—for a variety of elections: the presidential election of 1964, the state general elections in the off-year of 1966; and the municipal elections to choose the mayor and city council of Houston in 1965 and 1967. Through this effort, we will have the opportunity to draw conclusions concerning the impact on voter turnout of two related factors: the type of registration system employed and the level of election stimulating electoral interest.

Voter Qualification for Electoral Contests

As a prelude to our discussion it is necessary to say a few words about the setting and methods involved in research. The metropolitan area of Houston, Texas, is particularly appropriate for exploring the relationship between alternate registration systems and electoral levels in shaping voting rates. Aside from the fact that the potential electorate in the area is a large and diversified one—permitting us to examine the sociodemographic factors normally related to variations in turnout—the methods of voter qualification in the area have recently undergone modification. During the four-year period under investigation Houston (as did Texas generally along with three other Southern states), shifted from a poll tax system to a free registration arrangement for qualifying voters. Thus the case of Houston affords the opportunity for examining the types of people in a community who both qualify and actually vote under each system at three different electoral levels.

To be eligible to vote in Texas a person must be a U.S. citizen, 21 years of age or

106

older, a resident of the state for one year and of the county for six months, and not deprived of the franchise by reason of felony conviction or mental illness. All persons with these characteristics comprise the *potential* electorate in Texas elections—presidential, state, or local. Prior to February, 1966, these potential voters were required to qualify to vote either (1) by paying a $1.50 poll tax within a four-month period ending January 31 of the election year; or (2) by obtaining an exemption certification in the same period of time (exempted were those 60 years of age or older, and those whose residence and age made them temporarily eligible to vote before they became liable for the poll tax); or (3) by qualifying under the provisions of the Twenty-Fourth Amendment to the U.S. Constitution. The bulk of voters qualified by paying the poll tax, and most of the remainder qualified under the exemption procedure, with only a tiny handful utilizing the Twenty-Fourth Amendment. However, when the federal courts in 1966 invalidated the poll tax as a prerequisite to voting in those states still using it in state and local elections,[5] the Texas legislature enacted the state's first registration law. Since the court decisions came after the close of the normal poll tax deadline, a special fifteen-day period in mid-March was established for potential voters in 1966 who had not qualified under the poll tax system. For the years following 1966, members of the potential electorate were to establish their voting eligibility by registering prior to January 31 of each year. Thus for the presidential election of 1964 and the mayoralty election of 1965, Houstonians qualified through the poll tax and exemption system. For the state elections of 1966 the bulk of citizens (approximately 377,375 persons in Harris County) qualified under the poll tax and exemptee arrangements, while a smaller group (96,405) entered the qualified electorate by free registration. Finally, for the 1967 mayoralty elections all 372,483 members of the qualified electorate in Houston were free registrants.

In order to obtain information on the characteristics of the members of the

qualified electorate for each election, 1964 through 1967, a simple random sample was drawn by strict probability methods from the lists of eligibles for each year.[6] In 1964 a sample of 4,123 qualified voters was drawn from the poll tax and exemptee lists in Harris County. In 1965 a sample of 742 was drawn from those on the poll tax and exemptee lists in the city of Houston. In 1966 a total sample of 1,013 persons was drawn from the county lists, with 777 of these having qualified under the poll tax system and 236 being free registrants. Finally in 1967 a total of 732 names was drawn from those on the city's registration rolls.

For each qualified elector sampled, the following sociodemographic data could be obtained directly from the poll tax, exemption, or registration lists: place of residence; age; sex; length of residence in the state, county, and city; state (or country) of birth; voting precinct; and method of qualification. In addition, for voters listed on poll tax and exemptee rolls, occupation was also available; however, the lists for free registrants in 1967 did not include this information, thus making it necessary to obtain such data through direct contact with the persons listed. Finally, since critical information on race and ethnicity were missing from all listings, it was necessary to utilize admittedly imperfect indicators. Mexican-Americans were identified through use of the list of Spanish surnames developed by the U.S. Census Bureau for its census of the Spanish-speaking population of the Southwest. Black electors were first identified in a number of voting precincts as "Negro" on the basis of (1) demographic data on Houston precincts utilizing the Shevky–Bell technique (as described in Selection 8); (2) designations from the county clerk's office; and (3) precinct voting records in elections where there had been pronounced Negro bloc voting. All electors in these precincts were classified as

"Negro" unless previously designated as "Spanish surname." In accordance with Southwestern custom, all those in the samples who were not identified as Negroes or Mexican-Americans were classified as "Anglos."

Utilizing the data obtained by the above procedures it was possible to construct a profile of the *qualified electorate* for each election year: in the discussion that follows we shall compare the characteristics of those qualified electorates with both the *potential* and *actual electorates*. Our profiles of the potential electorate are based upon projections of census statistics for the population 21 years of age and older; the county-wide profile is projected to 1964 and the profile of the potential electorate for city-wide contests is projected to 1965. To ascertain the characteristics of the actual electorate in each election the name of every member of the qualified electorate in our sample was checked against the poll list used by election officials to verify voters entering the polls. In this way, it was possible to determine which qualified electors participated in the presidential, statewide, and municipal elections.

Since there is reason to believe that the composition of the qualified and actual electorates is affected by the salience and the competitiveness of the elections involved, brief mention should be made of the nature of the contests in the years under consideration. In 1964 of course, the major interest was focused on the presidential race between President Lyndon Johnson and his Republican challenger Barry Goldwater. Also capturing considerable attention was the race for U.S. Senator between incumbent Ralph Yarborough and Republican George Bush of Houston. In 1966 the principal statewide contest stimulating interest was between Republican Senator John Tower and his challenger, State Attorney-General Waggoner Carr.

As is the case with most Texas cities, and elsewhere in the nation, Houston selects its municipal officials through nonpartisan elections.[7] The resulting contests are frequently waged between personalities prominent in local politics.[8] This was the case in 1965 and 1967 when the principal candidates for mayor were the same in both elections. Houston's Mayor Louis Welch, running for re-election, defeated former Mayor Louis Cutrer (the man Welch had won the office from in 1963) in 1965. Again in 1967 Welch faced Cutrer and easily defeated the challenger; a third candidate in 1967, Joe Pirano garnered only 2.5 per cent of the total vote.

In sum the campaign of maximum salience during this period was that for President in 1964; the contest for U.S. Senator in 1966 had at best only medium salience and those for Mayor of Houston in both 1965 and 1967 attracted considerably less interest among the local electorate.

The Filtering Effects of Registration Systems

Our first concern in analyzing the data from the four samples is to determine the extent to which the qualified electorate that results from a registration system differs from the potential electorate. Table 1 presents the relevant data. In it we find a profile of the qualified electorates produced by the poll tax system in 1964 and 1965 and by free registration in 1967; moreover, for 1966 the profiles indicate the characteristics of the qualified electorate resulting from the poll tax period, free registration, and the combination of both.

From a consideration of Table 1 it is apparent that there are differences in the compared characteristics of the potential and the qualified electorates. Such a finding is not unexpected, for other studies have generally indicated that any registration system will to some extent act as a filter through which some potential voters pass and others do not.[9] But Table 1 enables us to extend the analysis further toward a determination of the filtering effects of the registration system and enables us as well to note the interaction of that system with the level of election.

So far as sex is concerned, the data in Table 1 indicate that men are consistently overrepresented in the qualified electorate, where they constitute a slim majority despite being outnumbered by women in the potential electorate. Furthermore, this male overrepresentation among qualified voters appears to be largely independent of the registration system or the level of the election, for there is no significant variation from 1964 to 1967.

The same cannot be said of the other three variables considered. Our findings regarding occupation, for example, are mixed or contradictory. One reason may be that the data themselves are "soft" and undifferentiated. The occupational categories for qualified and potential electorates were based on the Census Bureau's Classified Index of Occupations and Industries; our coding is subject to error due to the peculiarities of the occupational listings on the poll tax and registration lists and the fact that 1967 data on occupations had to be obtained directly from those sampled. Allowing for these limitations, however,

Dan Nimmo
Clifton McCleskey

certain patterns are clear. Professional, technical, and managerial occupations are always overrepresented in the qualified electorate, usually very substantially so. Their overrepresentation was greatest in the most salient election (the 1964 presidential) and least in the low-visibility municipal elections. However, blue-collar and white-collar workers are not greatly different from each other or in the rates of qualification, with both categories reflecting considerable correspondence between their potential and qualified shares of the electorate in all elections except 1967.

The data for age are more revealing. If we compare the various age categories of the qualified electorate in 1964 with the potential electorate, only minor differences are observed. This might indicate that the

TABLE 1. Characteristics of the Potential and Qualified Electorates in Harris County and Houston, Texas, 1964–1967

Characteristic	Potential Electorate		1964 Sample (N = 4123)	1965 Sample (N = 742)	1966 Sample			1967 Sample (N = 732)
	County 1964	City 1965			Combined (N = 1013)	Poll Tax and Exempt (N = 777)	Free Registration (N = 236)	
Sex:								
Male	47.6%	47.3%	51.3%	52.8%	53.1%	53.0%	53.4%	52.3%
Female	52.4	52.7	48.7	47.2	46.9	47.0	46.6	47.7
Age:								
21–29	18.5	20.4	18.7	14.6	20.2	15.6	35.2	20.0
30–39	27.0	26.7	25.4	22.8	23.3	22.5	25.8	26.6
40–49	21.5	20.3	23.2	24.0	21.1	21.1	21.0	21.4
50–59	16.4	16.2	16.4	18.1	17.8	19.6	12.0	17.5
60 +	16.3	16.4	16.3	20.5	17.6	21.2	6.0	14.5
Ethnicity:								
Anglo	75.5	71.4	81.5	73.7	82.5	82.8	81.8	76.3
Negro Precincts	18.9	22.5	15.4	23.0	14.5	15.6	11.0	20.2
Spanish Surname	5.6	6.1	3.1	3.2	3.0	1.6	7.2	3.4
Occupation:								
Prof./Mgr.	14.2	—*	28.2	19.9	27.0	27.4	25.4	21.2
White Collar	14.0	—	15.9	15.5	14.3	13.8	16.1	10.0
Blue Collar	28.4	—	28.9	27.3	30.9	28.8	33.4	18.9
Miscellaneous	43.4	—	27.1	37.2	28.8	30.0	25.1	49.8

*Not Computed.

poll tax was nondiscriminatory with respect to age, but a more likely explanation
is that the salience of the presidential
election overrode the filtering effects of the
poll tax where age is concerned. This is
borne out by examination of the qualified
electorate in 1966, for the youngest categories were clearly underrepresented among
the poll-tax payers but overrepresented
among the free qualifiers. Likewise, a
comparison of the qualified electorates in
1965 and 1967 reveals much more proportionality in the latter year, particularly with
respect to the age group 21–29 years. It thus
appears that the age distribution of the
qualified electorate varies most from that of
the potential when there is a less visible
election *and* a more restrictive registration
system (1965 municipal); it varies least
when there is a salient election (1964) *or*
when registration requirements are eased
through abandonment of the poll tax
(1966 free, 1967).

Because the use of the poll tax in the
South has always been linked in one
fashion or another to racial issues, we are
quick to perceive that when it was in effect
in 1964 and 1966 persons living in black
precincts were less likely than Anglos to
qualify to vote. As with age, however, one
must also take into account the impact of
the type of election involved. Thus in the
1965 municipal elections, with the poll
tax still in effect, Blacks were qualified to
vote in proportion to their potential,
whereas in the free registration period in
1966 their qualification dropped. In the
1967 municipal election—with free registration—Blacks were not quite as well
represented in the qualified electorate as
they had been in 1965. Apparently, then,
the efforts of black political organizations
to qualify potential voters enabled them to
offset the filtering effects of the poll tax
up to a point, but an over-all lower level
of achievable mobilization prevented them
from keeping pace with Anglo qualification in more salient elections.[10]

Whatever its consequences for Blacks,
the poll tax requirement shows more
discriminatory tendencies where Mexican-
Americans are concerned. Their proportion
of the qualified electorate was consistently
far below their potential strength, and the
only marked improvement in that relationship came in the free registration period
of 1966. Further indication of the beneficial consequences of the end of the poll
tax for Mexican-Americans is their slight
gain in registration in 1967 as compared
with 1965. Our data make it impossible to
determine why the poll tax should affect
differently two minority groups with such
similar social and economic conditions,
but in all likelihood the explanation will
have to be sought in differences in the two
political subcultures and in the poor political
organization of Mexican-Americans compared to Blacks.

From what has been said of black and
Mexican-American patterns of registration, it follows that Anglos are invariably
overrepresented in the qualified electorate,
regardless of type of registration and level
of election. In the short run at least their
overrepresentation has been increased by
the demise of the poll tax, for Anglos took
advantage of free registration in 1966 in
disproportionate numbers and increased
their 1967 share of the qualified electorate
over 1965 levels. Moreover, Anglo overrepresentation increased in the more salient
elections.

One final observation should be made
about the comparison of potential and
qualified electorates under two registration
systems before turning our attention to
actual voters. The "fit" of the qualified
electorate to the potential is generally
closer in 1964 than in 1966. Moreover, the
fit of the "combined" profile to the potential in 1966 is closer than for the "poll tax
and exempt" electorate, indicating free
registration may have reduced the filtering
effects of the over-all system for qualification. We might expect, of course, that the
differences between the two electorates
compared would be somewhat greater in
1966 than in the presidential election year
when the level of popular interest rises
higher and earlier than in the "off year." In
looking at the city-wide elections we find
the fit between qualified and potential

electorates closer in 1967 than 1965 (this being especially true if we include controls for age); this suggests again that the type of registration system does make a difference.

In sum, we may say that any registration system filters, and, given no change in the stimulus level of the elections, free registration tends to have less screening effect than a taxed system. But, we must qualify that by recognizing the fact that our data indicate that the filtering effects of even a poll tax system may be reduced in a high stimulus election, reduced perhaps even below that of free registration operating in contests having only marginal interest to most citizens. Registration system and electoral level interact in influencing qualification rates; does their impact also operate jointly in shaping turnout?

Voter Turnout, Registration, and Electoral Levels

By shifting our focus to Table 2 we are able to examine the profiles of qualified

Voter Qualification and Participation 111 in National, State, and Municipal Elections: The Case of Houston, Texas
Dan Nimmo
Clifton McCleskey

voters in our samples who actually participated in each of the major elections under study. At the outset it is obvious that our findings generally conform to the received notions regarding the sociodemographic characteristics of persons voting in national, state, and municipal elections. First, as one would expect from previous studies,[11] turnout is highest in presidential contests, markedly lower for general elections in the "off-year," and at its lowest point in municipal elections.[12] Secondly, women vote less than men, the intervening age groups between the very youngest and oldest comprise the highest proportions of the actual electorate. Finally, Anglos dominate turnout, and the upper-occupation categories usually make up twice the portion of the actual electorate that would be expected from their relative numbers among the qualified.

TABLE 2. Voting Turnout in Harris County and Houston, Texas, 1964–1967*

Characteristics	General Election 1964	Mayoralty Election 1965	General Election 1966 Taxed (N = 777)	General Election 1966 Free (N = 236)	General Election 1966 Combined (N = 1013)	Mayoralty Election 1967 (N = 732)
Sex:						
Male	51.4%	57.1%	56.7%	50.6%	55.7%	51.4%
Female	48.6	42.9	43.3	49.4	44.3	48.6
Age:						
21–29	18.1	11.4	13.3	44.2	18.6	12.8
30–39	26.9	21.5	21.7	20.9	21.6	23.2
40–49	24.1	28.5	24.6	19.8	23.67	25.4
50–59	17.0	19.3	21.4	10.5	19.6	22.1
60 +	13.9	19.3	19.0	4.6	16.6	16.5
Race Ethnicity:						
Anglo	81.5	77.8	84.3	84.9	84.4	79.6
Negro Precincts	15.5	19.8	13.8	4.6	12.3	18.2
Spanish Surname	3.0	2.4	1.9	10.5	3.3	2.2
Occupation:						
Professional/Managerial	29.7	25.0	30.9	30.2	30.8	27.1
White Collar	16.0	14.7	14.3	17.4	14.8	9.6
Blue Collar	29.0	25.1	26.9	30.2	27.5	18.7
Miscellaneous	25.3	35.2	27.9	22.1	26.9	44.6
Per cent of Qualified Voting	77.8	40.2	56.7	37.5	52.3	38.3

* Percentage turnout rates are computed on the basis of those persons in each sample of qualified voters actually voting in the general or mayoralty election.

Comparison of the data in Tables 1 and 2 will help us to draw inferences in two areas: (1) Does actual turnout show more resemblance to the qualified or to the potential electorate? (2) What is the influence of the type of election and of the registration system on the characteristics of the actual electorate?

With respect to the variable "sex," it appears that actual turnout typically is closer to the qualified than to the potential electorate. Male overqualification was lowest in 1964, and male strength in the actual electorate was the same as in the qualified electorate. In the 1965 and 1966 taxed electorates, male qualification was higher, and actual turnout even greater. However, in 1966 and 1967 with free registration there was a noticeable improvement in female voting, even though women did not much improve their rate of qualification. It thus appears that the tendency under the poll tax system for female registration and voting to decline in nonpresidential elections has been at least partially offset by free registration.

It is much harder to generalize with respect to age. In the presidential election of 1964 the rate of qualification and the actual turnout were roughly proportional to their potential for most age categories. For those age 21–29 and 30–39, the rate of actual turnout under the poll tax system in 1965 and 1966 worsened their underrepresentation in the qualified electorate. Free registration in 1966 and 1967 brought overqualification under 30, but their poor turnout, particularly in the municipal elections, kept them underrepresented in the actual electorate. Those age 30–39 improved their share but did not attain proportionality in either registration or actual turnout in 1966 and 1967. On the other hand, those persons age 40–49 and 50–59 turned out to vote in a way that tended pretty consistently to magnify the overrepresentation already achieved through the voter qualification process; free registration tended to have only minor impact on these groups. Persons age 60 and over

tended to overqualify under the poll tax system (from which they were exempt), but their turnout tended to be subnormal, so that their share of the actual electorate was typically greater than their potential but below their rate of qualification.

So far as race and ethnicity are concerned, Anglos were consistently overqualified and their actual turnout was always equal to or greater than their proportion of the qualified electorate. Their greatest overrepresentation in actual voting occurred in 1966; it was lowest in the 1965 municipal election. Blacks, who were substantially underqualified in all years except 1965, had an even smaller share of actual turnout in all elections except that of 1964. Their underrepresentation in the actual electorate was greatest in 1966, particularly in the free portion. They came closest to achieving parity in actual voting in 1965 and 1967. Mexican-Americans, who were grossly underqualified in all cases except the 1966 free electorate, were also underrepresented in the actual electorate, typically but not invariably below their qualified share. They had their poorest relative turnout in the 1966 paid electorate and their best in the 1964 presidential election.

What do these racial and ethnic patterns tell us about the impact of changes in the registration system and about the influence of the type of election? It appears, somewhat unexpectedly, that elections of medium salience (1966) tend to maximize the overrepresentation of Anglos and the underrepresentation of Blacks. Elections of low salience (the 1965 and 1967 municipal contests) bring Blacks closest to parity and improve the representation of Mexican-Americans. The most visible election (the 1964 presidential race) provided Mexican-Americans with their best relative turnout, even though it was still far below parity; that year was neither the best nor the worst for Anglos and Blacks.

So far as registration is concerned, the end of the poll tax improved Anglo representation in the actual electorate both in 1966 and 1967, while reducing that of Blacks in both years. Mexican-American participation was dramatically improved in

1966 by free registration, but their 1967 share of the actual electorate was slightly below that of 1965. It appears on balance that the type of election produces more variation in racial-ethnic turnout than does alteration of the registration system, at least in the short run.

The soft nature of our occupational data precludes any extended analysis, but a few impressions can be reported. Just as those in the professional–managerial group qualify in grossly disproportionate numbers, so they turn out to vote at an unusually high rate, invariably comprising 25–30 per cent of the actual voters although they account for only 14 per cent of the potential electorate. Though the variations are not great, they are most overrepresented in the medium-visibility elections and least so in the low-visibility contests—a pattern conforming to that just described for Anglos, who constitute the bulk of the professional–managerial class. The end of the poll tax requirement did not appear to reduce the strength of professionals and managers in the actual electorate.

For the white-collar and blue-collar workers, the actual turnout tended to conform roughly to the distribution of the qualified electorate. Those in the "miscellaneous" category usually voted somewhat below their strength in the qualified electorate. For our purposes, the most interesting thing about this is the fact that neither the change in the registration system nor the type of election seemed to have much effect on turnout by occupational categories, other than for the professional–managerial group, and even there the variations appear to be modest.[13]

Conclusions

Although the findings of this study are necessarily limited by the fact that we have examined only a single locale, a few conclusions can be drawn about the interplay of alternate registration requirements, voter qualification, and turnout at various electoral levels.

It can be said first of all that any

Dan Nimmo
Clifton McCleskey

registration system is discriminatory to the extent that it filters out, from the population of citizens eligible to vote in every other respect, those without the means and/or inclination to achieve formal qualification. It is at this point that such factors as age, sex, race-ethnicity, and occupation, and probably other social factors as well, exert their earliest and perhaps most decisive influence on voting participation.

But the registration system alone is not the only force structuring voter qualification and turnout. Even a restrictive registration system, such as that imposing a poll tax, does not generate a set of either qualified or actual voters grossly distortive of the potential electorate in every election. Moreover, there is no assurance that a free system will in each and every election produce qualified voters representing proportionately the characteristics of the eligible citizenry. The type and level of the electoral contest itself interacts with the registration system to stimulate or reduce interest in qualifying and voting. Free registration did not revolutionize turnout patterns in the senatorial race of 1966, nor were the characteristics of voters in municipal elections under the poll tax in 1965 greatly altered by free registration in 1967, although a few notable differences emerged in the profiles of the two qualified electorates. Initially, at least in comparatively low-stimulus elections, the consequences of the removal of the poll tax in the Houston area have hardly matched the optimistic predictions of its critics; it remains, of course, to be seen whether a presidential contest under conditions of free registration will generate an actual electorate similar in composition to that potentially eligible and formally qualified.

There are undoubtedly other reasons behind the failure of a change from the poll tax to a free registration system alone to work a radical modification in voting turnout. For one, the Texas registration system still retains other restrictive features, such as the necessity of qualifying anew each year with a deadline for registration (January 31) far in advance of the presidential, congressional, and municipal contests held in November. Secondly, the registration system is only one of many factors depressing voter interest in Texas politics: Party competition is muted (indeed, nonexistent in the nonpartisan municipal elections) except in presidential races; political organizations are weak; the level of education of the citizenry is low; and most people still see little relationship between their votes and the policies ultimately made. Third, it will be some time before the minorities and younger elements who have been most newly "enfranchised" by free registration develop the responses that condition them to register and vote. Finally, it may be several years before the change in registration affects the already extensive efforts to encourage Black participation and the less strenuous activity to mobilize the Mexican-Americans in Houston.

Hıghly organized urban political parties are generally conceded to be one of America's distinctive contributions to mankind's repertory of political forms. Just as the two major national parties in the United States are almost universally described in terms of their *dis*organization—their lack of an authoritative command structure—the municipal parties have, until recently, been characterized by most observers in terms of their hierarchical strength. E. E. Schattschneider once summarized this state of affairs in the memorable image of a truncated pyramid: a party system which is weak and ghostlike at the top and solid at the bottom.[1]

This essay deals with the disciplined, largely autonomous local political parties which sprang up in many American cities in the nineteenth century. Much of the literature on these political configurations is heavily pejorative, concerned more with excoriation than explanation. Even the basic nomenclature, "boss" and "machine," is laden with negative connotations, although recently there has been a turn toward nostalgic romanticization of the "vanishing breed" of city bosses.[2]

Here, for reasons which I shall indicate, the attempt shall be to delineate rather than to pass moral judgment: What was the nature of old-style urban party organization? Why did this political pattern develop and how did it operate? What contributed to its short-run persistence in the face of reform campaigns? Under what circumstances have such organizations disappeared and under what circumstances have they continued into the present day—or even undergone renaissances? What are the present-day descendents of old-style urban party organizations?

Analytic delineation invariably involves oversimplification. This is doubly necessary in the present case, because our knowledge of the distribution of types of local party organization is scant. We have no census of local political parties, either for today or for the putative heyday of bosses and

*Reprinted with permission of the author and publisher, from Fred I. Greenstein, "The Changing Pattern of Urban Party Politics," The Annals of the American Academy of Political and Social Science, 353 (May 1964), pp. 1–13.

The Changing Pattern of Urban Party Politics*

Fred I. Greenstein

Wesleyan University

machines. And there is reason to believe that observers have exaggerated the ubiquity of tightly organized urban political parties in past generations, as well as underestimated somewhat their contemporary prevalence.

Old-Style Party Organization: Definitional Characteristics

Ranney and Kendall have persuasively argued that the imprecision and negative connotations of terms like "boss" destroy their usefulness. What, beyond semantic confusion, they ask, can come from classifying politicians into "bosses" versus "leaders"? Such a distinction leads to fruitless preoccupation with the purity of politicians' motives rather than the actuality of their behavior; it overestimates the degree to which figures of the past such as Richard Croker, William Tweed, and Frank Hague were free of public constraints; and it obscures the fact that *all* effective political leaders, whether or not they are popularly labeled as bosses, use quite similar techniques and resources.[3]

Granting these points, it still seems that a recognizable and noteworthy historical phenomenon is hinted at by the venerable terms "boss" and "machine." If the overtones of these terms make us reluctant to use them, we might simply speak of an "old style" of party organization with the following characteristics:

1. There is a disciplined party hierarchy led by a single executive or a unified board of directors.

Notes to this selection will be found on pages 340–341.

2. The party exercises effective control over nomination to public office, and, through this, it controls the public officials of the municipality.

3. The party leadership—which quite often is of lower-class social origins—usually does not hold public office and sometimes does not even hold formal party office. At any rate, official position is not the primary source of the leadership's strength.

4. Rather, a cadre of loyal party officials and workers, as well as a core of voters, is maintained by a mixture of material rewards and *nonideological* psychic rewards—such as personal and ethnic recognition, camaraderie, and the like.[4]

The Rise of Old-Style Party Organization

This pattern of politics, Schattschneider comments, "is as American as the jazz band .... China, Mexico, South America, and southern Italy at various times have produced figures who played roles remotely like that of the American boss, but England, France, Germany, and the lesser democracies of Europe have exhibited no tendency to develop this form of political organization in modern times."[5] What then accounted for the development of old-style party organization in the United States?

The Crokers, Tweeds, and Hagues and their organizations probably could not have arisen if certain broad preconditions had not existed in American society and culture. These include the tradition of freewheeling individualism and pragmatic opportunism, which developed in a prosperous, sprawling new society unrestrained by feudalism, aristocracy, monarchy, an established church, and other traditional authorities. This is the state of affairs which has been commented on by countless observers, even before de Tocqueville, and which has been used to explain such disparate phenomena as the failure of socialism to take hold in the United States, the recurrence of popularly based assaults on civil liberties, and even the peculiarly corrosive form which was taken by American slavery.[6]

It also is possible to identify five more direct determinants of the form that urban party organization took in the nineteenth century, three of them consequences of the Industrial Revolution and two of them results of political institutions and traditions which preceded industrialization.

MASSIVE URBAN EXPANSION

Over a relatively brief span of years, beginning in the mid-nineteenth century, industrial and commercial growth led to a spectacular rise in the number and proportion of Americans concentrated in cities. A thumbnail sketch of urban expansion may be had by simply noting the population of urban and rural areas for each of the twenty-year periods from 1840 to 1920:

	Urban Population	Rural Population
	(in millions)	
1840	1.8	15.2
1860	6.2	25.2
1880	14.1	36.0
1900	30.1	45.8
1920	54.2	51.6

These statistics follow the old Census Bureau classification of areas exceeding 2,500 in population as urban. Growth of larger metropolitan units was even more striking. In 1840 slightly over 300,000 Americans lived in cities—or, rather, a single city, New York—with more than a quarter of a million residents; by 1920 there were twenty-four cities of this size, containing approximately 21 million Americans.

The sheer mechanics of supporting urban populations of this magnitude are, of course, radically different from the requirements of rural life. There must be transportation arrangements; urban dwellers are as dependent upon a constant inflow of food and other commodities as an infant is on the ministrations of adults. A host of new administrative functions must be performed as the population becomes urbanized: street construction and maintenance, bridges, lighting, interurban transportation, sanitary arrangements, firefighting, police protection, and so forth. Overwhelming demands suddenly are placed on governments which, hitherto, were able to operate with a minimum of effort and activity.

DISORGANIZED FORMS OF URBAN GOVERNMENT

The forms of government which had evolved in nineteenth-century America were scarcely suitable for meeting the demands of mushrooming cities. Governmental structures reflected a mixture of Jacksonian direct democracy and Madisonian checks and balances. Cities had a multitude of elected officials (sometimes they were elected annually), weak executives, large and unwieldy councils and boards. The formal organization of the cities placed officials in a position permitting and, in fact, encouraging them to checkmate each other's efforts to make and execute policies. Since each official was elected by appealing to his own peculiar constituency and had little incentive to co-operate with his associates, the difficulties caused by the formal limitations of government were exacerbated. In a period when the requirements for governmental action were increasing geometrically, this was a prescription for chaos.

NEEDS OF BUSINESSMEN

A third aspect of mid-nineteenth-century American society which contributed to the formation of old-style party organizations was the needs of businessmen. There was an increasing number of merchants, industrialists, and other businessmen, licit and illicit, who needed—and were willing to pay for—the appropriate responses from city governments. Some businessmen wanted to operate unrestrained by municipal authority. Others desired street-railway franchises, paving contracts, construction work, and other transactions connected with the very growth of the cities themselves.

NEEDS OF DEPENDENT POPULATIONS

The needs of the bulk of the nineteenth-century urban population were not for

profits but for the simple wherewithal to survive and maintain a modicum of dignity. It is difficult in the relatively affluent society of our day to appreciate the vicissitudes of urban life several generations ago: the low wages, long hours, tedious and hazardous working conditions, and lack of security which were the lot of most citizens. Even for native-born Americans, life often was nasty and brutish. But many urbanites were first- and second-generation immigrants who, in addition to their other difficulties, had to face an alien culture and language. Between the Civil War and the First World War, the United States managed somehow to absorb 25 million foreigners.

UNRESTRICTED SUFFRAGE

Urban dwellers were not totally without resources for their own advancement. The American tradition of unrestricted male franchise was, in the long run, to work to their advantage. Although it doubtless is true that few city dwellers of the day were aware of the importance of their right to vote, politicians *were* aware of this. Because even the lowliest of citizens was, or could become, a voter, a class of politicians developed building upon the four conditions referred to above: the requirements of organizing urban life, the inability of existing governments to meet these requirements, and the presence of businessmen willing to pay for governmental services and of dependent voting populations in need of security from the uncertainties of their existence.

The old-style urban party leader was as much a product of his time and social setting as was the rising capitalist of the Gilded Age. Building on the conditions and needs of the day, the politician had mainly to supply his own ingenuity and co-ordinating ability in order to tie together the machinery of urban government. If a cohesive party organization could control nominations and elect its own agents to office, the formal fragmentation of government no longer would stand in the way of municipal activity. The votes of large blocs of dependent citizens were sufficient to control nominations and win elections. And the financial support of those who sought to transact business with the city, as well as the revenues and resources of the city government, made it possible to win votes. The enterprising politician who could succeed in governing a city on this basis was a broker *par excellence*; generous brokers' commissions were the rule of the day.

The importance of out-and-out vote-buying on election day as a source of voter support can easily be overestimated. Party organizations curried the favor of voters on a year-long basis. In a day when "better" citizens espoused philosophical variants of Social Darwinism, urban politicians thought in terms of an old-fashioned conception of the welfare state. In the familiar words of Tammany sachem George Washington Plunkitt:

> What holds your grip on your district is to go right down among the poor families and help them in the different ways they need help. I've got a regular system for this. If there's a fire in Ninth, Tenth or Eleventh Avenue, for example, any hour of the day or night, I'm usually there with some of my election district captains as soon as the fire engines. If a family is burned out I don't ask whether they are Republicans or Democrats, and I don't refer them to the Charity Organization Society, which would investigate their case in a month or two and decide they were worthy of help about the time they are dead from starvation. I just get quarters for them, buy clothes for them if their clothes were burned up, and fix them up till they get things runnin' again. It's philanthropy, but its politics, too—mighty good politics. Who can tell how many votes one of these fires bring me? The poor are the most grateful people in the world, and, let me tell you, they have more friends in their neighborhoods than the rich have in theirs.[7]

With numerous patronage appointees (holders not only of city jobs but also of jobs with concerns doing business with the city), party organizations could readily administer this sort of an informal relief program. And, unlike many latter-day charitable and governmental relief programs, the party's activities did not stop with the provision of mere physical assistance.

> I know every man, woman and child in the Fifteenth District, except them that's been born this summer—and I know some of them, too. I know what they like and what they don't like, what they are strong at and what they are weak in, and I reach them by approachin' at the right side.
>
> For instance, here's how I gather in the young men. I hear of a young feller that's proud of his voice, thinks that he can sing fine. I ask him to come around to Washington Hall and join our Glee Club. He comes and sings, and he's a follower of Plunkitt for life. Another young feller gains a reputation as a baseball player in a vacant lot. I bring him into our baseball club. That fixes him. You'll find him workin' for my ticket at the polls next election day. Then there's the feller that likes rowin' on the river, the young feller that makes a name as a waltzer on his block, the young feller that's handy with his dukes—I rope them all in by givin' them opportunities to show themselves off. I don't trouble them with political arguments. I just study human nature and act accordin'.[8]

This passage reflects some of the ways in which party activities might be geared to the *individual* interests of voters. *Group* interests were at least as important. As each new nationality arrived in the city, politicians rather rapidly accommodated to it and brought it into the mainstream of political participation. Parties were concerned with the votes of immigrants virtually from the time of their arrival. Dockside naturalization and voter enrollment was not unknown.

But if the purpose of the politicians was to use the immigrants, it soon became clear that the tables could be turned. In Providence, Rhode Island, for example, a careful study of the assimilation of immigrant groups into local politics shows that, within thirty years after the arrival of the first representative of a group in the city, it began to be represented in the councils of one or both parties. Eventually, both of the local parties came to be dominated by representatives of the newer stocks. Thus, in 1864 no Irish names appeared on lists of Democratic committeemen in Providence; by 1876 about a third of the names were Irish; by the turn of the century, three-quarters were Irish. In time, the Republican party became the domain of politicians of Italian ancestry.[9] Perhaps the most dramatic example to date of urban party politics as an avenue of upward social mobility was in the antecedents of President Kennedy, whose great-grandfather was an impoverished refugee of the Irish potato famine, his grandfather a saloon keeper and a classical old-time urban political leader, his father a multimillionaire businessman, presidential advisor, and ambassador to the Court of St. James's.

When the range of consequences of old-time party organizations is seen, it becomes apparent why moral judgments of "the boss and the machine" are likely to be inadequate. These organizations often were responsible for incredible corruption, but they also—sometimes through the very same activities—helped incorporate new groups into American society and aided them up the social ladder. The parties frequently mismanaged urban growth on a grand scale, but they *did* manage urban growth at a time when other instrumentalities for governing the cities were inadequate. They plied voters, who might otherwise have organized more aggressively to advance their interest, with Thanksgiving Day turkeys and buckets of coal. But, by siphoning off discontent and softening the law, they probably contributed to the generally pacific tenor of American politics. It seems fruitless to attempt to capture this complexity in a single moral judgment. One can scarcely weigh the incorporation of immigrant groups against the proliferation of corruption and strike an over-all balance.

Why Reformers Were "Mornin' Glories"

Stimulated by high taxes and reports of corruption and mismanagement on a grand scale, antiboss reform movements, led by the more prosperous elements of the cities, became increasingly common late in the nineteenth century. Compared with the regular party politicians of their day,

reformers were mere fly-by-night dilettantes —"mornin' glories."[10] They lacked the discipline and the staying power to mount a year-long program of activities. Perhaps more important, the values of the reformers were remote from—in fact, inconsistent with—the values of the citizens whose support would be needed to keep reform administrations in office. Reformers ordinarily saw low taxes and business-like management of the cities as the exclusive aim of government. To the sweatshop worker, grinding out a marginal existence, these aims were at best meaningless, at worst direct attacks on the one agency of society which seemed to have his interests at heart.

The Decline of Old-Style Party Organization

Although in the short run old-style party organizations were marvelously immune to the attacks of reformers, in recent decades the demise of this political form has been widely acclaimed. Because of the absence of reliable trend data, we cannot document "the decline of the machine" with precision. The decline does seem to have taken place, although only partly as a direct consequence of attempts to reform urban politics. Events have conspired to sap the traditional resources used to build voter support and to make voters less interested in these resources which the parties still command.

DECLINE IN THE RESOURCES OF OLD-STYLE URBAN POLITICIANS

Most obviously, job patronage is no longer available in as great a quantity as it once was. At the federal level and in a good many of the states (as well as numerous cities), the bulk of jobs are filled by civil service procedures. Under these circumstances, the most a party politician may be able to do is seek some minor form

of preferment for an otherwise qualified
job applicant. Furthermore, the technical
requirements of many appointive positions
are sufficiently complex to make it inex-
pedient to fill them with unqualified
personnel.[11] And private concerns doing
business with the cities are not as likely to
be sources of patronage in a day when the
franchises have been given out and the
concessions granted.

Beyond this, many modern governmental
techniques—accounting and auditing requirements, procedures for letting bids,
purchasing procedures, even the existence
of a federal income tax—restrict the opportunities for dishonest and "honest"
graft. Some of these procedures were not
instituted with the explicit purpose of
hampering the parties. Legislation designed deliberately to weaken parties *has*,
however, been enacted—for example, nomination by direct primary and nonpartisan
local elections, in which party labels are
not indicated on the ballot. Where other
conditions are consistent with tight party
organization, techniques of this sort seem
not to have been especially effective; old-
style parties are perfectly capable of controlling nominations in primaries, or of
persisting in formally nonpartisan jurisdictions. But, together with the other party
weakening factors, explicit antiparty legislation seems to have taken its toll.

DECLINE OF VOTER INTEREST IN REWARDS
AVAILABLE TO THE PARTIES

Even today it is estimated that the mayor
of Chicago has at his disposal 6,000 to
10,000 city patronage jobs. And there are
many ways of circumventing good-government, antiparty legislation. An additional
element in the decline of old-style organization is the increasing disinterest of many
citizens in the rewards at the disposal of
party politicians. Once upon a time, for
example, the decennial federal census was a
boon to those local politicians whose party
happened to be in control of the White
House at census time. The temporary job
of door-to-door federal census enumerator

was quite a satisfactory reward for the
party faithful. In 1960 in many localities,
party politicians found census patronage
more bother than boon; the wages for
this task compared poorly with private
wages, and few voters were willing
to put in the time and leg work. Other
traditional patronage jobs—custodial work
in city buildings, employment with departments of sanitation, street repair jobs—
were becoming equally undesirable, due to
rising levels of income, education, and job
security.

An important watershed seems to have
been the New Deal, which provided the
impetus, at state and local levels as well
as the federal level, for increased governmental preoccupation with citizen welfare.
The welfare programs of party organizations were undercut by direct and indirect
effects of social security, minimum wage
legislation, relief programs, and collective
bargaining. And, as often has been noted,
the parties themselves, by contributing to
the social rise of underprivileged groups,
helped to develop the values and aspirations
which were to make these citizens skeptical
of the more blatant manifestations of
machine politics.

Varieties of Contemporary
Urban Politics

Nationally in 1956, the Survey Research
Center found that only 10 per cent of a cross
section of citizens reported being contacted
personally by political party workers during
that year's presidential campaign. Even if
we consider only nonsouthern cities of
over 100,000 population, the percentage is
still a good bit less than 20.[12] This is a far
cry from the situation which would obtain
if party organizations were well developed
and assiduous. But national statistics conceal a good bit of local variation. A survey
of Detroit voters found that only 6 per cent
of the public remembered having been
approached by political party workers; in
fact, less than a fifth of those interviewed
even knew that there *were* party precinct
officials in their district.[13] Reports from a

number of other cities—for example, Seattle and Minneapolis—show a similar vacuum in party activity.[14]

In New Haven, Connecticut, in contrast, 60 per cent of the voters interviewed in a 1959 survey reported having been contacted by party workers.[15] The continuing importance of parties in the politics of this municipality has been documented at length by Robert A. Dahl and his associates.[16] New Haven's Mayor Richard C. Lee was able to obtain support for a massive urban redevelopment program, in spite of the many obstacles in the way of favorable action on such programs elsewhere, in large part because of the capacity of an old-style party organization to weld together the government of a city with an extremely "weak" formal charter. Lee commanded a substantial majority on the board of aldermen and, during the crucial period for ratification of the program, was as confident of the votes of Democratic aldermen as a British Prime Minister is of his parliamentary majority. Lee was far from being a mere creative creature of the party organization which was so helpful to him, but he also was effectively vetoed by the party when he attempted to bring about governmental reforms which would have made the mayor less dependent upon the organization to obtain positive action.[17]

Further evidence of the persistence of old-style party activities came from a number of other studies conducted in the late 1950's. For example, in 1957 party leaders from eight New Jersey counties reported performing a wide range of traditional party services, in response to an ingeniously worded questionnaire administered by Professor Richard T. Frost.[18]

Services Performed by New Jersey Politicians

The Service	Percentage Performing It "Often"
Helping deserving people get public jobs	72
Showing people how to get their social security benefits, welfare, unemployment compensation, etc.	54
Helping citizens who are in difficulty with the law. Do you help get them straightened out?	62

There was even some evidence in the 1950's of a rebirth of old-style urban party activities—for example, in the once Republican-dominated city of Philadelphia, where an effective Democratic old-style organization was put together. Often old-style organizations seem to exist in portions of contemporary cities, especially the low-income sections. These, like the reform groups to be described below, serve as factions in city-wide politics.[19]

Why old-style politics persists in some settings but not others is not fully clear. An impressionistic survey of the scattered evidence suggests, as might be expected, that the older pattern continues in those localities which most resemble the situations which originally spawned strong local parties in the nineteenth century. Eastern industrial cities, such as New Haven, Philadelphia, and many of the New Jersey cities, have sizable low-income groups in need of traditional party services. In many of these areas, the legal impediments to party activity also are minimal: Connecticut, for example, was the last state in the Union to adopt direct primary legislation, and nonpartisan local election systems are, in general, less common in industrial cities than in cities without much manufacturing activity.[20] Cities in which weak, disorganized parties are reported—like Seattle, Minneapolis, and even Detroit (which, of course, *is* a manufacturing center of some importance)—are quite often cities in which nonpartisan institutions have been adopted.

Some New-Style Urban Political Patterns

In conclusion, we may note two of the styles of politics which have been reported in contemporary localities where old-style organizations have become weak or nonexistent: the politics of nonpartisanship and the new "reform" factions within some urban Democratic parties. Both patterns are of considerable intrinsic interest to

students of local government. And, as
contrasting political forms, they provide us
with further perspective on the strengths
and weaknesses of old-style urban politics.

THE POLITICS OF NONPARTISANSHIP

The nonpartisan ballot now is in force
in 66 per cent of American cities over
25,000 in population. Numerous styles of
politics seem to take place beneath the
facade of nonpartisanship. In some communities, when party labels are eliminated
from the ballot, the old parties continue to
operate much as they have in the past; in
other communities, new local parties spring
up to contest the nonpartisan elections.
Finally, nonpartisanship often takes the
form intended by its founders: no organized
groups contest elections; voters choose
from a more or less self-selected array of
candidates.

In the last of these cases, although nonpartisanship has its intended effect, it also
seems to have had—a recent body of
literature suggests[21]—a number of unintended side effects. One of these is voter
confusion. Without the familiar device of
party labels to aid in selecting candidates,
voters may find it difficult to select from
among the sometimes substantial list of
names on the ballot. Under these circumstances, a bonus in votes often goes to
candidates with a familiar sounding name—
incumbents are likely to be re-elected, for
example—or even candidates with a favorable position on the ballot. In addition,
campaigning and other personal contacts
with voters become less common, because
candidates no longer have the financial
resources and personnel of a party organization at their disposal and therefore are
dependent upon personal financing or
backing from interest groups in the community.

Nonpartisan electoral practices, where
effective, also seem to increase the influence
of the mass media on voters; in the absence
of campaigning, party canvassing, and
party labels, voters become highly dependent for information as well as advice on
the press, radio, and television. Normally,
mass communications have rather limited
effects on people's behavior compared with
face-to-face communication such as canvassing by party workers.[22] Under nonpartisan circumstances, however, he who
controls the press is likely to have much
more direct and substantial effect on the
public.

Ironically, the "theory" of nonpartisanship argues that by eliminating parties a
barrier between citizens and their officials
will be removed. In fact, nonpartisanship
often attenuates the citizen's connections
with the political system.

THE REFORM DEMOCRATS

The doctrine of nonpartisanship is
mostly a product of the Progressive era.
While nonpartisan local political systems
continue to be adopted and, in fact, have
become more common in recent decades,
most of the impetus for this development
results from the desire of communities to
adopt city-manager systems. Nonpartisanship simply is part of the package which
normally goes along with the popular city-
manager system.

A newer phenomenon on the urban
political scene is the development, especially
since the 1952 presidential campaign, of
ideologically motivated grass-roots party organizations within the Democratic party.[23]
The ideology in question is liberalism:
most of the reform organizations are led
and staffed by college-educated intellectuals,
many of whom were activated politically by
the candidacy of Adlai Stevenson. In a
few localities, there also have been grass-
roots Republican organizations motivated
by ideological considerations: in the Republican case, Goldwater conservatism.

New-style reformers differ in two major
ways from old-style reformers: their ideological concerns extend beyond a preoccupation with governmental efficiency alone
(they favor racial integration and improved housing and sometimes devote much
of their energy to advocating "liberal"
causes at the national level); secondly,
their strategy is to work within and take
control of the parties, rather than to
reject the legitimacy of parties. They do

resemble old-style reformers in their pre-occupation with the evils of "bossism" and machine politics.

There also is an important resemblance between the new reform politician and the old-style organization man the reformer seeks to replace. In both cases, very much unlike the situation which seems to be stimulated by nonpartisanship, the politician emphasizes extensive face-to-face contact with voters. Where reformers have been successful, it often has been by beating the boss at his own game of canvassing the election district, registering and keeping track of voters, and getting them to the polls.[24]

But much of the day-to-day style of the traditional urban politician is clearly distasteful to the new reformers: they have generally eschewed the use of patronage and, with the exceptions of campaigns for housing code enforcement, they have avoided the extensive service operations to voters and interest groups which were central to old-style party organizations. For example, when election district captains and other officials of the Greenwich Village Independent Democrats, the reform group which deposed New York Democrat County Leader Carmine De Sapio in his own election district, were asked the same set of questions about their activities used in the New Jersey study, strikingly different responses were made.

Services Performed by New York Reform Democrats[25]

The Service	Percentage Performing It "Often"
Helping deserving people get public jobs	0
Showing people how to get their social security benefits, welfare, unemployment compensation, etc.	5
Helping citizens who are in difficulty with the law. Do you help get them straightened out?	6

The successes of this class of new-style urban party politician have vindicated a portion of the classical strategy of urban party politics, the extensive reliance upon canvassing and other personal relations,

and also have shown that under some circumstances it is possible to organize such activities with virtually no reliance on patronage and other material rewards. The reformers have tapped a pool of political activists used by parties elsewhere in the world—for example, in Great Britain—but not a normal part of the American scene. One might say that the reformers have "discovered" the British Labor constituency parties.

It is where material resources available to the parties are limited, for example, California, and where voter interest in these resources is low, that the new reformers are successful. In practice, however, the latter condition has confined the effectiveness of the reform Democrats largely to the more prosperous sections of cities; neither their style nor their programs seem to be successful in lower-class districts.[26] The areas of reform Democratic strength are generally *not* the areas which contribute greatly to Democratic pluralities in the cities. And, in many cities, the reformers' clientele is progressively diminishing as higher-income citizens move outward to the suburbs. Therefore, though fascinating and illuminating, the new reform movement must at least for the moment be considered as little more than a single manifestation in a panorama of urban political practices.[27]

Conclusion

The degree to which *old-style* urban party organizations will continue to be a part of this panorama is uncertain. Changes in the social composition of the cities promise to be a major factor in the future of urban politics. If, as seems possible, many cities become lower-class, non-white enclaves, we can be confident that there will be a continuing market for the services of the service-oriented old-style politician. Whether or not this is the case, many lessons can be culled from the history of party politics during the years of growth of the American cities—lessons which are relevant, for example, to studying the politics of urbanization elsewhere in the world.[28] In the nineteenth century, after all, the United States was an "emerging," "modernizing" nation, facing the problems of stability and democracy which are now being faced by countless newer nations.

OUR CONCERN here is with the nature of the individual's attachment to the body politic and, more particularly, with the value premises underlying the choices made by certain classes of voters. Our hypothesis is that some classes of voters (provisionally defined as "subcultures" constituted on ethnic and income lines) are more disposed than others to rest their choices on some conception of "the public interest" or the "welfare of the community." To say the same thing in another way, the voting behavior of some classes tends to be more public-regarding and less private- (self- or family-) regarding than that of others. To test this hypothesis it is necessary to examine voting behavior in situations where one can say that a certain vote could not have been private-regarding. Local bond and other expenditure referenda present such situations: it is sometimes possible to say that a vote in favor of a particular expenditure proposal is incompatible with a certain voter's self-interest narrowly conceived. If the voter nevertheless casts such a vote and if there is evidence that his vote was not in some sense irrational or accidental, then it must be presumed that his action was based on some conception of "the public interest."

Our first step, accordingly, is to show how much of the behavior in question can, and cannot, be explained on grounds of self-interest alone, narrowly conceived. If all of the data were consistent with the hypothesis that the voter acts as if he were trying to maximize his family income, the inquiry would end right there. In fact, in turns out that many of the data cannot be explained in this way. The question arises, therefore,

Public-Regardingness as a Value Premise in Voting Behavior*

James Q. Wilson and Edward C. Banfield†

Harvard University

whether the unexplained residue is purposive or "accidental." We suggest that for the most part it is purposive, and that the voters' purposes arise from their conceptions of "the public interest."

1

We start, then, from the simple—and admittedly implausible—hypothesis that the voter tries to maximize his family income or (the same thing) self-interest narrowly conceived. We assume that the voter estimates in dollars both the benefits that will accrue to him and his family if the proposed public expenditure is made and the amount of the tax that will fall on him in consequence of the expenditure; if the estimated benefit is more than the estimated cost, he votes for the expenditure; if it is less, he votes against it. We assume that all proposed expenditures will confer some benefits on all voters. The benefits conferred on a particular voter are "trivial," however, if the expenditure is for something that the particular voter (and his family) is not likely to use or enjoy. For example, improvement of sidewalks confers trivial benefits to those voters who are not likely to walk on them.

Insofar as behavior is consistent with these assumptions—i.e., insofar as the voter seems to act rationally in pursuit of self-interest narrowly conceived—we consider that no further "explanation" is required. It may be that other, entirely different hypotheses would account for the behavior just as well or better. That possibility is not of concern to us here, however.

* Reprinted with permission of the authors and publisher, from James Q. Wilson and Edward C. Banfield, "Public-Regardingness as a Value Premise in Voting Behavior," American Political Science Review, 58 (December 1964), pp. 876–887.

† This is a preliminary report of a study supported by the Joint Center for Urban Studies of M.I.T. and Harvard University and the Rockefeller Foundation. The writers wish to acknowledge assistance from Martha Derthick and Mark K. Adams and comments from James Beshers, Anthony Downs, Werner Hirsch, Hendrick Houthakker, H. Douglas Price, and Arthur Stinchcombe. This paper was originally presented at the Second Conference On Urban Public Expenditures, New York University, February 21–22, 1964.

125

No doubt, our assumptions lack realism. No doubt, relatively few voters make a conscious calculation of costs and benefits. Very often the voter has no way of knowing whether a public expenditure proposal will benefit him or not. In only one state which we have examined (Florida) do ballots in municipal referenda specify precisely *which* streets are to be paved or *where* a bridge is to be built. Even if a facility is to serve the whole city (e.g., a zoo, civic center, or county hospital), in most cities the ballot proposition is usually so indefinite that the voter cannot accurately judge either the nature or the amount of the benefits that he would derive from the expenditure. Similarly, it is often difficult or impossible for the voter to estimate even the approximate amount of the tax that will fall upon him in consequence of the expenditure. Some states (e.g., Illinois and California) require that the anticipated cost of each undertaking be listed on the ballot (e.g., "$12,800,000 for sewer improvements"). Of course, even when the total cost is given, the voter must depend on the newspapers to tell, or figure out for himself—if he can—how much it would increase the tax rate and how much the increased tax rate would add to his tax bill. Ohio is the only state we have studied where the voter is told on the ballot how the proposed expenditure will affect the tax rate ("17 cents per $100 valuation for each of two years"). Almost everywhere, most of the expenditure proposals are to be financed from the local property tax. Occasionally, however, a different tax (e.g., the sales tax) or a different tax base (e.g., the county or state rather than the city), is used. In these cases, the voter is likely to find it even harder to estimate how much he will have to pay.

We may be unrealistic also both in assuming that the voter takes only *money* costs into account (actually he may think that a proposed civic center would be an eyesore) and in assuming that the only money costs he takes into account are *taxes* levied upon him (actually, if he is a renter he may suppose—whether correctly or incorrectly is beside the point—that his landlord will pass a tax increase on to him in a higher rent).

The realism of the assumptions does not really matter. What does matter is their usefulness in predicting the voters' behavior. It is possible that voters may act *as if* they are well informed and disposed to calculate even when in fact they are neither. If we can predict their behavior without going into the question of how much or how well they calculate, so much the better.

II

On the assumptions we have made, one would expect voters who will have no tax levied upon them in consequence of the passage of an expenditure proposal to vote for it even if it will confer only trivial benefits on them. Having nothing to lose by the expenditure and something (however small) to gain, they will favor it. In the *very* low-income[1] wards and precincts of the larger cities a high proportion of the voters are in this position since most local public

TABLE I.   *Relationship Between Percentage of Ward Voting "Yes" and Percentage of Dwelling Units Owner Occupied; Various Issues in Cleveland and Chicago*

Issue and Date	Simple Correlation Coefficient (r)
Cleveland (33 wards):	
Administration Building (11/59)	−0.86
County Hospital (11/59)	−0.77
Tuberculosis Hospital (11/59)	−0.79
Court House (11/59)	−0.85
Juvenile Court (11/59)	−0.83
Parks (11/59)	−0.67
Welfare Levy (5/60)	−0.72
Roads and Bridges (11/60)	−0.77
Zoo (11/60)	−0.81
Parks (11/60)	−0.57
Chicago (50 wards)	
County Hospital (1957)	−0.79
Veterans' Bonus (1957)	−0.49
Welfare Building (1958)	−0.67
Street Lights (1959)	−0.83
Municipal Building (1962)	−0.78
Urban Renewal Bonds (1962)	−0.79
Sewers (1962)	−0.79
Street Lights (1962)	−0.81

expenditures are financed from the property tax and the lowest-income people do not own property. We find that in these heavily non-home-owning districts the voters almost invariably support all expenditure proposals. We have examined returns on 35 expenditure proposals passed upon in 20 separate elections in seven cities and have not found a single instance in which this group failed to give a majority in favor of a proposal. Frequently the vote is 75 to 80 per cent in favor; sometimes it is over 90 per cent. The strength of voter support is about the same no matter what the character of the proposed expenditure.[2]

In all of the elections we have examined, non-homeowners show more taste for public expenditures that are to be financed from property taxes than do homeowners. Table I shows by means of product-moment (Pearsonian r) coefficients of correlation the strength and consistency of this relationship over a wide variety of issues in several elections in Cleveland and Chicago.[3] As one would expect, when an expenditure is to be financed from a source other than the property tax the difference between homeowner and non-homeowner behavior is reduced. This is borne out in Table II in which we have compared wards typical of four major economic groups in Cook County (Illinois) in their voting on two issues: first, a proposal to increase county hospital facilities and, second, a proposal to construct a state welfare building. The measures were alike in that they would benefit only indigents; they were different in that their costs would be assessed against different publics: the hospital was to be paid for from the local property tax, the welfare building from state sources, largely a sales tax. Middle-income homeowners showed themselves very sensitive to this difference; the percentage favoring the state-financed measure was twice that favoring the property-tax-financed one. Low-income renters, on the other hand, preferred the property-tax-financed measure to the state-financed one.

Let us turn now to the behavior of voters who do own property and whose taxes will therefore be increased in consequence of a public expenditure. One might suppose that

TABLE II. *Voting Behavior of Four Major Economic Groups Compared in Cook County*

Group	Per cent "Yes" Vote	
	County Hospital (1957)	State Welfare Building (1958)
	(%)	(%)
High-Income Homeowners*		
Winnetka	64	76
Wilmette	55	70
Lincolnwood	47	64
Middle-Income Homeowners†		
Lansing	30	54
Bellwood	21	55
Brookfield	22	51
Middle-Income Renters‡		
Chicago Ward 44	65	71
Chicago Ward 48	61	72
Chicago Ward 49	64	74
Low-Income Renters§		
Chicago Ward 2	88	73
Chicago Ward 3	87	76
Chicago Ward 27	87	78

*Three suburbs with highest median family income ($13,200 to $23,200) among all suburbs with 85 per cent or more home ownership.
†Three suburbs with lowest median family income ($8,000 to $8,300) among all suburbs with 85 per cent or more home ownership.
‡Three wards with highest median family income ($6,200 to $6,800) among all wards with less than 15 per cent home ownership (none of the three wards is more than 4 per cent Negro).
§Three wards with lowest median family income ($3,000 to $4,100) among all wards with less than 15 per cent home ownership (Negro population of wards ranges from 59 to 99 per cent).

the more property such a voter has, the less likely it is that he will favor public expenditures. To be sure, certain expenditures confer benefits roughly in proportion to the value of property and some may even confer disproportionate benefits on the more valuable properties; in such cases one would expect large property owners to be as much in favor of expenditures as the small, or more so. Most expenditures, however, confer about the same benefits on large properties as on small, whereas of course the taxes to pay for the expenditure are levied (in theory at least) strictly in proportion to the value of property. The owner of a $30,000 home, for example, probably gets no more benefit from the construction of a new city hall or the expansion of a zoo than does the owner of a $10,000 one; his share of the tax increase is three times as much, however. Very often, indeed, there is an inverse relation between the value of a property and the benefits that

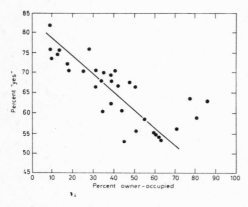

Figure 1. Relation between percentage voting "yes" on proposition to provide increased county hospital facilities (November 1959) and percentage of dwelling units owner–occupied in the 33 wards of Cleveland.

Source of housing data: U.S. Census of housing, 1960. Figure reprinted from Edward C. Banfield and James Q. Wilson, "City Politics" (Cambridge: Harvard University Press, 1963), p. 238.

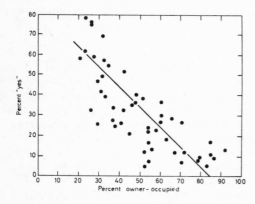

Figure 2. Relation between percentage voting "yes" on proposition to provide additional sewer facilities (1962) and percentage of dwelling units owner–occupied in wards of Chicago.

accrue to its owner from a public expenditure. The probability is certainly greater that the owner of the $10,000 house will some day use the free county hospital (patronized chiefly by low-income Negroes) than that the owner of the $30,000 house will use it. Since normally the *ratio* of benefits to costs is less favorable the higher the value of property, one might expect to find a positive correlation between the percentage of "No" votes in a neighborhood and the median value of homes there.

This expectation is not borne out by the facts, however. Table III gives partial correlation coefficients relating the per cent voting "Yes" in the wards of Cleveland and

TABLE III. *Partial Correlations Between Median Family Income of Ward and Percentage "Yes" Vote on Various Measures, Cleveland and Suburbs*

Area and Issue	Partial Correlation*
Cleveland (33 wards):	
Administration Building	+0.49
County Hospital	+0.64
Tuberculosis Hospital	+0.57
Court House	+0.49
Juvenile Court	+0.66
Parks	+0.48
Welfare Levy	+0.70
Roads and Bridges	+0.61
Zoo	+0.59
Cuyahoga County Suburbs (90 wards and towns):	
Administration Building	+0.47
County Hospital	+0.54
Tuberculosis Hospital	+0.43
Court House	+0.60
Juvenile Court	+0.59
Parks	+0.52
Welfare Levy	+0.35
Roads and Bridges	+0.60
Zoo	+0.62

*Controlling for proportion of dwelling units owner-occupied.

the suburban wards and towns of Cuyahoga County to the median family income in those wards and towns.[4] It shows that the higher the income of a ward or town, the more taste it has for public expenditures of various kinds. That the ratio of benefits to costs declines as income goes up seems to make no difference.[5]

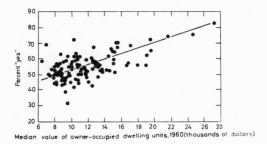

Figure 3. Relation between percentage voting "yes" on proposition to provide additional flood control facilities (November 1960) and median value of owner-occupied dwelling units in the precincts of Flint, Michigan.

Note: Only property owners and their spouses could vote. Source of housing data: U.S. Census of Housing, 1960. Figure reprinted from Banfield and Wilson, City Politics, p. 239.

The same pattern appears in a 1960 Flint, Michigan, vote on additional flood control facilities. This is shown graphically in Figure 3. Although there is a considerable dispersion around the line of regression, in general the higher the home value—and accordingly the more the expected tax—the greater the support for the expenditure.[6]

It may be argued that because of the phenomenon of the diminishing marginal utility of money these findings are not really anomalous. The richer a man is, perhaps, the smaller the sacrifice that an additional dollar of taxation represents to him. Thus, even though the well-to-do voter may get no more benefit than the poor one gets and may have to pay a great deal more in taxes, an expenditure proposal may nevertheless be more attractive to him. He may be more willing to pay a dollar for certain benefits than his neighbor is to pay fifty cents because, having much more money than his neighbor, a dollar is worth only a quarter as much to him.

Differences in the value of the dollar to voters at different income levels account in part for the well-to-do voter's relatively strong taste for public expenditures. They can hardly account for it entirely, however. For one thing, they do not rationalize the behavior of those voters who support measures that would give them only trivial benefits while imposing substantial costs upon them. The suburbanite who favors a county hospital for the indigent which

he and his family will certainly never use and for which he will be heavily taxed is not acting according to self-interest narrowly conceived no matter how little a dollar is worth to him.

Moreover, if the well-to-do voter places a low value on the dollar when evaluating some expenditure proposals, one would expect him to place the same low value on it when evaluating all others. In fact, he does not seem to do so; indeed, he sometimes appears to place a *higher* value on it than does his less-well-off neighbor. Compare, for example, the behavior of the Cook County (Illinois) suburbanites who voted on a proposal to build a county hospital (an expenditure which would confer only trivial benefits on them and for which they would be taxed in proportion to the value of their property) with the behavior of the same suburbanites who voted on a proposal to give a bonus of $300 to Korean War veterans (an expenditure from which the well-to-do would benefit about as much as the less-well-to-do and for which they would not be taxed disproportionately, since the bonus was to be financed from state, not local, revenues, and the state had neither an income tax nor a corporate profits tax). As Figures 4 and 5 show, the higher the median family income of a voting district, the larger the percentage voting "Yes" on the welfare building (the rank-order correlation was +0.57), but the *smaller* the percentage voting "Yes" on the veterans' bonus (the rank-order correlation was −0.71).

In Cuyahoga County, Ohio, the same thing happened. There the higher the median family income, the larger the percentage voting for all the expenditure proposals except one—a bonus for Korean War veterans. On this one measure there was a correlation of −0.65 between median family income and percentage voting "Yes."

Thus, although it is undoubtedly true that the more dollars a voter has, the more he will pay for a given benefit, the principle does not explain all that needs explaining.

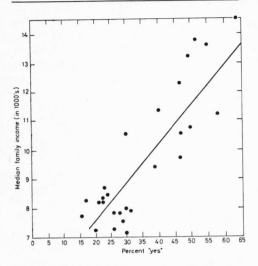

Figure 4. Relation between percentage voting "yes" on proposition to provide increased county hospital facilities (1957) and median family income in the suburban cities and towns of Cook County, Illinois, in which two-thirds or more of the dwelling units are owner-occupied.

When it comes to a veterans' bonus, for example, the opposite principle seems to

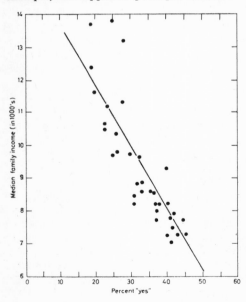

Figure 5. Relation between percentage voting "yes" on proposition to provide a $300 bonus for veterans of Korean War (1958) and median family income in the suburban cities of Cook County, Illinois, in which two-thirds or more of the dwelling units are owner-occupied.

work: the more dollars the voter has, the fewer he will spend for a given benefit of that sort.

That there is a positive correlation between amount of property owned (or income) and tendency to vote "Yes" does not, of course, imply that a majority of property owners at *any* income level favors expenditures: the correlation would exist even if the highest income voters opposed them, provided that at each lower level of income voters opposed them by ever-larger majorities. In fact, middle-income homeowners often vote against proposals that are approved by both the very poor (renters) and the very well-to-do (owners). Table IV gives a rather typical picture of the response of the various income groups to proposals that are to be financed from the property tax in Cuyahoga County (Ohio).

Not infrequently the highest-income districts support expenditure proposals by very

TABLE IV. Voting Behavior of Four Major Economic Groups Compared in Cuyahoga County

	Per cent "Yes" Vote	
Group	County Hospital (1959)	County Court House (1959)
	(%)	(%)
*High-Income Homeowners**		
Pepper Pike	69	47
Beachwood	72	47
Middle-Income Homeowners†		
Olmstead Township	51	28
Garfield Heights (Ward 4)	48	29
Lower Middle-Income Renters‡		
Cleveland Ward 31	76	66
Low-Income Renters§		
Cleveland Ward 11	73	63
Cleveland Ward 17	74	62

*Two suburbs with highest median family income ($15,700 and $19,000) of all suburbs with 85 per cent or more home ownership.
†Two suburbs with lowest median family income ($6,800 and $7,000) of all suburbs with 85 per cent or more home ownership.
‡The one ward with less than 15 per cent home ownership and which is less than 10 per cent Negro (median income: $4,700).
§Two wards with lowest median family incomes ($3,400 and $3,600) of all wards with less than 15 per cent home ownership (Negro populations of wards was 90 and 97 per cent).

large majorities—indeed, sometimes by majorities approaching those given in the propertyless slums. Table V compares the percentage voting "Yes" in the high-income, high-home-ownership precincts of three city–county areas with the percentage of all voters in the areas who voted "Yes."[7]

Except for Detroit and Dade County, where only property owners and their spouses may vote on expenditures, the city–county totals include large numbers of renters. Even so, the high-income precincts are comparatively strong in their support of all expenditures.

TABLE V. Percentage Voting "Yes" on Expenditure in Home-owning, Upper-income "Old-stock" Precincts in Various Counties

County, Issue, and Date	Per cent "Yes" Vote in Upper-Income Precincts	Per cent "Yes" Vote in County As a Whole
	(%)	(%)
Detroit–Wayne County		
Sewers (8/60)	83.6	64.3
Increase school tax limit	52.0	39.0
Build schools (4/63)	52.0	33.4
Increase sales tax (11/60)	78.6	47.8
Kansas City–Jefferson County		
Increase school taxes (11/60)	68.6	54.9
Build jails (3/62)	86.3	78.0
Sewage treatment plant (11/60)	93.2	81.6
Miami–Dade County		
Highways (5/60)	71.2	53.0
Schools (1955)	90.8	92.1

III

When we hold constant the percentage of home ownership, percentage of nonwhites, and median family income, a negative correlation appears between the percentage of voters in the wards of Cleveland who are of foreign stock and the percentage of the total vote in those wards that is "Yes." This is shown in Column 1 of Table VI.[8] Of the many foreign stocks in Cleveland, the Poles and Czechs have the strongest distaste for expenditures. Column 2 of Table VI shows how markedly the presence of Poles and Czechs in a voting district affects the "Yes" vote.[9] In the suburbs the correlation is only slightly weaker, but significant at the .001 level in all but two cases and in these at the .01 level. The complete correlation table shows that in all but three cases the percentage of Poles and Czechs is a more important influence on voting than

TABLE VI. Partial Correlations Between Selected "Ethnic" Variables and Percentage Voting "Yes" on Expenditures in Cleveland and Cuyahoga County Wards and Towns*

Issue	Foreign Stock		Polish-Czech		Negro	
	City	Suburbs	City	Suburbs	City	Suburbs
Admin. Building	−0.40	ns†	−0.54	−0.17	ns	ns
County Hospital	ns	ns	−0.79	−0.40	ns	ns
TB Hospital	ns	−0.22	−0.74	−0.46	ns	ns
Court House	−0.47	ns	−0.58	−0.28	ns	ns
Juvenile Court	−0.46	ns	−0.74	−0.40	ns	ns
Parks (1959)	−0.41	ns	−0.62	−0.31	−0.49	ns
Welfare Levy	−0.58	ns	−0.71	−0.49	ns	ns
Roads and Bridges	−0.48	ns	−0.66	−0.40	ns	ns
Zoo	−0.62	ns	−0.71	−0.40	ns	ns
Parks (1960)	ns	ns	ns	−0.50	ns	ns

* These are partial correlation coefficients derived from a regression analysis in which home ownership, median family income, and two "ethnic" variables have been held constant.
† If the correlations were not significant at the .05 level (Student's *t*), "ns" is entered in the table. The critical values were based on 27 degrees of freedom for the city data and 84 degrees of freedom for the suburban data.

median family income, and is second in influence only to home ownership. In two of the three exceptional cases, indeed, it was *more* important than home ownership.

The findings in Column 3 of Table VI are surprising. We expected a positive correla-

tion between percentage of Negroes and the strength of the "Yes" vote. Deficiencies in the data may possibly account for the absence of any correlation: there are not enough home-owning Negroes or enough very low-income whites in Cleveland to make a really satisfactory matching of wards possible.

In order to get a closer view of ethnic voting it is necessary to forego general

TABLE VII. *Percentage of Various "Ethnic" Precincts Voting "Yes" on Selected Expenditures in Chicago*

Ethnic Group and Number of Precincts	Per cent Voting "Yes" On:				
	Co. Hosp. (6/57)	Vet's Bonus (11/58)	Urban Renewal (4/62)	City Hall (5/62)	School (4/59)
	(%)	(%)	(%)	(%)	(%)
*Low-Income Renters**					
Negro (22)	84.9	80.2	88.6	82.3	97.8
Irish (6)	61.3	55.3	45.7	46.3	79.4
Polish (26)	60.1	54.6	57.1	53.8	81.8
Middle-Income Home-Owners†					
Negro (13)	66.8	54.9	69.6	49.8	88.9
Irish (6)	54.6	44.1	22.0	27.2	64.2
Polish (38)	47.4	40.0	14.6	15.2	58.3

* Average median family income under $6,000 per year; at least two-thirds of all dwelling units renter-occupied.
† Average median family income between $7,500 and $10,000 a year for whites; over $6,000 a year for Negroes. At least 80 per cent of all dwelling units owner-occupied.

TABLE VIII. *Percentage of Various "Ethnic" Precincts Voting "Yes" on Selected Expenditures in Cleveland and Cuyahoga County*

Ethnic Group and Number of Precincts	Per cent Voting "Yes" on:				
	Co. Hosp. (11/59)	Court House (11/59)	Parks (11/59)	Welfare Levy (5/60)	Vet's Bonus (11/56)
	(%)	(%)	(%)	(%)	(%)
*Low-Income Renters**					
Negro (16)	78.6	67.3	52.6	85.9	89.9
Italian (10)	68.8	53.3	43.5	49.9	74.8
Polish (6)	54.9	39.9	28.1	33.7	71.6
Middle-Income Home-Owners†					
Negro (8)	68.1	54.0	39.6	73.2	79.2
Italian (7)	59.3	49.7	41.1	56.8	66.8
Polish (12)	52.9	35.8	34.3	46.4	61.7
Upper-Income Home-Owners‡					
Anglo-Saxon (11)	70.6	51.4	57.2	64.8	53.7
Jewish (7)	71.7	47.1	48.4	64.5	56.8

* Average median family income less than $6,000 per year; at least two-thirds of all dwelling units renter-occupied.
† Average median family income between $7,000 and $9,000 a year for whites; over $6,000 a year for Negroes. At least 75 per cent of all dwelling units owner-occupied.
‡ Average median family income over $10,000 per year; over 85 per cent of all dwelling units owner-occupied.

In Tables VII and VIII we show how selected "ethnic" precincts belonging to two income and home-ownership classes voted in several elections in the Chicago and Cleveland areas.[10] There is a remarkable degree of consistency in the influence of both ethnicity and income or home-ownership, whether viewed on an intra- or inter-city basis. In Chicago, for example, the low-income renters in *every* case voted more favorably for expenditures than did the middle-income home-owners of the same ethnic group. Within the same economic class, however, ethnicity makes a striking difference. Low-income Negro renters are in *every* case more enthusiastic by a wide margin about public expenditures than low-income Irish or Polish renters. Middle-income Negro home-owners are in *every* case more enthusiastic about the same proposals than middle-income Irish or Polish home-owners. (In passing it is worth noting that Negroes are two or three times more favorable toward urban renewal—despite the fact that they are commonly the chief victims of land clearance programs—than Irish or Polish voters.)

Essentially the same relationships appear in Table VIII for Cleveland-Cuyahoga County. With one exception (Italians voting on the welfare levy), low-income renters in an ethnic group are more favorable to expenditures than middle-income home-owners in the same ethnic group. Low-income Negro renters are the most favorable to all proposals and middle-income Negro home-owners are more favorable to them than are the other middle-income ethnic groups. Aside from the veterans' bonus (a special case), both the "Anglo-Saxon" and the Jewish upper-income home-owners are more favorable to expenditures than any middle-income groups except the Negro.

IV

We have shown both that a considerable proportion of voters, especially in the upper

income groups, vote against their self-interest narrowly conceived and that a marked ethnic influence appears in the vote. Now we would like to bring these two findings together under a single explanatory principle.

One such principle—but one we reject—is that the voters in question have acted irrationally (either in not calculating benefits and costs at all or else by making mistakes in their calculations) and that their irrationality is a function of their ethnic status. According to this theory, the low-income Polish renter who votes against expenditures proposals that would cost him nothing and would confer benefits upon him and the high-income Anglo-Saxon or Jewish home-owner who favors expenditures proposals that will cost him heavily without benefiting him would both behave differently if they thought about the matter more or if their information were better.

A more tenable hypothesis, we think, is that voters in some income and ethnic groups are more likely than voters in others to take a public-regarding rather than a narrowly self-interested view of things—i.e., to take the welfare of others, especially that of "the community" into account as an aspect of their own welfare.[11] We offer the additional hypothesis that both the tendency of a voter to take a public-regarding view and the content of that view (e.g., whether or not he thinks a Korean war veterans' bonus is in the public interest) are largely functions of his participation in a subculture that is definable in ethnic and income terms. Each subcultural group, we think, has a more or less distinctive notion of how much a citizen ought to sacrifice for the sake of the community as well as of what the welfare of the community is constituted; in a word, each has its own idea of what justice requires and of the importance of acting justly. According to this hypothesis, the voter is presumed to act rationally; the ends he seeks are not always narrowly self-interested ones, however. On the contrary, depending upon his income and ethnic status they are more or less public-regarding.[12]

That his income status does not by itself determine how public-regarding he is, or what content he gives to the public interest, can be shown from the voting data. As we explained above, generally the higher a home-owner's income the more likely he is to favor expenditures. This is partly—but only partly—because the value of the dollar is usually less to people who have many of them than to people who have few of them. We suggest that it is also because upper-income people tend to be more public-regarding than lower-income people. We do not think that income *per se* has this effect; rather it is the ethnic attributes, or culture, empirically associated with it. It happens that most upper-income voters belong, if not by inheritance then by adoption, to an ethnic group (especially the Anglo-Saxon and the Jewish) that is relatively public-regarding in its outlook; hence ethnic influence on voting is hard to distinguish from income influence.

In the three scatter diagrams which comprise Figure 6 we have tried to distinguish the two kinds of influence. For this figure, we divided all wards and towns of Cleveland and Cuyahoga County in which 85 or more per cent of the dwelling units were owner-occupied into three classes according to median home value. Diagram 6a shows the voting where that value was more than $27,000; diagram 6b shows it where it was $19,000–27,000, and diagram 6c shows it where it was less than $19,000. The horizontal and vertical axes are the same for all diagrams; each diagram shows the relationship between the percentage of voters in the ward or town who are Polish-Czech (vertical axis) and the percentage of "Yes" vote on a proposal to expand the zoo (horizontal axis). In the group of wards and towns having the lowest median home value (diagram 6c), the presence of Polish-Czech voters made little difference; these wards and towns were about 65 per cent against the proposal no matter how many Poles and

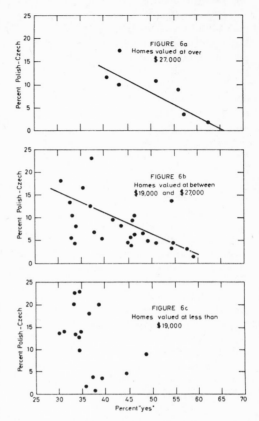

Figure 6. Relation between percentage voting "yes" on proposition to provide additional zoo facilities (1960) and proportion of ward or town population which is of Polish or Czech foreign stock in Cuyahoga County, Ohio; at three median home value levels (only wards and towns with 85 per cent or more owner-occupied dwellings used).

Czechs lived in them. In both groups of higher home-value wards and towns, however, Poles and Czechs were conspicuously less favorable to the proposal than were the rest of the voters. Among the non-Polish-Czech voters in these higher home-value wards and towns, Anglo-Saxons and Jews were heavily represented; therefore it seems plausible to conclude that, as compared to Poles and Czechs in these two income groups, the Anglo-Saxons and Jews were decidedly public-regarding.

Another interpretation of the behavior of the Poles and Czechs is possible, however. It may be that they had the welfare of the community in view also but defined it differently than did the Anglo-Saxons and the Jews. They may have thought that the particular expenditure proposed, or for that matter all public expenditures, would do the community more harm than good. (This would rationalize the behavior of those low-income renters—see Table VIII—who voted against proposals giving them benefits without any costs.)[13] Whatever may be true of the Poles and Czechs, it seems clear that upper-income Anglo-Saxons, and to a somewhat lesser degree Jews, tend to vote on public-regarding grounds *against* some proposals (notably those, like veterans' bonuses and city employees' pension benefits and pay increases) that they regard as serving "special interests" rather than "the community as a whole."

When we know more about each of the various subcultures—especially about the nature of the individual's attachment to the society, his conception of what is just, and the extent of the obligation he feels to subordinate his interest to that of various others (e.g., the community)—we should doubtless be able to make and test more refined hypotheses about voting behavior.

Appendix

We chose the "ethnic" precincts for Tables VII and VIII by inspecting census tract data and then visiting the precincts that appeared to be predominantly of one ethnic group to get confirmatory evidence from well-informed persons and from a view of the neighborhoods. We could have used

a less impressionistic method (e.g., counting the proportion of ethnic names on voter registration lists), but since we wanted only to identify precincts that are predominantly of one ethnic group, not to place them on a scale of ethnicity, this did not appear necessary.

Having identified the "ethnic" precincts, we divided them into two (sometimes three) income groups on the basis of census data. As we indicate on the tables, with one exception we used the same cutting points to separate the income levels of all ethnic groups. The exception was the Negro. The income distribution among Negroes is so skewed to the low end of the scale that "middle-income" has to be defined differently for Negroes than for whites. We identified "middle-income" Negro precincts by selecting from among all precincts that were at least 85 per cent Negro and had an owner-occupancy rate of at least 80 per cent those few with the highest median family incomes. Some of these precincts turned out to have median incomes as low as $6,000 a year, which is about $1,000 less than any of the "middle-income white" precincts had. If we had made the cutting point higher, however, we would not have had enough middle-income Negro precincts to work with. In our opinion, Negroes with incomes of $6,000 are about as likely to "feel" middle-income as are whites with incomes of $7,000.

Who Riots?*

Robert M. Fogelson

Massachusetts Institute of Technology

Robert B. Hill

Columbia University

Introduction

DURING the past four years the United States has experienced a series of extraordinary and probably unprecedented racial disorders. These disorders erupted first in Harlem and then—to mention only a few of the other communities—in southcentral Los Angeles, Cleveland's Hough District, Newark's Central Ward and Detroit's West Side. They left hundreds dead, thousands injured, and tens of thousands arrested, thousands of buildings damaged and millions of dollars of property destroyed, the Negro ghettos devastated and white society shocked. Though the long-term implications of the 1960s riots are not yet clear, their historic significance is already emerging. The riots have assumed a place in the course of American race relations perhaps more important than the East St. Louis, Chicago, and Washington, D.C. race riots of 1917 and 1919. They have also confronted the nation's urban centers with the gravest threat to public order since the terrible industrial disputes of the late nineteenth and early twentieth centuries.[1] And in view of the rioting in Washington, D.C., Baltimore, and about a hundred other cities after the assassination of Dr. Martin Luther King, Jr., in April, 1968, there is good reason to believe that the riots have not yet run their course.

A great many public figures—including the mayors and the governors of the stricken areas—have already given their views on the 1960s riots. This was their privilege and responsibility. That they have disagreed sharply on a number of crucial issues—among them, the degree of organization and advanced planning, the amount of violence and destruction, the conditions in the Negro ghettos, and, perhaps most important, the implications for public policy—is not surprising.[2] The differences between California Governor Ronald Reagan and New Jersey Governor Richard J. Hughes and between former Acting-Mayor of New York Paul Screvane and the late Los Angeles Police Chief William H. Parker were marked. And so were the differences between the Los Angeles (1965), Newark (1967), Detroit (1967), and Washington, D.C. (1968) riots, on the one hand, and the Rochester (1964), Chicago (1965), San Francisco (1966), and Boston (1967) riots, on the other. What is surprising is that most of these public figures (and, as the public opinion surveys reveal, most of their constituents) have agreed substantially on probably the most perplexing question raised by the 1960s riots: who riots?

Their answer is what we refer to as the "riffraff theory" of riot participation.[3] At the core of this "theory" are three distinct, though closely related, themes. First, that only an infinitesimal fraction of the black population (2 per cent according to some, including several prominent Negro moderates, and 1 per cent according to others) actively participated in the riots. Second, that the rioters, far from being representative of the Negro community, were principally the riffraff—the unattached, juvenile, unskilled, unemployed, uprooted, criminal—and outside agitators. Indeed, many public figues have insisted that outside agitators, especially left-wing radicals and black nationalists, incited the riffraff and thereby provoked the rioting. And third, that the overwhelming majority of the Negro population—the law-abiding and respectable 98 or 99 per cent who did not join in the rioting—unequivocally opposed and deplored the riots.[4]

* Reprinted from Supplemental Studies for the National Advisory Commission on Civil Disorders (Washington, D.C.: Government Printing Office, July 1968).

Notes to this selection will be found on pages 343–345.

The Extent of Participation

There is little hard evidence that supports the first point of the riffraff theory—that an infinitesimal fraction of the Negro population, no more than 1 or 2 per cent, actively participated in the 1960s riots. For, if only 1 or 2 per cent of the Negroes rioted in, say, Detroit or Newark, then, in view of the large number of persons arrested there, one would have to conclude that the police must have apprehended almost all of the rioters,[5] a conclusion which is sharply contradicted by the eye-witness accounts of these riots. Also, surveys of riot areas have obtained much higher rates of participation. According to the University of Michigan's Survey Research Center, for example, 11 per cent of the Negroes 15 years and older rioted in Detroit, and 45 per cent of the Negro males between the ages of 15 and 35 rioted in Newark.[6] It is, however, much harder to reach a more precise estimate of how large a segment of the Negro population actively participated in the riots. For any estimate depends on the answers to two very difficult questions: How many Negroes in a community might have joined in the riots? and how many Negroes there did join in the riots? Nonetheless, the survey research and arrest data provide the basis for tentative, if highly speculative, answers to these questions and for rough estimates of riot participation.

To determine how many Negroes in a community might have joined in the riots, it is incorrect to use the total number of Negroes living there. The reason why is well illustrated by a brief discussion of the McCone Commission report, which based its estimate of riot participation on all of Los Angeles County's 650,000 Negroes.[7] Such a base figure was wrong for at least two reasons. First, the 1965 riots occurred principally in southcentral Los Angeles, and not in Los Angeles County's other small and dispersed black enclaves. Negroes from these other communities should not have been counted any more than Negroes from Chicago's South Side should be counted to determine how many might have joined in the West Side rioting of 1966. Second, southcentral Los Angeles—like any other community—contains a sizable number of residents who, for a variety of reasons, could not possibly have participated in the 1965 riots. Neither the infants and the elderly, the lame, the halt, and the blind, nor the residents in prisons, hospitals, and the armed forces should have been counted either. Thus to determine how many Negroes in a community might have joined in the riots, it is essential to compute the number of potential rioters living there.

Who, then, are the potential rioters? They are, to begin with, the Negro residents of the riot area—not the metropolis, nor the city, and not necessarily even the poverty area, but rather the neighborhood which experienced the rioting. To chart the riot area—or, in effect, to fix the boundaries of the rioting, looting, arson, and assault—is an overwhelming task, and one well beyond the scope of this brief report. Fortunately, the Kerner Commission mapped the riot areas for several cities—among them,

TABLE 1.   *Age Distribution of Nonwhites in Riot Areas*

City	Total Nonwhite Population	Under 10	Over 59	Total Potential Rioters
Detroit	219,730	54,263	16,479	148,988
Newark	69,915	19,158	4,265	46,492
Cincinnati	65,676	17,809	5,845	42,022
Grand Rapids	9,068	2,814	512	5,742
New Haven	7,839	2,138	455	5,246
Dayton	4,700	1,028	575	3,097

Detroit, Newark, Cincinnati, Grand Rapids, New Haven, and Dayton—in the course of its investigation.[8] And it was on the basis of the Commission's maps that we computed the number of Negroes living in the riot areas. Only some of the Negroes living in the riot areas—namely, the males and females between the ages of 10 and 59 inclusive—are defined by us as the potential rioters. This definition is a rather broad one. It excludes children under 10 and adults over 59 not only for reasons of common sense, but, more important, because together they constitute only one per cent of the arrestees. It includes, however, the handicapped and the institutionalized, who are admittedly few in number, and women, even though they were less likely than men to join in the riots.[9]

This definition of potential rioters as all Negroes living in the riot areas between the ages of 10 and 59 inclusive tends to maximize the base of the population and thereby minimize the extent of participation. It is, if anything, biased in favor of the riffraff theory. In any event, if this definition is applied to the six cities for which the Kerner Commission mapped the riot areas, the number of Negroes who might have joined in the riots is, as Table 1 indicates, 149,000 in Detroit, 46,500 in Newark, 42,000 in Cincinnati, 5,700 in Grand Rapids, 5,200 in New Haven, and 3,100 in Dayton. It is important to point out, however, that since we are using 1960 census tract data, the total number of potential rioters presented in Table 1 for each city is much smaller than the total number of Negroes between the ages of 10–59 who resided in these areas when the riots occurred in 1967, because all of these cities have increased their Negro population since 1960. Thus, we will be sharply underestimating the actual number of rioters in our analysis.[10]

In order to derive estimates of the total number of Negro rioters in the above six cities we relied upon the three surveys of riot areas that were available to us—the 1967 Caplan surveys of Newark and

Detroit and the 1965 Sears survey of south-central Los Angeles.[11] Unfortunately, each of these surveys had either age or sex limitations for its respondents that hampered our efforts somewhat. The Newark survey, for example, was limited to Negro males between the ages of 15 and 35; the Detroit survey, while including both males and females, did not interview anyone under the age of 15. And, in the Los Angeles survey, which also included both males and females, the lowest age limit was never made explicit. Since each of these surveys contained only a segment of our potential riot population, we had to find a way by which we could calculate the rate of participation for all the Negro riot area residents between the ages of 10 and 59. We decided to select, wherever possible, an age category that was known to have a high proportion of arrestees (such as between 15 and 35 years old) and to use its reported rate of participation in our calculations.

The approach that we used to derive our estimates of riot participation (with the aid of survey, arrest and census data) requires two fairly simple, though not totally reliable, calculations. First, we obtain a "riot ratio" by dividing the number of potential rioters in a given age interval by the number of arrestees in the same age interval for each of the three cities (which are Detroit, Newark and Los Angeles) where surveys had been taken. Second, we apply the average of the three ratios to the other cities (where no surveys had been conducted) by multiplying the ratio times the total number of arrestees in each city— and so derive our estimates of the total number of rioters in each city.

Using the above approach, we obtained the following results. Of the 33,600 or so Negroes in the Los Angeles ghetto between the ages of 25 and 34, approximately 1,200 were arrested in the 1965 riots, and (according to the Sears survey) roughly 22 per cent, or 7,200, were active in the riots. Hence the ratio of rioters to arrestees for Los Angeles was about six to one. Of the 9,800 or so Negro males in the Newark riot area between the ages of 15 and 35, approximately 900 were arrested in the 1967 riots, and (according to the Caplan survey) roughly 45 per cent, or 4,400, participated in the riots. Hence the ratio of rioters to arrestees for Newark was about five to one. Of the 147,000 or so Negroes in the Detroit riot area 15 years and older, approximately 5,400 were arrested in the 1967 riots, and (again, according to the Caplan survey) roughly 11 per cent, or 16,200, joined in the riots. Hence the ratio of rioters to arrestees for Detroit was about three to one. Whether the ratios which hold for Los Angeles, Newark, and Detroit would also hold for the other cities is impossible to say. But we can say that the ratios are fairly similar in the three cities and that they are extremely conservative.[12]

Since Newark's five to one ratio fell between Los Angeles' six to one ratio and Detroit's three to one ratio, it was arbitrarily applied to the remaining four cities. Consequently, the total number of Negroes who participated in the riots is, as Table 2 indicates, 16,900 in Detroit, 6,900 in Newark, 1,800 in Cincinatti, 900 in Grand Rapids, 1,800 in New Haven and 800 in Dayton. As these figures do not reflect the rise in the Negro population of these cities since 1960, they are conservative estimates of the minimum number of rioters for each city. The Negro population in Newark, for example, increased from 34 per cent in 1960 to an estimated 47 per cent in 1965. Thus, our estimate of the total number of rioters in Newark is probably underestimating the true figure by at least 13 per cent. There is

Robert M. Fogelson
Robert B. Hill

probably less of an underestimation with regard to Detroit and Cincinnati, each of which experienced only slight increases in its Negro population since 1960; Detroit's Negro population rose by 4 per cent from 1960 to 1965 and Cincinnati's by 2 per cent over the same period.[13]

These estimates, to repeat, are highly speculative: our figures are based on 1960 census data, riot areas are not precise boundaries, ghetto residents are constantly on the move, the reliability of self-reports about deviant behavior in surveys is questionable, and police arrest practices differ from one city to another. But these estimates are no more speculative than the personal impressions of courageous, but terribly harried, newspaper reporters or the official statements of concerned, but hardly dispassionate, public figures.[14] Furthermore, these estimates far exceed the riffraff theory's estimates, and, perhaps even more noteworthy, nowhere, except in Cincinnati, do they even remotely approximate 1 or 2 per cent of the black population. Hence the rioters were a minority, but hardly a tiny minority—and, in view of the historic efficacy of the customary restraints on rioting in the United States, especially among Negroes, hardly an insignificant

TABLE 2. *Estimates of Rioters in Riot Areas for Six Cities*

City	Riot Ratio*	Total Number of Negro Arrestees	Total Number of Negro Rioters†	Per cent of Riot Area Residents who Rioted‡
Detroit	3 : 1	5,642	16,900	11
Newark	5 : 1	1,387	6,900	15
Cincinnati	5 : 1	350	1,800	4
Grand Rapids	5 : 1	189	900	16
New Haven	5 : 1	353	1,800	35
Dayton	5 : 1	160	800	26

* The "riot ratio" was derived by dividing the number of nonwhite residents within a particular age category by the number of Negro arrestees within the same age category.
† The total number of Negro rioters was derived by multiplying the total number of Negro arrestees by the riot ratio for each city.
‡ The per cent of residents who rioted was derived by dividing the total number of Negro rioters by the total nonwhite residents of the riot area who were between the ages of 10 and 59 inclusive.

minority either. And to characterize them otherwise, as the first point of the riffraff theory does, is not only to distort the historical record, but, even worse, to mislead the American public.

The Composition of the Rioters

The second component of the riffraff theory—that the rioters, far from being representative of the Negro community, were principally the riffraff and outside agitators—is perhaps the most difficult to test using arrest statistics because of their built-in biases in favor of this theory. For it is a fact that for similar offenses, lower-class persons (who tend to have most of the traits of the riffraff: unattached, uprooted, unskilled, unemployed and criminal) are much more likely to get arrested than middle-class persons.[15] Therefore, it is to be expected that the riffraff element would be over-represented among riot arrestees.

At the same time, however, since most Negroes are either lower- or working-class persons, it is also to be expected that these so-called riffraff traits can be found among large segments of the Negro community. Many Negroes, whether rioters or not, are single, or otherwise unmarried; many are juveniles or young adults, many are recent immigrants from the South, many unemployed or unskilled, and many have criminal records.[16] Hence to test the second point of the riffraff theory, it is not enough just to ask whether many of the rioters have these traits; the answer, obviously, is they do. It is also necessary to ask whether a greater proportion of the actual rioters than of the potential rioters possess these traits. But even if we do find that a higher proportion of actual rioters than potential rioters have certain riffraff characteristics, our task is not yet complete. We must still assess the proportion of the actual rioters that these traits account for.

Therefore, despite the built-in biases of the arrest statistics in favor of the riffraff theory, we shall use these data in conjunction with census data—and, whenever possible, survey data—to assist us in determining the social composition of rioters.

Before we examine the so-called riffraff traits it seems instructive to begin with a discussion of the sex distribution of riot arrestees and the potential rioters.

Since 90 per cent of those arrested for non-riot offenses in the general population are males, it should come as no surprise that riot arrestees are also predominantly male—and, by the same proportion of nine to one.[17] According to arrest statistics, therefore, it seems safe to conclude that men are much more likely to participate in riots than females.

A different picture of sex involvement in riots is obtained, however, when one observes the findings of survey reports of riot participation. In the Detroit survey 39 per cent of the self-reported rioters were females, whereas only 10 per cent of the Detroit riot arrestees were females. Thus, assuming the survey findings are reliable, the Detroit arrest data are under-representing the participation of women in riots by almost 30 per cent. A similar under-representation of the extent of female participation in riots was found in the Los Angeles survey of 1965. Fully one-half of those who reported they were "active" in the riot were females, whereas only 13 per cent of the Los Angeles arrestees were females. If the survey data are reliable, the Los Angeles arrest data are grossly under-representing the participation of females in the 1965 riot by almost 40 per cent.[18]

Since about 50 per cent of the potential rioters in the riot area are males, the 90 per cent for males among riot arrestees would indicate that males are heavily over-represented in riots. Yet, if the 60 per cent figure for males from the Detroit survey or the 50 per cent figure for males from the Los Angeles survey is compared to the 50 per cent figure for the potential rioters, one would have to conclude that males are only slightly over-represented, if at all, in riots.

Eye-witness accounts of the riots also indicate that a higher proportion of males participate in riots than females. In view of the above data, it appears that the safest conclusion that we can make about sex involvement in riots is that although males are more likely than females to participate in riots, their differential rates of participation are much closer than arrest statistics indicate. Policemen, for one reason or another, are permitting large numbers of female rioters to go unapprehended.

Although one may not ordinarily consider being young a riffraff characteristic, it is a trait that is commonly identified with the undesirable elements in riots. In fact, it is widely assumed in some quarters that teenagers are primarily responsible for most riots. In Table 3 we compare the relative proportions of juveniles (defined as youths between the ages of 10 and 17 inclusive) among the arrestees and the potential rioters (that is, the riot area residents between 10–59 inclusive) for each city. With the exception of two cities (New Haven and Boston), it is noteworthy that the proportion of juveniles is considerably higher among the arrestees than among the

potential rioters. Yet it is also important to note that in no city is the proportion of juveniles a majority of the arrestees. In fact, the highest proportion of juvenile arrestees is 32 per cent (in Cincinnati) and the lowest proportion is 8 per cent (in New Haven). Thus, the riot arrestees are overwhelmingly adults. It may very well be, however, that as with the case of female involvement in riots, higher proportions of juveniles are participating than are reflected by arrest statistics. Since we do not have survey data available on the rate of participation in riots of persons under the age of 15, we cannot draw upon that data to make generalizations about the participation of juveniles in riots. It would appear, however, that descriptions of the riots tend to indicate a higher degree of involvement by juveniles than is reflected in the arrest statistics. But even this degree of participation by juveniles appears to be much less than the involvement of adults in riots.

*TABLE 3. Proportion of Juveniles and Adults Among Arrestees and Residents**

City	Total Negro Arrestees†	Arrestees (Per cent)		Residents (Per cent)	
		Juveniles	Adults	Juveniles	Adults
Detroit	5,642	16.6	83.4	7.2	92.8
Newark	1,387	18.4	81.6	12.8	87.2
New Haven	353	8.1	91.9	12.0	88.0
Cincinnati	350	32.4	67.6	18.9	81.1
Buffalo	190	22.1	77.9	13.9	86.1
Grand Rapids	189	25.4	74.6	16.0	84.0
Plainfield	161	10.1	89.9	—	—
Dayton	160	15.2	84.8	11.9	88.1
Phoenix	111	—	—	—	—
Boston	62	11.3	88.7	15.0	85.0

* We define "juvenile" as those persons under the age of 18. This definition of juvenile is consistent with that employed by most police departments. For Detroit, however, juveniles refer to those persons 16 years and under. The arrestee data throughout this report will refer only to Negro arrestees.
† Although these base figures for Negro arrestees will not be presented in any of the succeeding tables, they should be used to compute the absolute frequencies of particular categories, when necessary.
‡ The residents (or the "potential rioters") refer only to the nonwhite persons between 10–59 years old residing in the riot area; whites residing in the area are excluded from our analysis. The juveniles among the residents are defined as those nonwhite youths between the ages of 10 and 17. The figures for the nonwhite residents were obtained from 1960 census tract data. See U.S. Bureau of the Census, "U.S. Censuses of Population and Housing: 1960. Census Tracts" U.S. Government Printing Office, Washington, D.C., 1962.

In Table 4 we are provided with a more detailed breakdown of the age distribution among the arrestees and potential rioters. It reveals that if any age-group is over-represented in the riots, it is not primarily the juveniles. It is rather the young adults between the ages of 15 and 24. Forty-five per cent to 73 per cent of the arrestees in the ten cities are between 15 and 24 years old. But only 13 per cent to 23 per cent of the potential rioters fall within that age category. Even among the arrestees, in only three of the ten cities (Cincinnati, Buffalo and Dayton) do those persons between the ages of 15 and 24 constitute a clear majority. However, the young people between the ages of 15 and 34 constitute an overwhelming majority of the arrestees: these proportions range from 70 per cent in Detroit to 93 per cent in Buffalo. Yet the similar proportions of those between 15 and 34 among the potential rioters—with the exception of one city (New Haven)—are all under 50 per cent. In all, those persons between 15-24 are highly over-represented among the arrestees, those between the ages of 25 and 34 are slightly over-represented, whereas the elderly (35–59) and the children (10–14) are under-represented in the riots.

Thus, we conclude that on the basis of the arrest data, individuals between the ages of 15 and 34 and especially those between the ages of 15 and 24 are most likely to participate in riots.

Since Table 4 revealed that the age category with the highest proportion of arrestees were young adults between the ages of 15 and 24, we would expect a large proportion of the arrestees to be single. And, if we can assume that single persons are more likely than married persons to participate in riots, then we would expect a higher proportion of the arrestees to be single than the potential rioters. And, indeed, Table 5 reveals this to be the case. In every city, there are at least twice as many arrestees who are single, as there are potential rioters who are single. In Detroit, for example, about one-fifth of the riot area residents are single, but almost half of the arrestees are single. On the other hand, between 56 to 60 per cent of the potential rioters are married, but only 23 to 48 per cent of the arrestees are married. Thus, arrestees are for the most part, more likely to be single, but less likely to be married, separated, widowed, or divorced than are the potential rioters. Yet it is also important to note that in only two out of the five cities (Cincinnati and Buffalo) do the single persons constitute a clear majority of the arrestees. In fact, when those two cities are excluded, the differences between the proportions of single arrestees and married arrestees vary from a low of 3 per cent to a high of 9 per cent. Consequently, there are

TABLE 4.   Age Distribution of Arrestees and Residents of Riot Areas (In per cent)

City	Arrestees				Residents			
	10–14	15–24	25–34	35–59	10–14	15–24	24–34	35–59
Detroit	3.6	49.7	27.1	19.6	12.4	17.1	22.7	47.8
Newark	5.3	45.2	29.0	20.5	29.4	13.4	17.2	40.0
New Haven	0	47.4	35.4	17.2	11.6	23.5	28.1	36.8
Cincinnati	7.0	73.4	15.6	4.0	14.2	20.1	22.1	43.6
Buffalo	0	71.7	21.0	7.3	13.7	19.8	25.0	41.5
Grand Rapids	19.7	51.8	19.0	9.5	15.8	22.0	23.7	38.5
Plainfield	1.2	45.2	35.1	18.9	—	—	—	—
Dayton	0	58.6	24.3	17.1	12.2	16.3	20.5	51.0
Phoenix	0	53.1	30.7	16.2	16.7	23.0	20.6	39.7
Boston	1.6	51.6	29.1	17.7	13.3	21.0	24.4	41.3

almost as many arrestees who are married as there are those who are single. Nevertheless, it is clear that single persons are over-represented among the arrestees, whereas married, separated, widowed, and divorced persons are under-represented among the arrestees. In short, one unattached group (the single persons) is over-represented, whereas the other unattached group (the formerly married) is under-represented among the arrestees.

One popular assumption about riot participation is that the rioters are primarily the uprooted—those immigrants from the rural South who have not been able to make a successful adjustment to the demands of urban life. According to this view we would expect the Southern-born to be over-represented among the arrestees. The data in Table 6, however, do not indicate this.

Robert M. Fogelson
Robert B. Hill

In each of the three cities (Detroit, Cincinnati, and Boston) for which we have comparative information on both arrestees and residents, we find that the arrestees are somewhat less likely to be Southern-born than are the potential rioters. Among the arrestees, however, we find that in three cities (Detroit, New Haven, and Grand Rapids) a majority were born in the South and in the remaining three cities (Cincinnati, Plainfield, and Boston) a majority were born in the North. Thus, it appears that southerners may be just as likely to participate in riots as northerners. But arrestees are more likely to be born in the state where the riot occurred than are the potential rioters. In

TABLE 5. Marital Status of Arrestees and Residents of Riot Areas* (In per cent)

City†	Arrestees			Residents		
	Single	Married	Other	Single	Married	Other
Detroit	48.4	38.4	13.2	19.2	60.1	20.7
Cincinnati	75.6	22.5	1.9	20.2	58.3	21.5
Buffalo	69.0	28.7	2.3	21.2	59.6	19.2
Grand Rapids	44.8	38.6	16.6	20.9	58.5	20.6
Boston	51.6	48.4	0	24.2	55.7	20.1

* The figures for marital status of both arrestees and residents are presented only for persons 14 years and over.
† Newark, Plainfield, Dayton, Phoenix and New Haven are omitted from the above table because marital status information on their arrestees was not available. It will be our practice to omit a city whenever we do not have arrest data information on the item in question. The Detroit figures were obtained from a study of 500 Detroit male Negro arrestees conducted for the U.S. Department of Labor. See Sheldon Lachman and Benjamin Singer, *The Detroit Riot of July 1967*, (Detroit, Michigan: Behavior Research Institute, 1968), p. 19.

TABLE 6. Birthplace of Arrestees and Residents of Riot Areas* (In per cent)

City	Arrestees			Residents		
	Born in State	Outside of State		Born in State	Outside of State	
		North	South		North	South
Detroit	35.5	5.7	58.9	26.9	8.2	64.9
New Haven	18.0	16.0	66.0	—	—	—
Cincinnati	72.4	8.5	19.1	44.5	2.5	53.0
Grand Rapids	21.5	20.3	58.2	—	—	—
Plainfield	53.2	8.2	38.6	—	—	—
Boston	41.0	16.4	42.6	40.5	11.1	48.4

* Our definition of "South" includes the following eleven states: Alabama, Arkansas, Florida, Georgia, Louisiana, Mississippi, North Carolina, South Carolina, Tennessee, Texas and Virginia. All the remaining states constitute the "North."
† Newark, Buffalo, Dayton, and Phoenix have been omitted from the above table because of lack of birthplace information on their arrestees.

Cincinnati, for example, whereas less than half (45 per cent) of the potential rioters were born in the state of Ohio, almost three-fourths (72 per cent) of the arrestees were native-born.

Therefore, we conclude that the "uprooted" thesis of riot participation is not supported by our data. Northerners are just as likely as southerners to participate in riots; and, more important, native-born residents of the state are more likely than those born in other states to become involved in riots.

Another important theme of the riffraff theory is that the rioters are recruited primarily from those who are poorly-trained and who lack the skills to obtain good-paying jobs. Thus, it would be expected that the unskilled are over-represented among the riot arrestees. This expectation is confirmed by the figures presented in Table 7. For we find that the arrestees are much more likely to be unskilled than are the potential rioters. The smallest difference between the proportions of the two groups

is 10 per cent (in Grand Rapids) and the largest difference is 29 per cent (in Newark). Among the arrestees, we find that in all the cities, except Boston, the proportion of unskilled persons is over 49 per cent; it ranges from 47 per cent in Boston to 67 per cent in Cincinnati. Among the potential rioters, however, the proportion of the unskilled goes from 28 per cent in Detroit to 48 per cent in Cincinnati. Although the arrestees are over-represented on the lowest skill level, there are, nonetheless, strong similarities between the occupational distributions of the arrestees and the potential rioters. In both groups, for example, the proportion of these holding either semi-skilled or unskilled jobs include (for the most part) more than 70 per cent of the members of each group. It is clear that the overwhelming majority of Negroes, whether rioters or not, hold low-skilled jobs. On the other hand, only a slightly smaller proportion of arrestees than potential rioters hold skilled or white-collar jobs.

Consequently, although our data clearly support the thesis that a large proportion of the rioters hold unskilled jobs, it must also be pointed out that about just as many

TABLE 7. *Occupation of Male Arrestees and Residents of Riot Areas** (In per cent)

City†	Arrestees				Residents			
	White collar	Skilled	Semi–skilled	Un–skilled	White collar	Skilled	Semi–skilled	Un–skilled
Detroit	10.2	10.7	29.0	50.1	18.4	12.8	41.2	27.6
Newark	18.0		23.0	59.0	24.6		45.6	29.8
Cincinnati	9.4	6.5	16.7	67.4	18.0	10.8	22.9	48.3
Buffalo	10.6	3.5	33.3	52.6	10.9	13.9	36.8	38.4
Grand Rapids	6.4	14.2	27.4	51.9	7.7	15.8	34.9	41.6
Boston	29.4	11.8	11.8	47.1	20.3	13.5	29.7	36.5

* The above figures for occupation among the arrestees refer only to those arrestees who are Negro males 18 years and older; similarly, among the residents, the figures are given for nonwhite males 14 years and older. The "unskilled" category includes both laborers and all service occupations; the "semi-skilled" grouping includes only operatives; the "skilled" category includes only craftsmen; and the "white-collar" category includes sales, clerical, managers and proprietors and professionals.

† Since the occupations of the Detroit and Newark arrestees were not available to us, the figures presented in the above table were obtained from other sources. The Detroit figures are based upon a sample of 500 male arrestees interviewed by the Behavior Research Institute. We recomputed their percentages after excluding the "miscellaneous" category. See Sheldon Lachman and Benjamin Singer, *The Detroit Riot of July 1967*, (Detroit, Michigan: Behavior Research Institute, 1968), p. 14. The figures for Newark were obtained from the Governor's Select Commission on Civil Disorder, *Report for Action*, State of New Jersey, February 1968, p. 271. Since the N.J. Commission included the "white-collar" figures in the "skilled" category, we have placed the figures midway between the two columns for both Arrestees and Residents to make them comparable.

potential rioters as arrestees have low-skilled jobs as operatives or laborers.

Closely related to the assertion that rioters consist primarily of the unskilled is the contention that a large proportion of the rioters are unemployed. Since we cannot use the 1960 employment figures of the riot areas, because of their sharp fluctuations from year to year, we can only make comparisons for the two cities for which we do have recent unemployment figures—Detroit and Newark. In the New Jersey riot report, *Report for Action*, it was indicated that while 27 per cent of the arrestees were unemployed, 12 per cent of the Newark Negro population in the city as a whole were unemployed.[19] Similarly, whereas our arrest data reveal that 24 per cent of the Negro adult males in Detroit were unemployed, the Bureau of Labor Statistics estimated that 10 per cent of the nonwhite residents in the central city were unemployed.[20] Thus, a higher proportion of the arrestees are unemployed than the potential rioters in the general population. But this discrepancy is not as large as it appears, for two reasons. First, since the Department of Labor includes in its count only those persons actively seeking a job, it severely underestimates the actual rate of unemployment. It excludes completely the "sub-employed," which consists of a large proportion of men in the ghetto who have given up looking for work.[21] Furthermore, since our arrestees are heavily over-represented by the young adults between the ages of 15 and 24, an age group which is itself greatly over-represented in the unemployed, it should not be surprising that our arrest data should indicate higher proportions of the unemployed than exist in the Negro population for the city as a whole. But, and more important, it should be noted that about three-quarters of the riot arrestees are employed. Hence the overwhelming majority of those who participate in riots are gainfully employed—even though it is usually in a semi-skilled or unskilled occupation. Thus, although unemployment may be a factor in riot participation, it does not account for the riot participation of the three-fourths who are employed.

At the heart of the riffraff theory is the

notion that rioters represent the criminal element of the Negro community. In fact, the arrest data tend to support this contention. With the exception of Buffalo and Newark, a sizable majority of the arrestees—ranging from 40 per cent in Buffalo, 45 per cent in Newark, 57 per cent in Detroit, 67 per cent in New Haven, 70 per cent in Grand Rapids and 92 per cent in Dayton—had prior criminal records.[22] But it is one thing to have a record and quite another to be a criminal; what is more, there are a number of reasons why these figures do not prove that the riot arrestees were principally criminals.

First, a criminal record in the United States simply means an arrest, as opposed to a conviction, record; probably no more than one-half of the arrestees with a record have been convicted, and probably no more than one-quarter for a major crime. Second, according to the President's Commission on Law Enforcement and Administration of Justice, which has made the only estimate we know of on the subject, roughly 50 to 90 per cent of the Negro males in the urban ghettos have criminal records.[23] Third, if the findings of the President's Commission on Crime in the District of Columbia are applicable elsewhere, convicted felons are much more likely to be unemployed and to have criminal records than riot arrestees.[24] Fourth, our inspection of the prior criminal records of the riot arrestees revealed that their past arrests were for offenses which, on the whole, were much less serious than the offenses committed by the typical non-riot felons. The Bureau of Criminal Records in California's Department of Justice arrived at a similar conclusion after inspecting the prior criminal records of those arrested for participating in the Los Angeles riot of 1965.[25]

Hence, to label most rioters as criminals is simply to brand most members of the Negro community—and, particularly, the majority of Negro males—as criminals. Therefore, the criminal element is not over-represented among the rioters. Since the close surveillance of the Negro community by the police results in a disproportionately high number of arrests among male Negroes, it is to be expected that a majority of the rioters—who are predominantly young Negro males—would have criminal records.

The riffraff theory also holds that the riots were primarily the result of demagogic agitation by outsiders. Many first-hand descriptions of the riots do indicate that a few individuals and organizations—radicals as well as nationalists—encouraged some rioters and tried to exploit the rioting. Indeed, it would have been surprising if they had done otherwise. According to the arrest data, however, whether agitators or not, the overwhelming majority of the rioters were not outsiders. In seven of the nine cities for which information is available the proportion of the arrestees who were residents of the cities involved was 97 per cent or more. Ninety-seven per cent of the arrestees in Boston, Detroit and Grand Rapids, 98 per cent in Buffalo and New Haven, and 100 per cent in Cincinnati and Dayton were residents of the cities that experienced the rioting. And in Newark and Plainfield 92 per cent and 77 per cent of the arrestees were residents of those cities.[26] With regard to the role of conspiracy in the riots, the arrest sheets are, of course, less informative. On the basis of other evidence, however, it is clear that, whether outsiders or not, the agitators did not plan or organize the 1960s riots. This was the conclusion reached by the F.B.I. in 1964 and reiterated by its director J. Edgar Hoover and Attorney-General Ramsey Clark in 1967. This was also the conclusion confirmed a year later by the Kerner Commission, which made a thorough survey of the federal, state, and municipal reports on the 1967 riots.[27]

In sum, we have found that many of the social traits predicted by the second component of the riffraff theory to characterize rioters were over-represented among the arrestees, and in some instances, decidedly so. Much of this, of course, was due to the biases of the arrest data. But "over-representativeness" is quite a different matter from saying that the arrestees had predominantly riffraff characteristics. In spite of the heavy over-representation of young, single males, the striking facts are—again in view of the historic efficacy of the customary restraints on rioting in the United States, especially among Negroes—that one-half to three-quarters of the arrestees were employed in semi-skilled or skilled occupations, three-fourths were employed, and three-tenths to six-tenths were born outside the South. So to claim, as the second point of the riffraff theory does, that the rioters were principally the riffraff and outside agitators—rather than fairly typical young Negro males—is to seriously misconstrue the 1960s riots.

The Sentiment of the Negro Community

The third point of the riffraff theory—that the overwhelming majority of the Negro population, the law-abiding and respectable 98 or 99 per cent who did not join in the rioting, unequivocally opposed and deplored the riots—also has a certain plausibility. First of all, a sizable majority of the potential rioters, not to mention the ghetto residents, refrained from rioting, and their restraint and respect for the law might be construed as a repudiation of the riots. In one city after another, too, a host of local Negro leaders—among them, James Farmer of New York, John A. Buggs of Los Angeles, James Threatt of Newark, and Nicholas Hood of Detroit—labored valiantly to restrain the rioters.[28] And a good many ordinary Negroes registered sharp protest against the violence while the rioting was underway and expressed extreme dismay at the consequences when it was over. From Washington, too, a group of national Negro leaders—including Martin Luther King, Jr., A. Philip Randolph, Roy Wilkins, and Whitney Young—criticized the riots as "ineffective, disruptive and highly damaging" and called on the Negroes to "forego the temptation to disregard the law."[29] This evidence, it could be argued, proves that the overwhelming majority of the Negro population un-equivocally opposed and deplored the 1960s riots.

And yet it could also be argued that this evidence proves nothing of the kind. After all, about one out of five potential rioters did join in the riots, and the other four-fifths might have refrained from rioting because they feared the local policemen, national guardsmen, and federal soldiers and not because they disapproved of the riots. Moreover, the local Negro leaders labored in vain to restrain the rioters: no matter how strongly committed to their race or how deeply concerned about their com-munity, they had little or no impact on the course of the riots.[30] By the same token, a good many ordinary Negroes objected to the violence not so much because they sympathized with the authorities as because they suspected that the blacks, not the whites, would suffer the worst losses. If Martin Luther King, Jr. and the other moderates appealed for non-violence, H. Rap Brown, Stokely Carmichael, and the other militants did not; and by the end of the summer of 1967 it was not clear which, if either, of the two groups spoke for the Negro people.[31] Hence this evidence proves nothing conclusively—except perhaps that to gauge community sentiment about the riots with any confidence it is essential to raise more revealing questions, probe more relevant sources, and offer more tentative answers.

To begin with the questions, it is not particularly enlightening simply to ask whether the Negro population supported or opposed the riots. For to do so is to assume that the Negroes felt clearly one way or another about the rioting when, in all probability they had mixed feelings, and second, that the Negroes agreed basically about the rioting when, in all likelihood, they had sharp disagreements. Hence, it is more valuable to ask whether the Negroes believed that the riots were beneficial or essential or, even if not, inevitable, and then whether the Negroes objected to the rioting mainly on principled or pragmatic grounds. One may also ask what proportion of Negroes (and especially of the Negroes who did not participate as rioters or coun-

ter-rioters) and which groups of Negroes considered the rioting beneficial, essential, and/or inevitable. To phrase the questions in these ways is to allow for the ambiguities in the Negroes' positions and the dif-ferences among the ghettos' residents and to make it possible to gauge the black com-munity's sentiment about the 1960s riots with a fair degree of confidence.

But not with much more than a fair degree. For, to turn from the questions to the sources, the information available is extremely scanty. The position of the mod-erate Negro leaders is, of course, well documented; so, for that matter, is the ideology of the militant black leaders. The activities of the rioters are also well known; and so, to a lesser extent, are the efforts of the counter-rioters. But the leaders—moderates and militants—and the partici-pants—rioters and counter-rioters—are a minority, even if a substantial one, of the Negro population. And about the Negro rank-and-file and the uninvolved Negroes, very little is known and not much informa-tion is available. The studies of arrest sheets are not particularly helpful either, except perhaps for comparative purposes. There are, however, a handful of opinion surveys —some local and others national, a few illuminating but none comprehensive—made throughout the 1960s.[32] There are also first-hand descriptions of the riots and on-the-spot interviews with the ghetto residents reported during or shortly after the rioting.[33] Notwithstanding their limita-tions, the opinion surveys and impressionis-tic accounts convey—with reasonable ac-curacy—the black community's sentiment about the 1960s riots.

According to the opinion surveys, the black community's attitude towards rioting is ambivalent. Of the Negroes in Los Angeles interviewed by U.C.L.A.'s Institute of Government and Public Affairs in 1965, only one-third favored the rioting, yet two-thirds believed that it would increase the white's awareness and sympathy and im-prove the Negro's position; only one-

eighth thought that violent protest was the
Negro's most effective weapon, yet two-
thirds believed that the riots had a purpose
and five-sixths that the victims deserved
their treatment; three-fourths preferred
negotiations and nonviolent protests, yet
only one-fourth believed that there would
be no more riots in Los Angeles.[34] Of the
blacks interviewed across the nation by
Louis Harris and Associates in 1966, 68
per cent felt that Negroes stood to lose by
the rioting; yet 34 per cent thought that it
has helped their cause, 20 per cent that it
has hurt, and 17 per cent that it has made
no difference; 59 per cent were confident
that Negroes will win their rights without
violence, but 21 per cent were convinced
that violence will be necessary and 20 per
cent were not certain; in any event, 61 per
cent predicted that there will be further
rioting, 31 per cent were not sure, and 8 per
cent predicted that there will be no riots in
the future.[35]

These surveys indicate that, in addition to
the large number of people who felt the
riots were inevitable, a large minority or a
small majority of the Negro community
regards them as beneficial, essential. According to the Institute of Government and
Public Affairs, moreover, the Negroes in
Los Angeles objected to the rioting mainly
on pragmatic rather than principled
grounds; they disapproved of the violent
consequences of the riots rather than the
riots themselves. Whereas 29 per cent dis-
liked the burning and 19 per cent the
looting, 21 per cent protested the shooting
and the killing and 13 per cent the police
action, and only 1 per cent objected to the
Negro rioting and 1 per cent to the Negro
assault.[36] According to the Institute of
Government and Public Affairs, too, the
relatively well-to-do and well-educated
supported the Los Angeles riots as much as
the less well-off and poorly-educated,
though, according to the University of
Michigan's Survey Research Center, the
counter-rioters in Detroit tended to be
more affluent and better educated than the
rioters. And according to the Harris orga-

nization, lower- and lower-middle-income
Negroes were somewhat more likely to
regard the riots favorably than middle-
and upper-middle-income Negroes; and
Negroes 34 years and younger were considerably more likely to do so than Negroes
50 years and older and even more than
Negroes between the ages of 35 and 49.[37]

These findings are consistent with the
impressionistic accounts of the 1960s riots.
The first-hand descriptions of the riots and
the on-the-spot interviews with ghetto
residents revealed a great deal of tacit
support for the rioters among the non-
rioters. Apparently many of them also saw
the rioting as a protest, and a successful one
at that, against the grievances of the Negro
ghettos—a protest which, if need be,
would be delivered again. Their feelings
were well articulated by a middle-age
Negro woman who ran an art gallery in
southcentral Los Angeles: "I will not take
a Molotov cocktail," she said, "but I am
as mad as they (the rioters) are."[38] Nor
are these findings inconsistent with a
commonsense approach to the 1960s riots.
After all, is it conceivable that (as the third
point of the riffraff theory holds) several
hundred riots could have erupted in nearly
every Negro ghetto in the United States
over the past five years against the opposition of 98 or 99 per cent of the black community? And is it conceivable that militant
young Negroes would have ignored the
customary restraints on rioting in the
United States, including the commitment
to orderly social change, unless they en-
joyed the tacit support of at least a sizable
minority of the black community?

If the survey research, arrest data, and
impressionistic accounts are indicative, the
rioters were a small but significant minority
of the Negro population, fairly representative of the ghetto residents, and especially
of the young adult males, and tacitly
supported by at least a large minority of
the black community. Which, to repeat,
means that the 1960s riots were a manifestation of race and racism in the United States,
a reflection of the social problems of
modern black ghettos, a protest against
the essential conditions of life there, and an
indicator of the necessity for fundamental

changes in American society. And if the riffraff theory has not been accurate in the past, its accuracy in the future is seriously questioned. The riots appear to be gaining recruits from all segments of the Negro community. Of the Negroes asked by Louis Harris in 1966 if they would or would not join in riots, 15 per cent replied that they would, 24 per cent that they were unsure, and 61 per cent that they would not. Thus, fully 39 per cent of the Negroes either would join a riot or were uncertain about what they would do. Moreover, the lower-middle-, middle-, and upper-middle-income

Negroes were more likely to respond affirmatively than the lower-income Negroes. And of the Negroes 34 years and younger, the current generation, fully 19 per cent said that they would join a riot, 24 per cent that they were uncertain, and 57 per cent that they would not. On the eve of the summer of 1968, these responses are anything but reassuring.[39]

Who Can Activate The Poor? One Assessment of "Maximum Feasible Participation" [*1]

Warner Bloomberg, Jr.

University of Wisconsin at Milwaukee

Florence W. Rosenstock

Albert Einstein College of Medicine

WHATEVER its original authors intended it to convey, the phrase, "maximum feasible participation" of the poor, has become a troubling and troublesome ideological projective test for social scientists and social critics, as well as for planners and protesters. To some it has been read as simply one of several pieties included in the legislation for the "war on poverty" and applicable to only one of its titles, an exhortation not subject to any very precise policy prescriptions. In sharp contrast, militant activists, whose contemporary strategy and style are best expressed in the direct mass action techniques of certain civil rights groups such as SNCC, heard it as an unequivocal call for a modern populism of the poor, the beginning of a political reconstruction that would eventually institutionalize participative democracy as the form and process of the urban polity. Many local officials in city halls and community chest agencies reacted with predictable anger and alarm, some of the more paranoid among them suspecting that this

* *Excerpt from "Who Can Activate the Poor: One Assessment of Maximum Feasible Participation" by Warner Bloomberg, Jr., and Florence W. Rosenstock, is reprinted from* Power, Poverty and Urban Policy, Vol. II, *Urban Affairs Annual Reviews (1968), pp. 313–314, 317–330, edited by Bloomberg, and Henry Schmandt, by permission of the publisher, Sage Publication, Inc.*

was but one more ploy in federal expansionist gamesmanship, others fearing a possible increase of independent political power on the part of the people of the central city ghetto.[2] Administrators in the Office of Economic Opportunity, especially in regional branches, in sheer self-defense often sought to shove such basic issues at least temporarily into the background by reducing them to questions of percentage representation of the poor, however selected, on the local boards or commissions that review and provide overall supervision of OEO projects, tending to urge one-third as a kind of *ad hoc* numerical embodiment of social justice. That effort failed as the 1967 Congress combined the "one-third poor" formula with other stipulations that would emasculate the authority of the board on which the poor sat. . . .

Participation: Correlates and Causes

What, then, determines whether or not people participate in politically relevant associations, organize on behalf of one or another institutional or community decision, and seek access to the actual decision-making roles? In attempting to answer this question, first for the American population in general and then with respect to the poor in particular, it is important to remember that we are considering unusual rather than typical behavior.[3] Contrary to a fairly popular stereotype, the majority of American citizens belong to only one or two organizations, if any, and for the most part are passive members rather than part of the active core of any associations to which they belong. Moreover, only a small proportion of those associations are normally relevant to or in any way affect the kind of decision-making with which "maximum feasible participation" is concerned; usually they serve other individual and institutional goals, most often those having to do with religion, job security, and recreation and sociability. And when actual involvement in roles most directly concerned with making community decisions apart from elections is examined, the proportions drop below the 10 per cent level. As Dahl has said, "The first fact, and it

Notes to this selection will be found on page 345.

overshadows almost everything else, is that *most citizens use their political resources scarcely at all.*"[4]

The point has already been made that the poor are least evident, by any of the usual indices, among the minority who are "participators." It should be added that the correlation of participation with education, income, and other generally valued characteristics is probably curvilinear, with a rapid increase in memberships, politically relevant activity, and participation in direct decision-making roles as the shift is made into what we usually refer to, albeit somewhat vaguely, as the "upper middle" and "upper" strata. But the meaning of the available correlations is far from clear.

Three Theoretical Models for Participation

Many, especially schoolmen and educational psychologists, seem to conclude that any group's place on the socioeconomic class ladder determines the extent of their political participation. They hold that this is true at least in part because the relevant cultural patterns themselves are associated with social level. Therefore, eliciting extensive and continuing social action from the poor becomes a practical goal only if segments of the poor can be "leapfrogged" upward along some of the status continua, or if changed cultural patterns can somehow be developed among people whose locations in the social structure remain relatively fixed. In short, since political participation is believed to derive from social structural and cultural variables, it is not itself a means of changing the place of the poor in society or the values and action norms which the poor display. Education and other means of deliberate cultural change may be used to affect the latter, and programs such as those which relocate people a number of jumps upward in employment status may be used to begin to break up the "status crystallization" of the poor.

Unfortunately, a majority of the adult poor are not employable, or continue to be chronically underemployed, given current

standards and institutional patterns.[5] Job retraining and placement programs inevitably have had only limited impact. Efforts to remake the subcultures of the slums or of individual poor families through educational and training programs have been meager, but their results have been so negligible that one must doubt the utility of such projects, unless truly massive resources could be brought to bear. As a result, those who believe the most evident correlations actually denote causal factors for participation, who use cultural and social structural patterns to *explain* the absence of participation by the poor, tend to emphasize programs for children and youth. "Compensatory education" is proposed as a means both for developing values and overt behavior norms that depart from the parental models and for creating skills that will leapfrog high school or job corps graduates into good jobs.

A second model, shared in large part by a variety of reformers and organizers of what might best be called the "social action–social protest school," in effect reverses the direction of causation associated with the frequently reiterated percentages and correlations.[6] Those who lack money income also rank low on all the other status hierarchies, according to this view, precisely because they have no other power resources with which to enforce claims for more goods and services, better neighborhoods, and access to other kinds of opportunities and pleasures associated with the American version of the "good life." Most aspects of what we have been calling the "culture of poverty" are seen as reflections of this powerlessness, the habits inculcated by being continuously subject to others' decisions and the emotional adjustments and rationalizations that make this condition as bearable as possible for people who also learn from the larger society that dependency and helplessness among adults are signs of personal worthlessness.

Only the experience of individual and group potency through organization on behalf of their own needs and interest and through the exercise of power against those who have excluded and exploited them, will enable a majority of the poor, especially the most deprived, to break through the "bind" of their own cultural and psychological patterns at the same time that they break down the institutional barriers that are the sources of their impoverishment. An inevitable part of this "sociotherapeutic" process, and a necessary component for its full success, is the clarification of the conflict between the poor and the presently powerful and affluent segments of the society, and the mobilization of the emotional and intellectual energies of the poor around this frequently concealed but now fully revealed nexus of antagonistic interests and purposes.

A third model, the "community development" approach, largely disregards the usual correlations and does not impute any special and especially entrenched incapacities for action to any segment of the population.[7] It assumes that there are enough capacities for leadership and action distributed among all, or almost all, human communities or subcommunities to make possible development of effective self-help programs and projects. Though these are to be based in the locality, they may be developed cooperatively with supralocal agencies and organizations that are part of "the establishment." To elicit action organizers must enable residents with leadership and activist capabilities to articulate the needs felt by themselves and the others in their community, to understand what can be changed and how such changes can be brought about, and to realize the resources that they do have and how their resources can be expanded so as to be able to effect desired changes. The problems of a cultural nature confronting the organizer are not so much those of alienation in the face of opportunity and apathy in the face of perceived needs, but patterns of evaluation that produce contentment with the *status quo* and habitual interpretations that prevent understanding or acceptance of

available means for successful problem-solving, such as new technology or formal procedures for political and legal action.

Community development personnel, therefore, see education techniques as useful, not to change the "basics" of a culture or subculture, but to inculcate cognitive and judgmental patterns, especially in selected leadership personnel, that are specifically relevant to a definite project to be undertaken, whether it is to clean up a well in a village in an underdeveloped nation or to petition and create political pressure for a road in an Appalachian hollow or a park and recreation center within an urban slum. These particular patterns of perception and evaluation may link into and therefore elicit change in more basic cultural components, but that is not necessarily a goal and there may even be some concern for preserving as much of the old culture as is compatible with meeting the people's perceived needs in their present historic circumstances. However, educational techniques depart drastically from the typical and fairly formal classroom procedures of most American programs of adult education. They are intermixed and interwoven with the ongoing projects and the organizer-educator often participates directly in the project. He also may act as an intermediary between those whom he serves and those with whom they must deal, usually local decision-makers, until his "clients" gain the necessary skills and understanding to do so themselves.

Some Implications of the Alternative Models

These three statements of theory and strategy are, of course, only "models.' Actual projects and organizations may and do combine elements from more than one. Nevertheless, each has a certain logic which is likely to affect both who utilizes it and the scale and locale of its most effective utilization.

For example, the first approach, seeking to change the habits of enough individuals or families to amount to an alteration of culture and trying to promote a forced-draft movement of a great many poor persons up some one or two relevant status dimensions, such as employment or school achievement, requires very large resources unless it is to be merely a research experiment or another pilot demonstration. Programs such as Head Start, Job Corps, and Manpower Retraining usually require substantial plant, professional staff, large organizational structures, and relatively substantial allocations of money. There is a tendency for them to be undertaken on at least a ghetto-wide, if not city-wide, basis; to be developed through existing institutions that already have some staff, buildings, and so on; to require federal or foundation fiscal support; and to have "successes" contingent upon decision-makers in other institutional sectors or at least outside of the direct influence of those in the business of changing habits and achievement skills: Head Start gains tend to be washed out unless relevant reforms take place at subsequent grade levels; job training programs do not succeed in "leapfrogging" the impoverished unless both initial placements and subsequent opportunities for advancement make this possible. Finally, the focus on individuals and families, as has already been pointed out, is largely irrelevant to other kinds of changes in community and institutional patterns that presently contribute to dependency and deprivation.

While both the social protest–social action model and the community development model address themselves directly to issues involving the institutional *status quo* in the community and to overcoming conditions of dependency, their respective logics can yield quite different action strategies and to some degree different resource and personnel requirements. The social action–social protest model is embodied in the work of SNCC in the South and in IAF developed and influenced organizing efforts in some Northern slums. The community development approach has been most evident in rural areas and smaller cities and towns.

Social action theory assumes the existence of a profound but often disguised

conflict between a class and/or racial-ethnic minority and a majority who support or acquiesce in the existing institutional regime, the "establishment" in each institutional sector. Cooperation and collaboration with most existing agencies is, therefore, likely to confuse rather than clarify this underlying conflict. Authentic cooperation, from this viewpoint, would be possible only if the poor could approach the established political and private welfare institutions from positions of power and thereby bargain with them on behalf of aims and projects proposed by the poor themselves. Organizers, therefore, must use every opportunity to bring latent conflict to the surface, to intensify it, and to aid the poor in developing and using whatever power resources can be developed by those who have little money: the capacity to disrupt the community's "peace and tranquility," to develop bloc voting, to investigate and disclose practices disadvantageous to the poor, to consolidate such economic power as the poor can muster through action such as boycotts, and to obtain from sympathetic supralocal sources of community funds, such as the federal government, conditions to the granting of those funds.

Frequently, some "quick and easy" victories are sought in order to give the poor initial experience and to overcome their sense of impotence and helplessness before "the establishment." The dramaturgy of conflict which the organizer seeks to create and maintain around these often minor initial demands is a necessary part of this "sociotherapy." Any who seek to organize the poor or develop projects meeting their needs through means which neglect or bypass this "sociotherapeutic" process of protest, conflict, and the direct experience of power are seen, at best, as digressive and in the long-run ineffective, and, at worst, as part of "the enemy," albeit inadvertently. Efforts, therefore, may be made to eliminate or co-opt "competing" organizations.

Finding starting points for the generation of protest is the way this form of social
action usually begins, often with a handful
of angry and determined people and their
organizer. They can be living in a housing
project, or located within a few city blocks
in a metropolitan slum, or inhabiting the
shacks along a dirt road in the southland's
agrarian, tenant-farmer black belt. Initial
smallness of scale does not necessarily
reduce the effort to a research or demonstration project, for a sequence of organization-
building actions is assumed. Only modest
physical and monetary resources may be
required, at least at first. Frequently, these
resources are obtained only as programs
develop and by such means and in such
locations as the poor themselves can manage, though they may be aided by sympathetic private or public agencies that are
supralocal and, therefore, not part of the
community "establishment" that is increasingly being identified as "the enemy."
Except for a few organizers, or even just
one, no professional staff is required and
little or no formal organization. It is
anticipated that eventually a large-scale
organization of the poor, perhaps an
"organization of organizations," will be
developed, but it will be largely self-staffed
by indigenous personnel who have acquired
new skills.

As Frank Riessman has pointed out,
there are important differences between
Alinsky's IAF and the "New Left," and
these should not be neglected even though
they may usefully be seen as variants
within this social action–social protest
type.[8] The IAF will utilize any and all
existing organizational bases actually located within poor communities and willing
to be consolidated into (and in decisional
terms merged with) the new organization;
the New Left tends to involve only the
poor themselves, to develop among them
a thoroughly new leadership, and to try to
reach the most alienated. Since participation is an end as well as a means, those
operating within the framework of the New
Left ordinarily would not sacrifice "democratic process" for a desired "product,"
that is, an immediate victory; IAF organizers seek to develop an indigenous leadership capable of planning and carrying out
successful action, but they use many
techniques of manipulation and control
within the developing organization to make
sure that "right decisions" are made, sometimes asserting that local leaders can have
their own way only when they can "pay the
bills." Alinsky and his orthodox followers
are rather anti-ideological and determinedly
unromantic, emphasizing and normally
approving of whatever works to build a
lasting local organization which can get
what its members and their constituents
want by the usual exercise of interest-
group power politics within the local
polity; the New Left is oriented to a rather
unsystematic ideology stressing a "new
society" utopianism built up around hu-
manistic values, a militant rejection of the
upper-strata and the older-generation cultural *status quo*, and a rather romantic view
of the powerless and exploited—the poor
and racial minorities ("the hope is in the
proles"). The most ambitious effort to
bring these two variants together into a
single approach was Warren Haggstrom's
effort in Syracuse and his writings partake
of parts of both perspectives.

The community development model leads
to action strategies which are in some ways
more pragmatic than Alinsky's even though
reflecting an idealism as intense and often
as naive as the New Left's. Once the client
population (which may be but does not
have to be the poor or minority groups) has,
with the aid of the professional organizer,
arrived at its own goals and set some
realistic priorities, any legitimate means for
achieving those goals may be utilized so
long as it does not negate the development
of a more and more participative and competent citizenry. Anyone may help who can
accept the means and ends required for
such community development; so can any
agency, private or public, that is acceptable
to the participating personnel and amenable
to the imperatives and constraints of community development. Conflict is not sought
as a necessary part of the process, but its
possible or even probable emergence is

recognized and accepted as one of the "facts of life." No special dramaturgical procedures are prescribed for therapeutic purposes, and the first projects undertaken often are of the "self-help" variety that neither engender emotional demonstrations nor bring into the open hostility from or toward other segments of the community. Indeed, there may be some effort to avoid conflict until the developing organization has gained internal strength and greater competence and self-confidence through completion of initial projects.

Community development theory is rooted in the communal utopianism of the eighteenth and nineteenth century, but it draws easily upon the jargon of contemporary sociology and anthropology. Its proponents do not, as is the case with so many in the New Left, view academic social scientists as corrupted servants of the various establishments; nor do they reject them as sissified quasi-liberals who panic and run for home when the going gets rough, which is Alinsky's usual portrayal of them. Involvement of social scientists in community development projects is often sought where their skills seem relevant to the undertaking. As with the social action-social protest model, initial organizing efforts may be small in scale (this is probably typical) without rendering the effort ineffective. Each project should enable the organization to develop greater skills among its participants and to add new participants. As organizational size and competence increase, the scale of operation can expand. Eventually projects of very substantial scope intended to bring more and more basic changes to the community may be undertaken, and an increasingly participative local democracy is continuously sought as a deliberate by-product. But no unified overall organization is necessary and no effort is envisioned to launch a social movement or build an institutional structure supralocal in its boundaries and impact.

In Search of More Clues to Causation

The differences among the three models of explanation and action just described

have very practical consequences for any university whose leadership, like that at the University of Wisconsin, has asserted a commitment to making the institution relevant to an authentic "war on poverty." For the resources a university can actually assign to such efforts are very limited, and the role it can play through an equally limited number of relevant and willing faculty also is normally constrained by political considerations as well. For example, if alienation were a major cause of citizen inaction, requiring the sociotherapy of the social action–social protest model, then members of the faculty would have to be involved mainly on their own time as volunteers. If differences between subcultures and one's place in the social structure were the main determinants, then only large-scale efforts involving much greater commitments of university personnel than could be realistically anticipated, in conjunction with institutions providing elementary and secondary education, vocational training, and employment, would have meaningful impact on existing patterns. But if participation were significantly linked to variables subject to change through the techniques and strategies of community development, such as perception of needs and the skills and competences for action, then even a few university personnel might make consequential contributions through their professional roles.

In spring and summer of 1964 students and faculty of the Department of Urban Affairs undertook an extensive study of "Northtown A," a fifty-block area within Milwaukee's "inner core north," the segment of the inner city which includes the Negro ghetto and the areas of transition produced by the movement of Negroes north and northwest and the exodus of whites along the ghetto's expanding periphery. A questionnaire survey included many items dealing with the perception of neighborhood and community problems by respondents and forms of participation that were or could be relevant to taking action on those problems. Special emphasis was placed on determining, to the extent that survey procedures permitted, the correlates of participation within this particular population.

The area sampled was particularly useful for this inquiry because it included census tracts with many deprived neighborhoods characterized by low income, a large proportion of Negroes (some representing mainly an influx between 1950 and 1960), substantial unemployment, a large proportion of low-income families, many unskilled workers, many broken homes, and less than average education; while those on the periphery of the ghetto were still predominantly middle class and white with social pathology indicators similar to or less than those of the city as a whole (see Table A in the Appendix).

The dependent variable, political participation (with a broad interpretation of "political"), was indexed by a crude but serviceable "action score" indicating how many of the following kinds of participation each respondent claimed for himself.

1. Registering complaints about community or commercial services, politics, or civil rights.
2. Requesting assistance from an alderman.
3. Attending meetings or public hearings.
4. Belonging to a neighborhood committee, civic group, or improvement association.
5. Voting in local elections.

The matrix of correlations among these kinds of participation is shown in Table 1.

All correlations are, not surprisingly, positive; but all are low enough (though two achieve statistical significance) that one can feel comfortable about treating the items as separate dimensions of participation. Each respondent could, therefore, receive an action score ranging from 0 to 5. As can be seen in Table 2, about two-thirds of the respondents reported engaging in either none or only one of these forms of participation. Only about 15 per cent could be considered strongly oriented to action, reporting three or more types of participation. This pattern is compatible with other studies of participation and political action by the general citizenry.

TABLE 2. Number of Respondents
Receiving Each Action Score

Score	Number	Per Cent of Total Sample
0	45	27.6
1	66	40.4
2	28	17.3
3	11	6.7
4	7	4.3
5	6	3.7
	163	100.0

Nineteen variables were assessed as determinants of greater or lesser action tendencies among the persons in the sample. Those used to indicate place in the social structure and probable involvement in any

TABLE 1

	Complaining	Requesting Assistance	Attending Meetings	Belonging to Groups	Voting
Complaining	1				
Requesting Assistance	.12	1			
Attending Meetings	.13	.21*	1		
Belonging to Groups	.23*	.10	.17	1	
Voting	.02	.13	.12	.05	1

* Significant at .05 level.

related subcultures include race, age, education, family income, financial dependency (indexed by the number of kinds of financial aid being received), and occupation. Those which seemed to have the most direct relevance to the assumptions about causes of participation built into the social action–social protest model included feelings of personal political efficacy, group potency, alienation, perceived commonality of discontent, and personal potency in family relationship during adolescence. Those most related to causes of participation as posited by the community development model included perceived need for improvement of the neighborhood and community, political competence, home ownership, length of residence in the neighborhood and desire to stay in the neighborhood, and preference for neighborhood as against more distant sources of means of decision-making. (Table B in the Appendix presents the matrix of correlations among all of these variables.)

Within this sample, social structural variables were correlated in the usual way, though the relatively small size of the correlations (except for age and dependency) indicates less status crystallization than suggested by stereotypes of inner core populations held by those whose image of the ghetto is shaped more by journalism and fantasy than by personal familiarity or research. Race was not correlated significantly (the highest correlation is .13) with any of the other social structural variables, reflecting both the poor whites, mainly older people, "trapped" in the slum, and a disproportionate representation of middle-income Negroes who tend to be found in the expanding fringe areas of the ghetto and who have more education, better jobs, and higher income than is characteristic of the Negro population as a whole.

Variables relating to sociotherapeutic needs of the sort posited by the social action–social protest model were indexed by responses to questionnaire items taken directly or derived from relevant published research. (Items are summarized in the Appendix.) Except for the correlation between doubts about personal political efficacy and alienation (.50), all correlations are quite low.

The variables suggested by the community development model fall into two main categories. Four of them—home ownership, length of residence, desire to remain in the neighborhood, and preference for neighborhood decision-making—were intended to index what might be thought of as a kind of neighborhood-level "localism" which in turn might be conducive to participation on behalf of improving conditions in the area. The other category included an index of perceived need for improvement and one of political competence relevant to participating in action on community problems. The two highest correlations among these variables, not surprisingly, were between length of residence and home ownership (.46), but other correlations were relatively low.

The simple correlations of each of all 19 variables with action score are arrayed in Table 3. Nine of the eleven most highly correlated variables were selected for inclusion in a computation of multiple correlation and multiple determination coefficients, as shown in Table 4. Because of the

TABLE 3. *Simple Correlations with Action Score*

Competence	.49
Perceived need	.33
Income	.25
Home ownership	.24
Length of residence	.24
Financial dependency	−.20
Group potency	.20
Alienation	.18
Education	.17
Occupation	.16
Decision locus	−.15
Adolescent freedom to complain	.14
Political efficacy	.10
Desire to remain	.09
Perceived commonality	.09
Adolescent family influence	.08
Race	.06
Adolescent decision success	.03
Age	.01

correlations among income, financial dependency, education and occupation, only income and education were included as indicators of "place" in the social structure; financial dependency designates a rather small set of sampled families and many of the multiple aid cases are on old age assistance (thus the high correlation—.47—with age).

Table 4 emphasizes most of all how little —about one-third—of the variation in participation, at least as it is indexed in this study, can be statistically accounted for

TABLE 4.   Relative and Cumulative Effectiveness of Nine Variables as Predictors of Action Score

Variable	Multiple Determination Index (R^2)	Correlation With Action Score (R)
Competence	.25	.50
Felt need	.30	.54
Home ownership	.32	.57
Group potency score	.32	.57
Income	.33	.57
Residence length	.33	.57
Decision means	.33	.57
Alienation	.33	.57
Education	.33	.57

by the variables considered here, mainly by those relevant to the community development model. Other combinations (see Tables C, D, and E in the Appendix) continue to emphasize perceived need and political competence as the two most important variables in accounting for action. Both are presumably subject to change by

experience and continuing formal education. Competence is positively correlated with present income and education (combined correlation of .43), with respect to the development (up to the time of the survey) of relevant cognitive skills and actual experiences.

The following conclusions seem warranted by this study:

1. In Milwaukee the patterns of participation in politically relevant activities by residents of the area known as inner city north tend to reflect the perception of problems and their discontent over them, on the one hand, and the political understandings and organizational experience they already have, on the other hand.

2. However, independence or dependency, in terms of available income and its source, operates as an important constraint on or facilitation of such participation: those with less income tend to be less likely to participate, but this withdrawal from or avoidance of participation is more pronounced when income is derived from assistance, especially in families with more than one type of assistance.

3. Social psychological variables such as alienation and belief in personal efficacy or in group potency may to some degree reduce or increase participation beyond what one would expect given the perceived needs, action competences, and income-dependency statuses of any group or category of adults.

4. So much of the variation in participation among these people remains unexplained that no one model or theory can be held exclusively as doctrine on how to activate the poor among them and facilitate their continuing and "maximum feasible" participation.

Elites and Power Structures

Introduction

The juxtaposition of central themes from the two sections preceding this one yields the observation that, in spite of the extremely large number of formal governmental structures at the local level, the number of individuals exerting influence through or on these structures is relatively small. Direct participation in making key community decisions is (except through referenda) of course even smaller, yet we should keep in mind that voters and others may or may not exercise influence on community leaders and how issues are resolved. Once a distinction is made between a *power structure* as the potential ability of various actors to achieve their goals, and a *decision-making structure* as the patterns by which such goals have been achieved in past decisions,[1] then many of the selections which follow may be seen as analyses of how power structures become decision-making structures. Specifically, two aspects of decision-making structures are accorded most attention: centralization and leadership. *Centralization* refers to the degree to which decisions in a large number of issue areas are made by a small number of actors. *Leadership* is used here to designate the distinctive characteristics of actors centrally involved in community decision-making. Both may be seen as dimensions of the stratification of power as discussed in Selection 3.

There was a general tendency in the 1950s for studies of community decision-making to portray a relatively centralized structure. Floyd Hunter's well known study of Atlanta, Georgia, *Community Power Structure*,[2] was especially influential in these years, and its conclusions that the most important decisions were taken by a relatively small number of business, professional, and civic leaders—not the elected political officials—were often supported by other studies that used

159

the same type of method to study the power structure. The method, subsequently termed the reputational approach, starts by asking a panel of informants to provide the names of the most influential persons in the community. The persons named are interviewed in turn and asked the same question, as well as questioned about certain basic social background information (occupation, education, etc.).

Hunter's general approach came under attack in the late 1950s as increasing numbers of social scientists began to inquire if Hunter's results about community leadership were in part a consequence of his method. By the early 1960s, this criticism was supported in the results of studies by Edward Banfield of Chicago and by Robert Dahl of New Haven, Connecticut, which suggested that elected political officials, especially the mayor, played a much more important role in community leadership than the reputational studies had suggested.[3] Banfield and Dahl, in contrast, used a variety of methods—interviewing, clipping newspapers, participant observation—that were generally structured around the history of a few specific decisions, such as where to build a new public hospital, or the planning of an urban renewal program. The assertion that elected officials were centrally involved in many decisions provided greater support for a more "pluralistic" view of decision-making: the electorate could make its views felt through its votes, and these elected leaders were the major participants from one decision to the next; most community decision-makers were involved in only a few specific decisions. Bonjean and Olson discuss the reputational and decisional methods and the major issues that emerged from the confrontations of their respective proponents in Selection 16.

There was considerable disagreement between researchers studying community decision-making in the early 1960s on both these methodological and substantive issues. As increasing numbers of studies of individual communities were completed, however, with many of them differing in their results, it came to be generally recognized (as noted by Bonjean and Olson) that it was perhaps somewhat naive to inquire who governs, and then to assume that an answer for many or most American communities could result from a case study of a single community. If important differences were found from one community to the next, then it became an interesting problem to isolate those aspects of a community which led it to have a more centralized or decentralized pattern of decision-making. Most of the chapters in this section deal with this basic theme.

In Selection 17, Clark elaborates a series of 34 propositions using basic community-structural characteristics to specify "where" and "when" different patterns of centralization and leadership are likely to emerge. *Basic demographic variables* suggest that large communities are likely to have more decentralized (or pluralistic) power structures than smaller communities, for several reasons: larger communities tend to have a larger number of full-time roles, more autonomous political institutions, and (as suggested in Selection 1) a more socially heterogeneous population. These provide the bases for a larger number of potential elites able to compete with one another for leadership. A fundamental *economic characteristic* of a community is industrialization, which tends to lead to decentralization. Industrialization generally means greater economic diversification and consequently a larger number of potential community leaders. It also often means absentee-ownership, which implies industrial leaders oriented more toward the central office than the local community. It implies a larger proportion of such industrial inputs as capital and management from outside the community, and redirection of industrial outputs toward a national market; both lead to withdrawal of industrial executives from community decisions. Among *governmental characteristics*, it is suggested that nonpartisan elections and reform government lead to greater control by the wealthy. The larger the number and competition among *political parties and voluntary organizations*, the more decentralized the community. Such *cultural and educational characteristics* as a highly educated population subscribing to a democratic, participatory ideology also tend toward decentralization. Several of these propositions are subsumed under a more "general formulation" and tested using data from a national sample of 51 communities in Selection 28 by Clark.

Walton, in Selection 18, is concerned with analyzing a different set of causes of decentralization, those related to the "vertical axis" of community organization. He reports that such community characteristics as absentee ownership, adequate economic resources, satellite city status, and competitive political parties were found to be related to decentralization in a reanalysis of 55 case studies. He argues that each of these empirical relationships suggests that communities which are more closely integrated into the national society through private and public channels—those with strong vertical ties—tend to develop conflict with the local normative order and to generate more decentralized patterns of decision-making.

Roland Warren offers a generally favorable critique of the Walton paper in Selection 19, but he suggests that the discussion of normative structures adds little to the argument, and that it is unclear that these four particular indicators are the most representative of "vertical integration." He adds that decentralized decision-making patterns and community autonomy, two frequently desired goals, may be inherently incompatible.

The interrelationships between vertical and horizontal integrative structures and the ways that changes in each lead to shifts in community decision-making patterns are examined in Selection 20. Phillip E. Present studied the adaptations of the leadership in two California communities to the rise of aircraft installations. Leaders in the smaller, more cohesive community resisted the changes demanded by the new residents for increased services and eventually were replaced by a more educated, cosmopolitan group of leaders. The larger community, with a more diversified economic base, incorporated changes more easily as the more decentralized leadership expanded and adapted to the new residents and technological changes. Gradually, the more cosmopolitan leaders in both communities came to co-operate and to formulate plans for more balanced expansion of the region.

These articles assessing shifting patterns of vertical and horizontal differentiation and integration in communities deal with some of the basic sources of change in recent years. Such an historical perspective may be linked with a more structural orientation if the conditions making for structural change over time are specified. Gilbert, in Selection 21, moves in this direction in considering changes in decision-making and leadership patterns in the United States by comparing case studies conducted in 166 communities over various time periods. The results are necessarily limited by the availability of case studies for earlier periods and the absence of control for community-structural characteristics, but they are nonetheless provocative.[4] She finds trends toward a reform government orientation, more decentralized decision-making structures, increasing leadership by nonofficials, more participation by economic leaders, a greater role played by informal groups, and a lesser role performed by governmental officials and their agencies.

We are under no illusions that the selections included here will provide final and unambiguous answers to Dahl's query, "who governs?". They do, however, indicate the pace and progress of studies of community power structure over the past several years. Trends toward comparative analysis, quantification, and longitudinal analysis are all reflected in these writings. While each of these trends produces a pattern of ever greater complexity, they also generate richer data and more searching conceptualization in the important study of community power structure.

ALTHOUGH social scientists have attempted for quite some time to answer the question, "Who governs at the community level?" methodological and theoretical progress in this area of investigation has moved rapidly only within the past decade.

Prior to 1953 and publication of Floyd Hunter's *Community Power Structure*, the question, "Who governs?" was answered in much the same manner by both social scientists and the lay public. Those persons occupying important offices—elected political officials, higher civil servants, business executives, officials of voluntary associations, heads of religious groups, leaders of labor unions and others—were assumed to be those making key decisions affecting directly or indirectly the lives of most other community residents.[1] Political scientists made this same assumption by focusing on interest groups in studies of state and national governments. Their studies of community governments tended to concentrate on the structure and manifest tasks of the governmental units, while largely ignoring the private organizational positions.

Although a little-known study of the Chicago Board of Education in 1928 seemed to indicate that organizational officers may not, in fact, make the key decisions,[2] it was Hunter who first seriously challenged the assumed relationship between office holding and decision making at the community level. Hunter's study of Atlanta indicated that institutions and formal associations played a "vital role in the execution of determined policy, but the formulation of policy often takes place outside these formalized groupings."[3] In other words, Hunter concluded that Atlanta (and possibly other communities) was governed by a covert economic elite.

Hunter's conclusions stimulated interdisciplinary interest in community leadership patterns resulting in a large number of

Community Leadership: Directions of Research*

Charles M. Bonjean

University of Texas at Austin

David M. Olson

University of Georgia

uncoordinated case studies (and later a few comparative analyses), some supporting and some negating his answer to the question, "Who governs?"[4] Different investigators have used different research techniques, have focused on different features of community leadership structures, and have criticized one another's methods and conclusions.[5] This presentation re-examines many of these investigations and their criticisms in order to assess current theory, methods, problems, and the emergent trends over the last decade. Comparability, continuity, and direction will be sought by attempting to answer the following three questions: (1) How is community leadership studied, or how are leaders identified? (2) What are the salient characteristics of leadership structures in the various communities that have been investigated? (3) What, if anything, may be related to leadership structure characteristics?

Identifying Leaders

Most studies of community leadership have used one of three techniques (or a combination or modification of the three) to identify community leaders—the positional approach, the reputational approach, or the decisional approach.

* Reprinted with permission of the authors and publisher, from Charles M. Bonjean and David M. Olson, "Community Leadership: Directions of Research," Administrative Science Quarterly, 9 (December, 1964), pp. 278–300. The authors gratefully acknowledge the valuable suggestions made by S. Dale McLemore and Ivan Belknap who read an earlier draft of this paper.

163

Notes to this selection will be found on pages 346–349.

THE POSITIONAL APPROACH

As was indicated above, this was the most widely used technique prior to 1953. It consists of the use of extensive lists of formal positions or offices to help define leadership. Those individuals holding the greatest number and most important offices in the community are considered to be the key decision makers in the community.[6] Sometimes indexes are computed in an attempt to make the procedure even more precise.[7] Each potential leader is given a total score consisting of a sum of scores for all offices he holds. Top leaders are those with the highest scores.[8]

One variation of the positional approach is by way of a general institutional description of a local government such as that used in the study of New York by Sayre and Kaufman in which they described the major positional actors, their characteristics, their goals, and their strategies. In that instance neither was a set of issues isolated for special study nor was a set of leaders located by reputation; rather, all actors were examined on all issues generally.[9] A similar method was used in a comparative study of ten cities of varying sizes in Florida.[10] Also similar was Adrian's examination of the leadership roles of city managers, elected mayors, and interest groups in a comparative study of three cities.[11]

The validity and utility of the positional approach has been criticized from many standpoints—for example, because of the variation in terminology characteristic of different associations in designating similar offices.[12] But, in fact, the success or failure of this approach to the identification of community decision makers depends upon the degree to which its basic assumption is valid: those holding positions of authority actually make key decisions while those who do not occupy such positions do not make key decisions.

This assumption may be tested if results of the positional approach are compared with those of the other two approaches discussed below. Considering the relationship between office holding and decision making as a hypothesis, rather than as an a priori assumption, some investigations yield data that support the relationship while others contradict it.[13] It has been suggested that the hypothesis is usually supported in small communities, and thus in such communities the formal technique of leader identification is the quickest, most efficient, and the most reliable method.[14] Two recent investigations indicate that even this may not be the case. Laskin and Phillett, using both the positional and reputational techniques, studied leadership in four small Canadian communities (ranging in size from 500 to 4,000 inhabitants) and found that only 38 per cent to 77 per cent of the reputational leaders were also formal or positional leaders.[15] Bonjean studied four communities, ranging in size from 33,000 to 202,000 persons, and found fewer reputational leaders holding public or associational office in the two smaller communities (62 per cent and 65 per cent) than in the two larger communities (75 per cent and 77 per cent).[16]

In short, although the positional approach has been widely used, it cannot stand alone because the assumption upon which it is based may not be valid for all communities. The use of this approach precludes accepting the legitimacy of leadership structures as problematic.

THE REPUTATIONAL APPROACH

This approach was first used in a study of community power by Hunter but was, of course, used earlier by Warner, Hollingshead, and others to study another dimension of social stratification—status.[17] Although this technique has numerous variations, essentially it consists of asking informants to name and rank the leaders in their community.[18] The informants may be a predesignated panel of experts or a random sample of community members, or they may be selected by what is known as the "snowball" or "cobweb" technique. The final list of leaders usually consists either of those individuals who have received the greatest number of nominations by the informants or of all leaders whose average ranking is above a certain arbitrarily set limit.

Although the reputational approach has probably been the most widely used technique in the study of community leadership, it has been criticized from several standpoints:

1. It does not measure leadership *per se*, but rather the reputation for leadership. Critics do not feel that a reputation for power is a valid index of power.[19] They have suggested, as an alternative way to determine who "runs things," studying a series of concrete decisions in order to find out who specifically dominates those decisions (this approach will be discussed in detail below). Just as there may or may not be agreement on positional and reputational leaders, these criticisms indicate that there may or may not be agreement on decision-making dominants and reputational leaders. The most salient rebuttals to this criticism focus on the relationship between perception and behavior: "If we can ascertain that the way in which people perceive the power structure of the local political system affects the way in which they behave towards and in that system, then surely we are dealing with very meaningful and very useful considerations."[20]

2. The reputational approach incorporates an a priori assumption of a monolithic power structure. Some critics believe that different groups of elites probably have different scopes of interest, and thus there may be several structures of influence rather than merely one as the reputational approach may imply.[21] Associated with this general criticism are the related criticisms that "no study considers the full range of issues which come before a particular decision maker" and that "those [issues] that have been studied have been on the more dramatic side."[22] To the degree that some reputational studies have considered decision areas and have built this consideration into their techniques of investigation (for example by asking informants not only to name and rank leaders but also to specify those issues or institutions in which the nominee is active), this criticism has been met by some reputational analyses.[23] Another way to meet this objection is to ask what the earlier reputational studies assumed: Is there a small group which runs things in this town?[24]

Charles M. Bonjean
David M. Olson

A related problem is that the examples of power roles in reputational studies are too general and vague. Not enough evidence of action is present to permit a validation of the reputed and self-confessed leadership roles. Both Hunter in Atlanta and Thometz in Dallas give examples of elite action, but both also stress the long and complex bargaining process through which the elite reached agreement within itself and with external elements in the community. If other elements than the reputed elite can force that elite to negotiate and modify positions, those elements possess at least some kind of power.

3. This approach sometimes incorporates an a priori assumption about group structure. The critics indicate that even though some individuals have been designated by the reputational approach as having more power than other members of the community, one cannot assume that these highest ranking individuals make up a ruling *group* rather than merely an aggregate of leaders.[25] This criticism has been met by some investigators by incorporating sociometric and interaction checks.[26]

4. Even if the above criticisms are met and even if there is a high correlation between power reputation and power *per se*, the reputational approach may not accurately identify leaders because (1) of inaccuracies in respondent perceptions—that is, private citizens may be unreliable sources of information,[27] (2) interviewer and respondent may not agree on what is meant by power—that is, the questions may not be valid,[28] and (3) when nominations and rankings are tabulated, the arbitrary cut-off points may be too high (and thus not include all of the leaders) or too low (and thus include some of the followers, as well).[29] The first problem may be handled to some extent by using a panel of experts (themselves perhaps determined by the snowball variation of the reputational technique) rather than by a random sample of community members.

Other reputational studies have begun with a panel of nominators selected for their knowledge of different sectors of community life. Both Hunter and Miller began with a diversified panel and both found a predominantly business-based elite.[30] Booth and Adrian, using the same method, found a diversified reputational elite which included not only businessmen, but also unionists and government officials who were professed leaders of the working class.[31] The second problem is common to all forms of survey research and has been answered adequately elsewhere (validity checks may be incorporated in this form of survey research as readily as in any other form of it). The third problem can be handled to some degree by using conventional tests of statistical significance (for example, including in the leadership category those nominees whose total number of nominations is significantly greater than the mean number of nominations of all nominees), by noticing clusters or conversely gaps in the frequency distribution of leadership scores, or by comparing the nominations of leaders themselves with those of other informants, to determine whether a specific individual should be included as a leader or not.

In short, the reputational approach, which has been the most widely used technique over the last decade, has been criticized on the counts cited above, but it has survived the wave of criticism. Why it has survived, in spite of its shortcomings, will be more apparent after a discussion of the third major approach to the study of community leadership.

THE DECISIONAL APPROACH

Also known as the "Event Analysis" or the "Issue" approach, this alternative is preferred by most of the critics of the reputational approach. It involves tracing the actions of leaders in regard to decision making and policy formation within the context of specific issues.[32] The tracing may be done by gathering data from extensive interviews, from attendance at committee and organizational meetings, from reports,

speeches, and newspaper accounts, and so on.[33] The approach has as its major advantage the possibility of identifying overt power rather than power potential; it also provides a more realistic viewpoint of power relations as processes rather than as fixed structures. On the other hand, this approach also has several inherent limitations:

1. Given certain issues, where does the investigator start? Observing committee and organizational meetings appears to involve accepting the same relationship between authority positions and decision making assumed by the use of the positional approach. How does the investigator know whether or not the decisions have already been made informally some time before the meeting, and how does he know if the committee or organizational members who appear to wield influence are not themselves being influenced by others who may, in fact, be covert? Decisional studies usually involve interviews to ascertain prior informal acts, motives, and influences. In that an attempt is made to identify informal influences, these interviews come close to the reputational approach, and to some degree meet this criticism. Presthus, for example, concluded that the decisional approach identified several government officials as powerful who, he concluded by also using a reputational approach, were only exercising ministerial or purely formal roles rather than actually making decisions.[34] It appears, then, that the decisional approach should be supplemented to some degree by the reputational approach.

2. To establish the rapport and gain the confidence necessary to be permitted to attend informal meetings (if they are a part of the influence structure) is quite time-consuming. Burgess, for example, spent three years in and out of Crescent City while she was "interviewing, observing, listening and occasionally participating in subcommunity activities."[35] Similarly, Dahl relied upon a collaborator who spent a year's internship in the New Haven city hall in "highly strategic locations."[36] It thus appears that the use of this approach would also include the decision to conduct an intensive study and description of

influence patterns in a single community or subcommunity rather than perhaps a less intensive description and comparison based on the reputational or positional approaches in several communities. In short, this method is less expedient than either of the others.

3. By what criteria are the decisions or issues selected for study? Some agree that focus should be upon the "most important" areas, however they may be defined. At times the decisions are arbitrarily selected by the investigator. An alternative method is to ask respondents which they consider the most important community decisions. In effect, this alternative uses the reputational method to begin a study of issue resolution. A start toward sampling of issues has been made by the suggestion that issues vary along five important dimensions: unique or recurrent, salient or nonsalient to leadership, salient or nonsalient to community publics, effective action possible or effective action impossible, and local or cosmopolitan.[37] Decisions have also been categorized into five subject-matter fields which are said to "differ in personnel, style of operation, and significance for public policy": race relations and interfaith activity, good-government activities, welfare and fund-raising activities, cultural and hospital work, and business promotion, construction, and planning activities.[38]

4. Another criticism is that the study of decision making ignores those actors who may be able to keep latent issues from emerging into open controversy. The most important issues in a community may be submerged. To focus on the actual events and controversies is to assume the importance of the decisions selected and does not provide a means of examining nondecisions and the people who can keep them latent.[39] To examine this aspect of community power, research must seek the origins and rationale of the status quo. Studies with a historical dimension are better designed to probe the origins of the status quo than studies concerned mainly with recent events or reputations.[40]

Certainly a combination of methods (any two or all three) appears to be the most

Charles M. Bonjean
David M. Olson

satisfactory means for the study of community leadership at our present stage of development. Apparently, some consensus exists in regard to this in that most of the more recent investigations have, in fact, used a combination of techniques.[41] In fact, it has been suggested that perhaps the different methods locate different types of leaders.[42]

Leadership Structure Characteristics

The answers to the question, "Who governs?" show even more variation than the techniques used to seek the answers.

At one extreme are Hunter's conclusions.[43] He allegedly found a monolithic power structure consisting of about forty individuals, most of whom were wealthy and important in business. These forty leaders all knew one another and all belonged to one of five cliques which were coordinated by about twelve leaders who wielded even more influence than the other twenty-eight. These individuals, according to Hunter, informally determined policy, which in turn was carried out by lower level leaders (including public officials and associational officers).

Other investigators have asserted that the administrators and politicians are the decision makers and furthermore are influenced, more or less, by a sizeable proportion of the rest of the community (the electorate). At least one of these investigators has even indicated that "politicians innovated policy choices and had their acceptability certified by the visible support of top businessmen."[44]

Leadership structures vary in many ways. In some communities, for example, leaders were found to be active in all decision areas, while in other communities the leaders varied with the decision. In still others, leaders of both types were found. In some communities, the leaders were found to know one another and act in concert, while in others they know one another and are rivals. In still others, they do not even know one another. Apparently no single descriptive statement—not even a very general one—applies to community leadership in general in the United States today (unless the statement includes variability itself).

Early investigators often studied one community, described its patterns of leadership, and then generalized (usually with some caution) to other communities.[45] Their critics responded in a similar manner, implying that such a pattern of leadership could be found in no American community.[46] Both investigators and critics are more tentative today, and although numerous issues are still at stake, a more realistic perspective appears to be emerging. Today, no one would deny the existence of different patterns of leadership in different communities or in the same community over time. Therefore, the focus is shifting to a concern with the range of possibilities. In other words, the types of questions that appear to be most salient to the study of community leadership today are concerned with (1) the various types of power structures that could function in contemporary American communities, (2) the important dimensions that differentiate these types of structures, and (3) the manner in which these dimensions can be measured.

The types of power structures that could function in American communities (and, in fact, have been described by the investigators cited in this paper) are many, and, indeed, little would be gained here from a brief description of each of them. Rather, what is needed is a means by which their main characteristics can be summarized and compared. One approach that has been successful in describing and comparing other types of social structures is the use of sets of ideal-type constructs.[47] Entire societies, for example, have been described and compared by the degree to which they approximate folk societies or urban societies.[48] Complex organizations are said to approximate the Weberian model of bureaucracy or the human relations model.[49] There is no reason why this same

approach could not be used in the study of community leadership.[50] For example, using Hunter's findings and exaggerating the main characteristics of the leadership structure he found, an ideal type may be constructed that would logically fall at one extreme on our hypothetical yardstick and therefore could be used as a rough measure that would enable comparison and thus give some meaning to data that have been and will, no doubt, be found by others. One possible leadership model, then, is the Covert Power Elite, identified by the following characteristics: (1) leaders do not hold political offices or offices in associations, (2) they are not recognized by the community at large as key decision makers, (3) they are active in a wide range of decision areas, and (4) they work together as a group, rather than independently or in opposition.

Most ideal-type constructs have logical opposites, which, in this case, would be a leadership model where: (1) leaders hold political or associational office, (2) leaders are recognized by the community at large as key decision makers, (3) leaders are concerned only with those decisions related to official areas, and (4) group structure may not be present (certainly, at least, primary relations would be absent). These characteristics, of course, probably best describe that type of leadership structure most consistent with the political formula of our society— legitimate pluralism.[51] Between these two extremes one would find independent sovereignties (covert subgroupings concerned with one or a few decision areas), rival sovereignties (visible, though not legitimate, subgroupings competing on any number of decisions), and interest groups (leaders may hold associational, but not political, office; concern is with one or a few decisions; and leaders are recognized by the community).[52]

In short, the following four characteristics appear to be the most important in identifying the two ideal-type leadership structures and thus perhaps any structure falling between these two:

1. *Legitimacy.* Where leaders hold public or associational office, the leadership structure is, in fact, an authority structure. Legitimacy is easily measured by collecting

information on each leader (identified by either the reputational or decisional approach) in regard to political or associational offices. One measure of the leadership structure's legitimacy, then, is simply the proportion of leaders who hold or have recently held such offices.[53] The use of a percentage score enables the comparison of different communities that may have different numbers of leaders.

2. *Visibility.* This is a dimension separate from legitimacy. If all community leaders held political or associational offices, perhaps the leadership structure would be clearly visible. But the reverse is not equally as true. Leaders who do not hold positions of authority may or may not be covert. Thus legitimacy tells us nothing about visibility unless all leaders *are* public or associational officers. To measure visibility necessitates the use of the reputational approach, at least to some degree. Visibility may be roughly measured if the nominations and rankings of a panel of judges (or better, the leaders themselves) are compared with the nominations and rankings of a sample of the general public or some other segment of the community. Comparing the rankings by sets of informants yields three possible types of leaders: *visible* (those recognized by both the judges and the general public), *concealed* (those recognized by the judges but not by the general public), and *symbolic* (those recognized by the general public, but not by the judges).[54] The differential visibility of community leadership structures could be assessed by comparing the proportions of visible leaders.

3. *Scope of Influence.* One leader or set of leaders may participate in decision making in a wide range of issues in a community, or different leaders or sets of leaders may be active in different areas. Both types of leaders, in fact, could be found within the same community. Scope of influence could be measured in at least two different ways:

a. A list of actual or possible decisions in the community could be presented to each leader (or each informant), and he, in turn, could be asked to specify those

Charles M. Bonjean
David M. Olson

decisions in which he (or his nominee) had participated in policy formation. Each leader could then be assigned a percentage score based on the number of decision areas in which he participated compared to the total number of decision areas. Scores within and between communities are important here, in that a summary score for any given community may be misleading if leaders of both types have been identified. A problem arises from the fact that the number of salient decisions may vary from community to community. If *possible* rather than *actual* decisions are used as the denominator, the total score will be affected by the number of actual decisions. The problem is minimized, of course, if the investigator limits his concern to actual decisions.

b. The second method of measuring scope of influence is possible only if the decisional approach is used to identify leaders. If several different types of decisions are analyzed, each leader's role in each type of decision may be carefully assessed. Indeed, participation in decision making in four different types of issues, for example, would be evidence of *general* leadership.[55] Perhaps one criterion for selection using the decisional approach (or for inclusion on an interview schedule using the reputational approach) to assess scope of influence should be variability along the dimensions suggested by Barth and Johnson or by Banfield and Wilson.[56]

4. *Cohesiveness.* Given legitimate or nonlegitimate, visible or concealed, and general or issue leaders, they may or may not interact as members of a group (or perhaps several groups). It is possible that cohesiveness, certainly one characteristic of a group, could be measured, at least roughly, by the degree to which leaders nominate one another. Indeed, one sociometric statistic, the ratio of interest, purports to measure this group characteristic in precisely such

a manner.[57] Interaction patterns, themselves, may be investigated by asking respondents to indicate those with whom they have worked (and in regard to which decisions). Cohesiveness has been treated in a particularly precise way by Scoble. After finding three major factions by sociometric techniques, he determined that each was internally divided on policy preferences by using Rice's index of cohesion to measure their answers to a set of public opinion questions. Nevertheless, the factions possessed sufficient agreement for at least some members of each to participate as identifiable cliques on most decisions.[58] Other similar techniques, for example an acquaintanceship scale, have also been used to attempt to assess the group structure of leadership elites.[59] Such techniques appear to identify unitary, bifactional, multifactional, and amorphous patterns. These patterns may be found within either a general- or issue-oriented elite. The analysis of clique or factional patterns is very similar to that used in discussion of political parties (one-, two-, or multi-party systems), intraparty factions (one-faction, two-faction, or multifactional parties), and industrial competition (monopoly, oligopoly, or competition).

In summary, legitimacy, visibility, scope of influence, and cohesiveness appear to be the most significant dimensions of community leadership structures in that (1) they have been the major sources of disagreement and criticism, (2) a review of leadership studies indicates that variation may, in fact, be found along all four dimensions, and (3) they are useful in the identification of different types or models of leadership structures.

Antecedents and Consequences of Leadership Structure Characteristics

Given the tentative conclusion that community leaders may be identified and that leadership structures vary along certain dimensions from community to community, what has been found to be related to leadership structure characteristics? The search for such relationships is a fairly recent trend. Most of the earlier investigations were simply case studies attempting to describe the leadership structure or processes in one community. Explanation, of course, usually requires the examination of two or more cases and an attempt to account for their differences or similarities. Only through a comparative approach—studies of large numbers of decisions on comparable issues within one community over time or in many different communities—is it possible to make generalizations in regard to those phenomena which might be related to leadership structure characteristics.[60] The few comparative analyses of community leadership structures that have been undertaken usually deal with possible antecedents of community leadership structures or possible consequences of the same, but seldom, if ever, both. Many of these investigations have not been concerned with visibility, legitimacy, cohesiveness, or scope of influence as leadership structure characteristics *per se*; some, however, do offer insights into relationships between these characteristics and antecedents and consequences.

ANTECEDENTS

That the characteristics of influence structures may be dependent on the nature of the society or community of which they are a part has been the basic relationship investigated by those concerned with antecedents of community leadership structures.

A number of comparative analyses have been cross-cultural comparisons seeking to test the hypothesis that leaders represent those institutions that are the most powerful and influential in the society at large. Thus, as might be expected, Miller found that businessmen exerted a predominant influence in community decision making in two United States cities, but in a British city other institutions were better represented.[61] According to Miller, this is in part a consequence of the higher social status of industry and its captains in the United States; in part a function of city government in the British city—specifically an active community council requiring much time and work of its 112 members.

D'Antonio and his colleagues compared institutional and occupational representations in eight United States cities, the British city studied by Miller, and two Mexican cities.[62] They found that business provided the largest number of top influentials in all the United States cities as well as in the two Mexican cities. The two Mexican cities, however, gave the strongest evidence of a challenge to business by another sector of the community—government. They explain this as a consequence of the dominance of the PRI (*Partido Revolucionario Institucional*) in Mexico. The role of economic dominants over time in one community was studied by Schulze.[63] He noted, for example, that as the economic structure of the community changed, so did its leadership structure. As the community economic system became absorbed into the larger industrial complex of a nearby large city, local economic dominants participated less in community decision making, leaving it almost wholly in the hands of a group of middle-class business and professional men. The same relationship was observed by Clelland and Form in a more recent investigation of another community.[64] One implication of those studies concerned with the relationship between the community's institutional structure and leadership structure is the greater probability of legitimate, visible structures with limited scopes of influence in communities with complex institutional structures, or at least in those where a single institution or organization is not dominant.

Not only may the relative importance of different institutions influence the nature of the leadership structure, but characteristics of a single institution may also be important. Perhaps the most obvious, as suggested by Miller above, is the political institution itself. The perceptions and values of public officials may, of course, vary between communities. While they may play merely formal ministerial roles,[65] and therefore be rated low in reputation for power, they may also actively exercise independent and real power. On at least

those issues which require government decision, government officers occupy potentially strategic positions. Studies of state legislators show that they vary considerably in their role orientations toward their jobs and toward other participants in the legislative process, and that these variations are linked systematically with their behavior as public officials.[66] City officials, both elected and appointed, might also be expected to vary in these respects.[67] One would expect, then, a positive relationship between activist role perceptions of public officials and the legitimacy, visibility, and definite scope of decision making.

Another institutional factor affecting community power is the party system. The boss of a cohesive political party who is also mayor has considerable independent power, though he, of course, does not lack external constraints on his behavior.[68] Rossi has suggested that professionalization of political roles and electoral competition in a diverse electorate lead to an independence of government actors from economic influence.[69]

The locale and procedures of decision making may have an important impact on leadership patterns. Some issues are public and are resolved only through a referendum. The referendum is potentially the least capable of control by a small covert elite. To have power, the leaders must be able to control both voter turnout and their voting.[70] Power is not subjected to this test if the issue is resolvable through private means, such as fund raising for an auditorium or hospital.[71] Decisions resolvable through formal positions occupy an intermediate category. The holders of formal positions may actually exercise power, or they may be open to degrees of influence from either covert elites or segments of the public.

The institutional structure of the community includes but one set of variables that may influence the nature of a community's leadership structure. Eighty-eight different community variables, ranging from population density to socioeconomic status, have been factor analyzed by Jonassen and Peres.[72] Seven factors were identified that accounted for most of the variation: urbanism (population size, density, and heterogeneity), welfare (health, wealth, employment, education), influx (population growth), poverty (low income, dependent population), magnicomplexity (social, economic, and governmental complexity), educational effort, and proletarianism (propertyless, relatively poor, low-skilled and poorly paid workers). Bonjean examined four communities to see if any of these community factors were associated with any of the leadership structure characteristics discussed above.[73] It was found that those characteristics most closely associated with the Covert Power Elite type of structure were population influx (for example, the greater the influx, the less visible the leadership structure), poverty (for example, the greater the community poverty, the less visible the leadership structure), and magnicomplexity (for example, the less complex the community, the less visible the leadership structure). Although the same factors *per se* were not used, Presthus studied similar relationships in two communities. His conclusions show a relationship between magnicomplexity and the presence of a Covert Power Elite (in the same direction as was found in the investigation cited above),[74] a relationship between poverty and Covert Power Elite characteristics (also consistent with the findings set forth above),[75] and a negative relationship between urbanism and Covert Power Elite characteristics.[76]

CONSEQUENCES

Even fewer studies have been concerned with consequences of leadership structure characteristics than with antecedents. Sociologists' interest here seems to be relating leadership structure characteristics to the effectiveness, efficiency, or quality of community projects, organizations, or institutions. Belknap and Steinle, for example, studied relationships between hospital systems and community leadership in two communities and found that the quality of hospital facilities, services, and so forth was higher in the community where the hospital board-members were also community leaders.[77] Hunter, of course, was concerned with the same types of relationships, noting for example, that community agencies were extremely careful not to incur the displeasure of top leaders and thereby be excluded from their interest and beneficence.[78] The same general type of relationship was studied by Dakin who was concerned with the relationship between variations in leadership structure and differences in the effectiveness with which four areas were organized for action on some area problem.[79] He also found that group structure and legitimacy were positively related to effective organization.[80]

The major consequence studied by political scientists is the "public interest." Interest group studies, and now community power-structure studies, cause political scientists to ask if a given distribution of power is in the public interest. While most investigators in this field distrust a monolithic power structure, especially if it is composed of economic rather than political actors, political scientists are generally content to raise the issue of the public interest without pronouncing a definitive answer.[81]

Conclusions

Basic changes have taken place in the study of community leadership over the past decade. The changes seem to indicate that there have been perhaps more continuity and direction in this area of investigation than would appear to be the case at first glance. Briefly, the basic trends have been: (1) a shift in preference and use from the positional to the reputational to the decisional method, and finally to a combination of methods for the identification of leaders; (2) growing consensus in regard to the variability of leadership structure over time and place, and thus more concern with the salient dimensions along which the variation takes place—legitimacy, visibility, scope of influence, and cohesiveness; and finally, (3) less concern with descriptive case studies and greater interest in comparative analyses of explanatory utility—that is, more concern

Charles M. Bonjean
David M. Olson

with those factors that may be related to variations in leadership structure.

Power and Community Structure: Who Governs, Where, and When?*

Terry N. Clark

The University of Chicago

THE MOST influential single postwar study on community power (both positively and negatively) has unquestionably been Hunter's *Community Power Structure*, published in 1953.[1] Hunter concluded that Regional City (Atlanta, Georgia) was dominated to a large degree by a small number of business leaders who could be said to constitute a power elite. Although the reception of Hunter's work among social scientists could hardly be described as one of uncritical acclaim,[2] it was not until 1961, with the publication of *Who Governs?* by Robert Dahl, that there appeared in the literature a theoretical alternative to that of Hunter along with the supporting intellectual ballast of a carefully executed empirical study.[3] Dahl's central thesis was that a "pluralistic" conception of community power—one where several competing groups vie with one another for control of community resources in various areas—is more useful than the power elite model. *Who Governs?* is the most incisive and challenging community power study of recent years.

The works of Hunter and Dahl have tended to serve as opposite poles in the

rather vigorous discussions on community power which have been largely stimulated by their influential contributions. Much of the initial exchange has tended to be uncompromising in character and acrimonious in tone; with time, however, the intensity of the cross fire seems to be diminishing. This paper is based on the assumption that enough of the smoke has cleared to reevaluate the situation and move forward once again.

One salient characteristic of the majority of community power studies is the acceptance of a common conception of the community: although it is seldom explicitly stated—for the weakness of the position then becomes difficult to justify—most writers assume an undifferentiated conception of the community. Rural villages, commuter suburbs, central cities, vacation hamlets, and entire metropolitan regions all tend to be carelessly thrown together under the general rubric of "community." It is only through accepting such an undifferentiated conception that methodological legitimation can be granted to studies which, after examining the distribution of power in generally only one, but perhaps two, three, or even four communities, conclude with such statements as ". . . community power structures [perhaps 'in contemporary America' is added as a qualification] tend to be . . . characterized by the dominance of business leaders"; or, "are pluralistic," or "bifurcated." When exposed to examination, the inadequate foundation of this assumption becomes only too apparent; nevertheless, it has been implicitly or explicitly accepted in dozens of community case studies conducted over the past two decades.

This broad acceptance of an undifferentiated central concept is all the more remarkable when one considers some of the work going on during the same two decades in relatively near-by subject matters within the disciplines of sociology and political science. The literature of urban sociology, demography, and ecology contains numerous classifications for different types of social units which may be designated communities; political scientists for centuries have been speculating on the general

* Reprinted by permission from The Sociological Quarterly, *Vol. 8, No. 3 (Summer 1967), pp. 291–316. This is a revised and expanded version of a paper read at the meetings of the American Sociological Association in Chicago, 1965. For comments and suggestions, and for reading an earlier draft of this paper, I must thank Bernard Barber, William Goode, Raymond Glazier, Terence Hopkins, Juan Linz, Nelson Polsby, David Rogers, Peter Rossi, Immanuel Wallerstein, and Raymond Wolfinger.*

Notes to this selection will be found on pages 349–352.

consequences of adopting different types of constitutions for the functioning of the political system, and during the last decade in particular have expended great effort in developing more abstract typologies of "political systems" and "political culture"; families, small groups, organizations, and national societies have been classified and typologized almost *ad nauseum*. Why, then, should students in the field of community power suffer in such acute typological poverty when surrounded on all sides by general wealth?

It would appear that the predominance of case studies has been a major factor hindering the development of typologies, for in studying a population of one, contrasts that almost inevitably present themselves in comparative research are not readily apparent. As more comparative studies are undertaken, it is likely that typologies of communities will be developed, and the regrettable poverty of the field in this respect should gradually disappear.[4]

So as not to defile this close to virgin soil for future typologists, however, in this paper a truly new typology will not be developed; instead, one which has already served to differentiate aspects of a broad variety of other social systems will be adapted for use

on communities. This typology, generally associated with the names of Bales and Parsons, has become known as "AGIL," or, in certain other quarters, "LIGA," each letter referring to one of the following general functions: Adaptation, Goal-Attainment, Integration, and Latent Pattern-Maintenance and Tension-Management.[5]

The fourfold classification may be utilized in community studies in at least two different ways. First, it is possible to analyze the extent to which any given community does or does not perform each of the four functions. If one considers that a community may be classified as either performing or not performing each of the functions, a typology may be constructed such as is shown in the accompanying diagram.

A large number of problems are raised when the four AGIL functions are utilized in this way, such as the precise "level" of analysis, the social units for which the functions are performed, overlapping of functions, and difficulties in finding meaningful and available empirical indicators

Partial Typology of Communities Classified According to Function

Example	A Economy	G Polity	I Legal Profession Political Parties Interest Groups	L Family Education System
Functionally autonomous community	+	+	+	+
Residential community, politically autonomous, economically dependent	—	+	+	+
Residential community, economically and politically dependent	—	—	—	+
Residential community, politically dependent, economically autonomous	+	—	—	+
Nonresidential community, economically autonomous, politically dependent	+	—	—	—
Nonresidential community, economically and politically autonomous	+	+	+	—

for each of the functions. Because of the amount of space demanded for an adequate treatment of these and associated problems, and because they have already been dealt with elsewhere,[6] they will simply be signaled as problems demanding treatment, but treatment which will not be accorded in the present discussion.

A second way of utilizing the typology does not concentrate on whether or not a particular function is performed by a community, but instead asks what particular structural arrangement exists for the performance of each function. Assuming at least minimal performance of a given function, this mode of inquiry will then try to determine how these structures influence the degree and type of performance of each function. It is in this second way that the typology will be employed in the following sections.

The central thesis underlying the present paper is that previous investigations of community power structure have started by asking if not the wrong questions, at least not very challenging ones. To first inquire, as Dahl has argued, whether there is a power elite is certainly an important question that must be satisfactorily answered before asking, following Hunter, who constitutes the power elite. Nevertheless, as intimated in the writings of virtually all students of the problem, there have been, and probably still are, different types of power structures in different communities under different conditions. To admit that there can be a variety of legitimate answers to the question, "Who governs?" depending on the community studied suggests a reformulation of the problem in less absolutist terms. An adequate analysis must answer a series of three questions: *Who governs?*—what is the nature of the community power structure; *Where?*—in what kinds of communities; and *When?* —under what conditions. Restating the problem in this fashion focuses on the variables distinguishing one community from the next which tend to be associated with one or another type of power structure. Finally, to relate decision-making patterns to outputs, one should inquire *With What Effects?*[7]

An effort will be made to answer the questions thus reformulated by developing a series of propositions relating tendencies toward different types of power structure with crucial community variables. The variables focused on include general demographic characteristics and those associated with the structural arrangements for performing each of the four AGIL functions. The following statements, although worded as propositions, should be viewed as a set of hypotheses. Some have been quite consistently found to hold in numerous empirical investigations; others are without any empirical support whatsoever. To the degree that the statements form an interrelated set of propositions, their aggregate plausibility is greater than if each is considered in isolation.[8]

Frequently, an empirical study supporting one or more propositions will be cited, but the purpose of such citation is only illustrative; a good deal more comparative empirical work must be completed before it will be possible to substantiate many of the propositions.

The propositions are of several different types. Most state a relationship between two variables. All are *stochastic* (if *x*, then probably *y*); none is *deterministic* (if *x*, then always *y*); most are *sequential* (if *x*, then later *y*), and may be considered to be causal statements as opposed to simply reported associations; most are *irreversible* (if *x* then *y*; but if *z*, then also *y*) and *contingent* (if *x*, then *y*, but only if *z*).[9] Several have as their dependent variable the type of community power structure; others may be viewed as intermediate links in a chain that eventually terminates in a statement about the type of power structure likely to be found. Most propositions about the power structure are stated in terms of a pluralistic-monolithic continuum.

The propositions are grouped according to their principal type of independent variable in the following order: (1) basic demographic variables; (2) adaptation: economic variables; (3) goal attainment: legal and political structural variables; (4) integration: voluntary organizations and political parties; (5) latent pattern-maintenance and tension management: cultural and educational variables. (A summary list of all propositions is appended at the end of the paper.)

Basic Demographic Variables

1. The larger the number of inhabitants in the community, the more pluralistic the power structure.[10]

This is one of the most frequent comparative observations about community power structure found in the literature.[11]

If it is correct that larger communities tend to have more dispersed power structures,[12] the next question is Why? What sort of intervening variables can be specified? One important factor is the high amount of integration characteristic of elites in small, closely knit communities.[13] In such a community, the divisions among the elite characteristic of a two-party system are practically impossible to maintain. Thus,

2. The larger the community, the larger the number of potential elites that can democratically compete for power.

Accompanying the increase of the number of inhabitants in a community is an increase in the size of the governmental bureaucracy.

3. The larger the community, the greater the number of full-time political roles.

As political institutions increase in size, they are likely to become less dependent on other community institutions and less easily dominated by the elites of other institutions (primarily the economic). Thus,

4. The larger the community, the more autonomous its political institutions;
and

5. The more autonomous the political institutions of a community, the more pluralistic the power structure.

The implications of propositions 3, 4, and 5 will be developed further below, in the section on legal and political structural variables.

A second important demographic variable in addition to size is the amount of

social homogeneity or heterogeneity of a community's inhabitants in terms of such fundamental characteristics as ethnicity, national background of immigrants, religion, occupation, income, education, etc. Variations in such factors may influence the power structure in a number of ways. First, to relate size to the variable of social homogeneity, it is likely that

6. The larger the community, the more socially heterogeneous its population;
and

7. The more heterogeneous a community, the greater the possibilities for interlocking memberships and cross-cutting status-sets;[14]

8. The greater the density of cross-cutting status-sets, the more controlled the community conflicts.

This last idea has been developed at length by Coleman.[15] The relation between conflict and power structure arrangements is a problem which will be explored further in the section on voluntary organizations and political parties. At this point only a few additional demographic variables influencing the development of cross-cutting status-sets will be considered.

9. The larger the community, the less dense the cross-cutting status-sets.

This proposition is based on the assumption that a smaller community is more closely knit and forces a larger number of its citizens to interact with one another in more diverse situations than is the case in larger communities. Although Proposition 9 may hold true *ceteris paribus*, at least two fundamental demographic variables are important conditioning factors in addition to community size in determining the density of cross-cutting status-sets.

10. The fewer the fundamental lines of cleavage within the community (ethnic, national, etc.), the more extensive the cross-cutting status-sets.

11. The stronger the intracommunity ties of a community's residents, the more extensive the cross-cutting status-sets.[16]

The relation of community conflict and cross-cutting status-sets to community power structure will be elaborated further in the section on integration—voluntary organizations and political parties.

Adaptation: Economic Variables

12. The more diverse the economic structures within the community, the more pluralistic the power structure.[17]

13. The greater the percentage of absentee-owned enterprises in a community, the more pluralistic the power structure.[18]

These two propositions are among the most frequently asserted comparative statements relating community differences to varying power structures.

Searching for intervening variables for Proposition 13, the widely discussed phenomenon of the nationalization of industry leads to the following hypothesis:

14. The executives of absentee-owned enterprises tend to withdraw from instrumental community activities and apply their talents to more consummatory activities.

For example, participation is deflected from internecine political battles to relatively nonpolitical voluntary organizations or social activities.

Many studies have documented this trend in the northern and eastern parts of the United States, as well as in Great Britain.[19] Other studies generally in the American South or Southwest, have not found a withdrawal on the part of the economic elite.[20]

The differences in findings could be interpreted as the consequence of cultural differences between the various areas, but several economic structural factors also seem to impinge upon the situation. It is likely that

15. The more immobile a community's enterprises, the more likely their management to participate actively in instrumental as well as consummatory community activities (whether ownership of the enterprise is local or not local).

Immobility may result from two sets of factors.

16. The more geographically stationary the inputs for an enterprise, the more immobile the enterprise.

A stationary input would be one deriving from a specific geographical region—e.g., the relatively inexpensive labor in the South, or, as is the case for all extraction industries, crucial raw materials.

17. The more outputs from an enterprise are directed toward a fixed region, the lower the mobility of the enterprise.

This is the case, for instance, when the principal market of an enterprise is both limited and stationary, as for coke and alfalfa. If the mobility of an enterprise is low, its managerial representatives are likely to be more concerned with the outcome of local political decisions and their possible impact on the enterprise than if the location of the enterprise is only of marginal importance.[21]

On the other hand, in enterprises which are both relatively mobile and relatively uninfluenced by most local political decisions, it is likely that the policy followed by the management will be one of engagement in local community activities of a more consummatory nature, designed to help develop good will and create a favorable public image for the enterprise in the eyes of the community. As active involvement of its management in political affairs could lead to possible antagonism toward the enterprise, it is likely that engagement in local political activities, which could lead to thorny situations for the enterprise, will be discouraged.

Labor union organization as a possible influential variable is a topic that has been comparatively neglected in studies of community power structure. Still, the few studies that have examined the community impact of labor organizations offer evidence to suggest that such organizations can perform an important role in balancing the distribution of community power.[22] Such findings imply an additional proposition.

18. The better organized and more active the labor movement in the community, the more pluralistic the power structure—up to the point where the labor organizations exert such extensive influence that other groups withdraw from community activities.

Presthus has described a community—Riverview—where labor oganizations allied with other groups had become so dominant in community affairs that the upper economic and social groups withdrew from community politics and many other local activities. The result was a less pluralistic distribution of community power.[23]

19. The lower the involvement of business elites in community activities beyond a certain minimal point, the smaller the number of competing elites and the less pluralistic the power structure.

This proposition probably holds true *ceteris paribus*, but it has seldom been reported that the business elite withdraws completely from community activities, and other factors accompanying a withdrawal of business elites from politics are likely to minimize the effect of this situation. It appears more likely that business leaders, especially the more cosmopolitan, tend to withdraw from local community governmental activities but still continue to engage in relatively nonpolitical voluntary organizations, social activities, etc. Moreover, the withdrawal of the business elite from local government generally takes place in association with a general decline of crucial decision-making at the community level. As increasingly more decisions—within private and public enterprises, trade unions and government—are made on nonlocal levels, there tends to be a decline of instrumental involvement at the local level.

20. The smaller the proportion of instrumental decisions made at the local level within private and public enterprises, labor organizations and government, the more

consummatory and pacific the general nature of community relations.

The difficulties involved in operationalizing the variables involved in this proposition may be greater than for most of the others, but because it isolates important theoretical elements, it should not be discarded for this reason alone. One step toward operationalizing the instrumental-consummatory distinction is to consider it in terms of the number of subsequent decisions affected by a single decision. An instrumental decision would affect a large number of subsequent decisions; a consummatory decision, only a smaller number.

The same proposition may be broken down for the various subgroups of the community as well.

21. The smaller the proportion of instrumental decisions made on the local level within any one institution in the community —public or private enterprises, labor organizations, or government—the more consummatory the behavior of the members of that institution with respect to community life.

For example, consider the case of a community where the employees of a large national corporation or members of one of the armed forces residing in the community rely upon the national organization for educational facilities, health insurance, medical care, and recreational facilities, while a second group of other community residents not employed by the national corporation or the armed forces relies upon the local community government to provide these same facilities.[24] In such a community it is probable that those persons not employed by a national organization will participate more actively in instrumental community affairs than the others.

A crucial variable generally intertwined with the extent of economic diversification, the percentage of absentee ownership, the nonlocal character of inputs and outputs, the development of labor organizations and the nationalization of many economic decisions is the degree of industrialization. Indeed, some writers have focused on industrialization and the accompanying bureaucratization and rationalization of economic life as the central independent economic variable underlying these other changes. [25] Thus,

22. The higher the degree of industrialization in a community, the more pluralistic the power structure.

may be considered a higher level proposition from which, in most cases, the others may be derived (to use the term "derived" in a loose sense). Nevertheless, as the changes accompanying industrialization do not occur in the same order in all situations, it is useful to break down the general process of industrialization into the various components that impinge most directly on community power relationships. In this way it is possible to specify the differential impact of the various individual factors on the changes in community power structure.

Goal-Attainment: Legal and Political Structures

A third and important class of variables relate to the performance of the goal-attainment function: these are primarily the legal and political arrangements of the community. (Political parties and voluntary organizations, although involved to some degree in the goal-attainment function, are more directly related to the problem of integration and will therefore be considered in the next section.)

One legal arrangement that appears to be of importance in structuring the distribution of power within communities is the nonpartisan election. Sixty-one per cent of American communities with more than 5,000 inhabitants presently have nonpartisan elections.[26] Although nonpartisan electoral procedures have to date been largely neglected by students of community power, there is evidence suggesting that

nonpartisanship tends to favor the better organized (and generally more wealthy) segments of the community population over the amorphous (and generally less well-to-do) segments.[27] At least three factors would seem to offer support for this assertion.

First, in partisan elections, it is more likely that the issues and candidates will be more clearly distinguished from one another because of candidates' ties with political parties which are in turn characterized by relatively enduring ideological differences and which repose on relatively distinct social bases. Voting turnout is likely to be higher than if the issues at stake and the candidates' positions on these issues remain vague and imprecise to the majority of the electorate. With lower over-all rates of voter turnout characterizing nonpartisan elections, and as voters from the more privileged social strata generally need less inducement to bring them to the polls than do those of the poorer strata, the candidates supported by the active and better organized middle classes will tend to fare proportionately better than if there were partisan elections.

Second, candidates for office are more likely to be dependent on business organization and wealthy private individuals for campaign contributions than if the alternative possibility of deriving financial support from a political party were open to them.

Third, in the absence of a party label distinguishing candidates from one another when the voter actually enters the voting booth, information about the individual candidates to which the electorate is exposed before election day takes on a more important role than is the case in partisan elections. As the means of communication are generally disproportionately controlled by the wealthier segments of the population, the poorer voters are once more disadvantaged.

For these reasons and others, one would expect conservative candidates to fare better in nonpartisan elections than in partisan elections. The available empirical evidence seems to offer support for this assertion. For example, in twenty-six California communities of over 50,000 inhabitants, it was found that 80 per cent of the mayors and 68 per cent of the city councilmen were registered Republicans although the great majority of the registered voters in these same communities were Democrats.[28]

This brief review of the effects of nonpartisanship suggests the following proposition:

> 23. The larger the number of governmental statuses in a community filled according to nonpartisan electoral procedures, the more dominant are the wealthy in decision-making.

Another proposition relating governmental structure to the distribution of community power is

> 24. The larger the number of full-time nonelected officials in the community government, the more pluralistic the community (up to a certain point).

This proposition can be subsumed under the more general statement set forth above, Proposition 5.[29]

Several examples of (generally small) communities have been reported where the political institutions are dominated by individuals whose primary occupation may be nonpolitical, e.g., business or one of the professions.[30] Such persons fill the vacuum created by the absence of any autonomous political institutions and full-time occupational roles associated with them in larger communities. Persons who actively participate in local political life frequently report that it is a "sense of civic responsibility" that motivates them. Still, if a community government must rely upon the efforts of an elite group of citizens acting solely in a voluntary capacity to perform many of its central tasks, it is likely to be more susceptible to monolithic domination than if it has a more autonomous core of full-time officials whose principal function is to serve the entire community. Demands from minorities are more likely to be heard by a community official whose specific job it is to listen to such grievances than by "leading citizens" who must be approached directly by the minority.

Because the communities whose power structures have been studied to date have

been in Western nonsocialist countries, it has frequently been a latent assumption that communities are likely to be dominated by economic elites. A strong and autonomous set of governmental institutions has consequently been seen as a means of forestalling economic domination of local communities. Consideration of a hypothetical socialist community, however, where the political institutions would tend to dominate community affairs unless there were some sort of countervailing power, should serve as a warning to the limitations of Propositions 5 and 24.[31] A general model of the interrelations between divers community institutions that should lead to an optimally pluralistic situation will be considered in the next section.

Integration: Political Parties and Voluntary Organizations

One important aspect of a community is its relative homogeneity along a number of dimensions: basic demographic characteristics of its population, the diversity of its economic enterprises, and the number and variety of voluntary organizations and political parties and factions. This aspect of community life was involved to some degree in Propositions 2, 5, 12, 18, and 19 delineated above. These five propositions can be subsumed under a single more general one.

> 25. The greater the structural support within the community for a plurality of competing elites, the more pluralistic the power structure.

This general idea has been advanced innumerable times in varying forms and contexts.[32] In most previous applications of the principle to community power, however, the independent variable has been stated in terms of homogeneity of the community population with regard to standard demographic variables. A typical formulation is the following: homogeneous middle-class communities are likely to have monolithic power structures.[33]

Although social heterogeneity can serve as one type of structural support for competing elites, two qualifications should be emphasized. The first is that there are a sufficient number of latent issues and areas of potential conflict ready to be mobilized in almost any community; the social heterogeneity of the population is far from being the only basis for political differences. In other words, political cleavages need not only reflect social ones. The example of the political career of Mayor Lee as documented by Dahl demonstrates this point rather well. From the turn of the century into the 1950's, New Haven politics were largely ethnic politics. Candidates were assessed by political machines and the electorate alike largely in terms of being Irish, Jewish, Italian, Old Yankee, or Negro. Slates were balanced to a large degree so as to reflect the nationality distribution of the New Haven population. (During this period, it might be pointed out, these nationality and ethnic cleavages overlapped to a large degree with social class divisions, although not completely.)

By 1950, however, the previously cohesive and distinct ethnic groups had become relatively assimilated, economically, socially and politically. Richard C. Lee took advantage of this situation in his campaigns during the 1950's by emphasizing the collective benefits that would accrue to all citizens of New Haven if the extensive urban renewal program he supported were implemented. In contrast to his opponent, who tried to mobilize the traditional ethnic voting patterns, Lee appealed to all groups as citizens of New Haven. His victory marked a deep shift in New Haven political alignments.[34]

A second point that should not be neglected is that the minimal amount of structural support necessary for an individual or group of citizens to challenge effectively the policies of the community leadership in many cases need not be very large, especially in smaller communities. In a homogeneous middle-class suburb, for example, a single group of active citizens and a single party may dominate community politics and general community affairs year after year. It is possible, however, that a dynamic housewife could almost singlehandedly mobilize enough support in a relatively short amount of time to alter significantly the policy of the community leadership in a given area, or even to displace several established leaders from office.[35]

If individual citizens can potentially exert such extensive influence on the community *status quo*, it seems inappropriate to term such a situation as monolithic or undemocratic, even if there is not active competition between candidates at every election.

The crucial variable for the maintenance of a pluralistic system, from this point of view, then, is some type of structural support for competing elites. The simple factor of size in a small enough community (in an industrial, democratic society) may lower what might be termed the "influence threshold" to a point where almost any active and interested citizen could exert a substantial amount of influence and perhaps even become entrenched in the community power structure.[36]

In larger communities, however, a pluralistic power structure is more likely to emerge only if there is more solid and permanent structural support for a plurality of competing elites. Such support can be provided, for example, by ethnic, national, linguistic, subregional or economic solidarity. If within the community there exist dividing lines in terms of the basic demographic characteristics of the population or of their positions in the economic system, these lines of cleavage can be articulated with the political system through various integrative structures, such as voluntary organizations or political parties, performing what Almond has termed the functions of interest articulation and interest aggregation.[37]

Such factors as heterogeneity of the population along basic demographic lines or diversity of economic structures can provide a structural context favorable to a pluralistic community power structure, but in themselves are by no means determinant.

From this point of view, integrative structures can be seen as intervening variables between the more fundamental community factors and the type of power structure. Two propositions on this level which can be derived from Proposition 25 are the following.

> 26. *The greater the density of voluntary organizations in the community, the more pluralistic the power structure.*

> 27. *The greater the number of effective competing political parties (or factions within a single party in a one-party community), the more pluralistic the power structure.*

At this point, it is appropriate to comment, especially apropos of Proposition 27, that pluralism, when carried to extremes, can lead to anarchy. If the dependent variable in these propositions were, for example, "responsible democratic government," Proposition 27 might be rephrased with just two parties or factions as the ideal number.[38]

The analysis relating to competing elites as developed thus far highlights one important aspect of the functional contributions of integrative institutions to the maintenance of a pluralistic power structure. The aspect emphasized heretofore has been the necessity of the existence of different competing elite groups within the community. A second vital aspect of the problem that must not be neglected, however, is that in order for effective competition to be maintained, there must be a certain minimal consensus between the competing groups concerning the "rules of the game," tolerance of opposition groups, etc. If this minimal consensus among various community groups does not exist, as soon as one group is able to seize control of certain community institutions it may seek to dominate other groups by expanding its jurisdiction of authority through illegitimate means. In such a situation, the community will become fragmented into warring groups so hostile to one another that application of the term pluralistic as commonly used would no longer be appropriate—no longer is there fair competition, but instead, violent conflict.

It is this second general theme concerning

the necessity of restraining conflict between integrative structures that underlies discussions on rates of citizen participation, cross-cutting status-sets and the dampening of community conflicts.

Examining first citizen participation, it would appear that

> 28. *The greater the participation of community members in political parties and voluntary organizations, the greater their ego-involvement in community life.*[39]

> 29. *The greater the ego-involvement in community life, the more complete the internalization of community values, norms, and traditions.*

> 30. *The more complete the internalization by community members of community values, norms, and traditions, the less likely is violent community conflict to occur.*

Approaching this same general problem from the standpoint of status-set analysis, two relevant propositions stated above were 8 and 10.

Most previous discussions of the functional contributions to the dampening of community conflict provided by such factors as high rates of citizen participation and the high density of cross-cutting status-sets have been phrased so as to apply to the entire population of the community.[40] It would appear that such analysis is founded on an unrealistic view of most communities. It is more likely that only a relatively small minority of the population (in most contemporary democratic societies) ever becomes sufficiently involved in any community issue to do more than vote or perhaps attend a few meetings a year.

Empirical studies of voting behavior have demonstrated the extensive amount of apathy characterizing the great majority of American voters.[41] According to the classical model of an ideal democracy, such widespread apathy is to be deplored. In actual practice, however, it appears that the apathetic citizen performs an important function for the maintenance of a democratic system: he changes his position and voting preference with a great deal more facility than the actively involved citizen who is generally far more inflexible.[42]

These findings imply that a more realistic model of the ideal pluralistic system may consist of an elite of citizens whose rate of participation in community activities is relatively high, whose ego-involvement is great, and whose internalization of community-wide values, norms, and traditions is extensive. This elite will ideally be characterized by a network of cross-cutting status-sets sufficiently dense to transcend to some degree the potential lines of fundamental community cleavage: e.g., ethnic, national, religious, and economic divisions. On the other hand, only a minority of citizens is deeply involved in community affairs; the majority of others is relatively uninvolved, has unfirm opinions on most community issues, and is capable of being persuaded in one direction or another without undue effort on the part of the more active citizens. Thus, according to this model of the ideal pluralistic community, the apathetic members are just as important as the active ones.

Latent Pattern-maintenance and Tension-management: Cultural and Educational Variables

Using the term culture to refer to the transmitted patterns of values, norms, and ideas, as distinct from social structure, which refers to the system of interaction,[43] two variables on a cultural level may be distinguished that have important consequences for the structuring of community power.

Proposition 20 analyzed the consequences of the general process of structural-functional differentiation according to the theoretical formulation as normally delineated.[44] There is a remarkable similarity in the dynamics of change associated with industrialization for two social systems infrequently classified together: the family

and the community.[45] Both institutions have been affected in such a way that they tend to perform certain functions only at a reduced level: specifically those of adaptation, goal-attainment, and integration, to use Parsons' categories. At the same time, their relative (and perhaps absolute) importance in performing the latent pattern-maintenance and tension-management function has greatly increased. Social structural as well as cultural modifications are closely interwoven and generally tend to develop together. Still, in certain cases changes develop more rapidly in one of these two areas, and a disjunction between the two results. This general situation has been identified by social scientists in a number of different substantive areas;[46] Ogburn has termed one manifestation of this general phenomenon "cultural lag."[47]

It is possible to consider the paternalistic value system of *noblesse oblige* that characterizes the community elites of certain areas as a cultural value that is lagging behind the broad structural changes associated with the general processes of centralization and bureaucratization taking place in most modern industrial societies. This value system has had an influence on certain elite groups, especially in small, rural, isolated communities (as are frequently found in the American South). It helps explain the continual involvement of industrial managers of such communities in local politics and other community activities even when their enterprises have become absentee-owned and the majority of important decisions are no longer made on the community level.[48] Analyzing the paternalistic value system as an independent variable, the following proposition may be formulated.

31. The more paternalistic the value system of elite groups in the community, the greater their involvement in community affairs.

To a certain degree, the paternalistic value system is the antithesis of the pluralistic value system. Considering the pluralistic system in relation to the power structure we would expect that

32. *The more pluralistic the value system of members of the community, the more pluralistic the power structure.*

The degree of internalization of the pluralistic value system in countries where general democratic values are inculcated into students through the educational system will tend to be positively associated with the level of education of the members of the community, implying

33. *The higher the educational level of community residents, the more pluralistic the power structure.*

The isolation of the pluralistic value system from other values and skills generally associated with education doubtless poses a problem for the empirical testing of this proposition. Cross-national comparison of countries which differ in their degree of emphasis on the democratic value system in the educational institutions can, however, provide a test.[49]

Another cultural variable that may influence the distribution of power in a community is the prestige hierarchy of social statuses within the community. If, for example, a community judges its clergymen and teachers as important as its businessmen, it is likely that clergymen and teachers will play a more significant role in community affairs than if they are considered in the same category as skilled workers.[50] Thus, our last proposition.

34. *The higher the prestige of a social status, the more likely are its occupants to rank high in the community power structure.*

Further Research

The inventory of propositions presented above contains many statements that are reasonably well established. Others, however, were formulated in this paper for the first time and have little or no empirical evidence to support them. There are two ways of correcting this imbalance between the development of theory and research. First, it is possible to extract more information from the existing community power literature. This paper has been mainly

concerned with the conceptual problems associated with the study of community power, and consequently has not concentrated on systematically reviewing the empirical studies that would help lead to the validation, refinement, or rejection of the above propositions. One method for proceeding is to evaluate the supporting evidence for the propositions delineated above by systematically classifying the variables reported in the empirical studies of community power that are available and testing the inventory of propositions against this bank of evidence.[51]

The second avenue toward correcting the imbalance is to conduct more empirical research. Probably the most important single research implication of this paper is that the day of the isolated case study has passed. It is unlikely that advancement could have been made toward developing as generalizable a theory of community power as we now have without building on the foundation laid by the numerous case studies. And, for someone deeply interested in answering the question, "Who governs in my community?" (and ignoring most broader considerations), the case study of the individual community is still appropriate. Still, for the further advancement of the general conceptual framework that has been developed in the study of community power thus far, comparative studies of a large number of communities differing on theoretically relevant variables are indubitably called for.[52]

In addition to collecting data from different communities, future empirical studies should also attempt to obtain information on more community variables than has generally been the case in the past. The imbalance in the amount of data available for support of the various propositions suggests that future research might fruitfully be conducted so as to examine the interrelations among various community variables which appear to be crucial in influencing the distribution of community power, but which have been relatively neglected in previous empirical work. Outstanding in this respect are different types of legal and political arrangements relating to community government. For example, the consequences of such administrative arrangements as the city manager system, of nonpartisan electoral procedures and of varying types of representational institutions on the distribution of community power remain practically unresearched questions. In addition, an entire area of research that needs to be explored concerns the relationship between different types of power structure and the ways in which they influence the actual content of community decisions. What types of political outputs are associated with different power structures? Virtually no systematic work has been produced which can provide answers to this question. This curious gap in the present body of knowledge can probably be explained at least in part as a consequence of the fissure between the disciplines of sociology and political science. For years, sociologists have been studying community power structure, and, at the same time, political scientists have been studying local government and public administration. The sociologists have generally overlooked the various types of local governmental structures as independent variables in studying community power, and students of local government have often been content to analyze hypothetical consequences of different types of governmental structures without reference to the broader social structural characteristics of the community, and without conducting actual empirical studies.

A somewhat analogous situation is to be found concerning the varying impact of community roles played by labor organizations. Economists and industrial sociologists have written a great deal on the relations between labor and management, but they have generally ignored the impact of these disputes on the broader community structure.

The mutual benefits of cooperation in this field to the several social science disciplines should be obvious, and perhaps there can be more of the much pleaded for, but seldom achieved, "cross-fertilization" between the brother and sister disciplines. Hopefully the universal incest taboo may be relaxed for these purposes.

List of Propositions

1. The larger the number of inhabitants in the community, the more pluralistic the power structure.

2. The larger the community, the larger the number of potential elites that can democratically compete for power.

3. The larger the community, the greater the number of full-time political roles.

4. The larger the community, the more autonomous its political institutions.

5. The more autonomous the political institutions of a community, the more pluralistic the power structure.

6. The larger the community, the more socially heterogeneous its population.

7. The more heterogeneous a community, the greater the possibilities for interlocking membership and cross-cutting status-sets.

8. The greater the density of cross-cutting status-sets, the more controlled the community conflicts.

9. The larger the community, the less dense the cross-cutting status-sets.

10. The fewer the fundamental lines of cleavage within the community (ethnic, national, etc.), the more extensive the cross-cutting status-sets.

11. The stronger the intracommunity ties of a community's residents, the more extensive the cross-cutting status-sets.

12. The more diverse the economic structures within the community, the more pluralistic the power structure.

13. The greater the percentage of absentee-owned enterprises in a community, the more pluralistic the power structure.

14. The executives of absentee-owned enterprises tend to withdraw from instrumental community activities and apply their talents to more consummatory activities.

15. The more immobile a community's enterprises, the more likely their management

to participate actively in instrumental as well as consummatory community activities (whether ownership of the enterprises is local or not local).

16. The more geographically stationary the inputs for an enterprise, the more immobile the enterprise.

17. The more the outputs from an enterprise are directed toward a fixed region, the lower the mobility of the enterprise.

18. The better organized and more active the labor movement in the community, the more pluralistic the power structure—up to the point where the labor organizations exert such extensive influence that other groups withdraw from community activities.

19. The lower the involvement of business elites in community activities beyond a certain minimal point, the smaller the number of competing elites and the less pluralistic the power structure.

20. The smaller the proportion of instrumental decisions made at the local level within private and public enterprises, labor organizations, and government, the more consummatory and pacific the general nature of community life.

21. The smaller the proportion of instrumental decisions made on the local level within any one institution in the community—public or private enterprises, labor organizations, or government—the more consummatory the behavior of the members of that institution with respect to community life.

22. The higher the degree of industrialization in a community, the more pluralistic the power structure.

23. The larger the number of governmental statuses in a community filled according to nonpartisan electoral procedures, the more dominant are the wealthy in decision-making.

24. The larger the number of full-time nonelected officials in the community

government, the more pluralistic the community (up to a certain point).

25. The greater the structural support within the community for a plurality of competing elites, the more pluralistic the power structure.

26. The greater the density of voluntary organizations in the community, the more pluralistic the power structure.

27. The greater the number of effective competing political parties (or factions within a single party in a one-party community), the more pluralistic the power structure.

28. The greater the participation of community members in political parties and voluntary organizations, the greater their ego-involvement in community life.

29. The greater the ego-involvement in community life, the more complete the internalization of community values, norms, and traditions.

30. The more complete the internalization by community members of community values, norms, and traditions, the less likely is violent community conflict to occur.

31. The more paternalistic the value system of elite groups in the community, the greater their involvement in community affairs.

32. The more pluralistic the value system of the community, the more pluralistic the power structure.

33. The higher the educational level of community residents, the more pluralistic the power structure.

34. The higher the prestige of a social status, the more likely are its occupants to rank high in the community power structure.

The Vertical Axis of Community Organization and the Structure of Power[*][1]

John Walton

Northwestern University

IN THE RELATIVELY BRIEF PERIOD since its inception, the study of community power structure has attracted a wide range of enthusiasts. Researchers of diverse backgrounds have found their particular interests coalesce around the assumption that local leadership processes are of central importance to the explanation of community action. The research implications of this approach have been explored in a variety of areas including urban renewal, social welfare, health and hospital services, community conflict and ethnic relations.[2] Though often divided on issues of how the leadership process is organized and the extent to which power is effectively exercised, investigators are in agreement concerning the viability of research problems suggested by the approach.

In addition to these fertile substantive applications, much has been done to develop the research methods of power-structure studies.[3] The conflict which prevailed a few years ago between proponents of rival methods seems to have subsided with the recognition that different methods tap different dimensions of the total power scene. Investigators now appear to agree on the need for methodologically balanced, comparative, and longitudinal studies. This

* Reprinted with permission of the author and publisher, from John Walton, "The Vertical Axis of Community Organization and the Structure of Power," (Southwestern) Social Science Quarterly, 48 (December 1967), pp. 353–368, and in Terry N. Clark (ed.), Community Structure and Decision Making: Comparative Analyses, (San Francisco: Chandler Publishing Co., 1968), pp. 441–459.

trend is manifest in several notable works that have appeared recently.[4]

In spite of these convergences, however, there has been almost no progress in one vital respect; the development of theoretical explanation of the reported findings. Elaborate documentation of the atheoretical character of the field hardly seems necessary. One has only to peruse a portion of the literature to discover that the principal issues are almost entirely concerned with method and conflicting interpretations of how broadly power is distributed. Only rarely do we find some of the initial steps in theorizing represented by conceptual considerations and the development of propositional inventories.[5]

The purpose of this paper is to develop a theoretical explanation of how power is distributed in local communities, and to consider briefly how various power arrangements may account for different forms of community action. The analysis incorporates earlier theoretical discussions of the community and a systematic review of the power-structure literature. Anticipating the conclusions for a moment, it will be argued that as communities become increasingly interdependent with extracommunity institutions, changes in the local normative order ensue producing more competitive power arrangements.

Starting with a review of previous research, the argument moves on to consider the adequacy of certain theoretical approaches and, finally, to develop the propositions concerning power structure and community action.

Findings of Previous Research

In an earlier paper the findings of thirty-three power-structure studies dealing with fifty-five communities were analyzed in order to determine the relationship between a number of substantive and methodological variables and the dependent variable, type of power structure.[6] Subsequently that analysis was replicated using a somewhat larger number of studies.[7] The selection of studies was intended to be exhaustive of the published literature in social science

Notes to this selection will be found on pages 352–355.

devoted specifically to the study of community power structure. By dealing with the published literature the examination excluded some unpublished studies, especially dissertations. Confining the analysis to the social science literature excluded journalistic reports. Finally, the criterion that the research be specifically concerned with community power excluded a number of community studies dealing with stratification, local government and related aspects of social and political life. These criteria were employed in a screening of the literature, and the resulting list of studies was checked against several lengthy bibliographies to insure its inclusiveness. Thus the studies are regarded as a universe, defined by the above criteria, rather than a sample.

Each study was reviewed and, when sufficient information was available, coded in terms of a number of self-explanatory independent variables (e.g., region, population

The Vertical Axis of Community   **189**
Organization and the Structure of Power
John Walton

size, industrialization, economic diversity, etc.). Similarly, the type of power structure identified in each report was coded in terms of four categories: (1) Pyramidal—a monolithic, monopolistic, or single cohesive leadership group; (2) Factional—at least two durable factions that compete for advantage; (3) Coalitional—leadership varies with issues and is made up of fluid coalitions of interested persons and groups: (4) Amorphous—the absence of any persistent pattern of leadership or power exercised on the local level. Table 1 indicates those few associations which were found to be significant or meaningful. [8]

In contrast to these positive findings, a large number of variables, including region,

TABLE 1.[9] *Community Characteristics and Community Power Structure*[10]

	Pyramidal	Factional, Coalitional and Amorphous	Total
Absentee Ownership[11]			
Present	2	18	20
Absent	12	9	21
Total	14	27	41
	$Q = -.85$ $.01 > p > .001$		
Economic Resources[12]			
Adequate	9	17	26
Inadequate	6	5	11
Total	15	22	37
	$Q = -.39$ $.30 > p > .20$		
Type of City[13]			
Independent	14	22	36
Satellite	2	10	12
Total	16	32	48
	$Q = -.52$ $.20 > p > .10$		
Party Competition			
Competitive	0	10	10
Noncompetitive	10	12	22
Total	10	22	32
	$Q = -1.0$ $.02 > p > .01$		
Change in Power Structure			
Dispersion	2	17	19
Concentration	0	0	0
No Change	3	4	7
Oscillation	2	1	3
Decline Locally	1	2	3
Total	8	24	32

population size, population composition, industrialization, economic diversity, and type of local government, were *not* found to be related to type of power structure.

Taking these results as a summary of the present status of research, it appears that no firm generalizations are suggested. The findings fail to conform to any neat pattern such as an association between competitive power structures and greater complexity of local social and economic organization. The inadequacies of such an explanation are underscored by the negative findings. The evidence may, however, be suggestive of some less obvious explanation. In order to explore that possibility we shall look at some implicitly theoretical positions in the area of community power and a major theoretical work on American communities, asking, in both cases, how they square with the above findings and how they might inform the present analysis.

Theoretical Approaches

In one of the first attempts to bring some order out of the confusion of results, David Rogers developed a series of propositions concerning community political systems.[14] His dependent variable, type of political system, was made up of the categories monolithic and pluralistic. In stating the relationship between these and a number of characteristics of community social structure, Rogers hypothesized that the following would be associated with a pluralistic system: a high degree of industrialization, a large population, a socially heterogeneous population, a policy differentiated from the kinship and economic systems, a local government of extensive scope, two or more political parties, and the unionization, or other political and economic organization, of working-class groups. The underlying theme in this series of propositions, what has been referred to as the implicit theory, centers on the effects of industrialization, and attendant processes of urbanization and bureaucratization, the outcome of these being structural differentiation which contributes to a pluralistic power situation. The

approach is, of course, central to contemporary social science whether stated in terms of *gemeinschaft* and *gesellschaft* or any other of a variety of polar types.

Amos Hawley has presented a somewhat more specific approach.[15] Here power is defined as a system property whose distribution can be measured by the ability to mobilize resources and personnel. In any total system, such as a community, this ability lies in the various component subsystems and is exercised through their managerial functions. Hence, operationally, the greater the number of managerial personnel, the greater the concentration of power. If we grant that success in a collective action requires the mobilization of resources and personnel, and that this ability is greatest where power is most highly concentrated, then it follows that the greater the concentration of power in a community the greater the *probability* of success in any collective action. In a recent paper, inspired in part by the Hawley piece, Edgar Butler and Hallowell Pope have suggested another measure of power concentration, the number of profile or key industries and the concentration of managerial functions within these.[16]

It should be noted that the Hawley and Butler and Pope papers are concerned chiefly with community action; for each the premise is that more concentrated power situations are conducive to concerted action. Unlike Rogers they are not trying to explain patterns of power distribution but, rather, employ these to explain community action. Nevertheless, they are pertinent here because they imply a theoretical position involving the saliency of managerial functions in the determination of community power structures.

How do these explanatory schemes square with the findings culled from the existing literature? Considering first the hypotheses formulated by Rogers, the evidence runs counter to his notions of the effects of industrialization, population size and population heterogeneity. On the positive side, his proposition about political parties, though not entirely equivalent to party competition, is supported. Unfortunately, no data are available on the remaining three propositions. What evidence we have, however, indicates that Rogers' propositions do not fare very well within the present context, though they may have greater predictive power in a cross cultural or historical perspective. For our purposes the implication is that the theoretical approach implicit in these propositions is in need of revision. Perhaps it will be necessary to abandon the simplified notion of a unilinear relationship between the growing complexity of industrial society and more pluralistic local power arrangements, in favor of a more limited, yet more discriminating explanation.[17]

The evidence presented previously is not directly relevant to the Hawley and Butler and Pope approaches since these attempt to explain community action. If, however, we assume with these authors that concentrated power structures are associated with community action, and then examine the antecedent link in their chain of reasoning, we find that those community characteristics allegedly conducive to power concentration (i.e. ones engendering a large number of managerial functions)—industrialization, economic diversity, proportion of absentee ownership, and economic resources—are either unrelated or associated with the less concentrated power structures in our data. This fact can hardly be taken as a refutation of the positions presented. What it does indicate is that the number of managerial functions appears to be a poor indicator of type of power structure (though it may indicate the number of potentially powerful people in community action).

In short, the analysis thus far demonstrates the need for theoretical statements which are both more explicit and account better for the available data.

As we shall see, Roland Warren's analysis of *The Community in America*[18] provides a pertinent general framework for dealing theoretically with the specific questions of power structure. Warren's central thesis is that American communities are undergoing a drastic transformation of their entire structure and function; "[this] 'great change' in community living includes the increasing orientation of local community units toward extra-community

systems of which they are a part, with a decline in community cohesion and autonomy."[19] Although Warren analyzes these changes along seven fundamental dimensions of community life, a summary statement indicates their relevance for present purposes:

> In the first place, they signalize the increasing and strengthening of the external ties which bind the local community to the larger society. In the process, various parts of the community—its educational system, its recreation, its economic units, its governmental functions, its religious units, its health and welfare agencies, and its voluntary associations—have become increasingly oriented toward district, state, regional, or national offices and less and less oriented toward each other.
>
> In the second place, as local community units have become more closely tied in with state and national systems, much of the decision-making prerogative concerning the structure and function of these units has been transferred to the headquarters or district offices of the systems themselves, thus leaving a narrower and narrower scope of functions over which local units, responsible to the local community, exercise autonomous power.[20]

On the basis of these observations concerning the "great change" and with the simultaneous recognition that communities (i.e. "combinations of social units and systems which perform the major functions having locality reference") do persist as meaningful units, Warren finds useful a distinction between the *horizontal* and *vertical axes* of community organization. The vertical axis refers to connections between community organizations and extra-community centers, and the horizontal axis refers to connections between community organizations. The "great change" involves an increase in the former type of connections often at the cost of the latter.

In what follows several propositions will be developed which relate Warren's approach specifically to the question of how power is distributed on the local level. We will find that his concept of a vertical axis of community organization has particular importance for this analysis.

An Explanation of Differential Patterns of Community Power Structure

Power is defined here as *the capacity to mobilize resources for the accomplishment of intended effects with recourse to some type of sanction(s) to encourage compliance.*[21] This definition includes the elements of both potential and actualized power in that capacity for mobilizing resources refers to potential while the application of sanctions refers to actualized power. *Capacity* also implies a distinction from *right* such that *authority* is not confused with the definition. Following Lasswell and Kaplan, the threat of sanctions, positive or negative, distinguishes *influence* from power—i.e. influence refers only to the capacity to mobilize resources.

Power structure is defined as *the characteristic pattern within a social organization whereby resources are mobilized and sanctions employed in ways that affect the organization as a whole.*

For the sake of simplicity we will deal here with competitive and monopolistic power structures.[22] Monopolistic power structures characterize social organizations in which the capacity for mobilizing resources and recourse to sanctions are the exclusive property of a group with similar interests. In competitive situations the capacity for mobilizing resources and recourse to sanctions are possessed by two or more groups with different interests.

The basic assumption of the theoretical statement to be developed here is that a monopoly of power produces a situation in which consensus is the most important factor underlying the use of power. This consensus may, but need not imply agreement on values and objectives. What it does imply is agreement concerning the capabilities of those holding power to realize their own intentions over a wide range of community relevant issues. In such a monopolistic situation expectations concerning the norms prescribed by the existing power arrangement tend to be widely recognized. That is, the limits of allowable (nonsanctionable) deviance and opposition are narrow and clear. As a result of these congruent expectations, potential rather than manifest power is more commonly the mechanism by which compliance is encouraged; overt conflict and coercion are relatively infrequent occurrences because compliance can be realized without them. Merriam captured the sense of this assumption when he wrote "Power is not strongest when it uses violence, but weakest."[23]

By contrast, in competitive situations the exercise of power moves from a reliance on consensus to more overt applications of sanctions. This becomes necessary to the extent that competing groups become capable of restricting the scope of each other's sanctions. Claims to power must be supported by effective action. Greater normative diversity, with attendant diversity in expectations, characterizes this situation. Such circumstances result in a greater incidence of conflict stemming from the fact that those who would exercise power are required to make evident their claim through the use of sanctions.

It should be added that each of these circumstances contains elements of the other. Monopolistic power arrangements do, at times, generate divergent norms and expectations just as they occasionally have recourse to overt applications of coercion. More importantly, the role of consensual expectations and potential power are critical to all forms of social organization and can be observed in many of the transactions carried on in competitive power settings. In this connection conflict is probably most characteristic of those transitional periods in which power is becoming more or less diffused since it is at this point that the normative order is most uncertain and expectations least clear.[24] In the event that this transition is one from monopolistic to competitive it may culminate in a new set of rules defining community power arrangements which, while more conducive to conflict than the monopolistic situation, produces less conflict than the transitional phase.

Because at first glance this assumption may appear to be a truism, its nontrivial character will be demonstrated. Presthus' study of two New York communities which differed on a pluralistic-elitist continuum is valuable here. Discussing the more elitist of the two, Presthus reasons:

> In Riverview sharper class and economic differences and resulting disparities in expectations, values and consensus seem to have placed a premium on more centralized, imperative leadership. As organizational theory and studies of group behavior suggest, social support, shared values, and common expectations make possible the minimization of overt power and authority. When community consensus is limited, leaders tend to function in a more unilateral manner.[25]

Here the minimization of overt power and authority is equated with a more pluralistic (competitive) power situation. The present argument agrees with the prior notion that common expectations result in a minimization of overt power (and conflict), but this is taken to be characteristic of a monopolistic situation. Thus, when community consensus is limited the leadership process tends to be more competitive.[26]

Obviously the relationship identified in my assumption may operate in either direction—i.e. changes in the competitiveness of the power situation can produce changes in norms and expectations and, similarly, changes in norms and expectations can lead to changes in power arrangements. In this approach we are concerned with developing an explanation of the change in power structures, that is, in the latter direction of the causal complex.

In this section we have reasoned that normative expectations bear a particular relationship to power structure and that conflict can be taken as an indicator of that relationship.[27] In what follows an attempt will be made to elaborate the connection between normative expectations and types of power structure in terms of the data drawn from existing community studies.

Returning to the data in Table 1, we can now raise the question of how the ideas presented would account for the findings. It

will be recalled that the data indicate a relationship between competitive power structures and the presence of absentee-owned corporations, competitive party politics, adequate economic resources and satellite status. Further, in those communities where change was studied, the trend was in the direction of a greater dispersion of power. Do these findings suggest some underlying explanation?

Upon closer examination the evidence does point to such an explanation. Each of the variables associated with competitive power structures reflects the interdependence of the community and extracommunity centers of power or increased emphasis on the vertical axis. For example, a high proportion of absentee-owned industry suggests that many community relevant decisions are controlled by the personnel and interests of national corporate bodies whose influence may stem from either a deliberate intervention in local affairs or from the more characteristic aloofness to local responsibility.[28] Similarly competitive political parties may often reflect the involvement of county, state and national party organizations in a struggle for control of local constituencies.[29] While it could be reasonably argued that inadequate economic resources result in substantial intervention and control by state and federal agencies which extend aid to local bodies, the position taken here is that communities with more adequate economic resources maintain a greater number of interdependent ties to extra-community institutions such as suppliers, markets, investors and other economic units. Finally, in the case of type of city, the connection is apparent. Suburban municipalities and smaller towns which form satellites of larger urban centers are interdependent in a variety of economic and political activities including municipal services, jobs, consumer behavior, etc. If, at points, the relationship between each of the variables and community interdependence is not unambiguous, the position taken here is enhanced by the pattern they suggest when taken together.

Drawing together all that has been said up to this point, the proposition which seems best to account for the findings can be stated as follows: to the extent that the local community becomes increasingly interdependent with respect to extra-community institutions (or develops along its vertical axis) the structure of local leadership becomes more competitive.[30]

Theoretically this proposition derives from the more general statement concerning norms and power arrangements: That is, the mechanism by which interdependence, or increasing relevance of the vertical axis of community organization, affects the distribution of community power is the disruption of the local normative order associated with the existing power structure. Development along the vertical axis involves the introduction of new interests and new institutional relationships implying new definitions of the community, and these have the effect of disrupting consensual normative expectations.

In addition to a differentiation of allegiances, these changes include the introduction of new *resources* and *sanctions* into the community. Local organizations with vertical ties to extracommunity institutions frequently share in the capital and human resources of the larger entity making it possible for them to sustain a broader scope of activities than would otherwise be the case. For example, absentee-owned corporations may receive funds and skilled personnel for a desired expansion of local operations making them more important as local tax contributors, employers and suppliers. Such resources carry with them potential sanctions. In the above example some of these would include the threat to locate elsewhere,[31] threat of cutbacks or other actions having an adverse effect on the local economy, support or nonsupport in local elections. What has been said here of absentee-owned corporations could also be said, though perhaps in less dramatic ways, of other vertical community organizations. The point to be emphasized is that these organizations introduce new sources of power into the local picture and, being interdependent, they also have stakes in the local decision-making process which occasionally must be defended. The greater the number of community organizations with vertical ties, the more frequent and the more inclusive are contests surrounding the decision-making process.

In summary, the theoretical statement advanced here states that the introduction of organizations with vertical ties produces a greater interdependence between community and extracommunity centers of power. This interdependence brings changes in the local normative order, as well as new resources and sanctions, creating circumstances conducive to the emergence of competing power centers. Accordingly, variables which reflect the interdependence of the community and the "carrying society"—absentee ownership, party competition, adequate economic resources and satellite status—are associated with competitive power structures; whereas those variables which reflect only intracommunity change—economic diversity, population increase, etc.—are not as associated.[32]

Parenthetically, it is instructive to note certain parallels between this argument and Banfield's theoretical treatment of the exercise of power. Defining power as "the ability to establish control over another" (i.e. "the ability to cause another to give or withhold action"),[33] Banfield states that any actor has a limited stock of power which he spends or invests in ways that he believes will maintain and enhance his ability to control. When "investment opportunities" change so does the structure of influence. For example, he offers the following proposition; "As the number of autonomous actors increases, control tends to become less structured. Structures of control—i.e. relationships which are stable from proposal to proposal—are expensive to maintain. The value of a structure—and thus the amount that will be invested in it—tends to decline as the outcome of the process becomes less and less subject to control."[34] In the present context the number of "autonomous actors" increases as a result of changes in normative expectations and the effectiveness of sanctions. Similarly, the result here is a less concentrated structure of power.

Returning to our own explanatory scheme, one loose end can be tied up. The findings on change in Table 1 indicated that community power structures are tending to become more competitive. This trend is a predictable consequence of the spread of "metropolitan dominance"[35] and its implications for greater community interdependence. That is, if Bogue and others are correct—and there seems to be ample evidence that they are—the spread of metropolitan dominance would lead one to predict a corresponding trend toward competitive power arrangements. Such is, in fact, what the findings indicate.

Discussing the effects of increasing interdependence, Greer summarizes the consequences for the "locality group" in terms of a loss of autonomy, exposure to conflicting norms and the fragmentation of local normative order. In connection with the latter he identifies many of the events and explanations embodied in the theoretical statement developed here.

> Fragmentation of the local normative order is a predictable consequence; some of the members of the local group must conform to patterns from afar, since they are dependent upon the large, extended organization for their livelihood. Others take advantage of the local group's loss of coercive power to exploit added degrees of freedom; they experiment with new means to old ends, they exercise freedom of choice. Others, still, are dependent upon the local order for social position and rewards; their life is controlled by its norms, but with the attrition of dependence (and therefore the basis for order), they find it impossible to communicate or to enforce compliance. (The cutting edge of the sanctions depended, after all, upon the interdependence of the local group.) When individuals become committed to groups centering outside the locality, the new dependence brings a measure of independence from their neighbors.[36]

This fragmentation of the local normative order, accomplished through changes in expectations concerning power leads, according to this theoretical statement, to changes in the structure of community power; specifically it leads to more competitive power arrangements.

Metropolitan Politics and Community Action

Since the purpose of this paper was to develop an explanation of how power is distributed in local communities, *and* how power arrangements may account for community action, some comments on the latter question are called for. This may be particularly useful for two reasons; first, the foregoing analysis bears directly on the subject of community action and, second, the discussion serves to integrate another perspective on power and decision-making into this explanation.

In his well known essay describing the local community as an "ecology of games,"[37] Norton Long argues that the concept of "power structure" suffers from misplaced concreteness, that when we look more closely at cities we find no such structured decision-making institution.

> What is characteristic of metropolitan areas is the lack of overall decision-making institutions. This does not mean that there are not institutions with power in metropolitan areas. It does mean that there are no institutions with sufficient power and overall responsibility to make decisions settling metropolitan issues and solving metropolitan problems . . .[38]

Rather, Long conceives of metropolitan issues as having careers in which interested and powerful parties—governments, groups, and institutions—interact and "develop a system of largely unintended cooperation through which things get done. . . ."[39] In this process actors deal with metropolitan problems from a limited point of view: i.e. one confined to their particular interest and institutional base.

There are at least two reasons why Long's empirically persuasive approach has stymied students of community power. One would appear to be the fact that much of this research has been conducted in places other than metropolitan areas where decisions settling local issues are possible.

Second, the well known controversy over pluralism and elitism in the literature—because it is a debate over who makes local decisions, a small, cohesive group or a large, diverse one—may have obscured the possibility that no one makes such decisions.

In the present explanation metropolitan areas are prototypes of interdependent, vertically organized communities. Here we would expect a highly fragmented and competitive power arrangement in which the scope of any group or institution would be limited to prime interest areas. That is, the competitive process would militate against generalized influence and require that actors work to maintain their position within the system. Long and Banfield concur with this prediction in the stress they put on metropolitan politics as going systems in which institutions and groups seek to maintain and enhance their power in particular areas, public policy representing the results of their cooperation.[40]

Under these circumstances we would expect to find a fragmented and competitive pattern of community action. Community action in American cities seems increasingly to fit this pattern. The most apparent illustrations are found in the activities of civil rights, anti-poverty, and peace groups which often possess resources conferred by extracommunity institutions and which are beginning to seriously involve themselves in the local political process. Here, of course, they encounter opposition from other local and vertically organized groups. As a result coordinated community action becomes more problematic and public policy represents less a reflection of consensus than a byproduct of the competitive process in which power is differentially exercised. Discussing the resurgence of radical politics in Chicago, Cleveland, Pittsburg, Gary, and several other cities, one author concludes "In the midwest, this tendency is general, and holds promise of becoming the outstanding fact of urban political life in America by the end of the decade."[41] In another vein, several studies which have touched on the consequences of increasing involvement of the federal government in local affairs find, contrary to political folklore, an enhancement of competitive, democratic processes.[42]

Notable among deviant cases is the Vidich and Bensman study[43] where involvement of state and county governments resulted in an abdication of responsibility on the part of local leaders. While it is significant that these changes diluted the power of Springdale's elite, it is also recognized that the consequences of extracommunity involvement were not those we would predict. In this regard the theory presented here may be in need of modification. Recalling that Springdale is a town of 2,500 people and that its extracommunity ties center chiefly around state subsidies, it is reasonable to infer that both the nature of the community and of the vertical ties are contingent elements in the theory presented here. Perhaps it is the case, for example, that changes along the vertical axis lead to greater competitiveness only in those communities which possess a certain minimum of institutional viability and that without this the same changes spell the demise of local leadership.

Conclusions

The explanation offered here represents an attempt to push the study of community power beyond a disproportionate emphasis on technique and toward a concern for testing propositions derived from explicit theoretical statements. There seems little doubt that this alternative is best suited for resolving the controversies over how power is distributed in local communities, and for generalizing research in this area to the larger problems of social organization and change.

The theory developed in this paper states that the introduction into the local community of the institutions and influence of national-urban culture produces a "fragmentation of local normative order" or a disruption of consensual expectations concerning the norms prescribed by existing power arrangements. As expectations are altered and interests are differentiated, new resources are exploited for the creation of competing power groups.

The theory, as we have said, focuses on one direction of influence in what is undoubtedly a complex process. In so doing, however, it has the virtue of generating a number of testable propositions. Future comparative studies could evaluate, on the basis of first-hand data, the fundamental proposition regarding community interdependence and the advent of competitive power arrangements. A sampling of related propositions includes:

1. Changes, other than interdependence, which challenge the local normative order lead to more competitive power arrangements.
2. Intracommunity change which does not challenge the normative order does not lead to greater competitiveness.
3. Vertical ties which do not alter the normative order do not lead to the exploitation of new resources and more competitive power arrangements.
4. Normative diversity within a community leads to a greater frequency of application of overt sanctions (Presthus).

5. The greater the number of vertical ties in a community, the smaller the scope of local power groups.
6. The greater the number of vertical ties (and competitiveness) the more difficult (less frequent) is coordinated community action.

In addition to suggesting propositions the theory implies a new direction for research in that it locates the source of local change in the relationship between the community and extracommunity institutions. It is expected that researchers will find this theory informative as they become increasingly aware of what it implies for the choice of an appropriate unit of analysis in future community power studies. If the theory is correct the appropriate unit of analysis is not the community per se but, rather, the relationship between the community and the institutions of national-urban culture.

A Note on Walton's Analysis of Power Structure and Vertical Ties*

Roland L. Warren

Brandeis University

JOHN WALTON'S analysis of community power structures is important not only in that it goes beyond a mere equating of competitive power structures with size of population, but also because it suggests a theoretical explanation for competitiveness in power structures which is both plausible and fraught with substantive implications. Although the analysis is plausible and significant, the variables on which it is based can be challenged on the basis of their validity as indicators of interdependence; and, of course, additional, more deliberately designed research would be needed to establish firmly the relationship between community interdependence and competitive power structures which is derived from the present analysis.

But that is for the future. Let us examine the analysis itself, in relation to the data on which it is based, and then go on to consider some of the implications of the relationship, if it is corroborated by subsequent research.

Walton concludes that four variables show a statistically significant relationship to competitive power structures. These are absentee ownership, adequate economic resources, satellite status, and political party competition. These otherwise purely empirical relationships are given theoretical meaning by the observation that they are

* Reprinted with permission of the author and publisher, from Roland L. Warren, "A Note on Walton's Analysis of Power Structure and Vertical Ties," (Southwestern) Social Science Quarterly, 48 (December 1967), pp. 369–372.

all indicators of a community's dependence on the surrounding society. Such dependence, linking community units to extra-community systems, introduces new resources and sanctions into the community and brings about a fragmentation of the local normative order and, through this, a number of competing power centers.

Consequently, those communities with the greatest dependence on vertical ties, as indicated by these four variables, will show the greatest pluralism, or diversity, or competitiveness of power structures. In oversimplified terms, the greater and more numerous the vertical ties, the more pluralistic the power structure; the fewer and weaker the vertical ties, the more monolithic the power structure.

Because of the great significance of this thesis, it is doubly important to note that reasoning on which it is based, though entirely plausible, is still extremely tenuous. A key point in the analysis is the extent to which the four indicators actually constitute valid and powerful operational measures of strength of vertical ties. Taken individually, both absentee-owned industry and competitive political parties would seem to be plausible indicators of community interdependence, for the reasons which Walton suggests. On the other hand, he is understandably temperate in assertions about the variable of adequate economic resources. I doubt strongly that this variable would have occurred to him in advance as something especially to test for, had it not been one which showed an empirical relationship to competitive power structures in the direction indicated. It certainly would not have occurred to me. Probably on this one, we should simply reflect on the note written in the margin of a preacher's sermon: "Weak point. Pound the pulpit!" and then go on to the next point.

The fourth variable, or attribute, is that of being a satellite community. Here again, the reasoning is plausible, but would require more refined consideration of whether the dimensions of interdependence which satellite status indicates are relevant to the dimensions of interdependence which could be the basis for a plausible theoretical association between interdependence and

Notes to this selection will be found on page 355.

competitive power structures. Those aspects of interdependence which could be theoretically derived from satellite status would have to be specified, operationalized, and then tested for degree of association with competitive power structure, before one could draw a valid conclusion on this question.

Yet, taken all in all, the distributions would indicate the plausibility of the theoretical explanation, and would strongly support the desirability of pursuing this new, rich vein.

One other aspect of the analysis suggests the need for greater clarification in the theoretical explanation of the data. This has to do with the use of the community's "normative order" as an important variable, a variable which is sometimes treated as an independent variable, at other times as an intermediate variable. The question is whether this variable is not superfluous. It does not seem to be necessary to the theoretical explanation, and rather seems to have the status only of a theoretical construct, not too clearly defined, which accounts for nothing and simply clutters the analysis. Further, it lends itself to reification and what, it would seem to me at least, is a deliberate reversal of the direction of the imputed relationship.

Thus, we get the statement: "In the present context the number of 'autonomous actors' increases as a result of changes in normative expectations and the effectiveness of sanctions." But there is nothing in either the data or in the theoretical reasoning to lend support to normative expectations as an independent variable. Put quite simply, ties to extracommunity systems give local community units access to resources and sanctions which may be relatively independent of other local community units, and often subject them to constraints which are determined by extracommunity systems. Both of these aspects quite plausibly operate to fragmentalize the community power structure. In doing so, they may also fragmentalize the community's "normative expectations," all depending on what this term means. But it is the existence of independent sources of resources and sanctions, and of independent constraints,

which fragmentalizes the community power structure—not the fragmentalizing of the community's normative structure as such.

Hence, in my judgment, the concept of fragmentation of normative structure should either be abandoned or clarified. Incidentally, the work of Levine and his associates lends both data and analysis which support this thesis. Their analysis of the health field indicates among other things that those health agencies which are least dependent upon other local community agencies for their necessary resources are least likely to collaborate with them.[1]

But let us examine briefly some of the substantive implications of the thesis which Walton presents, for in acknowledging the above difficulties I do not mean to minimize either the brilliance of the analysis, the plausibility of the theoretical aspects, or the importance of the assertion.

Some time ago, I presented a seminar of graduate students with three values, or desiderata, which appear frequently in the literature of those who participate in community development as a social movement. These three values are: (1) Community autonomy (the community is master of its own fate), (2) Community viability (the community is capable of confronting its problems and making decisions and taking appropriate action) and (3) Citizen participation (there is broad participation in community organizations and in decision-making on community matters).

The assignment was to take, abstractly, a city of some 100,000 people in the continental United States, with a surrounding fringe population of perhaps another 100,000. What would a community of this size look like, in its social structure and behavior, which maximized these three values which are so often championed by "community-development" advocates? The students worked in three subgroups, each sketching out the implications for such a community of the maximization of *one* of these three values. In a subsequent plenary session, as each group reported and a general discussion ensued, two things became strikingly apparent.

The first was that each value could be maximized only at a price (in terms of the jeopardization of other values) which most communities would probably find excessive.

The second was that these three values could not be maximized simultaneously, for beyond a certain threshold they impeded each other. This was especially the case with viability and autonomy. One can be approximated only at increasing costs to the other.

Walton's thesis is of great substantive importance in this respect. For it implies that you must take your choice between autonomy and a democratic fragmentation of power structures. Those communities which are most autonomous are the most monolithic in their power structures. Those communities which are the least autonomous are the most pluralistic in their power structures. Thus, two different expectations or value aspirations for the "good" community in the eyes of many community-development advocates are found to be incompatible. One must therefore choose. Which do you want: Community autonomy at the sacrifice of broad distribution of power? or a democratically broad distribution of community power at the sacrifice of autonomy?

In this connection, a friend and colleague of mine was recently engaged in developing a series of seminars in a fairly large metropolis, in which his explicit goal was to bring together top leadership from different segments of community interests and organizations so that they could jointly confront community problems at a more inclusive level. I asked him whether, inadvertently, he was not trying to convert a pluralistic power structure into a monolithic one, and how he could be sure that the community would benefit by the concerted decision-making and action he hoped to further, rather than be harmed by it. The works of

political scientists such as Banfield and economists such as Lindblom make a strong case for a plurality of decision-making centers at the community level. Likewise, sociologists have indicated an implicit value preference for pluralistic power structures, without being so analytically specific as to the fact that they are making this judgment and the reasons why they make it.[2]

My friend responded by stating that his effort would not be justifiable if it were not accompanied by an equal stress on community-wide values, as opposed to the selfish values of this or that particular power group. Yet works such as *Political Influence* and the *Intelligence of Democracy* make a strong case that the community's inclusive interests are furthered by a fragmented power structure rather than by a monolithic one (although Banfield, especially, acknowledges that there may be a plausible justification for centralized decision-making, and even enumerates situations in which the juxtaposition of opposing power centers may produce an inferior aggregate utility as compared to a unified decision-making context).[3]

It is somewhat ironic that many of us tend to criticize the advocates of decentralization, of "market choice" as opposed to centralized planning, as somehow being nineteenth-century characters who do not adequately appreciate the obvious desirability of centralized planning, while at the same time we continue to make an implicit and largely unexamined value judgment against the very monolithic power structures which are empirical examples of centralized planning.

In the immediately preceding remarks, it is quite apparent that many of the terms are being used in ambiguous senses, and that their full implications have not been precisely delineated. All the more reason why we should welcome the kind of coldly analytical study which Walton has produced, especially since his findings are so imbued with implications for social theory and social policy.

For THE PAST two decades, emphasis has been placed on defense contracting in the United States as a means of meeting our military and aerospace requirements. While many citizens have tended to relate defense contracting only to national and international issues, there are those who are concerned with its impact on local communities. These people recognize that the implementation of defense contracting may cause a community to undergo considerable transformation. The changes are often rapid and jarring, and the communities which have experienced this phenomenon have become aware, often too late, that government contracting has great significance and consequence for them.

Defense Contracting and Community Leadership: A Comparative Analysis*

Phillip Edward Present

San Fernando Valley State College

The Problem

Social scientists have recorded and analyzed some of the general reactions of local communities to the sudden introduction of government spending and activity.[1] A more specific type of investigation, however, was conducted by the author in 1966. An attempt was made to treat defense contracting as both an independent and a dependent variable with respect to local community political systems in order to examine the relationship between defense contracting and two local communities in Southern California.[2] Other studies have related community politics and economics,[3] but by isolating defense contracting as a specific variable, a particular set of questions and hypotheses was developed which could be used to explain in more detail the relationship between politics and economics within a community setting.

This article will report on one aspect of the larger study: the relationship between defense contracting and community leadership structures. Certain basic questions arose which needed to be answered concerning leaders, politics and economics in a defense-oriented community political

system. For example, in what ways do defense activities influence the growth, decline or change in the community leadership structures? Conversely, how do local leaders and their policies influence the growth, decline or change in defense contracting activities?

These general questions and the subsequent investigation suggested the following hypotheses:

1. The greater the dependence of a community on government defense contracting, the greater the probability that a specific group in the community will be formed to cope with this dependency.

2. The more rapid the impact of defense contracting upon the community, the more rapidly will there occur a change in the overall leadership structure of the community.

3. The greater the dependence of a community on defense contracting, the greater the probability the community and its leaders will be in agreement on community policies relating to defense contracting.

4. The greater the dependence of a community on defense contracting, the more cohesive the community's leadership will be.[4]

Because of limited time and resources, these hypotheses could not be rigorously

* Reprinted with permission of the author and publisher, from Phillip Edward Present, "Defense Contracting and Community Leadership: A Comparative Analysis," (Southwestern) Social Science Quarterly, 48 (December 1967), pp. 399–410.

201

Notes to this selection will be found on page 355.

tested. Rather, they provided the basis for a comparative study of the two local communities by suggesting possible causal relationships. Through the use of hypotheses which indicate cause and effect, researchers can make comparative studies which may lead beyond case studies to general explanatory theories about political phenomena. Even though the conclusions from this study are tentative at this time, they may provide some insights and explanations for various relationships found within local community political systems.

Methodology

Over a period of five months, interviews and other field research were conducted in the two communities and the surrounding areas. To identify community leaders in general and those leaders connected with defense contracting issues in particular, three methods of leadership identification were used. Initially, the positional approach was employed to quickly indicate the individuals who held the key public offices in the communities, such as the mayor, council members, and other civic leaders.

Because of the limitations of the positional approach, the next step was to use a reputational approach. Eight community "informants" were chosen from individuals who had resided in the area during the time under study, and who would have been in a position to observe and to know the inner-workings of the contracting process. Among the informants were a social science professor from the local college, the business managers from the chambers of commerce, and a newspaper editor from one of the local papers. Separately, each of the eight informants offered names and rankings (in most cases) of individuals considered to be influential in both community and contracting issues. By cross checking names, plus using information obtained from other interviews, it was possible to construct lists of the most frequently mentioned names for the two communities, the area, and the contracting issues.

A final method of identification was to examine specific issues connected with defense contracting in order to determine who the individuals were that played a part in the decision-making process. In some cases, the activities of already identified individuals were traced, while at other times, events were examined to see which persons were associated with these events. A cross check of these findings revealed a pattern of names which suggested frequency of personal associations and connections with defense contracting issues.

The use of these three methods tended to increase the validity and reliability of the findings on the community leaders. An examination of influence was made on the basis of position, reputation and issue-events, and from this, a final list of leaders was drawn up. Interviews were then held with these people for further information about their roles and relationships to the contracting process.

Two methodological difficulties encountered should be mentioned for they provide background information on the communities, their leaders and the findings. There was a reluctance by many community residents to name or discuss the influential members of the communities even though the respondents were assured of anonymity. There was also a reticence to speak openly about most contrasting issues, especially about the degree of dependence of the communities upon defense contracting.[5] Three reasons for this attitude can be advanced. First, both communities have a small, homogeneous population with close personal relationships within the leadership structures. Second, a political sensitivity surrounds defense contracting activities. The respondents were cautious to avoid criticizing or offending any person or group that might be of assistance to the communities in their efforts to resolve the problems created by defense contracting. Finally, the respondents apparently wished to convey the idea that the communities were no longer as closely tied economically to contracting as they once were although at times the evidence indicated the contrary.

A second general methodological difficulty stemmed from the fact that one of the communities was unincorporated and had no precise boundaries for a clear delineation of its labor market and economic activity. Often there was a lack of readily available data, as statistical information was usually grouped into figures for the entire area. In order to make comparable studies, it was necessary to cull from the aggregate tables the specific data for each community.

This study also required the measurement of the terms "dependence" and "cohesion." "Dependence" upon defense contracting by the communities referred to the extent to which defense contracting influenced the economy or conditioned the activities of the communities. To make an operational definition for "dependence," the following economic variables were used: the per cent of residents employed in defense contracting work; the number and types of businesses and industries within each community; and the amount of payroll generated by defense contracts within each community.

"Leadership structure" was considered to be the identifiable network of relationships among the influential members connected with an issue, or a geographic area.

The "cohesiveness" of the leadership structures was measured by the degree of unity of purpose on community policies held by the community leaders, the incidence of activity by the same community leaders on different community projects, and the extent of overlapping membership in community groups by the community leaders.

The Setting

The two neighboring communities studied are called Elmwood and Centerville and are located in the Southern California area known as Belhaven Valley.[6] The incorporated city of Elmwood has a population of 10,000 while unincorporated Centerville consists of approximately 30,000 residents. The valley contains about 120,000 people. It has remained relatively isolated from the Los Angeles metropolitan area, and as a result, Belhaven has developed primarily as a self-contained economic unit. The introduction of defense contracting

has been the only major economic force upon Belhaven and the two communities during the past seventeen years. Because of the area's isolation and the absence of other economic influences, the researcher is better able to measure precisely the effect of this defense contracting.

Both Elmwood and Centerville, and most of the valley, are economically dependent either directly or indirectly upon companies and industries doing defense contract work for the government in the military and aerospace fields. The work force of the valley numbers about 37,000. About 40 per cent of all employed residents in Belhaven are on payrolls dependent upon defense contracting. Using a 1 : 1 ratio, another 40 per cent of the labor force can be assumed to be employed in non-basic activities indirectly supported by the basic industry. This means that from 40 to 80 per cent of the labor force and their families in Belhaven Valley are dependent in varying degrees upon defense contracting employment.

There are two major centers of defense employment in the valley. DeLong Air Force Base, located thirty miles north of the two communities, has about 12,000 military and civilian employees. The second defense installation is the Air Force Facility in Elmwood. This employs around 3,000 people. In both cases, approximately 75 per cent of the employees are civilian.

Of the two communities, Elmwood is more dependent upon defense contracting than is Centerville for employment and general economic support. The primary reason is that Elmwood is much more closely tied to the Air Force Facility than is Centerville to either of the two defense installations. Of Elmwood's total work force of approximately 3,000, about 40 per cent are employed at the Facility, with an additional 10 to 15 per cent employed at DeLong Air Force Base.

On the other hand, no more than about 30 per cent of Centerville's total work force is employed directly at either the Air Force base or the Facility. It is significant that more of these residents are employed at DeLong Air Force Base which has a record of being a more stable employer. The base is engaged in long-range space and military programs which have been subject to fewer Congressional and Pentagon cancellations than those programs carried out at the Facility. In short, Centerville has fewer of its residents engaged in defense employment than Elmwood, and those who are are generally in more stable jobs. Elmwood is tied more closely to a particular installation which by its function is subject to more economic fluctuations.

Another distinction between the two communities should be noted. Centerville is the primary retail and commercial center for the entire Belhaven Valley. For example, the largest stores, some of which are part of national chains, and the automobile franchises for most of the Valley are found in Centerville. In contrast, Elmwood has only small, local merchants, and many of its residents prefer to shop in the larger community. Centerville also has a greater number and variety of businesses and services than Elmwood, including a significant agricultural base. All of these factors tend to make Centerville more diversified and less dependent economically on a single industry than is Elmwood. This is not to minimize Centerville's relationship to defense contracting, but by comparison, it is less dependent than Elmwood.

The first time Elmwood and Centerville became connected with defense contracts was at the beginning of the Korean conflict in 1950. With the entrance of the United States into the fighting, there was an urgent demand for additional aircraft. Belhaven Valley possessed ample land, air space and favorable weather for the testing of planes, while Elmwood had an airport which could be made suitable for final assembly of airplanes. The Air Force bought the airport, redesignated it as the Air Force Facility, and leased it to four contractors.

There was an immediate influx of skilled and unskilled labor with their families into Elmwood and the surrounding area. Building construction and air-frame manufacturing became the dominant economic activities replacing agriculture. After the Korean armistice in August of 1953, the demand for aircraft and the use of the Facility continued, and the entire area prospered from 1950 to 1957. Then, abruptly, the boom halted.

In the closing months of 1957, the United States began to shift its military strategy and emphasis from manned bombers to missiles. As a result, government contracts for the construction of airplanes were cancelled or drastically reduced. The airplane manufacturers either moved their Elmwood operations to other sites where rocket and missile developments were being established or they shutdown their local plants. Employment at the Facility was cut in half—by about 3,000 employees—within the first six months of 1958. Additional layoffs soon followed.

The economic situation remained extremely critical for the entire valley until 1961 when a new contract for a supersonic bomber was in progress. Two years later this contract was cancelled and the area received another setback. This jolt, however, was less severe than the one in 1957. Since 1963, the communities and the valley have been able to establish a more stable and diversified economy, although defense contracts are still the primary basis for the economy of the area. DeLong Air Force Base has provided much of the contract stability to the area the past few years while the valley has been attempting to diversify. A great deal of the economic stabilization and diversification which have resulted since 1957 can be attributed to the community and valley leaders.

The Findings

The leadership structures of Elmwood and Centerville were found each to be composed of two to five top influentials with a layer of subleaders exerting lesser control. In terms of the models suggested by Form and Miller, the leadership structures of the two communities are characterized by a "stratified pyramidical structure centering in a top group of policy-makers."[7]

Centerville, however, has a more diffused leadership structure, especially in the sub-leader layer. This can be attributed to three factors. First, Centerville, unlike Elmwood, is unincorporated and has no local government of its own. There is less opportunity therefore, for a visible leadership structure to exist and to be recognized. Second, Centerville has been concerned with a greater number of community issues than Elmwood because it has been historically a relatively more diversified community. This has provided, therefore, more opportunities for leadership openings.

A third reason is related to both the size of the communities and the defense contracting environment. Fewer people in Elmwood are able to participate in community affairs because the pool of potential leaders is considerably smaller. Elmwood has about one-third the population of Centerville, but size alone does not explain the difference. Rather, individuals employed by companies doing defense contracting work find it difficult to establish themselves in a community either because they are constantly subject to transfers to other areas or they are prevented by company or agency policy from participating in political or controversial community programs.[8] As a result, the number of residents in Elmwood that might normally be leaders is significantly reduced. Based upon their educational, social and economic characteristics, these individuals would be expected to be more active than they are.

In addition to the community leadership structures, a separate leadership group was identified for defense contracting issues. This was accomplished by using the issue-event approach mentioned previously in the section on methodology. This group consisted of six to ten leaders of the Belhaven Valley Development Association (BVDA), a group formed in 1957 to deal specifically with the economic crisis. Since then, the BVDA has been instrumental in alleviating some of the valley's economic problems related to defense contracting.

Significantly, this group consists of individuals from the entire valley and not

just from Elmwood and Centerville. Those individuals most often cited as being active in defense contracting issues were invariably identified as valley leaders as well. In contrast, only two or three individuals were recognized as working on the contracting problem exclusively for one of the two communities.

The emergence since 1957 of the BVDA to handle problems related to defense contracting has had a profound effect on community leadership. Initially, the communities fought many of the suggestions of the valley group for it was felt local interests would suffer. Eventually, the communities and their leaders saw the advantage in terms of resources and strategies of thinking and working as a group of valley residents rather than as individuals. With limited resources, Elmwood's leaders realized that there was little their community could do by itself to prevent economic disruption every few years.

Hypotheses

1. The findings did not confirm what might have been expected. Elmwood, with its greater dependence on defense contracting, did not initially form a group specifically to handle defense problems. In the crucial 1957 period, the residents of Elmwood were apparently no more inclined to take organized steps to solve mounting economic problems than the people in Centerville. Only after the BVDA was operating and initiating programs did Elmwood form a local group. For the most part, the community group's role has remained secondary to the BVDA. It appears, therefore, that factors other than the degree of economic dependency will determine whether a community will form a special group for its defense contracting problems. Reasons why Elmwood did not immediately form a group can be traced to the community's size, the nature of its

existing leadership structure, and the resources of the community. At least until the time of the economic crisis in 1957, most of the economic and business developers of the valley resided in Centerville. Generally they thought in terms of Belhaven rather than a specific community, especially Elmwood. This attitude, coupled with the much smaller number of potential leaders in absolute and relative terms for Elmwood to draw upon, accounts for its inability to establish a dynamic group to meet the challenges brought on by defense contracting.

2. A comparison of Elmwood and Centerville tends to support this hypothesis. The former community did experience a more rapid change in its overall leadership structure as a result of the impact of defense contracting. As Elmwood became more involved with a defense contracting environment, new demands were made upon its leaders. Generally, one of two reactions occurred: either the leaders were unable or unwilling to handle the new types of community problems and they were replaced, or the community issues related to defense contracting multiplied so rapidly that it became necessary to increase the size of the leadership structures. The net result was about the same: a change in the composition of the structures. Elmwood replaced more of its leaders as the size of the structure increased, while Centerville retained more of the existing leaders as it added to their number.

Of the two communities, Elmwood underwent a greater and more rapid change in the nature and composition of its leadership structure than did Centerville during the years 1954–1960. Before the 1957 economic decline, Elmwood, then unincorporated, was governed informally through its Chamber of Commerce composed mainly of small retail merchants. These tended to resist the community changes resulting from the influx of new residents. As the community grew, it became evident that additional services such as schools, utilities, recreation, sewers and streets were needed and that revenues would have to be raised to pay for these. The traditional leaders of Elmwood refused to move in the direction of higher taxes and additional services. When conditions became critical, other citizens became active in the Chamber. These people wanted Elmwood to change with the times and were willing to pay for the change. Eventually, by 1960, the former leadership structure had been replaced by the new group and Elmwood has taken a different approach to its problems since then.

Centerville also saw the emergence of new leaders during this period, but there were significant reasons for the differences in the rate and degree of turnover in the leadership structure. Because of Centerville's historical importance in the valley as the trading and commercial center, it had attracted most of the founding families of Belhaven as residents. Long-established families were more prevalent in Centerville than in Elmwood. In contrast to the traditional leaders in Elmwood, those in Centerville were firmly rooted in community positions by virtue of their length of residence and economic control.

Another difference between the two communities' leaders should be noted. There was not the attempt in Centerville to replace the traditional leaders as there was in Elmwood. This was not necessary for two reasons. First, the number of leadership positions in the community expanded enabling the leadership structure to absorb new leaders. Second, the traditional leaders of Centerville were more flexible and more willing to accept or to initiate changes than were their counterparts in Elmwood. Their economic investments were more secure whether the community grew or remained the same. If Centerville expanded, it would yield them huge profits through their landholdings; if the community remained static, it still would be the commercial center of the valley. They were, therefore, in a more favorable position to accept either outcome.

In addition to the general replacement or increase in the number of individuals within the leadership structures, there also has been an improvement in the caliber of leaders. The present leaders, when compared to their predecessors, are perceived by defense contractors and other government officials to be more knowledgeable about economic, social and political problems and the means available to solve these. Because of the increasing complexity of the issues facing the communities, the most able individuals are sought and recruited into the leadership structures. Before defense contracting activity began in the valley, there was much less active recruitment of individuals with any kind of technical, military or governmental background.

3. The leaders of Elmwood are more in agreement on matters relating to contracting than are the leaders in Centerville. Thus, this hypothesis was tentatively confirmed. The reason appears to stem from the limited number of alternatives open to the former community. Practically all the community's leadership efforts are concerned in some way with government defense contracting. On one hand, attempts are made to ensure that Elmwood and the Air Force Facility obtain all the defense contracts they can. Yet, at the same time, every effort is being made to diversify the economy and to move Elmwood away from a one-industry relationship.

In contrast, Centerville's leaders are more divided on the kind of community they want to see developed and the kinds of issues they wish to emphasize. Some leaders want no further connection with defense contracting activities. Others, however, believe that Centerville can afford additional defense activity without danger to the overall well-being of the community. The data suggest there is some direct relationship between the degree of community dependency upon defense contracting and the amount of agreement among community leaders concerning contracting policies. In the case of Elmwood, little choice is left to the leaders except to diversify. For Centerville, there is room for debate on the question of the kind of community and its economic base that ought to be encouraged.

4. There appeared to be some relationship

between dependency and leadership cohesiveness although this hypothesis can only be tentatively confirmed at this time. Cohesiveness in both community leadership structures can be attributed to the geographic isolation and the common bond and experience of having faced economic disruption. Other reasons for the differences in the cohesiveness of the two community structures have already been given. These included the size and the homogeneity of the structures. Yet, despite these variables which do influence the nature of the leadership structures, it does appear that defense contracting itself creates a more cohesive structure in Elmwood than in Centerville. This is due to the reduction of alternative policies available to the leaders (noted in Hypothesis Three), and to the need to provide a favorable business climate to attract new industries. Elmwood discovered that it was essential to avoid community splits which could disrupt normal business activities. This had happened in the early stages of the 1957 crisis. The community leadership, it was found, must appear to be united and to speak for the entire community when confronting business or other governmental officials in discussions on contracting issues. Apparent dissention among community leaders does not induce businesses to settle and it weakens the pressure on other governmental officials to follow through on needed programs. For these reasons, it is suggested that the defense contracting environment has a direct influence upon the cohesiveness of community leadership structures.

Conclusions

The findings suggest that the defense contracting environment caused changes in the composition, size and rate of turnover in the leadership structures examined. Because of the relative geographic isolation of the communities, and because of the sudden introduction of new economic activity as a result of defense contracting, it appears that no intervening variables accounted for the events and conditions described. The analysis of two communities divorced from the economic influence of other areas enables the researchers to examine more precisely the influence of economic variables, such as defense contracting, within the communities.

Defense contracting also precipitated the creation of a new leadership structure to cope with related contracting issues. Barth indicated the impact community growth has on issues which then in turn influence community leadership systems and the distribution of power: "A rapid rate of urban growth is associated with a rapid increase in the number of issues facing community leaders and also with the complexity of these issues. At the same time, the expansion produces new positions of influence and new sources of power."[9] The relationships observed by Barth were very similar to the ones studied in the two communities. Elmwood and Centerville have each experienced marked increases in population. Both communities, particularly Centerville, have been required to increase the size of their leadership groups in order to meet the newer and more complex demands resulting from changes in economic activity within the communities.

The people coming into Elmwood and Centerville because of defense employment tended to bring with them a more cosmopolitan view of life than existed in the valley before. They were often upper managerial and ranking military officers who did not wish to be suddenly isolated culturally and socially from the type of life they knew in other communities. These new residents expected—as did their employers —that there would be living conditions reasonably comparable to those found in large cities. Demands were made for increased educational, recreational and cultural facilities. The people wanted these activities in Belhaven and not many miles away in other areas. Because of these demands and the need to attract additional business and industry into the valley, it became necessary for the communities to establish problem-solving mechanisms such as local community groups and committees.

To do this, the community leaders were required to work more actively than before in the larger political process. Contact was made with all levels of government, for in many instances the communities could not solve their problems alone. The leaders' knowledge of issues and techniques had to increase in order for them to be competitive with other communities with similar goals. As one congressional administrative assistant observed, there is a growing "maturity" in the actions of leaders in the valley. They are more "politically alert and organized" than they were before 1958 when dealing with issues concerned with defense contracting. These changes in the modes of operation by the community leaders, it is believed, can be traced primarily to the initial and continuing impact of defense contracting activities, for without defense contracting there might have been very little reason for the community leaders to have as frequent contact as they have had with county, state and national officials.

The findings also suggest that the leadership structure functions as an adjustment mechanism for a community. This mechanism must reflect and adapt to its changing environment if it is to remain vital and dynamic. The community leaders in this study were able to control and direct some of the political, economic and social activities related to defense contracting, but the leaders also had to be able to react and to adjust to events over which they had little or no control.

Further questions remain to be answered about leadership structures in defense-oriented communities. What are the essential characteristics needed for effective community leaders in defense environments? What is the role of social backgrounds, previous training and experience? Other questions might relate community political institutions and leaders. For example, are certain kinds of political arrangements more effective in promoting community stability?

This examination of community leaders and defense contracting has suggested the interdependence of politics and economics in two contract-oriented communities. While some of the conclusions and explanations are only tentative at this time, it is believed that a relationship between the influence of defense contracting and community leadership structures was shown to exist. Additional research might measure more precisely the strength of the relationship, but because of the relative geographic isolation and the freedom from other

external economic forces in the communities, some indication was noted of the probable effect that defense contracting has on community leadership structures. It is hoped that the hypotheses and findings presented here can be used as a guideline for future investigation in order to understand more completely the interrelationship between the consequences of defense contracting and the dynamics of community politics.

Some Trends in Community Politics: A Secondary Analysis of Power Structure Data from 166 Communities[*][1]

Claire W. Gilbert

Florida Atlantic University

THE ONE FIRM generalization emerging from a review of the community power and local politics literature is that scholars have been unable to agree on interpretations of research and theory.[2] The purpose of this article is to attempt to find some order among the data presented by others by comparing the findings of studies conducted before 1944 and 1954 with the findings of studies conducted after these dates.[3] Given the assumption that changes in local political structure and function may be a consequence of societal changes, then time itself—and consequently trends or changes over time—may be a variable largely overlooked in the study of community power. This paper is based on a larger study, the underlying assumption of which was that generalizations could be formulated from and hypotheses could be tested with data gathered by means of inventorying existing knowledge.

Conceptualization

The term *community power* is used here as a blanket or umbrella concept:[4] community

* *Reprinted with permission of the author and publisher, from Claire W. Gilbert, "Some Trends in Community Politics: A Secondary Analysis of Power Structure Data from 166 Communities,"* (Southwestern) Social Science Quarterly, *48* (*December 1967*), *pp. 373–381.*

power refers to political processes, decision-making on the local level and many related phenomena. No assumptions are made about the stability or integration of any power structure. In other words, *structure* is regarded as a variable (or as made up of several variables). It may be used to identify four conceptual dimensions of community power:

1. The political organization involving party structures, councils, departments, elected and appointed officials, government employees, and experts.

2. The parapolitical[5] organizations which include businesses, newspapers, and religious, educational, voluntary, and formal organizations, and all of their leaders.

3. Informal organizations, including *ad hoc* groups formed around particular issues, and their leaders.

4. The population of the city in terms of masses, minorities, economic classes, publics, and voters.

These dimensions of power structure may be related to or may be a consequence of underlying variables of the following types:

1. Theorists such as Wirth suggest social variations among cities which differ in any of the following ways: industrial makeup, location in a metropolitan region, age, national region, growth characteristics, size, density, and functional type.[6]

2. Political theorists tend to stress the importance of the local constitutional form: ward or at-large elections, partisan or nonpartisan elections, council or commission form of local government, and presence or absence of a city manager.[7]

3. Theorists such as Durkheim, Mills, and Shevky and Bell indicate that the temporal dimension is important because national changes are reflected in local communities.[8]

It is the temporal dimension, of course, that is the focus here.

Notes to this selection will be found on page 356.

Trends

Some Trends in Community 211
Politics: A Secondary Analysis
of Power Structure Data from
166 Communities
Claire W. Gilbert

Social theorists agree that the scale of the United States is increasing: i.e., there is greater functional interdependence between and among local communities than before.[9] Rather than finding all or most human communities in the United States homogeneous, we find them differentiated from each other in an ever-increasing myriad of ways—along economic, social, educational, normative, and other lines. Differences include growth rates and population sizes. Some communities are highly specialized, some are diversified, and some contain both large numbers of specialities and are diversified along any of the several objective dimensions mentioned (or other dimensions, or many dimensions). There is increasing consolidation of business enterprises as manifested in increasing disappearance of local firms and an increasing proportion of nationally (or internationally) owned economic enterprises. Many functions of government are increasingly carried out on federal levels. Communications are also increasingly concentrated and have wider spans of influence. Along with these and other changes, it is fair to expect that people today hold different ideas from their forebears regarding local politics.

Taking as given the increasing societal differentiation and functional interdependence, we can then ask what are some of the concomitant changes that can be expected in community power structures? In attempting to answer this question, we begin by taking generalizations from 166 community power studies dating from 1900 and subjecting them to a comparative analysis from which we will draw conclusions regarding the existence of trends or changes in community power structures and the nature of these trends.

FUNCTION OF LOCAL GOVERNMENT

Political scientists call our attention to the function of local government and have distinguished between two functions or orientations: *political* and *"good" government*.[10] Where the former is dominant, government is seen as mediating conflict between various interests in the community.

Cities characterized by the political orientation tend to have partisan elections, ward electoral structure, and political machines. All of the above-mentioned characteristics are thought to be congenial to the "self-serving" immigrant, ethnic, or working-class ideal—and to machine style, conflict-oriented politics. The "good" government function stresses businesslike efficiency, absence of graft and "corruption," and often assumes that no conflicts of interest exist in the community. Good government cities tend to have nonpartisan and at-large electoral procedures and a manager form of government. These characteristics are considered as conducive to the "public-serving" interests of the Protestant Anglo-Saxon or middle-class ideal.[11]

Of the cities analyzed here, one-fourth were classified as having a mixture of both functions, fewer than one-fourth as having a political function (conflict orientation), and slightly more than one-half as having a good government function.

Banfield and Wilson have noted a general trend away from the machine-style ethos as a result of changes in the social-class composition of the urban electorate. Increasingly, rule is by the "qualified" rather than by the "politicians." Although the population holding Anglo-Saxon Protestant values is increasing in the fringe areas of cities, and although central cities remain homes for the "immigrants," the Protestant values are nevertheless expected to prevail because state and federal governments take patronage away from the central cities—thereby undermining machine politics.[12]

THE SHAPE OF POWER STRUCTURE

The structure of political control is expected to change also because the functional relationship of the community to the larger society has changed. On the basis of the work of Booth and Adrian, and Schulze, one would expect that the communities involved most extensively in the larger economic, social, and ecological systems are becoming more pluralistic in structure.[13] Communities with few commitments beyond their borders are becoming rare; thus one would expect a decrease in simple power structures that are quite concentrated (such as an elite or a single pyramid of power). Though evidence will be shown to support these notions, it should be pointed out that some of the most "pluralistic" contemporary cities are so diffuse or fragmented that in order to get things done, a chieftain arises who is capable of pulling together (for some purposes) all of the disparate elements or interest groups. The overall pattern of such a structure might resemble a "pyramid" or an "elite" but is quite different in process from what these terms usually connote.

CONFLICT

Another change in power structure concerns their levels of conflict or abilities to manage conflict when it arises. Potential conflict may be increasing in at least some cities because of sharper differentiation along many lines among their populations. In addition, the spread of the middle-class ideal and turning away from conflict orientations may reduce the ability of local governments to manage conflict. On the other hand, the spread of the middle-class ideal may also reduce the amount of conflict requiring management, because the value of particular issues—not generalized class antagonisms—would be under consideration: "The ideal includes willingness to settle matters on the basis of reasonable discussion and to make sacrifices of immediate and private interest for the sake of the longer-run 'larger good of the community as a whole'."[14]

TOP LEADERSHIP

With increasing urbanization and fragmentation, it might be expected that economic leaders are withdrawing from their former political activities.[15] The idea that political bosses are on the decline has also been suggested.[16] The juxtaposing of the two foregoing statements creates a conceptual dilemma for two reasons: (1) a long-standing polemic has revolved around the question of whether it is really the economic elites or the officials who "run" things and (2) if you grant that the type of leader who controls policy (to the extent anyone does control policy) varies from community to community, it has still been traditionally either the officials or the business elites who predominate. Now, it is plausible to believe that both types of leaders are declining in importance. The examination of data here sheds some light on this problem.

ASSOCIATIONS AND INSTITUTIONS

Banfield and Wilson predict that civic leaders, paid executives of associations, and the press are increasing in influence. (For coding purposes, newspapers are classified with businesses, schools, churches, and voluntary associations as "community institutions or organizations.") The institutions mentioned speak for, or claim to speak for, the public interest and their claim is founded on their expertise with regard to "objective facts."[17]

EXPERTS

Due to the spread of the middle-class ideal, politicians may try to appear as detached and impartial "experts." Yet the professionals, such as city managers, are expected to be drawn more frequently into politics as opposed to administration.[18] Perhaps the experts, the associations, and the professionals will take up the void in the power structures which will occur if political bosses *and* dominant businessmen are reduced in influence.

Hypotheses

The trends suggested above can be summarized as hypotheses, to be tested below:

1. "Good" governments have proportionately increased.

2. Power structures have become more pluralistic.

3. Community conflict has increased because of increased divisions—*or* it has

decreased because of the spread of the conciliatory middle-class ideal.

4. Political bosses and economic dominants have decreased as important community power leaders.

5. Community institutions and organizations have increased in importance.

6. Experts have become increasingly important in the local political process.

Method

From 166 cities, data were obtained for the current inquiry. This was done by a secondary analysis of community power studies. Sometimes data in the original work were incomplete for the purposes outlined above, or they were unclear. Therefore, the number of cases for any particular attribute studied is less than 166.

Cities were not really sampled. The research design was intended to be exhaustive of all published works on local power structures within political units defined as cities, towns, or villages (rather than wards, counties, states, school districts, etc.). For impressionistic reasons, it was further decided to exclude studies of cities in Mexico, England, Japan, Italy, India, and other nations because it was believed that "culture" might introduce an uncontrollable variable within the framework of the inquiry.[19] When coding was completed, it was noted that forty-six states were included and cities with larger population concentrations were over-represented, although the range includes villages of fewer than 1,000 inhabitants as well as great central cities of over 1,000,000. The sample, development of the content analysis coding schedule, measures of concepts, interrelations of measures, estimates of validity, reliability, and replicability, are discussed in detail.[20]

Since scholars do not agree on the validity of community power research, one may wonder how it is possible to learn about communities using data based on "doubtful" sources. Naroll developed data quality control to deal with a similar problem.[21]

Some Trends in Community Politics: A Secondary Analysis of Power Structure Data from 166 Communities
Claire W. Gilbert

His basic theory is applied to data here in order to lend assurance that the current findings are "real" and not simply the correlated errors of previous research. For example, several controls are used in regard to methods of investigation used in the 166 studies surveyed. Thus it is unlikely that the findings reported below represent trends in the *study* of community politics rather than changes in the political structure and activities themselves. Controls are also used in regard to coder bias. Where systematic distortion (measurement error) exists, a flag (so to speak) is attached to the probability value to indicate this.

Findings

Table 1 summarizes the relevant findings:

1. Cities appear to be decreasingly oriented toward the political function of government. It would, however, be fairer to say that cities that were formerly oriented to machine politics are adding good government to their functions.

2. There is very strong evidence that political processes are tending to be more pluralistic. Though only one measure is included in the table, several measures were included in the larger investigation—all obtained the same results.

3. Data show no relationship between conflict and the time-dimension. It is plausible to interpret this finding as an indication of tendencies in the society which push toward increased conflict but are mitigated by other factors which tend to minimize conflict, thus erasing any measurable effects of time.[22]

4. Structures are decreasingly headed by officials, but an increasingly large proportion of cities have economic dominants as upper-level power leaders. An interpretation of the increase of economic dominants

TABLE 1.   Trends in Community Politics ‖

Political Characteristics	Cities in the Year: 1944 or Earlier		1945 and Later	Cities in the Year: 1954 or Earlier		1955 and Later
76.* Local Government Is Oriented toward:						
1. Good government, or mixed good government and machine politics	61%		85%	70%		86%
2. Machine politics	39%	P = .008‡	15%	30%	P = .034	14%
	N = 36		N = 91	N = 63		N = 64
85. Decision-Making Structure Is:						
1. Least pluralistic†	90%		56%	72%		57%
2. Most pluralistic	10%	P = .000	44%	28%	P = .068	43%
	N = 39		N = 117	N = 81		N = 75
102. Structure Is Headed By:						
1. Officials	54%		28%	43%		25%
2. Nonofficials or officials and nonofficials	46%	P = .006§	72%	57%	P = .026§	75%
	N = 39		N = 111	N = 79		N = 71
105. Upper-Level Power Leaders Are:						
1. Economic dominants	13%		28%			
2. Politicians and/or other than economic dominants	87%	P = .080§	72%			
	N = 38		N = 102			
106. Upper-Level Power Leaders Are:						
1. From all sectors or pressure groups and aldermanic blocs	00%		08%			
2. Other than from all sectors or pressure groups and aldermanic blocs	100%	P = .116	92%			
	N = 38		N = 102			
124. Innovation Comes From:						
1. Informals, *ad hoc* groups, or varying sources depending on the issues	31%		55%	38%		57%
2. Experts, the city council, or organizations and pressure groups who may work through government and voters	69%	P = .032	45%	62%	P = .059‡	43%
	N = 29		N = 84	N = 52		N = 61
125. Innovation Is Enforced by:						
1. Government officials and their agencies	66%		38%			
2. Pressure groups, the electorate, informals, or various segments depending on issues	34%	P = .012‡	62%			
	N = 32		N = 84			

* Attribute number is given for each dichotomy for the purpose of cross-reference to the other work of the author.
† *Least pluralistic* refers to a single or multi-pyramidal or fractional structure. *Most pluralistic* refers to fluid group alliances or a variable structure which fluctuates with issues. Eight additional measures of power structure have been evaluated. All of them show differences along the 1944/1945 split and all but two show these for the 1954/1955 split even when measurement biases are evaluated.
‡ Data are biased systematically on both measures here.
§ Measures share systematic biases. When one data quality control factor is held constant, the relationship continues to hold.
‖ P-values are from Fisher's Exact Test of Probability, two-tailed.

is that it reflects changes in smaller communities that are dominated by a few industries. Table 1 also shows that since the end of World War II, 8 per cent of the cities have leadership composed of representation from *all* sectors within the city *or* from pressure groups and aldermanic blocs —a phenomenon not noted prior to 1945. Seven of these cities (of a total of eight) are metropolitan central cities.

Data also show that, while politicians tend less to be the sole figures dominating politics, it is rare today to find a city where politicians and their parties are totally emasculated. That is, in earlier decades, it was possible to find more towns that were run by informal processes in which control by politicians and/or political parties was *totally absent*. (These data are not presented here.)

5. The importance of associations and institutions in shaping local policy shows no difference over time.

6. No trend appears for policy to be increasingly recommended by experts. However, two related measures in Table 1 show that a larger percentage of cities have innovative policies as a result of the activities of informal *ad hoc* groups, or because various groups get involved in innovation depending on the issues at hand.

Some Trends in Community   **215**
Politics: A Secondary Analysis
of Power Structure Data from
166 Communities
Claire W. Gilbert

Fewer innovations in these cities are initiated by experts in government or by the machinations of pressure groups working through governmental procedures. A similar statement can be made for the enforcement of innovation: It is increasingly the work of pressure groups, the electorate, informals, or other segments depending on what is at stake; less and less innovation enforcement is the sole province of the officials.

Conclusions

The evidence supports the notion that increasing scale of society is reflected in the political structure of local communities. It appears that power—i.e., the ability to make binding decisions for the community —is less and less in the hands of a privileged few and is increasingly dependent upon the broker, be he elected official or not, who can bring together (to the extent he can bring together) the various elements in the *community*.

V

Attitudes and Values of Community Leaders

Introduction

The vast majority of the community leadership studies conducted since Hunter's *Community Power Structure*[1] are similar to the articles in the preceding section in that they have been more concerned with *structure* than *content*. Even the pluralists who investigate specific issues and the directions in which they are resolved do so primarily to identify how leadership is structured and at best are only incidentally concerned with the implications of the substance of decisions and how leaders' orientations towards issues may be indicators of their attitudes and values. The importance of investigating the nature of leaders' attitudes, values, and ideologies is demonstrated by all four of the selections which follow. Although a large number of research questions are posed and answered by these articles, three themes are dominant throughout the section:

1. Since most political leaders are drawn from the upper social strata, their orientations may reflect the political perspectives of these strata and differ in particular ways from those of the masses.

2. Related to the first theme is the degree to which attitudes and values among community leaders are congruent or divergent. As will be explained below, their divergence may be one of the most valid indicators of the degree to which pluralism exists.

3. To what degree are leader attitudes and values related to their activity and to public policy in their communities?

That political leaders are drawn from the upper social strata in our society has been documented elsewhere[2] and is again confirmed by data presented by Kuroda and Wells in Selections 23 and 24. Historically, of course, there has been one major exception to this pattern in the

Notes to this introduction will be found on page 357.

United States—the party machine (see Selection 12). This fact may help explain the opposition to "machine politics" by upper-middle-class reformers. Although reformers may not have achieved all of their stated goals, the data presented in Selection 24 suggest they were at least successful in making the city managership a position where their own pragmatic, conservative values would be held by position incumbents. Wells sent questionnaires to all city managers in a single state (Missouri) and then interviewed each. His data confirm the hypothesized pro-business conservatism of city managers, but he also notes that the managers' conservatism is of the moderate, pragmatic, middle-of-the-road variety.

Another difference between elites and masses is the much richer conceptualization of political affairs exhibited by the former. Even in the United States, where popular literacy is much greater than most nations, the level of ideological sophistication among the mass public is quite limited. Studies by the University of Michigan's Survey Research Center, for example, found that only about ten per cent of the adult population could, by a rather generous definition, be described as ideological in their political thinking. Twice as many respondents indicated no issue content whatsoever than demonstrated some degree of ideological thinking.[3] Nonleaders thus tend to respond to politics, not in terms of grand ideologies with well-integrated issue positions, but in terms of party identifications, candidate attractiveness, or transitory issues. Elites, on the other hand, possess (as Kuroda demonstrates in Selection 23) a greater *cognitive capacity* for evaluating political stimuli. Thus, the various ideologies set forth by Agger, Goldrich, and Swanson in Selection 22 may be useful in describing the political orientations of leaders, but not those of the masses. Still, to the degree that even the uninformed voter displays a consistent party preference (in those elections where he has the opportunity to do so), he may be voting for or against an ideology even though he is not aware of it.

Other attitudinal differences between leaders and rank-and-file citizens are discussed in Kuroda's study of the Japanese community of Reed Town. Some of these differences are remarkably parallel to differences which have been found in the United States. For example, studies in the United States have shown, as in Reed Town, leaders are more tolerant and less authoritarian than the public at large.[4] Yet the reader should be cautioned that some findings may be culture-bound. Kuroda, for example, found no difference in economic liberalism between leaders and rank-and-file citizens of Japan, while Wells found that city managers were quite conservative in regard to economic welfare—a finding consistent with other studies of leadership values in the United States.[5] Similarly, Jacob (in Selection 25) notes that American leaders are strongly opposed to economic egalitarianism, while leaders in India were strongly in favor of it and leaders in Poland and Yugoslavia were (surprisingly) only lukewarm toward this ideology

The importance of assessing the *congruency* of leaders' values and attitudes *within* communities is noted in several of the selections which follow and especially by Agger, Goldrich, and Swanson in Selection 22. They note that the content of ideologies must be considered to establish the existence of pluralism. If all leaders' values are highly congruent, then it makes little difference whether or not there is elite competition or a division of labor in regard to decision-making. Only in communities with competing elites possessing divergent ideologies can a "developed democracy" be nearly assured. Ideologies are described by these authors in terms of five component variables: conception of the community, preferences as to "who shall rule," the sense of socioeconomic class, the sense of cultural class or caste, and attitudes toward the legitimate method of allocating values. The discussion of ideologies resulting from various combinations of these variables is the most sophisticated attempt to date to describe leadership ideology at the local level.

Philip Jacob presents a sampling of results from what is probably the most ambitious study of community leaders undertaken to date: the International Studies of Values in Politics. This five-year research program involved interviewing almost four thousand community leaders in India, Poland, Yugoslavia, and the United States. Extensive aggregate data were also compiled, case studies of decision-making conducted, and content of leaders' speeches and communications analyzed. An effort was made throughout to compare leaders along nine basic dimensions: concern for economic development, conflict avoidance, participation, selflessness, national commitment, action propensity, honesty, change orientation, and economic equality. Honesty and selflessness were important everywhere, and the commitment to national groups generally similar internationally. But the differences were interesting. The American leaders were the most prone to act, to want to "do something," but the least inclined to accept changes in their ways of doing things. The Poles were at the other extreme—the least ready to act, but most ready for changes. The Yugoslavs and Americans were most in favor of wide-spread community participation, but whereas the Americans were most ready to accept conflict as part of the legitimate decision-making process, the Yugoslavs preferred more orderly processes of change, while the Indians were most concerned to avoid conflict. The Americans were the least concerned with economic development, the Indians most concerned. Economic equality of all citizens was most important for the Indians and least important for the Americans. Jacob also relates value patterns to resource mobilization in various communities and to community policies.

Without denying that the structure of leadership is a critical question in community politics, these four studies emphasize the importance of the content of leader's values, attitudes and ideologies. They suggest that studies of content are not substitutes for studies of structure in community leadership analysis, but rather that the two complement one another.

Scope of Government and Leaders' Ideologies*

Robert Agger

McMaster University

Daniel Goldrich

University of Oregon

Bert E. Swanson

Sarah Lawrence College

P OLITICAL IDEOLOGY is viewed here as, in brief, a constellation of beliefs and preferences about the nature of the constituent elements in social or community life: Who should rule in the polity? What should the relationship of the government to private institutions be? Where is or should a person be located in the socio-economic-cultural orders of the society and polity? This conception of political ideology, which is discussed more fully later here, proved useful in understanding the workings of the political systems of the four research communities.

During periods of social, economic, and intellectual change, diverse political interests and divergent ideologies are likely to emerge from what was a more homogeneous set of values. All four communities have experienced currents of change in recent years, particularly since the Second World War. The forces of urbanization and industrialization and the currents and crosscurrents that shaped national politics in the first half of the twentieth century have affected the four communities and the two regions, the West and the South, in which they are located.[1]

* Reprinted with permission of the authors and publisher, from Robert Agger, Daniel Goldrich and Bert E. Swanson, The Rulers and the Ruled (New York: John Wiley & Sons, Inc., 1964), pp. 4–11 and 17–32.

220

The political demands and decisions in the four cities were thus shaped by the larger national and international environment. The general conditions of life throughout the United States at the time of this study resulted in similarities in the potential for political conflict in the four communities. Regional and other special conditions, including the particular historical development of the individual communities, also affected the potential issues. All these conditions that shaped political decision-making can be analyzed in relation to the perspectives and behavior of people in local politics. Thus this analysis is concerned with understanding the conditions—particularly the political conditions—under which potential conflict became actual conflict. It is concerned also with how the variations in the structure and functioning of the four political systems affected the outcomes of political decision-making, whether these outcomes were conflictive or not.

The scope of local government may be considered to affect human values. These values can be grouped under four categories that have psychological as well as social significance. The four categories refer to the institutionalized ways of organizing the production, distribution, and consumption of (1) wealth; (2) civic amenities; (3) social status, respect, affection, or prestige; and (4) governmental rights and obligations of citizenship.

Economic institutions in American communities involve those relationships primarily concerned with the production, distribution, and consumption of goods and services. Social institutions, such as the family, the friendship group, and the voluntary "social" association, more or less specialize in such areas as social status, respect, affection, or prestige. Institutional processes devoted to civic amenities and livability include housekeeping services, so-called public works and services, and preserving public order; planning and guiding development of the uses of land and buildings, including design and aesthetics; recreation, particularly out-of-doors; and health facilities, for example, chlorination and fluoridation of the water supply, and

Notes to this selection will be found on pages 357–358.

hospitalization. This category of "civic improvement" is a mixture of both public and private goods and services; whereas the areas of economic and social institutions tend to be generally thought of in America as private, even though government itself performs important economic and social functions.[2]

The patterned sets of relationships that constitute the rights and obligations of citizenship are within the institution of government itself. For example, the jurisdiction and boundaries of local government determine who has the right to vote in local elections. Certain groups of citizens, such as Negroes, lower class people of any color, or union officials, may be ineligible, in fact if not in theory, to serve as elected or appointed officials. Citizens serving in government have rights and obligations relative to each other and to citizens at large.

The pattern of these relationships constitutes the organization of the particular institutional area. Local government has direct or indirect effects on other types of institutions at all times. Thus, demands or decisional processes involving shifts in the way government functions in reference to these relationships are classified into four categories: (1) Economic Reorganization, (2) Social Reorganization, (3) Civic Improvement Reorganization, and (4) Governmental Reorganization.

These categories are convenient, heuristic devices used for analytic purposes. Consequently, classifying a political decisional process under these frequently nondiscrete categories is not a simple matter. People have many values; they pursue social, economic, and civic livability and citizenship values simultaneously. Thus, the sentiments of those most active in promoting a shift in the functioning of local government are at the focus of attention. Even so, arbitrary classifications are sometimes necessary. For example, a decisional question about annexation of a fringe area may involve other considerations than governmental reorganization. Such a decision might affect levels of services and civic improvements, as well as social and economic relations between urban and rural citizens. A demand for school desegregation

Robert Agger
Daniel Goldrich
Bert E. Swanson

may be more a demand for social dignity or respect than for knowledge or income; but it may be both. More will be said about the multiplicity of values when the meaning of political decisions in community life is discussed later here.

The Scope of Government: The Core of Politics

It is useful at this point to present in summary form an analogue model of the political process on which the foregoing considerations have been based. This model will be elaborated on throughout the book. A government may be viewed at a moment in time as being more or less involved in people's lives. We may picture two opposite ideal states: one where there is no governmental functioning and one where governmental functioning is ever-present or total. In the one case private institutions meet all citizen needs; in the other a total—totalitarian—government is the sole value-producing, distributing, and consuming institution. The first would best characterize a pre-political society or community; the latter a postpolitical one. Both societies or communities would actually be apolitical. In order to evaluate the analysis that follows, it is essential to understand the rationale for the seeming paradox that these two opposites represent a single condition: the absence of politics.

As we have said, political history may be viewed as a series of large or small movements of government along a continuum of expansion and contraction. Governments may move in one or the other direction or they may alternate, making little net progress in either direction. The extremes of this continuum are situations in which (1) there is no government activity and consequently no governmental intervention in the other institutions of organized life, and (2) government is total. In the second case, government is so pervasive in the organized life of the community that its activities cannot be distinguished from nongovernmental activities. At either extreme, then, it would presumably be impossible, theoretically or empirically, to characterize a functionally distinct government.

There are thus two ways to attain such an apolitical condition. One is to reduce the functions of government; the other is to extend them. The former alternative is preferred by some people who are called reactionaries: they want to return to a previous era or to a state of nature where government is minimal.[3] Most "romantic" philosophical anarchists consider this the preferable path to a society without government. Point A in Figure 1.1 represents this condition as a result of the contraction of the scope of local government.

If life in "nature" is not considered brutish, nasty, and short, if it is considered idyllic instead, the society is pictured as being cohesive and organic, without conflicting social divisions. Philosphical reactionaries may advocate doing away with social antagonisms by returning to the imagined social harmony of earlier epochs.

Other philosophical anarchists prefer the second path: the extension of the scope of government to the point where its functioning cannot be distinguished from "private" sectors of organized life. Points $B-B'$ in Figure 1.1 represent the condition at the end of this path. Marx advocated a political utopia without government, to be achieved through a purposeful, planned extension of government's scope. He believed that the state or government with its monopoly of force would "wither away" when the dictatorship of the proletariat was established, rather than at some distant time after the revolution. Some Marxists, particularly Engels, have envisaged the withering away of government as an historical stage that begins after the dictatorship

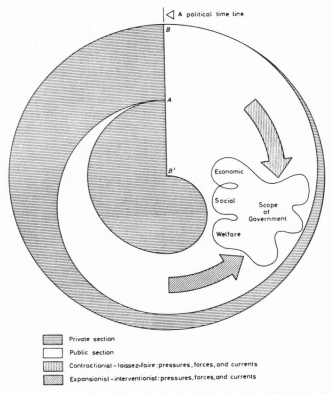

Figure 1.1. Expansion–contraction continuum of the local scope of government.

destroys economically based classes which are the reason government exists. Khrushchev blames internal and external capitalist conspiracies for the failure of the Soviet government to begin to wither away. A more paradoxical but intellectually consistent view of Marxist thinking, in some ways more consistent than Engels', would propose that the increasing scope of government is an integral part of the withering-away process, and is in being as soon as, if not before, the revolution. At some undefined point in time, a distinctive or distinguishable government presumably could disappear if it had become inextricably mingled with the day-to-day living patterns of people.

The Marxist philosophical school sees man as historically locked in social conflict. Social antagonisms are expected to increase as history unfolds; it is only after a period of intensive economic, social, and political conflict among classes that the class struggle will end once and for all. The job of preparing for utopian social harmony can then be undertaken by the government of the proletariat. Engels has qualified Marx's view of the beginnings of organized life as being a condition of class struggle: he saw "primaeval communities" to be socially cohesive, cooperative, and harmonious.[4] The suggested model would be closer to Engels' than to Marx's view in that it indicates a return to a hypothetical earlier *agovernmental* condition by the juxtaposition or interpenetration of Points A and $B-B'$ of Figure 1.1.

In order to understand national and international political movements in the nineteenth and twentieth centuries, this belief in the possibility of a withering away of government by expanding or contracting its net scope is of critical importance. Whether either alternative can be realized is irrelevant for the student of politics. But the existence of these as conceptual possibilities shapes the model of politics for the analyst of community, national, and international politics. Although it would be virtually impossible to reach either extreme, pressures for or actual movements in one direction or the other are possible; these pressures constitute

Robert Agger
Daniel Goldrich
Bert E. Swanson

part of the basic forces of politics, local or otherwise, whether or not so intended.

The analogue model of politics may be pictured in the following way. Local government, or any government, is considered to be located in a public space. The boundaries of this public space (curves $A-B$ and $A-B'$ on Figure 1.1) are represented by the extent to which government can actively function in the day-to-day lives of people. The activities of people may be viewed as a community space (the innermost and outermost circles). The private space is represented by the shaded portion of the total community space. In the public space are the currents, forces, or pressures directed toward moving government in the direction of expansion and intervention or that of contraction and laissez-faire, an increase or decrease in the scope of government. Movement in the former direction may result in a greater overlapping of the community space by the public space; movement in the latter direction may result in a relative decrease in the proportion of public to community space. This ratio of public to private space is what we mean by the words "net scope" of government.

The mixed public and private character of activities in which purposeful government regulation is a manifest factor makes any set of curves for such a model of the real world difficult to construct. Further conceptualization and research are needed to make such models more useful and to establish the character of general and particular social–psychological distinctions between governmental and private institutions, as well as the conditions under which such conceptions undergo various kinds of reorganization. It may or may not be that, in social–psychological terms, as government extends its programs into formerly nongovernmental areas and apparently moves toward points $B-B'$, people extend their activities and, hence, community space, so that the ratio of public to private space remains relatively constant.

The action units in this model are people; it is the demands of people that constitute the pressures for a shift in government's scope. It is through the actions of government officials that shifts in local government's scope finally occur. A demand that government act in a particular way may be made by any unit or group of units—any private citizen or government official—in the political system.

Every demand that government act in one way rather than another, or that it function in some way different from the way it has in the past, is a pressure for a shift in government's scope. For example, people may demand a higher level of welfare services. This constitutes a pressure on government to expand. If such demands are made at a time when the level of government services has been declining, it is, nevertheless, a demand for a move back toward the expansionist pole. Suppose a person suggests that his street be paved and the community paves it instead of someone else's. This is not an increase in the net scope of government; the total street paving resources of government are held constant. But for the man whose street is paved, there has seemed to be an increase in government's scope. The scope actually has been balanced by a decrease for those others whose streets were not paved. The petitioner was, in effect, demanding an increased scope of government for himself, but the decisional outcome balanced this demand by reducing someone else's scope of government. Thus, the total or net scope of local government may remain the same, as a result of two, sometimes simultaneous, movements. Such decisional outcomes are regarded as changes in the scope of government wherein there is an *internal* although no *net* shift in scope.

Suppose a question arose as to whether local government ought to build a civic center. Those urging that this be done would be demanding an increased scope of government, whether it was a matter of replacing an existing facility that was in poor condition or in a poor location, or one of extending government's recreational functions. If the most appropriate location became a decisional question, the proponents of one or another site would be demanding that government increase its scope to satisfy *their* needs. In effect, they are saying that government will be serving them more fully by providing a convenient facility that will enable them to consume a greater amount of recreational resources than if the facility were located on some other site. If a proponent of one site asks that a civic center be built or moved there for aesthetic reasons or because it will take most people, but not himself, less time to reach the facility, his request is still a demand for an increased scope of government. Such a person would be urging government to expand its function to satisfy his aesthetic or altruistic need, needs as genuine as that for food.

Conflict may be generated by demands for an internal shift of government that would result in the deprivation of other citizens, or by demands that require a shift in the net scope of government. A demand for school desegregation is a case in point. Opposition to desegregation may be understood as opposition to the increased functioning of government to satisfy a multiplicity of needs of Negroes. Opponents of desegregation might cast the issue in terms of an undesirable increase in the net scope of government, or as a novel and unwarranted intervention of government in the social system. But since government has already exercised its authority to decide whose children should be educated, and how and where, these demands and counter-demands may be more appropriately viewed as involving a redistribution of government's need-satisfying functions, rather than a change in the ratio of public to private space. Only when there has been a change in the ratio of governmental to private satisfaction of human needs in the community has a net shift in scope occurred. If there is no such net shift, all other changes in the way government functions that result in the satisfaction of different needs of different people constitute internal shifts in the scope of local government . . . .

The decisional preferences of most citizens in the four communities seemed to be more influenced by group and personal interests than by ideology. Some citizens were found to be apolitical—they did not see that local government affected personal or group interests to any great degree in either general or particular decisions. These people tended to be politically nonpartici-pant. Among those who did participate were people who had neither a nationally nor a community-oriented political ideology but did have personal or group interests; people who had a national ideology which they did not think had local relevance; and people whose political interests were more central and compel-ling than their ideologies. The proportion of citizens in any of the four communities whose ideologies were of equal or greater importance than their interests was very small. What, then, was the im-portance of ideology?

First of all, community politics was found to be largely group politics. Relatively enduring groups of people were found to be actively involved in the political decision-making of all four communities. Some of these groups followed or overlapped party or factional lines and some cut across them and were irrelevant to the local parties. They tended to be differentiated along ideological rather than interest lines.

These political groups were of special importance in community politics because they included those who were considered to be the leaders in decision-making by others in the community. The impulse to become a leader and obtain power appeared to be a manifestation of interest in proposed local government programs and of a desire to maintain or impose an ideology on the leaders of the community power structure. The latter desire was most intense in the key members of these political groups.

The key men were important because they had extraordinary political status and influence, at least within their own groups. Very small "inner cliques" were made up of articulate ideologists. These were the active

Robert Agger
Daniel Goldrich
Bert E. Swanson

spokesmen for the people who wanted interest-based decisional preferences filtered through the proper ideological sieve. They were the men who in their intimate sub-group operations constituted "a firmly established, authoritative, and continuing organizational center empowered to decide questions of doctrine and discipline."[5] McClosky, *et al.* found this to be so, to a greater degree than many analysts suspected among the leaders of the two major national parties.

In every community some active partici-pants in politics did stand outside the dominant ideologically bounded group or groups; some belonged to more than one of them. Yet much of the variation in the politics of the four communities is under-standable only in the light of the variations within the ideological dimension.

Of special concern in this analysis is an examination of the conditions that produce varying degrees of citizen participation and conflict in political decision-making. Most American communities have complex econ-omies and social structures. A potential exists in communities for the politicizing of group interests through existing voluntary associations or through new political organizations. With the organization of political interest groups, a community may experience extreme political group conflict or cooperation. Whether there is conflict or consensus along interest lines, citizen political participation can be either high or low. While these are all logical possibilities, what we actually find is that the informal political organization of ideologically differ-entiated groups is a necessary although in-sufficient condition for both extensive citizen participation in politics and inten-sive conflict in decision-making. Competi-tive ideological groups give rise to both situations, whereas the competition among groups lacking ideological interests is insufficient to produce "mass" participation of either a cohesive or conflicting character.

Ideologists indoctrinate others with their system of beliefs in order to enlist political participation as a means of achieving their ideological ends. When there is a competition of such political idea systems, each protagonist has to enlist more citizen support than if there were a consensus. Militant ideologists activate interests which become subject to the appeals of the protagonists. Political interests sometimes conflict with the ideological precepts even among the leaders of ideological groups. The extent to which this happens affects the strength of the group in political decision-making. The conditions under which conflict among leaders occurs are also an important subject for political analysis. Ideological groups also differ in the degree to which there is both potential and actual divergence and conflict between ideology and interest in the formation of decisional preferences.

In all four communities ideologists spent some of their time trying to bring together the ideology and the political interests of their members and citizens at large. A lesser degree of doctrinaire orthodoxy within political groups than otherwise might have been the case resulted. Neither this nor the fact that the ideologies had a quality of contingency when used to evaluate decisional options does away with the significance of ideology as an explanatory variable in the analysis that follows.

The five component variables of political ideologies are: (1) conception of the community, (2) preferences as to "who shall rule," (3) the sense of social (socioeconomic) class, (4) the sense of cultural class or caste, and (5) attitudes toward the legitimate method of allocating values.

In Figure 1.2, a combination of the first two variables yields 18 possible cells when the conception of the community is treated as a threefold classification, and the answer to "who shall rule?" as a sixfold one. Only seven of these 18 cells were found to have empirical referents in the form of at least one actual political group in the leadership of at least one of the communities. One political group which aspired but failed to attain a leadership position in one community during the postwar period occupies an eighth cell.

The label "conservative" is found in four of these seven cells. Conservative ideologists feel that political leaders should be recruited from among the more affluent citizens. They differ from one another concerning the particular category of affluence from which they feel the political leadership should come—industrialists–financiers, proprietors–professionals, or the propertied generally; they differ also from ideologists—Community Conservationists, Liberals, Radical Leftists, and Supremacists—who consider as qualifying characteristics other dimensions than affluence or property. The Radical Right is treated at this point as a conservative ideology; it will be differentiated from other ideology in the same cell, labeled Jeffersonian Conservatism later. The Liberals and the Radical Leftists, as well as businessmen–labor minorities, believe that political leadership should come from the disadvantaged sectors of the community. The Supremacists' requisite condition for leadership is the appropriate race.

Conservatives can also be internally distinguished by their conception of the community. Orthodox Conservatives view their communities as being composed of sections of people having different needs, values, or interests. The leaders should rule in the interests of their sectors and must expect that other sectors will advocate policies that need to be opposed.

Jeffersonian Conservatives, as well as Radical Rightists, view the community as being early Jeffersonian: the community is a collection of individuals and not a set of potentially or actually conflicting interest groups. They distinguish two broad categories of individuals, the propertied and the propertyless, and, like Jefferson, are concerned with preserving the particular virtue that belongs to the propertied. They regard the propertyless as being not so much an interest group as a collection of individuals who have been lazy or who lack the personal capabilities that qualify men of property for

Who shall rule?

Conception of community	Industrialists-financiers	Proprietors-professionals	Public officials-administrators	Propertied — Jeffersonian Conservatives / Radical Rightists	Disadvantaged — Businessmen / Labor, minorities	Races
Individuals				Jeffersonian Conservatives / Radical Rightists		
Interests and interest groups	Orthodox Conservatives	Orthodox Conservatives			Liberals	
Collectivity(ies)	Progressive Conservatives		Community Conservationists		[Radical Leftists] *	Supremacists

*Perforated box indicates that the Radical Leftists did not actually attain political leadership positions in any of the four communities from the end of the Second World War to 1961 even though there was an aspiring group in one community, Metroville, for a short time during those years.

Figure 1.2. Matrix of ideologies : two dimensions.

a ruling voice in community affairs. The Jeffersonian Conservative strongly defends the small rural community, where virtuous men may acquire property and live the good life; the big city is a place where alien philosophies of life and civic corruption deplorably, but inevitably, prevail.

Progressive Conservatives are fundamentally "collectivists" in outlook. They view the community as a collectivity—an organism with a common interest. The welfare of one person depends upon the welfare of others; they recognize that interdependency is the keystone of a naturally ordered community. Since they believe in rule by the industrialists and financiers, they view this rule as necessarily operating in the interest of the collectivity. This political leadership must be benevolent; the attitude of "what's good for the 'X' Corporation is good for the community" indicates an innate complement of self-interest and the common good.

Community Conservationists are also collectivists. They view the community as a complex of mutually interdependent parts where the individual good and the common good are naturally compatible, if not identical. They see the values of community life maximized when political leadership is exercised by men representing the public at large, rather than "special interests." They believe in a "public interest" that may differ from the shortsighted, limited interest of a portion of the community. Elected public officials and appointed professional public administrators must be the guardians, as well as the architects and builders, of this public interest.

Liberals believe that disadvantaged people or those who identify themselves with the disadvantaged should be the political leaders in communities which are complexes of interest groups. Organized labor is one of the major, fundamental interests of Liberalism. In addition, Liberals see racial minorities and even small businessmen as disadvantaged interests. Liberals want public officials to accord the needs of the disadvantaged the highest political status.

These needs will be defined by the leaders of the disadvantaged. Community Conservationists want public officials to be accorded the highest political status by all interests, including the disadvantaged.

The Radical Left's ideology advocates rule of the community by those disadvantaged under capitalism. Adherents of that ideology see the community as a collectivity in the Marxist sense and as having a single natural interest in the collective good of the proletariat. This single interest is to be implemented through the political leadership of the intelligentsia. The relatively large, disadvantaged proletariat would rule the community through the very small minority of progressive true believers who may work from the offices they hold in organizations of the disadvantaged, such as labor unions and racial groups.

Finally, the Supremacists believe that race should be the primary criterion for community rule. Race becomes the necessary and sufficient condition for participation as a political leader. Therefore, the appropriate racist sentiment tends to qualify any citizen for a position of political leadership. Supremacists can be either Whites or Negroes.[6]

The third component variable of these political ideologies is the "sense of social class." Social class not only adds depth to the picture of each ideology but also suggests bases for cooperation and conflict among different ideologies and among groups within one ideology. The sense of social class refers to people's self-images with regard to how much social status, respect, and affection they receive from others in the community. These feelings tend to be affected by the occupations people hold, their income or wealth, and their educational attainments. The sense of social class may be based on accurate perceptions of differential social status arising from admission to or exclusion from groups, associations, or organizations, although such admission or exclusion may be based on personal rather than socioeconomic characteristics.[7]

The political ideologies in the matrix in Figures 1.2 and 1.3 were set up to range

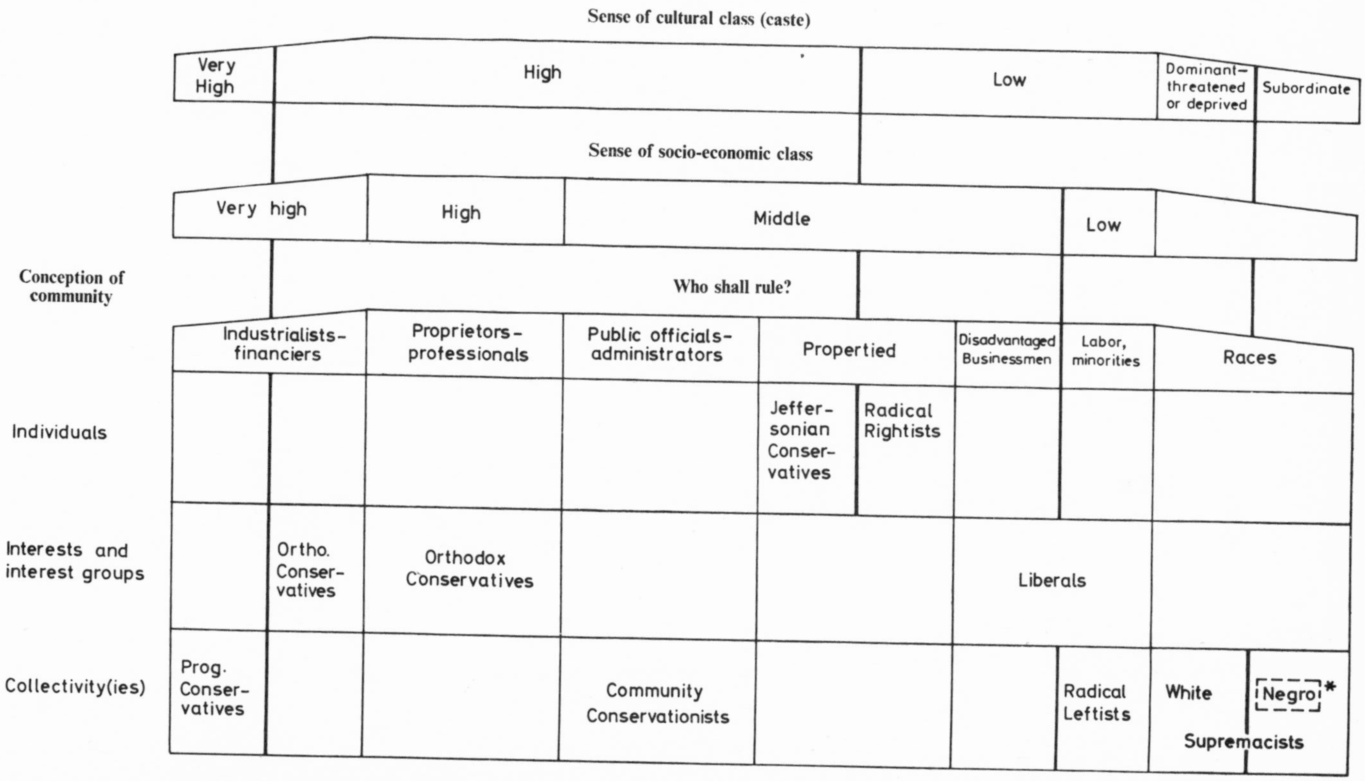

Sense of cultural class (caste)

Sense of socio-economic class

Conception of community	Very High	High			Middle		Low		Dominant-threatened or deprived	Subordinate
	Very high	High		Who shall rule?						
	Industrialists-financiers	Proprietors-professionals	Public officials-administrators	Propertied		Disadvantaged Businessmen	Labor, minorities	Races	
Individuals				Jeffersonian Conservatives	Radical Rightists				
Interests and interest groups	Ortho. Conservatives	Orthodox Conservatives					Liberals		
Collectivity(ies)	Prog. Conservatives		Community Conservationists				Radical Leftists	White	Negro*
								Supremacists	

*The perforated box enclosing Negro Supremacists indicates there was no political group of this ideology aspiring to community leadership in any of the cities although there were individual Negro Supremacists in both southern cities.

Figure 1.3. Matrix of ideologies: four dimensions.

from very high to low in the measurement of social class, reading from left to right. The Orthodox Conservatives and Progressive Conservatives believe that the industrialists–financiers should rule, because they are the most important, or even superior, men in the community; they deserve their social and political status. The attainment of their high-income-producing occupational positions, whether by birth or through their own efforts, is seen as reason enough for the community to accord them the lion's share of respect or deference. Their wealth alone, apart from their manners or morality, leads naturally to places on boards of directors, or to the organization of country clubs which provide exclusive social settings for the development and maintenance of a sense of high social position.

The Orthodox Conservatives who believe that proprietorial–professional occupations should rule have a sense of high social class, as compared to groups they perceive as their protagonists in the community. They appear not to have quite the same feelings of social superiority as are evidenced by the aforementioned conservative ideologists. The Community Conservationists, the Jeffersonian Conservatives, and the Radical Rightists tend to perceive themselves as properly middle class; this is a matter of some pride and significance to them. Liberals include some people who feel they belong to the middle class and others who feel that they are members of the lower class. Blue-collar and Negro Liberals tend to think that they receive a disproportionately small share of social status. Liberal businessmen and professionals tend to think of themselves as belonging to the middle class. The Radical Leftists have the strongest sense of receiving few social—and economic—gratifications in the community; they feel such gratifications belong to them by right because of the nature of the world and its inevitable historical forces. To Supremacists social class is irrelevant and racial purity is all important.

Another defining characteristic of ideologies is the sense of cultural class, or caste. This refers to the people's self-images and feelings concerning how much status or respect their values, beliefs, opinions, judgments, and ideas receive from others. Sense of cultural class may follow, to a greater or lesser degree, the sense of social class, but there are important differences in the two concepts.

The sense of cultural class may be very general and refer to a host of matters or phenomena: political values, political beliefs, political opinions, political judgments, and ideas about the polity—the political culture—as well as matters of manners, morals, money, and music. Just as we treat theoretically distinct senses of social and economic class as a single dimension, so too do we deal with these various "senses" as a single, composite, general sense of cultural class.[8]

The three sets of political ideologists characterized by a high sense of social class—both kinds of Orthodox Conservatives and the Progressive Conservatives—have a comparably high sense of cultural class (Figure 1.3). The Progressive Conservatives have an extremely high sense of cultural superiority which extends throughout most areas of life. Their sense of cultural class makes them the most aristocratic of any set of Conservatives. When born to the highest social and economic positions, they accept their roles as cultural leaders as a matter of course. They have unquestioned faith that the cultural trends and heritage they oversee are superior to any alternatives. On occasion, they may be influenced by such men of lower cultural class as their professional advisors; but they regard themselves as without peer in the realm of judgment. The two sets of Orthodox Conservatives appear—in our communities at least—less certain that their cultural superiority is infallible, particularly in such peripheral cultural areas as the arts and letters.

Both Community Conservationists and Jeffersonian Conservatives, who identify themselves with the middle social class, have a high sense of cultural class which is comparable to that of the Orthodox

Conservatives. Although the Community Conservationists believe their wisdom is superior in civic and political affairs, in some areas they assume that one man's values are as good as another's. For example, Community Conservationists do not see business success as an indication of cultural superiority; they view its attainment as a function of unimportant or chance factors. Their upper-cultural-class feelings derive in part from their awareness that they are currently well informed and highly educated and that they have the most modern, progressive view of what is good for the community. This is in contrast to the old-fashioned, regressive views of most of their articulate opponents, of professional politicians, and, perhaps, of many of the citizens. This sense of high cultural class characterizes Community Conservationists whether they are Harvard intellectuals, city managers or planners, or leaders of the League of Women Voters. Community Conservationists value professionally trained public administrators and stress public planning; they tend to hold in disrepute the professional politician and "dirty politics." They are the most recent of a long line of "reformers," but differ in at least one major aspect: earlier reformers tended to concentrate on eliminating particular evils so that the political system might return to a sort of laissez-faire operation in cooperation with private institutions. The Community Conservationist, in contrast, stresses the need for and the duty of the government to provide long-range planning in the public interest by nonpolitical administrators. There is a socialist-like emphasis on community planning without the socialist objective of increased public ownership of the means of production.[9]

Jeffersonian Conservatives differ sharply from the Radical Rightists in respect to cultural class. The Jeffersonian Conservatives' sense of belonging to the upper cultural class appears to be based in part on their images of themselves as being men of some affluence when compared to the propertyless, and as being believers in eternal verities rather than in the misconceived modern notions of the good life to which eccentrics adhere. In sharp contrast, Radical

Rightists sense that they belong to the cultural class which is lowest in regard to community affairs. They feel deprived—not necessarily of social status or access to prestigious social organizations—because they are treated by a frequently subversive community leadership as part of a "lunatic fringe," as people with destructive ideas.

Both Liberals and Radical Leftists have a sense of being members of a low cultural class. The Radical Leftists, much like the Radical Rightists, feel that they are treated unjustly. Moral indignation seems stronger on the part of the Radical Rightists than on that of the Radical Leftists; this may be because the Leftists' belief in historical necessity accords them security, and the Rightists fear that history is constantly moving in the wrong direction. The Radical Leftists resemble in a sense Progressive Conservatives in their elite outlook because the cultural class to which each group feels it belongs is extremely small. Radical Rightists, if elitists, are of a Populist variety. They feel that there are many people in this same low cultural class position who would become associated with the Radical Right if they recognized the truth of the Rightist diagnosis of, and prescription for, the current illness in the body politic.

The Liberals, somewhat split on the basis of their sense of social class—some identify with the middle and some with the lower class—are united in their sense of a common cultural-class plight. They may feel as deprived as either the Radical Right or the Radical Left by the disregard of their cultural standards, but they seem more confident that a change in their relative cultural class position is attainable in the relatively near future.

White and Negro Supremacists may now be treated as separate groups. The White Supremacists see themselves as the racial caste which is currently dominant. However, they feel threatened by an overturn in the "natural order" of caste-control relations. Negro Supremacists feel they are treated as inferior, subordinate people. They feel that their destiny, and that of dark-skinned peoples throughout the world, is to reverse the traditional master–serf relationship.

Two important aspects of political culture are beliefs about the good regime and the good power structure. Of these ten political ideologies—including both types of Orthodox Conservatives and both types of Supremacists—six have as their ideal type of good regime a "developed democracy." . . . The ideal regime of all the Conservative, the Liberal, and the Community Conservationist ideologies is one wherein the citizens correctly believe that they have full access to the political decision-making process, including the ballot. Radical Rightists feel that an oligarchy is the desirable regime for the foreseeable future. Such a regime exists when some categories of citizens are aware that they do not have access to the political decision-making process. Until utopia is reached, Radical Leftists prefer a situation called "guided democracy." Under this system citizens believe that they have full access to the political decision-making process, but are in error: should certain demands be made for shifts in the scope of government, illegitimate sanctions would be effectively applied to those making the demands. Such a situation prevails where there is a widespread sense of democracy with perhaps some of its forms, but without the necessary conditions to give it substance. Supremacists favor oligarchy for the other race; they vary in their preferences for the good regime for the master race.

All four conservative ideologies prefer a type of power structure wherein power is in the hands of a relatively small proportion of the citizens and the political leadership agrees on one set of values for the general scope of government. Although Jeffersonian Conservatives believe that the relatively large propertied segment should participate in ruling, the actual political leadership will naturally be relatively small in size. Relatively large numbers of shiftless, propertyless people and some misguided people with property are disqualified from sharing in political power and leadership positions because of their attachment to an alternative ideology. The Orthodox Conservatives think politics is necessary in the competition with other interests for scarce resources; they try to attain or preserve a consensual power structure, in which Orthodox Conservatism is the prevailing political ideology.

The ideal power structure of Community Conservationists, Liberals, and Radical Leftists is more of a mass and less of an elite distribution of political power. The Radical Leftists understand that such a distribution of political power is necessary if they are to move from their present powerless position, in what they consider oligarchies run by and for their enemies, to a position of power in a pseudodemocracy that is guided by them. Community Conservationists prefer to see the masses share in political power through extensive electoral participation in support of the Conservationists and their policies; Liberals envisage the development of a complex of more active political roles for the rank-and-file. Supremacists tend to support a consensual elite power structure as the only safe way of preserving the oligarchy and the dominance of their race.

The fifth factor among political ideologies is a principle of community organization, which, in its most extreme form, may be stated in this way: The good community is a natural product of governmental non-interference with private allocation of social, economic, or other resources according to the individual's ability to compete for them, tempered by mercy and charity. The Radical Rightists adhere to this principle in a most uncompromising fashion. In their political ideology, almost all governmental action is seen as a dangerous violation of this natural law principle. Jeffersonian Conservatives also tend to view the growth of government as unwarranted interference, but they view this somewhat less rigidly.

The major difference between the two is that the Radical Right is restorationist in outlook whereas the outlook of Jeffersonian Conservatives is preservationist. Jeffersonian Conservatism may be strongest in small or rural communities where government is minimal, and the Radical Right tends to be strong in communities where government has grown larger. But Jeffersonian Conservatism places its greatest emphasis on preventing further increases in the net scope of government, whereas the Radical Right stresses the need to decrease the net scope of government. Jeffersonian Conservatives may accept shifts in the functioning of government if the shifts accord with their cultural values, but the Radical Rightist consistently views government as evil. One of the cultural aims of Jeffersonian Conservatism is a community undivided by political controversy. Since the Jeffersonian Conservative has a sense of upper cultural class status and a duty to preserve the community consensus, he is more likely than the Radical Rightist to accept a governmental program if resistance will result in extensive or intensive community conflict. This would be particularly true if the Jeffersonian Conservatives were the political leaders of the polity and able to control administrative decision-making for any governmental program. The Radical Rightist has the hostility that goes with believing oneself treated as a member of an inferior cultural class; he also feels, as a political–cultural value, the need for conflict and extreme forms of political warfare to reestablish the principle of community organization in its pure form and to establish the desired oligarchic type of polity.[10] Both the Radical Right and Jeffersonian Conservatism are hostile to a professional, independent governmental bureaucracy; they see these professionals as men who are, by their very occupations, dedicated to the subversion of this basic principle of community life.

Conservatives other than Jeffersonians tend to have the latter's rhetoric, but differ in their interpretations of what constitutes governmental interference with the private distribution of goods, services, and other values. Alexander Hamilton's advocacy of certain national governmental programs made him no less conservative than Calvin

Robert Agger
Daniel Goldrich
Bert E. Swanson

Coolidge's negative sentiments toward government. If governmental programs are seen to serve the interests of the rulers, they may be thought to strengthen rather than weaken the rule of private allocations of values. The result of this qualification is that Conservatives have a contingent or dependent outlook toward the appropriate scope of government.[11] Primary among these contingent factors is whether or not particular governmental programs hurt or help conservative socioeconomic interests, and the extent to which their adversaries, the Liberals, are likely to use shifts or expansions in the scope of government for antibusiness ends. Since these liberal shifts have been a national trend, the conservative political ideology tends to be more in favor of the *status quo* and retrenchment than of expansion.[12]

Progressive Conservatives are less opposed to the use of government where private collectivities are unable or less able to act effectively. Since they view their rule as benevolent and in the interests of the entire community, they find it easier than do other conservative groups to accept government's role as one of the mechanisms for resource distribution along with the major private corporations and the voluntary civic and social organizations. This is particularly the case when Progressive Conservatives are in dominant political leadership positions. Thus, they also have a contingent position on the preferred scope of government. Progressive Conservatives sometimes see such programs as organized, large-scale charity in everyone's interest, and government as an efficient welfare-dispensing institution; they may approve of public welfare programs that are anathema not only to the Radical Right and Jeffersonian Conservatives but also to Orthodox Conservatives.

Community Conservationists tend to see government as the most important institution for producing in the good community values that are neither produced by private efforts nor actually inspired by private activities. Community Conservationists do not advocate as general principles either the circumscription of the private sectors of the community or a particular scope of government. Their cultural values are such that the programs of civic improvement and repair which they favor tend to make them advocates of vigorous, expansionist government. These programs include a stress on the improved distribution of knowledge through the public schools, cleanliness and beauty in architecture, planning and guided development of land use and of the size and character of the community's population, and a spirit of harmonious cooperation on the part of the citizenry. They value civic pride, a strong sense of public spirit, and an efficient, corruption-free, integrated city government. They believe "good government" is possible only where small, inefficient, multiple jurisdictions do not exist to obstruct nonpartisan, professional public administrators, officials, and civic-minded citizens in their work of building the good community. Since the property tax is still the primary fiscal base of local government, their relative unconcern with the costs and the tax requirements of their programs makes them particularly unacceptable to both Jeffersonian Conservatives and the Radical Rightists. Furthermore, the tax-conscious, property-oriented Rightists are considered members of an extremely inferior cultural class by Community Conservationists. Community Conservationists are not adverse to accepting federal funds for programs of civic improvement. When they do receive such funds they become the mortal enemies of the Radical Rightists who see socialism and the triumph of the Radical Left as the inevitable consequence of the extension of federal funds and planning controls into the local community.

Liberals agree, in general, with the principle that resources should be distributed according to the ability of individuals to compete in the distribution process. They believe that, with the passive or active cooperation of government, the affluent have unfair advantages that only counter-organization of the disadvantaged can overcome. They distrust local government officials whom they do not control for their traditional alliance with the business community; they also look with some hostility on nonbusiness-oriented Community Conservationists and their "modern" conception of good government. Liberals may advocate shifts in local government's scope either internally or in an expansionist direction. They may even advocate contraction in the scope of government if this seems a way to reduce the advantages of the affluent in the competition for scarce resources. Liberals tend to have a very pragmatic approach to the scope of government, particularly at the local level. Although their rhetoric often stresses expansion of local government, their pragmatism and their fear of government when their opponents have power give the Liberal's political ideology the same contingent character as that of the Conservative ideologies.

The Supremacists, both White and Negro, see the appropriate scope of local government in relation to the implementation of their interests in racial supremacy and a rigid caste system. Under some conditions, they see local government as their strongest force against enemies who advocate desegregation, either from without or from within the community. Under other conditions, they try to reduce the scope of local government to repair or prevent breaches in the wall between the races. Their attitude toward the scope of government is variable, therefore, rather than fixed and determinate.

The only political ideology that rejects this principle of community organization completely is that of the Radical Left. To the Leftist, the good community is one wherein government, during the pre-utopian period, distributes resources. Even here there is a quality of contingency about the Radical Leftists' position on the appropriate scope of government. Marxists may work with Liberals or with Conservatives to generate resentment and rebellion among the disadvantaged; the international communist movement often has used this strategy. The flexibility of the Radical Leftists' tactics and strategy, within the framework of fixed long-range goals, lends even to this political ideology a quality of contingency shared by all of the aforementioned political ideologies except that of the Radical Right.

We may return to the earlier point that political ideology may range from a deeply rooted personality trait to a surface attitude. It appears that while any group of ideologists may be deeply committed to ideological precepts, Radical Rightists, Supremacists, and Radical Leftists—the Leftists are currently least important in numbers and political significance in community politics —are people whose ideologies seem to play a more central role in their lives than do the ideologies of other groups. These are "deviant" political ideologies—ideologies subscribed to by relatively few people and in which the preferred type of regime differs markedly from that in most other American political ideologies. Furthermore, Radical Rightists express open hostility to, and engage in open warfare with, the cultural classes they consider their enemies; they use tactics that the latter believe are as radical and as undesirable as are the ends of that ideology. The term "radical" for both left and the right has three connotations. It signifies that these ideologies advocate relatively sharp shifts in the scope of government although such shifts would be in different directions. It also signifies that these ideologies envisage the best political regime as being quite different from the regime desired by other ideologists. Finally, consistent with their preferences for other than developed democratic regimes, the Radical Rightists and Leftists advocate "radical" political tactics such as slander, smears, and secret societies which other ideologists view with disdain.

We purposely refer to government rather than to "local" government in the foregoing section. This suggests what may have been apparent all along: the taxonomy constructed for these political ideologies is relevant for national as well as for local American politics. By a consistent substitu-

Robert Agger
Daniel Goldrich
Bert E. Swanson

tion of the word "nation" for the word "community," the Progressive Conservatives have their analogue in the Eisenhower administration and the Community Conservationists in Kennedy's New Frontier.[13] These counterparts are not perfect equivalents, of course. Furthermore, some people adhere strongly to one ideology at one level and to another ideology at another.[14] This alone will explain some of the apparent paradoxes of current American politics, both locally and nationally. But our basic point is that political ideology did not disappear at the national level with the end of the Depression or the end of the New or Fair Deal; nor has it been as absent from local politics as many observers seem to think.

Important dimensions of a community's power structure are the extent to which a political leadership is characterized by single or by multiple ideologies and the extent to which there is ideological convergence or divergence. . . . From the foregoing descriptions, it would seem that some political ideologies diverge substantially from others. If their proponents attained political leadership positions, the extent of the divergence would seem to be clearly established. However, this is problematical; such factors as the strength of the leaders' ideological commitment affect the degree of divergence. This chapter closes with the suggestion that the great ignorance about political ideology in the United States at the community, state, and national levels of government and politics should be reduced by additional research. Except for two follow-up sample surveys in one community, which was revisited several years after the first sample survey for the purpose of testing specific hypotheses, little systematic, comparative information is available on the political ideologies of the citizens at large in our four communities. Even fewer data are available at this time on the genesis and development of ideological orientation.[15]

We have included this discussion of ideology in our analysis because we do have some comparative data on its nature and functions, particularly at the political leadership level of the power structure in our four communities, despite the many facets left unexplored.[16]

CENTRAL to any empirical test of the extent of democracy is the concept of representation,[2] or the extent to which a government or the political leadership in a political system represents the will of the people.[3]

The roll-call voting record has been used by Miller and Stokes and others in the United States as the dependent variable or as a major indicator of the representatives' preferences. To use the same method, however, in studying politics elsewhere without a careful examination of the political culture is bound to fail, for the roll-call vote may have nothing to do with a representative's value preference. In small communities in many countries where consensus-building prior to the formal announcement of a decision is an accepted way of making decisions, open cleavages are not allowed to appear in public. Most of the minutes of Japanese town assemblies show that practically all decisions are made without even one dissenting voice.[4] One cannot very well use the roll-call vote as the dependent variable when all decisions are made unanimously.

An alternative method used in this study to examine the extent to which and the areas in which leaders of Reed Town represent the will of the people is to review value orientations of a general population sample of Reed Town and those of a leadership sample.

In short the purpose of this study is to scrutinize the relationship between the rank-and-file citizens in Reed Town and their leaders with respect to their value orientations. By so doing, I hope to be able to make more meaningful statements about the question of whether leadership of a power-elite variety or a democratic type of leadership structure exists in Reed Town, Japan.

The Data

This study is based on data gathered under the author's direction in Reed Town,

* Reprinted with permission of the author and publisher, from Yasumasa Kuroda, "Psychological Aspects of Community Power Structure: Leaders and Rank-and-File Citizens in Reed Town, Japan," (Southwestern) Social Science Quarterly, 48 (December 1967), pp. 433–442.

Psychological Aspects of Community Power Structure: Leaders and Rank-and-File Citizens in Reed Town, Japan[*1]

Yasumasa Kuroda

University of Hawaii and East–West Center

a Japanese community, in the summer of 1963. The total population of Reed Town, located near Tokyo, was 16,500 at the time of the survey. Two different samples, the Leadership sample and the General Population sample, are used in this analysis. The Leadership sample was secured through a variant of the reputational technique.[5] The sample for the rank-and-file citizens was obtained from a list of registered voters, through the systematic interval system.[6]

These two different samples of respondents' responses to a battery of scale items plus current issues are examined in the present analysis. The scale items in the survey included the SRC's political efficiency and other scale items in addition to scales which were devised for this particular research project. Respondents were asked to choose one of the following six possible answers: agree strongly, agree somewhat, agree slightly, disagree slightly, disagree somewhat, and disagree strongly for each item on the questionnaire.[7] An English version of all items is listed in Table 1. On several items as many as one-third of the respondents (General Population) failed to provide us with a definite response, whereas the leaders answered almost all questions with only a few exceptions.

The Findings

Table 1 presents mean responses of the General Population sample and the Leadership sample to fifty-nine items included in

237

our questionnaire. A t-test was performed on each item to see if there were any statistically significant relationships between these two samples. Statistically significant differences between the mean responses of the two groups were observed for thirty-eight out of the fifty-nine items.

TABLE 1. Answers to Various Scaling Items by General Population and Leadership Samples

Item*	Means General Population ($N = 287$)	Leaders ($N = 18$)	P†
1. What youth needs most is strict discipline, rugged determination and the will to work and fight for family and country (F).	2.06	2.56	NS‡
2. Most of our social problems could be solved if we could somehow get rid of the immoral, feeble-minded and crooked people (F).	2.22	2.28	NS
3. People ought to pay more attention to new ideas even if they seem to go against the Japanese way of life (F).	2.28	1.78	S§
4. The findings of science may some day show that many of our most cherished beliefs are wrong (F).	2.96	2.81	NS
5. I don't blame anyone for trying to grab all he can get in this world (SS).	3.79	3.72	NS
6. The most important things to me are my duties to my job and to my fellow man (SS).	1.85	1.50	NS
7. A person does not need to worry about other people if only he looks after himself (SS).	4.08	5.33	S
8. I chose my life work primarily because I wanted to help make a better society (SS).	1.94	1.33	S
9. So many other people vote in the general elections that it doesn't matter much to me whether I vote or not (PO).	5.56	6.00	S
10. It is not so important to vote when you know your party does not have any chance to win (PO).	5.07	5.94	S
11. If cities and towns around the country need help to build more schools, the government ought to give them the money they need (I).	1.65	1.39	NS
12. The government ought to see to it that everybody who wants to work can find a job (I).	1.56	1.17	S
13. A good many local elections are not important enough to bother with (PO).	4.96	5.94	S
14. The government ought to help people get doctors and hospital care at low cost (I).	1.52	1.11	S
15. If a person doesn't care how an election comes out he shouldn't vote in it (PO).	4.20	5.72	S
16. The government should leave things like electric power and housing for private businessmen to handle (I).	3.92	3.50	NS
17. I prefer being with other people rather than by myself (S).	2.44	2.28	NS
18. If "Burakumin" (an ethnic minority) are not getting fair treatment in jobs and housing, the government should see to it that they are (I).	1.69	1.50	NS
19. I would rather not have very much responsibility for other people (S).	3.27	5.17	S
20. The government ought to cut taxes even if it means putting off some important things that need to be done (Tax).	2.16	3.00	S
21. When in a group of people, I have trouble thinking of the right things to talk about (S).	3.08	3.72	NS

TABLE 1. *(cont.)*

Item*	Means General Population ($N = 287$)	Leaders ($N = 18$)	P†
22. Voting is the only way that people like me can have any say about how the government runs things (PE).	2.65	2.83	NS
23. When I think something is good for someone, I frequently try to persuade him that this is the case (S).	2.13	2.00	NS
24. Sometimes politics and government seem so complicated that a person like me can't really understand what's going on (PE).	2.79	3.72	S
25. It is hard for me to find anything to talk about when I meet a new person (S).	3.08	4.53	S
26. People like me don't have any say about what the government does (PE).	3.09	3.94	S
27. In social conversation, I frequently have definite ideas and try to convince others (S).	2.98	1.42	NS
28. I don't believe that public officials care about what people like me think (PE).	2.93	4.06	S
29. In a group I usually take the responsibility for getting people introduced (S).	3.77	2.00	S
30. In order to get nominated, most candidates for political offices have to make basic compromises and undesirable commitments (PC).	4.42	5.50	S
31. The major goal of our nation should be to obtain peace at any price (PW).	1.72	1.94	NS
32. Politicians spend most of their time getting re-elected or reappointed (PC).	2.52	1.78	S
33. We should not fight any war even though it may be to our advantage (PW).	1.52	1.94	NS
34. Money is the most important factor influencing public policies (PC).	2.26	1.56	S
35. Peaceful coexistence (U.S. and U.S.S.R.) is our best bet for survival (PW).	1.67	1.18	S
36. A large number of city and county politicians are party hacks (PC).	3.07	4.28	S
37. In this atomic age, we must not proclaim peaceful negotiation as a means of national policy (PW).	4.39	4.72	NS
38. People are often manipulated by politicians (PC).	2.69	2.33	NS
39. We should rearm our country at once (PW).	4.40	4.33	NS
40. Politicians represent the general interests more frequently than they represent special interests of groups (PC).	1.96	1.33	S
41. The United Nations is just a plot by the "one worlders" to sacrifice the sovereignty of Japan on the altar of world government (IN).	4.44	5.33	S
42. Most politicians in the community are probably more interested in getting known than in serving the needs of their constituents (PC).	2.57	3.22	S
43. I am not willing to surrender my allegiance to Japan in order to give it to a world government (IN).	2.67	2.11	NS
44. International students, scientists, farmers and other exchanges of personnel should be encouraged and expanded (IN).	1.52	1.06	S
45. I would prefer to be a citizen of the world first, and a citizen of one country second (IN).	3.28	2.89	NS
46. I'm for my country, right or wrong (IN).	2.52	3.94	S

TABLE 1. *(cont.)*

Item*	Means General Population (*N* = 287)	Leaders (*N* = 18)	P†
47. The United States is a democratic nation in general (A).	2.12	1.89	NS
48. The United States is imperialistic (A).	4.09	4.83	S
49. The United States is by and large the best country I can find in the world today (A).	2.84	2.78	NS
50. The United States is not really trying to bring about peace in the world (A).	3.86	4.72	S
51. The Soviet Union is a democratic nation in general (R).	4.11	5.83	S
52. The Soviet Union is imperialistic (R).	3.55	2.78	S
53. The Soviet Union is by and large the best country I can find in the world today (R).	4.31	5.17	S
54. The Soviet Union is not really trying to bring about peace in the world (R).	3.25	2.89	NS
55. The Shushin should be revived (C).	2.10	2.50	NS
56. I am opposed to the Japan-Korea Conference (C).	3.70	5.00	S
57. The United States should withdraw its troops and bases (from Japan) (C).	2.51	2.61	NS
58. Japan should trade with Communist China (C).	1.96	1.39	S
59. The Atomic-powered submarine should not be allowed to visit Japan (The U.S. Submarine F 104) (C).	4.25	3.44	S

* F = F scale: SS = Self–society: PO = Political Obligation: I = Ideological Orientation: S = Sociability: PE = Political Efficacy: PC = Political Cynicism: PW = Peace–War: IN = Internationalism: A = Anti-Americanism: R = Anti-Russianism: C = Current Issues.
† P = Level of significance (Student t-test).
‡ NS = Not Significant.
§ S = Difference significant beyond the .05 level.

However, one can easily see that the significant differences found in Table 1 are not distributed equally among different scale items. For example, statistically significant differences are found in the mean responses to all four items on the Political Obligation or the "sense-of-civic-duty" scale. Also we find more than one-half of the items included per scale to which these two groups responded differently in the following scale items: Political Efficacy, Internationalism, and Anti-Russianism.

It is reasonable to assume that the rank-and-file citizens have a lower sense of political obligation and feel less efficacious in influencing the decisional outcomes of government than the leaders. These variables are generally associated with higher political involvement in the United States as well as in Japan.[8]

The leaders seemed to be more internationally oriented than the general population—the leaders' responses were signifi- cantly different from those of the general population respondents in three out of five items on the internationalism scale. V. O. Key reports a positive correlation between the level of education and internationalism which coincides with our finding.[9] Those who receive more formal schooling may see things in a wider perspective than those who are less educated, as Key implies. Furthermore if a qualification of a politician or a leader is to be able to see things as others see them, the leaders certainly should be more favorably inclined toward internationalism.

The leaders are somewhat more pro-American and anti-Russian than the general population; responses of the leaders were significantly so inclined in two out of four items in the anti-Americanism scale and in three out of four items in the anti-Russianism scale. One explanation for this is that most of the leaders selected are conservative in their party identification. They are in fact almost exclusively Liberal-Democracts (the ruling conservative party) with few exceptions.

An interesting finding is that the leaders were more cynical than the general population on two (item 32 and 34) out of seven items in the Political Cynicism scale which showed significant differences between the mean responses of the two groups.[10] One possible explanation for this is that individuals selected through the use of a variant of the reputational technique as leaders included some who did not occupy either elected or appointed political positions in the local government. Those leaders without any official position in the local government may not regard themselves as being politicians. As a result, they agreed with a statement (item 34) that "politicians spend most of their time getting re-elected or re-appointed." A second explanation could be that some of the leaders are so distrustful of other politicians that their cynicism causes the sample to exceed that of the general population. The relationship between political cynicism and political involvement is complicated since the relationship will vary from one policy to another.

There is considerable agreement between the leaders and the general population with regard to the scope of government on questions of social welfare. However, on the five items which dealt with current issues at the time of the survey the leaders are shown to be more conservative on three out of the five questions. On the other hand, they are more liberal on the question of government expenditures and taxes. They do not wish to see tax cuts "if it means putting off some important things that need to be done."[11] Boskoff and Zeigler report that people of high SES (socioeconomic status) are more likely to accept various bond issues than the public as a whole.[12] At least in these two studies the leaders at the local level show their willingness to continue with the existing social welfare, school, and other important programs, whereas the people would rather have tax cuts at any price. The general population in Reed Town desires just as much government service as leaders do, but at the same time it desires a tax cut. What the general population wants

is impossible: trying to get something for nothing. The leaders, on the other hand, are more realistic: they realize that what the government provides for the people costs money that must come from the people in one way or another. Of course, one can argue that the people feel that the cost of government operation must be paid by those who are rich and not by people like those who are included in this survey. We must conclude then that one's ideological orientation depends largely upon specific areas of government decision-making.[13] In other words, we must specify that one is conservative with reference to some areas of legislation.

Sociability has been said to induce people to get involved in politics.[14] The mean responses of the general population on sociability indicate that they consistently score lower on sociability items although statistical differences between the leaders and the general population are significant only on three out of seven items.

Although there were not many statistically significant differences between the mean responses of the general population and the leaders, the leaders scored consistently low on authoritarianism.[15] Furthermore, this finding is in agreement with Stouffer's finding that civic leaders are more tolerant than the rank-and-file citizens.[16] As Milbrath reasons, politics in a nonauthoritarian political culture is filled with uncertainty, which may discourage authoritarians from taking an active part in politics.[17]

The last two scales to be discussed are those measuring self–society and peace–war attitudes. Even though there were few statistically significant differences between mean responses of the leaders and the general population, the leaders persistently responded toward society and peace orientations. They are more society-oriented and peace-oriented than the general population. This finding in a way is consistent with an earlier finding on the leaders' responses to items on internationalism. One conclusion reached on peace–war orientation indicates that liberals are peace-oriented regardless of the extent of political involvement but conservatives are peace-oriented only if they are involved in community politics.[18] Our finding in this report, thus, coincides with the above empirical report.

Summary and Conclusions

To sum up our findings, empirical evidence supports the following hypotheses: (1) The leaders have a higher sense of political obligation and political efficacy than the general population; (2) The leaders are more internationally minded; (3) The leaders tend to be more pro-American and anti-Russian than the general population; (4) There are no appreciable differences between the leaders and the general population as far as economic liberalism is concerned; (5) On the other hand, the general population is more inclined to favor the policy of tax cuts "even if it means putting off some important things that need to be done"; (6) The leaders are more sociable than the general population; and (7) The leaders are less authoritarian than the general population.

These findings suggest a few points of theoretical importance:

1. The differences we find between the leaders and the general population are not strictly differences in value orientations as such but are also related to *cognitive capacity*. The leaders respond differently to some of the items[19] because of their capacity to see things beyond their shoes or wooden clogs. To be actively involved in politics requires not only an interest in politics but also the ability to perceive things in a variety of ways.[20] This would explain a number of findings such as the leaders' proclivity to be more internationally oriented and less authoritarian.

2. The difference between the two groups stems not only from value differences and cognitive differences but also from personality differences, as evidenced in the case of sociability.

3. From the findings in this report, we must conclude that we find a mixture of the first two models of what Miller and Stokes refer to as the "Burkean, instructed delegates, and responsible party models"[21] in this Japanese community. The leaders share some values with the rank-and-file citizens but certainly not all. The leaders probably play the role of the "instructed delegates" in areas of representation in which they have least intense opinions. Indeed, as Miller and Stokes so aptly pointed out, what was seriously lacking in normative theorists' discourse was the question of whether or not one model should be applied to all areas of legislation or only in some areas.

4. This study is far from comprehensive. Future research should include a number of areas that have not been covered in the past. This would require some paradigm which includes all relevant areas we wish to examine. This study as well as other studies point to the need of at least separating domestic issues from international issues, since there are very definite differences between leaders and the general population on these issues. The future normative political theorists must specify areas in which they have reason to believe there ought to be an agreement between the rulers and the ruled. Such an attempt should contribute to the development of more useful definitions of pluralistic democracy, the power elite, and other forms of community power structure.

5. As for the controversial question of community power structure, evidence presented in this short article is sufficient for one to conclude that the leaders do not have the power elite type of mentality.[22] It is important to point out that the power elite type of community power structure was not found in Reed Town, Japan, despite the employment of the reputational technique.

This study points to the need for examining psychological aspects of the leaders in any study of community power structure. Roll-call vote analysis too should be included where appropriate. *It is my contention that those who study community power structure should not only examine structural aspects of the leadership or several cases of important decision-making*

Psychological Aspects of   **243**
Community Power Structure:
Leaders and Rank-and-File Citizens
in Reed Town, Japan
Yasumasa Kuroda

but should also scrutinize the psychological dimension of the leadership structure.

Social Values and Political Orientations of City Managers: A Survey Report*[1]

Lloyd M. Wells

University of Missouri

THIS BRIEF ARTICLE is based on research designed to explore certain hypotheses advanced by Charles Adrian and others concerning the social values and political orientations of city managers. These hypotheses, which have rarely been treated empirically,[2] assert the probability that city managers, for a variety of reasons relating to their social experience, are likely to be "pro-business" in their social values and "conservative" in their political outlook.[3] In one of Adrian's textbook formulations:

> Very many managers are engineers, and some are trained in schools of business administration. This means that they received much of their education in the most conservative colleges of our universities. They are likely to be personally conservative in political views. They are business-oriented in their social values. Many of them have had experience in private business before becoming managers; others may hope to move into good positions in private business after serving a number of years in city government.[4]

Since Adrian presumably was generalizing about city managers in the nation as a whole, the present research, based on questionnaires and interviews with all

* Reprinted with permission of the author and publisher, from Lloyd M. Wells, "Social Values and Political Orientations of City Managers: A Survey Report," (Southwestern) Social Science Quarterly, 48 (December 1967), pp. 433–450.

city managers in a single state, can neither directly confirm nor refute his observations. It can, however, present a variety of empirical evidence of a kind heretofore unavailable which bears directly on the above statement and upon similar assumptions in the literature. We shall proceed to deal briefly with the methodological limitations of this study, with the social values and social style of our respondents, and finally with their political orientations.

Methodology

Reliance on a survey of the twenty-six incumbent managers in the state of Missouri rather than upon a national sample was dictated by limitations of time and resources. Such a procedure has its obvious disadvantages and constitutes the major limitation on the findings here reported. One obviously cannot generalize far on the basis of such limited evidence. The smaller sample, however, permitted attitudinal exploration which otherwise would not have been possible. It also suggested hypotheses about the nature of the larger universe of the city-management profession.

City managers within the state were readily accessible and available for intensive interview. An examination of their social characteristics reveals that, in general, they are very much like other administrative elites in the United States. The city managers of this study are a highly educated group. They are white, male, native born, predominantly Anglo-Saxon and overwhelmingly Protestant. Over one quarter of our sample claims affiliation with one of the "high status" Protestant denominations. There were few Catholics and no members of the Jewish faith among the managers interviewed. One other fact is worth mention. The managers of this study were distributed among the various cities of the state in the following population ranges: 475,000—1; 50,000 to 100,000 —3; 25,000 to 50,000—3; 10,000 to 25,000 —7; 5,000 to 10,000—8; 2,700 to 5,000—4.

In the research design the usual distinctions were made between "economic

244

Notes to this selection will be found on page 360.

liberalism," "free speech liberalism" and "civil (Negro) rights" liberalism on the assumption that what are commonly designated as "liberal" and "conservative" responses in one dimension do not necessarily carry over into other spheres.[5] Questionnaires were first mailed to all incumbent managers as of 1963–1964 when research began. Extensive interviews followed. Whenever possible questions previously used in other studies were employed.

Several different instruments were used to explore managerial values and attitudes. Imbedded in the questionnaire were five scalable welfare items developed by the Survey Research Center at the University of Michigan to derive one measure of economic liberalism along with two questions previously tested by other survey organizations to elicit attitudinal responses toward labor unions and large-scale business enterprises.[6] Martin Trow's three-item measure of political tolerance was employed in the free-speech dimension.[7] Finally, a series of open-ended interview questions relating to political and ideological self-identification were used as springboards for additional discussion of the Negro revolution and other controversial issues.

To gain a composite picture of economic liberalism, a crude but serviceable index was derived by assigning one point for each liberal response to the scalable welfare item questions and dividing respondents into four groups on the basis to total scores. Those who scored from 0 to 1 were designated as "conservative." Those with a score of 2 were designated as "moderately conservative," those with a score of 3 were labelled "moderately liberal" and those who gave four or five liberal responses were designated as "liberal." A similar index was devised for the political tolerance or free-speech dimension. The specific application of these techniques as presented subsequently in this report should serve further to clarify the approach taken.

Social Values and Social Style

One of the most striking aspects of the city manager's value system as revealed in this survey is the predominance of his orientation toward public service rather than toward private business. This orientation was revealed in a variety of ways. One rough measure was derived from respondents' free-ranging answers to the following questions: "If you were to leave the city management profession, what kind of job would you prefer? Why?" In response to the first question some 65 per cent of respondents indicated a preference for teaching, governmental service or politics. Only about 30 per cent indicated a preference for a career in business. Two themes ran through the subsequent discussion with a majority of the managers. One was the theme of personal commitment to public service; the other involved an appraisal of other occupations, in terms of the transferability of managerial knowledge and skills. The following comments are illustrative and revealing:

"I am not interested in any profession or occupation where the profit making motive is king."

"Teaching would come closer to giving me the same sense of personal satisfaction . . . through service to others that city management provides."

"Politics would not be much of a jump from my current job."

"I would probably stay in some sort of public administration work because it would be less of a switch."

"Going into business would be less of a leap from my current job."

"I would go into some field where I could occasionally step out of line without reading about it in the headlines next day."

A substantial majority of the respondents drew sharp contrasts between the roles of city manager and business executive. They frequently stressed the public-service *vs.* private-profit theme and with about equal frequency alluded to the political environment within which the city manager must operate as contrasted with the privatization of business decision-making. Most of the managers displayed many of the same attitudes and values which Warner, *et al.*, found to be characteristic of the "American federal executive." For a majority of the city managers there was the same expression of lofty aspiration which Warner and associates found with the federal executives, the same high evaluation of public service, the same emphasis on the significance of public problems, and the same high estimate of professional associates.[8]

The public-service orientation of the managers is, however, tinged with strong hues of pragmatism. While respondents employed a public-service rhetoric and espoused a public-service ideology, only a small minority displayed an obvious distaste for personal involvement in predominantly commercial operations. The esthetic, cultural and intellectual interests which Warner and associates found to undergird the preferences of many federal executives for noncommercial employment is not readily apparent in the city manager population subject to this study. The "average" manager would hardly be classified as an intellectual. He frequently seeks out contact with academicians and looks to the campus for assistance; but he tends to stress the instrumental, the vocational and the utilitarian aspects of education.

The managerial style of life, moreover, brings him into close association with segments of the business community. Most managers, some 76 per cent of our sample, report civic club membership. The majority, about 56 per cent, belong to only one such organization with the Rotary Club the overwhelming choice.[9] Local Chambers of Commerce attract only a scattering of city managers and some 24 per cent of our sample report no civic club membership whatsoever. For a few respondents the demands of the professional role cast doubt on the propriety of such organizational attachments.

There are other respects in which city managers and businessmen display similarity of style and taste. The leisure-time reading habits of city managers bear a striking resemblance to the reading of small businessmen as reported in studies by Bauer, *et al.*, and elsewhere.[10] In both instances, the reading of one or more daily newspapers is virtually unanimous and the reading of trade and technical journals is widespread. A very few businessmen and none of the city managers reported reading any of the liberal magazines of commentary such as *The Reporter*, *The Nation*, and the *New Republic*. A very few businessmen and a mere scattering of city managers reported reading any of the "high brow" magazines such as *Atlantic Monthly*, *Harper's*, *The Saturday Review* or *The New Yorker*. Some 50 per cent of the city managers and "slightly over half" the business executives[11] read *Time* magazine. Second in popularity with both city managers and businessmen is *U.S. News and World Report*. It is read by about half the city managers and by about one-third of the business executives. Finally, *Reader's Digest* was "checked with some frequency" (23 per cent)[12] by the heads of the smallest business firms in the Bauer study but only infrequently (6 per cent) by men from the largest corporations,[13] and by 50 per cent of the city managers. While the city manager appears to read somewhat more than his small business counterpart, the quality of his literary intake outside his field of specialization is very similar.

Political Orientations

The city managers divide about equally in their political party identification or lack of it. Approximately one third of our sample consider themselves Democrats, another one third indicate a preference for Republican party identification, and the final one-third classified themselves as Independents. A majority of respondents shied away from liberal and conservative labels and pictured themselves as "moderates," "middle of the roaders," "progressive-conservatives," "practical liberals," etc.

Conservative responses were given by a majority of respondents on three out of five of the scalable welfare items. They were most nearly unanimous in their rejection of the proposition that "The government in Washington ought to see to it that everybody who wants to work can find a job." About 77 per cent of the sample disagreed with the proposition, some because of the role which it assigned to "the government in Washington," others because of a more basic commitment to individual rather than collective responsibility. About 62 per cent rejected the notion that "The government ought to help people get doctors and hospital care at low cost," and a rather surprising 58 per cent refused to accept as a general rule the proposition that "If cities and towns around the country need help to build more schools, the government in Washington ought to give them the money they need."

On two of the scalable welfare items the managers gave predominantly liberal responses. Bare majorities agreed with the proposition that "If Negroes are not getting fair treatment in jobs and housing, the government in Washington ought to see to it that they do," and rejected the proposition that "The government should leave things like electrical power and housing for private businessmen to handle."

Analyzed on the basis of the liberal-conservative index mentioned earlier, it appears that some 73 per cent of the managers fall into the "conservative" (42 per cent) or the "moderately conservative" (31 per cent) category while only 27 per cent fell into the "liberal" (8 per cent) or "moderately liberal" (19 per cent) category. Thus it would appear that the managers tend to cluster toward the conservative end of the economic welfare scale.

Much the same kinds of attitudes were reflected in answers to questions relating to labor unions and large-scale business corporations. The majority of respondents indicated general acceptance of both institutions. On balance, however, the views expressed were more favorable toward the business corporation. A substantial minority, some 42 per cent of the total, expressed the view that "although we need labor

unions in this country, they do more harm than good the way they are run now."

Attitudes slightly more liberal in nature characterized managerial response to the problems of free speech and Negro rights. While eschewing blanket endorsement of governmental activity in the realm of civil rights, some 54 per cent of respondents indicated general sympathy for federal and state efforts to promote equality of treatment, while 23 per cent displayed ambivalence and avoided taking a stand and the remainder expressed a general lack of sympathy for governmental involvement. Except in a very few instances the managers displayed little intensity of feeling about the issue.

In the realm of free speech, a majority of the managers again indicated a moderate and restrained liberalism. They unanimously agreed that newspapers should be allowed "to criticize our form of government" and 88 per cent would allow socialist parties to publish newspapers. These measures of political toleration may seem modest, indeed, unless one recalls the results from national samples on the same questions. As summed up by Samuel Stouffer, those who would prohibit newspapers from criticizing our form of government has varied from 30 per cent to 42 per cent of national samples and those who would deny socialists the right to publish has ranged between 25 per cent to 45 per cent.[14] In this respect, then, the city managers of our sample appear relatively more tolerant than do general cross sections of the population.

The limits of managerial toleration are quickly reached, however, as one begins to explore attitudes toward Communism. Whether avowed Communists should be allowed to speak on the radio and appear on television proved to be a troublesome and divisive question for our sample. About half the respondents gave conservative answers to the question while 38 per cent supplied the liberal response and the remainder evaded the question. A modicum of latent but intense conservatism was brought to the surface in connection with the question of Communists, but, for the most part, respondents displayed moderation in their assessments. No evidence of a broad conspiratorial theory of Communist infiltration was apparent.

Using an index similar to that devised for economic liberalism and assigning one point for each unequivocal liberal response on free speech questions, we find that 35 per cent of the sample ranked as "more liberal," that only 7 per cent ranked as "more conservative," and that 58 per cent may be classified as "moderates" who are either ambivalent or opposed to allowing Communists access to the mass media but who otherwise accept the rationale of freedom of speech.

Conclusions

In most respects the present study, given its limitations, tends merely to confirm, to document and to elaborate upon hypotheses relating to the supposed pro-business conservatism of city managers. In other respects, however, it suggests the need for qualifying, refining and restating these hypotheses. The "average" manager as he appears in this study is a Protestant, a Rotarian, an avid reader of technical journals relating to his job, a devotee of *Time, U.S. News and World Report* and *Reader's Digest*. He does not regularly expose himself to publications which espouse a liberal point of view and his attitudes on economic welfare policy tend to be conservative. He is slightly more liberal, however, when liberalism is defined in terms of free speech and Negro rights. He takes a more or less instrumental view of education and tends to support the propagation of knowledge which has some kind of a practical pay-off.

The manager's conservatism is, however, a conservatism of the moderate, pragmatic, middle-of-the-road variety. His ideology,

if such it may be called, is quite unlike the "pre-industrial agrarian spirit" which Bunzel finds to be characteristic of the ideology of small business.[15] The average manager of this sample is, in the main, positively oriented toward both labor unions and large business corporations although he is more skeptical of the former than the latter.

The manager's public-service orientation sets him apart from the business executive. Our manager does not, contrary to some expectations, regard city management as a mere stepping stone to more lucrative employment in private business. While a considerable number have had some kind of prior business experience, few express a desire to return to the commercial world. The dominant rhetoric is that of the public-service professional.

The potential thrust of a public-service ideology should not be overlooked. Grounded in perceptions as to the exigencies of contemporary social life, such an ideology contains implicit within it a tendency to justify a central role for government in the life of society.[16] Men do not ordinarily become career public executives, it may be assumed, in order to preside over the liquidation or curtailment of governmental functions for which they have been made responsible. Economy and efficiency in the public-service idiom do not require absolute reductions in the size of governmental budgets but rather the more effective utilization of resources so as to produce more and better services. "Progress," a word much on the lips of professional managers, is not likely to be defined in terms of the withering away of the state.

The question remains as to whether or not the kind of pragmatic, middle-of-the-road conservatism here delineated is best described as a "pro-business" conservatism. If the city manager shares certain attitudes and values with businessmen, so do other segments of American society. Commercial values tend to permeate all social structures including those of the church and the academy. If we follow Janowitz, Huntington[17] and others, the conservatism of the military establishment seems to rest on an ideological structure which, in some respects, is the very antithesis of commercial values; and yet the businessman and the military leader may find themselves in frequent agreement, for different reasons, on particular issues of public policy. On the basis of the present study it is merely suggested that a more precise formulation of hypotheses and propositions relating to the conservatism of city managers in the nation as a whole will probably have to

take into account the public service orientation of the managers along with their political sensitivity and their pragmatic inclinations.

Leaders' Values and the Dynamics of Community Integration: A Four-Nation Comparative Study*

Philip E. Jacob

University of Hawaii and East-West Center

WHY DO SOME communities grow and others stagnate? Why do some demonstrate a common purposefulness and an ability to act vigorously to satisfy social needs, while in others people split apart, nurse separate interests, and fail to respond to civic goals? Why are some more parochial, preoccupied with local problems, while others are persuaded to tie themselves closely to broader regional or national concerns, either functional or political?

Such questions, relating to the phenomenon of community integration or the lack thereof, have been the subject of the International Studies of Values in Politics, a five-year program of comparative cross-national research now nearing completion in India, Poland, Yugoslavia, and the United States.[1]

The immediate objective of the project was to determine *the influence of leaders' values on the integration of local communities.*

Underlying this set of studies was the thesis that values, i.e., norms or standards, are so important a component of human behavior, that no explanation of social behavior and institutions can be adequate if it does not demonstrate the extent to which people's actions reflect particular values or patterns of value they hold and profess. This is especially the case with the study of communities and their development. Emphasis on the structure of status and power as an overwhelming, almost independent force shaping the conduct of men in society has tended to conceal the reverse process. Social structures are themselves molded by the dispositions, normative and otherwise, of the human stuff to which they are composed and through which they must function.

On the other hand, the design of the project providing that the role of leaders' values in community integration would be challengeable by alternative explanations, based on environmental variables, such as the level of affluence or resource base, the character of the political system (especially the amount of local autonomy prevailing), and certain features of the structure of influence in the community. Control for these factors was secured through the selection of four countries with sharply divergent political, cultural, and economic conditions and the amassing of a substantial body of aggregative data on social and economic conditions, permitting differentiation within a sample of thirty localities chosen in each country.

Essential to the success of this kind of study was its distinctive pattern of organization. The project became, in effect, an international cooperative in which design, execution, and analysis of the studies were jointly planned and conducted by teams of social scientists from the four countries under sponsorship of the International Social Science Council (the official coordinating body of the international social science professional organizations). This experience has confirmed the feasibility—indeed an essentiality—of applying the joint enterprise pattern to the organization of cross-cultural comparative research, especially for studies of political decision-making and community integration.[2]

Design and Methods

The evolution of the design and operational procedures was governed by mutual commitment to meet three requirements:

1. All concepts should be defined in such a

Published for the first time in this volume.

Notes to this selection will be found on pages 360–361.

way that they could be identified by empirical indicators using accessible data in each of the countries;

2. Measurement of the concepts should be cross-nationally equivalent (though not necessarily using identical indicators, as will be explained below);

3. Analytical procedures should take account of the multiplicity of possible determinants in a complex interactional situation such as that confronted in this research (even though experimental manipulation of variables over time was not possible).

As finally matured, the design called for examination of the interrelationships of two main sets of variables—leaders' values and community "activeness," which was conceived as a major expression of community integration.

Values were defined operationally as the norms or principles which people apply in decision-making, that is, the criteria they use in choosing which of alternative courses of action to follow (or whether to make no decision at all).[3] Values, as we have explored them, include broadly based concepts of legitimacy prevalent throughout a society; role-expectations of the general public or influence groups perceived by a decision-maker to be specifically applicable to his conduct; or personal convictions of what is right or wrong (which may conflict with the social norms to which the individual is exposed). It is quickly apparent that political decision-making involves a process not only of applying particular values to the issue at hand, but of ordering priorities among inconsistent or conflicting values. So the study probed for the composition of leaders' value-*profiles*, in which they linked one value to another in a well-defined "syndrome" of interrelated commitments and priorities.

The principal concept of *integration* applied in this study was, as indicated, a performance concept. It assumes that the output of a community—what it does—is a powerful indicator of how well integrated it is. Investigation revealed at least two dimensions of such activeness—decisions of the local government to allocate or mobilize

resources for various types of community needs and voluntary popular participation in organizations or activities directed toward the accomplishment of social goals (including political as well as cultural and functional activities).

Two other forms of integration were included as supplementary variables: (1) the congruence of values among local leaders, or the extent to which they shared the same or compatible values, and (2) integration of the local community with the nation, in the sense of responsiveness to national goals and values and specifically to policies and programs initiated by the national leadership.[4]

Linking leaders' values to community activeness is the process variable of *political decision-making* within the going system of government and structure of influence in the community. Patterns of interpersonal relations among leaders in live decisional situations proved difficult to investigate. Consequently attention was focused first on the formal characteristics of the system and especially on the degree of autonomy to make decisions possessed by the local leaders; second on the leaders' perceptions of influence and support groups affecting their political role; and third on the interplay of opposing interests within and outside the community as they wrestled to determine the outcome of critical issues.

Control variables, as previously mentioned, included the resource base of the community (economic level), certain ecological and demographic features, and additional personal characteristics of the leaders such as age, eduation, political career and mobility.

The design is summarized in Table 1.

BASES FOR CROSS-NATIONAL COMPARISONS

Fundamental to the whole project, of course, has been the comparison of these relationships across countries, on the assumption that societal characteristics might make a crucial difference in determining the dynamics of community integration on the one hand, or the values of leaders on the other. The selection of India, Poland, Yugoslavia, and the United States as the participating countries was guided in part by the desire to provide for important differences in socioeconomic conditions, cultural background, and political ideology and system. At the same time in all four countries there was a common preoccupation with the problem of relating political system to economic development and social mobilization, as witnessed by variety and experimentation in the patterns of local–national relationships—pan-chayati raj in India, people's councils in Poland, the radical decentralization of powers in Yugoslavia to communes and workers' councils, and the shifting kaleidoscope of local–state–federal relations in the United States. The ultimate stage of analysis envisages a direct comparison between the amount of *intra*-national variation and *inter*-national differences in the major variables, leading to conclusions as to the over-all effect of distinctively *national* characteristics.

In India and Yugoslavia, it will be possible to examine regional differences as well, at least with regard to leadership characteristics, the sample of respondents having been chosen from three states and republics respectively. (It should be made clear that for India, findings cannot be generalized beyond the three states of Gujarat, Maharashtra, and Uttar Pradesh in which most of the field work was concentrated. The selection of units in the other countries may have been sufficiently representative to warrant conclusions about the nation as a whole.)

It should be emphasized that in developing the project, precisely parallel lines of inquiry were pursued in each country, so as to maximize the comparability of the results. This did not mean that identical bits of information were gathered to serve as indicators of the variables. Considering the vast differences among the four countries, it would have been neither possible nor appropriate to do so. Instead, a strategy of multiple observation was undertaken to establish the conceptual equivalence of the variables and the reliability of their indicators. Each variable was identified and measured by a whole set of items which were demonstrated statistically (usually by factor analysis) to be homogeneous.

In the case of values, an innovative method was devised to increase the cross-national reliability of scales by combining with identical items asked in all countries, a set of nation-specific items demonstrated to be homogeneous.[5]

TABLE 1. *Variables*

Explanatory Variables	Linkage Variables	Dependent Variables
1. Principal independent variable: leaders' values	Process of political decision-making:	1. Community activeness (Integration "A") Dimension I—resource mobilization (by the local government) Dimension II—popular involvement
2. Control variables— community characteristics: (a) economic base (b) ecological/social features	a. Autonomy—formal b. Autonomy—as perceived by leaders c. Support reference groups—perceived by leaders	
3. Control variables— leaders' characteristics: (a) biographical (b) perceptions of community (c) perceptions of role	d. Influence/interest group conflict structure in the community e. Inter-personal influence in the local governing bodies	2. Congruence of local leaders' values (Integration "B") 3. Local responsiveness to nation (Integration "C")

Furthermore, the study deliberately used a variety of techniques of inquiry, so as to "triangulate" the variables, checking results derived by one method against those produced by another. The importance of such built-in controls, to verify accuracy both of data and analysis, cannot be over-emphasized. The immense potentiality for error in this kind of broad-gauged empirical research, which requires the manipulation of large quantities of data, was so repeatedly demonstrated that the principal investigators now look with suspicion on the results of any studies which have not incorporated effective means of control.

THE LINES OF INQUIRY

Four main types of research were undertaken:

1. An intensive interview survey of 3929 political leaders, virtually all the major political position-holders in a sample of local governmental units in each country (blocks in India, powiats in Poland, communes in Yugoslavia, municipalities in the U.S.). The instruments, which underwent three to four pretests, included (a) forced-choice questions from which were derived ten scales of politically relevant values; (b) a set of open-ended questions concerning desirable leadership traits, and national aspirations, which helped to locate the horizons of the leaders' universe of values; (c) probes which elicited perceptions of the leaders' areas of influence, roles, reference groups, and loyalties; (d) queries concerning the scope and nature of community cleavages and conflicts; and (e) an assessment of attitudes toward the proper scope of government responsibility and local autonomy.

The leaders on whom the study focused were those who held governmental or political authority in the community (in other words the formal political power structure—both elected and administrative), plus party leadership outside as well as inside the government establishment, and some other political influentials. Approximately thirty were interviewed in each locality, assuring considerable stability in comparing communities within a country as well as between countries.

2. Compilation of a massive volume of aggregative data to secure measures of the level and rate of local economic development and the degree of social mobilization in the community. Much of this material had to be collected on-the-spot, first-hand, in default of relevant, reliable local data at central sources.

3. Case studies of political decision-making, reconstructing the life-history and social context of controversial issues in a cross section of communities. A total of 27 cases were completed in the four countries, of which 16 are final studies and the others pretests. Data for the final reports were derived from records, interviews with informants, and interviews with participants.

This led to the selection of the following general variables: (a) *power and influence structure* and how elements of the informal structure bear on decisions made by the formal political structure; (b) *mobilization and organization of support*, both with respect to particular individuals and groups and with respect to the public; (c) *exercise of roles*, how the participants perform according to self-expectations and expectations of others as well as clear identification of the place of the participant in the decisional process (initiator, promoter, opponent, supporter, decision-maker); (d) *communication, information and cognition*, how communication channels among levels affect decisions and how leaders acquire information about the decisions; (e) *local autonomy* and the ways in which real and perceived autonomy are influential—what are the formal–legal restrictions and how do leaders deal with them?

Finally, an over-all attempt was made to relate particular values identified in a case to specific output actions, especially whether leaders felt it necessary to modify or compromise their values and if so, how and with what justifications.

4. Systematic content analysis of the values expressed by leaders in speeches, other public communications, and in

the survey interviews. Content analytic techniques, especially developed to identify, classify and measure the emphasis placed on values, were applied to limited selections of major policy statements by national leaders.

Briefly, the approach involved clear specification of substantive (rather than syntactical) elements which distinguish value-laden themes as the units for analysis. The components of a value theme or thought-unit include some or all of the following: a standard of evaluation, an object being evaluated, a referent or beneficiary of the value asserted, and certain terms denoting an evaluative act. Various formats in which an evaluate communication might be conveyed by political leadership were empirically derived from the material and set forth as guidelines for coding. These procedures permitted identification of some values conveyed by inference, or reference to the common-knowledge context in which the statement was delivered, thus widening the value content beyond explicit expressions of approval, justification and the like, and coming closer to the intentions of the author.

Classification categories were also empirically derived directly from the material analyzed: value references were clustered into conceptually distinct groups, defined quite precisely, usually in the author's own terms. On examination, many categories appear cross-nationally comparable, but some are unique for particular countries, at least on the basis of statements so far analyzed.[6]

SOURCES OF INDICATORS

As a result of these investigations, the bodies of data shown in Table 2 were secured from which to compose indices of the different variables.

Value Scales

One of the important results of the ISVIP is a set of nine multi-item scales which reliably measure the strength of leaders' commitments to values relevant to political

conduct and public policy in very diverse countries.[7]

The scaled values, with their predetermined definitions, and those scale items which were identical and reliable for all countries are as follows (the additional nation-specific items included in the scales are reported in ISVIP Doc. No. RT/IV/3):

1. *Concern for Economic Development*, combining a general interest in material progress and well-being with a readiness to place future economic growth ahead of immediate consumption.

The economic development of the nation should take precedence over immediate consumer gratification.

A high standard of living should be the most important (ultimate) goal of a society.

The long term economic development of the nation should be considered as its most important goal.

Only economic development will ultimately provide the things required for the welfare and happiness of the people.

2. *Conflict Avoidance*, emphasizing particularly the extent to which a desire for consensus, and the avoidance of conflict limit the willingness of leaders to proceed with programs in the community.

If there is disagreement about a program, a leader should be willing to give it up. Public decisions should be made with unanimous consent.

Preserving harmony in the community should be considered more important than the achievement of community programs.

A good leader should refrain from making proposals that divide the people even if these are important for the community.

3. *Participation:* this scale includes two elements—a general concern for citizen involvement in public policy formation and decision-making; and a specific readiness to subordinate expertise and professional competence to the value of public participation in the decisional process.

The complexity of modern day issues requires that only the more simple questions should be considered publicly.

*TABLE 2.** *Indicators*

Variables	Data Sources
I. Leaders' characteristics:	
A. Values	(1) Responses to survey (Parts II and III)
	(2) Content analysis (Indian and U.S. national policy statements)
	(3) Case studies of decisions— informants' observations; leader interviews (supplementary to survey)
B. Perceptions and attitudes:	
1. community problems	(4) Survey (Part I, q. 1)
2. community conflicts and cleavages	(5) Survey (Part IV, q. 1, 2, 3)
3. spheres of local autonomy	(6) Survey (Part IV, q. 7)
4. areas of governmental responsibility	(7) Survey (Part IV, q. 6)
5. support and reference groups	(8) Survey (Part IV, q. 4, 5)
6. areas of leaders' activity and influence	(9) Survey (Part I, q. 2, 3, 4)
7. obstacles to leadership	(10) Survey (Part I, q. 5)
C. Personal and political background	(11) Survey (Part V)
II. Community Characteristics:	
A. Economic resources and level of development	(12) Production and income data
B. Political structure and decisional processes	(13) Substantive inventories of local government research
	(14) Local government manuals and reports
	(15) Decisional case studies
	(16) Survey: (see items 6, 7 above)
C. Ecological and social characteristics	(17) Survey: Leaders perceptions (see items above 4, 5, 8, 9, 10)
	(18) Decisional case studies
	(19) Supplementary information secured by field investigators
	(20) Census data (demographic)
III. Community Integration:	
A. Activeness	(21) Aggregative data on:
	(a) local expenditures
	(b) other resource commitments of local government
	(c) political participation
	(d) functional participation (in social organizations, etc.)
	(e) programmatic involvement
	(22) Decisional case studies
B. Responsiveness to national policies and programs	(23) Survey: Part II (local–national items) and Part IV, q. 4, 5, 6.
	(24) Selected activeness indicators (see item 21 above)
	(25) Comparisons of indicators 1 and 2 above.
C. Congruence of leaders' values	(26) Analysis of indicators 1, 2 and 3 above.

* Note: The decisional case studies furnish extensive additional material on leaders' perceptions derived from interviews with leaders and informants.

Most decisions should be left to the judgment of experts.

Only those who are fully informed on the issues should vote.

Only those who are competent on an issue should speak about it.

Participation of the people is not necessary if decision-making is left in the hands of a few trusted and competent leaders.

To have decisions made by people who are experts on the matter under consideration.

Participation by everyone in decision-making regardless of their knowledge of the issues involved.

4. *Selflessness:* Willingness to sacrifice for others.

A leader should not be concerned about his own status, only about doing a good job.

Sacrificing oneself for others is the highest value a man can achieve.

One should work to the best of his ability regardless of whether his services are adequately rewarded.

Sacrificing oneself for the benefit of others.

Subordination of one's own interest in the interest of a higher cause.

5. *National Commitment:* orientation to national as against local interest and goals, indicating readiness to give precedence to the former when there is conflict between them.

National goals should not be obtained at great costs to local communities.

Although national affairs are important, people here should first worry about their own community problems.

Community progress is not possible if national goals always have priority.

We should not worry so much about national problems when we have so many in our own community.

Local leaders should always be prepared to adjust their programs to national goals and policies even if this is disadvantageous for the community.

It is necessary to forego development of one's own community to help the development of the rest of the country.

6. *Action Propensity:* disposition to act, despite risks, uncertainties or lack of knowledge about consequences.

I prefer to stop and think before I act even on trifling matters.

I usually check more than twice to be sure that I am not overstepping my tasks.

One should be concerned with what he has rather than with what he could get.

The secret of happiness is not expecting too much out of life and being content with what comes your way.

Action should be delayed until it is certain that it will bring the desired results.

7. *Honesty:* truthfulness and the value of public disclosure by public officials.

Honesty and truthfulness must never be compromised at any cost.

Leaders should present the truth no matter what the consequences are.

If a person is requested by his superiors to present a false impression of certain matters, he should be willing to comply.

If a leader knows that the truth will harm someone, he should conceal certain facts.

Local officials should cover up situations which may embarrass their superiors.

In order to achieve community goals, it is permissible for leaders to present facts in a one-sided way.

It is not necessary for a leader to be strictly honest in public dealings if he knows this will interfere with getting his work done.

If a leader in local government is highly skilled, one should overlook minor instances of dishonesty.

8. *Change Orientation:* disposition to accept and support "new things," especially in the solution of community problems.

If society is to progress, newer solutions to problems are essential.

The people in this community must continually look for new solutions to problems rather than be satisfied with things as they are.

Even if the newer ways conflict with the way things were done in the past, they are absolutely necessary and desirable.

Changes are desirable even if they do not seem to contribute as much as one might expect.

9. *Economic Equality:* concern for reducing differences between rich and poor and improving the position of the underprivileged.

There should be an upper limit on income so that no one earns very much more than others.

The government has the responsibility to see that nobody lives well when others are poor.

In every situation poor people should be given more opportunities than rich people.

Philip E. Jacob

Avoiding spending on luxuries is necessary to minimize distance between social groups.

Discrepancies in salaries should be continually reduced.

CROSS-NATIONAL COMPARISONS

The following findings emerged from preliminary analysis of mean scores on nine value scales for the total group of leaders interviewed in all four countries. (See Table 3.)

1. There is substantial similarity across countries in the importance attached to

TABLE 3.* Political Values of Local Leaders
Means and Standard Deviations on Nine Value Scales for Total Leadership Samples in Four Countries

	India n = 946	Poland n = 889	U.S. n = 905	Yugoslavia n = 1,178
Economic Development				
Mean	3.64	3.11	2.83	3.45
S.D.	.367	.437	.417	.354
Conflict Avoidance				
Mean	3.13	2.42	2.13	2.85
S.D.	.566	.468	.351	.392
Participation				
Mean	2.13	2.26	2.74	2.74
S.D.	.457	.390	.417	.435
Selflessness				
Mean	3.41	3.23	3.15	3.21
S.D.	.307	.422	.374	.386
National Commitment				
Mean	2.57	2.70	2.29	2.34
S.D.	.604	.382	.346	.383
Action Propensity				
Mean	1.60	2.15	2.48	2.06
S.D.	.469	.393	.407	.357
Honesty (Truthfulness)				
Mean	3.38	3.13	3.28	3.48
S.D.	.466	.351	.374	.322
Change Orientation				
Mean	3.47	3.33	2.83	3.27
S.D.	.420	.386	.388	.375
Economic Equality				
Mean	3.50	2.74	1.72	3.03
S.D.	.429	.463	.428	.496

* Note: Mean scores are adjusted so that maximum commitment to a value equals 4.00 and maximum rejection of a value equals 1.00.

honesty and selflessness as standards of public conduct.

2. These local leaders, taken as composite national groups, are square in the middle when it comes to committing themselves as between national or local interests when the two are in conflict.

3. They are on the same side of the fence in being favorably disposed toward change, but American leaders as a whole are significantly less so than the others.

4. On the other hand, these leaders are *not* prone to act. That is, they want to calculate the risks before jumping. Indian leaders are particularly cautious (while being the most eager for change). The Americans are just the reverse.

5. A marked difference appears in concern for public participation in political decision-making. Indian leadership is strongly opposed. In contrast, Yugoslav leadership tends to favor participation.

6. As might have been expected, American leaders are strongly opposed to economic egalitarianism. Indian leaders are as strongly committed in favor. Curiously, local leadership in the Communist countries is not overly enthusiastic about leveling off economic differences.

7. Finally, the national groups diverge on the issue of conflict resolution. The Indians and Yugoslavs are clearly concerned to avoid conflict; Poles and Americans tend not to be upset over the possibility of conflict.

It should be emphasized that these conclusions are based on *mean* scores for each country, and do not constitute a profile characteristic of individual leaders. Indeed variances are so large within nations that a full-scale analysis is being undertaken of the nature and sources of individual differences.

On the other hand, variation is not great *among communities* in any country. While individual leaders differ markedly in the values they profess, they appear to cancel out each other at the community level, so that as a group leaders espouse much the same collective commitments, community to community, within each country.

What one gets is a picture of differences within community leadership but differences so evenly balanced throughout the local officialdom of these countries, that they present a deceptive appearance of universal homogeneity when compared as entities.

In fact, there is virtually no statistically significant difference between communities or between countries in the degree of leaders' consensus or dis-sensus on values, as measured by a composite index of the mean standard deviation on all nine values. This remarkable finding indicates that community integration in the sense of over-all sharing of values by leaders, i.e., integration "B" in the research design, is simply not a variable which has to be explained in these countries. Rich communities are as integrated in this sense as poor; community leaders are as united or disunited under one political system, as another; the amount of their over-all agreement or disagreement on political values is the same whatever the type of community power structure or whatever its status system.

Patterns of Activity

Such is not the case, however, with integration, when conceived as the outputs or social mobilization of a community. Using measures of activeness as described before (specific to each country), it is apparent that communities differ greatly from one another in every one of the four countries involved in the study.

While analysis has not been fully completed preliminary findings indicate that communities differ not only in the degree of activeness but in the pattern or *kind* of activity they engage in.

This would obviously be the case between countries where conditions of life are so different. Contrast, for instance, the measures of activeness which were found by factor analysis to be most indicative in the U.S. and India (see Tables 4, 5, and 6).

But within the same country communities may differ in the basic way they function, as well as in the degree of their vitality. In the Indian sample, for instance, there was a clear distinction between communities which were receptive to new techniques (Table 5) and those which were committed to conventional ways of life (Table 6). Communities might be highly active in *either* pattern but *not on both*.

The implication of this finding is that the quality of community dynamism may *not* be unidimensional. We must be on guard against the temptation to categorize community performance in terms of one measure of activeness only. Although it is

quite possible that a single dimension may be appropriate in some countries, this must be demonstrated empirically. In the case of India, the evidence from this study is that there is at least a dual pattern of activeness.[8]

Leadership in the Dynamic Community

The central issue of the entire study, it will be recalled, was to determine how

TABLE 4. U.S. Activeness Measures

Hypothesized Dimension	Indicator	Factor Loading
RM = resource mobilization		
PI = popular involvement		
RM	(1) Change in intergovernmental revenue, 1959–64, per capita	+.715
PI	(2) Boy Scout adult volunteers, 1965, pop. over 21	−.701
PI	(3) Mean turnout of voters in local elections, 1959–66, pop. 21 and over	+.636
RM	(4) Change in revenue from property taxes, 1959–64, per capita	+.619
PI	(5) Per cent change in Boy Scout members, 1960–65	−.521
PI	(6) Mean turnout of voters on referenda, 1960–66, pop. 21 and over	+.514
RM	(7) Expenditure: law and order, 1965, per capita	−.473
PI	(8) Mean turnout of voters in presidential elections, 1960–64, pop. 21 and over	+.452
PI	(9) Change in turnout of voters in presidential elections, 1960–64, pop. 21 and over	−.393
RM	(10) Non-patient hospital revenue, 1965, per capita	+.385
RM	(11) Value poverty program, 1965, per capita	+.384
PI	(12) United Fund contributions raised, 1965, per capita	−.285
RM	(13) Change in expenditure: public health and hospitals, 1960–65, per capita	+.256
PI	(14) YMCA—total number of board and committee members, 1965, total pop.	+.237
RM	(15) Change in expenditure: law and order, 1960–65, per capita	−.193
RM	(16) Expenditure: parks and recreation, 1965, per capita	−.189
RM	(17) Total general expenditure, 1964, per capita	−.136
RM	(18) Change in expenditure: parks and recreation, 1960–64, per capita	+.121
RM	(19) Increase in per pupil expenditure, 1960–65	+.113
PI	(20) Change in United Fund contributions raised, 1960–65, per capita	+.103
RM	(21) Expenditure; public health and hospitals, 1965, per capita	+.079
RM	(22) Change in expenditure: libraries, 1960–65, per capita	+.061
RM	(23) Expenditure: libraries, 1965, per capita	+.048
PI	(24) Members League of Women Voters, 1965, pop. over 21	−.044
PI	(25) Per cent change in the number of YMCA volunteer group leaders, 1960–65	−.025
RM	(26) Per pupil expenditure, 1965	+.006
PI	(27) YWCA contributions, 1965, per capita	+.004
PI	(28) YMCA contributions, 1965, per capita	+.001

* This is the second largest of four factors rotated, accounting for 12.7 per cent of the variance.

much of the variance in community activeness (i.e., integration "A") can be explained by leader characteristics, particularly leaders' values.

To reach this conclusion (with proper regard for alternative explanations), approximately 180 variables were intercorrelated with the various measures of activeness which were produced for each country. A set of the best correlated variables was selected and several different types of multivariate analysis then performed.[9]

Interpretation of the results is still in process, but it is already clear that *the pattern of explanation differs greatly among countries.* Leaders' values (especially the concern to avoid conflict and the sense of commitment to nation) are far more significantly associated with community

activeness in India than in the U.S.; the level of economic resources much less so. Certain aspects of the demographic, social, and cultural composition of leadership in the U.S. bear on the issue but have little apparent force in India. The caste composition of leadership in particular seems to have no relevance to the amount of social mobilization at the block level.

In India, there turns out to be an extraordinary dovetailing of the two main patterns of activeness on the one hand with clearly distinguishable sets of leader characteristics on the other. Two kinds of community leadership emerge, one the opposite of the other. Each tends to be associated with a different kind of community.

INNOVATORS

Those who lead in communities which are most active in adopting scientific improve-

TABLE 5. *Indian Activeness Measures – I**

Hypothesized Dimension	Indicator	Factor Loading*
RM = resource mobilization		
PI = popular involvement		
RM	(1) Average supply of chemical fertilizer per year—1962–65	+.940
PI	(2) Average number of adults made literate per year—1962–65	+.909
PI	(3) Average number of inoculations of cattle per year—1962–65	+.843
PI	(4) Average number of sterilizations (male and female) per year—1962–65	+.744
RM	(5) Average increment of village radios per year 1962–65 (base year 1961–62)	+.708
PI	(6) Average number of smallpox vaccinations per year 1962–65	+.605
RM	(7) Average increment of motor-run pumping sets per year 1962–65 (base year 1961–62)	+.540
PI	(8) Average number of artificial inseminations per year 1962–65	+.439
PI	(9) Average number of drinking wells constructed per year 1962–65	−.178
RM	(10) Average increment of area irrigated per year, 1962–65 (base year 1961–62)	−.157
RM	(11) Average number of improved ploughs distributed per year, 1962–65	−.150
PI	(12) Average increment in the proportion of paid-up share capital of cooperative societies, 1962–63/1965–66 (base year 1961–62)	−.120
RM	(13) Average increment in proportion of the supply of improved seeds, 1962–63/1965–66 (base year 1961–62)	−.104
RM	(14) Average number of new schools opened per year, 1962–65	−.077
PI	(15) Average increment in school enrollment 1962–65 (base year 1961–62)	−.053
PI	(16) Average increase in the proportion of members of cooperative societies, 1962–63/1965–66 (base year 1961–62)	−.042
PI	(17) Average number of latrines built per year, 1962–65	+.019
PI	(18) Average number of manure pits dug per year, 1962–65	+.012
PI	(19) Number of loops inserted, 1965–66	.004

* This is the largest factor of four factors rotated, accounting for 23.4 per cent of the variance.

ments and programs of social development (activeness measure I) look as follows:

1. They place priority on national goals and development; worry less about immediate local needs and problems.

2. They are less inclined to hold up action for the sake of harmony and consensus in the community.

3. The search for new solutions to problems appears to them more urgent; leaving "things as they are," less tolerable.

4. They are politically conscious, in at least two senses: they see political conflicts in the community as a concrete obstacle to effective leadership and an impediment to the development of the community; and at the same time, they are more personally committed to advance political party interests.

5. They are governmentally oriented, in at least two senses: they take a dim view of

leaving community problems up to "the people," rather than turning to government for action; and they are more keenly aware of the *lack of power* for local government to function effectively in such areas as housing and health.

6. They profess less attachment in their leadership role to local reference groups, such as local officials, influential people and even personal friends.

7. They tend to be more active and influential than others in the area of industrial and general economic development.

8. They are younger.

9. They are more educated and more homogeneous in their level of education than the leaders of other communities.

TABLE 6. Indian Activeness Measures – II*

Hypothesized Dimension	Indicator	Factor Loading
RM = resource mobilization		
PI = popular involvement		
RM	(1) Average number of improved ploughs distributed per year, 1962–65	+.877
PI	(2) Average increase in the proportion of members of cooperative societies, 1962–63/1965–66 (base year 1961–62)	+.805
RM	(3) Average increment of area irrigated per year, 1962–65 (base year 1961–62)	+.744
PI	(4) Average increment in the proportion of paid-up share capital of cooperative societies, 1962–63/1965–66 (base year 1961–62)	+.568
PI	(5) Average number of artificial inseminations per year, 1962–65	+.374
PI	(6) Average number of manure pits dug per year, 1962–65	+.253
RM	(7) Average number of new schools opened per year, 1962–65	+.241
PI	(8) Average number of inoculations of cattle per year, 1962–65	+.210
RM	(9) Average increment in proportion of the supply of improved seeds, 1962–63/1965–66 (base year 1961–62)	+.036
RM	(10) Average supply of chemical fetilizer per year, 1962–65	−.042
PI	(11) Average number of adults made literate per year, 1962–65	−.119
PI	(12) Average number of latrines built per year, 1962–65	−.143
PI	(13) Average number of sterilizations (male and female) per year, 1962–65	−.145
PI	(14) Average number of drinking wells constructed per year, 1962–65	−.155
PI	(15) Average increment in school enrollment, 1962–65 (base year 1961–62)	−.252
RM	(16) Average increment of motor-run pumping sets per year, 1962–65 (base year 1961–62)	−.314
PI	(17) Average number of smallpox vaccinations per year, 1962–65	−.337
RM	(18) Average increment of village radios per year, 1962–65 (base year 1961–62)	−.535
PI	(19) Number of loops inserted, 1965–66	−.605

* This is the second factor of four factors rotated accounting for 19.0 per cent of the variance.

HARMONIZERS

Those leaders who are attached to communities which are active in the conventional ways of a manual agricultural society (activeness measure II) have the following attributes:

1. They are greatly concerned to avoid conflict, secure consensus and maintain unity in their communities. There is wide homogeneity on this value; all leaders tend to be harmonizers in this kind of community.

2. These same leaders are unusually *conflict-conscious*, asserting more than others, that conflicts beset their communities and interfere with their development.

3. They are also cleavage-conscious, noting many differences which divide people in their communities.

4. They are far less convinced of the desirability, or necessity of changing the established ways of coping with community problems.

5. They attach less importance to expertise in making decisions on public matters.

6. They are less insistent on leaders adhering strictly to principles, such as truthfulness in public conduct, or placing public interest above self-interest.

7. They blame and they shun government; they see "bureaucracy," maladministration, corruption (outside, or up above) as a major obstacle in their leadership; and they favor leaving problems up to the people to resolve, rather than calling upon any level of government, even local, to take a hand.

8. Somewhat paradoxically, they also deplore public apathy and ignorance as an obstacle to leadership.

9. They are usually attached to local bases of support—official and non-official (including "poor people" as well as the "respected and influential").

10. Conversely, they are allergic to political party and political life: they profess not to seek support from higher party leaders; they state minimal concern for advancing party interests; far fewer than in other communities claim membership in the Congress Party; they don't recognize or admit partisan conflict to be an obstacle to their leadership; and an unusually small number indicate that they are either active or influential in political organizations.

11. These people are preeminently agriculturalists; and they quite clearly concede they are neither active nor influential in general economic development. They do take a lively hand in the area of community services.

12. Their age has no bearing on the activeness of their communities, but in education, they are more heterogeneous.

These relationships, of course, cannot justify inferences that leader characteristics "cause" activeness in a local community. The data do not permit a determination of sequence, what follows what. Based on a multivariate pattern of explanation, however, the evidence from this study is that leader values and other characteristics can have a critical place in the hierarchy of variables related to the level of resource mobilization and popular involvement in local governmental units. This relationship is stronger in areas which are less industrialized and economically developed, so strong, as a matter of fact, that knowing the kind of leaders a community has may make it possible to predict the vigor and character of that community's development and its potential for social integration.

VI

Community Politics and Public Policies

Introduction

IN SOME respects, this entire volume has concerned public policies and the socioeconomic and political variables which shape them. The four selections in this section, however, have explicitly centered their analyses upon particular policies taken as dependent variables. Included are the specific arenas of taxing, transportation, urban renewal and spending. Raymond A. Bauer has suggested that the study of public policy in the social sciences has moved through two rather distinctive traditions. The first, described as "normative decision theory," was "concerned with how people should act in order to achieve better (or best) results. The other tradition, so-called descriptive or behavioral decision-theory, is concerned with how people actually go about handling such problems, whether the outcomes be admirable or not. The distinction may be thought of as parallel to the contrast between the natural sciences and engineering in the physical world."[1] Utilizing Bauer's distinction, the selections included in Section VI could be most accurately described as behavioral rather than normative policy studies.

Although there are some quite important divergences in methodology (as illustrated by contrasting the intensive analysis of two cities' transportation policies by Colcord and the extensive 200-city study by Lineberry and Fowler), most of these authors probably agree at least upon the general nature of public policy. Austin Ranney's recent formulation of the "main components" of a public policy is probably as succinct, yet comprehensive, as any other:[2]

A particular object or set of objects—some designated part of the environment (an aspect of the society or physical world) which is intended to be affected.
A desired course of events—a particular sequence of behavior desired in the particular object or set of objects.

263

Notes to this introduction will be found on page 361.

A selected line of action—a particular set of actions chosen to bring about the desired course of events; in other words, not merely what the society happens to be doing toward the set of objects at the moment, but a deliberate set of one line of action from among several possible lines.

A declaration of intent—whether broadcast publicly to all who will listen or communicate secretly to a special few, some statement by the policy-makers as to what they intend to do, how and why.

An implementation of intent—the actions actually undertaken *vis-a-vis* the particular set of objects in pursuance of the choices and declaration.

One of the most difficult problems in policy analysis is that, while each analyst perceives something related to this set of components, readily comparable data are very difficult to obtain for any large sample of cities. While census bureau data are available for a variety of variables (and constitute the primary sources of data for Lineberry and Fowler in Selection 27 and Masotti and Bowen in Selection 29), these data obviously are silent on such matters as the distribution of power and the attitudes of community elites. Colcord in (Selection 26) grappled with the data-gathering problem by conducting an in-depth analysis of Baltimore and Seattle and their transportation policies. Clark (in Selection 28) reports findings based upon both standard data sources and data gathered by the NORC's Permanent Community Sample in 51 communities. The PCS was described in some detail in Selection 1.

Colcord, who studied a pair of large cities experiencing transportation problems, points to the importance of two factors discussed earlier in this book as determinants of transportation policies. First, as Walton and Warren (see Selection 18 and 19) have indicated, the community's capacity to manipulate its environment is heavily determined by the presence of extra-community forces or its "vertical axis"—in the case of transportation decisions, by the federal government. Second, the metropolitan complexity of local governments (see Section II of this book) is intimately intertwined in policy choices which affect more than one unit of local government. In both Seattle and Baltimore the controversy over transportation seems to polarize central city and suburban interests, the former being much more interested in what they call "balanced transportation" than the latter.

The other three studies in this section, those by Lineberry and Fowler, Clark, and Masotti and Bowen, are all primarily concerned with the matter of municipal spending and taxing policy, although Clark has an additional concern with urban renewal expenditures. Lineberry and Fowler develop the concept of "responsiveness" in order to explain the congruence of policy variations and socioeconomic composition of communities. Using a sample of 200 American cities, they found that reformed cities (i.e., those with manager or commission governments, nonpartisan elections, and at-large constituencies) were less responsive in their policy choices to variations in the social and economic structure of the city, than were unreformed cities. This indicated to them that the reformers' ambitions of making policy more a product of bureaucratic than political premises had been partially fulfilled. Clark is similarly concerned with expenditure variations, as well as with urban renewal commitment, but he also had available extensive data gathered through the Permanent Community Sample. The principal concern of his research is to test empirically the propositions about community power laid down in earlier work on community power structure (see, for example, the writing in Section IV and Clark's summary in Selection 17). As such, it represents one of the relatively few efforts to relate the structure of community power to policy outcomes.

Masotti and Bowen studied communities in Ohio in order to describe and explain the "sociology of municipal expenditures." Using factor analysis, a technique discussed by Bonjean in Selection 1, the findings of that analysis parallel remarkably the community factor analysis studies described in Selection 1. The three most important factors identified by Masotti and Bowen, labeled Socioeconomic Status, Age and Population Mobility, parallel three of the major community factors discussed by Bonjean. The authors then relate these factors and specific variables to two indicators of budget expenditures, the per capita amounts spent, and the per cent of the total budget consumed by each budget item.

All of the studies in this section present examples of both some promising trends in urban research and some complex problems. One of the most thorny problems lies in the gap between urban research and urban policy-making. Most of the studies in this volume and this section in particular are examples of what Bauer described as behavioral or descriptive research rather than normative or applied research. Since policy analysis in the study of urban polities is just now emerging out of its infancy, few students of community policy would claim the expertise needed to apply boldly existing research to social problems.[3] There are, however, continuing demands upon urban decision-makers that do not await the painstaking research of the urban scholars. It is no criticism of the dozens of social scientists who have trekked to Washington and to the city halls to note that their professional research served them at best only adequately. The gap between pure and applied research is further complicated by the gap between theory and hypothesis-construction and the available data and methods to test them. Still, there are more promising trends in policy research indicated by the materials included here. One of these is the effort to move beyond case studies to comparative studies. While the case study can highlight research problems and illustrate the infinite variety of urban systems, comparative studies alone are able to test hypotheses and build theories.

Another trend indicated by most of these studies of public policy is a renewed concern for the political system taken as a whole. Instead of treating the study of community power in a vacuum, Clark's study, for example, attempts to assess both the causes and the consequences of power distributions. The other studies similarly focus upon the inter-relationship among system components, rather than upon a description of one part of the system taken in isolation. There is probably no more important question asked in all of social science than that of "why and how does a political system serve one set of goals rather than another?" It is toward that question that Section VI is directed.

THE PURPOSE of this paper is to formulate some generalizations about the way political decisions are made with respect to the transportation problems of large urban areas.

The movement of people and goods has been a major public issue in America's large urban areas since the Second World War.[1] It has absorbed increasing amounts of the attention of political actors—both public and private—and increasing amounts of the nation's financial resources. Transportation problems have been the product of continuing urbanization, rapid decentralization and a steady growth of motor vehicle ownership and use.

The characteristic response to the "transportation crisis" during most of the postwar period has been the construction of more and more highways (best demonstrated by the passage in 1956 of the Federal Interstate and Defense Highway Act, which provided 90 per cent federal financing for the major expressway system, much of which was intended for urban areas). Until recently, alternatives to this response were not seriously considered.

However, as more and more highways were actually completed, an increasingly vocal skepticism has developed among significant public officials and influential private citizens and organizations in many larger cities. The first became audible late in the 1950's in the handful of cities with large rapid transit systems and/or commuter railroads (New York, Philadephia, Chicago and Boston). These facilities had been allowed to languish, and their financial difficulties and declining patronage raised them to the status of a major public issue. The dependence of large segments of the population on these facilities made their discontinuance unimaginable, and the first response of the cities and their states was to adopt various stop-gap measures (tax exemption, subsidies, loans, etc.) to prevent their demise.[2] However, by the early 1960's serious efforts at finding long-range solutions were being pressed. By 1967 significant

Decision-Making and Transportation Policy: A Comparative Analysis*

Frank C. Colcord, Jr.

Tufts University

programs to extend and improve the rail systems, involving major capital investments, were underway in all of these urban areas. In large part because of pressures from these cities and states,[3] Congress in 1961 and 1964 passed two measures to provide new programs of assistance to transit and commuter systems. Also, by the mid-1960's, both the San Francisco and Washington, D.C., areas had committed themselves to the construction of new and expensive mass-transit networks.

Less obvious than these cases have been the later but similar responses of many other large urban areas in the United States which lack rapid transit or commuter rail facilities. Indeed, there appears to be a major reconsideration of urban transportation policy underway in most of our larger centers throughout the country, including Seattle, Baltimore, Denver, Detroit, Pittsburgh, Atlanta, and even Miami, Los Angeles and Houston.

Urban transportation has become a matter of *public* policy in all large urban areas, and is a case of *metropolitan* political decision-making in every area because of the very nature of the function. Since the federal government has now chosen to intervene in all aspects of the field, it has also become the subject of one of the numerous recent experiments in the "new federalism." Thus its study explores some rather new territory which will unquestionably be illustrative of other urban public problems lying before us. Because of the many political actors involved and the

* Reprinted with permission of the author and publisher, from, Frank C. Colcord, Jr., "Decision-Making and Transportation Policy: A Comparative Analysis," (Southwestern) Social Science Quarterly, 48 (December 1967), pp. 383–397.

267

Notes to this selection will be found on pages 361–363.

absence of a government with sole responsibility for the problem, it is an extremely complex case in political decision-making.

Urban transportation decisions can be divided into several subcategories, all of which must be explored to comprehend the totality. Broadly, these include decisions relating to (1) the structure of government for transportation, (2) transportation planning, and (3) financing, construction and operation of facilities. Included in all of these are (4) decisions concerning the extent to which transportation will be handled comprehensively or piecemeal. Furthermore, transportation decisions are not made in a vacuum. Other closely related decisions bearing directly on transportation include those concerning (5) the general structure of metropolitan government, (6) metropolitan land-use planning, (7) home rule, and the distribution of powers between state and local government, and (8) financing and taxes.

Transportation policy-making in all large U.S. urban areas occurs in the same objective context. Relevant federal legislation applies to all, including the several highways acts, the 1958 Transportation Act (relating to Federal regulation of intra-state common carriers), the 1961 amendments to the Housing Act (providing for demonstration grants and loans to urban transit), the Urban Mass Transportation Act of 1964 (which authorized $375 million in matching grants for urban transit), as well as other relevant sections of the Housing Act provided for urban renewal, planning grants, community-facilities grants, etc. Also, all states have the same basic constitutional powers; everywhere the states have the primary responsibility for planning and building major highways, and have agencies for the regulation of common carriers. And everywhere with rare exceptions, there exists no true metropolitan government.[4]

Given these uniformities and the universal requirement of providing facilities for movement of persons and goods within large urban regions, and armed with some scattered and limited information about transportation politics in a few urban areas,[5] several hypotheses were constructed. (1) The "dynamics" of transportation politics will be similar in all large urban areas—i.e., roughly the same public and private political actors (see definition below) will be involved in the decision-making process; they will take roughly the same positions on issues, and much the same political alliances will be forming. (2) The outcome of the political process (i.e., the decisions) will depend upon (a) the extent of influence of the alliances and their members, (b) the degree of cohesiveness among the members of the alliances, and (c) the degree of intensity with which these members view the actual or potential impact of transportation policies on their own interests.[6] (3) The major membership of the alliance seeking alternatives to the prevailing "highways only" policy will be heavily concentrated in the central city, with some assistance from "metropolitan" organizations, where they exist. (4) Because of the absence of metropolitan government, the primary arena in which political controversies will be fought will be the state political system, since state officials control the roads program and must approve most other metropolitan transportation decisions.

Method of Investigation

This article represents a preliminary report of a larger study of transportation policy in seven large U.S. metropolitan areas. Baltimore and Seattle were the first two studied and were thus chosen for discussion herein. The study is being made possible by a grant to M.I.T. by the General Motors Corporation.[7]

The basic research method involves open-ended interviews with all significant "political actors" (or their staffs) concerned with urban transportation policy. These are defined as: (1) the general policy-makers (governors, mayors, county commissioners, selected suburban executives and relevant state legislators and city councilmen), (2) public officials directly or indirectly concerned with transportation policy (e.g., city, county and state public works directors, planning heads, and police chiefs, state motor vehicle and traffic safety directors, city urban renewal, traffic management and transit chiefs, metropolitan agency directors, locally based federal officials, etc.), and (3) private organizations and individuals actively interested in transportation policy (e.g., newspapers, chambers of commerce, labor unions, downtown business groups, transit operating companies, Negro organizations, Leagues of Women Voters, planning associations, automobile clubs, associations of contractors, truckers, etc.). The private actors were initially chosen from a standardized list of "transportation interests" but were expanded from information received from respondents. These interviews were augmented by interviews with knowledgeable academics and newpapermen, and by review of newspaper clipping files, published documents and papers, as well as historical and political literature relating to each urban area and its state (or states).

Baltimore and Seattle: A Profile

THE HISTORY AND THE ECONOMY

Baltimore became a major city in the early nineteenth century, Seattle in the early twentieth. In both cases, the initial spur to growth was the port: in both the port remains an important aspect of the economy, but manufacturing has become the major growing point.[8] Industry is highly diversified in the Baltimore area, and largely absentee-owned; in Seattle, there is a heavy concentration in aircraft manufacture, with Boeing employing over half the total industrial workers of the region. Both areas have experienced substantial industrial expansion in the past few decades.

Population, industry, and commerce have been steadily decentralizing since World War II, in accord with the national pattern. In both places, the central city now has approximately half the total metropolitan population, but still employs around two thirds of the total metropolitan work-force. However, the central business

districts (CBD) have experienced absolute declines. In the case of Baltimore, this decline was rather precipitous until 1963, when a major downtown renewal program began to take effect and the decline was arrested and later reversed. It appears to have stabilized in Seattle as well, although urban renewal has not been a major factor there. Employees working in the CBD in both places now constitute less than 20 per cent of the total area employment figure.

Both areas have experienced substantial population growth since World War II, although the central city remained stable in the decade of the 1950's.[9] There are major differences in the socioeconomic characteristics of the two areas. Baltimore is typical of cities in the eastern half of the nation, in that its central city population exhibits distinctly lower socioeconomic status characteristics than the suburban areas. Population size has remained stable, but the city has lost heavily in white population and gained many Negroes. In 1960 the latter constituted 33 per cent of the total, and their numbers have grown substantially since. The Seattle area, on the other hand, is remarkably homogeneous. Socioeconomic measures show little difference between city and surrounding suburban areas. Negroes constituted less than 5 per cent of the total in 1960, although they were also concentrated in the central city. Also, the Seattle area population is substantially richer and better educated than that of the Baltimore area, with the differences, of course, most extreme between the two central cities. For example, 1960 median family income in the Seattle Standard Metropolitan Statistical Area (SMSA) was 11 per cent higher, and in the city 23 per cent higher, than in Baltimore.

GOVERNMENT

There are major differences both in the structure of government and in the character of the politics of the two urban areas. Structurally, the Baltimore area is probably the simplest in the continental United States. The urban population lives in only four jurisdictions: Baltimore City, Annapolis (the state capital) and two counties (Baltimore County and Anne Arundel). Baltimore City is actually a city-county, and is totally separated from Baltimore County. There are no other municipalities in the urban area.[10] Seattle, on the other hand, lies within King County, and the SMSA spreads into a second county, Snohomish. Including Seattle, there are 48 municipalities in the SMSA, as well as literally hundreds of special districts, many of them with their own taxing powers. The counties have relatively little authority over the incorporated municipalities. In both places, the states have rather strong powers relative to the local jurisdictions; most major decisions must be approved by the state legislatures, particularly decisions of a metropolitan nature. In addition to the counties and municipalities, the two areas have a number of metropolitan agencies relevant to transportation.

The character of politics in the two areas differs significantly. Although an attempt at a brief summary within the constraints of this paper risks over-simplification and thus inaccuracy, nonetheless it is impossible to understand transportation policy-making without some appreciation of the nature of the political system and character of the political culture. Baltimore and Maryland politics are partisan and professional, demonstrating an odd admixture of Southern rural and Northern urban styles.[11] Despite the fact that the state and all the local governments of the Baltimore region are overwhelmingly Democratic, Republicans now occupy the governor's and mayor's chairs, as well as that of county executive of Anne Arundel County. Democrats control Baltimore County and the legislative bodies of the city, the state and Anne Arundel County. The two counties seem to be in something of a state of transition from the old-fashioned machine government typical of Maryland's rural counties to modernized urban systems; they have been reformed in structure, but the transition is not yet complete. The city still has vestiges of localized political machines within it, but there has not been a city-wide machine for several decades. In the city, the mayors D'Alesandro and McKeldin—who have dominated that office for many years—have worked effectively and cooperatively with the major business organizations in developing city programs.

The political systems of Seattle and the State of Washington provide a strong contrast to the Maryland systems. They tend to be highly "service-oriented." Evidence of corruption is rare, but both governments tend to be weak and disinclined to activism. Indeed, both governments are structured in such a way as to make political leadership exceedingly difficult. The city has a "weak-mayor" system with non-partisan voting, large numbers of commissions, and a strong merit system (thus limiting the mayor's appointment powers). The governor is similarly limited; particularly in the field of transportation, there is a long-standing tradition of highway commission independence. Major program changes in both city and state must generally go before the voters in referenda, which has meant that program leadership originates with citizens' groups. The county governments are traditional in form and politics; they do not have merit systems, and generally lack the service-orientation of the city and state. Their structure and traditions are not conducive to program innovation, and they are poorly equipped to carry on urban functions. In general, the Washington political systems are far more "open" than those of Maryland; they are less dominated by professional politicians, which has allowed more direct intervention by individual citizens and organized groups. This type of system carries with it the disadvantage of extreme difficulty in accomplishing change, a problem which is less severe in the Maryland-Baltimore system.[12]

Transportation Decisions in Baltimore and Seattle

Baltimore and Seattle are currently in an almost identical stage of development in their transportation planning. In this respect, they are well behind San Francisco and Washington (D.C.), which have made the crucial financing decisions, and are proceeding with construction. But they are well ahead of any other cities which do not now have rapid transit.

STRUCTURAL DECISIONS

Because metropolitan government does not exist in most U.S. urban areas, an important decision that must be made prior to the development of a transportation program is to establish the structure through which the program can be planned, developed and carried out. Baltimore and Seattle have both developed rather elaborate arrangements to accomplish these purposes. As they entered the post-war era, both were equipped with only the traditional agencies for transportation: state roads commissions and regulatory agencies for utilities, city departments of public works and planning boards, as well as bus transit operators. It was not until the late 1950's that new institutions began to develop.

In the Baltimore area, the first major development was the creation in 1958 of the Baltimore Regional Planning Council as a semi-autonomous unit within the state Planning Council. This was later (1963) established as an official representative body separate from the state unit, with its own assured financing from state and local sources. In 1961 the Maryland General Assembly created the Metropolitan Transit Authority with regulatory powers over all Baltimore area public carriers, a directive to prepare a long-range master plan, and authority to purchase the private bus lines. In 1966 two additional organizations were established: the Metropolitan Area Council, which is a voluntary intergovernmental coordinating body of local public officials, and a special organization (ACCORD) of similar makeup created to meet the 1962 requirement of the federal highway act that all transportation planning be based upon comprehensive regional plans. In 1967 a "Governor's Steering Committee for Mass Transit," composed of representatives of the state and local governments, was

created to spearhead the planning for rapid transit. Within the city, a Department of Traffic and Transit and the Baltimore Urban Renewal and Housing Authority were established in the mid-1950's.

The mid-1950's also saw the establishment of a number of private organizations of importance to transportation planning. The chief of these are the Committee for Downtown, Inc., and the Greater Baltimore Committee (both businessmen's groups primarily concerned with the renewal of the downtown), the Citizens Planning and Housing Association and Baltimore Heritage, Inc. The last named is concerned particularly with preservation of historic areas and buildings.

In the Seattle area, the first major postwar step was the authorization by the state legislature in 1957 of the Municipality of Metropolitan Seattle, with a wide variety of permissive "metropolitan" functions, including transportation planning and transit. Establishment of the agency, and the decision as to which functions would be performed, were made subject to approval of the voters through referenda. Only the function of sewage disposal was approved in the 1958 election. Also in 1957, five counties in the Seattle-Tacoma region agreed to establish the Puget Sound Governmental Conference, a voluntary coordinating committee, which has evolved into a regional planning agency with its own staff. Within the city, Mayor Braman has established an advisory committee for rapid transit, which is spearheading efforts to gain public support and working with interested private groups. In 1967 at the request of the governor, the Washington legislature approved a bill to authorize the Municipality of Metropolitan Seattle to assume responsibility for planning a rapid transit system for King County; that body has in turn established a rapid transit committee.

During the 1950's and 1960's, a number of private organizations relevant to

transportation were established: the Central
Association, a businessmen's group concerned with the downtown area, the Citizen's Planning Council, Allied Arts, the
Washington Roadside Council, and Design
for Washington. All of these groups are
concerned with aspects of planning, including aesthetics. Finally, in 1966, a new
group called Forward Thrust was established with a broad membership representing most elements in the metropolitan area,
whose objective is to raise funds through a
major bond issue for necessary capital
investments in the region (including rapid
transit).

Thus, by 1967 both areas had developed,
with the cooperation of their states, a
whole array of new metropolitan and
regional agencies with at least the theoretical capability of planning, constructing and
operating transportation facilities on a
comprehensive, metropolitan basis.

PLANNING DECISIONS

Before transportation programs can
become operable, there must be a plan of
action agreed to by the effective decision-
makers. In the case of major highways, in
most states this is the state highway commission, with advice (but rarely a veto) from
the local jurisdictions, varying amounts of
influence from the governor and legislature,
and final approval by the Federal Bureau of
Public Roads. This is an accurate description in the Seattle area, but Baltimore has
an almost unique situation. The city builds
and maintains all roads itself, except Federal
Interstate Highways, and has an effective
veto over the latter.

Since 1962 the Federal Highway Act has
contained language requiring that urban
highway plans be consistent with a comprehensive plan for the region. This has been
interpreted to mean, among other things,
that all transportation planning (roads and
public transportation) must be done in an
integrated fashion. Baltimore's present
highway "master plan" was completed in
1961[13] before this requirement took effect,
and thus did not fully consider mass

transportation requirements. It is based on
land-use projections developed by the
Regional Planning Council.[14] Following
creation of the MTA, that agency engaged a
consulting firm to prepare a long-range
transit plan, and required that it use the
same land-use projections as well as assume
that the total highway plan would be built.
The firm concluded that Baltimore needed
a rapid transit system, but was forced to
limit it to filling the interstices between the
proposed highways. The result is a plan
calling for a "downtown loop" (a subway)
and two suburban legs. The plan was presented to the MTA in 1965, and endorsed in
principle by that body in 1966.[15]

The Seattle–Tacoma area went through a
rather similar process, although the first
plan was intended to be comprehensive in
compliance with the 1962 amendment.
Unlike the Baltimore case, this plan was
developed "in-house" by a special staff
attached to the Puget Sound Governmental
Conference (PSGC), whose director was
borrowed from the State Highway Commission. The report, published in 1966,
proposed a highway network for the region,
but concluded that a rapid transit system
would not be necessary for the foreseeable
future.[16] Because of dissatisfaction with
this latter finding, the City of Seattle persuaded the PSGC to sponsor a special
transit study. This was completed in 1966
by the consultants, who proposed a "two-
leg" rapid transit system meeting in a downtown subway line. "Metro" in Seattle and
The Governor's Steering Committee in
Baltimore have now engaged consultants
to prepare comprehensive plans for the two
transit networks.

FINANCING

Federal Interstate Highways are financed
with 90 per cent federal participation, the
funds for both federal and state shares
coming largely from gasoline taxes. While
these are never sufficient to meet all demands for highways, nonetheless highway
officials have a steady and dependable
income for their programs, which is raised
relatively painlessly. Such is not the case
for public transit needs. Although modest
federal assistance has been available since

1964,[17] most of the costs must come from local and state sources, usually the property tax or other general revenue. Thus, decisions to engage in major capital programs for transit are much more difficult and controversial.

These decisions are all the more difficult because many persons, including transportation experts, express serious doubts about the viability of rail rapid transit in highly decentralized urban regions, such as Baltimore and Seattle.[18] The proposals for these two regions, both providing for minimal systems, involve the expenditure of hundreds of millions of dollars. In both places, the question will undoubtedly have to be presented to the voters for their approval. In neither case has the state made any commitment to participate in the construction cost, so the non-federal share may have to come entirely from the local jurisdictions.

Thus, while significant steps have been taken in both places toward the development of a "balanced" transportation system, these have all been relatively inexpensive steps, largely financed by the federal government. It will remain to be seen whether such "auto-oriented" populations will be willing to assume such a major financial burden.

Meanwhile, despite noisy objections from private planning and aesthetically oriented groups to various aspects of the program, highway construction is proceeding apace in the Seattle area. In Baltimore, after many years of delay, agreement has been reached on routes for two major interstate highways through the city. The major elements of the suburban highway networks are now complete.

The Politics of Transportation

These events in the Baltimore and Seattle areas have not yet resulted in commitments to build rapid transit systems, but they do represent rather dramatic changes in the political system for transportation decision-making. Whether transit comes or not, the cast of characters involved in the political process has changed radically since the early 1950's, and the transportation deci-

Decision-Making and Transportation Policy: A Comparative Analysis
Frank C. Colcord, Jr.

273

sions that are made will be different as a result. The mere relation of these events is of relatively little interest, however; what does interest us is how they occurred. What were the forces which influenced these political decisions? A few preliminary conclusions can be suggested on the basis of our study of these two large urban areas, which may outline the typical metropolitan political process in this age of the "new federalism."

First, federal policy has clearly been a major influence. In 1954 the Federal Housing Act was broadened in two important ways relevant to transportation: Section 701 was added, providing federal grants for metropolitan planning, and sections relating to urban renewal programs were liberalized. Metropolitan planning programs of the Baltimore Regional Planning Council and the Puget Sound Governmental Conference were almost wholly supported by 701 grants during their early years, thus giving impetus to the first major efforts at metropolitan planning in both areas. After demonstrating their usefulness, these two agencies were able to attract local funds to add to this source, and both now have full-time staffs and are statutorily more secure. Furthermore, 701 funds were the major component of both transit studies.

Liberalization of federal urban renewal legislation was instrumental in assuring the success of Baltimore's downtown reconstruction program. The imposing Charles Center project—the first downtown program—has reversed the downward trend of the central business district, and given new strength and confidence to its business leadership. It and later CBD projects have played a major role in bringing a strong sense of cohesiveness to the business groups and the city's political leadership. These groups have devoted much of their new-found political strength to metropolitan planning and transportation issues as well.

The Federal Interstate and Defense Highway Act of 1956 gave great impetus in both metropolitan areas to their highway construction programs. The regional highway master plans, developed largely with federal funds, have identified more clearly the program issues and provided the grist for appropriate debate among the interested actors. Actual progress on construction of these roads has even more dramatically raised these issues by their very visibility. In both cities, the secondary effects of highway construction on social units, the economy of the downtown historic sites and aesthetic considerations, have become the subject of active debate, and have fostered the establishment of new civic organizations.

The 1962 amendment to the Federal Highway Act requiring comprehensive planning has had mixed results, but has at least forced recognition by some in both communities of the desirability of this approach and provided ammunition to the opponents of the "roads only" approach. In Seattle the transportation study was in large part a product of this amendment and the study has been found by the Bureau of Public Roads, if not by some of its local critics, to be in compliance with it. In Baltimore the amendment had the direct effect of causing the establishment of a new metropolitan institution. While this organization (ACCORD) has never gotten off the ground, the amendment has given added strength to other metropolitan institutions, with more direct action responsibilities in their negotiations with the State Highway Commission.

Finally, the Urban Mass Transportation Act of 1964 has offered the first glimmer of hope to mass transit enthusiasts for a feasible and dramatic change in the mass transit arrangements for the regions. While the funds are still limited, the proponents in the two areas are obviously relying on the hope that appropriations will be increased in the future, and the local share thus reduced to manageable proportions. The sharp imbalance of federal aid between alternative transportation programs, however, continues to distort the local decision-making process.

Second, the local stimulus for a rethinking of existing policy and for innovative action in the field of transportation has come almost entirely from central city actors. Prior to the mid-1950's there was relatively little concern for public transportation and there existed a broad consensus in both regions favorable to the highways approach, including the downtown. In 1955 and 1958 the City of Baltimore made two studies of its languishing bus transit system; the major recommendation of each was the creation of a metropolitan transit authority. Following a third study, this time by the state legislature, which reached the same conclusion, legislation was introduced to establish the MTA.[19] The evidence indicates clearly that this bill and the bill to establish a permanent independent Regional Planning Council, as well as a third bill to create a study commission to study the metropolitan governmental structure and tax problems, were all results of initiatives from the central city's public officials and private organizations. More recently (winter 1966–1967), this type of initiative was demonstrated again by the joint efforts of the mayor and the Greater Baltimore Committee to get rapid transit planning off dead center, where it had been since the 1965 publication of the consultants' report. Through their initiative, agreement was reached with the two suburban counties and the governor (a) to alter the plan to make it more politically feasible,[20] (b) to obtain a state contribution for the costs of the detailed engineering studies, and (c) to remove the planning function from the MTA and place it in the new Governor's Steering Committee, working with the Regional Planning Council and the MTA. The state contribution was approved by the General Assembly, and a proposal has been sent to Washington for a federal contribution.

Transportation policy-making in the Seattle area has exhibited very similar characteristics, although differing in detail. From the mid-1950's until about 1965, a Seattle attorney carried on almost single-handedly a crusade for rapid transit. He was the leading figure in the unsuccessful effort of 1958 to gain voter approval for inclusion of rapid transit as a function of the new "Metro" organization, and participated in a second unsuccessful effort in 1962. In 1965, however, he gained a major ally, the new mayor, who then appointed him chairman of his special committee on rapid transit. The mayor and his committee were largely responsible for persuading the PSGC to sponsor a transit study, and for gaining approval of the detailed engineering studies which have just begun. The same attorney is one of the organizers of Forward Thrust, which is expected to take the leadership in creating a favorable public opinion for a major 1968 bond issue referendum to include capital costs for the transit program.

In both areas, political action regarding highways has taken a different course, and the role of central city actors has been less concerted. One generalization about both can be made: the business and political communities of the central cities favor "balanced transposition." What this means for highway construction, however, is a matter of controversy. In Baltimore, the CBD businessmen and the mayor have publicly supported new highways, but they have not exerted themselves strongly. Support has come chiefly from such groups as the local automobile clubs and bureaucrats responsible for roads and traffic. Opposition seldom takes the form of negativism on roads in general, but rather on particular routes—from city councilmen, neighborhood organizations, public and private planning groups, historic societies, etc. But, since the key decisions have to be made within the city, this particularistic opposition has been crucial; Baltimore's highway program is hardly off the ground. Now, thanks to pressure from the state and federal roads agencies and leadership from a few city councilmen, the impasse seems to be ending, and two major roads should be under construction in the near future. In the suburban counties, no such obstruction has occurred or been feasible since they have no veto.

In Seattle similar opposition has arisen to particular roads on social, aesthetic, and economic grounds, but, lacking a veto, city groups have not effectively stopped construction. Two other factors may explain the difference between the two cities: (1) traffic congestion is patently worse in

Seattle than in Baltimore, in part because of the topography of the city, but also because Baltimore in the late 1950's employed Mr. Henry Barnes[21] and invested substantial sums (and continues to do so) to establish the latest in traffic management techniques; and (2) auto ownership in the city of Seattle is substantially greater than in Baltimore.[22]

Third, it seems clear from our own study of these two areas that the creation of new metropolitan institutions has resulted in new allies for the central city proponents of "balanced transportation." It is a cardinal tenet of the planners' catechism that transportation planning should be "comprehensive" and should serve general land-use objectives.[23] Since metropolitan planning agencies and commissions are the only metropolitan actors in any position to identify these objectives, they naturally seek to play an influential role in determining transportation policy, so that those objectives can be better served. Traditional highway planning methods contradict these tenets and thus tend to be opposed by regional and metropolitan planners. It is thus not surprising that these new regional agencies—or at least their professional staffs—have developed alliances with the central city interests promoting "balanced" transportation. While they have little formal power in either urban area, their influence derives from their professional skill and their position as spokesmen for the whole metropolitan region. Federal policy, if not always practice, also supports these views, adding greater weight to the argument.[24]

The evidence of the above two sections tends to demonstrate the validity of our third hypothesis. Another factor which tends to effectuate this position is the fact that, despite the declining proportion of the SMSA represented by the central city, it remains the most highly organized jurisdiction politically, and contains (either as employees or residents) the major portion of the area's professional skills relevant to transportation and planning.

Fourth, there is considerable evidence in these two states that the governor's office is becoming a more important source of initiative for innovations in transportation planning and programming. In largely urban states, the governors have little choice but to at least appear to be responsive to urban needs. We have observed in this study two Maryland governors and one in Washington. The incumbent governor in Maryland at the time of our interviews (1966), J. Millard Tawes, was a product of prereapportionment Maryland. He was from a rural district, but like all Maryland governors, he could not ignore the city of Baltimore, which is a major center of Democratic political strength. It was during his term of office that most of the new metropolitan agencies were created. The present governor, Spiro T. Agnew, a Republican from Baltimore County, has already demonstrated his responsiveness to the needs of the central city, as expressed by the business-community and its Republican mayor, by supporting state assistance to transportation planning and by strongly and successfully promoting a tax reform beneficial to urban areas. In Washington, Republican Governor Evans, who comes from Seattle, was instrumental in staking a major conference soon after his election, called "Design for Washington," which laid great stress on the importance of improving the quality of the environment, particularly in urban areas. Both Governor Agnew and Governor Evans have urged the establishment of Departments of Transportation at the state level, in order to achieve better coordination of transportation planning, an objective which is only meaningful in urban areas. In March 1967, at Governor Evans' request, the Washington legislature approved establishment of a new "Planning and Community Affairs Agency."[25]

The wide variety of legislation approved in recent years relevant to metropolitan transportation and the increasingly active role of the governors suggests the validity of our fourth hypothesis. Most of this activity to date, however, has been "instru-mental" rather than creative or participatory. Specifically, so far there has been little in the way of financial participation. Whether this will develop in these two highly urban states will no doubt depend on the fruits of reapportionment, the character of which it is too early to tell.

Conclusions

Transportation policy-making in these two areas has experienced major and important changes in the past decade. Numerous new actors are now on the scene, both public and private, both central city and metropolitan, thus creating essentially an entirely new bargaining system. Concepts of metropolitan planning have been accepted in theory, by practically all actors, even those who oppose it in practice. The central cities have demonstrated their substantial influence in affecting metropolitan decision-making. The issues relating to transportation have been more clearly delineated, and, whether or not either area ever builds a rapid transit system, a new awareness of the need for making "metropolitan" and "comprehensive" decisions and new mechanisms for accomplishing these have been created.

Despite the many changes in the last decade or so, the highway agencies have not lost their power, nor are they likely to in the near future. Their programs serve a vital and ever-growing need to meet the demands of the motoring public, which is the vast majority of the population. They are very strongly supported by many powerful interests and by the driving public. However, particularly within the central cities, their power is being modified. Those responsible for decisions in these cities are taking vigorous actions, both locally and in the state and national political arenas, to find ways of making the cities more viable and attractive. Through the devices suggested above, they have already succeeded in improving their chances of accomplishing this. While more roads will no doubt be built in these cities, they are now more likely to be built in a manner consistent with these general objectives.

A DECADE ago, political scientists were deploring the "lost world of municipal government" and calling for systematic studies of municipal life which emphasized the political, rather than the administrative, side of urban political life.[1] In recent years, this demand has been generously answered and urban politics is becoming one of the most richly plowed fields of political research. In terms originally introduced by David Easton,[2] political scientists have long been concerned with inputs, but more recently they have focused their attention on other system variables, particularly the political culture[3] and policy outputs of municipal governments.[4]

The present paper will treat two policy outputs, taxation and expenditure levels of cities, as dependent variables. We will relate these policy choices to socioeconomic characteristics of cities and to structural characteristics of their governments. Our central research concern is to examine the impact of political structures, reformed and unreformed, on policy-making in American cities.

Reformism and Public Policies in American Cities*

Robert L. Lineberry

University of Texas at Austin

Edmund P. Fowler

York University

Political Culture, Reformism and Political Institutions

The leaders of the Progressive movement in the United States left an enduring mark on the American political system, particularly at the state and municipal level. In the states, the primary election, the referendum, initiative and recall survive today. The residues of this *Age of Reform*,[5] as Richard Hofstadter called it, persist in municipal politics principally in the form of manager government and at-large and nonpartisan elections. The reformers were, to borrow Banfield and Wilson's phrase, the original embodiment of the "middle class ethos" in American politics. They were, by and large, White Anglo-Saxon Protestants reacting to

the politics of the party machine, which operated by exchanging favors for votes.[6]

It is important that we understand the ideology of these reformers if we hope to be able to analyze the institutions which they created and their impact on political decisions. The reformers' goal was to "rationalize" and "democratize" city government by the substitution of "community oriented" leadership. To the reformers, the most pernicious characteristic of the machine was that it capitalized on socioeconomic cleavages in the population, playing on class antagonisms and on racial and religious differences. Ernest S. Bradford, an early advocate of commission government with at-large elections, defended his plans for at-large representation on grounds that

> ... under the ward system of governmental representation, the ward receives the attention, not in proportion to its needs but to the ability of its representatives to "trade" and arrange "deals" with fellow members.... Nearly every city under the aldermanic system offers flagrant examples of this vicious method of "part representation." The commission form changes this to representation of the city as a whole.[7]

The principal tools which the reformers picked to maximize this "representation of the city as a whole" were the commission, and later the manager, form of government, the nonpartisan election and the election at-large. City manager government, it was argued, produced a no-nonsense,

* Reprinted with permission of the authors and publisher, from Robert L. Lineberry and Edmund P. Fowler, "Reformism and Public Policies in American Cities," American Political Science Review, 61 (September 1967) pp. 701–716.

277

Notes to this selection will be found on pages 363–365.

efficient and business-like regime, where decisions could be implemented by professional administrators rather than by victors in the battle over spoils. Nonpartisan elections meant to the reformer that state and national parties, whose issues were irrelevant to local politics anyway, would keep their divisive influences out of municipal decision-making. Nonpartisan elections, especially when combined with elections at-large, would also serve to reduce the impact of socioeconomic cleavages and minority voting blocs in local politics. Once established, these institutions would serve as bastions against particularistic interests.

Banfield and Wilson have argued that the "middle class ethos" of the reformers has become a prevalent attitude in much of political life. The middle class stands for "public regarding" virtues rather than for "private regarding" values of the ethnic politics of machines and bosses. The middle class searches for the good of the "community as a whole" rather than for the benefit of particularistic interests.[8] Agger, Goldrich and Swanson, in their study of two western and two southern communities have documented the rise of a group they call the "community conservationists," who "see the values of community life maximized when political leadership is exercised by men representing the public at large, rather than 'special interests.'"[9] Robert Wood has taken up a similar theme in his penetrating analysis of American suburbia. The "no-party politics of suburbia" is characterized by "an outright reaction against partisan activity, a refusal to recognize that there may be persistent cleavages in the electorate and an ethical disapproval of permanent group collaboration as an appropriate means of settling disputes."[10] This ideological opposition to partisanship is a product of a tightly-knit and homogeneous community, for "nonpartisanship reflects a highly integrated community life with a powerful capacity to induce conformity."[11]

Considerable debate has ensued over both the existence and the consequences of these two political ethics in urban communities. Some evidence has supported the view that reformed governments[12] are indeed found in cities with higher incomes, higher levels of education, greater proportions of Protestants and more white-collar job-holders. Schnore and Alford, for example, found that "the popular image of the manager city was verified; it does tend to be the natural habitat of the upper middle class." In addition, manager cities were "inhabited by a younger, more mobile population that is growing rapidly."[13]

More recently, Wolfinger and Field correlated socioeconomic variables—particularly ethnicity and region—to political structures. They concluded that "the ethos theory is irrelevant to the South ... inapplicable to the West ... fares badly in the Northeast ..." and that support for the

TABLE 1. Independent Variables

1. Population, 1960
2. Per cent population increase or decrease 1950–60
3. Per cent non-white
4. Per cent of native population with foreign born or mixed parentage
5. Median income
6. Per cent of population with incomes below $3000
7. Per cent of population with incomes above $10,000
8. Median school years completed by adult population
9. Per cent high school graduates among adult population
10. Per cent of population in white collar occupations
11. Per cent of elementary school children in private schools
12. Per cent of population in owner-occupied dwelling units

theory in the Midwest was "small and uneven."[14] Region proved to be a more important predictor of both government forms and of policy outputs like urban renewal expenditures than did the socioeconomic composition of the population.

In our view, it is premature to carve a headstone for the ethos theory. It is our thesis that governments which are products of the reform movement behave differently from those which have unreformed institutions, even if the socioeconomic composition of their population may be similar. Our central purpose is to determine the impact of both socioeconomic variables and political institutions (structural variables) on outputs of city governments. By doing this, we hope to shed some additional illumination on the ethos theory.

II. Research Design

VARIABLES

The independent variables used in this analysis, listed in Table 1, consist of relatively "hard" data, mostly drawn from the U.S. census.[15] These variables were selected because they represent a variety of possible social cleavages which divide urban populations—rich vs. poor, Negro vs. White, ethnic vs. native, newcomers vs. old-timers, etc. We assume that such social and economic characteristics are important determinants of individual and group variations in political preferences. Data on each of these independent variables were gathered for each of the two hundred cities in the sample.[16]

Our principal theoretical concern is with the consequences of variations in the structural characteristics of form of government, type of constituency and partisanship of elections. The variable of government form is unambiguous. Except for a few small New England towns, all American cities have council-manager, mayor-council or commission government. There is, however, somewhat more ambiguity in the classification of election type. By definition, a "nonpartisan election is one in which no candidate is identified on the ballot by party affiliation."[17] The legal definition of nonpartisanship conceals the wide variation between Chicago's and Boston's nominal nonpartisanship and the more genuine variety in Minneapolis, Winnetka and Los Angeles.[18] We will quickly see, though, that formal nonpartisanship is not merely an empty legal nicety, but that there are very real differences in the political behavior of partisan and nonpartisan cities, even

though we are defining them in legal terms only.[19]

Our classification of constituency types into only two groups also conceals some variation in the general pattern. While most cities use either the at-large or the ward pattern of constituencies exclusively, a handful use a combination of the two electoral methods. For our purposes, we classified these with district cities.

The dependent variables in this study are two measures of public policy outputs. A growing body of research on local politics has utilized policy measures as dependent variables.[20] The present research is intended to further this study of political outputs by relating socioeconomic variables to expenditure and taxation patterns in cities with varying political structures.

The dependent variables are computed by a simple formula. The measure for taxation was computed by dividing the total personal income of the city into the total tax of the city, giving us a tax/income ratio. Similarly, dividing expenditures by the city's aggregate personal income gave us an expenditure/income ratio as the measure for our second dependent variable. These measures, while admittedly imperfect,[21] permit us to ask how much of a city's income it is willing to commit for public taxation and expenditures.

HYPOTHESIS

Much of the research on city politics has treated reformed institutions as dependent variables. Although we shall briefly examine the social and economic differences between reformed and unreformed cities, our principal concern will be to explore the *consequences* for public policy of political institutions. From our earlier discussion of the political culture of cities we hypothesized that:

1. The relationship between socioeconomic cleavages and policy outputs is stronger in unreformed than in reformed cities.

This hypothesis focuses on the intention

of the reformers to minimize the role of
particularistic interests in policy making.

III. Reformed and Unreformed
Cities: A Comparison

The economic and social contrasts between reformed and unreformed cities have
been the subject of much research,[22] and
for our purposes we may be brief in our
treatment. We divided the independent
variables into three groups, one measuring
population size and growth, a second containing social class indicators and a third
including three measures of social homogeneity. The means and standard deviations
for each variable by institutional category
are found in Table 2.

It should initially be noted that population size and growth rate fairly clearly
separate the reformed from the unreformed
cities. As Alford and Scoble have amply
documented,[23] the larger the city, the

greater the likelihood of its being unreformed; the faster its growth rate, the more
likely a city is to possess manager government, nonpartisan and at-large elections.
These differences are largely accounted for
by the fact that very large cities are most
likely to (1) have unreformed institutions
and (2) be stable or declining in population.
Since neither of these variables emerged as
particularly important predictors of our
output variables, we relegated them to
secondary importance in the rest of the
analysis.

The data in Table 2 indicate that reformed
cities (at least those over 50,000) do not
appear to be "the natural habitat of the
upper middle class." While reformed cities
have slightly more educated populations
and slightly high proportions of white collar
workers and home ownership, unreformed
cities have generally high incomes. In any
case, whatever their direction, the differences are not large. What is striking is not
the differences between the cities but the
similarities of their class composition.

Homogeneity is easily one of the most
ambiguous terms in the ambiguous language

TABLE 2. *Comparison of the Means (and Standard Deviations) of Socioeconomic Characteristics of
Reformed and Unreformed Cities*

Independent Variable	Government Type					
	Mayor-Council		Manager		Commission	
Population:						
Population (10³)	282.5	(858.6)	115.7	(108.0)	128.6	(115.2)
% Change, 1950–60	36.4%	(118.8)	64.1%	(130.4)	18.5%	(36.7)
Class:						
Median Income	$6199.	(1005.0)	$6131.	(999.6)	$5425.	(804.4)
% under $3000	15.3%	(7.0)	17.3%	(6.9)	21.5%	(7.9)
% over $10,000	16.9%	(7.2)	17.5%	(6.7)	12.5%	(3.7)
% High School Graduates	40.7%	(10.8)	48.1%	(8.9)	41.6%	(10.4)
Median Education (yrs.)	10.7	(1.1)	11.4	(.89)	11.0	(2.1)
% Owner-Occupied Dwelling Units	54.9%	(15.1)	57.3%	(13.6)	54.6%	(13.7)
% White Collar	44.1%	(9.0)	48.1%	(7.1)	44.2%	(7.6)
Homogeneity:						
% Nonwhite	10.6%	(11.5)	11.6%	(10.8)	16.5%	(14.9)
% Native with Foreign Born or Mixed Parentage	19.7%	(9.9)	12.4%	(8.3)	11.7%	(10.7)
% Private School Attendance	23.5%	(11.9)	15.3%	(11.8)	16.6%	(11.8)
	N = 85		N = 90		N = 25	

Table 2. (cont.)

Independent Variable	Election Type			
	Partisan		Nonpartisan	
Population:				
Population (10^3)	270.8	(1022.1)	155.8	(198.7)
% Population Increase 1950–1960	17.1	(40.1)	58.3%	(136.1)
Class:				
Median Income	$5996	(904.5)	$6074	(1045.5)
% under $3000	16.8%	(7.1)	17.2%	(7.2)
% over $10,000	16.1%	(6.1)	16.7%	(7.0)
% High School Graduates	40.5%	(9.2)	45.3%	(10.6)
Median Education (yrs.)	10.6	(1.1)	11.2	(1.2)
% Owner-Occupied Dwelling Units	51.5%	(14.4)	57.7%	(13.8)
% White Collar	43.5%	(7.5)	46.7%	(8.3)
Homogeneity:				
% Nonwhite	13.0%	(11.9)	11.5%	(11.8)
% Native with Foreign Born or Mixed Parentage	17.5%	(10.7)	14.7%	(9.6)
% Private School Attendance	24.1%	(13.6)	16.9%	(11.3)
	N = 57		N = 143	

Independent Variable	Constituency Type			
	District		At-Large	
Population:				
Population (10^3)	246.9	(909.8)	153.6	(191.2)
% Population Increase 1950–1960	23.1%	(36.4)	59.1%	(143.7)
Class:				
Median Income	$6,297	(965.2)	$5,942	(1,031.9)
% under $3,000	14.7%	(6.5)	18.2%	(7.6)
% over $10,000	17.7%	(7.1)	16.0%	(6.6)
% High School Graduates	43.6%	(10.9)	44.4%	(10.4)
Median Education (yrs.)	10.9	(1.1)	11.2	(1.2)
% Owner-Occupied Dwelling Units	55.1%	(14.4)	56.9%	(14.5)
% White Collar	45.2%	(9.4)	46.3%	(7.5)
Homogeneity:				
% Nonwhite	9.8%	(10.6)	13.0%	(12.3)
% Native with Foreign Born or Mixed Parentage	18.9%	(9.4)	13.4%	(9.7)
% Private School Attendance	23.2%	(12.5)	16.6%	(11.7)
	N = 73		N = 127	

of the social sciences. We have followed Alford and Scoble who used three measures of homogeneity: for ethnicity, the per cent of population native born of foreign born or mixed parentage; for race, the per cent nonwhite; and for religious homogeneity, the per cent of elementary school children in private schools. The last measure, while indirect, was the only one available, since data on religious affiliation are not collected by the Census Bureau.

With the exception of race, reformed cities appear somewhat more homogeneous than unreformed cities. While the differences in homogeneity are more clear-cut than class differences, this hardly indicates the reformed cities are the havens of a socially homogeneous population. Although the average nonpartisan city has 16.9 per cent of its children in private schools, this mean conceals a wide range— from 2 to 47 per cent.

Our findings about the insignificance of class differences between reformed and unreformed cities are at some variance with Alford and Scoble's conclusions. There is, however, some support for the argument that reformed cities are more homogeneous. While we used cities with populations of over 50,000, their sample included all cities over 25,000; and varying samples may produce varying conclusions. The only other study to analyze cities over 50,000 was Wolfinger and Field's and our conclusions are generally consistent with theirs. We differ with them, however, on two important questions.

First, Wolfinger and Field argued that what differences there are between unreformed and reformed cities disappear when controls for region are introduced: "The salient conclusion to be drawn from these data is that one can do a much better job of predicting a city's political form by knowing what part of the country it is in than by knowing anything about the composition of its population."[24] Since regions have had different historical experiences, controls for region are essentially controls for history, and more specifically, historical variation in settlement patterns. The problem with this reasoning, however, is that to "control" for "region" is to control not only for history, but for demography as well: to know what region a city is in *is* to know something about the composition of its population. Geographical subdivisions are relevant subjects of political inquiry only because they are differentiated on the basis of attitudinal or socioeconomic variables. The South is not a distinctive political region because two surveyors named Mason and Dixon drew a famous line, but because the "composition of its population" differs from the rest of the country.

It is therefore difficult to unravel the meaning of "controlling" for "region" since regions are differentiated on precisely the kinds of demographic variables which we (and Wolfinger and Field) related to reformism. Cities in the Midwest, for example, have a much higher proportion of

home ownership (64 per cent) than cities in the Northeast (44 per cent), while northeastern cities have more foreign stock in their population (27 per cent) than the Midwest (16 per cent). Hence, to relate ethnicity to political reformism and then to "control" for "region" is in part to relate ethnicity to reformism and then to control for ethnicity. Consequently, we have grave reservations that the substitution of the gross and unrefined variable of "region" for more refined demographic data adds much to our knowledge of American cities. "Controlling" for "region" is much more than controlling for historical experiences, because region as a variable is an undifferentiated *potpourri* of socioeconomic, attitudinal, historical and cultural variations.[25]

We also differ with Wolfinger and Field in their assertion that their analysis constitutes a test of the ethos theory. As we understand it, Banfield and Wilson's theory posits that particular attitudes are held by persons with varying sociological characteristics (ethnic groups and middle class persons, in particular) and that these attitudes include preferences for one or another kind of political institution. But relating the proportion of middle class persons in a city's population to its form of government says nothing one way or another about middle class preferences. An important part of understanding, of course, is describing, and it is certainly useful to know how reformed cities differ from unreformed cities.

In our view, however, such tests as Wolfinger and Field used cannot logically be called explanations, in any causal sense. The most obvious reason is that they violate some important assumptions about time–order: independent variables are measured with contemporary census data, while the dependent variables are results of decisions made ten to fifty years ago. Moreover, this problem is multiplied by the difficulty of inferring configurations of political power from demographic data. Presumably, their assumption is that there is a simple linear relationship between sheer numbers (or proportions) of, say, middle class persons and their political power: the larger the size of a group in the city's population, the easier it can enforce its choice of political forms. At least one prominent urban sociologist, however, has found empirical support for precisely the opposite proposition. Hawley concluded that the smaller the proportion of middle class persons in a city, the greater their power over urban renewal policies.[26] Similarly, it may also be dubious to assume that the size of an ethnic population is an accurate indicator of influence of ethnic groups. Although we recognize the importance of describing the socioeconomic correlates of political forms, the logical problems involved suggest the need for a good deal of caution in interpreting these differences as explanations.[27]

In any case, the question of why the city adopts particular structures is of less interest to us than their consequence for public policy. It is to this analysis that we now turn.

IV. Policy Outputs and the Responsiveness of Cities

We are now in a position to take three additional steps. First, we can compare the differences in policy outputs between reformed and unreformed cities. Second, we can assess the cumulative impact of socioeconomic variables on these policy choices. Finally, we can specify what variables are related in what ways to these output variables. In essence, we can now treat political institutions, not as dependent variables, but as factors which influence the *level* of expenditures and taxation and the *relationship* between cleavage variables and these outputs.

DIFFERENCES BETWEEN REFORMED AND UN-REFORMED CITIES' OUTPUTS

Contrary to Sherbenou's conclusions about Chicago suburbs,[28] our data indicate that reformed cities both spend and tax less than unreformed cities, with the exception of expenditures in partisan and nonpartisan cities. It appears that partisan, mayor-council and ward cities are less willing to commit their resources to public purposes

than their reformed counterparts. What is of more importance than the difference in outputs, however, is the relative responsiveness of the two kinds of cities to social cleavages in their population.

TABLE 3. *Mean Values of Tax Income and Expenditure/Income Ratios, by Structural Characteristics*

Structural Variables	Taxes /Income	Expenditures /Income
Election type:		
Partisan	.032	.050
Nonpartisan	.030	.053
Government type:		
Mayor-Council	.037	.058
Manager	.024	.045
Commission	.031	.057
Constituency type:		
Ward	.036	.057
At-large	.027	.049

THE RESPONSIVENESS OF CITIES

We have argued that one principal goal of the reform movement was to reduce the impact of partisan, socioeconomic cleavages on governmental decision-making, to immunize city governments from "artificial" social cleavages—race, religion, ethnicity, and so on. As Banfield and Wilson put their argument, the reformers "assumed that there existed an interest ('the public interest') that pertained to the city 'as a whole' and that should always prevail over competing, partial (and usually private) interests."[29] The structural reforms of manager government, at-large, and nonpartisan elections would so insulate the business of governing from social cleavages that "private regarding" interests would count for little in making up the mind of the body politic. But amid the calls of the reformers for structural reforms to muffle the impact of socioeconomic cleavages, a few hardy souls predicted precisely the opposite consequence of reform: instead of eliminating cleavages from political decision-making, the reforms, particularly the elimination of parties, would enhance the conflict. Nathan Matthews, Jr., a turn-of-the-century mayor of Boston, issued just such a warning:

> As a city is a political institution, the people in the end will divide into parties, and it would seem extremely doubtful whether the present system, however illogical its foundation be, does not in fact produce better results, at least in large cities, than if the voters divided into groups, separated by property, social or religious grounds.[30]

Matthews recognized implicitly what politi-

cal scientists would now call the "interest aggregation" function of political parties.[31] Parties in a democracy manage conflict, structure it, and encapsulate social cleavages under the rubric of two or more broad social cleavages, the parties themselves. "Parties tend to crystallize opinion, they give skeletal articulation to a shapeless and jelly-like mass . . . they cause similar opinions to coagulate . . ."[32] The parties "reduce effectively the number of political opinions to manageable numbers, bring order and focus to the political struggle, simplify issues and frame alternatives, and compromise conflicting interests."[33] Since parties are the agencies of interest aggregation, so the argument goes, their elimination makes for greater, not lesser, impact of

DIAGRAM 1. *Proportion of Variation Explained (R²) in Taxation Policy with Twelve Socioeconomic Variables, by Institutional Characteristics**

Independent Variables	Structural Variables		Dependent Variable
	Reformed Institution:		
	Government: Commission	62%	
	Government: Council-Manager	42%	
	Election: Nonpartisan	49%	
	Constituency: At-Large	49%	
Twelve Socioeconomic Variables			Tax/Income Ratio
	Unreformed Institution:		
	Government: Mayor-Council	52%	
	Election: Partisan	71%	
	Constituency: Ward/Mixed	59%	

* In the total sample, the twelve independent variables explained 52 % of the variation in taxes.

DIAGRAM 2. *Proportion of Variation Explained (R²) in Expenditure Policy with Twelve Socioeconomic Variables, by Institutional Characteristics†*

Independent Variables	Structural Variables		Dependent Variable
	Reformed Institution:		
	Government: Commission	59%	
	Government: Council-Manager	30%	
	Constituency: At-Large	36%	
	Elections: Nonpartisan	41%	
Twelve Socioeconomic Variables			Expenditure/Income Ratio
	Unreformed Institution:		
	Government: Mayor-Council	42%	
	Constituency: Ward/Mixed	49%	
	Elections: Partisan	59%	

† In the total sample, the twelve independent variables explained 36 % of the variation in expenditures.

social cleavages on political decisions.

Political scientists have recently confirmed Matthews' fears, at least with regard to electoral behavior in partisan and nonpartisan elections. Evidence points to the increased impact of socioeconomic cleavages on voting when a nonpartisan ballot is used than when the election is formally partisan. Gerald Pomper studied nonpartisan municipal elections and compared them with partisan elections for the New Jersey State Assembly in Newark. He concluded that the "goal of nonpartisanship is fulfilled, as party identification does not determine the outcome. In place of party, ethnic affiliation is emphasized and the result is 'to enhance the effect of basic social cleavages.' "[34] If (1) this is typical of other American cities and if (2) electoral cleavages can be translated effectively into demands on the government in the absence of aggregative parties, then we might assume that the reformed institutions would reflect cleavages more, rather than less, closely than unreformed ones.

Essentially, then, there are two contrasting views about the consequences of municipal reform. One, the reformers' ideal, holds that institutional reforms will mitigate the impact of social cleavages on public policy. The other argues that the elimination of political parties and the introduction of other reforms will make social cleavages more, rather than less, important in political decision-making.

THE MEASUREMENT OF RESPONSIVENESS

We have hypothesized that socioeconomic cleavages will have less impact on the policy choices of reformed than unreformed governments. Thus, one could do a better job of predicting a city's taxation and expenditure policy using socioeconomic variables in partisan, mayor and ward cities than in nonpartisan, manager and at-large cities. Operationally, we will test this hypothesis by using multiple correlation coefficients. Squaring these coefficients, called "multiple R's," will give us a summary measure of the total amount of variation in our dependent variables explained by our twelve independent variables.[35] The results of the correlation

analysis are summarized in Diagrams 1 and 2.

On the whole, the results of the correlation analysis strikingly support the hypothesis, with the exception of commission cities. Thus, we can say, for example, that our twelve socioeconomic variables explain 71 per cent of the variations in taxation policy in partisan cities, and 49 per cent of the variation in nonpartisan cities. In commission cities, however, socioeconomic variables predict substantially more variation in both taxes and expenditures than in the unreformed mayor-council cities.[36] The anomaly of commission governments is interesting, for they present, as we will see, marked exceptions to virtually every pattern of relationships we found. The substantial explanatory power of these socioeconomic variables is not altered, but confirmed, by examining the variables independently. The rest of the correlations show a consistent pattern: reformed cities are less responsive to cleavages in their population than unreformed cities.

If one of the premises of the "political ethos" argument is that reformed institutions give less weight to the "private regarding" and "artificial" cleavages in the population, that premise receives striking support from our analysis. Our data suggest that when a city adopts reformed structures, it comes to be governed less on the basis of conflict and more on the basis of the rationalistic theory of administration. The making of public policy takes less count of the enduring differences between White and Negro, business and labor, Pole and WASP. The logic of the bureaucratic ethic demands an impersonal, apolitical settlement of issues, rather than the settlement of conflict in the arena of political battle.

V. To Spend or Not to Spend

If efforts to expand or contract the scope of government stand at the core of municipal political life,[37] they are nowhere better reflected than in the taxation and expenditure patterns of cities. A generation ago, Charles Beard wrote, "In the purposes for which appropriations are made the policies of the city government are given concrete form—the culture of the city is reflected. Indeed, the history of urban civilization could be written in terms of appropriations, for they show what the citizens think is worth doing and worth paying for."[38] Pressures to expand and contract government regulations and services are almost always reflected one way or another in the municipal budget. Labor, ethnic groups, the poor and the liberal community may press for additional services and these must be paid for; the business community may demand municipal efforts to obtain new industry by paring city costs to create a "favorable business climate"; or businessmen may themselves demand municipal services for new or old business. In any case, few political conflicts arise which do not involve some conflict over the budget structure.

CLASS VARIABLES AND PUBLIC POLICIES

Part of the political rhetoric associated with the demand for a decrease in the scope of the national government is the argument that the initiative for policy-making should rest more with the state and local governments. Opposition to high federal spending

levels, as V. O. Key has demonstrated, is found more often among persons with middle class occupations than among blue-collar workers.[39] It is not inconceivable that the middle class argument about state and local responsibility might be more than political rhetoric, and that at the local level, middle class voters are willing to undertake major programs of municipal services, requiring large outlays of public capital. Wilson and Banfield have argued that the "public regarding" upper-middle class voters in metropolitan areas are often found voting for public policies at variance with their "self-interest narrowly conceived," and that "the higher the income of a ward or town, the more taste it has for public expenditures of various kinds."[40] Similarly a longitudinal study of voting patterns in metropolitan Cleveland found that an index of social rank was positively correlated with favorable votes on welfare referenda.[41] If these data reflect middle class willingness to spend on a local level, they might indicate that the "states' rights" argument was more than ideological camouflage: middle class voters stand foursquare behind public expenditure at the local level even when they oppose those expenditures from the national government. Therefore, we hypothesized that:

2a. The more middle class the city, measured by income, education and occupation, the higher the municipal taxes and expenditures.

TABLE 4.   Correlations Between Middle Class Characteristics and Outputs in Reformed and Unreformed Cities

Correlations of	Government Type			Election Type		Constituency Type	
	Mayor-Council	Manager	Com-mission	Partisan	Non-Partisan	Ward	At-Large
Taxes with:							
Median income	−.13	−.24	−.19	.03	−.19	−.17	−.22
White collar	−.23	−.12	−.62	−.21	−.33	−.30	−.32
Median education	−.36	−.22	−.08	−.45	−.24	−.48	−.18
Expenditures with:							
Median income	−.19	−.32	−.43	−.04	−.32	−.23	−.34
White collar	−.24	−.23	−.58	−.18	−.39	−.32	−.35
Median education	−.32	−.36	−.26	−.36	−.38	−.44	−.32

In line with our general concern of testing the impact of political structures on municipal policies, we also hypothesized that:

2b. Unreformed cities reflect this relationship more strongly than reformed cities.

With respect to hypothesis 2a, the data in Table 4 on three middle class indicators are unambiguous and indicate a strong rejection of the hypothesis. However we measure social class, whether by income, education or occupation, class measures are negatively related to public taxes and expenditures.

It is possible, however, that income does not have a linear, but rather a curvilinear relationship with municipal outputs. Banfield and Wilson argue that "In the city, it is useful to think in terms of three income groups—low, middle, and high. Surprising as it may seem to Marxists, the conflict is generally between an alliance of low-income and high-income groups on one side and the middle-income groups on the other."[42] If the relationship between income and expenditure is curvilinear, then we should expect to find that proportions of both low and high income groups were positively correlated with outputs. Our data, however, lend no support to this notion of a "pro-expenditure" alliance. Rather, the proportion of the population with incomes below $3000 is positively correlated with expenditures in all city types (although the relationships are small) and the proportion of the population in the above $10,000 bracket is negatively correlated with expenditures. Summing the two measures and correlating the combined measure with outputs produced no correlation greater than .15 and the relationships were as likely to be negative as positive. Tests for non-linearity also suggested that

Robert L. Lineberry
Edmund P. Fowler

no such coalition exists in the cities in our analysis.

To be sure, aggregate data analysis using whole cities as units of analysis is no substitute for systematic survey data on middle class attitudes, but it is apparent that cities with larger middle class population have lower, not higher expenditures. As we emphasized earlier, the "ethos theory" deals with attitudes and the behavior of individuals, while our data deal with cities and their behavior. The coalition suggested by Banfield and Wilson, however, is not discernible at this level of aggregation in these cities.

Hypothesis 2b is not consistently borne out by the data. In fact, the relationships between middle class variables and outputs are, if anything, stronger in the reformed cities than in their unreformed counterparts. One would not want to make too much of the data, but a large body of literature on city politics, which we discuss below, suggests that reformed institutions maximize the power of the middle class.

We originally assumed that the proportion of owner-occupied dwelling units constituted another measure of middle class composition, but it soon became apparent that it was only weakly related to income, occupation and education measures. Nevertheless, it emerged as the strongest single predictor of both expenditure and taxation policy in our cities. We hypothesized that:

3a. Owner-occupancy and outputs are negatively correlated, and
3b. Unreformed cities reflect this relationship more strongly than reformed cities.

TABLE 5. *Correlations Between Owner Occupancy and Government Outputs in Reformed and Unreformed Cities*

Correlations of Owner Occupancy with:	Government Type			Election Type		Constituency Type	
	Mayor–Council	Manager	Com–mission	Partisan	Non–Partisan	Ward	At–large
Taxes	−.57	−.31	−.73	−.64	−.45	−.56	−.48
Expenditures	−.51	−.23	−.62	−.62	−.40	−.50	−.40

Hypothesis 3a is consistently borne out in the data presented in Table 5. These relationships were only slightly attenuated when we controlled for income, education and occupation. No doubt self-interest (perhaps "private regardingness") on the part of the home owner, whose property is intimately related to the tax structure of most local governments, may account for part of this relationship. Moreover, home ownership is correlated (almost by definition) with lower urban population density. High density, bringing together all manner of men into the classic urban mosaic, may be itself correlated with factors which produce demands for higher expenditures—slums, increased needs for fire and police protection, and so on.

In confirmation of hypothesis 3a, the unmistakable pattern is for unreformed cities to reflect these negative relationships more strongly than the manager, nonpartisan and at-large cities, although commission cities show their usual remarkably high correlations.

HOMOGENEITY VARIABLES AND PUBLIC POLICIES

Dawson and Robinson, in their analysis of state welfare expenditures, found strong positive relationships between the ethnicity of a state's population and the level of its welfare expenditures.[43] If this is symptomatic of a generalized association of ethnic and religious minorities with higher expen-

ditures, we might find support for the hypothesis that:

4a. The larger the proportion of religious and ethnic minorities in the population, the higher the city's taxes and expenditures.

And, if our general hypothesis about the impact of political institutions is correct then:

4b. Unreformed cities reflect this relationship more strongly than reformed cities.

The correlations between ethnicity, religious heterogeneity and outputs (see Table 6) are, with one exception, positive, as predicted by hypothesis 4a. These associations may reflect the substantial participation by ethnic groups in municipal politics long after the tide of immigration has been reduced to a trickle.[44] The relatively intense politicization of ethnic groups at the local level,[45] the appeals to nationality groups through "ticket balancing" and other means, and the resultant higher turnout of ethnic groups than other lower status groups,[46] may produce an influence on city government far out of proportion to their number.

We found when we related all twelve of our independent variables to outputs in various city types that the associations were much weaker in cities we have labeled reformed. The correlations for ethnicity and religious homogeneity show a generally similar pattern, with commission cities exhibiting their usual erratic behavior. The data, then, show fairly clear support for hypothesis 4b.

TABLE 6. *Correlations Between Ethnicity and Religious Heterogeneity and Outputs in Reformed and Unreformed Cities*

Correlations of	Government Type			Election Type		Constituency Type	
	Mayor–Council	Manager	Com–mission	Partisan	Non–Partisan	Ward	At–large
Taxes with:							
Ethnicity	.49	.26	.57	.61	.43	.56	.40
Private School Attendance	.38	.15	.37	.33	.37	.41	.25
Expenditures with:							
Ethnicity	.36	.02	.21	.48	.21	.44	.13
Private School Attendance	.34	−.01	.07	.25	.24	.40	.05

The third variable of our homogeneity indicators—per cent of population non-white—had almost no relationship to variation in outputs, regardless of city type. We found the same weak correlations for the poverty income variable, which was, of course, strongly related to the racial variable. An easy explanation suggests that this is a consequence of the political impotence of Negroes and the poor, but one should be cautious in inferring a lack of power from the lack of a statistical association.

We have dealt in this section with factors which are positively and negatively related to spending patterns in American cities. While social class variables are associated negatively with outputs, two measures of homogeneity, private school attendance and ethnicity are related to higher taxes and spending. Examining the strengths of these correlations in cities with differing forms, we found some support for our general hypothesis about the political consequences of institutions, especially about the political consequences of institutions, especially for the homogeneity variables and the home ownership variable. Interestingly, however, this was not the case with class variables.

VI. Reformism as a Continuous Variable

The central thrust of our argument has been that reformed governments differ from

Reformism and Public Policies in American Cities   289
Robert L. Lineberry
Edmund P. Fowler

their unreformed counterparts in their responsiveness to socioeconomic cleavages in the population. Logically, if the presence of one feature of the "good government" syndrome had the impact of reducing responsiveness, the introduction of additional reformed institutions should have an additive effect and further reduce the impact of cleavages on decision-making. We therefore decided to treat "reformism" as a continuous variable for analytic purposes and hypothesized that:

5. The higher the level of reformism in a city, the lower its responsiveness to socio-economic cleavages in the population.

We utilized a simple four-point index to test this hypothesis, ranging from the "least reformed" to the "most reformed." The sample cities were categorized as follows:

1. Cities with none of the reformed institutions (i.e., the government is mayor-council, elections are partisan and constituencies are wards).

2. Cities with any one of the reformed institutions.

3. Cities with two of the reformed institutions.

4. Cities with three reformed institutions (i.e., the government is either manager or commission, elections are nonpartisan and constituencies are at-large).

TABLE 7. *Correlations Between Selected Independent Variables and Output Variables by Four Categories of Reformism*

Correlations of	Reform Scores			
	1 (least reformed)	2	3	4 (most reformed)
Taxes with:				
Ethnicity	.62	.41	.50	.34
Private School Attendance	.40	.32	.28	.25
Owner-Occupancy	−.70	−.39	−.54	−.44
Median Education	−.55	−.27	−.32	−.13
Expenditures with:				
Ethnicity	.51	.27	.41	.05
Private School Attendance	.46	.23	.16	.08
Owner-Occupancy	−.67	−.30	−.54	−.38
Median Education	−.49	−.19	−.38	−.37

We can not overemphasize the crudity of this index as an operationalization of the complex and abstract concept of "reformism." Nonetheless, we think some of the relationships we found are strongly suggestive that reformism may in reality be a continuous variable.

To test this hypothesis, we took four variables which had moderate-to-strong correlations with our dependent variables and computed simple correlations in each reform category. If our hypothesis is correct, the strength of the correlations in Table 7 should decrease regularly with an increase in reform scores. While there are some clear exceptions to the predicted pattern of relationships, there is some fairly consistent support for the hypothesis. Even when the decreases in the strengths of the correlations is irregular, there is a clear difference between cities which we have labeled "most reformed" and "least reformed."

Again, we would not want to attach too much importance to the results of this rough-and-ready index. But, the patterns support our previous argument about the impact of reformism: the more reformed the city, the less responsive it is to socioeconomic cleavages in its political decision-making.

VII. A Causal Model and Interpretation

A CAUSAL MODEL

The implicit, or at times explicit, causal model in much of the research on municipal reformism has been a simple one: socioeconomic cleavages cause the adoption of particular political forms. A more sophisticated model would include political institutions as one of the factors which produce a given output structure in city politics. We hypothesize that a causal model would include four classes of variables: socioeconomic cleavages, political variables (including party registration, structure of party systems, patterns of aggregation, strength of interest groups, voter turnout, etc.), political institutions (form of government, type of elections and types of constituencies), and political outputs. Diagram 3 depicts one possible causal model.

This study has of necessity been limited to exploring the linkages between socioeconomic cleavages, political institutions and political outputs. We found that political institutions "filter" the process of converting inputs into outputs. Some structures, particularly partisan elections, ward constituencies, mayor-council governments and commission governments, operate to maximize the impact of cleavage indicators on public policies. We conclude by discussing some of the reasons why different structures have varying impacts on the conversion process.

AN INTERPRETATION

1. Cities with reformed and unreformed institutions are not markedly different in terms of demographic variables. Indeed, some variables, like income, ran counter to the popular hypothesis that reformed cities are havens of the middle class. Our data lent some support to the notion that reformed

DIAGRAM 3.   A Hypothesized Causal Model

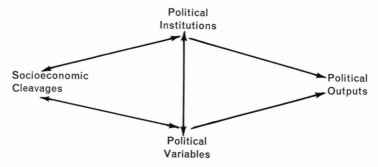

cities are more homogeneous in their ethnic and religious populations. Still, it is apparent that reformed cities are by no means free from the impact of these cleavages.

2. The more important difference between the two kinds of cities is in their behavior, rather than their demography. Using multiple correlation coefficients, we were able to predict municipal outputs more exactly in unreformed than in reformed cities. The translation of social conflicts into public policy and the responsiveness of political systems to class, racial, and religious cleavages differs markedly with the kind of political structure. Thus, political institutions seem to play an important role in the political process—a role substantially independent of a city's demography.

3. Our analysis has also demonstrated that reformism may be viewed as a continuous variable and that the political structures of the reform syndrome have an additive effect: the greater the reformism, the lower the responsiveness.

Through these political institutions, the goal of the reformers has been substantially fulfilled, for nonpartisan elections, at-large constituencies and manager governments are associated with a lessened responsiveness of cities to the enduring conflicts of political life. Or, as Stone, Price and Stone argued in their study of changes produced by the adoption of manager governments, the council after the reform "tended to think more of the community as a whole and less of factional interests in making their decisions."[47]

The responsiveness of a political institution to political conflicts should not be confused with the "responsibility" of a political system as the latter term is used in the great debate over the relative "responsibility" of party systems.[48] In fact, the responsiveness of political forms to social cleavages may stand in sharp contrast to "responsible government" on the British model. Presumably, in American cities, partisan elections, ward constituencies, and mayor-council governments maximize minority rather than majority representa-

tion, assuring greater access to decision-makers than the reformed, bureaucratized and "de-politicized" administrations.

Partisan electoral systems, when combined with ward representation, increase the access of two kinds of minority groups: those which are residentially segregated, and which may as a consequence of the electoral system demand and obtain preferential consideration from their councilmen; and groups which constitute identifiable voting blocs to which parties and politicians may be beholden in the next election. The introduction of at-large, nonpartisan elections has at least five consequences for these groups. First, they remove an important cue-giving agency—the party—from the electoral scene, leaving the voter to make decisions less on the policy commitments (however vague) of the party, and more on irrelevancies such as ethnic identification and name familiarity.[49] Second, by removing the party from the ballot, the reforms eliminate the principal agency of interest aggregation from the political system. Hence, interests are articulated less clearly and are aggregated either by some other agency or not at all. Moreover, nonpartisanship has the effect of reducing the turnout in local elections by working class groups,[50] leaving office-holders freer from retaliation by these groups at the polls. Fourth, nonpartisanship may also serve to decrease the salience of "private regarding" demands by increasing the relative political power of "public regarding" agencies like the local press.[51] And when nonpartisanship is combined with election at-large, the impact of residentially segregated groups or groups which obtain their strength from voting as blocs in municipal elections is further reduced.[52] For these reasons, it is clear that political reforms may have a significant impact in minimizing the role which social conflicts play in decision-making. By muting the demands of private regarding groups, the electoral institutions of reformed governments make public policy less responsive to the demands arising out of social conflicts in the population.

The structure of the government may serve further to modify the strength of minority groups over public policy. It is significant in this respect to note that commission governments, where social cleavages have the greatest impact on policy choices, are the most decentralized of the three governmental types and that manager governments are relatively the most centralized.[53] From the point of view of the reformer, commission government is a failure and their number has declined markedly in recent years.[54] This greater decentralization of commission and of mayor-council governments permits a multiplicity of access points for groups wishing to influence decision-makers.[55] It may also increase the possibilities for collaboration between groups and a bureaucratic agency, a relationship which has characterized administrative patterns in the federal government. As a result of this decentralization, group strength in local governments may be maximized.

It is important in any analysis of reformism to distinguish between the factors which produce the *adoption* of reformed institu-tions and the *impact* of the new political forms once they have been established. We can offer from our data no conclusions about the origins of reformed structures, for it is obviously impossible to impute causation, using contemporary census data, to events which occurred decades ago. Once a city has institutionalized the reformers' ideals, however, a diffused attitude structure may be less helpful in explaining the city's public policy than the characteristics of the institutions themselves. With the introduction of these reforms, a new political pattern may emerge in which disputes are settled outside the political system, or in which they may be settled by the crowd at the civic club at the periphery of the system.[56] If they do enter the political process, an impersonal, "non-political" bureaucracy may take less account of the conflicting interests and pay more attention to the "correct" decision from the point of view of the municipal planner.

These conclusions are generally consistent with the ethos theory developed by Banfield and Wilson. If one of the components of the middle class reformer's ideal was "to seek the good of the community as a whole" and to minimize the impact of social cleavages on political decision-making, then their institutional reforms have served, by and large, to advance that goal.

DURING MUCH of the 1950s and early 1960s, studies of community decision-making were largely concerned with conceptualizing and measuring the leadership and influence patterns within local communities. The central question of the research tended to be a variation of Who Governs?[1]

Almost all empirical investigations took the form of case studies of individual communities. However, by the end of the 1950s, some researchers began to undertake comparative studies of two or more communities. There were several reasons for this new trend: discontent with the limited generalizations possible from case studies, a persuasion that the methodological difficulties of measuring "power structures" could be at least partially resolved by comparative research, and—not a negligible factor—increased research funds. Initially, the questions posed by these comparative studies were essentially the same as those in the earlier case studies. Nevertheless, systematic differences emerged between the decision-making patterns of various communities, and a broader range of questions gradually came to be perceived as essential for understanding community decision-making processes. To comprehend

Community Structure, Decision-Making, Budget Expenditures, and Urban Renewal in 51 American Communities*

Terry N. Clark

University of Chicago

adequately Who Governs, it is necessary to ascertain not only Who Governs, but also Where, When, and With What Effects?[2] This series of questions focuses attention on those structural characteristics of a community which predispose it toward one or another pattern of decision-making. It also meets one particularly well taken criticism of the earlier studies: their failure to portray the impact of one or another pattern of decision-making on concrete community outputs. The influence structure of a community is best understood by examination of its *causes* as well as its *consequences*.

With the guiding questions reformulated in this fashion, researchers began to elaborate a series of comparative propositions to specify answers for these general questions under varying conditions.[3] Although until very recently it has been easier to elaborate propositions than to test them, a number of procedures for "testing" propositions have been devised.

A first, admittedly crude, procedure is to compare two or three case studies of individual communities which have been conducted by different persons, focusing on the concomitant variations in community structures, decision-making patterns, and outputs.[4] But although superior to generalizing from a single case, this procedure has definite limitations. Besides the problem of whether varying research methods can yield comparable results, the simple lack of

* Revised and expanded from a paper with the same title published in the American Sociological Review, 33 (August 1968), pp. 576–593.

Sections of this paper were presented at the Colloque Yougoslave du Programme Méditerranéan du Centre de Sociologie Européene, Belgrade, December 1966; at the International Conference on Electoral Behavior, Survey Research Center, University of Michigan, Ann Arbor, Michigan, April 1967; at the Second Lecture Series on Fundamentals of Urban and Regional Planning, American–Yugoslav Project in Urban and Regional Planning Studies, Ljubljana, Summer, 1967; and at the annual meeting of the Southwestern Social Science Association in Dallas, Texas, April 11–13, 1968.

I am grateful to Harold Bloom, William Kornblum, and David Monsees for assistance in data processing, and to Leo A. Goodman, Robert W. Hodge, Jack Sawyer, Joe L. Spaeth, and Donald B. Treiman for suggestions on statistical matters.

General support for the research leading to this report was generously provided by the McNeil Foundation of Philadelphia and the National Science Foundation. Support for preparation of the manuscript was made available by the Social Science Research Committee of the University of Chicago and the American–Yugoslav Project in Urban and Regional Planning Studies in Ljubljana.

This is research paper No. 5A of the Comparative Study of Community Decision-Making, supported by grant GS-1904 from the National Science Foundation.

293

Notes to this selection will be found on pages 365–367.

information on theoretically important variables constitutes a formidable obstacle.

A second, improved variation of this procedure is the comparison of results from two, three, or four communities that have been investigated by the same researcher, or team of researchers, using directly comparable results and collecting identical data.[5] While this procedure has been more successful than the first, significant advances have been made by using both procedures, as well as by combining them. But, while contrasting results from a small number of communities may provide excellent stimulation for generating propositions as well as illustrative support for them, such a limited number of cases make it virtually impossible to sort out the complex interplay of variables.

A third type of procedure is the quantitative comparison of relatively large numbers of case studies.[6] Here, as when examining smaller numbers of studies, problems of comparability loom large, while, to compound the difficulty, missing information inevitably lowers the n of any given correla-

tion. But despite its drawbacks, this procedure permits more systematic comparisons than do the first two.

A fourth procedure, and the most satisfactory one for testing comparative propositions, is the quantitative study of large numbers of communities, collecting identical data in each case using directly comparable research methods. While the value of this procedure has been recognized for some time, only quite recently has it been possible to mobilize the necessary human and financial resources for an undertaking utilizing this approach.

The 51 Community Study

This article is a first report on a study in which 51 American communities were investigated using the field staff of the National Opinion Research Center (NORC) at the University of Chicago. To date this is by far the largest study of its kind. The background history of the study has already been reported elsewhere[7] and will be passed over here except to note that it was a joint undertaking of the International

TABLE 1. Selected Characteristics of 51 Communities

Characteristics	Mean	N	Minimum Value	Maximum Value
Total Population*	250,786	51	50,498	750,026.
Median Income*	6,186.04	51	4,232.00	9,132.00
Median School Years Completed*	11.05	51	8.80	13.30
Per cent Foreign Born*	7.82	51	1.00	19.00
Per cent Nonwhite*	11.82	51	0.00	41.00
Per cent Income Under $3,000*	15.86	51	4.00	33.00
Per cent Unemployed*	5.04	51	2.00	8.00
Per cent Jewish†	2.44	49	0.04	17.69
Per cent Catholic†	18.57	51	1.02	56.91
Per cent Protestant†	23.67	51	7.60	65.30
League of Women Voters Membership‡	268.33	49	0.	995.
General Budget Expenditures, 1957§	33,633.039	51	1,537.00	217,110.00
Urban Renewal Expenditures, 1965‖	39,148.636	51	0.	167,627.00

   * Source: *County City Data Book* (Washington, D.C.: U.S. Government Printing Office, 1966). Data are for central cities and independent cities in 1960.
   † Source: *Churches and Church Membership in the United States* (New York: National Council of the Churches of Christ in the USA, 1956). Figures are for members of religious institutions; in some cases they are only estimates.
   ‡ Supplied by Washington headquarters of the League of Women Voters. Data are for cities, as of January 1, 1967. Thanks are due to Mrs. Paul Cleveland for making these data available.
   § Source: *U.S. Census—Compendium of Municipal Finances* (Washington, D.C.: U.S. Government Printing Office, 1960).
   ‖ Source: *Urban Renewal Project Characteristics* (Washington, D.C.: Department of Housing and Urban Development, 1965).

Studies of Values in Politics and the NORC Permanent Community Sample, financed by the National Science Foundation and the McNeil Foundation of Philadelphia.

The 51 communities were sampled on the basis of region and population size. Table 1 presents some of the basic characteristics of the 51 cities. Representing 22 different states, their population size ranged from 50,000 to 750,000; the mean was 250,786. Cities in this range were selected in order to eliminate the somewhat unique metropolises and the smaller communities for which basic census-type statistics were not readily available. Median income ranged from $4,323 to $9,132, and median school years completed from 8.8 to 13.3. The percentage of foreign-born ranged from 1 to 19. The extent to which cities included a sizable poor, uneducated, and often nonwhite population sector also varied a good deal: the per cent with incomes under $3,000 ranged from 4 to 33; those having completed fewer than five years of formal education varied from 1 to 14 per cent; nonwhites were less than one per cent in one city, but represented 41 per cent of the population in another.

These are the rankings of the communities on a few of the approximately 300 variables obtained for each community. Principal sources for these data were the U.S. Census and such derivative publications as the *County City Data Book* and the *Compendium of Municipal Finances*, as well as various urban renewal and public health reports, and *The Municipal Yearbook*. Certain data, however, were obtained from less conventional sources. For example, we were interested in the possible importance of the religious affiliation of the population and procured religious data from a relatively little known source: the the reports of the National Council of the Churches of Christ. These data are less precise than one might desire: in some cases they are only estimates; they generally were compiled in 1952; and they are not reported by city but by county. Because the religious figures were obviously crude, we initially had strong doubts about using them at all; we decided to include them provisionally, however, because they varied so

much from one place to another. The percentage of Roman Catholic, for example, ranged from 1 to 56. As will be shown below, the number of Catholics residing in an area seems to lead to some very interesting consequences. Then because of the extensive discussions from de Tocqueville to the present about the role of voluntary organizations in community life, we sought membership figures on as many organizations as possible that might conceivably influence community decision-making patterns. In certain communities, such as Dallas and Pittsburgh, there is a single organization that reputedly brings together many leading citizens of the community and that plays a leading role in public affairs. In a case study of such a community, information on this kind of organization is of course vital. But since such organizations are not found everywhere and since their composition and functions vary considerably from one community to the next, information on such organizations is extremely difficult to interpret meaningfully for a systematic comparative study. Ideal are membership figures for an organization that is found in virtually all communities, and which undertakes generally comparable activities everywhere. The Parent–Teachers Association was one candidate, but as primarily local organizations, they are organized around individual school districts. There is no national PTA organization in a position to supply membership figures. We considered several other voluntary organizations, but either they were not comparable across communities or membership figures for our sample were impossible to obtain. The League of Women Voters, however, was ideal from several standpoints. It is perhaps the most important single civic voluntary organization in American communities. It frequently becomes involved in significant local issues. While not identical, the activities of the League from one community to the next are carefully circumscribed by the national organization: the local chapter in at least one of our communities had been disbanded after involvement in activities beyond those sanctioned by the national leadership. The national headquarters also maintains careful membership figures on the local organizations and generously made them available to us for analysis. In our 51 communities membership ranged from zero to 995.

Data Collection Procedures

In addition to these data from central sources, we conducted a series of interviews to collect additional information on matters such as political organization and decision-making.

In earlier studies[8] and on the basis of preliminary field work in several communities, we found about a dozen persons from different community sectors particularly well informed about community affairs. These were not necessarily the most active *participants*, but were generally knowledgeable *informants*. Attempting to collect as much information as possible but to maximize reliability and validity while minimizing costs, we decided to interview eleven strategically placed informants in each community[9]: the mayor, chairmen of the Democratic and Republican parties, the president of the largest bank, the editor of the newspaper with the largest circulation, the president of the chamber of commerce, the president of the bar association, the head of the largest labor union, the health commisisioner, the urban renewal director, the director of the last major hospital fund drive.

Interview schedules for the various informants concentrated on their particular institutional realms, but most interviews also contained a core set of items dealing with general community issues.

The professional field staff of NORC conducted the interviews in January, 1967, generally with one interviewer in each community. In an effort to maximize reliability, interviewers were provided with a general report about the study as well as detailed interview instructions, including a list of substitutes for unavailable interviewees.

Issue Areas and Decision-Making

To maintain intercommunity comparability, in each community these same informants were interviewed about the same four issues: urban renewal, the election of the mayor, air pollution, and the antipoverty program. These four particular issues were selected because they tend to involve different types of community actors in differing relationships with one another.[10] A mayoral election, for example, tends to mobilize the various community sectors along traditional lines of political cleavage as detailed by studies of voting behavior: income, education, religion, etc.

Urban renewal, on the other hand, is an issue that varies considerably. It may divide a community along traditional political lines, but, due to the importance of outside funds, it may also become a general distributive issue, whereby virtually all members of the community benefit from funds supplied largely by the Federal government.

The antipoverty issue is similar to urban renewal in reliance on outside funds, thus necessitating no reallocation of community resources. But unlike urban renewal, which may be turned toward diverse subsectors of the community depending on the content of the program, the antipoverty program is largely oriented toward assisting the poorer sectors of the community (although there may be substantial indirect benefits to other sectors).

Air pollution, on the other hand, requires direct and often expensive sacrifices by the industrial sector of the community for the benefit of the community as a whole.

Two issues, mayoral elections and air pollution, are largely local and tend to involve the redistribution of local resources, although the directions and amounts of reallocation are subject to varying definitions. The two other issues, urban renewal and poverty, principally involve distribution within the community of resources supplied from outside. The latter two issues also imply close relationships with higher level governmental officials outside the community.

All four issue areas need the support of local government to implement basic decisions. Of course, insofar as any decision-making structure exists within a community it will channel and redirect the activities within these various areas.[11]

But it is just this decision-making structure which is illuminated by comparison of the patterns of influence in the four different issue areas. We attempted to measure the community decision-making structure by using what we termed "the ersatz decisional method."

We examined the number of major actors involved in each issue area, and the degree to which decision-makers overlapped from one issue area to the next: for each issue area, we posed a series of questions inquiring essentially:

1. Who initiated action on the issue?
2. Who supported this action?
3. Who opposed this action?[12]
4. What was the nature of the bargaining process; who negotiated with whom?
5. What was the outcome? Whose views tended to prevail?

The cross classification of the five

TABLE 2. Communities in Which Issue Areas Were Absent

Issue Area	Number of Communities in which Absent
Air Pollution	5
Urban Renewal	2
Poverty Program	1

TABLE 3. Index Scores of Decentralized Decision-making Structure for the 51 Committees*

0. Akron, Ohio	7.50	26. Milwaukee, Wisconsin	7.75
1. Albany, New York	6.63	27. Minneapolis, Minnesota	8.00
2. Amarillo, Texas	3.33	28. Newark, New Jersey	9.13
3. Atlanta, Georgia	6.50	29. Palo Alto, California	6.50
4. Berkeley, California	5.92	30. Pasadena, California	5.50
5. Birmingham, Alabama	5.88	31. Phoenix, Arizona	7.75
6. Bloomington, Minnesota	4.45	32. Pittsburgh, Pennysylvania	7.75
7. Boston, Massachusetts	7.25	33. Saint Louis, Missouri	8.00
8. Buffalo, New York	8.67	34. Saint Paul, Minnesota	8.50
9. Cambridge, Massachusetts	8.67	35. Saint Petersburg, Florida	6.75
10. Charlotte, North Carolina	6.25	36. Salt Lake City, Utah	7.13
11. Clifton, New Jersey	5.90	37. San Francisco, California	7.75
12. Duluth, Minnesota	5.25	38. Santa Ana, California	6.50
13. Euclid, Ohio	6.93	39. San Jose, California	5.63
14. Fort Worth, Texas	6.75	40. Santa Monica, California	6.33
15. Fullerton, California	6.45	41. Schenectady, New York	5.75
16. Gary, Indiana	6.75	42. Seattle, Washington	7.50
17. Hamilton, Ohio	6.00	43. South Bend, Indiana	7.00
18. Hammond, Indiana	7.75	44. Tampa, Florida	8.25
19. Indianapolis, Indiana	9.00	45. Tyler, Texas	7.67
20. Irvington, New Jersey	7.67	46. Utica, New York	9.38
21. Jacksonville, Florida	6.25	47. Waco, Texas	3.25
22. Long Beach, California	4.75	48. Warren, Michigan	5.50
23. Malden, Massachusetts	8.50	49. Waterbury, Connecticut	8.75
24. Manchester, New Hampshire	4.97	50. Waukegan, Illinois	7.67
25. Memphis, Tennessee	6.38		

* Mean score for the 51 communities = 6.792.

decisional stages with the four issue areas
generated a twenty-cell matrix for each
community. From this was constructed our
index of centralization. Most theoretical
discussions of centralization of authority,
pluralism (here understood as decentralization), and related concepts[13] have isolated
two basic dimensions, both of which are
included in our index. The first is *participation*: the larger the number of actors
involved in community decision-making,
the greater the decentralization. Second is
overlap: the less similar the cluster of actors
in one issue area to those in adjoining issue
areas, the greater the decentralization. To
combine these conceptual dimensions in a
single index, we counted the number of
actors named by our informants, but we
counted each actor only once even if he was
named in more than one issue area. Then,
because in a few communities a particular
issue area did not exist (see Table 2), when
we obtained the number of actors by
summing as described above, we divided by
the number of issue areas present in the
community.

A few examples may clarify this procedure. Consider first a situation that most
writers would label highly centralized or
monolithic: a community where the mayor
initiated action on a decision, was supported
by the downtown businessmen, and opposed
by the labor unions and the newspaper. The
mayor was the major "entrepreneur" in
bargaining between the various groups. And
the mayor-businessmen coalition prevailed.
Under such circumstances, the total number
of actors in the issue would be four: mayor,
businessmen, labor unions, and newspaper.
If these same four actors, again playing the
same roles, were the only ones involved in
the other three issues, there would still only
be a total of four actors in all issue areas,
which, dividing by the number of issue areas,
yields a final score for the community of
one. This centralized community would
thus rank near the bottom of our scale of
decentralization. On the other hand, if we
consider a situation generally regarded as
more decentralized, where, for example,

five different actors were involved in each
issue area, the total number of actors would
be twenty, and, dividing by the number of
issue areas, the community score comes to
five. Applying this same procedure, we
computed a decentralization score for each
of the 51 communities. These scores are
presented in Table 3.

A few comments are perhaps in order on
some of the points of ambiguity we confronted in operationalizing centralization of
decision-making, and the solutions we
finally decided upon. One is the problem of
identifying distinct actors. For example, in
one community three labor leaders might be
named as actors, while in another only "the
labor unions" would be specified. We
reasoned that different individuals closely
similar in status should not be counted the
same as three individuals from three
differing sectors of the community. Therefore we devised a code of some 73 community
statuses, and we considered that a separate
actor would be counted for each status
named. But two persons occupying the
same status were counted only once. A
single individual could thus be counted as
two actors if he were named in two different
issue areas as occupant of two distinct
statuses (e.g., county judge and chairman
of a neighborhood organization). Some
might disagree with this interpretation but
we reasoned that it was more logical to
weight by the involvements of community
institutions than by individual persons.

Another ambiguity concerns conflicting
or missing information from different informants. Our solution was to count each new
status mentioned by any informant as a new
actor, but if a status were mentioned several
times by different informants, it was still
counted only once. There was, however,
slight but systematic differences in the
number of actors which our different informants would name. For this reason, we
constructed weights for the mean number of
different actors they named that were not
mentioned by any other informant. The
weights were constructed for the informants
in the 36 communities in which there were
no missing informants, and are presented
in Table 4. Then in the 15 communities where
one or more informants were unavailable

for an interview, the centralization index score for that community was increased by the amount of the weight for the missing informant(s).

TABLE 4. Mean Number of Community Actors Named by Each Informant in Addition to Those Named by All Other Informants, and Number of Communities in Which the Informant Was Not Able to be Interviewed

Informant	Mean No. of Actors	No. of Communities Unavailable
Chamber of Commerce President	2.08	0
Labor Council President	2.14	3
Newspaper Editor	1.81	1
Bar Association President	2.69	6
Democratic Party Chairman	1.50	2
Republican Party Chairman	1.53	1
Mayor	1.53	6

Another point relates to what might be termed the dynamics of the decision-making process: within a given issue area, how should one conceive of the relationships between the various stages of a decision? Is initiating action more important than supporting it, or does a heavy involvement of actors at the opposition stage imply greater conflict and a more decentralized decision-making process? If the answer to these last two questions were a clear affirmative, it would imply, methodologically, a disproportionate weighting of the actors involved at the initiation and opposition stages. But given the absence in this area of any theory sufficiently rigorous to permit the researcher to assign specific weights, we followed the conservative alternative of assigning equal value to every actor in the issue area regardless of the stage at which he became involved.[14]

Community Structure, Decision-Making and Outputs

An earlier article[15] formulated a series of 34 propositions relating community structural characteristics (demographic, economic,

legal–political, cultural, etc.) to centralized and decentralized patterns of decision-making. Subsequently[16] refining certain of these propositions, we added several others relating decision-making patterns to outputs, and subsumed a number of the discrete propositions under a more general formulation:

The greater the horizontal and vertical differentiation in a social system, the greater the differentiation between potential elites, the more decentralized the decision-making structure, which, without the establishment of integrative mechanisms, leads to less coordination between sectors and a lower level of outputs.'

The empirical analysis reported in the present paper was primarily oriented toward testing the earlier propositions and the general formulation. We therefore focused on variables for which some theoretical propositions had already been elaborated, although we were prepared to include other variables that might account for significant variance in any of the dependent variables. A large zero-order correlation matrix was inspected, and variables isolated about which we had specific hypotheses or which correlated highly with the measure of centralization of decision-making. Due to the high intercorrelation of many variables we performed a series of factor analyses to isolate clusters of variables and then from each cluster selected one or two with high factor loadings. Performance of regression analyses reduced the number of independent variables still further. We finally ended with eight, which together generated multiple correlation coefficients of .475 to .840 with centralization of decision-making and the two policy output variables. To briefly review each of these variables and the output measures utilized[17]:

X_1 = *Population Size* refers to the total number of community inhabitants.

X_2 = *Community Poverty* was reflected in per cent of population with incomes under

$3,000, per cent with fewer than five years education, per cent unemployed, and per cent nonwhite. Since all four measures were highly intercorrelated, to simplify the analysis we used simply per cent with income under $3,000 as an indicator for this cluster.

X_3 = *Industrial Activity* was represented by the per cent manufacturing establishments in the community with more than 20 employees.

X_4 = *Economic Diversification* comprised a dichotomous classification of communities ranked by Nelson[18] as diversified or financial, and all other communities.[19]

X_5 = *Highly Educated Population* was simply the median number of years of schooling completed by the community residents.

X_6 = *Catholic Population* was the number of members of the Roman Catholic Church in the county, standardized by the county population.

V = *Civic Voluntary Organization Activity* was based on membership in the League of Women Voters. Community membership figures were standardized by community population size.

W = The Index of Governmental Reformism was constructed from three govern-mental characteristics traditionally associated in the United States with "reform" government: the professional city manager, nonpartisan elections, at-large electoral constituencies.[20] Communities with varying combinations of these characteristics were scored as follows[21]:

3 = manager government, nonpartisan elections, at-large electoral constituencies;
2 = any two of these characteristics;
1 = any one of these characteristics;
0 = none of these characteristics.

Y = *Decentralized Decision-Making Structure* has already been discussed.

Z_1 = *General Budget Expenditures* were the total budget expenditures of the local community government on all items, standardized by population size.

Z_2 = *Urban Renewal Expenditures* were the total expenditures from Federal and local sources on urban renewal projects in the community up to 1965, standardized by the size of the population.

Table 5 presents the zero-order correlation matrix (of product moment correlations) for these twelve variables.

To test our propositions and evaluate the relative importance of each variable in the model, we computed the relationships among all variables utilizing a graphic variation of multiple regression analysis, path analysis.[22] We refer the reader to the works cited for a more general consideration

TABLE 5. Zero-order Correlation Matrix of Eleven Variables of the Model

Variables	X_1	X_2	X_3	X_4	X_5	X_6	V	W	Y	Z_1	Z_2
X_1 Population Size	...	...	...	...	...	...	...	...	...	...	...
X_2 Community Poverty	.276	...	...	...	...	...	...	...	...	...	...
X_3 Industrial Activity	−.104	−.141	...	...	...	...	...	...	...	...	...
X_4 Economic Diversification	−.516	.334	−.154	...	...	...	...	...	...	...	...
X_5 Highly Educated Population	−.238	−.339	−.339	.027	...	...	...	...	...	...	...
X_6 Catholic Population	.037	−.441	.204	−.236	−.322	...	...	...	...	...	...
V Civic Voluntary Organizations	−.427	−.269	.049	−.335	.490	.083	...	...	...	...	...
W Reformist Government	−.199	.077	−.332	.143	.625	−.425	.276	...	...	...	...
Y Decentralized DMS	.384	−.031	−.008	.347	−.332	.254	−.275	−.548	...	...	...
Z_1 General Budget Expenditures	.310	−.100	−.062	−.045	−.057	.610	.042	−.015	.237	...	...
Z_2 Urban Renewal Expenditures	.392	.136	.119	.050	−.297	.454	−.051	−.308	.350	.464	...

of the method, and note here only that path analysis is a procedure for representing a causal model of the relationships among a number of different variables. Arrows pointing in the direction of assumed causation connect the variables to one another. Straight arrows represent lines of causation, while double-headed bowed arrows indicate simple intercorrelations not implying dependency relationships. The numerical figure above each arrow leading away from a variable represents the separate contribution made by that variable in each of the directions indicated. Path coefficients may vary from $+1$ to -1, a negative sign indicating a negative contribution. In addition to those arrows connecting interrelated varables, there is an arrow for a residual error term for each variable dependent on others in the model. Residual error terms may vary from 1 to 0; the larger the error term the smaller the amount of variance in the dependent variable explained by the model.[23]

Although over a long enough period none of the variables is without some influence on the others, at any given point in time we may, without undue simplification, order most of the variables in a causal sequence.[24] Six variables relate to the demographic composition and economic base of the community and, for the present analysis, may be conceived as generally constant: population size, community poverty, industrial activity, economic diversification, educational level of the population, and percentage of Catholic population. We shall examine in turn the impact of each

Terry N. Clark

of these independent variables on five dependent variables: the level of civic voluntary organization activity, the form of government, patterns of community decision-making, general budget expenditures, and urban renewal expenditures.

CIVIC VOLUNTARY ORGANIZATION ACTIVITY

As one would fully expect from the literature on voluntary organizations[25] the

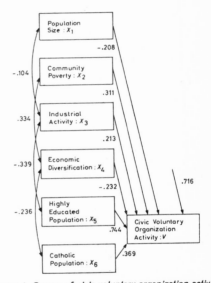

Figure 1. Causes of civic voluntary organization activity

TABLE 6. Correlations and Path Coefficients for Civic Voluntary Organization Activity

Dependent Variable: Civic Voluntary Organization Activity: V		
Independent Variable	Zero-Order Correlation	Path Coefficient
Highly Educated Population: X_5	.490	.744
Catholic Population: X_6	.083	.369
Community Poverty: X_2	−.269	.311
Economic Diversification: X_4	−.335	−.232
Industrial Activity: X_3	.049	.213
Population Size: X_1	−.427	−.208

$R = .699 \qquad$ Variance Explained $= 43\%$

$$V^* = -1031.8581 - 0.000122\ X_1 + 5.8659\ X_2 + 3.5166\ X_3 - 58.3283\ X_4 + 85.2983\ X_5 + 3.0859\ X_6$$
$$\quad\ (0.000079) \qquad (2.9738) \qquad (2.0055) \qquad (33.8527) \qquad (17.6693) \qquad (1.2286)$$

*Regression coefficients unstandardized; standard errors in parentheses.

educational level of the population strongly influences the level of civic voluntary organization activity. The next most influential variable was not so predictable: the size of the Catholic population. While the per cent of the community residents who were Roman Catholics shows no zero-order correlation with voluntary organization activity, when the other variables are controlled in the model, the influence becomes quite sizable. The impact of the extent of poverty in the community changed even more

radically from the zero-order relation— from a −.269 correlation to a +.311 path coefficient.

REFORM GOVERNMENT

Our findings about the socioeconomic correlates of reform government characteristics are generally similar to those reported by earlier students of the subject.[26] The most influential variable by far is the educational level of the population: more highly educated populations tend to have reform governments. As Wolfinger and Field point out, this is most characteristic of Western communities: our index correlated

TABLE 7. *Correlations and Path Coefficients for Index of Reform Government*

Dependent Variable: Index of Reform Government: W

Independent Variable	Zero-Order Correlation	Path Coefficient
Highly Educated Population: X_5	.625	.617
Community Poverty: X_2	.077	.265
Population Size: X_1	−.199	−.182
Economic Diversification: X_4	.143	.110
Industrial Activity: X_3	−.332	−.075
Catholic Population: X_6	−.425	−.062
Civic Voluntary Organization Activity: V	.276	.012

R = .716   Variance Explained = 51%

$W^* = -5.744202 - .000001\ X_1 + .0469\ X_2 - .0116\ X_3 + .2592\ X_4 + .6645\ X_5 + .0001\ V$
          (.000001)   (.0122)   (.0192)   (.3243)   (.2026)   (.0014)

*Regression coefficients unstandardized; standard errors in parentheses.

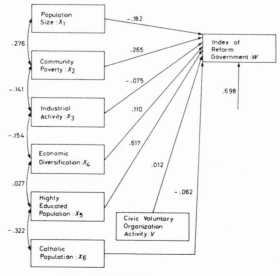

Figure 2. Causes of reform government.

.645 with a dummy variable for communities in the Western states. We should call attention, however, to the relationships between reformism and two variables not utilized by earlier authors. The correlation (zero-order) with reformism of per cent Catholic is $-.425$, and that of civic voluntary activity is .276. Both of these relationships would seem to offer support for the traditional "public regardingness" thesis. However, when the other variables (but not region) are introduced in the model, the relationships between these two variables and reformism virtually disappear. This should presumably be interpreted as implying that when Catholics move into communities (in the West or elsewhere) with highly educated populations, they assimilate a political culture of reformism. Correspondingly, potential League members in such communities may become less active as they are reasonably content that the victory for reform has already been won. Still, the present data force these interpretations to remain highly tentative.

THE DECISION-MAKING STRUCTURE

As we remarked above, the present study was oriented principally toward investigating the causes and consequences of community decision-making patterns. Correspondingly, a larger number of specific propositions had been formulated in this area than for the others. Because the more general theoretical considerations relating

to each proposition have been treated in detail elsewhere[27] we here limit the presentation to the propositions themselves and a discussion of the extent to which they were or were not supported by the empirical findings.

An idea that has been advanced on several occasions[28] is:

The larger the number of inhabitants in the community, the more decentralized the decision-making structure. But the proposition has not been substantiated on several occasions when it has been subjected to empirical test, to the great dismay, generally, of those forced to present the results.[29] It is therefore heartening to be able to report that the earlier theory seems to have been stronger than its empirical tests: we found a firm zero-order correlation between community population size and decentralization of decision-making.

But for most of us who have theorized about population size, size *per se* is not generally thought of as the crucial variable; rather various associated phenomena, among which the foremost is perhaps structural differentiation, are likely to be of more central importance. With increasing size, differentiation tends to advance in the

TABLE 8. Correlations and Path Coefficients for Decentralized Decision-Making Structure (Y)

Dependent Variable: Decentralized Decision-Making Structure: Y

Independent Variable	Zero–Order Correlation	Path Coefficient
Index of Reform Government: W	$-.548$	$-.586$
Economic Diversification: X_4	.347	.477
Industrial Activity: X_3	$-.008$	$-.213$
Community Poverty: X_2	$-.031$	$-.220$
Highly Educated Population: X_5	$-.332$	$-.061$
Civic Voluntary Organization Activity: V	$-.275$	.105
Population Size: X_1	.384	.066
Catholic Population: X_6	.254	.000

$R = .738$ Variance Explained = 47%
$$Y^* = 11.5429 + .0000\, X_1 - .0462\, X_2 - .0393\, X_3 + 1.3340\, X_4 - .2062\, X_5 + .0012\, V - .6959\, W$$
$$(.000001)\quad (.0273)\quad (.0219)\quad (.3751)\quad (.2254)\quad (.0015)\quad (.1748)$$

*Regression coefficients unstandardized; standard errors in parentheses.

whole range of community institutions:
economic, political, cultural, etc. Differentiation in the economic sphere has led to the
following proposition[30]:

*The more diverse the economic structures
within a community, the more decentralized
the decision-making structure.* Here too,
however, empirical support has often been
lacking. But once again our findings provide
strong support for the theorized relationship; the more economically diversified
communities definitely have more decentralized decision-making structures.

Although differentiation of governmental
institutions is less clear than differentiation
in the economic sector, the characteristics
of reform government may be interpreted as
tending toward a less differentiated pattern
than the "unreformed" alternatives of our
index. Reform government is less differentiated when the set of political institutions
are considered as a distinct subsystem of the
total community. But if we consider the
general functions performed by the political
subsystem for the rest of the community
system, we must recognize the political
subsystem generally, and reform government
institutions more specifically, as an important mechanism of integration. These
considerations[31] suggest that reform governmental characteristics should lead to
more centralized patterns of decision-
making, as indeed they do. Reform
government has the strongest relationship
with centralization of any variable in the
model.

Reform government, in turn, is strongly
correlated with a highly educated community population. But, the zero-order correlation of education with decentralization
is negative. This would seem, at first, to
contradict our proposition that:

*The higher the educational level of com-
munity residents, the more pluralistic the
decision-making structure.*[32] When the other
variables in the model are introduced, however, the negative association disappears.
But the proposition is still not supported.

Another variable closely related to a
highly educated population is the level of
civic voluntary activeness. We had postulated that:

*The greater the density of voluntary
organizations in the community, the more
decentralized the decision-making structure.*[33] The negative zero-order correlation
between civic activeness and decentralization implies rejection of the proposition;
but in the causal model, the relationship

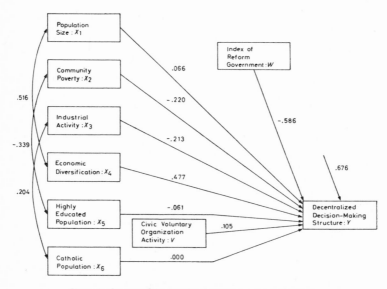

Figure 3. Causes of decentralized decision-making structure

although quite weak, was positive. Highly educated populations thus tend to lead to both reform governments and higher levels of civic activity. But while the first tends toward centralization of decision-making, the second tends, it seems, toward decentralization. Correspondingly, the general proposition about higher education leading to decentralization is not supported by the present evidence; still, the intermediate links in the causal chain need to be specified more precisely before the proposition can be verified or rejected.

A final proposition which we were able to test suggested that:

The higher the degree of industrialization in a community, the more decentralized the decision-making structure.[34] The path coefficient in our model, while not very strong, suggests exactly the opposite relationship. Even if strongly negative, however, the substantive meaning of such a finding would not be self-evident. By international standards, the United States is obviously a highly industrialized country. But the effects of industrialization such as those implied by the proposition do not necessarily make themselves felt in the areas immediately surrounding large industrial installations. The more indirect consequences of industrialization—wealth, leisure

time, education, more harmonious social relations—are apparently more important in effecting a decentralized pattern of decision-making than industrial activity *per se*. And when these indirect benefits are separated ecologically from industrial establishments, the relationship stated in the proposition will no longer strictly hold. One solution would be to reformulate the proposition and apply it to larger ecological units—Standard Metropolitan Statistical Areas or regions. But here, the differences within the United States are so small when compared to those between the United States and communities in other countries that it seems preferable provisionally to retain the proposition as it stands, but to seek comparable data from communities in less industrialized countries in order to test it. Several projects are presently underway which should make this feasible in the near future.[35]

POLICY OUTPUTS

Until quite recently, neither theoretical

TABLE 9. Correlation and Path Coefficients for the Dependent Variable: Urban Renewal Expenditures (Z_2)

Dependent Variable: Urban Renewal Expenditures: Z_2

Independent Variable	Zero-order Correlation	Path Coefficient
Catholic Population: X_6	.454	.620
Community Poverty: X_2	.136	.527
Population Size: X_1	.392	.341
Decentralized Decision-Making Structure: Y	.350	.291
Highly Educated Population: X_5	−.297	.282
Economic Diversification: X_4	.050	−.235
Industrial Activity: X_3	.119	.181
Index of Reform Government: W	−.308	.052
Civic Voluntary Organization Activity: V	−.051	.025
Residual	...	.708

R = .705 Variance Explained = 50%

$$Z_2{}^* = -581.9180 + .001\ X_1 + 6.7657\ X_2 + 2.0347\ X_3 - 40.1232\ X_4$$
$$(.00006) \quad (2.2836) \quad (1.5096) \quad (28.0434)$$
$$+ 22.0305\ X_5 + 3.5293\ X_6 + .0169\ V + 3.8038\ W + 17.7491\ Y$$
$$(17.2175) \quad (.9209) \quad (.1061) \quad (13.4547) \quad (10.0208)$$

* Regression coefficients unstandardized; standard errors in parentheses.

nor empirical work on community decision-making has been concerned with systematically relating decision-making patterns to policy outputs.[36] Consequently, the number of propositions in this area was smaller than those predicting patterns of decision-making from community structural characteristics.

One basic proposition, however, referred to in the general formulation above and for which some support exists,[37] is the more centralized the decision-making structure, the higher the level of outputs. But our findings with regard to both general budget and urban renewal expenditures were precisely the opposite of those predicted by this proposition. The fact that certain studies have supported the proposition suggests that it is not necessarily wrong, but more likely incomplete; it may apply only to certain types of decisions.

The types of decisions that have been the subject of earlier studies that have supported the proposition have been fluoridation, school desegregation, and urban renewal. One characteristic of these types of decisions, which apparently differentiates them from our two policy outputs, is their *fragility*. Fluoridation studies have con-tinually stressed the difficulty of successfully implementing fluoridation programs after they have come under general attack from outspoken local community groups. The same is true of school desegregation. And, if we are to judge from the earlier case studies of urban renewal programs, and the quantitative data for the 1950s presented by Hawley, this would seem to have been the case for urban renewal as well, at least until recently. As an important component of fragility is the newness of any particular program to a community, fragility, *ceteris paribus*, should decrease over time. For with time, community residents become increasingly accustomed to the presence of a particular activity; the personnel associated with the program establish continuing relationships with other community sectors; initial projects have a chance to be completed and later projects improved through experience from the earlier ones: the program activities become legitimated. School desegregation and urban renewal both seem to have become less fragile issues than they were a decade ago.

In a decentralized community, a small but discontented group is much more likely to be able to find a sympathetic ear of at least one of the leaders, or potential leaders, of the community than it would be in a

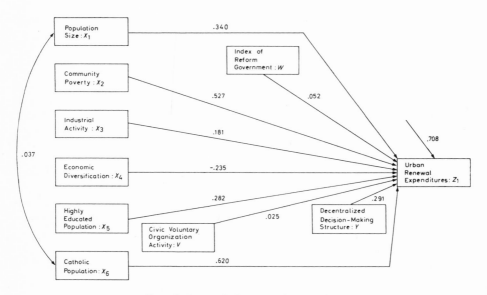

Figure 4. Causes of urban renewal expenditures.

more centralized community where the leadership is strong enough to be able to ignore mild opposition. In the case of a sufficiently fragile issue, active opposition by even a small discontented group may delay or even halt action on the issue. A weak government, or at least one which must govern with participation and active consent of many supporting groups, is more likely to have difficulty in carrying out fragile decisions than a stronger one. Or,

slightly restated, *for fragile decisions, the more centralized the decision-making structure, the higher the level of outputs.*

But if the effects of decentralization may be to lower the level of outputs in fragile

TABLE 10. *Correlations and Path Coefficients for General Budget Expenditures*

Dependent Variable: General Budget Expenditures: Z_1

Independent Variable	Zero-order Correlation	Path Coefficient
Catholic Population: X_6	.610	.922
Index of Reform Government: W	−.015	.521
Community Poverty: X_2	−.100	.422
Economic Diversification: X_4	−.045	−.408
Decentralized Decision-Making Structure: Y	.237	.394
Highly Educated Population: X_5	−.057	.382
Population Size: X_1	.310	.369
Civic Voluntary Organization Activity: V	.042	−.126
Industrial Activity: X_3	−.062	.097

$$R = .840 \qquad \text{Variance Explained} = 66\%$$
$$Z_1{}^* = -459.3432 + .0001\,X_1 + 3.8870\,X_2 + .7850\,X_3 - 50.0548\,X_4$$
$$(.5064) \qquad (1.2558) \qquad (.8301) \qquad (15.4211)$$
$$+\ 21.4175\,X_5 + 3.7679\,X_6 - .0618\,V + 27.1004\,W + 17.2776\,Y$$
$$(9.4679) \qquad (.5064) \qquad (.0584) \qquad (7.3988) \qquad (5.5105)$$

* Regression coefficients unstandardized; standard errors in parentheses.

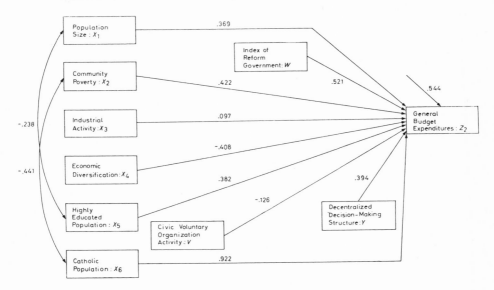

Figure 5. Causes of general budget expenditures.

decisions, by no means is this necessarily the case in less fragile decisions. Although compromise on a fragile issue may result in a complete stalemate, compromise on a less fragile issue is likely simply to lead to its modification. For such less fragile issues as budget construction or (established) urban renewal programs, as increasing numbers of outside pressures develop, each pleading for an increase in a particular section of the budget, or special treatment in the urban renewal program, compromise is likely to be in the direction of further expansion of these programs. And in more decentralized communities, where more pressure can be brought to bear by a larger number of groups, the expansion of outputs should be greater. These last considerations suggest, then, that *for less fragile decisions, the more centralized the decision-making structure, the lower the level of outputs.*

Insofar as budget construction and more established urban renewal programs may be classified as less fragile decisions, their size should increase with decentralization of the decision-making structure. And this we found in fact to be the case.

Decentralization of decision-making, however, is not the only factor behind budget and urban renewal expenditures in American communities. By far the most influential variable was one which has been virtually ignored by every major study of factors affecting community budget expenditures of which we are aware: the per cent of the community residents who are members of the Roman Catholic Church. The zero-order correlation of per cent Catholic and budget expenditures was high—.610—but instead of declining in importance when other variables in the model were introduced as one might have expected, a phenomenally strong path coefficient of .922 was generated. This was the strongest single path coefficient in our entire analysis. The path coefficient from per cent Catholic to urban renewal expenditures was not quite so impressive, but it was still easily the strongest single path in Figure 5. As we suggested above, the figures that we used for religious affiliation have remained unknown to most social scientists although they are not new. That they are somewhat old and necessarily somewhat inexact should simply lower their correlations with other variables. But that such strong relationships persist even with a crude measure seems remarkable testimony to the importance of a hitherto neglected variable.

How are we to explain these findings? Our first reaction was that there may have been errors in the data, but all figures were checked twice and found to be correct. Our second concern was multicollinearity. We thus examined the zero-order correlations between per cent Catholic and other variables in order to search out possible strong associations between Catholicism and some other unanalyzed factor. Zero-order correlations show that communities with large numbers of Catholic residents are often in the Northeast, less often in the South, reasonably high in population density, slightly more industrialized, and have populations that are somewhat less educated, and less frequently protestant, but have a relatively *small* per cent of the population with incomes under $3,000. From these findings, one might infer that the Catholic communities tend toward the private-regarding ideal-type of Banfield and Wilson, but although per cent Catholic correlated −.425 with reform governmental institutions, strongly Catholic communities only tend slightly toward having a Democratic mayor (.378).

Searching for factors that might be more significant than Catholicism in explaining high community expenditures, we introduced into our standard regression model, one or two at a time, region, population density, various measures of industrial activity, per cent Protestants and Jews in the population, the party of the mayor, and per cent Democratic vote in the SMSA in 1960. But none of these factors—to our surprise— seriously decreased the impact of per cent Catholic membership—the path coefficient from per cent Catholic to budget expenditures never dropped below .680. Per cent Catholic was also quite consistently influential when, instead of the general budget figures, expenditures on separate budget items were analyzed: for a total of 23 separate items, it was the most influential single variable for nine items, and second or third most influential for five others. Its influence was virtually zero for six items (highways, highway capital outlays, sewerage, parks and recreation, libraries, and general public buildings), and negative for just two (sewerage capital outlays and total utility expenditures). Thus the impact of Catholics on budget expenditures derives not from just a few items, but is found quite consistently on about two thirds of all budget items.

We then tried to specify what kinds of Catholics were most likely to spend public funds. Much of the literature on ethnic politics suggests that, among Catholics, it is the Irish who have been most consistently involved in politics. But there is little support in the literature for the proposition that Irish Catholics spend more than other national groups.[38]

To evaluate the relative importance of the various national groups, we computed sixteen measures based on the number of foreign born persons and persons with at least one parent born in Ireland, Germany,

Poland, Mexico, Italy, Western Europe (UK, Ireland, Norway, Sweden, Denmark, Switzerland, France), Central Europe (Germany, Poland, Czechoslovakia, Austria, Hungary, Yugoslavia), and Southern Europe (Greece, Italy, Yugoslavia). (The countries with low rates of immigration were grouped, and others were not included because the immigration rates were so small.) These eight figures for each community were then standardized in two different measures, by dividing by (1) the total number foreign born and persons with foreign or mixed parents, and (2) the total community population. As the figures we used were from the 1960 census, we were concerned that certain groups, especially Irish and Germans, would be underrepresented because these figures would reflect immigration only after the last part of the nineteenth century. But although the Irish were probably more underrepresented in these figures than most other national

TABLE 11. Budget Expenditures Model with Irish as a Per Cent of the Total Community Population Included

Dependent Variable: General Budget Expenditures: Z_1

Independent Variable	Zero-order Correlation	Path Coefficient
Index of Reform Government: W	$-.004$	.542
Per cent Irish: X_7	.679	.501
Population Size: X_1	.330	.365
Per cent Catholic: X_6	.573	.362
Economic Diversification: X_4	$-.007$	$-.255$
Community Poverty: X_2	.007	.243
Decentralized Decision-Making Structure: Y	.216	.208
Civic Voluntary Organization Activity: V	$-.045$	$-.047$
Highly Educated Population: X_5	$-.166$	$-.039$
Industrial Activity: X_3	$-.013$	.030

$$R = .848 \qquad \text{Variance Explained} = 65\%$$
$$Z_1{}^* = 3.5899 + .0000\,X_1 + .0162\,X_2 + .0018\,X_3 - .2257\,X_4 - .0159\,X_5$$
$$\qquad (.0000) \quad (.0091) \quad (.0059) \quad (.1075) \quad (.0658)$$
$$+ .0107\,X_6 + .1779\,X_7 - .0260\,V + .2036\,W + .0658\,Y$$
$$(.0058) \quad (.0618) \quad (.0667) \quad (.0531) \quad (.0409)$$

* Regression coefficients unstandardized; standard errors in parentheses.

groups, they still emerged as the most important national group. When the sixteen standardized figures were introduced one at a time into our path analysis model for general budget expenditures (see Table 10 and Figure 5), only the two Irish figures were significant.[39] With Irish as a percentage of the total community population included in our model, the path coefficient for per cent Catholic dropped to .362; the path coefficient for Irish was .501 (see Table 11). No other national group or combination of national groups significantly decreased the per cent Catholic relationship. The distinctiveness of Irish Catholics, at least with regard to this issue, suggests that the currently widespread practice in discussions of city politics of lumping together persons under such categories as "ethnics," "immigrants," or even "private regarding" groups may be highly misleading.

It has been abundantly documented in public opinion studies that Catholics prefer the Democratic over the Republican party,[40] that they are well disposed toward increased governmental activities,[41] and that they support more extensive welfare state activities.[42] However, the importance of Catholicism, especially Irish Catholicism, in influencing actual policy outcomes to our knowledge has not been previously demonstrated in such striking fashion. It is to be hoped that future studies will more often include religious and national background variables in their analysis.

But let us compare our findings somewhat more systematically with those reported by earlier research on community budget expenditures.[43] Probably the most frequently analyzed variables, not surprisingly, are those associated with wealth. When data from individuals are aggregated, most often in national studies, personal income has generally been strongly associated with budget expenditures.[44] Studies of a state or a region have been able to make use of locally compiled figures for per capita assessed value of property of individual communities and have found strong relationships with budget expenditures.[45]

These findings concur with our .382 path coefficient from education (which is highly associated with measures of wealth) to budget expenditures; the coefficient was .337 from education to urban renewal expenditures. (The path coefficient for median income, when it was used in the model instead of median education, was lower than that for education.)

Most of the rest of our findings, however, are interesting in the ways in which they differ from earlier research. Studies of New York and Philadelphia suburbs, for example, showed that measures of the industrial activity of the community were extremely important in explaining governmental expenditure levels.[46]

Our findings suggest that the tendency of a community to spend more than others nearby by taxing its industries is more a suburban than a general phenomenon. Various measures of industrial activity—the per capita number of manufacturing establishments with more than 20 employees, per capita value added by manufacturing, per cent of industrial establishments with 20 or more employees—were introduced one at a time into our model, but all were of minimal importance.

Hawley observed several years ago that the proportion of the SMSA population residing in the central city was more important in predicting budget expenditures than the city population, and Brazer reported the same relationship for large American cities.[47] This proportion was not important for our sample, however, presumably because of the inclusion of more independent and smaller communities than in the studies by Hawley and Brazer.

The other variables included in our model which exercised some influence on budget expenditures were reform government (positively), economic diversification (negatively), the size of the poverty sector (positively), and the total population size (positively). Voluntary organization activity, however, showed no impact on budget or urban renewal expenditures.

The strong positive contribution of reform government to general budget expenditures in the causal model was unanticipated by the literature on the subject. Rather, many studies have suggested that a major rationale for reform government was the increased efficiency and decreased cost that would presumably result, and which apparently did result in the years immediately following adoption of reform government in a number of cities in the 1920s and 1930s.[48] It would seem at least very possible, however, that earlier studies which have reported negative relationships between reform government and budget expenditures have been misled by the high association of other community characteristics with reform government, and there may have been substantial changes in more recent years. Then the most recent statistical studies of reform government, for example by Wolfinger and Field and by Lineberry and Fowler,[49] have focused on interaction effects associated with reform government and relatively neglected the importance of other factors associated with the reform characteristics. Several variations of the models we have experimented with have not shown interaction effects of the sort reported by Lineberry and Fowler. Studies of budget expenditures using multivariate causal models and including reform government characteristics are still few in number, and direct comparisons are virtually impossible with those with which we are most familiar.

The weak contribution of reform government to urban renewal expenditures, and the possibilities of distortion in our path coefficients due to specification of this particular model, initially led us to remain circumspect in interpreting the result. Subsequently, however, we have essentially replicated the system of models reported here using near-orthogonal variates deriving from a factor analysis of socioeconomic characteristics of American communities.[50] Including the reform government index in a model with fourteen such variates still shows a very strong contribution from the reform characteristics to budget expenditures. Clearly, further study is called for to investigate more carefully the many implications of reform government. At this point we can only suggest that much of the traditional thinking on the subject seems in need of careful re-examination.

It is also perhaps not superfluous to comment, apropos of the explanatory importance of many of our variables which are not specifically economic, that some of the recent studies by economists and economically-oriented political scientists would be more useful if they considered more systematically certain noneconomic variables.

Conclusions

Without following Comte too closely, we suggest that the study of community decision-making has developed in a series of three stages. After a power elitist stage inspired by Hunter and Mills, and a pluralist stage influenced by Dahl, a comparative stage now seems to be in the offing. This third stage does not just pose new questions but new types of questions: no longer content with Who Governs?, the query is extended to Who Governs, Where, When, and With What Effects? A body of propositions specifying answers to these questions under varying conditions is growing, inspired by theoretical advances in several substantive areas as well as by empirical studies of decision-making employing a broad variety of methods. For example, small numbers of separate case studies conducted by separate persons are compared qualitatively, or larger numbers quantitatively, or a single person may investigate three or four communities using comparable research procedures. But while any source of inspiration for a theory may be in some sense legitimate, if propositions are to be verified, reformulated, or rejected, it is imperative that somewhat more rigorous procedures be utilized to "test" them. And to sort out interrelationships among many variables, a reasonably large number of communities must be studied.

This paper reports on the most extensive systematic investigation of community decision-making undertaken to date: 51

communities of varying sizes and dimensions throughout the United States were studied using directly comparable research methods. Ranging in population size from 50,000 to 750,000, the communities also varied a good deal in income, education, religion, civic voluntary association activity, form of government, budget expenditures, and urban renewal expenditures. A professional interviewer from NORC collected information about the decision-making structure of each community by interviewing about a dozen persons whom earlier research had identified as particularly knowledgeable informants about community affairs. In each community occupants of homologous positions were questioned about decision-making in four contrasting issue areas: urban renewal, mayoral elections, air pollution control, and antipoverty programs. An "ersatz decisional method" was used to collect information about the initiators, supporters, opponents, and other actors involved in decision-making in each issue area. An index of centralization of decision-making was computed, based on the amount of overlap of actors from one issue area to the next and on the total number of actors involved in all issue areas.

Using these data, it was possible to test a series of previously formulated propositions relating community structural characteristics to decision-making patterns and to community outputs. The procedure used to specify interrelationships among the variables in the statistical model was a graphic variation of multiple regression analysis: path analysis.

These findings, on the whole, supported our general formulation:

The greater the horizontal and vertical differentiation in a social system, the greater the differentiation between potential elites, the more decentralized the decision-making structure, which, without the establishment of integrative mechanisms, leads to less coordination between sectors and a lower level of outputs.

Horizontal differentiation of basic community structures was best reflected in the economic sphere in *economic diversification* and to some extent in the political sphere in the *index of reform government*. Differentiation was also generally associated with *population size*.

Differentiation between potential elites, although not measured very precisely, was to some extent indicated by active *civic voluntary associations*, these in turn reflecting the degree of development of a potential elite group outside of and in addition to leaders of political parties, higher civil servants, and leaders of other community institutions who may rather easily become involved in community decision-making.

Decentralized decision-making was positively associated with *economic diversification, population size*, and (very slightly) active *civic voluntary associations*, and negatively associated with the *index of reform government*. All of these relationships are consistent with our reasoning that the greater the structural support for a plurality of potential elites, the more decentralized the decision-making structure.

Our best indicator of the strength of *community integrative mechanisms* was the index of *reform government*, which did tend to lead to higher outputs.

Where specification and revision of the general formulation seemed most necessary was in the relationship of the antecedent variables to the *level of outputs*. In contrast with our expectations, *decentralization of decision-making* was positively associated with both *budget expenditures* and *urban renewal expenditures*. We suggested one alternative interpretation of this finding, but further study of community outputs is certainly imperative before we can formulate more precise propositions relating community characteristics to various types of community outputs. It is necessary here, as for the other causal mechanisms suggested, to specify the actual content and structure of the processes involved, using all kinds of procedures. At this point we may turn to the highly detailed case study which can once more perform an indispensable function. Content analysis and attitude questionnaires also can be profitably employed to relate political cultural variables to the largely structural variables utilized in our model.

In this regard, analysis of social and cultural characteristics of community leaders should be especially profitable. Then, too, replication of these findings is no doubt in order: in small and larger American communities and in societies outside the United States marked by differing structural and cultural local community decision-making patterns. Only in this way will it be possible to

Terry N. Clark

generate and verify a more general theory of decision-making, to which this paper may have made a modest contribution.

Communities and Budgets: The Sociology of Municipal Expenditures*

Louis H. Masotti and

Don R. Bowen

Case-Western Reserve University

THIS PAPER reports the findings of a preliminary investigation of the extent to which municipal budget expenditures reflect various measures of the socioeconomic environment within which budgetary decisions are made. The study was undertaken on the premise that the community budget can be viewed as public policy spelled out in dollars and cents, and that budget decisions represent the allocation of certain kinds of values. The initial hypothesis was that these allocations are made, not in a vacuum, but in response to the characteristics of the community involved. More specifically it was hypothesized that the budget of a community would vary with the socioeconomic characteristics of the population.[1]

Since the hypothesis was fairly straightforward, but the factors which might influence budget allocations were not known it was decided to employ a factor analysis—a research technique which demanded the minimum prior commitment to specific relationships.[2] Following this decision, a "sample" of cities was selected. The sample was composed of all cities in

* "Communities and Budgets: The Sociology of Municipal Expenditures" by Louis H. Masotti and Don R. Bowen is reprinted from Urban Affairs Quarterly, Vol. 1, No. 2 (December 1965), pp. 39–58, by permission of the Publisher, Sage Publications, Inc.

Ohio with a population of over 50,000 in 1960 ($N = 18$). The sample was limited to Ohio in an effort to minimize differences in the reporting of expenditures which might vary with state statutory regulations.[3] Cities over 50,000 population were selected because the sources of data yielded considerably more information on the socioeconomic characteristics of these cities than it did for those under 50,000. Since the sample was in no sense random, it is impossible to speak of generalizing in any rigorous sense, from the findings presented below to comparable cities. Hence the research must be seen as merely exploratory, but hopefully provocative.

Methodology

There were eighteen cities in Ohio which fitted into the initial definition. For these cities twelve categories of expenditure were adapted from data found in the *Compendium of City Government Finance in 1961.*[4] Education was omitted because the problem of overlapping and/or independent jurisdictions precludes comparable data. The eighteen cities were then ranked according to the amount they spent on each of the twelve budgetary items measured by (a) per capita expenditure, and (b) the per cent of their total budget expended on each item. Two different measures of expenditures were used to ascertain what, if any, differences might be found using differing ways of ranking expenditures.

Following the selection of the categories of budgetary expenditures, thirty-eight items were chosen as socioeconomic characteristics of the eighteen communities.[5] The cities then were ranked for each of these thirty-eight characteristics (Table 1). Thus each of the eighteen cities in the sample were described by fifty items of information— thirty-eight socioeconomic characteristics and twelve items of budgetary expenditure. However, because of the two different ways of measuring expenditures there were actually two lists of fifty items each which described the cities. One consisted of thirty-eight socioeconomic characteristics

Notes to this selection will be found on pages 367–369.

and twelve budgetary items measured by per capita expenditure; the other was made up of thirty-eight socioeconomic characteristics plus twelve budgetary items measured by the per cent of the total city budget devoted to each item. At this point the two lists were coded, punched and reduced to

two 50 by 50 matrices on which separate factor analyses were run.[6]

TABLE 1. *Eighteen Ohio Cities Ranked (High to Low) for Thirty-Eight Selected Socioeconomic Characteristics Used in Per Capita Expenditure and Per Cent of Budget Factor Analyses*

Characteristics* included in both per capita and per cent analyses	Akron	Canton	Cincinnati	Cleveland	Cleveland Hts	Columbus	Dayton	Euclid	Hamilton	Kettering	Lakewood	Lima	Lorain	Parma	Springfield	Toledo	Warren	Youngstown
1. Population	5	8	2	1	15	3	6	14	11	17	13	18	12	9	10	4	16	7
2. Area	4	12	3	2	17	1	6	15	13	9	18	16	10	8	11	5	14	7
3. Density	12	3	7	2	5	13	4	8	10	18	1	9	17	16	14	6	11	15
4. % Population growth, 1950–60	8	—	—	—	11	4	7	2	5	13	—	12	3	1	9	10	6	—
5. Pop. change, 1950–60 (±)	8	13	17	12	11	4	7	2	5	18	14	15	3	1	9	10	6	16
6. % Pop. non-white	7	11	3	1	14	5	2	17	13	16	18	10	12	15	6	8	9	4
7. % Pop. over 21 yrs.	10	7	3	4	2	11	9	13	15	18	1	14	16	17	12	6	8	5
8. % Pop. over 65 yrs.	11	3	4	9	2	13	10	16	14	18	1	7	15	17	6	5	12	8
9. Deaths/1,000	12	3	8	6	1	13	2	16	14	17	8	10	15	18	5	4	11	7
10. Median family income	7	15	16	12	1	11	9	4	10	2	5	18	13	3	17	8	6	14
11. % Pop./fam. income under $3,000	12	5	1	4	14	8	6	16	10	18	15	2	13	17	3	9	11	7
12. Median years schlg./pop. 25 yrs.+	8	15	17	18	1	6	12	4	15	2	3	7	13	4	10	11	9	14
13. % Pop. 25+ / w/ 5 yrs. schl. or less	10	5	4	2	13	11	9	15	8	18	17	14	3	15	12	7	6	1
14. % Pop. 25+ / compld. HS	9	16	17	18	2	6	12	4	14	1	3	7	13	5	10	11	8	15
15. % total labor force unemployed	7	2	9	1	17	12	11	14	6	18	16	13	10	14	5	4	7	3
16. % civ. lab. force emplyd. mfg. dur. gds.	1	14	4	9	10	11	5	13	2	6	7	8	17	3	16	12	18	15
17. % tot. labr. force using pub. trans.	11	10	3	1	4	6	5	12	16	17	2	18	13	8	14	9	15	7
18. % Pop. in single fam. d.u.'s	10	13	18	17	12	15	11	3	6	2	16	9	4	1	8	14	7	5
19. % Pop. living in strcts. blt. 1950–60	8	16	15	17	14	5	10	3	6	2	18	12	4	1	11	13	7	9
20. % h.u.s. w/2+ persons/rm.	12	11	1	5	18	6	4	13	2	16	17	10	3	15	8	14	9	7
21. % h.u.s. newly occupd., 1958–60	11	13	2	6	18	1	4	16	3	5	9	8	12	15	7	14	10	17
22. % h.u.s. owner occupd.	6	12	18	17	4	15	14	3	9	2	16	11	5	1	13	10	8	7

TABLE 1 (cont.)

Characteristics included in both per capita and per cent analyses	Akron	Canton	Cincinnati	Cleveland	Cleveland Hts	Columbus	Dayton	Euclid	Hamilton	Kettering	Lakewood	Lima	Lorain	Parma	Springfield	Toledo	Warren	Youngstown
Characteristics* included in both per capita and per cent analysis cont.																		
23. % Pop. in sound strcts.	9	14	18	12	2	15	10	4	11	3	5	17	6	1	16	7	8	13
24. % occd. units w/ wash. mach.	7	10	18	14	11	17	15	6	9	2	16	12	5	1	8	13	4	3
25. % occd. units w/ food freezer	11	12	17	18	2	13	7	4	5	1	14	8	9	3	6	10	15	16
26. % occd. units w/ TV	7	15	17	16	6	14	8	3	12	2	4	18	5	1	10	9	11	13
27. % occd. units w/ phones	6	9	18	17	1	16	13	4	11	3	5	15	14	2	12	8	10	7
28. % occd. units w/ 1 auto	9	10	18	17	16	12	14	2	3	7	6	4	8	1	5	13	15	11
29. % occd. units w/ 2 autos or more	7	14	17	18	2	11	16	4	12	1	8	13	6	3	15	9	5	10
30. % RTE† service stas.	4	6	18	17	12	8	5	16	10	1	14	12	15	2	3	7	9	11
31. % RTE† apparel, accessories	16	10	9	6	1	14	15	4	12	17	13	3	5	18	8	11	2	7
32. % RTE† furn., furnishgs.	16	8	18	14	11	10	7	3	9	1	17	5	6	15	4	13	2	12
33. % RTE† eating, drinkg.	5	4	8	2	17	6	3	11	7	16	15	13	14	18	9	1	10	12
Characteristics* included in per capita analysis only																		
34. % Pop. decrease, 1950–60	—	2	5	1	—	—	—	—	—	—	3	—	—	—	—	—	—	4
35. % Fams. w/ income over $10,000	7	16	10	14	1	12	9	4	11	2	3	18	13	5	17	8	6	15
36. % employed persons/white col. jobs	11	14	9	17	1	6	12	4	13	3	2	8	18	5	10	7	15	16
37. % RTE† lumber, hdwr., bldg. matls.	12	7	18	13	17	11	9	16	6	2	3	4	5	10	8	14	15	1
38. % RTE† general merchandise	14	15	7	7	9	5	18	1	9	16	3	4	2	5	17	13	11	12
Characteristics* included in per cent analysis only																		
34. Median age	9	5	6	7	1	17	12	7	16	18	2	14	15	13	11	3	10	4
35. % Pop. w/ for. or mixed parentage	11	10	12	7	3	14	15	2	16	13	4	17	6	1	18	9	8	5
36. % labr. force empd. wholesl./ret'l. trade	12	6	10	15	2	5	14	17	16	13	8	3	1	9	11	4	18	7
37. % serve estmts.—personal services	11	7	14	13	1	10	8	18	4	16	2	15	3	17	12	9	5	6
38. % serve estmts.—hotels, motels	4	5	14	10	13	9	12	—	8	—	15	2	3	—	7	6	1	10

*Data adapted from U.S. Bureau of the Census, *County and City Data Book, 1962* (Washington: GPO, 1962) Table 6.
†"Retail Trade Establishments."

The factor analysis technique was employed for several reasons. First it was suspected that all or some of the fifty different items of information were actually measures of the same underlying factors. If these basic factors could be discovered, the project could be conceptually simplified by reducing fifty items to a few factors. Second, as previously indicated, the technique did not require an advance prediction or commitment to a set of hypotheses about the kinds of factors which would be uncovered. Third, since the project was conceived with a particular interest in expenditures, it was hoped that the budgetary items would exhibit strong associations with the factors uncovered.

General Findings

Three underlying factors were uncovered which account for approximately sixty-five per cent of the variance in each of the two factor analyses. Additional factors could be adduced but they were not judged to be as significant as the first three.[7] Most of the fifty items of information in each of the two analyses turned out to be measures of at least the first three factors. In both analyses there is little doubt that the first and most explanatory underlying factor (approximately 40 per cent of the total variance) is socioeconomic status (SES).[8] The second most important factor (i.e., percentage of variance explained) appears to be the age of the residents, and the third seems to be population mobility, whether budget items are analyzed in terms of the per cent of total budget or per capita expenditure. A more detailed comparison of the per capita and per cent of budget analyses will be made below, but the specific findings for each will be reported first.

Findings: Per Capita Expenditure Analysis

As noted above, when budgets are compared by per capita expenditure the single most important underlying factor was socioeconomic status (41.7% of the variance). The best measures of high SES for the

Louis H. Masotti
Don R. Bowen

eighteen Ohio cities are measures of consumption, e.g., the possession of more than one car, home food freezers or television sets. Direct measures of higher income and education are also strong indicators of this factor. Conversely, such items as low incomes and a high proportion of non-whites in the community indicate a lower socioeconomic level in the city. Table 2 summarizes and compares the per capita and per cent of budget factor loadings for the expenditure categories and selected socioeconomic variables used in this study.

Among the budgetary items included with the first factor, Table 2 indicates relatively high positive factor loadings for high expenditures on police, fire protection, general control, water, housing and urban renewal, parks and recreation, and employee retirement. The positive factor loadings in this case are indications that lower SES communities spend a relatively greater amount of money on these items. Hence, in treating other community budgets we would expect that greater than average expenditures on the above items would be a reflection of a community ranked low in socioeconomic status. While this "expectation" cannot be taken as a reliable prediction because of the non-random character of the sample in both space and time, it does constitute a guideline for further inquiry.

On the other hand, such items of expenditure as highways, health and hospitals, sewers and sanitation, and interest do not appear to be related in any significant way to the socioeconomic class factor although, as will be seen, they are indicators of other factors.

Finally, what is perhaps one of the most interesting findings relates to per capita expenditures on welfare. The factor loading is positive indicating that higher expenditures on welfare are a measure of lower SES, as might be expected. However, it is not as high as some of the other items related to this factor. Welfare expenditures are commonly thought to be the most obvious fiscal consequence of a lower socioeconomic class city. However the analysis argues that it is not as responsive to variations in socioeconomic status among these cities nor is it as good an indicator of low socioeconomic status as are such items as police, fire or any of five other expenditure categories.[9]

The second most important factor, when budgets are compared on the basis of per capita expenditure, was judged to be the age

TABLE 2. *Variable Loadings of Per Cent of Budget and Per Capita Factor Analyses Compared*

Variable	Factor I "SES"		Factor II "Age"		Factor III "Mobility"	
	Per Cent	Per Capita	Per Cent	Per Capita	Per Cent	Per Capita
1. % families w/ income under $3,000	.917	.909				
2. % housing units owner occpd.	−.896	−.891				
3. % occpd. units w/ TV	−.893	−.867				
4. % occpd. units w/ 2 autos or more	−.876	−.887				
5. % pop. in structures built 1950–60	−.868	−.810	.387	.321		.414
6. % occpd. units w/ telephone	−.857	−.859	−.414	−.368		
7. % pop. in sound structures	−.843	−.840	−.441	−.423		
8. % occpd. units w/ food freezers	−.836	−.870				
9. Median family income	−.802	−.804	−.470	−.503		
10. % pop. non-white	.800	.867	.309			
11. % RTEª—eating, drinking	.778	.784				
12. Median yrs. schling./ pop. 25 yrs. +	−.778	−.800	−.473	−.497		
13. % total labor force—unemployed	.764	.770	.308	.469		
14. % occpd. units w/ washing machine	−.757	−.740		.445	−.392	
15. % pop. in sngl. fam. dwelling units	−.747	−.746	.371	.536	−.425	
16. % pop. 25 yrs. +/ completed high school	−.737	−.780	−.505	−.524		
17. EMPLOYEE RETIREMENT EXPENDITURE	.711	.756	−.616	−.477		
18. Deaths/1,000	.705	.647	−.493	−.425		−.465
19. % occpd. units w/ 1 auto	−.698	−.700				
20. % RTEª—service stations	−.686	−.687	.302			
21. GENERAL CONTROL EXPENDITURE	−.661	.686			−.316	
22. HOUSING/URBAN RENEWAL EXPENDITURE	.648	.705			.493	.529
23. % pop. 25 yrs. +/ w/ 5 yrs. or less schling.	.641	.684			−.359	
24. Population	.615	.695			.497	.512
25. Population growth, 1950–60	−.608	−.539			.421	.565
26. Population change (+ or −), 1950–60	−.598	−.529				.568
27. % pop. over 65 yrs. old	.589	.511	−.725	−.642		−.440
28. % service establhmts.—hotels, motels	.580				−.600	
29. SEWER/SANITATION EXPENDITURE	−.573				−.311	
30. % housing units w/ 2+ persons per room	.553	.599	.697	.624		
31. Area	.541	.616			.500	.552
32. HIGHWAY EXPENDITURE	−.523		.409			
33. WATER UTILITY EXPENDITURE	.522	.725			−.595	−.323
34. INTEREST EXPENDITURE	−.495					.750
35. Density	.486	.471	−.636	−.712	.310	

TABLE 3 (cont.)

Variable	Factor I "SES" Per Cent	Factor I "SES" Per Capita	Factor II "Age" Per Cent	Factor II "Age" Per Capita	Factor III "Mobility" Per Cent	Factor III "Mobility" Per Capita
36. % RTE[a]—furniture, home furnishings	−.440	−.441	.346		−.446	−.357
37. % pop. w/ foreign or mixed parentage	−.430		−.484			
38. % total labor force using public transport'n	.379	.426	−.516	−.658	.534	.415
39. POLICE EXPENDITURE	−.359	.817			−.342	
40. % housing units newly occpd., 1958–60	.358	.355	.426		.507	
41. % pop. over 21 yrs. old	.356	.310	−.905	−.881		
42. % service establhmts.—personal services			−.560		−.350	
43. WELFARE EXPENDITURE		.440			−.325	
44. % RTE[a]—apparel, accessories			−.418		−.665	−.494
45. HEALTH/HOSPITAL EXPENDITURE			−.471	−.531		
46. Median age			−.946			
47. PARKS & RECREATION EXPENDITURE		.604	−.437	−.465		
48. % total labor force empld. mfg. non-durables					.508	.342
49. % total labor force empld. wholesale/retail					−.481	
50. FIRE EXPENDITURE		.794			−.691	
51. % families w/ income over $10,000		−.698		−.618		
52. % RTE[a]—general merchandise						
53. % employed persons/ white collar jobs		−.597		−.720		
54. Population decrease, 1950–60		−.407		.353		
55. % RTE[a]—lumber, hrdwr., building materials						−.426

[a] "Retail Trade Establishments."

of the residents of the community.[10] This factor explains 15.2 per cent of the total variance which when added to factor one (socioeconomic status) accounts for 56.9 per cent. The best single measures of this factor are direct measures of age (per cent of the population over twenty-one, and over sixty-five) and the mortality rate. All three of these have high negative factor loadings indicating that they are measures of an older community; positive factor loadings in this factor are related to a younger community. Here the measures indicate that such items as population in single family dwelling units (a characteristic strongly associated with new suburbs, whose population is generally younger), houses built since 1950, and unemployment (which tends to be disproportionately concentrated among younger persons) are all indications or measures of a relatively younger population.

In terms of the specific items of expenditure, allocations for health and hospitals, employee retirement, and parks and recreation have high negative factor loadings. This simply means that increasing expenditures on these items reflects an increasingly older community. The other nine categories of expenditure do not appear to be significantly related to this factor.

An examination of the loadings for the third underlying factor led to the conclusion that it was population mobility.[11] This factor by itself accounts for nine per cent of the total variance, making the cumulative variance explained by factors one, two, and three 65.9 per cent. Relatively high factor loadings for such items as population change, population growth, and percentage of the 1960 population living in structures built between 1950–1960 indicate that a community is experiencing high mobility. On the negative side, certain businesses appear to be peculiarly associated with low mobility which suggests the conclusion that only in relatively settled communities are businesses such as apparel stores or furniture stores likely to account for a relatively high percentage of the total number of retail firms. In addition, items such as population over 65 and the mortality rate also appear to be negative indicators of mobility (i.e., relative immobility) in the community. These are, of course, also measures of the factor we have called age, but there is an obvious relationship between communities with older residents and communities with a relatively less mobile population.

Of the expenditure items, three appear to be measures of the mobility factor.[12] Interest and housing-urban renewal have high positive loadings on this factor, i.e., they are measures of relatively greater mobility in the community. High expenditure on interest is characteristic of newer communities which experience mobility. Greater expenditure on public housing and urban renewal is associated with larger cities with relatively poor neighborhoods where mobility is also likely to be high. In the direction of less mobility, the only budgetary item with a significant factor loading is water utility expenditure. This suggests that relatively greater expenditures on a water utility would indicate an older, more settled community.

To summarize the findings for the twelve categories of budgetary expenditure: when measured by the per capita amount spent by the eighteen communities, such things as police, fire protection, general control, and welfare are measures of lower socio-economic status.[13] Generally speaking, we would expect that relatively higher expenditures on these items, discovered in other cities, would reflect this underlying factor. Moreover, these items do not appear to be measures of other factors; the loadings for these expenditures on the remaining two factors were not statistically significant.

One expenditure item, health and hospitals, is related only to the age factor. The direction of the loading indicates that rising expenditures for this function in comparison to other communities is a reflection of an older community. Similarly in the mobility factor, interest expenditure is the one item unambiguously related to this factor alone. The sign of the loading shows that higher expenditures on interest is an indicator of relatively higher mobility.

Four of the twelve expenditure categories, housing and urban renewal, water supply, parks and recreation, and employee retirement, are significant measures of more than one factor. However, in two cases, employee retirement and water supply, it appears that they are better measures of SES than of any other factor. Employee retirement is a measure of both lower SES (.756) and old age ($-$.477). Water supply is related to lower SES (.725) and greater stability ($-$.323). In both cases the loading for SES is considerably higher than for the competing factor and leads to the conclusion that higher city expenditures on these items are primarily a reflection of a less affluent community.

The remaining two cases, parks and recreation and housing and urban renewal, are not so clear. Parks and recreation is related to lower SES (.604) and to old age ($-$.465). Housing and urban renewal is related to lower SES (.705) and to greater mobility (.579). Although in both cases the loading for SES is higher than those for other factors they are not enough higher to justify assigning these expenditures to the first factor alone. Hence, comparatively greater allocations of funds for both of these latter functions must be interpreted as a reflection of either underlying factor.

Finally, the factor analysis of per capita expenditures revealed no discernible significant relation between two of the twelve functions, highways and sewers and sanitation, and any of the three underlying factors.

Findings: Per Cent of Budget Analysis

For comparative purposes, a second factor analysis was made using municipal budget expenditures as a percentage of the total budget. As in the first analysis, socio-economic status, age, and mobility (in that order) emerge as the three most significant underlying factors (Table 2). Together they account for 65.3 per cent of the variance.

When budgets are compared on the basis of the proportion spent on each of the budgetary categories, the single most important factor is again SES, which accounts for 38.0 per cent of the variance. However, despite this general similarity, there are some striking differences which need to be explained.

As in the case of the per capita analysis, the best indicators of high socioeconomic status communities are measures of consumption (e.g., possession of cars, food freezers and televisions) and direct measures of income (median family income). Conversely, the best measures of lower socioeconomic status are income, unemployment, and the percentage of the population which is non-white. However, for two budget items the direction of the factor loadings is the reverse of that found in the per capita analysis. Expenditures on police and general control have negative factor loadings, i.e., they are associated with high socioeconomic class rather than low as was the case when budgets were compared on a per capita expenditure basis.

To explain this reversal it is necessary to introduce an additional consideration about the size of the cities. Most of the cities which were ranked high on the various measures of socioeconomic class were among the smaller cities in the sample.[14] Expenditures on police and general control are a necessary item in any city's budget and are likely to appear as a greater percentage of a small city's budget, which often does not include the range of expenditure found in the budgets of the larger cities.[15] While per capita expenditures on police are less for the smaller and generally more wealthy cities, what they do spend on this item assumes a large proportion of a relatively limited budget. Thus in the per capita factor analysis both police expenditure and general control are a reflection of lower socioeconomic status and in the per cent of budget analysis they indicate higher status. This apparent contradiction is explained by the fact that per capita expenditure controls for the differences in the size of the cities, while per

Communities and Budgets: **321**
The Sociology of Municipal
Expenditures
Louis H. Masotti
Don R. Bowen

cent of budget expenditure does not.[16]

A comparison of the two analyses also reveals that on a per cent of budget basis expenditures for highways, interest, and sewers and sanitation are indicators of relatively more affluent communities while on a per capita basis these categories are unrelated to socioeconomic standing. Again the explanation seems to lie in the fact that these are major expenditures which will almost certainly loom large in a smaller city budget as a per cent of allocations. Since the smaller cities tend to be disproportionately more affluent, these expenditure items are related to high SES.

The second most important per cent of budget factor, as in the per capita expenditure analysis, is age (16.3 per cent of the variance explained). The community characteristics which measure this factor are comparable to the same factor in the first analysis. Such variables as the percentage of the population over sixty-five, the percentage over twenty-one, and median age have high negative factor loadings meaning that they reflect an older community. High positive loadings on items such as persons living in houses built since 1950, newly occupied houses, single family dwelling units, and the proportion of unemployed reflect a younger community.

As for specific expenditure items, significant negative factor loadings for employee retirement and health and hospitals indicate that these two items are measures of greater age. They also appear as measures of an older community in the per capita analysis. One additional expenditure item—highways —emerges as a reflection of age variations among the communities studied, which did not appear in the per capita analysis. Younger and newer cities will spend a greater percentage of their budgets on roads but the per capita expenditure analysis indicates that the amount spent does not vary significantly ($> \pm .300$). The younger communities also happen to be the smaller ones and expenditure on highways will appear as a greater proportion of a more limited budget.

The third per cent of budget factor, which explains eleven per cent of the variance, was again labeled mobility. Although there is some similarity between the items which appear as good indices in this and the per capita analysis, they were somewhat stronger in the latter. Housing units newly occupied and population growth both reflect a relatively high rate of population turnover. Although the age indicators (e.g., population over 65, mortality rate) of relative immobility disappeared in this analysis, retail and service establishments (e.g., furniture, apparel, hotels-motels) again emerged as significant indices of community stability.

Among the budgetary items, two show up here which also appeared in the per capita factor analysis. These are expenditures on housing and urban renewal, associated with higher mobility, and expenditures on water supply, associated with lower mobility. Precisely the same relations were noted in the per capita analysis. Two additional items which appear only in the per cent of budget analysis are welfare and fire expenditure. The first emerges as a weak and the second as a strong measure of low mobility. The latter finding can be explained by the interrelationship of the age and mobility factors. The less mobile communities also tend to be the older ones where the older buildings require a considerable amount of money to be spent on fire protection. However, the fact that fire expenditures are not associated with stability in the per capita analysis, where the size of the community and the budget are controlled, argues that the relationship between them in the per cent of budget analysis is perhaps deceptive.

To summarize the twelve categories of budget expenditure for the per cent of budget analysis: relatively high expenditures on employee retirement, housing and urban renewal and water supply indicate a lower socioeconomic status city. All three of these items are measures of lower SES

whether budgets are ranked on a per capita expenditure basis or on the per cent of budget basis.

Expenditures on general control, police, sewers and sanitation and interest, when relatively high, indicate an upper socioeconomic status community when budgets are compared on the per cent of total base. For two of these items, police and general control, the per cent of budget analysis contradicts the per capita analysis, i.e., on a per capita basis they measure lesser affluence, and on a per cent of budget basis they reflect a relatively greater affluence. This was judged to be due to the fact that these items are necessary expenditures for any city, and hence would loom larger as a per cent of comparatively limited small city budgets, which also happen to be associated with the richer communities in the sample. The same explanation was offered for the other two items, which appear in this analysis as measures of higher socioeconomic status (higher expenditures on interest and sewers and sanitation), but which do not appear at all related to this factor in the per capita analysis.

In the case of the second factor (age), higher expenditures on health and hospitals, employee retirement, and parks and recreation indicate an older community, and higher expenditures on highways appear to be a measure of a relatively younger city. The first three are also measures of an older community when budgets are compared on the per capita basis. Highways does not appear to be related to age when the size of the community is controlled in the per capita analysis.

The last factor, mobility, is best measured by higher budgetary allocations for fire protection, housing/urban renewal and water supply. Increasing expenditures on fire and water supply indicate a more stable community and, for housing/urban renewal, greater population mobility. Two of these, water supply and housing/urban renewal measure the same thing in the same direction in the per capita expenditure analysis. The third, higher expenditures on fire protection, is not significantly related to the mobility factor when expenditures are compared on a per capita basis.

Among the twelve categories of budgetary items in the per cent of budget analysis there are three which are measures of more than one factor. Employee retirement is a measure of both lower socioeconomic class communities (.711) and older communities (.616). These do not differ enough to justify a conclusion that high employee retirement expenditures are an indication of either factor alone and, for the time being, such a finding must be accepted as indicating either lower socioeconomic class cities or older cities. A second item which overlapped was water supply. Higher expenditures on water appear to be a reflection of both a more stable community ($-.595$) and a lower socioeconomic class community (.522). Again the factor loadings are ambiguous and high expenditures on this item must be taken to indicate the presence of either factor. The third ambiguous case was expenditure on housing and urban renewal which indicated both lower class (.648) and higher mobility (.483). In this case it would seem that greater expenditures on housing and urban renewal are a better indicator of socioeconomic class than of mobility. However, such a conclusion can only be tentative at best.

Conclusion

This study began with the assumption that at least a certain degree of variation in city expenditure patterns was a reflection of the environment of the city. Budget-makers, like other decision-makers, do not operate in a social vacuum. They respond to those pressures and opportunities which they perceive, and when these forces are large and gross, such as the characteristics we have been discussing in this paper, the responses of different decision-makers to similar stimuli are likely to be similar. That assumption seems borne out by the results reported here for eighteen Ohio cities. Variations among the cities in the levels of expenditure for twelve functional categories are associated with variations in three underlying factors—socioeconomic status, age and mobility.

In large part these results are comparable

to other investigations. The exact similarities and differences have been pinpointed and need not be repeated here. Suffice it to say that we do not consider our results significantly enough at variance with other reported findings to conclude that either they or we are mistaken. The positive way of putting this is that, despite differences of sample and analytic technique, the results here by and large confirm other investigations of the relations between socioeconomic characteristics and levels of expenditure. We have included a larger number of socioeconomic characteristics than other studies but the number of cities used is smaller.[17] The gains and losses of this procedure have not made any significant difference between the outcomes here and those of other studies.

There is one significant independent variable which other investigations have included that is omitted here; namely, the size of the community. Both of our ways of measuring expenditures, per capita expenditure and per cent of total budget expenditure, were designed to control for the size of the community. There is disagreement in the existing literature about the relation of size to total expenditures.[18] However, there seems to be general agreement (confirmed here) that size is unrelated to variations in per capita expenditure rates.[19] We did, of course, include total population as one of the socioeconomic characteristics in the analysis. It turned out to be significantly associated with lower SES and higher mobility as a single item measuring those two underlying factors,[20] but it was not one of the identifiable factors by itself.

As a side comment on the various ways of measuring city expenditures, it developed that the per cent of budget measure is an imperfect instrument for controlling for the size of the community when compared with per capita expenditure. This is so because there are certain functions, e.g. police, which

all cities undertake and which demand a
certain fixed level of initial expenditure. If
the total community budget is relatively
small, as it tends to be for the smaller cities,
then this expenditure appears as a larger
percentage of the total budget for the
smaller city than it does for a larger city.
This distortion, while possible for per capita
expenditures, is not nearly so important for
this latter way of measuring money spent.
Another point influencing this relation is
that the larger cities undertake to furnish a
greater range of functions, hence the per
cent of their total budgets devoted to any
one is smaller than for the smaller cities
which do not undertake so many activities.

In general we conclude that we would
expect that variations in city expenditures,
however measured, would be in part
accounted for by differences in the three
factors discussed here. This expectation is
in no sense a rigorous prediction. The
limitations of the sample in both space and
time preclude that degree of methodological
sophistication. However, the comparability
between our results and those of other
investigations (also suffering from similar
sample limitations) encourage us in the
belief that there is a sociology of municipal
budget-making, i.e., that expenditure rates
do respond to differences in the socioeconomic environment. Hopefully the
direction and degree of this relation has
been in part delineated by the above
findings.

Notes

Notes

PREFACE

1. (*Southwestern*) *Social Science Quarterly*, 48 (December) 1967.

THE COMMUNITY AS RESEARCH SITE AND OBJECT OF INQUIRY
Charles M. Bonjean

1. Albion W. Small and George E. Vincent, *An Introduction to the Study of Society* (New York: American Book Co., 1894).
2. Robert E. Park, Ernest W. Burgess and Roderick D. McKenzie, *The City* (Chicago: University of Chicago Press, 1925).
3. Louis Wirth, *The Ghetto* (Chicago: University of Chicago Press, 1928).
4. Harvey W. Zorbaugh, *The Gold Coast and Slum* (Chicago: University of Chicago Press, 1929).
5. Frederick M. Thrasher, *The Gang* (Chicago: University of Chicago Press, 1927).
6. Clifford R. Shaw, F. M. Zorbaugh, H. D. McKay and L. S. Cottrell, *Delinquency Areas* (Chicago: University of Chicago Press, 1929).
7. E. Franklin Frazier, *The Negro Family in Chicago* (Chicago: University of Chicago Press, 1932).
8. R. D. McKenzie, *The Metropolitan Community* (New York: McGraw-Hill, 1933).
9. That the range of Chicago sociology went beyond the study of the community is made explicit in Robert E. L. Faris, *Chicago Sociology, 1920–1932* (San Francisco: Chandler Publishing Co., 1967).
10. Robert E. Park, "Human Ecology," *American Journal of Sociology*, 42 (July 1936), pp. 1–15.
11. Two other national associations still have program sections dealing with the community *per se*. These are the Society for the Study of Social Problems and the Rural Sociological Society.
12. The problems of concern to the social pathologist manifested themselves, of course, at the community or local level. See most of the Chicago school sources cited above as well as Charles Booth, *Life and Labour of the People of London* (New York: Macmillan and Co., 9 Vols., 1891–1904).
13. See for example, Charles M. Bonjean, "Mass, Class and the Industrial Community: A Comparative Analysis of Managers, Businessmen and Workers," *American Journal of Sociology*, 72 (September 1966), pp. 149–162; Norval D. Glenn and Jon Alston, "The Cultural Distance Among Occupational Categories,"

The American Sociological Review, 33 (June 1968), pp. 365–382 and in Norval D. Glenn, "Massification Versus Differentiation: Some Trend Data from National Surveys," *Social Forces*, 46 (December 1967), pp. 172–180; Michael Aiken, Louis A. Ferman, and Harold L. Sheppard, *Economic Failure, Alienation, and Extremism* (Ann Arbor: University of Michigan Press, 1968); and James D. Preston, "Community Norms and Adolescent Drinking Behavior," *Social Science Quarterly*, 49 (September 1968), pp. 350–359.
14. Floyd Hunter, *Community Power Structure* (Chapel Hill: University of North Carolina Press, 1953).
15. Robert Dahl, *Who Governs?* (New Haven: Yale University Press, 1961).
16. See, for example, the number published since 1953 in the bibliographies in Section VII of this anthology. The community study approach in anthropology in contrast with sociology, has sustained itself over the years and, in fact, may be even more widespread now than earlier. See Conrad M. Arensberg and Solon T. Kimball, "Community Study: Retrospect and Prospect," *American Journal of Sociology*, 74 (May 1968), pp. 691–705.
17. Severyn T. Bruyn, A Call for Papers for the A.S.A. Meeting on Community, mimeographed, January 1969.
18. Peter H. Rossi and Robert Crain, "The NORC Permanent Community Sample," *Public Opinion Quarterly*, 32 (Summer 1968), p. 265.
19. George A. Hillery, Jr., "Definitions of Community: Areas of Agreement," *Rural Sociology*, 20 (June 1955), pp. 111–123.
20. William Petersen, *Population* (New York: The Macmillan Co., 1961), p. 186. For more precise definition of this and related terms (including exceptions) see Petersen, any of the other standard introductory population texts, or U.S. Bureau of the Census publications.
21. Lewis Mumford, *The Culture of Cities* (New York: Harcourt, Brace and Co., 1938). The summary here is based primarily on pp. 283–292.
22. Robert Redfield, "The Folk Society," *American Journal of Sociology*, 52 (January 1947), pp. 293–308.
23. Louis Wirth, "Urbanism as a Way of Life," *American Journal of Sociology*, 44 (July 1938), pp. 1–24.
24. Gideon Sjoberg, *The Preindustrial City: Past and Present* (New York: The Free Press, 1960).
25. Donald J. Bogue, *The Structure of the Metropolitan Community: A Study of Dominance and Subdominance* (Ann Arbor: Horace H. Rackham School of Graduate Studies, University of Michigan, 1949).
26. William F. Ogburn, *Social Characteristics of Cities* (Chicago: The International City Managers' Association, 1937). See Chapter 9, "Different Types of Cities."
27. E. L. Thorndike, "American Cities and

States," *Annals of the New York Academy of Science*, 39 (1939), pp. 213–298.

28. See Jeffrey Hadden and Edward Borgatta, *American Cities: Their Social Characteristics* (Chicago: Rand McNally and Co., 1965).

29. *Ibid.*, p. 16.

30. *Ibid.*, pp. 15 and 17.

31. Bureau of the Census, *County and City Data Book* (U.S. Government Printing Office, 1967).

32. Daniel O. Price, "Factor Analysis in the Study of Metropolitan Centers," *Social Forces*, 20 (May 1942), p. 449.

33. For a brief, but informative, discussion of factor analysis see Gwyn Collins, "Factor Analysis," *Journal of Advertising Research*, 1 (September 1961), pp. 28–32. For a detailed discussion, see Harry F. Harmon, *Modern Factor Analysis* (Chicago: University of Chicago Press, 1960).

34. In addition to the three discussed below, see Price, *op. cit.*, pp. 449–455; Peter R. Hofstaetter, "Your City—Revisited: A Factorial Study of Cultural Patterns," *American Catholic Sociological Review*, 13 (October 1952), pp. 159–168; Byron Munson, *Interrelationships of Community Variables* (Columbus: Center for Community and Regional Analyses, Ohio State University, forthcoming), and Glenn H. Johnson, "A Search for Functional Unities: An Analysis of U.S. County Data," Unpublished Ph.D. Dissertation, New York University, 1958.

35. Christen T. Jonassen and Sherwood H. Peres, *Interrelationships of Dimensions of Community Systems: A Factor Analysis of Eighty-two Variables* (Columbus: Ohio State University Press, 1960). A summary of major findings may be found in Christen T. Jonassen, "Functional Unities in Eighty-eight Community Systems," *American Sociological Review* 26 (June 1961), pp. 399–407.

36. Hadden and Borgatta, *loc. cit.*

37. Charles M. Bonjean, Harley L. Browning, and Lewis F. Carter, "Toward Comparative Community Analysis: A Factor Analysis of United States Counties," *Sociological Quarterly*, 10 (Spring 1969), pp. 157–176.

38. Jonassen and Peres, *op. cit.*, p. 8.

39. *Ibid.*, p. 18.

40. *Ibid.*, p. 23.

41. Hadden and Borgatta, *op. cit.*, p. 5.

APPROACHES TO THE STUDY OF COMMUNITY POLITICS
Robert L. Lineberry

1. Popularly called the Kerner Commission, after its Chairman, former Governor Otto Kerner of Illinois, the *Report* of the Commission was published by the Government Printing Office on March 1, 1968. An edition is also available from Bantam Books.

2. Cited by Ithiel de Sola Pool, in his "Foreword" to *Contemporary Political Science: Toward Empirical Theory* (New York: McGraw-Hill, 1967), p. ix.

3. This is a central argument in Amitai Etzioni, *The Active Society* (New York: The Free Press, 1968), especially pp. 43–56. This chapter has benefited enormously from Etzioni's wide-ranging and perceptive analysis, although our argument is much more simplified than his. Etzioni is somewhat more conservative about the possibility of moving readily from the macro to the micro level of analysis. Our concept of "linkages" thus opens the possibility of fruitful movement from one level to the other, while his notion of "emergent properties" denies, by and large, that possibility. We are most strongly in agreement with Etzioni, however, in opposition to the reductionist position, which denies the existence of macrolevel properties.

4. "Ecological Correlations and the Behavior of Individuals," *American Sociological Review*, 15 (June 1950), pp. 351–357.

5. Hubert M. Blalock, *Causal Inferences in Nonexperimental Research* (Chapel Hill: University of North Carolina Press, 1961), p. 98.

6. Etzioni, *The Active Society, op. cit.*, p. 47.

7. *Ibid.*, p. 50.

8. Kerner Commission, *Report*, pp. 359–407 (Government Printing Office version).

9. Stanley Lieberson and Arnold R. Silverman, "The Precipitants and Underlying Conditions of Race Riots," *American Sociological Review*, 30 (December 1965), pp. 887–898; Bryan T. Downes, "The Social and Political Characteristics of Riot Cities: A Comparative Study," *Social Science Quarterly*, 49 (December 1968), pp. 504–520.

10. Downes, *op. cit.* There are a number of other relevant conclusions in Downes' article, but these four will serve for illustration of the macro approach.

11. This is no place to explore the complex question of causality in social research. One of the most imaginative treatments is found in Blalock, *op. cit.*

12. Kerner Commission, *Report*, pp. 74–75. The italics in the second quotation are supplied.

13. See, e.g., Robert E. Lane, *Political Life* (New York: The Free Press, 1959), Chapter 16.

14. Lester Milbrath, *Political Participation* (Chicago: Rand McNally, 1965), p. 116.

15. John C. Bollens *et al.*, *Exploring the Metropolitan Community* (Berkeley and Los Angeles: University of California Press, 1961), Chapter 11.

16. Etzioni, *op. cit.*, pp. 45–47.

17. *Ibid.*, p. 669.

18. *Ibid.*, p. 68.

19. The concept of "nondecision" is discussed by Peter Bachrach and Morton Baratz,

"Decisions and Non-Decisions: An Analytic Framework," *American Political Science Review*, 57 (1963), pp. 632–642.

Notes for pages 20 to 26 **329**

20. Donald E. Stokes, "Analytic Reduction in the Study of Institutions," A Paper Presented at the 1966 Annual Meeting of the American Political Science Association, New York City, p. 3.

21. Alan K. Campbell and Seymour Sacks, *Metropolitan America: Fiscal Patterns and Governmental Systems* (New York: The Free Press, 1967), Chapter 5.

22. The three definitions, respectively, are from David Easton, *A Framework for Political Analysis* (Englewood Cliffs, New Jersey: Prentice-Hall, Inc., 1965), p. 50; Robert Agger, Daniel Goldrich, and Bert E. Swanson, *The Rulers and the Ruled* (New York: John Wiley and Sons, 1964), pp. 6–14 (included in this volume, Selection 22); and Harold D. Lasswell, *Politics: Who Gets What, When and How* (New York: McGraw-Hill, 1936).

23. See, e.g., Thomas R. Dye, *Politics, Economics and the Public* (Chicago: Rand McNally, 1968); and Richard E. Dawson and James A. Robinson, "Economic Variables, Inter-Party Competition and Welfare Policies in the American States," *Journal of Politics*, 15 (November 1963), pp. 265–289.

24. The micro counterpart of the macro-integration approach explores integration within subcommunity units, e.g., neighborhood groupings or ethnic groups. In part, the difference between macro- and micro-integration turns upon the boundaries of the observer-defined community.

25. See Philip E. Jacob and Henry Teune, "The Integrative Process," in Philip E. Jacob and James V. Toscano (eds.), *The Integration of Political Communities* (Philadelphia: Lippincott, 1964), especially p. 5.

26. See Harold Kaplan, *Urban Political Systems* (New York: Columbia University Press, 1967), on Toronto Metro; Brett Hawkins, *Nashville Metro* (Nashville, Tennessee: Vanderbilt University Press, 1966), on Nashville-Davidson County; and Edward C. Sofen, *The Miami Metropolitan Experiment* (Bloomington: Indiana University Press, 1963), on Miami-Dade County.

27. Jacob and Teune, *op. cit.*, p. 18.

28. Amos Hawley, "Community Power and Urban Renewal Success," *American Journal of Sociology*, 68 (January 1963), pp. 422–423.

29. Robert C. Wood, *1400 Governments* (Cambridge, Massachusetts: Harvard University Press, 1961), pp. 67–83.

30. Robert A. Dahl, *Who Governs? Democracy and Power in an American City* (New Haven, Connecticut: Yale University Press, 1961), p. 305.

31. For a good summary of research on participation, see Milbrath, *Political Participation, op. cit.*

32. Lester Milbrath, "Political Participation in the States," in Herbert Jacob and Kenneth N. Vines (eds.), *Politics in the American States* (Boston: Little, Brown and Company, 1965), p. 43.

33. Agger, Goldrich, and Swanson, *The Rulers and the Ruled*, pp. 655–657.

34. Certainly the best treatment of this perspective on community politics is Edward C. Banfield and James Q. Wilson, *City Politics* (Cambridge, Massachusetts: Harvard University Press and M.I.T. Press, 1963).

35. John C. Bollens and Henry J. Schmandt, *The Metropolis* (New York: Harper and Row, 1965), p. 243.

36. Max Weber, *The Theory of Social and Economic Organization*, edited by Talcott Parsons (New York: The Free Press, 1957), p. 152.

37. Robert D. Putnam, "Political Attitudes and the Local Community," *American Political Science Review*, 60 (September 1966), pp. 640–654.

38. Heinz Eulau and Robert Eyestone, "Policy Maps of City Councils and Policy Outcomes: A Developmental Analysis," *American Political Science Review*, 62 (March 1968), p. 125.

39. Ted Gurr, "Psychological Factors in Civil Violence," *World Politics* 20 (January 1968), p. 254.

40. *Ibid.*, p. 253.

41. See Nathan S. Caplan and Jeffrey M. Paige, "A Study of Ghetto Rioters," *Scientific American*, 219 (August 1968), pp. 15–21. Although Caplan and Paige reject one version of the relative deprivation theory, their support of an explanation of rioting which they call the "blocked-opportunity" theory could usefully be combined with Gurr's notion of relative deprivation.

THE CONCEPT OF POWER: SOME OVEREMPHASIZED AND UNDERRECOGNIZED DIMENSIONS
Terry N. Clark

1. A number of persons aided the development of this paper through their informed criticism and helpful suggestions. Especially important were Robert A. Dahl, William J. Goode, Raymond Glazier, Terence K. Hopkins, Juan J. Linz, Nelson W. Polsby, Peter H. Rossi, and Raymond E. Wolfinger.

2. For three recent review articles of the more theoretically abstract formulations of the concept of power, see Robert A. Dahl, "The Power Analysis Approach to the Study of Politics," draft of article for the *International Encyclopedia of the Social Sciences*; James G. March, "The Power of Power," in David

Easton (ed.), *Varieties of Political Theory* (Englewood Cliffs, New Jersey: Prentice-Hall, Inc., 1966); William H. Riker, "Some Ambiguities in the Notion of Power," *American Political Science Review*, 58 (June 1964), pp. 341–349.

3. See Dahl, *op. cit.*, for a comprehensive review of the concept of this level of analysis.

4. Carl J. Friedrich, *Constitutional Government and Democracy* (New York: Ginn and Company, 1950), p. 49.

5. Peter Bachrach and Morton S. Baratz, "Two Faces of Power," *American Political Science Review*, 56 (Dec. 1962), pp. 947–952.

6. Roland J. Pellegrin and Charles H. Coates, "Absentee-Owned Corporations and Community Power Structure," *American Journal of Sociology*, 61 (March 1956), pp. 141–149; and Linton C. Freeman, *et al.*, *Metropolitan Decision-Making* (Syracuse: University College of Syracuse University, 1962).

7. See Herbert A. Simon, "Notes on the Observation and Measurement of Political Power," *Journal of Politics*, 15 (Nov. 1953), pp. 500–516; James G. March, "An Introduction to the Theory and Measurement of Influence," *American Political Science Review*, 49 (June 1955), pp. 431–451; and Dahl, *op. cit.*, p. 8. It should be obvious that the phenomenon of anticipated reaction is a special case of the more general concept of reciprocity.

8. The term "mobilization of bias" is from Schnattschneider. See Bachrach and Baratz, *op. cit.*, p. 952, for further discussion.

9. Peter Bachrach and Morton S. Baratz, "Decision and Non-Decisions: An Analytical Framework," *American Political Science Review*, 57 (Sept. 1963), pp. 632–642.

10. Parsons' formulations of power have generally taken this point of view. See Talcott Parsons, "The Distribution of Power in American Society," *World Politics*, 10 (Oct. 1957), pp. 123–143, also published in *Structure and Process in Modern Societies* (New York: The Free Press of Glencoe, 1960), pp. 199–225; "On the Concept of Influence," *Public Opinion Quarterly*, 27 (Spring 1963), pp. 37–62; "On the Concept of Political Power," *Proceedings of the American Philosophical Society*, 107, No. 103 (June 1963), pp. 232–262; an article in Harry Eckstein and Klous Knorr (eds.), *On Internal War* (New York: The Free Press of Glencoe, forthcoming); and " 'Voting' and the Equilibrium of the American Political System," in Eugene Burdick and Arthur J. Brodbeck (eds.), *American Voting Behavior* (Glencoe, Illinois: The Free Press, 1959), pp. 80–120.

11. See Bert E. Swanson (ed.), *Current Trends in Comparative Community Studies* (Kansas City, Missouri: Community Studies, Inc., 1962), especially "Conference Notes," pp. 4–17; Marshall N. Goldstein, "Absentee Ownership and Monolithic Power Structures:

Two Questions for Community Studies," pp. 49–59; and Robert C. Stone, "Power and Values in Trans-Community Relations," pp. 69–80 (all in Swanson) for discussions of the role of values in the analysis of community power. Gaetano Mosca also offered a number of sophisticated remarks on the social and political implications of value differences between leaders and followers—see *The Ruling Class* (New York: McGraw-Hill, 1939), esp. pp. 120–153.

12. Floyd Hunter, *Community Power Structure* (Chapel Hill: University of North Carolina Press, 1953).

13. Peter H. Rossi, "Community Decision-Making," *Administrative Science Quarterly* 1 (March 1957), pp. 415–443.

14. Robert E. Agger, *et al.*, *The Rulers and the Ruled* (New York: John Wiley and Sons, 1964), esp. pp. 69–155.

15. Robert A. Dahl, *Who Governs?* (New Haven: Yale University Press, 1961).

16. See, for example, Max Weber, *The Theory of Social and Economic Organization* (New York: Oxford University Press, 1947), pp. 148–154, 327–407.

17. See Terry N. Clark, "The Communist Take-Over and Consolidation of Power in Yugoslavia: An Empirical and Conceptual Analysis," Department of Sociology, Columbia University, 1964, for an analysis of the different types of legitimacy accorded the Tito regime by different subgroups within the Yugoslav population as well as by various foreign governments.

18. Swanson (ed.), *Current Trends*, pp. 8–13; and James S. Coleman, *Community Conflict* (Glencoe, Illinois: The Free Press, 1957), for discussions of the different types of forces operating to bring about a decision when increasingly larger segments of the population demand active participation in a decision.

19. See Robert A. Dahl, "The Concept of Power," *Behavioral Science*, 2 (July 1957), pp. 210–215; and Dahl, "The Power Analysis Approach," *International Encyclopedia of the Social Sciences*.

20. Dahl, *Who Governs?* pp. 169–189.

21. Robert A. Dahl, "Equality and Power in American Society," William V. D'Antonio and Howard J. Ehrlich (eds.), *Power and Democracy in America* (Notre Dame: University of Notre Dame Press, 1961), pp. 73–89; and Nelson W. Polsby, *Community Power and Political Theory* (New Haven: Yale University Press, 1963), p. 114.

22. Dahl, "Equality and Power," *Power and Democracy in America*, p. 102. In the New Haven study, Dahl apparently relaxed the criteria for testing the existence of a ruling elite set forth in 1958:

"The hypothesis of a ruling elite can be strictly tested only if:

(1.) The hypothetical ruling elite is a well-defined group;

(2.) There is a fair sample of cases involving key political decisions in which the preferences of the hypothetical ruling elite run counter to those of any other likely group that might be suggested;
(3.) In such cases, the preferences of the elite regularly prevail." See Robert A. Dahl, "A Critique of the Ruling Elite Model," *American Political Science Review*, 52 (1958): 463–469.

23. Polsby, *Community Power and Political Theory*, p. 98.

24. Linton Freeman, *et al.*, *Local Community Leadership* (Syracuse: University College of Syracuse, 1960), pp. 7–8.

25. See Peter H. Rossi, "Theory, Research, and Practice in Community Organization," in Charles A. Adrian (ed.), *Social Science and Community Action* (East Lansing: Institute for Community Development and Services, 1960), for a list of five bases; Floyd Hunter and his associates in *Community Organization* (Chapel Hill: University of North Carolina Press, 1956), pp. 37–39, present a list of thirteen factors on the basis of which "a man was considered for top power billing." The thirteen are comparable to Dahl's list. See also William H. Form and Delbert C. Miller, *Industry, Labor, and Community* (New York: Harper Brothers, 1960), pp. 516–551.

26. Robert A. Dahl, "The Analysis of Influence in Local Communities," *Social Science and Community Action*, p. 32. See also Dahl, *Who Governs?* pp. 266 ff.; and Dahl, "Equality and Power," *Power and Democracy in America*, pp. 79 ff.

27. J. C. Harsanyi, "Measurement of Social Power, Opportunity Costs, and the Theory of Two-Person Bargaining Games," *Behavioral Science*, 7 (Jan. 1962), pp. 67–80.

28. See Dahl, "The Analysis of Influence," *Social Science and Community Action*, p. 33, for a discussion of "pyramiding" of power resources, and *Who Governs?* *passim*, for a case study of the process by which the mayor of New Haven was able to pyramid his power.

29. Merton has called attention to a similar phenomenon in analyzing interpersonal influence. See Robert K. Merton, "Patterns of Influence: Local and Cosmopolitan Influentials," *Social Theory and Social Structure* (Glencoe, Illinois: The Free Press, 1957), pp. 387–420.

30. See Talcott Parsons' works listed in footnote 10.

31. See Dahl, "The Analysis of Influence," *Social Science and Community Action*.

32. There has also been a debate of a terminological nature. One term that pluralistically oriented writers have often found particularly objectionable is "power structure." They have argued that "the term structure refers to a fairly stable, repetitive pattern of interactive events," further specifying that "stability in power structure appears to refer to repetition of the same pattern both over time

and over a wide range of issues." Nelson W. Polsby, "Three Problems in the Analysis of Community Power," *American Sociological Review*, 24 (Dec. 1959), p. 798.
Jennings has pointed out that:

the concept "power structure" has two general referents. In more popular parlance it refers to the people and institutions which have the potential power to obtain the outcomes they desire. City planners and other "staff" people are wont to speak of manipulating the "power structure" to achieve certain goals. Used this way the term is more synonymous with the concept of a power elite. A second meaning, however, is analogous to the way structure is used in such terms as "social structure," "economic structure," and "political structure" ··· power *structure* may be conceived of as consisting of all the more or less patterned elements which are involved in a power configurationship or relationship. For consistency of terminology in the social sciences, if for no other reason, it is preferable to use the terms in this sense. Just as we would not define "social structure" as the social elite, so there seems no apparent reason for denoting "power structure" in terms of the power elite. (Kent Jennings, "Study of Community Decision-Making," in Swanson (ed.), *Current Trends*, p. 92.)

Polsby has still used the concept in a fashion that would fall under Jennings' second usage, but seems to have extrapolated the meaning of the term to imply the "power elite" orientation of the first usage. That the term need not imply a "power elite" hypothesis should be obvious from the usage of such writers as Rossi, for example, who speaks of four types of "community structure": pyramidal, caucus rule, polylith, or amorphous. Miller has also set down a typology of five community power structures, only two of which could be called power elite models. (See note 35 for further discussion of typologies of community power structures.)

One might remark that controversy has also occasionally been raised concerning the use of the term "social structure," to which A. L. Kroeber, among others, objected especially vigorously. Providing that a term is used with a certain minimum of analytical specificity, there does not seem to be any strong reason for not using practically any term for any referent. The inevitable problem that arises is the confusion of analytical terminology with the language of everyday discourse, but short of adopting mathematical symbols (as Pareto once suggested) there seems no easy solution to the problem except for a writer to define the important terms of his analysis in as clear and precise a manner as possible. See Carl G. Hempel, *Fundamentals of Concept Formation in Empirical Science* (Chicago: University of Chicago Press, 1952), for a systematic consideration of such problems.

33. Dahl, "Equality and Power," *Power*

and Democracy in America, pp. 81 ff. See also Dahl, "The Analysis of Influence," *Social Service and Community Action,* pp. 40–42.

34. Dahl, *Who Governs?* pp. 163–164. Note that Dahl's "indirect influence" differs from that of section 3. His usage is closer to section 2, "anticipated reactions."

35. See Delbert C. Miller, "Decision-Making Cliques in Community Power Structures: A Comparative Study of an American and an English City," *American Journal of Sociology,* 64 (Nov. 1958), pp. 299–310; Miller, *Industry, Labor, and Community,* pp. 529–543; and Delbert C. Miller, "Democracy and Decision Making," *Power and Democracy in America,* pp. 52–70, for closely similar presentations of Miller's types.

Other typologies of community power structure are to be found in Peter H. Rossi, "Power and Community Structure," *Midwest Journal of Political Science,* 4 (Nov. 1960), p. 398, who speaks of "pyramidal" structures with one man or a small number of persons at their apices; "caucus rule" where decisions are made in caucus size group, through discussion among the participants; a "polylith" with separate structures for different spheres of community activity; and an "amorphous" structure where there is no enduring pattern of power.

Dahl has discussed situations of "parallel hierarchies," "dual leadership," "overlapping leadership," "strictly nonoverlapping leadership," and "weak hierarchies." See Dahl, "The Analysis of Influence," *Social Science and Community Action,* pp. 30–31.

Seasholes has presented models for "Monolithic Leadership," "Leadership Specialized by Issue Area," and "Specialized Leadership, Obscured." Bradbury Seasholes, "Patterns of Influence in Metropolitan Boston: A Proposal for Field Research," in Swanson (ed.), *Current Trends,* pp. 61–62.

Williams has presented a typology of the "roles of government" that may be used either to classify a set of abstract value orientations or to describe actual government structures. The four roles are 1) promoting economic growth, 2) promoting or securing life's amenities, 3) maintaining (only) traditional services, 4) arbitrating among conflicting interests. See Oliver P. Williams, "A Typology for Comparative Local Government," *Midwest Journal of Political Science,* 5 (May 1961), pp. 150–165, and, in more extended form, Oliver P. Williams and Charles R. Adrian, *Four Cities* (Philadelphia: University of Pennsylvania Press, 1963), esp. pp. 185–268.

Schulze has discussed self-contained community structures where ownership and control of industry is local, and contrasted them with "bifurcated" communities where local industries are absentee owned. Robert O. Schulze, "The

Role of Economic Dominants in Community Power Structures," *American Sociological Review,* 13 (1958): 290–296; and his "The Bifurcation of Power in a Satellite City," in Morris Janowitz (ed.), *Community Political Systems* (Glencoe, Illinois: The Free Press, 1961), pp. 19–80.

Agger, Goldrich, and Swanson have suggested a fourfold typology based on dichotomizing the political leadership's ideology as "convergent" and "divergent" and distribution of political power among citizens as "broad" or "narrow": "Consensual Mass" (broad distribution of political power, convergent leadership ideology); "Consensual Elite" (narrow distribution of power, convergent leadership ideology); "Competitive Mass" (broad distribution of power, divergent leadership ideology); and "Competitive Elite" (narrow distribution of power, divergent leadership ideology). See Agger, *et al., The Rulers and the Ruled,* pp. 73 ff.

A number of other writers discuss more or less absolutist or monocratic and more or less pluralistic or democratic structures.

36. Terry N. Clark, "Power and Community Structure: Who Governs, Where, and When?", Selection 17 in this anthology.

37. This perspective is evident in a number of recent studies reviewing work in the field and suggesting the strategy of cross-community comparative research. See, for example, Charles M. Bonjean and David M. Olson, "Community Leadership: Directions of Research," Selection 16 in this volume and Wallace S. Sayre and Nelson W. Polsby, "American Political Science and the Study of Urbanization," in Philip M. Hauser and Leo F. Schnore (eds.), *The Study of Urbanization* (New York: John Wiley and Sons, 1965), pp. 115–156.

38. See the work reported in Terry N. Clark, (ed.), *Community Structure and Decision-Making: Comparative Analyses* (San Francisco: Chandler, 1968).

39. Research under Jean Cuisenier with the Programme Mediterranéen of the Centre de Sociologie Européene in Paris, Robert Crain with the National Opinion Research Center, and myself with the International Studies of Values in Politics is in process in a total of more than two hundred communities in nine countries.

40. See Terry N. Clark, "Comparability in Community Research," paper presented to the session on Comparability in Community Research at the Sixth World Congress of Sociology, International Sociological Association, September 4 to 11, 1966, Évian, France.

41. Two committees are the Committee on Community Research and Development of the SSSP, chaired by Charles Bonjean, and the Committee for Comparability in Community Research, chaired by the writer.

42. See Clark, "Comparability in Community Research."

THE CONCEPT OF POWER: A SOCIOLOGIST'S PERSPECTIVE
Richard L. Simpson

1. I wish to thank Ida Harper Simpson and Benjamin Walter for commenting on an earlier draft of my comments.
2. Arthur F. Bentley, *The Process of Government* (Chicago: University of Chicago Press, 1908), p. 271 *et passim*.
3. Floyd Hunter, *Community Power Structure* (Chapel Hill: University of North Carolina Press, 1953), pp. 103–104.
4. Arthur J. Vidich and Joseph Bensman, *Small Town in Mass Society* (Princeton: Princeton University Press, 1958), Ch. 5.

THE CONCEPT OF POWER: A POLITICAL SCIENTIST'S PERSPECTIVE
David M. Olson

1. Some of the more adventurous scholars have attempted to generalize both theory and method from the community to national levels. Floyd Hunter, *Top Leadership, U.S.A.* (Chapel Hill: University of North Carolina Press, 1959); C. Wright Mills, *The Power Elite* (New York: Oxford University Press, 1957); and Robert A. Dahl, *Modern Political Analysis* (Englewood Cliffs, New Jersey: Prentice Hall, Inc., 1963).
2. The generic problem of power and especially the notion of community power structure has a seductive attraction for undergraduate students and for community professional workers at institutes.
3. George Belknap and Ralph Smuckler, "Political Power Relations in a Mid-West City," *Public Opinion Quarterly*, 20 (Spring 1956), pp. 73–81.
4. Robert Presthus, *Men at the Top* (New York: Oxford University Press, 1964, (pp. 221–234; and Arthur J. Vidich and Joseph Bensman, *Small Town in Mass Society* (Princeton, New Jersey: Princeton University Press, 1958), Ch. 8.
5. Robert A. Dahl, *Who Governs?* (New Haven: Yale University Press, 1961); Vidich and Bensman, *Small Town*; and Presthus, *Men at the Top*. The impact of external linkage on electoral events within a locality has been discussed by the author in "The Structure of Electoral Politics," *Journal of Politics*, 29 (May 1967), pp. 352–367.
6. Robert Agger, *et al.*, *The Rulers and the Ruled* (New York: John Wiley, 1964), pp. 102, 200 and 487 ff.
7. This term, from Schattschneider, is a good example of how concepts formulated for one level of government (national) are useful at another (local). E. E. Schattschneider, *The Semi-Sovereign People* (New York: Holt, Rinehart and Winston, 1960), p. 30.

8. Vidich and Bensman, *Small Town*, p. 217.
9. A similar set of cycles is used by Agger, *The Rulers*, pp. 40–51; and by H. Kent Jennings, *Community Influentials* (New York: The Free Press of Glencoe, 1964), pp. 107–109.
10. These interviews were conducted in Fall, 1964 in Austin, Texas, by students under the author's direction.
11. An example is Edward C. Banfield and James Q. Wilson, *City Politics* (Cambridge, Massachusetts: Harvard and M.I.T. Presses, 1963), pp. 248–250.
12. Clark, Selection 3, footnotes 18–23.
13. Ernest A. T. Barth, and Stuart D. Johnson, "Community Power and a Typology of Social Issues," *Social Forces*, 38 (Oct. 1959), pp. 29–32.
14. Terry N. Clark, Selection 3, footnotes 38–40; and Peter H. Rossi and Robert Crain, "The NORC Permanent Community Sample," in Thomas R. Dye (ed.), *Comparative Research in Community Politics* (Athens, Georgia: Proceedings of the Conference on Comparative Research in Community Politics, 1966), pp. 109–132.
15. Discussion on this point at a recent conference is summarized in Dye, *Comparative Research*, p. 142.

II.
INTRODUCTION

1. Martin Meyerson and Edward C. Banfield, *Boston: The Job Ahead* (Cambridge, Massachusetts: Harvard University Press, 1966), p. 17.
2. A Standard Metropolitan Statistical Area (SMSA), as defined by the United States Bureau of the Census, ordinarily consists of a central city containing a population of at least 50,000, the county in which it is located, and contiguous counties which are economically and socially integrated with the central city.
3. Arthur J. Vidich and Joseph Bensman, *Small Town in Mass Society* (Garden City, New York: Doubleday Anchor Books, 1960; originally published by Princeton University Press, 1958), p. 110.
4. Bernard Brown, "Municipal Finances and Annexation: A Study of Post-War Houston," *(Southwestern) Social Science Quarterly*, 48 (December 1967), p. 339.

METROPOLITAN AMERICA: SOME CONSEQUENCES OF FRAGMENTATION
The Advisory Commission on Intergovernmental Relations, Washington D.C.

1. James B. Conant, *Slums and Suburbs* (New York: McGraw-Hill, 1961), p. 3.

2. For a full discussion of the criteria used in delineating standard metropolitan statistical areas, see Executive Office of the President, Bureau of the Budget, *Standard Metropolitan Statistical Areas* (Washington: Government Printing Office, 1964). An even broader designation, the *Standard Consolidated Area*, is used to cover a group of adjacent SMSA's around New York and Chicago.

3. "Nassau Protesting Queens Mosquitoes," *New York Times*, Sept. 12, 1965, p. 1.

4. Roscoe C. Martin, *Metropolis in Transition: Local Government Adaptation to Changing Urban Needs* (Washington: Government Printing Office, 1963), p. 141.

5. Edward C. Banfield and Morton Grodzins, *Government and Housing in Metropolitan Areas* (New York: McGraw-Hill, 1958), p. 18.

6. Robert C. Wood, *Metropolis Against Itself* (New York: Committee for Economic Development, 1959), p. 38.

7. Norton E. Long, "Citizenship or Consumership in Metropolitan Areas," *Journal of the American Institute of Planners*, 31 (February 1965), pp. 4–5.

LIFE STYLE VALUES AND POLITICAL DECENTRALIZATION IN METROPOLITAN AREAS
Oliver P. Williams

1. The copyright for this manuscript has been assigned to the Chandler Publishing Company, San Francisco, Calif. as the article will appear in Terry N. Clark (ed.), *Community Structure and Decision Making: Comparative Analyses* (San Francisco: Chandler, 1968). An earlier version of this manuscript was presented at the Conference on Comparative Research in Community Politics at Athens, Georgia, November 16–19, 1966, under sponsorship of the National Science Foundation and the University of Georgia.

2. The Organization of a Metropolitan Region," *University of Pennsylvania Law Review*, 105 (Feb. 1957), pp. 538–552.

3. "The Governance of the Metropolis as a Problem in Diplomacy," *Journal of Politics*, 26 (Aug. 1964), pp. 627–647.

4. Philip E. Jacob and James V. Toscano (eds.), *The Integration of Political Communities* (Philadelphia: J. B. Lippincott Co., 1963), Ch. 4.

5. *Ibid.*

6. See also Oliver P. Williams, Harold Herman, Charles S. Liebman and Thomas R. Dye, *Suburban Differences and Metropolitan Policies* (Philadelphia: University of Pennsylvania Press, 1965), Ch. 9.

7. Wilbur R. Thompson, *A Preface to Urban Economics* (Baltimore: The Johns Hopkins Press, 1965), Ch. 7.

8. Vincent Ostrom, Charles M. Tiebout and Robert Warren, "The Organization of Government in the Metropolitan Area: A Theoretical Inquiry," *American Political Science Review*, 55 (Dec. 1961), pp. 385–387. The "polycentric" model presented in this article is not strictly an economic one.

9. *Community Power Structure* (Chapel Hill: University of North Carolina Press, 1953).

10. Roscoe C. Martin, Frank Munger and others, *Decisions in Syracuse* (Bloomington: Indiana University Press, 1961).

11. "The Local Community as an Ecology of Games," *American Journal of Sociology*, 64 (Nov. 1958), pp. 251–266.

12. A classic statement upon which many subsequent elaborations rest is R. M. Haig, *Major Economic Factors in Metropolitan Growth and Arrangements* (New York: The Regional Plan of New York and Its Environs, 1928).

13. Pioneering work in this area was contributed by Walter Firey. See his "Sentiment and Symbolism as Ecological Variables," *American Sociological Review*, 10 (April 1945), pp. 140–148.

14. *The City of History* (New York: Harcourt, Brace and World, Inc., 1961), p. 99.

15. *The Death and Life of Great American Cities* (New York: Random House, Inc., 1961). Mrs. Jacobs advocates a mixed land-use pattern and feels that zoning as presently practiced leads to undesirable blocks of single-usage land-developing patterns.

16. Williams, *et al., op. cit.*

17. Richard L. Stauber, *New Cities in America* (Lawrence: Government Research Bureau, the University of Kansas, 1965). The largest number of SMSA incorporations of any state in the decade 1950–1960 was in Texas (83).

18. *The Evolution of a Community* (London: Routledge and Kegan Paul, 1963).

LIFE STYLE, DEMOGRAPHIC DISTANCE, AND VOTER SUPPORT OF CITY–COUNTY CONSOLIDATION
Brett W. Hawkins

1. The author is indebted to several scholars for their helpful comments and suggestions on an earlier draft of this study. A particular debt is owed to Ira Sharkansky. I am also indebted to Thomas R. Dye and Oliver P. Williams. In addition, Ray N. Danner, of the University of Georgia's Computer Center, instructed the author in some of the subtleties of the biomedical computer programs, and Miss Alisa S. Norris collected most of the data. The research was made possible by grants from the University's Social Science Research Institute and Office of General Research. The author, of course, is responsible for any errors that may remain.

2. Terms may cause some confusion here. "Life style" is used to indicate general ways of living, especially those based on social status and familism. "Demographic distance" refers to indicators of life-style differences between aggregates of people living in proximity and is here treated as indicative of separatist, or life-style-protective, values. The term "social distance" is sometimes used in the literature on political integration, but because of its common usage in attitudinal research "demographic distance" is substituted here.

3. *The Integration of Political Communities* (Philadelphia: J. B. Lippincott, 1964), p. 18. See also Thomas R. Dye, "Urban Political Integration: Conditions Associated With Annexation in American Cities," *Midwest Journal of Political Science*, 8 (Nov. 1964), pp. 430–446; and Karl Deutsch, *et al.*, *Political Community and the North Atlantic Area* (Princeton: Princeton University Press, 1957).

4. The St. Louis consolidation referendum of 1962 is omitted because it did not require local approval; it was attempted by means of a state constitutional amendment. Nevertheless, the author made a separate computer analysis that included the St. Louis City—St. Louis County votes (local vote on the amendment) and social statistics. The result showed no directional change at all, and virtually no change in the magnitude of the various simple, partial, and multiple correlation coefficients.

5. Referendum did not require two local majorities, one in the city and one in the county outside the city. A single area-wide majority was required. The author broke down the area-wide vote into central city and fringe components.

6. At the time of this referendum Warwick was a city. It had incorporated in 1952, but it is included here because of its still (in 1958) suburban and rural character and because it was Warwick County six years before the referendum. The author might also have included a 1956 proposal to consolidate the cities of Newport News, Hampton, and Warwick. However, the three-way nature of the referendum, plus the fact that two of the three units had been municipalities for many years, suggested to this author that the 1956 proposal was not sufficiently comparable with the other referenda to warrant inclusion.

7. Referendum did not require two local majorities, one in the city and one in the county outside the city. A single area-wide majority was required. The author broke down the area-wide vote into central city and fringe components.

8. Walter C. Kaufman and Scott Greer, "Voting in a Metropolitan Community: An Application of Social Area Analysis," *Social Forces*, 38 (March 1960), pp. 196–224.

9. *Ibid.*, pp. 199, 200.

10. Dye, "Urban Political Integration," pp. 437–439.

11. *Ibid.*, pp. 440–442.

12. Eshref Shevky and Wendell Bell, *Social Area Analysis* (Stanford: Stanford University Press, 1955).

13. See Thomas R. Dye, "City-Suburban Social Distance and Public Policy," *Social Forces*, 44 (Sept. 1965), pp. 100–106.

14. In a few cases, such as the Virginia cities and counties, census figures are reported separately because the city and the county are separate units of government.

15. The variables analyzed here were plotted on a scattergram and examined visually. The simple relationships were linear. Also, the distribution of most statistics approximated a normal curve.

16. The technique used was as follows: under each life-style variable a listing was made of the referenda in which social distance favored the fringe. Then the percent YES and NO votes in these referenda was recorded. Finally, a count was made under each variable of the number of times fringe and city voted alike and the number of times they voted differently. Adding the number of similar votes (both NO) when social distance favored the fringe produced a total of twenty-two times. There were eighteen dissimilar votes, all with the city voting YES and the fringe NO.

17. There were ten similar votes and two dissimilar votes.

18. For example, Oliver P. Williams, "Life Style Values and Political Decentralization in Metropolitan Areas," (*Southwestern*) *Social Science Quarterly*, 48 (Dec. 1967), pp. 299–310. Reprinted as Selection 7 in this volume.

19. Dye, "Urban Political Integration," *op. cit.*

20. The author made a separate computer analysis that deleted extreme votes. Obviously there are many criteria that one might use to identify extreme votes. Considering the size of this universe, however, the author decided to delete all cases in which the fringe YES vote (fringe support seemed more crucial in this study) was more than one and one-half standard deviations from the mean. Using this criterion eliminated Hampton–Elizabeth City County and Virginia Beach–Princess Anne County. The computer run deleting these two cases produced a few changes in the correlation coefficients, but on the whole the findings reported in the body of the paper were not weakened. In the cities, for example, familism was still negatively related to the YES vote and R for familism increased from .68 to .71. However, R for social rank was reduced from .37 to .29 and the predominant direction became negative when it had been irregular.

In the fringes—using the fringes' own characteristics—there was virtually no change in the coefficients, either as to direction or magnitude. The fringes' own social characteristics remained just as weakly related to the fringe vote. Also fringe–city social distance, along both social rank and familism dimensions was still positively related to the fringe's YES vote. And R for fringe–city social rank plus familism was strengthened from .81 to .86. However, R for familism was weakened from .65 to .45 while R for social rank was greatly strengthened from .17 to .67.

The major negative result of this separate analysis, therefore, was that R for fringe–city social distance along the familism dimension was weakened to the point where fringe–city social rank became more strongly related to the YES vote than fringe–city familism. Nevertheless, this relationship still constituted a deviant finding since the hypothesis stated that social rank increasingly in favor of the fringe should be negatively related to the YES vote and both analyses showed a positive relationship—along both dimensions.

21. David G. Temple, "The Tidewater Mergers: The Politics of Local Government Consolidation in Virginia," Unpublished Ph.D. dissertation, Department of Government and Foreign Affairs, University of Virginia, 1966.

OPINIONS ON SCHOOL DISTRICT REORGANIZATION IN METROPOLITAN AREAS: A COMPARATIVE ANALYSIS . . .
Basil G. Zimmer and Amos H. Hawley

1. A version of this paper was presented at the annual meeting of the Society for the Study of Social Problems, San Francisco, 1967. This study was sponsored by the United States Office of Education, Cooperative Research Project No. 1044.

2. Philip M. Hauser, *Population Perspectives* (New Brunswick: Rutgers University Press, 1960); and Leo F. Schnore, *The Urban Scene* (New York: The Free Press, 1965).

3. In St. Louis County, for example, "one school district has an assessed valuation (the basis for all property taxes) which is twenty-eight times the tax base per capita of another. The first suburb pays one of the lowest tax rates in the area, the second one of the highest. But the school systems are far apart in quality. The first is a superior school system, the second is struggling to maintain its accreditation" (Scott Greer, *Governing the Metropolis* [New York: John Wiley and Sons, Inc., 1962], p. 116).

4. This is the type of problem one observer referred to as the "segregation of resources from needs." See Robert Wood, *1400 Governments: The Political Economy of the New York Metropolitan Region* (with assistance of Vladimir V. Almendinger) (Cambridge:

Harvard University Press, 1961). In St. Louis County, it was reported that "one school district spends $308 per pupil in average daily attendance, others attend school in a district where the comparable expenditure is $337, and still others go to school in a district that spends $615 per pupil" (John C. Bollens [ed.], *Exploring the Metropolitan Community* [Berkeley and Los Angeles: University of California Press, 1961], p. 44). See also, Roscoe C. Martin, *Government and the Suburban School* (Syracuse: Syracuse University Press, 1962).

5. James B. Conant, *The American High School Today* (New York: McGraw-Hill Book Co., 1959).

6. B. G. Zimmer and A. H. Hawley, "Approaches to the Solution of Fringe Problems: Preferences of Residents in the Flint Metropolitan Area," reprint from George A. Theodorson (ed.), *Public Administration Review in Studies in Human Ecology* (Evanston: Row Peterson, 1961), pp. 595–606. See also, Hawley and Zimmer, "Resistance to Unification in a Metropolitan Community," in Morris Janowitz (ed.), *Community Political Systems* (New York: The Free Press, 1961), pp. 146–184; and Henry S. Shryock, Jr., "The Natural History of Standard Metropolitan Areas," *American Journal of Sociology*, 63 (Sept. 1957), pp. 163–170.

7. For a discussion of this problem, see Amos H. Hawley, *Human Ecology: A Theory of Community Structure* (New York: The Ronald Press, 1950), pp. 425–426. The local government problem will be examined in a forthcoming monograph.

8. Bureau of the Census, *Local Government in Metropolitan Areas* (Washington D.C.: Census of Government, United States Department of Commerce, 1962).

9. For a discussion of the relative costs of education by size of enrollment, see Washington State Planning Council, *A Study of the Common School System of Washington* (Olympia: The Council, 1938); Iowa State Department of Public Instruction, *A Report to the People of Iowa on the Present Problems and Future Goals of Reorganization in Your School District* (Des Moines: The Department, 1952).

10. This figure does not include the more than 200,000 members of local school boards. The economic magnitude of public education is discussed in Charles S. Benson, *The Economics of Public Education* (Boston: Houghton Mifflin Co., 1961), Appendix A.

11. The general expenditures for education in all metropolitan areas exceeded the amount for all of the following functions combined: highways, public welfare, sanitation, health and hospitals, police and fire protection, housing and urban renewal, and park and recreation. See Bureau of the Census, *Local Government*, Table D, p. 10.

12. For a discussion of the general problems of school district reorganization, see C. O.

Department of Health, Education, and Welfare, Special Series No. 5, United States Government Printing Office, 1957).

13. This paper is based on a larger study by the authors which is concerned with the general and basic question: "What are the roots of the resistance to the establishment of a single administrative unit for the larger area?"

14. "In most states the procedures for reorganization of school districts have been cumbersome and difficult to set in motion. With few exceptions a favorable majority vote has been required in each of the districts in the proposed new district—that provision alone has always been sufficient to restrain reorganization progress to a snail's pace" (Fitzwater, *School District Reorganization*, p. 7).

15. The number of incorporated cities and unincorporated townships in each of the areas are: Buffalo, 7, 5; Milwaukee, 8, 5; Dayton, 3, 6; Rochester, 2, 8; Rockford, 1, 5; and Saginaw, 0, 7.

16. Greer, *Governing*, p. 109.

17. Robert C. Wood, *Suburbia: Its People and Their Politics* (Boston: Houghton, Mifflin Company, 1958), p. 19.

18. In actual practice, this does not make reform any easier because lower taxes would not necessarily result under a single district. And further, even if this were the case, the opposition would put up such a campaign as to confuse the issue and would make the claim that taxes would increase. This is a standard format for any resistance group concerning any issue where public funds are involved. This invariably proves to be a very effective defense against change, because people are always suspicious concerning what will happen to taxes. Also, the general opinion as reported here is that reorganization would not result in reduced taxes.

19. It is highly significant that a substantial majority of the suburban officials reported that they would not occupy such positions if they lived in the city. Thus, their leadership roles, as perceived by themselves, depend on the segmentation of school districts and governments in metropolitan areas.

20. A point worthy of emphasis here is the marked similarity between the views held by school officials and the residents in their areas in the higher socioeconomic status groups. This similarity is particularly significant since it is found in both city and suburban areas even though the officials in the two areas represent entirely different and frequently directly opposite views. With rare exceptions and regardless of the issue, officials more closely represent the views of the higher status residents than the general population. This is to be expected, since it is from this group that such officials are largely recruited. It would seem then, that suburban officials in particular,

oppose change not only because of their vested interest as officials but also because this is the general climate of opinion that is most frequently shared by persons in the community in the same general social class position.

III.
INTRODUCTION

1. The concept of "scope of government" is discussed more extensively by Agger, Goldrich, and Swanson, in Selection 22.

2. Some support for this argument has been offered by Stanley Lieberson and Arnold S. Silverman, "The Precipitants and Underlying Conditions of Race Riots," *American Sociological Review*, 30 (December 1965), 896.

3. Daniel Patrick Moynihan, *Maximum Feasible Misunderstanding: Community Action and the War on Poverty* (New York: The Free Press, 1969).

VOTING TURNOUT IN AMERICAN CITIES
Robert R. Alford and Eugene C. Lee

1. Charles R. Adrian and Charles Press, *Governing Urban America*, 3rd ed. (New York: McGraw-Hill Book Company, 1968), p. 95.

2. Alvin Boskoff and Harmon Ziegler's study, *Voting Patterns in a Local Election*, provides a brief review of the state of the literature (Philadelphia: J. B. Lippincott Company, 1964), Chapter 1. See also Lester W. Milbrath, *Political Participation* (Chicago: Rand McNally, 1965); but note that references to city elections are infrequent.

3. Eugene C. Lee, *The Politics of Nonpartisanship* (Berkeley: University of California Press, 1960), Chapters 9 and 11.

4. Eugene C. Lee, "City Elections: A Statistical Profile," in *Municipal Year Book* (Chicago: International City Managers' Association, 1963), 74–84.

5. Robert R. Alford and Harry M. Scoble, "Political and Socioeconomic Characteristics of American Cities," in *Municipal Year Book* (Chicago: International City Managers' Association, 1965), p. 95. See also Leo F. Schnore and Robert R. Alford, "Forms of Government and Socioeconomic Characteristics of Suburbs," *Administrative Science Quarterly*, 8 (June 1963), 1–17; and John Kessel, "Governmental Structure and Political Environment: A Statistical Note about American Cities," *American Political Science Review*, 66 (September 1962), pp. 615–620. Robert L. Lineberry and Edmund P. Fowler present data at some

variance with the above and suggest that there are not significant class differences between reformed and unreformed cities, although there is "some support for the argument that reformed cities are more homogeneous." However, as they suggest, varying samples may produce varying conclusions. In any event, the differences between these studies are not central to this analysis of voting participation. See their "Reformism and Public Policies in American Cities," 61 (September, 1967), p. 706. [See Selection 27 in this volume.]

6. Ruth B. Dixon, "Predicting Voter Turnout in City Elections," unpublished M.A. thesis in Sociology, University of California, Berkeley, 1966; Ruth B. Dixon, "The Reform Movement in American City Government: Has Democracy Been Sacrificed to Efficiency?", unpublished paper, Department of Sociology, University of California, Berkeley, 1965.

7. Maurice Pinard, "Structural Attachments and Political Support in Urban Politics: The Case of Fluoridation Referendums," *American Journal of Sociology*, 68 (March 1963), p. 518. A similar study reported that in cities with high levels of citizen participation, associated with a well-educated population, the local government was frequently immobilized from making decisions on such issues as bond referenda and fluoridation controversies. Robert L. Crain and Donald B. Rosenthal, "Community Status as a Dimension of Local Decision-Making," *American Sociological Review*, 32 (December 1967), 970–984.

8. See Robert R. Alford, "The Comparative Study of Urban Politics," in Leo F. Schnore and Henry Fagin (eds.), *Urban Research and Policy Planning* (Beverly Hills: Sage Publications, 1967), 263–302, for an analytic scheme which distinguishes "situational" from "cultural" and "structural" factors in explaining decisions, policies, and roles of government in urban politics. Situational factors themselves have causes and may be patterned, of course, but, by definition, are not predictable from structural or cultural factors. Voting turnout figures for four Wisconsin cities in April and November elections from 1950 to 1964 ranged from 14 per cent to 91 per cent, which is partly explainable by situational factors. See Robert R. Alford, with the collaboration of Harry M. Scoble, *Bureaucracy and Participation: Political Cultures in Four Wisconsin Cities* (Chicago: Rand McNally, forthcoming), Chapter VII.

9. V. O. Key, Jr., "The Politically Relevant in Surveys," *Public Opinion Quarterly*, 24 (1960), 54–61; and Austin Ranney, "The Utility and Limitations of Aggregate Data in the Study of Electoral Behavior," in Ranney (ed.), *Essays in the Behavioral Study of Politics* (Urbana: University of Illinois Press, 1962), p. 99.

10. Crain and Rosenthal, *op. cit.*, p. 984.

11. The following table compares characteristics of American cities above 25,000 population in 1960 and the cities used in this study.

12. Lee, "City Elections . . . ," *op. cit.*, p. 81.

13. Charles E. Gilbert and Christopher Clague, "Electoral Competition and Electoral Systems in Large Cities," *The Journal of Politics*, 24 (May 1962), p. 330.

14. We use "mayor-council" and "nonmanager" interchangeably, although the category includes some 30 commission cities, 10.6 per cent of the total of nonmanager communities with nonconcurrent elections.

15. Lineberry and Fowler, *op. cit.*, p. 715. This article provides a succinct summary of these hypotheses.

16. Lee, "City Elections . . . ," *op. cit.*, 74–84. Ecological data from Des Moines, Iowa, show a similar pattern; see Robert H. Salisbury and Gordon Blake, "Class and Party in Partisan and Non-Partisan Elections: The Case of Des Moines," *American Political Science Review*, 57 (September 1963), 589–590.

17. Michael Parenti, "Ethnic Politics and the Persistence of Ethnic Identification," *American Political Science Review*, 61 (September 1967), p. 717. An earlier statement of this thesis is found in Raymond E. Wolfinger, "Some Consequences of Ethnic Politics," in M. Kent Jennings and Harmon Ziegler (eds.), *The Electoral Process* (Englewood Cliffs, N.J.: Prentice-Hall, 1966). See also Raymond E. Wolfinger, "The Development and Persistence of Ethnic Voting," *American Political Science Review*, 59 (December 1965), 896–908. Robert Lane has suggested that "the seat of ethnic politics is the local community, not the national capitol." See his *Political Life* (New York: The Free Press, 1959), p. 239.

18. See, for example, Lane, *op. cit.*, p. 222; Boskoff and Ziegler, *op. cit.*, p. 16: Milbrath, *op. cit.*, p. 122.

19. Lineberry and Fowler, *op. cit.*, p. 707.

20. For an example of the use of "political culture" as a variable in categorizing American states, see Daniel J. Elazar, *American Federalism: A View from the States* (New York: Thomas Y. Crowell Company, 1966).

21. We are indebted to Raymond Wolfinger for bringing this point to our attention.

22. David Rogers, "Community Political Systems: A Framework and Hypothesis for Comparative Studies," in Bert E. Swanson (ed.), *Current Trends in Comparative Studies* (Kansas City, Mo.: Community Studies, Inc., 1962), p. 39.

23. Stanley Kelley, Jr., Richard E. Ayres and William G. Bowen, "Registration and Voting: Putting First Things First," *American Political Science Review*, 61 (June 1967), 359–379.

24. Dixon, "The Reform Movement . . . ," *op. cit.*

25. Kessel, *op. cit.*, p. 617.

26. It should be noted that while these correlations are based upon measures of education as a continuous variable, the measure itself is not continuous for a given city, but rather a single proportion of persons who have achieved a given level of education. See Robert R. Alford and Harry M. Scoble, "Sources of Local Political Involvement," *American Political Science Review*, 62:1192–1206, for an analysis of the relative importance of a variety of factors, including education, for political involvement.

27. Dixon, "Predicting Voter Turnout . . . ," *op. cit.*, 50–52.

28. Lineberry and Fowler, *op. cit.*, p. 716.

29. Letter to one of the authors dated January 29, 1964.

30. Lee, *The Politics of Nonpartisanship*, *op. cit.*, Chapter 11.

31. Crain and Rosenthal, *op. cit.*, 970–984.

32. *Ibid.*

33. James Q. Wilson and Edward C. Banfield, "Public-Regardingness as a Value Premise in Voting Behavior," *American Political Science Review*, 58 (December 1964), 876–887 [see Selection 13 in this volume].

34. Raymond E. Wolfinger and John Osgood Field, "Political Ethos and the Structure of City Government," *American Political Science Review*, 60 (June 1966), p. 326. While we take full note of the Wolfinger-Field vs. Banfield-Wilson controversy as to the use and abuse of "ethos," we make no attempt here to enter into their discussion as to what the latter pair said or implied in *City Politics*. The issue is discussed in letters to the editor of each pair in the December 1966 issue of *American Political Science Review*. See "Communications," 998–1000.

35. Samuel C. Patterson, "The Political Cultures of the American States," *The Journal of Politics*, 30 (February 1968), 204–207; Alford with the collaboration of Harry M. Scoble, *op. cit.*, and Oliver P. Williams and Charles R. Adrian, *Four Cities* (Philadelphia: University of Pennsylvania Press, 1963).

VOTER QUALIFICATION AND PARTICIPATION IN NATIONAL, STATE, AND MUNICIPAL ELECTIONS: THE CASE OF HOUSTON, TEXAS
Dan Nimmo and Clifton McCleskey

1. This is true, for example, of studies of the national electorate like Angus Campbell, Philip E. Converse, Warren E. Miller, and Donald E. Stokes, *The American Voter* (New York: John Wiley & Sons, 1960) and *Elections and the Political Order* (New York: John Wiley & Sons, 1966). See also the earlier studies undertaken by the Survey Research Center of

the University of Michigan: Angus Campbell, Gerard Gurin, and Warren E. Miller, *The Political Profile of the American Electorate* (Ann Arbor, Michigan: Survey Research Center, undated). Somewhat more helpful in providing clues of how local electorates respond both to local and national contests are: Herbert Tingsten, *Political Behavior: Studies in Election Statistics* (London: P. S. King & Son, 1937); D. S. Hecock and H. A. Trevelyan, *Detroit Voters and Recent Elections* (Detroit: Detroit Bureau of Governmental Research, Inc., 1938); James K. Pollack, *Voting Behavior: A Case Study* (Ann Arbor: University of Michigan Press, 1939); and Bernard Berelson, Paul F. Lazarsfeld, and William McPhee, *Voting* (Chicago: The University of Chicago Press, 1954).

2. Typical of such efforts in studying local electorates are Walter C. Kaufman and Scott Greer, "Voting in a Metropolitan Community: An Application of Social Area Analysis," *Social Forces*, 38 (March 1960), pp. 196–204 and Eugene S. Uyeki, "Patterns of Voting in a Metropolitan Area," *Urban Affairs Quarterly*, 1 (June 1966), pp. 65–77; a multivariate analysis of voter turnout in cities of over 25,000 can be found in Robert R. Alford and Eugene C. Lee, "Voting Turnout in American Cities," *American Political Science Review*, 62 (September 1968), pp. 796–813 (reprinted in this volume).

3. A few of those studies that do contain data on this problem include Robert H. Salisbury and Gordon Black, "Class and Party in Partisan and Nonpartisan Elections: The Case of Des Moines," *American Political Science Review*, 57 (September 1963), pp. 584–592, which correlates class, party and turnout in charter elections, municipal elections, senatorial elections, and national elections from 1949–61 using aggregate data; and, Harry Holloway and David M. Olson, "Electoral Participation by Whites and Negroes in a Southern City," *Midwest Journal of Political Science*, 10 (February 1966), pp. 99–122, examining aggregate turnout figures in a variety of elections for the electorate of Austin, Texas.

4. These exceptions include Stanley Kelley, Jr., Richard E. Ayres, and William G. Bowen, "Registration and Voting: Putting First Things First," *American Political Science Review*, 61 (June 1967), pp. 359–377; Donald R. Matthews and James R. Prothro, *Negroes and the New Southern Politics* (New York: Harcourt, Brace and World, 1966), pp. 148–156; Richard A. Watson, "The Politics of Urban Change," *Public Affairs Monograph Series*, No. 3 (Kansas City, Missouri: Community Studies, Inc.); Kenneth N. Vines, "Republicanism in New Orleans," *Tulane Studies in Political*

Science. Vol. II (New Orleans: Tulane University, 1955); and, in the same volume, Leonard Reissman, K. H. Silvert, and Cliff W. Wing, Jr., "The New Orleans Voter."

5. See *Harper v. Virginia State Board of Elections, et al.*, 303 U.S. 663 (1966).

6. The following comparison of actual turnout of qualified voters in all four elections with the sample turnout in each indicates an acceptably close fit of each sample to the universe in question:

	Actual Turnout of Qualified Voters	Turnout of Sampled Voters	
1964 Presidential Election	382,985	80.1%	N = 4123 77.8%
1965 Mayoralty Election	112,982	45.5%	N = 742 40.2%
1966 Gubernatorial Election	237,364	50.1%	N = 1013 52.3%
1967 Mayoralty Election	143,407	36.1%	N = 732 38.3%

7. See David M. Olson, *Nonpartisan Elections: A Case Analysis* (Austin, Texas: Institute of Public Affairs, University of Texas, 1965).

8. Charles R. Adrian, "Some General Characteristics of Nonpartisan Elections," *American Political Science Review*, 46 (September 1952), pp. 766–776; Oliver P. Williams and Charles R. Adrian, "The Insulation of Local Politics Under the Nonpartisan Ballot," *American Political Science Review*, 53 (December 1959), pp. 1052–1063; and Phillips Cutright, "Nonpartisan Electoral Systems in American Cities," in Phillips Cutright (ed.), *Comparative Studies in Society and History* (January 1963), pp. 212–226.

9. Kelley, *et al.*, *op. cit.*, pp. 359–377.

10. These findings were foreshadowed by Holloway and Olson's study of registration and voting in Austin, Texas. They found that when the Twenty-Fourth Amendment gave Negroes (and all others) the opportunity to qualify to vote *in federal elections* without paying a poll tax, Negro registration increased by only 61 persons (from 6,601 to 6,662) and registration of all others by only 862 persons (from 61,042 to 61,904). Holloway and Olson, *op. cit.*, p. 106.

Our Houston data suggest that the end of the poll tax may have had more impact on the internal make-up of the Negro electorate than

on its share of total registration. Of all Negroes registered in 1965, 12% were age 21–29; the year 1967 and free registration doubled that figure to 24% for the youngest voters. (Anglo registration in the 21–29 age category increased from 14% in 1965 to 20% in 1967.)

11. See Robert E. Lane, *Political Life* (Glencoe: The Free Press, 1959); Lester Milbrath, *Political Participation* (Chicago: Rand McNally & Co., 1965); and Seymour Martin Lipset, *Political Man* (New York: Doubleday and Co., 1959).

12. Estimates of voter turnout in local elections along with summaries of findings of previous studies of the socio-demographic characteristics of local electorates are found in John C. Bollens and Henry J. Schmandt, *The Metropolis* (New York: Harper & Row, 1965), p. 223.

13. To the extent that the data on occupational categories can be related to social class, our findings are in accord with those of Salisbury and Black, *op. cit.*, 590:

> The class component remains significantly related to turnout, however. This in turn means that lower income voters will vote less regularly than upper income residents. This relationship holds somewhat more strongly in municipal elections than in national elections, although the effect is apparent in both.

THE CHANGING PATTERN OF URBAN PARTY POLITICS
Fred I. Greenstein

1. E. E. Schattschneider, *Party Government* (New York, 1942), pp. 162–169.

2. Among the better known accounts are Frank R. Kent, *The Great Game of Politics* (Garden City, N.Y., 1923, rev. ed., 1930); Sonya Forthall, *Cogwheels of Democracy* (New York, 1946); Harold F. Gosnell, *Machine Politics* (Chicago, 1937); and the many case studies of individual bosses. For a recent romanticization, see Edwin O'Connor's novel, *The Last Hurrah* (Boston, 1956).

3. Austin Ranney and Willmoore Kendall, *Democracy and the American Party System* (New York, 1956), pp. 249–252.

4. This last definitional criterion explicitly departs from the characterization of a "machine" in James Q. Wilson's interesting discussion about "The Economy of Patronage," *The Journal of Political Economy*, 59 (August 1961), p. 370n., "as that kind of political party which sustains its members through the distribution of material incentives (patronage) rather than nonmaterial incentives (appeals to principle, the fun of the game, sociability, etc.)." There is ample evidence that for many old-style party workers incentives such as "the fun of the game," "sociability," and even "service" are of central importance. See, for example, Edward J. Flynn, *You're the*

Boss (New York, 1947), p. 22; James A. Farley, *Behind the Ballots* (New York, 1938), p. 237; and the passage cited in note 8 below. The distinction between "material" and "nonmaterial" incentives would probably have to be discarded in a more refined discussion of the motivations underlying political participation. So-called material rewards, at base, are nonmaterial in the sense that they are valued for the status they confer and for other culturally defined reasons.

5. *Op. cit.*, p. 106.

6. See, for example, Edward A. Shils, *The Torment of Secrecy* (Glencoe, Ill., 1956) and Stanley M. Elkins, *Slavery* (Chicago, 1959), reprinted with an introduction by Nathan Glazer, New York, 1963).

7. William L. Riordon, *Plunkitt of Tammany Hall* (originally published in 1905; republished New York, 1948, and New York, 1963; quotations are from the 1963 edition), pp. 27–28.

8. *Ibid.*, pp. 25–26.

9. Elmer E. Cornwell, Jr., "Party Absorption of Ethnic Groups: The Case of Providence, Rhode Island," *Social Forces*, 38 (March 1960), pp. 205–210.

10. Riordon, *op. cit.*, pp. 17–20.

11. Frank J. Sorauf, "State Patronage in a Rural County," *American Political Science Review* 50 (December 1956), pp. 1046–1056.

12. Angus Campbell, Philip E. Converse, Warren E. Miller, and Donald E. Stokes, *The American Voter* (New York, 1960), pp. 426–427. The statistic for nonsouthern cities was supplied to me by the authors.

13. Daniel Katz and Samuel J. Eldersveld, "The Impact of Local Party Activity on the Electorate," *Public Opinion Quarterly*, 25 (Spring 1961), pp. 16–17.

14. Hugh A. Bone, *Grass Roots Party Leadership* (Seattle, 1952); Robert L. Morlan, "City Politics: Free Style," *National Municipal Review*, 38 (November 1949), pp. 485–491.

15. Robert A. Dahl, *Who Governs?* (New Haven, 1961), p. 278.

16. *Ibid.*; Nelson W. Polsby, *Community Power and Political Theory* (New Haven, 1963); Raymond E. Wolfinger, *The Politics of Progress* (forthcoming).

17. Raymond E. Wolfinger, "The Influence of Precinct Work on Voting Behavior," *Public Opinion Quarterly*, 27 (Fall 1963), pp. 387–398.

18. Frost deliberately worded his questionnaire descriptions of these services favorably in order to avoid implying that respondents were to be censured for indulging in "machine tactics." Richard T. Frost, "Stability and Change in Local Politics," *Public Opinion Quarterly*, 25 (Summer 1961), pp. 231–232.

19. James Q. Wilson, "Politics and Reform in American Cities," *American Government Annual, 1962–63* (New York, 1962), pp. 37–52.

20. Phillips Cutright, "Nonpartisan Electoral Systems in American Cities," *Comparative Studies in Society and History,* 5 (January 1963), pp. 219–221.

21. For a brief review of the relevant literature, see Fred I. Greenstein, *The American Party System and the American People* (Englewood Cliffs, N.J., 1963), pp. 57–60.

22. Joseph T. Klapper, *The Effects of Mass Communication* (New York, 1960).

23. James Q. Wilson, *The Amateur Democrat* (Chicago, 1962).

24. There is another interesting point of resemblance between old- and new-style urban party politics. In both, an important aspect of the motivation for participation seems to be the rewards of sociability. Tammany picnics and New York Committee for Democratic Voters (CDV) coffee hours probably differ more in decor than in the functions they serve. An amusing indication of this is provided by the committee structure of the Greenwich Village club of the CDV; in addition to the committees dealing with the club newsletter, with housing, and with community action, there is a social committee and a Flight Committee, the latter being concerned with arranging charter flights to Europe for club members. See Vernon M. Goetcheus, *The Village Independent Democrats: A Study in the Politics of the New Reformers* (unpublished senior distinction thesis, Honors College, Wesleyan University, 1963), pp. 65–66. On similar activities by the California Democratic Clubs, see Robert E. Lane, James D. Barber, and Fred I. Greenstein, *Introduction to Political Analysis* (Englewood Cliffs, N. J., 1962), pp. 55–57.

25. Goetcheus, op. cit., p. 138.

26. DeSapio, for example, was generally able to hold on to his lower-class Italian voting support in Greenwich Village; his opponents succeeded largely by activating the many middle- and upper-class voters who had moved into new high-rent housing in the district.

27. Probably because of their emphasis on ideology, the new reform groups also seem to be quite prone to internal conflicts which impede their effectiveness. One is reminded of Robert Michels' remarks about the intransigence of intellectuals in European socialist parties. *Political Parties* (New York, 1962, originally published in 1915), Part 4, Chap. 6.

28. On the significance of the American experience with old-style urban politics for the emerging nations, see Wallace S. Sayre and Nelson W. Polsby, "American Political Science and the Study of Urbanization," Committee on Urbanization, Social Science Research Council, mimeo, 1963, pp. 45–48.

PUBLIC-REGARDINGNESS AS A VALUE PREMISE IN VOTING BEHAVIOR
James Q. Wilson and Edward C. Banfield

1. Median family income under $3,000 per year. Needless to say, most voters in this category are Negroes.
2. The cities and elections examined are:
Cleveland-Cuyahoga County: Nov., 1956; Nov., 1959; May, 1960; Nov. 1960.
Chicago-Cook County: June, 1957; Nov., 1958; Nov., 1959; April, 1962.
Detroit-Wayne County: August, 1960; Feb., 1961; April, 1961; April, 1963.
Kansas City: Nov., 1960; March, 1962.
Los Angeles: Nov., 1962.
Miami: Nov., 1956; May, 1960.
St. Louis: March, 1962; Nov., 1962; March, 1963.
3. The degree of association was also calculated using a nonparametric statistic (Kendall's *tau*). The relationship persists but at lower values. Since we are satisfied that the relationship found by r is not spurious, we have relied on it for the balance of the analysis because of its capacity to produce partial correlation coefficients.
4. Only two measures of tax liability can be got from the Census: median home value and median family income. We have used the latter for the most part. The Census classifies all homes valued at over $25,000 together, thereby collapsing distinctions that are important for us. We think, too, that people are more likely to know their incomes than to know the current market value of their homes, and that therefore the Census information on incomes is more reliable. Finally, in neighborhoods populated mostly by renters, median home values are likely to be unrepresentative of the class character of the neighborhood: this is so, for example, where a few owner-occupied slums exist in a district of luxury apartments.
5. Other studies which suggest that upper-income groups may have a greater preference for public expenditures than middle-income groups include Oliver P. Williams and Charles R. Adrian, *Four Cities: A Study in Comparative Policy Making* (Philadelphia: University of Pennsylvania Press, 1963), ch. v; Alvin Boskoff and Harmon Zeigler, *Voting Patterns in a Local Election* (Philadelphia: J. B. Lippincott Co., 1964), ch. iii; Richard A. Watson, *The Politics of Urban Change* (Kansas City, Mo.: Community Studies, Inc., 1963), ch. iv; and Robert H. Salisbury and Gordon Black, "Class and Party in Non-Partisan Elections: The Case of Des Moines," *The American Political Science Review*, 57 (September, 1963), p. 591. The Williams-Adrian and Salisbury-Black studies use electoral data; the Boskoff-Zeigler and

Watson studies use survey data. See also Otto A. Davis, "Empirical Evidence of 'Political' Influences Upon the Expenditure and Taxation Policies of Public Schools," Graduate School of Industrial Administration of the Carnegie Institute of Technology, January 1964 (mimeo), and William C. Birdsall, "Public Finance Allocation Decisions and the Preferences of Citizens: Some Theoretical and Empirical Considerations," unpublished Ph.D. thesis, Department of Economics, Johns Hopkins University, 1963. A difficulty with the Davis and Birdsall studies is the size (and thus the heterogeneity) of the units of analysis—entire school districts in one case, entire cities in the other.
6. Michigan is one of the few states which restricts the right to vote on expenditures to property owners and their spouses. Because the Flint returns were tabulated on a precinct basis, demographic data had to be obtained from block rather than tract statistics; since median family income is given only for tracts, median value of owner-occupied homes had to be used.
Possibly the flood control benefits would be distributed roughly in proportion to the value of properties; about this we cannot say. However, it is worth noting that the vote in Flint on other expenditures which presumably would *not* distribute benefits in proportion to the value of properties (e.g., parks) followed the same pattern.
7. We isolated all precincts in Census tracts having median family incomes of at least $10,000 a year, with at least 70 per cent home ownership (the central city of Chicago was excepted here), and at least 70 per cent of the population third- (or more) generation native born.
8. A person is of "foreign stock" if he was born abroad or if one or both of his parents was born abroad. We believe that the reason why a significant relationship does not appear for the suburbs is that there is a considerable number of Jews among the foreign stock of the suburbs. In the central city, there are practically no Jews. Like other Jews, Jews of Eastern Europe origin tend to favor expenditures proposals of all kinds. Their presence in the suburbs, therefore, offsets the "No" vote of the non-Jews of foreign stock.
9. Since no home-owning ward or town in Cuyahoga County is more than 25 per cent Polish-Czech according to the 1960 Census, it may be that no inferences can be drawn from the voting data about Polish-Czech behavior. Three considerations increase our confidence in the possibility of drawing inferences, however. (1) Only first- and second-generation Poles and Czechs are counted as such by the Census, but third- and fourth-generation Poles and Czechs tend to live in the same wards and towns; thus the proportion of the electorate sharing Polish-Czech cultural values (the relevant thing from our standpoint) is con-

siderably larger than the Census figures suggest. (2) When other factors are held constant, even small increases in the number of Poles and Czechs are accompanied by increases in the "No" vote; nothing "explains" this except the hypothesis that the Poles and Czechs make the difference. (3) When we take as the unit for analysis not wards but precincts of a few hundred persons that are known to contain very high proportions of Poles and Czechs, we get the same results. Because we are using ecological, not individual, data, we are perforce analyzing the behavior of ethnic "ghettos" where ethnic identification and attitudes are probably reinforced. Poles in non-Polish wards, for example, may behave quite differently.

10. The same method by which these precincts were selected is given in the Appendix. Unfortunately, it proved impossible to identify relatively homogeneous precincts typical of other ethnic groups at various income levels and degrees of home-ownership. For example, middle-income Jews tend to be renters, not home-owners, and there are practically no low-income Jewish precincts in either city. A complete list of these precincts is available from the authors.

11. *Cf.* Anthony Downs, "The Public Interest: Its Meaning in a Democracy," *Social Research*, 29 (Spring 1962), pp. 28–29.

12. The proposition that "subculture" can be defined in ethnic and income terms is highly provisional. We are looking for other and better criteria and we think we may find some. But so far as the present data are concerned, ethnic and income status are all we have.

13. Two other explanations are possible and, in our opinion, plausible. One is that the low-income renters may have taken into account costs to them other than taxes—e.g., the cost (perhaps monetary) of changes in the neighborhood that would ensue from expenditures. (Irish objections to urban renewal in Chicago may have been due, not to a fear of higher taxes, but to fear of neighborhood "invasion" by Negroes displaced from land clearance projects.) The other is that in these precincts a much higher proportion of renters than of home-owners may have stayed away from the polls. In Cleveland (though not, interestingly, in Chicago) voter turnout is highly correlated with home ownership and almost all white renter precincts have at least a few home-owners in them. Conceivably—we think it unlikely—all those who voted in some "renter" precincts were actually owners.

WHO RIOTS?
Robert M. Fogelson and Robert B. Hill

1. *Report of the National Advisory Commission on Civil Disorders* (N.Y.: Bantam Books, March, 1968), Chapter 5 (hereafter referred to as the *Kerner Report*); Robert M. Fogelson, "Violence as Protest," *Urban Riots: Violence and Social Change*, Proceedings of the Academy of Political Science, XXIX, 1 (July 1968); Elliott M. Rudwick, *Race Riot at East St. Louis, July 2, 1917* (Carbondale, Illinois, 1964); Arthur Waskow, *From Race Riot to Sit-In* (Garden City, New York, 1966).

2. New York *Times*, June 30, July 12, 16, 19, 20, 22, 24–28, 1967.

3. Robert M. Fogelson, "White on Black: A Critique of the McCone Commission Report on the Los Angeles Riots," *Political Science Quarterly*, LXXXII, 3 (September 1967), p. 342.

4. New York *Times*, July 16, 20, 22, 26, 1967; New York *Times*, July 22, August 4, 1964; Newark *Evening News*, July 20, 1964; New York *Journal-American*, July 26, 1964. Some officials, like former Detroit police chief Ray Girardin, rejected the riffraff theory.

5. The 5,637 Negro arrestees in Detroit, themselves, constituted 1.2 per cent of the city-wide nonwhite population. Similarly, the 1,387 Negro arrestees in Newark were 1.0 per cent of the nonwhite population in the city.

6. Caplan and Paige in *Kerner Report*, fn. 112, p. 172.

7. Harry M. Scoble, "The McCone Commission and Social Science," (August 1966), unpublished paper written for the U.S. Office of Economic Opportunity; and Fogelson, "White on Black," p. 345.

8. *Kerner Report*, p. 113.

9. In his survey on riot participation in the Rochester riots of 1964, Schulman defined the "riot eligible" population as persons from 11 to 50 years old. We have used a slightly wider age range to define "potential rioters" than he did. Our data reveal that only one-tenth of one per cent of riot arrestees are less than 10 years old and only one per cent are 60 years and older. The census data indicate that about 27 per cent of the nonwhite residents in the riot areas are under 10 years old, whereas about 8 per cent of these residents are over 59 years old. Thus, we are subtracting about 35 per cent of the total nonwhite population in the riot areas from the base figures in our computations. The remaining 65 per cent constitute the "potential rioters." See Jay Schulman, "Ghetto Residence, Political Alienation and Riot Orientation," *Urban Disorders, Violence and Urban Victimization*, L. Masotti, ed. (Sage Publishers, July 1968) fn. 10, p. 32.

10. U.S. Bureau of the Census. *U.S. Censuses of Population and Housing: 1960. Census Tracts.* U.S. Government Printing Office, Washington, D.C. 1962. All of these figures are based on 1960 U.S. Census statistics because these are the only figures available by

census tracts. The census tracts that make up the riot area for the six cities are as follows: Cincinnati, Final Report PHC (1)–27, 19 tracts: 3, 8, 11, 14, 15, 21, 23, 34–39, 41, 66–68, 77, 86–B; Dayton, Final Report PHC (1)–36, one tract: 0008–1A; Detroit, Final Report PHC(1)–40, 74, tracts: 11–16, 20, 24, 28, 31–33, 40, 42, 120, 121, 151–157, 161–165, 167–169, 176–A, 176–N, 176–C, 176–D, 177–189, 211, 212, 301–B, 519, 525, 530–533, 545, 551–559, 759–764, 793; Grand Rapids, Final Report PHC(1)–55, 3 tracts: 23–25; New Haven, Final Report PHC(1)–102, 4 tracts: 6, 7, 15, 22; and Newark, Final Report PHC(1)–105, 22 tracts: 29–32, 37–40, 53, 55–57, 59, 61–67, 81–82.

11. Caplan and Paige in the *Kerner Report*, fn. 115, p. 172.

12. These ratios provide estimates of the proportions of the rioters not apprehended by the police. In Detroit, for example, two-thirds of the rioters escaped apprehension, whereas in Newark 80 per cent of the rioters were estimated to have avoided arrest. Caplan and Paige in the *Kerner Report*, fn. 112, p. 172.

13. For 1965 estimates of the Negro population in various cities, see *Kerner Report*, p. 248.

14. Because of their smaller Negro populations, the smaller communities have a higher per cent of residents who rioted than the larger communities; this result is partly due to the mathematical artifact of having a smaller base figure. The greater severity of the riot in the larger communities is undoubtedly due to the fact that although a small percentage of the populace rioted, the absolute number of rioters was extremely large.

15. Korn and McCorkle, *Criminology and Penology*. New York: Holt, Rinehart and Winston, 1959).

16. Caplan and Paige in the *Kerner Report*, pp. 172–175.

17. Korn and McCorkle, *Criminology and Penology*, pp. 23–24.

18. David O. Sears, "Riot Activity and Evaluation: An Overview of the Negro Survey" (1966), Table 4.

19. Governor's Select Commission on Civil Disorder, State of New Jersey, *Report for Action*, February 1968 (hereinafter referred to as *N.J. Riot Report*), p. 271.

20. The Detroit figures were obtained from "Unemployment in 15 Metropolitan Areas," *Monthly Labor Review*, 91: (January, 1968), v–vi; the Newark unemployment figures were obtained from *N.J. Riot Report*, p. 271.

21. Of course, our unemployment statistics are not really comparable to the U.S. Census' unemployment statistics since different criteria for inclusion are employed. All males 18 years and over who said that they were not working were classified as "unemployed." Whenever

possible, full-time students were excluded. But even the Bureau of Labor Statistics criteria for estimating unemployment rates are being challenged by some observers. In a door-to-door survey of three Chicago poverty areas, it was found that an "actual" unemployment rate for these areas was more than a third higher than it would have been under the definition of joblessness used by the BLS. See "New Jobless Count Ups the Figure," *Business Week*, Dec. 10, 1966, pp. 160–162. Also *Kerner Report*, p. 257.

22. Many of the Negroes with previous arrest records, technically, were not even arrested; as many were picked up for suspicious conduct and then later released. This is particularly true in the case of juveniles, many of whom were brought to the police station, but not arrested. Therefore, in many cases we are really referring to previous "contact records" and not actual arrest records. The percentage for Dayton is higher than it ought to be; it resulted from an ambiguity in the coding instructions for that city.

23. For nationwide estimates of the prevalence of arrest records, see President's Commission on Law Enforcement, *The Challenge of Crime*, p. 75 and R. Christensen, "Projected Percentages of U.S. Population with Criminal Arrest and Conviction Records" (August 18, 1966), report paper for the Commission. See also Jerry Cohen and William S. Murphy, *Burn, Baby, Burn* (New York, 1966), p. 208.

24. Eighty per cent of the "typical" felons in Washington (who are 80 per cent Negro) have previous arrest records whereas only 60 per cent of the riot arrestees (who are 90 per cent Negro) have previous arrest (or "contact") records. About 50 per cent of the typical felons are unemployed, whereas only half as many (26 per cent) riot arrestees are unemployed. Furthermore, the typical felons more often have unstable marital relationships than riot arrestees; about 27 per cent of the typical felons are either separated, widowed or divorced, while only 7 per cent of the riot arrestees are either separated, widowed or divorced. Many of these differences are probably due to the age disparity between the two groups; the average age of the typical felon in Washington is 29 years old, whereas the average age of the riot arrestee is about 25 years old. See the *President's Commission on Crime in the District of Columbia*, Chapter 3.

25. Bureau of Criminal Statistics, California Department of Criminal Justice, "Watts Riots Arrests: Los Angeles, August, 1965." (June 30, 1966), p. 37.

26. Altogether about 95 per cent of the 1967 arrestees were residents of the city in which the disorders took place; 4 per cent were residents of other cities within that state and only one per cent were residents of other states. Thus, the assertion that the riots were primarily the

work of out-of-towners or out-of-state agitators appears to be without empirical foundation. In fact, most of the rioters were not only residents of the riot city, but also were long-term residents of the city. See the *Kerner Report*, p.131.

27. Federal Bureau of Investigation, *Report on the 1964 Riots* (September 18, 1964), p. 9; *Kerner Report*, Chapter 2.

28. F.B.I., "Report on the 1964 Riots," pp. 5–6.

29. New York *Times*, July 27, 1967.

30. Fogelson, "Violence as Protest," p. 1.

31. New York *Times*, July 14–18, 26–29, August 1, 2, 7, 10, 11, 16, 1967.

32. William Brink and Louis Harris, *Black and White* (New York: Simon and Schuster, 1967), pp. 184–279; Hazel Erskine, "The Polls: Demonstrations and Race Riots," *Public Opinion Quarterly*, XXXI, 4 (Winter 1967–68), pp. 655–677; Sears, "Riot Activity." Schulman, "Ghetto Residence."

33. Frank Besag, *The Anatomy of a Riot: Buffalo, 1967* (Buffalo: State University of N.Y. Press, 1967), pp. 138–139, 180–181, 188–190.

34. Sears, "Riot Activity," table 35; Schulman, "Ghetto Residence," pp. 23–24, tables 5, 5.1.

35. Brink and Harris, *Black and White*, Appendix D, p. 264, question 18(f); p. 260, question 18(a); p. 266, question 18(h); Erskine, "The Polls," p. 671.

36. Sears, "Riot Activity," table 17.

37. Brink and Harris, *Black and White*, Appendix D, p. 264, question 18(f).

38. McCone Archives, XV, Interview 29; XVI, Interview 90; *Anatomy of a Riot*, pp. 138–139, 188–189.

39. Brink and Harris, *Black and White*, p. 266, question 18(i).

WHO CAN ACTIVATE THE POOR? ONE ASSESSMENT OF "MAXIMUM FEASIBLE PARTICIPATION"

Warner Bloomberg, Jr. and Florence W. Rosenstock

1. This is a revised version of a paper originally presented to the joint session on "Poverty and Progress" of the American Sociological Association and the Society for the Study of Social Problems, San Francisco, August 29, 1967.

2. Elinor Graham, "The Politics of Poverty" and "Poverty and the Legislative Process," in Ben B. Seligman (ed.), *Poverty as a Public Issue* (New York: Free Press, 1965), pp. 231–271.

3. Warner Bloomberg, Jr., "Community Organization," in Howard S. Becker (ed.), *Social Problems: A Modern Approach* (New York: John Wiley and Sons, 1966), pp. 387–390.

4. Robert A. Dahl, *Who Governs?* (New Haven: Yale University Press, 1961).

5. James N. Morgan, M. H. David, W. J. Cohen and H. E. Brazer, *Income and Welfare in the United States* (New York: McGraw-Hill, 1962); Philip Sokol, "Providing for the Dependent," in R. M. MacIver (ed.), *The Assault on Poverty: and Individual Responsibility* (New York: Harper and Row, 1965), pp. 9–19; and Joseph Zeisel, "A Profile of Unemployment," in Stanley Lebergott (ed.) *Men Without Work* (Englewood Cliffs, N.J.: Prentice-Hall, 1964), pp. 115–129.

6. Saul Alinsky, *Reveille for Radicals* (Chicago: University of Chicago Press, 1946); Saul Alinsky, "From Citizen Apathy to Participation," paper presented at the Sixth Annual Fall Conference, Association of Community Councils of Chicago, October 19, 1957 (Chicago: Industrial Areas Foundation, 1957); Saul Alinsky "Citizen Participation and Community Organization in Planning and Urban Renewal," paper presented to Chicago Chapter of the National Association of Housing and Redevelopment Officials, January 29, 1962 (Chicago: Industrial Areas Foundation, 1962); Saul Alinsky and Marion K. Sanders, "The Professional Radical," *Harper's*, 230 (June 1965), pp. 37–47; Saul Alinsky and Marion K. Sanders, "A Professional Radical Moves in on Rochester," *Harper's*, 231 (July 1965), pp. 22–29; Patrick Anderson, "Making Trouble is Alinsky's Business," *New York Times Magazine*, 6 (October 9, 1966), p. 28; Warren C. Haggstrom, "The Power of the Poor," in F. Riessman, J. Cohen, and A. Pearl (eds.), *Mental Health of the Poor* (New York: Free Press, 1964), pp. 205–223; Frank Riessman, "A Comparison of Two Social Action Approaches: Saul Alinsky and the New Student Left," unpublished manuscript (Mimeographed, 1965); Frank Riessman, "Self-Help Among the Poor: New Styles of Social Action," *Transaction* (September/October 1966), pp. 32–37; Dan Wakefield, *Revolt in the South* (New York: Grove Press, 1960).

7. Clarence King, *Working With People in Community Action* (New York: Associated Press, 1965); Murray G. Ross, *Community Organization* (2nd ed.; New York: Harper and Row, 1967); Carl C. Taylor, "Community Development Programs and Methods," *Community Development Review*, International Cooperation Administration, Washington D.C. No. 2 (December 1956), pp. 34–42; United Nations, *Social Progress Through Community Development* (New York: United Nations, 1955).

8. Riessman, "A Comparison . . . Student Left" (1965).

IV:
INTRODUCTION

1. This distinction is elaborated further in Terry N. Clark, ed., *Community Structure and Decision-Making: Comparative Analyses* (San Francisco: Chandler, 1968), pp. 45ff.

2. (Chapel Hill: University of North Carolina Press, 1953).

3. Edward C. Banfield, *Political Influence* (New York: The Free Press, 1961) and Robert A. Dahl, *Who Governs?* (New Haven: Yale University Press, 1961).

4. For another analysis of the same data, see Terry N. Clark, William Kornblum, Harold Bloom, and Susan Tobias, "Discipline, Method, Community Structure and Decision-Making: The Role and Limitation of the Sociology of Knowledge," *The American Sociologist*, 3 (August 1968), pp. 214–217.

COMMUNITY LEADERSHIP: DIRECTIONS OF RESEARCH
Charles M. Bonjean and David M. Olson

1. See, for example, Robert S. Lynd and Helen Merrell Lynd, *Middletown in Transition* (New York, 1937); W. Lloyd Warner *et al.*, *Democracy in Jonesville* (New York, 1949); August B. Hollingshead, *Elmstown's Youth* (New York, 1949); Christopher Smith, Social Selection in Community Leadership, *Social Forces*, 15 (1937), 530–535; and James E. White, Theory and Method for Research in Community Leadership, *American Sociological Review*, 15 (1950), 50–60. Investigations incorporating this assumption at the national level may be found in Wendell Bell, Richard J. Hill, and Charles R. Wright, *Public Leadership* (San Francisco, 1961), 6–13.

2. George S. Counts, *School and Society in Chicago* (New York, 1928).

3. Floyd Hunter, *Community Power Structure* (Chapel Hill, N.C., 1953), p. 82.

4. The studies have been too numerous to cite here in a single footnote. Most of those published in monograph or book form or reported in the major journals will be cited in footnotes below.

5. For example, Robert A. Dahl, A Critique of the Ruling Elite Model, *American Political Science Review*, 52 (1958), 463–469; Herbert Kaufman and Victor Jones, The Mystery of Power, *Public Administration Review*, 14 (1954), 205–212; Nelson Polsby, The Sociology of Community Power: A Reassessment, *Social Forces*, 37 (1959), 232–236; Raymond E. Wolfinger, Reputation and Reality in the Study of Community Power, *American Sociological Review*, 25 (1960), 636–644; Peter H.

Rossi, Community Decision Making, *Administrative Science Quarterly*, 1 (1957), 415–443; Nelson Polsby, *Community Power and Political Theory* (New Haven, 1963); Lawrence J. R. Herson, In the Footsteps of Community Power, *American Political Science Review*, 55 (1961), 817–830; Peter Bachrach and Morton S. Baratz, Two Faces of Power, *American Political Science Review*, 56 (1962), 947–952; Peter Bachrach and Morton S. Baratz, Decisions and Non-decisions: An Analytical Framework, *American Political Science Review*, 57 (1963), 632–642; Thomas J. Anton, Power, Pluralism, and Local Politics, *Administrative Science Quarterly*, 7 (1963), 425–457; and Morris Janowitz, Community Power and "Policy Science" Research, *Public Opinion Quarterly*, 26 (1962), 398–410.

6. Bell, Hill, and Wright, *op. cit.*, pp. 21–23, look at the "social participation approach" as a method distinct from the positional approach. Since, in most cases, participation involves occupying positions such as those described above (as well as less important positions such as "member" in an association or organization), the social participation approach is regarded here as simply a variation of the positional approach.

7. White, *op. cit.*, 54.

8. Studies that have used this technique exclusively or in combination with other techniques include those listed in n. 1 above as well as Robert O. Schulze and Leonard U. Blumberg, The Determination of Local Power Elites, *American Journal of Sociology*, 63 (1957), 290–296; Charles Freeman and Selz C. Mayo, Decision Makers in Rural Community Action, *Social Forces*, 35 (1957), 319–322; Robert O. Schulze, The Role of Economic Dominants in Community Power Structure, *American Sociological Review*, 23 (1958), 3–9; and M. Kent Jennings, Public Administrators and Community Decision Making, *Administrative Science Quarterly*, 8 (1963), 18–43.

9. Wallace S. Sayre and Herbert Kaufman, *Governing New York City* (New York, 1960).

10. Gladys M. Kammerer, Charles D. Farris, John M. DeGrove, and Alfred B. Clubok, *The Urban Political Community* (Boston, 1963).

11. Charles R. Adrian, A Study of Three Communities, *Public Administration Review*, 18 (1958), 208–213.

12. White, *op. cit.*

13. Studies lending at least some support to this hypothesis include White, *op. cit.;* Freeman and Mayo, *op. cit.;* Robert A. Dahl, *Who Governs?* (New Haven, 1961); Richard Laskin, *Leadership of Voluntary Organizations in a Saskatchewan Town* (Saskatoon, Saskatchewan, 1962); M. Elaine Burgess, *Negro Leadership in a Southern City* (Chapel Hill, N.C., 1960); Arthur J. Vidich and Joseph Bensman, *Small Town in Mass Society* (Garden City, N.Y., 1958); and Benjamin Walter, "Political Decision Making in Arcadia," in F. Stuart Chapin,

Dynamics (New York, 1962), 141–187. Data clearly contradicting this hypothesis may be found in Hunter, *op. cit.*; Schulze and Blumberg, *op. cit.*; Schulze, *op. cit.*; Robert Presthus, *Men at the Top: A Study in Community Power* (New York, 1964); and Charles M. Bonjean, Community Leadership: A Case Study and Conceptual Refinement, *American Journal of Sociology*, 68 (1963), 672–681.

14. Richard Laskin and Serena Phillett, "Formal Versus Reputational Leadership" (paper read at the annual meeting of the Pacific Sociological Association, Portland, Ore., April 1963).

15. Richard Laskin and Serena Phillett, "Formal Versus Reputational Leadership Identification: A Re-evaluation" (paper read at the annual meeting of the Pacific Sociological Association, San Diego, Cal., March 1964).

16. Charles M. Bonjean, "Community Leadership: A Conceptual Refinement and Comparative Analysis" (unpublished Ph.D. dissertation, University of North Carolina, 1963).

17. See, for example, August B. Hollingshead, *op. cit.*, and W. Lloyd Warner *et al.*, *op. cit.*

18. Among those investigations that have used the reputational approach exclusively or in combination with another approach are Hunter, *op. cit.*; Schulze and Blumberg, *op. cit.*; Schulze, *op. cit.*; Jennings, *op. cit.*; Laskin, *op. cit.*; Burgess, *op. cit.*; Presthus, *op. cit.*; Bonjean, *op. cit.*; Ernest A. T. Barth and Baha Abu-Laban, Power Structure and the Negro Sub-Community, *American Sociological Review*, 24 (1959), 69–76; William H. Form and William V. D'Antonio, Integration and Cleavage Among Community Influentials in Two Border Cities, *American Sociological Review*, 24 (1959), 804–814; William V. D'Antonio, William H. Form, Charles P. Loomis, and Eugene C. Erickson, Institutional and Occupational Representations in Eleven Community Influence Systems, *American Sociological Review*, 26 (1961), 440–446; A. Alexander Fanelli, A Typology of Community Leadership Based on Influence and Interaction Within the Leader Subsystem, *Social Forces*, 34 (1956), 332–338; Orrin E. Klapp and L. Vincent Padgett, Power Structure and Decision Making in a Mexican Border City, *American Journal of Sociology*, 65 (1960); 400–406; Delbert C. Miller, Industry and Community Power Structure: A Comparative Study of an American and an English City, *American Sociological Review*, 23 (1958), 9–15; Roland J. Pellegrin and Charles H. Coates, Absentee Owned Corporations and Community Power Structures, *American Journal of Sociology*, 61 (1956), 413–419; Ivan Belknap and John G. Steinle, *The Community and Its Hospitals* (Syracuse, N.Y., 1963); Robert E. Agger and Daniel Goldrich, Community Power Structures and

Partisanship, *American Sociological Review*, 23 (1958), 383–392; David A. Booth and Charles R. Adrian, Power Structures and Community Change, *Midwest Journal of Political Science*, 6 (1962), 277–296; Carol Thometz, *The Decision-Makers* (Dallas, Tex., 1963); George Belknap and Ralph Smuckler, Political Power Relations in a Mid-West City, *Public Opinion Quarterly*, 20 (1956), 73–80; and Harry Scoble, "Leadership Hierarchies and Political Issues in a New England Town," in Morris Janowitz, ed., *Community Political Systems* (Glencoe, Ill., 1961), pp. 117–145. Contrary to a common assumption, a number of political scientists are represented in this group of researchers using the reputational approach.

19. William V. D'Antonio and Howard J. Ehrlich, eds., *Power and Democracy in America* (Notre Dame, Ind., 1961), 92 ff. and 132 ff. See also, Wolfinger, *op. cit.*, and Raymond E. Wolfinger, A Plea for a Decent Burial, *American Sociological Review*, 27 (1962), 841–847.

20. Howard J. Ehrlich, The Reputational Approach to the Study of Community Power, *American Sociological Review*, 26 (1961), 926. See also William V. D'Antonio, Howard J. Ehrlich, and Eugene C. Erickson, Further Notes on the Study of Community Power, *American Sociological Review*, 27 (1962), 848–854.

21. See, for example, Polsby, *Community Power and Political Theory;* Wolfinger, Reputation; Dahl, Critique; and Rossi, *op. cit.*

22. Rossi, *op. cit.*

23. See, for example, Presthus, *op. cit.*, p. 443 and p. 451. One typology that could be incorporated in reputational analyses has been set forth by Ernest A. T. Barth and Stuart D. Johnson, Community Power and a Typology of Social Issues, *Social Forces*, 38 (1959), 29–32.

24. See, for example, Presthus, *op. cit.*; Scoble, *op. cit.*; and Thometz, *op. cit.*

25. See, for example, Nelson W. Polsby, Three Problems in the Analysis of Community Power, *American Sociological Review*, 24 (1959), 796–803; Dahl, Critique; and Wolfinger, Reputation.

26. See, for example, Bonjean, *op. cit.*, and Robert O. Schulze, "The Bifurcation of Power in a Satellite City," in Janowitz, ed., *Community Political Systems*, 50–53.

27. See, in particular, Wolfinger, Reputation; Charles M. Bonjean, in Class, Status and Power Reputation, *Sociology and Social Research* 49 (1964), 69–75, has also noted that some informants may confuse power with class and status characteristics.

28. Wolfinger, Reputation.

29. *Ibid.*

30. Hunter, *op. cit.*, and Miller, *op. cit.*

31. Booth and Adrian, *op. cit.*

32. Investigations that have used this approach include Dahl, *Who Governs?*; Warner Bloomberg, Jr. and Morris Sunshine, *Suburban Power Structures and Public Education* (Syracuse, N.Y., 1963); Burgess, *op. cit.*; Walter, *op. cit.*; Presthus, *op. cit.*; and Roscoe C. Martin, *et al.*, *Decisions in Syracuse* (Bloomington, Ind., 1961).

33. Burgess, *op. cit.*, pp. 5–6 and Appendix B.

34. Presthus, *op. cit.*, pp. 59–60 and 231.

35. Burgess, *op. cit.*, p. 6.

36. Dahl, *Who Governs?*, p. vi.

37. Barth and Johnson, *op. cit.*

38. Edward C. Banfield and James Q. Wilson, *City Politics* (Cambridge, Mass., 1963), 248–250.

39. Bachrach and Baratz, Two Faces, and Decisions; and Anton, *op. cit.*, 453–455.

40. Dahl, *Who Governs?*, chs. i–vii; Schulze, "The Bifurcation"; and Booth and Adrian, *op. cit.*

41. For example, Burgess, *op. cit.*, used all three techniques; Belknap and Steinle, *op. cit.*, used both the positional and the reputational; Presthus, *op. cit.*, used all three; Bloomberg and Sunshine, *op. cit.*, used all three; and Delbert C. Miller, Town and Gown: The Power Structure of a University Town, *American Journal of Sociology*, 68 (1963), 432–443, used both the reputational and event analysis approaches.

42. Linton C. Freeman, Thomas J. Fararo, Warner Bloomberg, Jr., and Morris Sunshine, Locating Leaders in Local Communities: A Comparison of Some Alternative Approaches, *American Sociological Review*, 28 (1963), 791–798.

43. Hunter, *op. cit.*

44. Walter, *op. cit.*, 186.

45. See, for example, Hunter, *op. cit.*, especially chs. i and ix.

46. Especially Dahl, Critique; and Kaufman and Jones, *op. cit.*

47. For a more complete discussion of constructive typology and its role in social research see John T. Doby, ed., *An Introduction to Social Research* (Harrisburg, Pa., 1954), 139–198.

48. Robert Redfield, The Folk Society, *American Journal of Sociology*, 52 (1947), 293–308.

49. Eugene Litwak, Models of Bureaucracy Which Permit Conflict, *American Journal of Sociology*, 67 (1961), 177–184.

50. Good starts in this direction have been made by William H. Form and Delbert C. Miller, *Industry, Labor and Community* (New York, 1960), 538–543; by Dahl, *Who Governs?*, 184–189; and by Roscoe Martin *et al.*, *op. cit.*, 10–12.

51. "Political formula" includes the system of beliefs and values which legitimize the democratic (or any other) system and specify the institutions (such as political parties, a free press, etc.) which allow for the distribution of power. See Seymour Martin Lipset, *Political Man* (New York, 1960), chs. ii and iii.

52. The types are suggested by Dahl, *Who Governs?*

53. Laskin and Phillett, *op. cit.*, have noted that it may be meaningful to chart formal leadership not only at the time of the study but also for several preceding years as well, because there may be a time lag of a few years between one's emergence as an organizational officer and his earning a general reputation for influence in the community.

54. For further elaboration see Bonjean, *op. cit.*, and Serena Phillett, "An Analysis of Community Influence: Some Conceptual and Methodological Considerations" (unpublished M.A. thesis, University of Alberta, Edmonton, Canada, 1963).

55. William V. D'Antonio and Eugene C. Erickson, The Reputational Technique as a Measure of Community Power: An Evaluation Based on Comparative and Longitudinal Studies, *American Sociological Review*, 27 (1962), 373–374.

56. See ns. 23 and 38.

57. For a discussion of the ratio of interest and other statistics of social configuration, see J. L. Moreno, ed., *The Sociometry Reader* (Glencoe, Ill., 1960), 19–51.

58. Scoble, *op. cit.*

59. Schulze, "The Bifurcation," p. 51.

60. See Rossi, *op. cit.*, 436–437, and Herbert Kaufman, The Next Step in Case Studies, *Public Administration Review*, 18 (1958), 52–59.

61. Miller, *op. cit.*, 13–15.

62. D'Antonio, *et al.*, Institutional and Occupational Representations, 442.

63. Schulze, "The Bifurcation."

64. Donald A. Clelland and William H. Form, Economic Dominants and Community Power: A Comparative Analysis, *American Journal of Sociology*, 69 (1964), 511–521.

65. Presthus, *op. cit.*, 423–424.

66. John Wahlke, Heinz Eulau, William Buchanan and LeRoy C. Ferguson, *The Legislative System* (New York, 1962).

67. Adrian, *op. cit.*; Gladys M. Kammerer and J. M. DeGrove, Urban Leadership During Change, *The Annals*, 353 (1964), 95–106; Gladys M. Kammerer, Role Diversity of City Managers, *Administrative Science Quarterly*, 8 (1964), 421–442; Karl A. Bosworth, The Manager *Is* a Politician, *Public Administration Review*, 18 (1958), 216–222; and Jennings, *op. cit.*

68. Edward C. Banfield, *Political Influence* (Glencoe, Ill., 1961).

69. Rossi, *op. cit.*

70. James S. Coleman, *Community Conflict* (Glencoe, Ill, 1957), found that voter turnout

and referendum defeats were positively correlated (p. 19).

71. Scoble, *op. cit.*, 136–138.

72. Christen T. Jonassen and Sherwood H.
Peres, *Inter-relationships of Dimensions of
Community Systems: A Factor Analysis of
Eighty-two Variables* (Columbus, Ohio, 1960).

73. Charles M. Bonjean, "Legitimacy and
Visibility: Influence Structure Characteristics
Related to Four Community Systems" (paper
read at the annual meeting of the Society for
the Study of Social Problems, Montreal,
Canada, August 1964).

74. Presthus, *op. cit.*, 413.

75. *Ibid.*, 413–414.

76. *Ibid.*, 415.

77. Belknap and Steinle, *op. cit.*, ch. viii.

78. Hunter, *op. cit.*, 198.

79. Ralph E. Dakin, Variations in Power
Structures and Organizing Efficiency: A
Comparative Study of Four Areas, *Sociological
Quarterly*, 3 (1962), 228–250.

80. Dakin's measure of organizing efficiency
was based on the amount of time it takes to
organize a given number of people.

81. Banfield, *op. cit.*, ch. xii, and Roscoe
Martin *et al.*, *op. cit.*, ch. xiv.

POWER AND COMMUNITY STRUCTURE: WHO GOVERNS, WHERE AND WHEN?
Terry N. Clark

1. Floyd Hunter, *Community Power Structure* (Chapel Hill: Univ. of North Carolina
Press, 1953). The degree to which Hunter's
formulations should be referred to as "power
elitist" will not be considered here.

2. For two important critiques of the study
see Herbert Kaufman and Victor Jones,
"The Mystery of Power," *Public Administration
Review*, 14:205–212 (1954); and Robert A.
Dahl, "A Critique of the Ruling Elite Model."
American Political Science Review, 52:463–469
(1958).

3. Robert A. Dahl, *Who Governs?* (New
Haven, Conn.: Yale Univ. Press, 1961).

4. It should perhaps be pointed out that we
are not referring here simply to typologies of
communities in terms of their power structures,
for several of this sort exist—most ranging from
monolithic to pluralistic ends of a continuum,
although these two specific terms are not
universally employed. And more important,
these typologies for the most part have not
influenced general thinking about community
power or the majority of empirical studies.
What is lacking is a typology permitting a
broader classification of communities into a
series of general types, considering communities in terms of some of their demographic,
economic, political, and other structural
characteristics. These problems are investigated

further in Terry N. Clark (ed.), *Community
Structure and Decision-Making: Comparative
Analyses* (San Francisco: Chandler, 1968).

5. For a brief exposition of AGIL, see
Talcott Parsons, "An Outline of the Social
System," in Talcott Parsons, Edward Shils,
Kasper D. Naegele, and Jesse R. Pitts, *Theories
of Society* (New York: The Free Press of
Glencoe; 1961), 1:30–79.

6. See Terry N. Clark, "Community or
Communities? A Dilemma for Studies of
Community Power," *Kansas Journal of Soci-
ology*, Winter, 1967, Vol. 3, No. 1, pp. 1–11.

7. The relationships between decision-making
patterns and outputs are investigated in more
detail in Clark, *Community Structure and
Decision-Making: Comparative Analyses*.

8. See Carl G. Hempel, *Fundamentals of
Concept Formation in Empirical Science* (Chica-
go: Univ. Press, 1952); Hans L. Zetterberg,
On Theory and Verification in Sociology, rev. ed.
(Totowa, N.J.: The Bedminster Press, 1963).
Five "General Formulations," from which
many of the following propositions may be
derived, are presented in Clark, *Community
Structure and Decision-Making: Comparative
Analyses*.

9. See Zetterberg, *op. cit.*, pp. 11–34, for a
discussion on types of propositions and patterns
of interrelationships.

10. See note 36 for a qualification of this
proposition.

11. See Form and Miller, *op. cit.*, in *n.* 50,
p. 348); David Rogers, "Community Political
Systems," in E. Swanson (ed.), *Current Trends in
Comparative Community Studies* (Kansas City,
Mo.: Community Studies, 1962), p. 47;
Bradbury Seasholes, "Patterns of Influence in
Metropolitan Boston," in Swanson, *op. cit.*,
p. 67; Robert Presthus, *Men At The Top*
(New York: Oxford Univ. Press, 1964), p. 412;
James S. Coleman, *Community Conflict* (Glen-
coe, Ill., The Free Press, 1957), p. 16. A recent
study of eleven communities using primarily
the reputational method to identify leaders
found no decrease in the percentage of businessmen among the "top decision makers" as size
of community increased. William V. D'Antonio,
William H. Form, Charles P. Loomis, Eugene
C. Erickson, "Institutional and Occupational
Representations in Eleven Community Influence
Systems," *American Sociological Review*, 26:
440–446 (1961). Robert E. Agger, Daniel
Goldrich, and Bert E. Swanson, *The Rulers
and the Ruled* (New York: Wiley, 1964), in a
study of four communities varying in size (one
under 2,000, one 10,000, and two approximately 100,000 inhabitants) found no relationship between size and type of power structure
(see pp. 682–683).

12. More recent studies based on larger
samples have, however, found substantial

support for the proposition. See the article by Claire W. Gilbert in Clark, *Community Structure and Decision-Making: Comparative Analyses*; and Terry N. Clark, "Community Structure, Decision-Making, Budget Expenditures and Urban Renewal in 51 American Communities" (selection 28 in this volume). Several other propositions which follow were supported by one or both of these studies.

13. Coleman, *op. cit.*, p. 16.

14. A cross-cutting status-set refers to a social structural situation where two or more persons occupy one or more *common* statuses, but they include a number of *differing* statuses in their status-sets as well. The cross-cutting status-set is thus a specifically *sociological* concept that is not to be confused with the closely related social psychological concept of cross pressure. The cross-cutting status-set must also be distinguished from the narrower concept of interlocking membership. An interlocking membership refers only to common *organizational* statuses and neglects non-organizational statuses that may be even more important than many organizational ones—for example, age, sex, ethnic, and religious statuses. The concept of cross-cutting status-set has been derived by Robert K. Merton in lectures at Columbia University. It grows out of his analysis of status-sets that may be found in *Social Theory and Social Structure* (Glencoe, Ill., The Free Press, 1957), pp. 368–386. See Paul F. Lazarsfeld, Bernard Berelson, and Hazel Gaudet, *The People's Choice* (New York: Columbia Univ. Press, 1944), pp. 52–64, for a classic analysis of cross pressures on voting behavior; and Coleman, *op. cit.*, for a discussion of the effect of cross pressures on community conflict.

15. Coleman, *op. cit.*

16. If some of the propositions about cross-cutting status-sets do not seem entirely consistent with one another, the reader should refer to the discussion in the section on political parties and voluntary organizations here.

17. This proposition is found, for example, in C. Wright Mills and Melville Ulmer, "Small Business and Civic Welfare," *The Report of the Smaller War Plants Corporation*, U.S. Senate Document No. 135, 79th Congress, 2nd Session (Washington, D.C.: U.S. Government Printing Office, 1946); Form and Miller, *op. cit.*, p. 504; Peter H. Rossi, "Theory Research and Practice in Community Organization," in Charles R. Adrian (ed.), *Social Science and Community Action* (East Lansing, Mich.: Michigan State University, 1960), pp. 20–21; Maurice R. Stein, *The Eclipse of Community* (Princeton, N.J.: Princeton Univ. Press, 1960), pp. 94ff.

18. Similar statements as well as empirical examples are found in Mills and Ulmer, *op. cit.*,

W. Lloyd Warner and J. O. Low, *The Social System of the Modern Factory* (New Haven, Conn.: Yale Univ. Press, 1947); Robert O. Schulze, "The Role of Economic Dominants in Community Power Structure," *American Sociological Review*, 13:3–9 (1958); and in more detail in Schulze, "The Bifurcation in a Satellite City," in Morris Janowitz, ed., *Community Political Systems* (New York: The Free Press, 1961); Peter H. Rossi, "The Organizational Structure of an American Community," in Amitai Etzioni (ed.), *Complex Organizations* (New York: Holt, Rinehart and Winston, 1961), pp. 301–312; Rossi, in Adrian, *op. cit.*, p. 21. For a review of evidence supporting this proposition, see Miller and Form, *op. cit.*, chap. 12; Robert E. Lane, *Political Life* (Glencoe, Ill., The Free Press: 1959), pp. 321ff.; David Rogers, "Community Political Systems: A Framework and Hypothesis for Comparative Studies," in Swanson, *op. cit.*; Agger, Goldrich, and Swanson, *op. cit.*, pp. 680–682.

19. Mills and Ulmer, *op. cit.*; Warner and Low, *op. cit.*; Schulze, in *ASR*, 13:3–9; and in Janowitz, *op. cit.*; Rossi, in Adrian, *op. cit.*

20. See Roland J. Pellegrin and Charles E. Coates, "Absentee-Owned Corporations and Community Power Structure," *American Journal of Sociology*, 61:413–417 (1956); Hunter, *op. cit.*; although the methodology of both studies may have biased the findings.

21. See Lane, *op. cit.*, for a review of crucial factors influencing political participation. Economic factors are the focus of chapter 21. Various patterns of involvement in decision-making are considered in Terry N. Clark, "The Concept of Power: Some Overemphasized and Underrecognized Dimensions," Selection 3 in this volume.

22. See C. W. M. Hart, "Industrial Relations Research and Social Theory," *Canadian Journal of Economics and Political Science*, 15:53–73 (1949); James B. McKee, "Organized Labor and Community Decision Making," unpublished doctoral dissertation, University of Wisconsin, 1953; William H. Form, "Organized Labor's Place in Community Power Structure," *Industrial Labor Relations Review*, 12:526–539 (1959); W. H. Form and Warren J. Sauer, "Organized Labor's Image of Community Power Structure, *Social Forces*, 38:332–341 (1960); Form and Miller, *op. cit.*, pp. 572–586; Charles R. Walker, *Steeltown* (New York: Harper, 1950).

23. Presthus, *op. cit.*, esp. chaps. 3 and 8.

24. For a discussion of a ship-building community dominated by the U.S. Navy during World War II, see Robert J. Havighurst and H. Gerthou Morgan, *The Social History of a War Boom Community* (London: Longmans, Green, 1951).

25. See Stein, *op. cit.*; Schulze, in *ASR*, 13:3, and in Janowitz, *op. cit.*; Rogers, in Swanson, *op. cit.*

26. See Edward C. Banfield and James Q.

Wilson, *City Politics* (Cambridge, Mass.: Harvard Univ. Press and M.I.T. Press, 1963), p. 151.

27. For discussions of the effects of non-partisanship, see Banfield and Wilson, *op. cit.*, chap. 12, and Seymour Martin Lipset, "Introduction: Ostrogorski and the Analytic Approach to the Comparative Study of Political Parties," in M. Ostrogorski, *Democracy and the Organization of Political Parties* (Garden City, N.Y.: Doubleday, 1964), pp. ix–xvii. Frank M. Steward offers a history of the National Municipal League, a group that was important in bringing about the acceptance of nonpartisan elections in American communities in the past half-century in *A Half Century of Municipal Reform* (Berkeley and Los Angeles: Univ. of California Press, 1950). See also Richard Hofstadter, *The Age of Reform* (New York: Knopf, 1965), esp. chap. 4.

28. Eugene Lee, *The Politics of Nonpartisanship* (Berkeley: Univ. of California Press, 1960), pp. 56–57.

29. Peter H. Rossi, "Power and Community Structure," *Midwest Journal of Political Science*, 4:390–400 (1960); Form and Miller (*op. cit.*, p. 505) and Rogers (in Swanson, *op. cit*), among others, have emphasized the importance of governmental autonomy for democratic government.

30. See, for example, Arthur J. Vidich and Joseph Bensman, *Small Town in Mass Society* (Princeton, N.J.: Princeton Univ. Press, 1958), and Oliver P. Williams and Charles R. Adrian, *Four Cities* (Philadelphia: Univ. of Pennsylvania Press, 1963). Both works offer perceptive analyses of the ideological support for weak governmental institutions found in American political mythology. See also Floyd Hunter, Ruth G. Schaffer, and Cecil G. Sheps, *Community Organization: Action and Inaction* (Chapel Hill: Univ. of North Carolina Press, 1956), esp. chaps. 3, 4, 7 and 13; and Harry Scoble, "Leadership Hierarchies and Political Issues in a New England Town," in Janowitz, *op. cit.*, pp. 117–145.

31. Some support is found in Albert Meister, *Socialisme et autogestion, l'experience yougoslave* (Paris: Seuil, 1964) and in unpublished materials by the author and William Kornblum concerning Yugoslav communes.

32. Examples of students of community power who have advanced this idea are Rossi, in *Midwest Jour. Pol. Sci.*, 4:394ff (1960); Robert C. Wood, *Suburbia* (Boston: Houghton Mifflin, 1958); and Rogers, in Swanson, *op. cit.*

33. Both Rossi and Wood have advanced similar assertions. See above, note 32.

34. See Dahl, *Who Governs?* pp. 32–61, for an account of the rise and fall of ethnic politics in New Haven.

35. Dahl reports such an example in *Who Governs?* pp. 192–199. Another case is reported in a town of 60,000, where a housewife was able to dislodge the party-supported candidate

and secure a position on the Board of Education by mobilizing the potential power bases available to most other individual residents of the community. See Alice H. Clark, "A Local School Board Election," unpublished manuscript. Another case where a housewife acting practically singlehandedly was able to bring to bear a great deal of influence on school redistricting in her community—Waukegan—and the rest of the state of Illinois, is examined in Terry N. Clark and James W. Wagner, Jr., "Community Values, Decision-Making, and Outputs: Configurations of Inactiveness," *International Studies of Values in Politics*, USA series, No. 83, April 1967.

36. For this reason it may be necessary to qualify proposition No. 1. Size may be related to the influence threshold of a community in such a way that the relationship between the number of inhabitants and the power structure is in reality *curvilinear*. Thus, a monolithic structure will be most likely to characterize medium-small communities instead of very small communities. At either extreme of the size continuum—in relatively large and relatively small communities—the factor of size will exert a tendency in the opposite direction, i.e., toward a pluralistic power structure. Precisely how small a "medium-small" community must be before the factor of size exerts an influence in a pluralistic direction is a question that can only be answered after further investigation. Some first steps in this direction have been taken by Ruth Moser in an unpublished master's essay completed with the writer at the University of Chicago.

37. See Gabriel A. Almond, "A Functional Approach to Comparative Politics," in Gabriel A. Almond and James S. Coleman, *The Politics of Developing Areas* (Princeton, N.J.: Princeton Univ. Press, 1960), pp. 3–64.

38. For an especially cogent and concise review of the classic discussions on the functional consequences of social structural cleavages, electoral arrangements, and party systems for the maintenance of democratic government, see Seymour Martin Lipset, "Party Systems and the Representation of Social Groups," *European Journal of Sociology*, 1:50–85 (1960).

39. Note that this refers to participation over *a certain minimal period of time*. Ego-involvement cannot be assumed to result from interaction until the relationships have become somewhat established. See George C. Homans, *The Human Group* (New York: Harcourt, Brace, 1951), for discussion of the development of social relationships through interaction. Coleman (*op. cit.*) has pointed out the disintegrating effects of short-term and active participation of normally uninvolved individuals in community affairs.

40. See Coleman, *op. cit.*, and Rossi, "Power

and Community Structure," in *Midwest Jour. Pol. Sci.*

41. See Lazarsfeld, Berelson, and Gaudet, *op. cit.*; Bernard Berelson, Paul F. Lazarsfeld, and William N. McPhee, *Voting* (Chicago: Univ. of Chicago Press, 1954); Angus Campbell, Gerald Gurin, and Warren E. Miller, *The Voter Decides* (Evanston, Ill.: Row, Peterson, 1954).

42. Almond and Verba's recent comparative study of the United States, Great Britain, Germany, Italy, and Mexico has pointed to the importance of participation for the maintenance of a democratic political system. Still, in their concentration on the differences in "political culture" among the five countries, the authors seem in general to have neglected the importance of the differences within single countries. In particular, it appears that the notion of the positive function of apathy for the maintenance of a flexible democratic system that has emerged from earlier empirical studies has been almost completely neglected. See Gabriel A. Almond and Sidney Verba, *The Civic Culture* (Princeton, N.J.: Princeton Univ. Press, 1963).

43. See A. L. Kroeber and Talcott Parsons, "The Concept of Culture and of Social Systems," *American Sociological Review*, 23:582–583 (1958).

44. For a theoretical statement of the process of structural-functional differentiation, see Talcott Parsons and Neil J. Smelser, *Economy and Society* (Glencoe, Ill.: The Free Press, 1956); and Talcott Parsons, "Some Considerations on the Theory of Social Change," *Rural Sociology*, 26:219–239 (1961), reprinted in Amitai Etzioni and Eva Etzioni (eds.), *Social Change* (New York: Basic Books, 1964), pp. 83–97.

45. The process of structural-functional differentiation as it affected the family under the impact of industrialization is analyzed in Neil J. Smelser, *Social Change in Industrial Revolution* (Chicago: Univ. of Chicago Press, 1959), esp. pp. 180–312.

46. Merton in *Social Theory and Social Structure*, pp. 131–160, analyzes the general consequences of disjunction between culture and social structure.

47. William F. Ogburn, *Social Change* (New York: Viking, 1922).

48. See Schulze, in *ASR*, 13:8; Pellegrin and Coats, in *AJS*, 61:413–417, and Swanson, Agger, and Goldrich, in Swanson, *op. cit.*, pp. 81–88, for discussions of the influence of the paternalistic value system on the involvement of business elites in community affairs.

49. Cf. Almond and Verba, *op. cit.*, for some data on this matter.

50. It is significant that it has been in cross-national (and cross-cultural) investigations of community power that the occupational prestige structure has been suggested as an important determinant of the distribution of community power. See Delbert C. Miller, "Industry and Community Power Structure: A Comparative Study of an American and an English City," *American Sociological Review*, 23:9–15 (1958). In studies comparing the power structures of American and Mexican communities, it has been found that more public officials are likely to be cited as key influentials in Mexican than in American communities. See William H. Form and William V. D'Antonio, "Integration and Cleavage among Community Influentials in two Border Cities," *American Sociological Review*, 24:804–814 (1959), and Orrin E. Klapp and Vincent L. Padgett, "Power Structure and Decision-Making in a Mexican Border City," *American Journal of Sociology*, 65:400–406 (1959). It should, of course be remarked that as these studies are based on reputational techniques, the methodological criticism that prestige and not power is actually being measured may have some influence on the outcome. Although the authors offer no separate measure of prestige, the results are still stimulating and point to the necessity of further comparative research.

51. Since this paper was written, studies of this nature have been completed. See Selections 18 and 21 in this volume; and Terry N. Clark, William Kornblum, Harold Bloom, and Susan Tobias, "Discipline, Method, Community Structure and Decision-Making: The Role and Limitations of the Sociology of Knowledge," *The American Sociologist*, 3 (August 1968), 214–217.

52. Progress in this direction is reported in Terry N. Clark, "Comparability in Community Research," presented at the session on Comparability in Community Research, Sixth World Congress, International Sociological Association, Evian, France, September, 1966; and in Clark, *Community Structure and Decision-Making: Comparative Analyses*.

THE VERTICAL AXIS OF COMMUNITY ORGANIZATION AND THE STRUCTURE OF POWER
John Walton

1. The copyright for this manuscript has been assigned to the Chandler Publishing Company, San Francisco, Calif. as the article appears in Terry N. Clark (ed.), *Community Structure and Decision Making: Comparative Analyses*, (San Francisco: Chandler, 1968) An earlier version of this paper was presented at the annual meeting of the Society for the Study of Social Problems, San Francisco, August 1967.

2. See, for example, Amos Hawley, "Community Power and Urban Renewal Success,"

pp. 422–431; Warner Bloomberg and Morris Sunshine, *Suburban Power Structures and Public Education: A Study of Values, Influence and Tax Effort* (Syracuse: University Press, 1963); Ralph B. Kimbrough, *Political Power and Educational Decision Making* (Chicago: Rand McNally and Co., 1964); Irving A. Fowler, "Local Industrial Structure, Economic Power and Community Welfare," *Social Problems*, 6 (Summer 1958), pp. 41–51; Ivan Belknap and John Steinle, *The Community and Its Hospitals* (Syracuse: Syracuse University Press, 1963); Floyd Hunter, Ruth Conner Schaffer and Cecil G. Sheps, *Community Organization: Action and Inaction* (Chapel Hill: University of North Carolina Press, 1956); James S. Coleman, *Community Conflict* (New York: The Free Press, 1957); William A. Gamson, "Rancorous Conflict in Community Politics," *American Sociological Review*, 31 (Feb. 1966), pp. 71–81; James McKee, "Community Power and Strategies in Race Relations," *Social Problems*, 6 (Winter 1958–1959), pp. 41–51.

3. L. Vaughn Blankenship, "Community Power and Decision Making: A Comparative Evaluation of Measurement Techniques," *Social Forces*, 43 (Dec. 1964), pp. 207–216; William V. D'Antonio and Eugene Erickson, "The Reputational Technique as a Measure of Community Power: An Evaluation Based on Comparative and Longitudinal Studies," *American Sociological Review*, 27 (June 1962), pp. 362–376; Linton C. Freeman, *et al.*, "Locating Leaders in Local Communities: A Comparison of Some Alternative Approaches," *American Sociological Review*, 28 (Oct. 1963), pp. 791–798.

4. Robert Presthus, *Men at the Top: A Study in Community Power* (New York: Oxford University Press, 1964); Robert E. Agger, Daniel Goldrich and Bert E. Swanson, *The Rulers and the Ruled: Political Power and Impotence in American Communities* (New York: John Wiley and Sons, 1964); William V. D'Antonio and William H. Form, *Influentials in Two Border Cities: A Study in Community Decision-Making* (Notre Dame: University of Notre Dame Press, 1965).

5. For some efforts in this direction see Agger, *et al.*, *The Rulers*; Presthus, *Men at the Top;* M. Herbert Danzger, "Community Power Structure: Problems and Continuities," *American Sociological Review*, 24 (Oct. 1964), pp. 707–717.

6. John Walton, "Substance and Artifact: The Current Status of Research on Community Power Structure," *American Journal of Sociology*, 71 (Jan. 1966), pp. 430–438.

7. John Walton, "A Systematic Survey of Community Power Research" in Michael T. Aiken and Paul E. Mott, *The Structure of Community Power: Readings* (in press).

8. A complete summary of the findings,

positive and negative, is to be found in Walton, *op. cit.*

9. The cell entries in the table represent communities, rather than studies, since a single study often dealt with two or more towns.

10. The variable power structure was originally coded in terms of four categories. The categories are collapsed here to avoid small N's and to provide a contrast between more and less concentrated power arrangements.

11. The N's in each of these subtables vary because the studies coded do not provide uniform data on each variable.

12. Operational definitions of the following three variables are indicated by the type of information coded under each category. Adequate economic resources–includes towns with reportedly prosperous business communities and low rates of poverty and unemployment; inadequate economically–underdeveloped with high rates of poverty and unemployment. Independent city–includes central cities of metropolitan areas and independent manufacturing, commercial or agricultural centers; satellite city–suburb or town dominated by a nearby city. Party competition–the existence of two or more local parties (or affiliates in formally nonpartisan cities) which regularly contend for public office; noncompetitive–a one-party town.

13. When the zero-order level findings on economic resources and type of city are examined controlling for research method, a factor associated with type of power structure identified, the differences here do not persist. The findings are reported here because they are suggestive and because the low quality of the data may be obscuring significant associations. That is, the lower the quality of the data, the more difficult it is to demonstrate statistically significant relationships and the more likely it is that such relationships may be obscured. In the present context I have gone beyond a strict interpretation of the earlier findings in an attempt to draw some meaningful generalizations.

14. David Rogers, "Community Political Systems: A Framework and Hypotheses for Comparative Studies," in Bert E. Swanson (ed.), *Current Trends in Comparative Community Studies* (Kansas City, Mo.: Community Studies, Inc., 1962).

15. Hawley, *op. cit.*

16. Edgar W. Butler and Hallowell Pope, "Community Power Structures, Industrialization and Public Welfare Programs," paper read at the 61st annual meeting of the American Sociological Association, Miami Beach, Florida, August 1966.

17. This conclusion applies to similar propositional inventories based on the "evolutionary" or "continuum" notion. See, for example,

Delbert C. Miller and William H. Form, *Industry, Labor and Community* (New York: Harper Bros., 1960).

18. Roland L. Warren, *The Community in America* (Chicago: Rand McNally, 1963), and "Toward a Reformulation of Community Theory," *Human Organization*, 15 (Summer, 1962), pp. 8–11.

19. Warren, *The Community in America*, p. 53.

20. *Ibid.*, p. 5.

21. This definition derives from a number of discussions of the concept of power. Some of the most relevant writings include Bertrand Russell, *Power: A New Social Analysis* (New York: Barnes and Noble, 1962); Max Weber, *The Theory of Social and Economic Organization* (trans. by A. M. Henderson and Talcott Parsons; New York: Oxford University Press, 1947); Talcott Parsons, "On the concept of Political Power," *Proceedings of the American Philosophical Society*, 107 (June 1963), pp. 232–262; Harold Lasswell and Abraham Kaplan, *Power and Society: A Framework for Political Inquiry* (New Haven: Yale University Press, 1950).

22. This is not meant to imply that such a dichotomy is the most useful framework, though it tends to pre-occupy the literature, e.g., Presthus, *Men at the Top;* D'Antonio and Form, *Influentials*. Etzioni has offered four types of control structures based on the means of control available to various positions within an organization; see *A Comparative Analysis of Complex Organizations* (New York: Free Press, 1961). Agger, et al., *The Rulers*, characterizes power structures with two variables, "distribution of power" and "convergence of leadership ideology" and a resulting fourfold table. Construing the second variable as an indicator of leadership cohesiveness, the formulation provides an important distinction between truly competitive systems and cases where power is shared among a number of groups but similarity of interests unites them in a monopolistic power arrangement. Many controversies in the field stem from a failure to make this distinction.

23. In a more elaborate statement Merriam writes, "In most communities the use of force is relatively uncommon in proportion to the number of regulations, and the success of the organization is not measured by the amount of violence in specific cases but by the extent to which violence is avoided and other substitutes discovered." Charles E. Merriam, *Political Power*, Collier Books Edition (New York: Macmillan, 1964), p. 36.

24. Although the present concern is with community conflict, this argument closely parallels Durkheim's thesis on suicide and changes in the normative order.

25. Presthus, *Men at the Top*, p. 427.

26. A more precise treatment of this relationship would specify types of conflict and how these are associated with various power arrangements. For example, monopolistic power structures may suppress dissent and conflict, they may manage it within innocuous limits, or they may engender revolutionary conflict. Competitive power structures, on the other hand, may encourage conflict which results in a stalemate or ineffective argument and nonrevolutionary change.

27. James S. Coleman, *Community Conflict* (New York: Free Press, 1957) accords with this point arguing that whenever the pattern of control is so complete that certain elements can see no way of moving into a position of power, there may be sporadic conflict but no organized opposition (nor, presumably, regular conflict).

28. For studies documenting this, see, Robert O. Schulze, "The Bifurcation of Power in a Satellite City" in Morris Janowitz (ed.), *Community Political Systems* (Glencoe: The Free Press, 1961), pp. 19–80; Roland J. Pellegrin and Charles H. Coates, "Absentee-owned Corporations and Community Power Structure," *American Journal of Sociology*, 61 (March 1956), pp. 413–419.

29. On this point there is little evidence pro or con, and I present it only as a plausible hypothesis.

30. It should be noted that the inferences about change are drawn primarily from cross-sectional data and thus run the risk of incorrectly inferring trends. Given the nature of available data, there is no alternative other than recommending future longitudinal studies following the lead of Agger, et al., *The Rulers*, and D'Antonio and Form, *Influentials*. Other studies which attempt to replicate earlier work include Delbert C. Miller, "Decision-Making Cliques in Community Power Structures: A Comparative Study of an American and an English City," *American Journal of Sociology*, 64 (Nov. 1958), pp. 299–310; David A. Booth and Charles R. Adrian, "Power Structure and Community Change: A Replication Study of Community A," *Midwest Journal of Political Science*, 6 (Aug. 1962), pp. 277–296; Donald A. Clelland and William H. Form, "Economic Dominants and Community Power: A Comparative Analysis," *American Journal of Sociology*, 69 (March 1964), pp. 511–521; M. Kent Jennings, *Community Influentials: The Elites of Atlanta* (New York: Free Press, 1964).

31. For a discussion of this ploy and other sanctions available to economic institutions, see Arnold Rose, *The Power Structure: Political Processes in American Society* (New York: Oxford University Press, 1967), Chapter 3.

32. The point to be emphasized here is that greater complexity and specialization are not

necessarily conducive to the changes under consideration, but only insofar as these developments produce greater interdependence. At some point, of course, complexity and specialization do necessitate greater interdependence, but it would seem that this is not always the case at every level of community development. We would expect that some of these variables are confounded in such a way that increasing size, for example, will be related to competitive power structures at that point in a community's development when size and interdependence vary together. According to this argument, such an association would be spurious. This may be the case though the available data are too crude and provide too few observations to allow an unequivocal solution.

33. Edward C. Banfield, *Political Influence: A New Theory of Urban Politics* (New York: Free Press Paperback Edition, 1965), p. 348.

34. *Ibid.*, p. 318.

35. Don J. Bogue, *The Structure of the Metropolitan Community* (Ann Arbor: Horace H. Rackham School of Graduate Studies, University of Michigan, 1949).

36. Scott Greer, *The Emerging City: Myth and Reality* (New York: The Free Press, 1962), pp. 50–51.

37. Norton E. Long, "The Local Community as an Ecology of Games," *American Journal of Sociology*, 44 (Nov. 1958), pp. 251–266.

38. Norton E. Long, *The Polity* (Chicago: Rand McNally, 1962), p. 157.

39. *Ibid.*

40. Also relevant to this characterization is Wallace S. Sayre and Herbert Kaufman, *Governing New York City: Politics in the Metropolis* (New York: Russell Sage Foundation, 1960).

41. Stephen A. Booth, "The New Politics Goes Local," *The Nation*, Vol. 204, No. 22 (May 29, 1967).

42. Presthus, *Men at the Top;* William V. D'Antonio, "Community Leadership in an Economic Crisis: Testing Ground for Ideological Cleavage," *American Journal of Sociology*, 71 (May 1966), pp. 688–700.

43. *Small Town in Mass Society* (Princeton: Princeton University Press, 1958).

A NOTE ON WALTON'S ANALYSIS OF POWER STRUCTURE AND VERTICAL TIES
Roland L. Warren

1. Sol Levine and Paul E. White, "Exchange as a Conceptual Framework for the Study of Interorganizational Relationships," *Administrative Science Quarterly*, 5 (March 1961), pp. 583–601; and Sol Levine, Paul E. White, and Benjamin D. Paul, "Community Interorganizational Problems in Providing Medical Care and Social Services," *American Journal of Public Health*, 53 (August 1963), pp. 1183–1195.

2. Edward C. Banfield, *Political Influence* (New York: The Free Press of Glencoe, 1961), pp. 324 ff.; and Charles E. Lindblom, *The Intelligence of Democracy: Decision Making Through Mutual Adjustment* (New York and London: The Free Press-Collier-Macmillan, Ltd., 1965), *passim*.

3. Banfield, *Political Influence*, pp. 355 ff.

DEFENSE CONTRACTING AND COMMUNITY LEADERSHIP: A COMPARATIVE ANALYSIS
Phillip Edward Present

1. Robert Havighurst and H. Gerthon Morgan, *The Social History of a War-Boom Community* (New York: Longmans, Green & Co., 1951); Charles Walker, *Steeltown: An Industrial Case History of the Conflict Between Progress and Security*. (New York: Harper & Bros., 1950); Raymond Bauer, Ithiel de Sola Pool, and Lewis A. Dexter, *American Business and Public Policy: The Politics of Foreign Trade* (New York: Atherton Press, 1963).

2. See the author's Ph.D. dissertation, "The Relationship Between Community Political Systems and Defense Contracting," (University of Southern California, 1966). Available also on microfilm from University Microfilms, Inc., Ann Arbor, Michigan. (Order No. 67–421).

3. Especially useful were: William Form and Delbert Miller, *Industry, Labor and Community* (New York: Harper and Bros., 1960); Ernest A. T. Barth, "Community Influence Systems: Structure and Change," *Social Forces*, 40 (Oct. 1961), pp. 58–63.

4. Yasumasa Kuroda, *et al.*, "The Relation of a Defense Environment to the Social and Political Structures of Communities," an unpublished research design, 1963, p. 13.

5. Fortunately, however, the informants and a few other individuals were very co-operative and open. This may be attributed to the fact that they generally were not actually within the leadership structures and also that they had, perhaps, a clearer understanding of the purpose of the study.

6. The names used in this article are fictitious, although the community locations are accurate.

7. Form and Miller, *Industry*, pp. 538–543.

8. For a comparison of participation by corporation employees in community politics, see Robert Schulze, "The Role of Economic Dominants in Community Power," *American Sociological Review*, 23 (Feb., 1958), pp. 3–9, and the author's dissertation, pp. 135–137.

9. Barth, *op. cit.*, p. 63.

SOME TRENDS IN COMMUNITY POLITICS: A SECONDARY ANALYSIS OF POWER STRUCTURE DATA FROM 166 COMMUNITIES
Claire W. Gilbert

1. Research for this study was partially supported by The International City Managers' Association, The National Science Foundation (Grant GS-800), and The Center for Metropolitan Studies at Northwestern University. Among all of those individuals to whom I am indebted, John F. Speight is acknowledged here.

2. See Arnold Rose, *The Power Structure* (New York: Oxford University Press, 1967), Chapter 8.

3. The cutting point 1954–1955 was selected because it divided the data into two nearly equal parts (N = 84, N = 82). The 1944–1945 cut was selected in order to explore trends further (N = 41 for 1944 or earlier; N = 125 for 1945 or later).

4. Suggestion of this use came from David A. Minar, personal communication.

5. *Parapolitical* refers to organizations which are not political in their primary function but can and often do perform political functions. See Scott Greer and Peter Orleans, "The Mass Society and the Parapolitical Structure," *American Sociological Review*, 27 (Oct. 1962), pp. 634–646.

6. Louis Wirth, "Urbanism as a Way of Life," in Paul K. Hatt and Albert J. Riess, Jr. (eds.), *Cities and Society* (Glencoe, Illinois: The Free Press, 1959), pp. 46–63.

7. For example, see Raymond E. Wolfinger and John Osgood Field, "Political Ethos and the Structure of City Government," *American Political Science Review*, 60 (June 1966), pp. 306–326; and Harry M. Scoble, "Some Questions for Researchers," in Robert S. Cahill and Stephen P. Hencley (eds.) *The Politics of Education in the Local Community* (Danville, Illinois; The Interstate Publishers and Printers, 1964), pp. 120–122.

8. Emile Durkheim, *The Division of Labor in Society*, trans. George Simpson (Glencoe, Illinois: The Free Press, 1947); Eshref Shevky and Wendell Bell, *Social Area Analysis* (Stanford: Stanford University Press, 1954); and C. Wright Mills, *White Collar* (New York: Oxford University Press, 1951).

9. For a discussion of the concept of societal scale, see Shevky and Bell, *Social Area Analysis*. Some other references dealing with related social changes are Mills, *White Collar;* and Wirth, "Urbanism." For a comparative national framework within which to conceptualize

local communities, see Claire W. Gilbert, "Community Power Structure: A Study in the Sociology of Knowledge," unpublished Ph.D. dissertation, Northwestern University, 1966, Ch. 2.

10. The term "good" is not intended by the author as an endorsement of such governments, but rather should be understood as a commonly used *label*. There are finer distinctions that can be made about the functions of local government, but for present purposes, two are adequate.

11. Edward C. Banfield and James Q. Wilson discuss these notions throughout their book, *City Politics* (Cambridge: Harvard University Press, 1965).

12. *Ibid.*, pp. 329–330.

13. David A. Booth and Charles R. Adrian, "Power Structure and Community Change: A Replication Study of Community A," *Midwest Journal of Political Science*, 6 (Aug. 1962), pp. 288, 291; Robert O. Schulze, "The Role of Economic Dominants in Community Power Structure," *American Sociological Review*, 23 (Feb. 1958), p. 4.

14. Banfield and Wilson, *City Politics*, p. 431.

15. Schulze, *loc. cit.*

16. Scoble, "Some Questions," p. 123.

17. Banfield and Wilson, *City Politics*, p. 334.

18. *Ibid.*, p. 333.

19. The reasoning—at first impressionistic—became increasingly sophisticated as the study progressed. (It was initiated in 1962.) An hypothesis emerged about the importance of national ideology (valuing of centralization or decentralization) and societal scale. The present writer would suggest that much of what we find locally in the way of power structures is related to national ideology and societal scale. The importance, in short, of the temporal dimension for the communities in the United States (and other places) is due to the increasing scale of our society. In a different sense, expectations about local governing (another kind of ideology referred to) is no doubt correlated with national scale-related changes.

20. Gilbert, "Community Power Structure," Appendices A, B, and C.

21. Raoul Naroll, *Data Quality Control: A New Research Technique* (Glencoe, Illinois: The Free Press, 1962). Using data quality control reasoning, measurement error is defined as: A group of reports made under one condition differs three standard deviation units from a group of reports made under another condition on their descriptions of a community power attribute. An association only tends to be spuriously created or inflated when two attributes in a correlation share an identical measurement error. Naroll's Chapter I explains this.

22. The many riots taking place in major cities in the United States (summer, 1967)

indicate the lowered ability of local communities to deal with conflicts although the data do not show such a trend.

V:
INTRODUCTION

1. Floyd Hunter, *Community Power Structure* (Chapel Hill: University of North Carolina Press, 1953).

2. See, for example, Donald R. Matthews, *The Social Backgrounds of Political Decision-Makers* (Garden City, N.Y.: Doubleday and Company, 1954).

3. Angus Campbell *et al.*, *The American Voter* (New York: John Wiley and Sons, 1960), Chapter 10.

4. Samuel A. Stouffer, *Communism, Conformity, and Civil Liberties* (Garden City, N.Y.: Doubleday and Company, 1955); James W. Prothro and Charles M. Grigg, "Fundamental Principles of Democracy: Bases of Agreement and Disagreement," *Journal of Politics*, 22 (Spring 1960), pp. 276–294.

5. Herbert McClosky, "Consensus and Ideology in American Politics," *American Political Science Review*, 58 (June 1964), pp. 361–382.

SCOPE OF GOVERNMENT AND LEADERS' IDEOLOGIES
Robert Agger, Daniel Goldrich, and Bert E. Swanson

1. See Delbert Miller and William Form, *Industry, Labor and Community* (New York: Harper & Bros., 1960), Ch. XIV. For an analysis of the situation of a rural community in the context of these modern currents, see Arthur J. Vidich and Joseph Bensman, *Small Town in Mass Society* (Garden City, New York: Anchor Books, Doubleday & Co., Inc., 1958).

2. For a fairly comprehensive theoretical analysis of five "major systems" in terms of which a community might be analyzed, see Irwin T. Sanders, *The Community* (New York: The Ronald Press Company, 1958).

3. A modern reactionary in this sense is Friedrich A. Hayek; see *The Road to Serfdom* (Chicago: University of Chicago Press, 1944).

4. Engels refers to the "natural simplicity," of such communities; he calls them "wonderful," "natural and spontaneous," and says they produce "splendid men and women." Frederick Engels, *The Origin of the Family, Private Property and the State* (Chicago: Charles H. Kerr & Co., Co-operative, 1902), pp. 117–119.

5. Herbert McClosky, Paul J. Hoffman and Rosemary O'Hara, "Issue Conflict and Consensus Among Party Leaders and Followers," *American Political Science Review*, LVI (June 1960), pp. 406–427.

6. It is common practice to capitalize the word "Negro" and not the word "white." We see no reason for unequal treatment in such a minor but symbolic matter and therefore capitalize both words.

7. For discussions of social class in the United States, see Joseph A. Kahl, *The American Class Structure* (New York: Rinehart, 1957); and W. Lloyd Warner, M. Meeker, and K. Eells, *Social Class in America* (New York: Harper Torchbooks, 1960).

8. The observations and instruments for evaluating and estimating the specific and general senses of cultural class were not precise enough to detect theoretically significant discrepancies between the specific and general sense of cultural class. While the senses of cultural and social class may be highly correlated under many conditions, we suspect that they diverge significantly in relatively open social class systems. By the use of such terms as "status frustrations" and "the dispossessed," Seymour Martin Lipset and Daniel Bell imply some aspects of what we mean by a sense of cultural class. Once the latter is conceptualized as a distinct analytic variable (of a multidimensional character), it becomes possible to test the degree to which cultural-class position is due to what Lipset and Bell both suggest is the cause of distance and hostility between upper- and lower-cultural-class groups, namely, psychological anxiety or confidence related to position in and understanding of the modern technological, corporate socioeconomic structure and international order. We would question a predominant stress on a differential distribution of needs for, and frustrations regarding, social status and would hypothesize more of a socialization in differentiated cultures as a central factor in the motivational complex of forces producing a stratified cultural-class system. Whatever the original cause of different belief systems, their existence provides for the maintenance or the development of cultural-class systems based thereon, related to social class only to the extent that cultural belief systems follow social-class lines. See *The Radical Right*, ed. by Daniel Bell (Garden City, N.Y.: Doubleday & Co., Inc., 1963), especially Chapters 1, 2, 13 and 14.

9. Some of these aspects of Community Conservation are well expressed in Catherine C. Bauer Wurster, "Framework for an Urban Society," in *Goals for Americans, The Report of the President's Commission on National Goals* (New York: A Spectrum Book, Prentice-Hall, Inc., 1960), pp. 223–247.

10. Classifying people as Jeffersonian Conservatives and Radical Rightists, as with

the classification of people as ideologists of any other kind, will sometimes result in the problem of marginal or borderline cases. Senator Barry Goldwater may be considered such a case.

11. The late Senator Robert Taft's shift in position from an "anti" to a "pro" stance on such matters as public housing and urban redevelopment illustrates the contingent outlook on the part of Orthodox Conservatives, or, possibly, a movement toward national Progressive Conservatism. For a description of a variant of Orthodox Conservatism at the community level which permits "quasi-public action by private groups for public collective ends" while at the same time maintaining a minimal scope of (public) government, see Stone's description of what he calls "social free enterprise" in Robert C. Stone, "Power and Values in Transcommunity Relationships," ed. by Bert E. Swanson, Public Monograph Series, No. 1 (Kansas City, Mo.: Community Studies, Inc., 1962), pp. 69–80.

12. A useful description of Conservative and Liberal ideology, as well as descriptions of the differences in attitudes toward various aspects of the scope of national government by Republican and Democratic party leaders, is to be found in McClosky *et al., op. cit.* For a discussion of some of the ideological premises of businessmen, see Francis X. Sutton *et al., The American Business Creed* (Cambridge, Massachusetts: Harvard University Press, 1956).

13. That differences between Progressive Conservatives and Community Conservationists, particularly at the national level, may be difficult to discern is evidenced by the fact that many of the objectives mentioned in *Goals for Americans* are held by Eisenhower Republicans and Kennedy Democrats, as well as by Stevenson Liberals.

14. It may be of interest to note at this point that leaders of the three community-oriented Radical Right movements found in our research communities belonged to and received literature from nationally organized Radical Right groups.

15. James S. Coleman stresses the importance in a large class of conflicts of "a few active oppositionists" who are "sometimes motivated by the hope of power, but often they are ideologically committed to a 'cause.'" *Community Conflict* (Glencoe, Illinois: The Free Press, 1957), p. 8.

16. For a useful discussion on how to study the importance of ideas in political systems, and an explanation of Max Weber's general comparative research design and logic of inquiry, see Talcott Parsons, *Essays in Sociological Theory, Pure and Applied* (Glencoe, Illinois: The Free Press, 1949), pp. 151–165.

PSYCHOLOGICAL ASPECTS OF COMMUNITY POWER STRUCTURE: LEADERS AND RANK-AND-FILE CITIZENS IN REEDTOWN, JAPAN

Yasumasa Kuroda

1. This article is part of a larger study on Community Political Life in Japan, which is supported by the Joint Committee on Asian Studies of the ASLS and SSRC (1966–7). I wish to thank Alice K. Kuroda and Robert B. Stauffer for their suggestions on an earlier draft of this paper.

2. Recently Miller and Stokes pointed out that three elements of representation are in practice in the United States—i.e., the "Burkean (non-instructed representative), instructed-delegate, and responsible party models." (Warren E. Miller and Donald E. Stokes, "Constituency Influence in Congress," *The American Political Science Review*, 57 [March 1963], pp. 45–56).

3. Those political scientists who studied the social backgrounds of political leaders lead us to believe that somehow the political leadership ought to be recruited from wide segments of a society if there is to be a democracy. Some social scientists contend that competition in leadership recruitment ought to help develop a democratic political system. They are correct in isolating some of the most important contributory conditions to the development of a democracy, but these two variables discussed above are not by themselves sufficient to test the extent of a democracy anywhere. Marx, Lipset, Duverger, Goldstein and others seem to suggest that the really crucial question in the test of a democracy is to examine the extent to which a government or the political leadership in a political system represents the will of the people. I would hypothesize that there are areas in which the leadership and the rank-and-file citizens disagree, just as there are areas of decision-making in which harmony between them prevails. See Seymour M. Lipset, *Political Man* (New York: Doubleday and Company, Inc., 1960), p. 45; Maurice Duverger, *Political Parties* (London: Methuen and Company Ltd., 1954), pp. 424–425; Marshall N. Goldstein, "Absentee Ownership and Monolithic Power Structures: Two Questions for Community Studies," in Bert E. Swanson (ed.), *Current Trends in Comparative Community Studies* (Kansas City: Community Studies, Inc., 1962), pp. 49–59.

4. I attended a few town assembly meetings of Reed Town. I observed at least one socialist assemblyman objecting to a proposal who went along with the majority when it came to a showdown. An examination of the minutes of the town assembly showed that all decisions in the past several years were reached without a single dissenting opinion. For this aspect of Japanese politics, see Chitose Yanaga,

Japanese People and Politics (New York: John Wiley and Sons, Inc., 1956), pp. 83–87; Nobutake Ike, Japanese Politics (New York: Alfred A. Knopf, 1957), pp. 265–267; Richard K. Beardsley, John W. Hall, Robert E. Ward, Village Japan (Chicago: University of Chicago Press, 1959), p. 355. For a similar observation by Robert B. Stauffer, see his forthcoming book Legislative Model of Political Development: The Philippine Congress.

5. For a detailed description of the use of a variant of Hunter's reputational technique, see Chapter 2 of my forthcoming work on Community Political Life in Japan. One respondent was eliminated at random from the Leadership Population after the survey was completed to make the universe into a sample for purposes of the t-test.

6. Voter registration is more rigorous and standardized in Japan than one finds in the United States.

7. The following scoring procedure was used for the purpose of calculating the means: Agree strongly ... 1: Agree somewhat ... 2: Agree slightly ... 3: Disagree slightly ... 4: Disagree somewhat ... 5: Disagree strongly ... 6. Those who failed to respond were eliminated from the calculation of the means.

8. For findings in the United States, see Lester W. Milbrath, Political Participation (Chicago: Rand McNally & Company, 1965), pp. 58–59, and the references therein. For findings in Japan, see Yasumasa Kuroda, "Political Role Attributions and Dynamics in a Japanese Community," Public Opinion Quarterly, 29 (Winter 1965–1966), pp. 602–613; and Yasumasa Kuroda, "Measurement, Correlates, and Significance of Political Participation in a Japanese Community," Western Political Quarterly, 20 (Sept., 1967), pp. 660–668.

9. V. O. Key, Public Opinion and American Democracy (New York: Alfred A. Knopf, 1961), pp. 336–338.

10. There seems to be no definite correlation between political involvement and political cynicism. An Oregon study showed that political participation increases with political trust among highly educated people in an Oregon community (Robert E. Agger, Marshall N. Goldstein, Stanley A. Pearl, "Political Cynicism: Measurement and Meaning," Journal of Politics, 23 [Aug. 1961], pp. 477–506). I found that campaign experience, social-class factors and other variables act as intervening variables in making Japanese law students politically cynical (Yasumasa Kuroda, "The Political Cynicism of Law Students in Japan," Monumenta Nipponica, 22, [1967], pp. 147–161).

11. This is a question from the SRC. For Americans' reactions to this question see Key, Public Opinion, pp. 159–160.

12. Alvin Boskoff and Harmon Zeigler, Voting Patterns in a Local Election (Phila-

delphia: J. B. Lippincott Company, 1964), pp. 45–59.

13. Recently, it has been pointed out by a number of social scientists that one's ideological orientation must be related to some issue area if it is to have any meaning (Lipset, Political Man, pp. 101–105). Earlier social scientists used to lump all sorts of liberalism into one scale. For example, see Herbert McClosky, "Conservatism and Personality," American Political Science Review, 52 (March 1958), pp. 27–45.

14. Lester W. Milbrath, "Predispositions toward Political Contention," The Western Political Quarterly, 13 (March 1960), pp. 5–18; Lester W. Milbrath and Walter W. Klein, "Personality Correlates of Political Participation," Acta Sociologica, 6 (1962), pp. 53–66; Elihu Katz and Paul F. Lazarsfeld, Personal Influence (Glencoe, Illinois: The Free Press, 1955), pp. 223–233, 287–289; Yasumasa Kuroda, "Sociability and Political Involvement," Midwest Journal of Political Science, 9 (May, 1965), pp. 133–147.

15. Three studies found an inverse relationship between authoritarianism and political participation: Morris Janowitz and Dwaine Marvick, "Authoritarianism and Political Behavior," Public Opinion Quarterly, 17 (Summer, 1953), pp. 185–201; Robert E. Lane, "Political Personality and Electoral Choice," American Political Science Review, 49 (March 1955), pp. 173–190; Yasumasa Kuroda, "Authoritarianism and Political Behavior in a Japanese Community," an unpublished paper presented at the 1968 Western Political Science Association Meetings. A summary of the paper appeared in The Western Political Quarterly (Supplement), 19 (1966), p. 16.

16. Samuel A. Stouffer, Communism, Conformity, and Civil Liberties (Garden City, New York: Doubleday and Co., 1955), pp. 26–57.

17. Milbrath, Political Participation, p. 86.

18. Yasumasa Kuroda, "Peace-War Orientation in a Japanese Community," Journal of Peace Research, 3 (1960), pp. 380–388.

19. E.g., self–society, internationalism, and tax-cut questions.

20. William A. Scott, "Cognitive Complexity and Cognitive Flexibility," Sociometry, 26 (March 1963), pp. 66–74.

21. Miller and Stokes, op. cit.

22. It goes far beyond the scope of this article to review the literature on community power structure. A recent summary of community power studies is John Walton, "Substance and Artifact: The Current Status of Research on Community Power Structure," The American Journal of Sociology, 71 (Jan. 1966), 430–438. For a comprehensive

treatment of this problem, see my forthcoming *Community Political Life in Japan*, Chs. 2, 4 and 5.

SOCIAL VALUES AND POLITICAL ORIENTATIONS OF CITY MANAGERS: A SURVEY REPORT
Lloyd M. Wells

1. The author is grateful to the University of Missouri Research Council and to the Business and Public Administration Research Center for grants which made this study possible.
2. For an empirical study which deals briefly and peripherally with the attitudes of city managers see Jeptha J. Carrell, *The Role of the City Manager*, Public Affairs Monograph Number 2 (Kansas City: Community Studies, Inc., 1962), pp. 30–33.
3. Such assumptions are sometimes pressed into service to help explain the frequent support of business groups for the council manager plan and the frequent opposition of organized labor to the plan.
4. Charles Adrian, *Governing Urban America* (New York: McGraw-Hill, 1961), p. 229.
5. Seymour Martin Lipset, *Political Man* (New York: Doubleday & Company, Anchor Books, 1963), pp. 92 ff.
6. Reprinted in the Appendixes of V. O. Key, Jr., *Public Opinion and American Democracy* (New York: Alfred A. Knopf, 1961).
7. Martin A. Trow, "Small Businessmen, Political Tolerance, and Support for McCarthy," *American Journal of Sociology*, 64 (Nov. 1958), pp. 279–280.
8. W. Lloyd Warner, Paul P. Van Riper, Norman H. Martin and Orvis F. Collins, *The American Federal Executive* (New Haven: Yale University Press, 1963), pp. 221 ff.
9. Over half our respondents reported membership in Rotary.
10. Raymond A. Bauer, Ithiel de Sola Pool, Lewis Anthony Dexter, *American Business and Public Policy* (New York: Atherton Press, 1963), pp. 156–162. See also Edward C. Bursk, "New Dimensions in Top Executive Reading," *Harvard Business Review*, 35 (Sept.–Oct. 1957), pp. 93–112.
11. Bauer, *American Business*, p. 158.
12. *Ibid.*
13. *Ibid.*, p. 159.
14. Samuel A. Stouffer, *Communism, Conformity and Civil Liberties* (New York: John Wiley & Sons, Science Editions, 1966), pp. 55–56.
15. John H. Bunzel, *The American Small Businessman* (New York: Alfred A. Knopf, 1962), p. 89.

16. For a perceptive analysis of American civil bureaucratic ideology see R. Joseph Monsen, Jr., and Mark W. Cannon, *The Makers of Public Policy* (New York: McGraw-Hill, 1965), pp. 222–257.
17. Morris Janowitz, *The Professional Soldier* (New York: The Free Press, 1964), pp. 241–250; Samuel P. Huntington, *The Soldier and the State* (New York: Random House, Vintage Books, 1964), pp. 79, 222.

LEADERS' VALUES AND THE DYNAMICS OF COMMUNITY INTEGRATION: A FOUR-NATION COMPARATIVE STUDY
Philip E. Jacob

1. For a preliminary report on certain aspects of this project, see Philip E. Jacob, Henry Teune, and Thomas Watts, "Values, Leadership and Development," *Social Science INFORMATION*, Vol. VII/2 (April 1968). International Social Science Council, Paris. pp. 49–92. Some of this material is included in the present chapter. A portion of the American data is reported and analyzed by Terry N. Clark, in Selection 28 of this volume. A comprehensive international volume by the principal participants from the four countries is scheduled for publication in 1970, as well as a series of country and topical studies.
2. The following institutions cooperated in the ISVIP: in India, the Indian Institute of Technology (Kanpur), the University of Poona, and the Centre for the Study of Developing Societies (New Delhi); in Poland, the Institute of Philosophy and Sociology of the Polish Academy of Sciences; in the U.S., the University of Pennsylvania, with the collaboration of the National Opinion Research Center (University of Chicago) and social scientists from other American universities; in Yugoslavia, the Institute of Social Sciences (Belgrade) with the collaboration of scholars from the Institute of Sociology, (Ljubljana), the Faculty of Political Science (Sarajevo), and the Faculty of Law (University of Zagreb). The program has been cost-shared with generous support from the National Science Foundation, the Department of State (Division of Cultural Affairs), the Robert L. McNeil Jr. Foundation, the Johnson Foundation, the Rockefeller Foundation, and other sources. Most important, the indigenous cooperating institutions in Poland and Yugoslavia have themselves financed the internal costs of their research staff and facilities; while in India, the Planning Commission of the Indian Government supported two extensions of the study.
3. This definition, in general conformity with that developed by Clyde Kluckhohn, must be distinguished from concepts of values

as goals or preferences which are currently in vogue in much political science literature. See Philip E. Jacob and James Flink, "Values and Their Function in Decision-Making," *The American Behavioral Scientist Supplement* (May 1962); also "The Influence of Values in Political Integration," in Philip E. Jacob and J. Toscano, (eds.) *The Integration of Political Communities*, (Philadelphia: J. C. Lippincott & Co., 1964). See Allen Barton, *Measuring the Values of Individuals*, Bureau of Applied Social Research, Columbia University, Reprint No. 354.

4. For a summary of these and alternative concepts of integration current in social science inquiry, see Philip E. Jacob and Henry Teune, "The Integrative Process: Guidelines for Analysis of the Bases of Political Community," in Jacob and Toscano, *op. cit.* Actually nine different concepts of integration were elaborated in the course of developing the research design, but resources permitted intensive concentration only on the variable of community activeness.

5. This approach is elaborated by A. Przeworski and H. Teune in "Equivalence in Cross-National Research," *The Public Opinion Quarterly*, Vol. 30, Winter 1966–67, but it proved not to be as critical in this survey as expected. Correlations between the two sets of questions, international and nation-specific, were high; and few of the nation-specific questions survived the process of "purification" whereby items which did not correlate significantly and positively with the other items in a scale were eliminated. However, this strategy makes it possible to have much more confidence in the validity of the final results, than if only common questions had been used to start with.

6. See K. Krippendorff, "A preliminary inquiry into the expression of values in political documents," ISVIP doc. USA/68 for elaboration of the technique. Coding instructions are available in ISVIP doc. USA/72. See also P. E. Jacob, "Progress Report on Value-Content Analysis of National Leadership, U.S., and India," ISVIP doc. USA/71. This report is based on analysis of ten major speeches on "Great Society" issues by President Johnson 1965–1966, and ten speeches on domestic issues by Prime Ministers Shastri and Gandhi during approximately the same period.

7. Reliability was demonstrated by the internal homogeneity of the purified scales, calculated separately for each country; conceptual validity across countries was indicated by the high correspondence of most scales to distinguishable factors emerging from factor analyses of responses in each country to all the scale items pooled together. The procedures followed and the results are reported in Jacob, Teune, and Watts, *op. cit.*

8. These data are reported in *The Inter-*

action of Social Values and Political Responsibility in Developing Countries, Final Report to Science Director, U.S. Agency for International Development, under contract AID/csd -719 with the University of Pennsylvania, 1967.

9. These are partially described in Jacob, Teune and Watts, *op. cit.*, and in Allen H. Barton, *Technical Memoranda for ISVIP*. Doc. No. USA/91.

VI:
INTRODUCTION

1. Raymond A. Bauer, "The Study of Policy Formation: An Introduction," in Raymond A. Bauer and Kenneth J. Gergen, *The Study of Policy Formation* (New York: The Free Press, 1968), p. 9.

2. Austin Ranney, "The Study of Policy Content: A Framework for Choice," in Austin Ranney (ed.), *Political Science and Public Policy* (Chicago: Markham Publishing Company, 1968), p. 7.

3. See the provocative treatment of the question in J. J. Spengler, "Is Social Science Ready?" *Social Science Quarterly*, 50 (December 1969), pp. 449–468.

DECISION-MAKING AND TRANSPORTATION POLICY: A COMPARATIVE ANALYSIS
Frank C. Colcord, Jr.

1. The major literature treating the general problem includes: Wilfred Owen, *The Metropolitan Transportation Problem* (Washington, D.C.: The Brookings Institution, 1956, revised 1966); Lyle C. Fitch, *et al.*, *Urban Transportation and Public Policy* (San Francisco: Chandler Publishing Company, 1964); J. R. Meyer, J. F. Kain, and M. Wohl, *The Urban Transportation Problem* (Cambridge: Harvard University Press, 1965); and Committee for Economic Development, *Developing Transportation Policies: A Guide for Local Leadership* (April 1965). Also, see The Editors of *Fortune*, *The Exploding Metropolis* (Garden City: Doubleday Anchor Books, 1957, 1958), pp. 32–61; Lewis Mumford, *The Highway and the City* (New York: Harcourt, Brace and World, Inc., 1963), pp. 234–246; and The Scientific American, *Cities* (New York: Alfred A. Knopf, 1965), pp. 133–155.

2. For a full treatment of the response in the New York área to these problems see Jameson W. Doig, *Metropolitan Transportation*

Politics and the New York Region (New York: Columbia University Press, 1966). Also, see Robert C. Wood, *1400 Governments* (Cambridge: Harvard University Press, 1961), particularly pp. 123–143. For Boston, see Frank C. Colcord, Jr., *Metropolitan Transportation Politics*, Unpublished Ph.D. dissertation, MIT, 1964. A portion of the Chicago story is told in Edward Banfield, *Political Influence* (Glencoe, Illinois: Free Press, 1961), pp. 91–125. Unfortunately, the activities in the Philadelphia area, which were the earliest and most extensive, have not been the subject of any research literature.

3. Michael N. Danielson, *Federal-Metropolitan Politics and the Commuter Crisis* (New York: Columbia University Press, 1965).

4. The *only* exception among the larger urban areas is Miami-Dade County (Fla.).

5. Refer to footnote 2, above.

6. This hypothesis is an adaptation of a theory advanced by Edward C. Banfield and James Q. Wilson in *City Politics* (Cambridge: Harvard University Press, 1963), pp. 272–276.

7. The other areas included in the study are Boston, St. Louis, Kansas City, Houston, and San Francisco Bay. The seven areas were selected to provide a regional distribution, a distribution by size (ranging from one million to almost three million) and by stage of development of their present and planned local transportation systems. In this study we have avoided the "urban giants" (New York, Los Angeles, and Chicago) because of a fear they might be atypical, or at least that such a charge could be made. In fact, however, the literature regarding New York and the limited information available on Chicago and Los Angeles suggest that they may not differ significantly from the urban areas studied. Metropolitan areas below one million were omitted because we believed the character of most of their transportation problems is significantly different.

8. Hamilton Owens, *Baltimore on the Chesapeake* (Garden City: Doubleday, 1941), pp. 33–41.

9. The Baltimore SMSA grew from 1.4 in 1950 to 1.7 million in 1960, a 22.9 per cent increase. The Seattle SMSA grew from 844,000 in 1950 to 1,107,000 in 1960, a 31.1 per cent increase. By 1960 the Baltimore SMSA constituted 56 per cent of Maryland's total population, while that of Seattle was 39 per cent of Washington's. Seattle's population growth from 1950–1960 is largely attributed to an annexation which took place during the decade (Source: U.S. Census materials).

10. The Baltimore SMSA consists of two additional counties, Howard and Carroll, containing a total of only 5 per cent of the SMSA population. Carroll County contains one small municipality: Westminster.

11. John H. Fenton, *Politics in the Border States* (New Orleans: The Hauser Press, 1957), pp. 171–221; Jean E. Spencer, *Contemporary Local Government in Maryland* (College Park: University of Maryland, 1965).

12. Edward C. Banfield, *Big City Politics* (New York: Random House, 1965), pp. 133–146; Donald H. Webster, Ernest H. Campbell, George D. Smith, *Washington State Government* (Seattle: University of Washington Press, 1962).

13. *Baltimore Metropolitan Area Transportation Study*, 1964 (prepared by Wilbur Smith & Associates for the Maryland State Roads Commission).

14. Baltimore Regional Planning Council, *Technical Report No. 9*, "A Projection of Planning Factors for Land Use and Transportation," March, 1963.

15. *Baltimore Area Mass Transportation Plan: Phase II—Long Range Program*, Oct., 1965.

16. *Puget Sound Regional Transportation Study: A Summary Report*, Seattle, (undated).

17. The Urban Mass Transportation Act of 1964 (P.L. 88–365) authorizes $375 million for three years for grants-in-aid for transit capital expenditures on a two-thirds federal, one-third local matching basis.

18. In the conclusions of their exhaustive study of the subject, Meyer, Kain, and Wohl state,

Rail transit remains economically attractive for the line-haul only where population densities are extremely high, facilities are to be constructed underground, or rail roadbed structures are already on hand and can be regarded as sunk costs. *It is therefore significant that most American cities with enough population density to support a rail transit operation, or even with prospects of having enough, usually possess rail transit already* (emphasis added) (Meyer, Kain, and Wohl, *Urban Transportation Problem*, p. 364).

Wilfred Owen similarly states, "The inflexibility of rail operations, . . . indicates that rail rapid transit and railroad commutation services will not be greatly expanded beyond facilities now in use" (Owen, *Metropolitan Transportation Problem*, p. 214).

19. *Report*, Baltimore Metropolitan Area Mass Transit Legislative Commission, Oct. 1960.

20. The original plan proposed by the consultants, based on economic, demographic, and engineering considerations, proposed that the two suburban "legs" extend into Baltimore County. Under the new tentative plan, one of these legs will go to Anne Arundel County.

21. Mr. Barnes is probably the nation's most famous traffic director. He established his reputation in Denver, whence he came to

Baltimore; he now holds this position in New York City. His reputation is based on a combination of traffic engineering skills and public relations techniques. There is general agreement in Baltimore that he "worked a miracle" with that city traffic, the effects of which are still decidedly being felt.

22. In the latter city, 41 per cent of the housing units in 1960 had no automobile, whereas the comparable figure for Seattle was 26 per cent. The figures for the two suburban areas were 11 per cent and 8 per cent respectively (Source: U.S. Census of 1960).

23. "An effective solution to the urban transportation problem ... should ... be functionally comprehensive ... should be comprehensive geographically ... , (and) ... should be comprehensive from a planning standpoint by assuring that transportation is used to promote community goals, and that community plans make satisfactory transportation possible" (Owen, *Metropolitan Transportation Problem*, p. 224). It is interesting to note that it is almost exactly his prescription that was added to the Federal Highway Act by the 1962 amendment.

24. Federal Highway Act of 1962; Section 701 of the Housing Act of 1954.

25. "Washington Creates Local Affairs Agency," *Metropolitan Area Digest*, 10:3 (May–June 1967), p. 4.

REFORMISM AND PUBLIC POLICIES IN AMERICAN CITIES
Robert L. Lineberry and Edmund P. Fowler

1. Lawrence J. R. Herson, "The Lost World of Municipal Government," *American Political Science Review*, 51 (June 1957), 330–345; Robert T. Daland, "Political Science and the Study of Urbanism," *ibid.*, 491–509.

2. David Easton, "An Approach to the Analysis of Political Systems," *World Politics*, 9 (April 1957), 383–400.

3. Edward C. Banfield and James Q. Wilson, *City Politics* (Cambridge: Harvard University Press and the MIT Press, 1963); see also James Q. Wilson and Edward C. Banfield, "Public-Regardingness as a Value Premise in Voting Behavior," *American Political Science Review* 58 (December 1964), 876–887. [Reprinted as Selection 13 in this volume.]

4. See, for example, Thomas R. Dye, "City-Suburban Social Distance and Public Policy," *Social Forces*, 4 (1965), 100–106; Raymond Wolfinger and John Osgood Field, "Political Ethos and the Structure of City Government," *American Political Science Review*, 60 (June 1966), 306–326; Edgar L. Sherbenou, "Class, Participation, and the Council-Manager Plan," *Public Administration Review*, 21 (Summer 1961), 131–135; Lewis A. Froman, Jr., "An

Analysis of Public Policies in Cities," *Journal of Politics*, 29 (February 1967), 94–108.

5. (New York: Alfred A. Knopf, 1955.)

6. John Porter East, *Council Manager Government: The Political Thought of Its Founder, Richard S. Childs* (Chapel Hill: University of North Carolina Press, 1965), p. 18.

7. Ernest S. Bradford, *Commission Government in American Cities* (New York: Macmillan, 1911), p. 165.

8. Banfield and Wilson, *op. cit.*, p. 41.

9. Robert Agger, Daniel Goldrich, and Bert E. Swanson, *The Rulers and the Ruled* (New York: John Wiley and Sons, 1964), p. 21.

10. Robert C. Wood, *Suburbia: Its People and Their Politics* (Boston: Houghton Mifflin Co., 1959), p. 155.

11. *Ibid.*, p. 154.

12. We refer to cities characterized by commission or manager government, nonpartisan elections, and at-large constituencies as "reformed." Our use of the term is historical and no value position on reformism's merits is intended. To refer to reformed cities as "public regarding" or "middle class" is, it seems, to assume what needs to be proved.

13. Leo Schnore and Robert Alford, "Forms of Government and Socio-Economic Characteristics of Suburbs," *Administrative Science Quarterly*, 8 (June 1963), 1–17. See also the literature cited in Froman, *op. cit.*

14. Wolfinger and Field, *op. cit.*, pp. 325–326.

15. The source for the first nine variables is *The City and County Data Book* (Washington: United States Bureau of the Census, 1962). For the last three variables, the source is Orin F. Nolting and David S. Arnold (eds.), *The Municipal Yearbook 1965* (Chicago: International City Managers' Association, 1965), pp. 98 ff.

16. We used a random sample of 200 of the 309 American cities with populations of 50,000 or more in 1960. All information on the forms of government and forms of election are drawn from *The Municipal Yearbook, 1965, op. cit.*

17. Banfield and Wilson, *op. cit.*, p. 151.

18. For Minneapolis, see Robert Morlan, "City Politics: Free Style," *National Municipal Review*, 48 (November 1949), pp. 485–490; Winnetka, Banfield and Wilson, *op. cit.*, p. 140; Los Angeles, Charles G. Mayo, "The 1961 Mayoralty Election in Los Angeles: The Political Party in a Non-partisan Election," *Western Political Quarterly*, 17 (1964), 325–339.

19. At least one other variable may produce a given institutional form in a city—the legal requirements of a state government, which vary from state to state and may even vary for different kinds of cities within the same state. We have not taken account of this

variable because systematic information on comparative state requirements in this area was unavailable to us. However, Wolfinger and Field consulted several experts and eliminated cities which are not given free choice over their institutions. Nevertheless, a comparison of our figures with theirs revealed no important differences.

20. See footnote 4, *supra.*

21. We recognize that these are only rough indicators of city finance policies. Definitions of taxation vary from city to city and what may be financed from taxes in one city may be financed from fees in another. Expenditures present a more complex problem because the types and amounts of state transfer payments vary from state to state according to state laws, the division of governmental labor in a state, the incomes and sizes of cities, not to mention political factors at the state level. We think it important, however, that our independent variables explain a large proportion of the variation in municipal outputs as we measured them. No doubt one could explain an even larger proportion of the variation in measures which specify different functional responsibilities of cities. At least these measures constitute a starting point, and we hope others will improve on them.

The source of our output measures was the *County and City Data Book, op. cit.*

22. See, for example, Robert Alford and Harry Scoble, "Political and Socio-Economic Characteristics of American Cities," *The Municipal Year Book 1965, op. cit.*, pp. 82–97; Sherbenou, *op. cit*; John H. Kessel, "Governmental Structure and Political Environment," *American Political Science Review* 56 (September 1962), 615–620.

23. Alford and Scoble, *op. cit.* The particularly large differences found between the populations of reformed and unreformed cities reflect the fact that New York City and several other urban giants are included in the sample.

24. *Op. cit.*, p. 320.

25. In statistical parlance, the problem with "region" as an independent variable might be described as treating a complicated background variable as the first variable in a specific developmental sequence. But, as Blalock argues, ". . . *one should avoid complex indicators that are related in unknown ways to a given underlying variable.* Geographical region and certain background variables appear to have such undesirable properties": Hubert M. Blalock, *Causal Inferences in Nonexperimental Research* (Chapel Hill: University of North Carolina Press, 1964), p. 164 (italics in original).

26. Amos Hawley, "Community Power and Urban Renewal Success," *American Journal of Sociology*, 68 (January 1963), 422–431.

27. See also the exchange between Banfield and Wilson and Wolfinger and Field in "Communications," 60 (December 1966), 998–1000.

28. Sherbenou, *op. cit.*, pp. 133–134.

29. *Op. cit.*, p. 139.

30. Quoted in Banfield and Wilson, *op. cit.*, p. 154.

31. For a discussion of the concept of interest aggregation, see Gabriel Almond, "Introduction: A Functional Approach to Comparative Politics," in Gabriel Almond and James S. Coleman (eds.), *The Politics of Developing Areas* (Princeton: Princeton University Press, 1960), pp. 38–45.

32. Maurice Duverger, *Political Parties* (New York: Science Editions, 1963), p. 378.

33. Frank J. Sorauf, *Political Parties in the American System* (Boston: Little, Brown and Co., 1964), pp. 165–166.

34. Gerald Pomper, "Ethnic and Group Voting in Nonpartisan Municipal Elections," *Public Opinion Quarterly*, 30 (Spring, 1966), p. 90; see also, J. Leiper Freeman, "Local Party Systems: Theoretical Considerations and a Case Analysis," *American Journal of Sociology*, 64 (1958), 282–289.

35. It is possible that the difference between any two correlations may be a function of very different standard deviations of the independent variables. A quick look at Table 2, however, suggests that this is not likely to affect the relationships we find.

36. Wolfinger and Field, *op. cit.*, p. 312, " . . . omit the commission cities from consideration since this form does not figure in the ethos theory." Historically, however, commission government was the earliest of the structures advocated by the Progressives and is quite clearly a product of the reform era. While history tells us that commission cities can not legitimately be excluded from the fold of reformism, they appear to be its black sheep, characterized by low incomes, low population growth and large proportions of non-whites. In fact, they present a marked contrast to both mayor-council and manager cities.

37. Agger *et al., op. cit.*, pp. 4–14.

38. Charles A. Beard, *American Government and Politics* (New York: Macmillan, 1924, 4th edition), p. 727.

39. V. O. Key, *Public Opinion and American Democracy* (New York: Alfred A. Knopf, 1961), p. 124.

40. Wilson and Banfield, *op. cit.*, p. 876. Footnote 5 in the same article conveniently summarized research supporting this proposition.

41. Eugene S. Uyeki, "Patterns of Voting in a Metropolitan Area: 1938–1962," *Urban Affairs Quarterly*, 1 (June 1966), 65–77.

42. Banfield and Wilson, *op. cit.*, p. 35.

43. Richard E. Dawson and James A. Robinson, "The Politics of Welfare," in Herbert Jacob and Kenneth Vines (eds.), *Politics in the American States* (Boston: Little, Brown and Co., 1965), pp. 398–401.

44. Raymond Wolfinger, "The Development and Persistence of Ethnic Voting," *American Political Science Review*, 59 (December 1965), 896–908.

45. Robert E. Lane, *Political Life* (Glencoe, Ill.: The Free Press, 1959), pp. 236–243.

46. *Ibid.*

47. Harold Stone, Don K. Price and Kathryn Stone, *City Manager Government in the United States* (Chicago: Public Administration Service, 1940), p. 238.

48. The standard argument for party responsibility is found in the works of E. E. Schattschneider, esp., *Party Government* (New York: Farrar and Rinehart, 1942) and in the report of the Committee on Political Parties of the American Political Science Association, *Toward a More Responsible Two-Party System* (New York: Rinehart, 1950).

49. See Pomper, *op. cit.*; and Freeman, *op. cit.*

50. Robert Salisbury and Gordon Black, "Class and Party in Partisan and Nonpartisan Elections: The Case of Des Moines," *American Political Science Review*, 57 (September, 1963), 584–592.

51. One newspaperman said of nonpartisan politics that "You can't tell the players without a scorecard, and we sell the scorecards": Banfield and Wilson, *op. cit.*, p. 157.

52. Oliver P. Williams and Charles Adrian, *Four Cities* (Philadelphia: University of Pennsylvania Press, 1963) pp. 56–57.

53. Alford and Scoble, *op. cit.*, p. 84.

54. In our view, the failure of the commission government to achieve the intended reforms is more plausible as an explanation of its demise than its administrative unwieldiness—the conventional explanation.

55. Williams and Adrian, *op. cit.*, pp. 30–31.

56. Carol E. Thometz discusses the role of the "Civic Committee" in decision-making in Dallas: see *The Decision-Makers* (Dallas: Southern Methodist University Press, 1963).

COMMUNITY STRUCTURE, DECISION-MAKING, BUDGET EXPENDITURE, AND URBAN RENEWAL IN 51 AMERICAN COMMUNITIES
Terry N. Clark

1. Robert A. Dahl, *Who Governs?* (New Haven: Yale University Press, 1961).

2. Terry N. Clark, "Power and Community Structure: Who Governs, Where, and When?" *The Sociological Quarterly*, 8 (Summer 1967), pp. 316–319 (Selection 17 in this volume).

3. *Ibid.*, and the works cited there.

4. Peter H. Rossi, "Power and Community Structure," *Midwest Journal of Political Science*, 4 (November 1960), pp. 390–400.

5. Robert Presthus, *Men at the Top* (New York: Oxford University Press, 1964). Robert E. Agger, et al., *The Rulers and the Ruled* (New York: John Wiley & Sons, Inc., 1964). Charles Adrian and Oliver P. Williams, *Four Cities* (Philadelphia: University of Pennsylvania Press, 1963).

6. John Walton, "Substance and Artifact: The Current Status of Research on Community Power Structure," *American Journal of Sociology*, 71 (January 1966), pp. 684–99. John Walton, "Differential Patterns of Community Power Structure: An Explanation Based on Interdependence," in *Community Structure and Decision-Making: Comparative Analyses*, ed. by T. N. Clark (San Francisco: Chandler Publishing Company, 1968), pp. 441–462 (Selection 18 in this volume). Claire W. Gilbert, "Community Power and Decision-Making: A Quantitive Examination of Previous Research," in T. N. Clark, ed., *Community Structure*, pp. 139–158. T. N. Clark *et al.*, "Discipline, Method, Community Structure and Decision-Making: The Role and Limitations of the Sociology of Knowledge," *American Sociologist*, 3 (August 1968), pp. 214–217.

7. T. N. Clark, "Present and Future Research on Community Decision-Making: The Problem of Comparability," in T. N. Clark, ed., *Community Structure*, pp. 463–478. Peter H. Rossi and Robert L. Crain, "The NORC Permanent Community Sample," *Public Opinion Quarterly*, 32 (Summer 1968), pp. 261–272.

8. Robert L. Crain *et al.*, *School Desegregation in the North* (Chicago: National Opinion Research Center, University of Chicago, 1966).

9. Various measures of reliability and validity for the study are presently being prepared which will be reported in subsequent papers.

10. See the theoretical discussions in T. N. Clark, ed., *Community Structure*, pp. 45–72, and Theodore J. Lowi, "American Business and Public Policy, Case Studies, and Political Theory," *World Politics*, 6 (September 1964), pp. 701–716.

11. We understand by *decision-making structure* the patterned distribution of *influence* exercised in a community, in contrast to the patterned distribution of *resources*, which is better referred to as a *power structure*. See T. N. Clark, ed., *Community Structure*, pp. 45–72.

12. If there were more than two "sides" to an issue, the third (or fourth) side was treated as a second (or third) distinct "opponent."

13. Dahl, *op. cit.* Presthus, *op. cit.* T. N. Clark, "The Concept of Power: Some Overemphasized and Underrecognized Dimensions," *(Southwestern) Social Science Quarterly*

(December 1967), pp. 271–286 (Selection 3 in this volume)

14. Ruth Moser has experimented with alternative weighting schemes. Ruth Moser, "Correlates of Decision-Making in Eighteen New England Communities," (unpublished Master's essay, University of Chicago, 1968).

15. Clark, "Power and Community Structure," pp. 291–316.

16. T. N. Clark, ed., *Community Structure*, pp. 91–122.

17. The source for information about each variable is indicated under Table 2, except for the governmental characteristics, taken from *The Municipal Yearbook, 1966* (Chicago: International City Managers Association, 1966).

18. Howard J. Nelson, "A Service Classification of American Cities," *Economic Geography*, 31 (July 1955), pp. 189–210.

19. A dummy variable format was used when correlating qualitative with quantitative variables. See N. R. Draper and H. Smith, *Applied Regression Analysis* (New York: John Wiley & Sons, Inc., 1966).

20. Edward C. Banfield and James Q. Wilson, *City Politics* (Cambridge: Harvard University Press and M.I.T. Press, 1963). Charles R. Adrian and Charles Press, *Governing Urban America* (New York: McGraw-Hill Book Co., 1968), Chapter VIII.

21. This same procedure was used by Lineberry and Fowler except that they included commission government as a reform characteristic. In a personal communication Lineberry agreed that our weighting scheme is probably more appropriate. Robert L. Lineberry and Edmund P. Fowler, "Reformism and Public Policies in American Cities," *American Political Science Review*, 61 (September 1967), pp. 701–716 (Selection 27 in this volume).

22. Path analysis, although developed by the geneticist Sewall Wright in the 1920s, has remained a seldom utilized statistical technique. The works of Simon and Blalock stimulated interest in causal models, while Duncan's recent article brought path analysis as used in genetics to the attention of contemporary sociologists. Raymond Boudon's outstanding study is to date the most thorough treatment of path analysis and its relationships to more traditional statistical procedures. With the increasing concern in the social sciences for specifically causal models, and the ease of data processing made possible by high-speed computers, path analysis may well become widely used in the near future. Herbert A. Simon, *Models of Man* (New York: John Wiley & Sons, Inc., 1957). Hubert Blalock, *Causal Inferences in Non-Experimental Research* (Chapel Hill: University of North Carolina Press, 1961). Otis Dudley Duncan, "Path Analysis:

Sociological Examples," *American Journal of Sociology*, 72 (July, 1966), pp. 1–16. Raymond Boudon, *L'analyse mathématique des faits sociaux* (Paris: Plon Press, 1967).

23. Figures 1 through 5, when superimposed upon one another, constitute a complete path analysis diagram with all traditional elements included. The difficulties of reading such a complex diagram led us to break it down into five separate parts, each of which corresponds to a single dependent variable.

Each of the five tables also contains the corresponding regression equation, including the intercept, the unstandardized regression coefficient for each variable, and (in parentheses) the standard error of each regression coefficient. Linear least squares regression was used in every case, except for ethnicity, for only a few were sufficiently skewed to justify transformation. See also footnote 39.

24. There are one or two cases that follow in which the causal sequence is not as clearcut as indicated by the path analysis diagrams. While fully recognizing this point, we felt that it was valuable to attempt causal statements wherever possible instead of speaking merely in terms of associations. Our interpretations may then be more directly validated or revised by future studies.

25. Murray Hausknecht, *The Joiners* (New York: Bedminster Press, 1962).

26. Robert Alford and Harry Scoble, "Political and Socio-economic Characteristics of American Cities," in *The Municipal Yearbook, 1965* (Chicago: International City Managers Association), pp. 82–97. John H. Kessel, "Government Structure and Political Environment," *American Political Science Review*, 56 (September, 1963), pp. 615–620. Raymond E. Wolfinger and John Osgood Field, "Political Ethos and Structure of City Government," *American Political Science Review*, 60 (June 1966) pp. 306–326. Lineberry and Fowler, *loc. cit.*

27. See T. N. Clark, ed., *Community Structure*.

28. For documentation, see Clark "Power and Community Structure" (Proposition 1).

29. See T. N. Clark, ed., *Community Structure*, p. 99ff.

30. *Ibid.*, p. 130.

31. *Ibid.*, p. 107ff, for further discussion.

32. *Ibid.*, p. 119.

33. *Ibid.*, p. 115.

34. *Ibid.*, p. 107.

35. *Ibid.*, pp. 463–476.

36. But see *Ibid.*, pp. 383–422.

37. Amos H. Hawley, "Community Power and Urban Renewal Success," *American Journal of Sociology*, 68 (January 1963), pp. 422–431. William A. Gamson, "Rancorous Conflict in Community Politics," *American Sociological Review*, 31 (February 1966), pp. 78–81. Donald Rosenthal and Robert L. Crain, "Structure and Values in Local Political

Systems: The Case of Fluoridation Decisions," *Journal of Politics*, 28 (February 1966), pp. 169–196. Crain *et al.*, *op. cit.* T. N. Clark, ed., *Community Structure*, p. 92ff.

38. Harold F. Gosnell, *Machine Politics: Chicago Model* (2d ed., Chicago: University of Chicago Press, 1968). Nathan Glazer and Daniel Patrick Moynihan, *Beyond the Melting Pot* (Cambridge: The M.I.T. Press, 1963). Edward M. Levine, *The Irish and Irish Politicians* (Notre Dame: University of Notre Dame Press, 1966).

39. Because the distributions for several variables were slightly skewed, a natural logarithmic transformation was used for thirteen of the nationality variables. In Table 11 the natural logarithms of variables X_6, V, and Z_1 were used.

40. Angus Campbell *et al.*, *The American Voter* (New York: John Wiley & Sons, Inc., 1964), Chapter XI. Phillip E. Converse, "Religion and Politics: The 1960 Election," in Angus Campbell *et al.*, *Elections and the Political Order* (New York: John Wiley & Sons, Inc., 1966), pp. 96–124.

41. Gerhard Lenski, *The Religious Factor* (Garden City, New York: Doubleday-Anchor, 1961), p. 154.

42. *Ibid.*, p. 154.

43. There are practically no studies which systematically examine the determinants of urban renewal expenditures. Duggar is a partial exception, but he included no community-structural characteristics in his analysis. George Duggar, "The Relationship of Local Government Structures to Urban Renewal," *Law and Contemporary Problems*, 26 (Winter 1961), pp. 49–69.

44. Harvey Elliot Brazer, *City Expenditures in the United States* (New York: National Bureau of Economic Research, 1959). Seymour Sacks and William F. Hellmuth, Jr., *Financing Government in a Metropolitan Area* (New York: The Free Press, 1961). Alan Campbell and Seymour Sacks, *Metropolitan America* (New York: The Free Press, 1967).

45. John C. Bollans, ed., *Exploring the Metropolitan Community* (Berkeley and Los Angeles: University of California Press, 1965). Sacks and Hellmuth, *op. cit.* Stanley Scott and Edward L. Feder, *Factors Associated with Variations in Municipal Expenditure Levels* (Berkeley: Bureau of Public Administration, University of California, 1957). Glenn W. Fisher and Robert P. Fairbanks, *Illinois Municipal Finance* (Urbana: University of Illinois Press, 1968).

46. Robert C. Wood, *1,400 Governments* (New York: Doubleday–Anchor, 1964). Oliver P. Williams *et al.*, *Suburban Differences and Metropolitan Policies* (Philadelphia: University of Pennsylvania Press, 1965), p. 91 ff.

47. Amos H. Hawley, "Metropolitan Population and Municipal Government Expendi-

tures in Central Cities," *Journal of Social Issues*, 7 (1951), pp. 100–108. Brazer, *op. cit.*

48. See, for example, Harold C. Stone, D. Price, Katheryn Stone, *City Manager Government in Nine Cities* (Chicago: Public Affairs Service, 1940).

49. Wolfinger and Field, *op. cit.*; Lineberry and Fowler, *op. cit.*

50. Terry N. Clark, "Urban Typologies and Political Outputs: Causal Models Using Discrete Variables and Orthogonal Factors, or Precise Distortion versus Model Muddling" in Brian J. L. Berry, ed., *Classification of Cities: New Methods and Evolving Uses* (International City Managers Association and Resources for the Future, forthcoming).

COMMUNITIES AND BUDGETS: THE SOCIOLOGY OF MUNICIPAL EXPENDITURES
Louis H. Masotti and Don R. Bowen

1. This hypothesis has been investigated by others using various data, samples and techniques. See, for example, Harvey E. Brazer, *City Expenditures in the United States* (New York: National Bureau of Economic Research, 1959); Seymour Sacks and William F. Hellmuth, *Financing Government in a Metropolitan Area* (New York: The Free Press of Glencoe, 1961); Robert C. Wood, *1400 Governments* (Garden City, New York: Doubleday and Co., 1964). References to similarities and differences in methodology and findings between this study and those preceding it will be alluded to where relevant.

2. Factor analysis is a method designed to facilitate the uncovering of basic underlying variables. It involves a series of operations based on mathematical theory to solve systems of equations. For an introduction to the technique and its mathematical theory see L. L. Thurstone, *Multi-Factor Analysis* (Chicago: University of Chicago Press, 1947): K. J. Holzinger and H. H. Harman, *Factor Analysis: A Synthesis of Factorial Methods* (Chicago: University of Chicago Press, 1941). Less technical presentations will be found in Benjamin Fruchter, *Introduction to Factor Analysis* (New York: D. Van Nostrand Co., Inc., 1954); H. H. Harman, *Modern Factor Analysis* (Chicago: University of Chicago Press, 1960); R. B. Cattell, *Factor Analysis* (New York: Harper & Bros., 1956).

3. Specifically, because some states distribute governmental functions in slightly different ways; in addition there are differences in accounting for and reporting expenditures

within the various functional categories. Cf. Brazer, *op. cit.*, p. 16.

4. U.S. Department of Commerce, Bureau of the Census (G-CF61—No. 2) (Washington, D. C.: GPO, 1962). Separate categories in this publication were combined in two instances (health and hospitals, sewers and sanitation) for purposes of the present analysis.

5. Originally, sixty-six socioeconomic characteristics selected from the 1960 population census and the 1958 Census of Business were used. These represented all the items thought to be at all relevant. The original sixty-six were reduced to thirty-eight on the basis of a simple correlation analysis. Items which did not yield a correlation of $\pm .5$ or better with at least one of the twelve expenditure categories were omitted.

6. Calculations were made on a Univac 1107. Our thanks are due to Mr. Gerry McNichols of Case Institute of Technology who rendered invaluable assistance in programming and interpreting the results. The authors would also like to thank the Graduate Council of Western Reserve University for making funds available to process the data used in this study.

7. The analyses isolated seven additional factors which together accounted for only about 20 per cent of the variance. Hence we concentrated on the three most significant factors and, for the present at least, dismissed the others.

8. Although his analysis employs a different sample and technique, this finding gains some support from Brazer's conclusion, *op. cit.*, pp. 29, 56, that income is the single most important variable for explaining variance in city expenditures both for his national sample of 432 cities and the subsample of thirty-two Ohio cities. Sacks and Hellmuth, *op. cit.*, p. 125, note that per capita wealth is important to the explanation of variance in such functional categories as police, fire and general control for all cities in the Cleveland Metropolitan Area. This latter finding, however, should be set alongside the general conclusion that two other independent characteristics, size and assessed valuation, are generally as important as wealth in explaining variations in per capita city expenditures. Wood, *op. cit.*, pp. 40–42, using the same analytic technique employed in the present study (factor analysis), found that several items, such as residential affluence and prevalence of low income families, are related to expenditures in all functional categories on a per capita basis for a subsample of 64 Northern New Jersey communities in the New York Metropolitan Area. Both of these items appear to us to be included within the factor we have called socioeconomic class. Wood has also observed that the names affixed to factors should be recognized for what they are— identification tags, not complete descriptions of the contents. *Op. cit.*, p. 35.

9. Cf. Sacks and Hellmuth, *op. cit.*, p. 125.

10. Wood, *op. cit.*, pp. 41–43, finds that age is generally more important in accounting for differing rates of per capita expenditures in all functional categories than are such items as low income prevalence, residential affluence or housing density. The contrast appears to us to be due to the fact, as noted above, that these three latter characteristics are all included within the factor we have called socioeconomic class.

11. Brazer, *op. cit.*, pp. 29, 46, 53, notes that rate of population growth is of little significance in explaining variation in per capita city expenditures for both his national sample and the subsample of Ohio cities. He does, however, note that it is important for his subsample of California cities where growth is an important characteristic. Insofar as the differences in findings are not due to differences in analytic techniques and samples, it appears that our sample of 18 Ohio cities in 1960 is comparable to Brazer's sample of California cities in 1950 in that the cities used here include a number of rapidly growing suburbs, hence we would suspect that the factor we have called mobility would now loom larger than it did when Brazer's study was made. In addition, of course, the factor we have called mobility includes other measures besides rate of population growth.

12. Sacks and Hellmuth, *op. cit.*, p. 105, note that a static population is associated with increasing total operating expenditures but since they do not break this down into functional expenditure categories the finding cannot be compared to the results obtained here.

13. Cf. Wood, *op. cit.*, pp. 42–43, for comparable findings.

14. The 1960 population of the eighteen cities used in this analysis (smallest to largest) are as follows (See Table 1 for the ranking of specific socioeconomic characteristics): Lima (51,037); Kettering (54,462); Warren (59,648); Cleveland Heights (61,813); Lakewood (66,154); Lorain (68,932); Euclid (69,998); Hamilton (72,354); Springfield (82,723); Parma (82,845); Canton (113,631); Youngstown (166,689); Dayton (262,332); Akron (290,351); Toledo (318,003); Columbus (471,316); Cincinnati (502,550); Cleveland (876,050).

15. All eighteen cities spent some of their funds on these two items whereas a few did not allocate funds for some of the other budget items, e.g., housing and urban renewal, public welfare, water. See Table 1.

16. On this point, see Glenn W. Fisher, "Revenue and Expenditure Patterns in Five Large Cities," *Economics and Business*, 3 (Autumn 1963), pp. 61–72.

17. Brazer, *op. cit.*, p. 25, uses six independent variables in analyzing variations in expenditures for a national sample of 432 cities and subsamples of 35 California cities, 30 Massachusetts cities and 32 Ohio cities. Sacks and

Hellmuth, *op. cit.*, p. 89, use three independent variables to explain variation for subsample of 20 cities and 42 villages in the Cleveland Metropolitan Area. Wood, *op. cit.*, pp. 39–40, included seven socioeconomic characteristics in his factor analysis for a sample of 64 New Jersey cities in the New York Metropolitan Area. In a sense, of course, we have used only three variables—SES, age and mobility—to explain variations in expenditures. The difference is that we began with a total of 38 socioeconomic characteristics and reduced these to three underlying factors as a result of the factor analysis rather than committing

ourselves to a single measure of such a factor as SES beforehand.

18. Sacks and Hellmuth, *op. cit.*, p. 93 and Wood, *op. cit.*, p. 39 both argue that community size is the single most important variable bearing on total operating expenditures. Brazer concludes that for his national sample size is not significantly related to total operating expenses. *Op. cit.*, p. 25.

19. Brazer, *op. cit.*, p. 28; Sacks and Hellmuth, *op. cit.*, p. 119: Wood, *op. cit.*, pp. 39–40.

20. See Table 2.

Bibliographies

Selected Bibliography on Community Power Structure*

Roland J. Pellegrin

University of Oregon

1. Abramson, E., H. A. Cutter, R. W. Kautz, and M. Mendelson. "Social Power and Commitment: A Theoretical Statement," *American Sociological Review*, 23 (Feb. 1958), pp. 15–22.

2. Abu-Laban, Baha. "Leader Visibility in a Local Community," *Pacific Sociological Review*, 42 (Fall 1961), pp. 73–78.

3. ———. "Self-Conception and Appraisal by Others: A Study of Community Leaders," *Sociology and Social Research*, 48 (Oct. 1963), pp. 32–37.

4. ———. "Social Origins and Occupational Career Patterns of Community Leaders," *Sociological Inquiry*, 33 (Spring 1963), pp. 131–140.

5. ———. "The Reputational Approach in the Study of Community Power: A Critical Evaluation," *Pacific Sociological Review*, 8 (Spring 1965), pp. 35–42.

6. Adrian, Charles R. "Leadership and Decision-Making in Manager Cities: A Study of Three Communities," *Public Administration Review*, 18 (Summer 1958), pp. 208–213.

7. ——— (ed.). *Social Science and Community Action*. East Lansing: Institute for Community Development and Services, Michigan State University, 1960.

8. ———, and David A. Booth. *Simplifying the Discovery of Elites*. East Lansing: Institute for Community Development and Services, Michigan State University, n.d. Reprint.

9. Agger, Robert E. "The Dynamics of Local Political Participation: Empirical Research and Theoretical Inquiry." Unpublished Ph.D. dissertation, University of Oregon, 1954.

10. ———. "The Politics of Local Education: A Comparative Study of Community Decision-Making," in Donald E. Tope (ed.). *A Forward Look: The Preparation of School Administrators, 1970*. Eugene: Bureau of Educational Research, University of Oregon, 1960. Pp. 131–172.

11. ———. "Power Attributions in the Local Community," *Social Forces*, 34 (May 1966), pp. 322–331.

12. ———, and Daniel Goldrich. "Community Power Structures and Partisanship," *American Sociological Review*, 23 (Aug. 1958), pp. 383–392.

13. ———, and Vincent Ostrom. "Political Participation in a Small Community," in Heinz Eulau, *et al.* (eds.). *Political Behavior*. Chicago: Free Press, 1957. Pp. 138–148.

14. ———, and Vincent Ostrom. "The Political Structure of a Small Community," *Public Opinion Quarterly*, 20 (Spring 1956), pp. 81–89.

15. ———, Bert E. Swanson, Daniel Goldrich, and Marshall N. Goldstein. "Emprical Considerations," in Bert E. Swanson (ed.). *Current Trends in Comparative Community Studies*. Public Affairs Monograph Series, No. 1. Kansas City: Community Studies, Inc., 1962. Pp. 81–88.

16. ———, *et al.* "Political Influence Structures in Four Communities." Paper read at the American Sociological Association meeting, September 1959.

17. ———, *et al. The Rulers and the Ruled: Political Power and Impotence in American Communities*. New York: John Wiley and Sons, 1964.

18. Anderson, William. "Political Influences of the Metropolis," in R. M. Fisher (ed.). *The Metropolis in Modern Life*. New York: Doubleday Inc., 1955. Pp. 57–65.

19. Andrews, W. H. "Some Correlates of Rural Leadership and Social Power among Intercommunity Leaders." Unpublished Ph.D. dissertation, Michigan State University, 1956.

20. Anton, Thomas J. "Power, Pluralism, and Local Politics," *Administrative Science Quarterly*, 7 (March 1963), pp. 425–457.

21. ———. "Rejoinder," *Administrative Science Quarterly*, 8 (Sept. 1963), pp. 257–262.

22. Babchuck, Nicholas, *et al.* "Men and Women in Community Agencies: A Note on Power and Prestige," *American Sociological Review*, 25 (June 1960), pp. 399–403.

23. Bachrach, P. "Elite Consensus and Democracy," *Journal of Politics*, 24 (Aug. 1962), pp. 439–452.

24. ———, and M. Baratz. "Two Faces of Power," *American Political Science Review*, 51 (Dec. 1962), pp. 947–952.

25. Bailey, Stephen K. "Leadership in Local Government," *Yale Review*, 45 (June 1956), pp. 563–573.

* Reprinted with permission of the author and publisher, from Roland J. Pellegrin, "Selected Bibliography on Community Power Structure," (Southwestern) Social Science Quarterly, 48 (December, 1967), pp. 451–465.

26. Banfield, Edward C. *Political Influence.* Glencoe, Illinois: The Free Press, 1960.
27. ——, and James Q. Wilson. *City Politics.* Cambridge: Harvard University Press and MIT Press, 1963.
28. Barkley, R. "Theory of the Elite and the Mythology of Power," *Science and Society,* 19 (Spring 1955), pp. 97–106.
29. Barth, Ernest A. T. "Air Force Base-Host Community Relations: A Study in Community Typology," *Social Forces,* 41 (March 1963), pp. 260–264.
30. ——. "Community Influence Systems: Structure and Change," *Social Forces,* 40 (Oct. 1961), pp. 58–63.
31. ——, and Baha Abu-Laban. "Power Structure and the Negro Sub-Community," *American Sociological Review,* 24 (Feb. 1959), pp. 69–76.
32. ——, and Stuart D. Johnson, "Community Power and a Typology of Social Issues," *Social Forces,* 38 (Oct. 1959), pp. 29–32.
33. Bassett, Raymond E. "Sampling Problems in Influence Studies," *Sociometry,* 12 (Nov. 1948), pp. 320–328.
34. Belknap, George M. "Methodological Problems in the Study of Urban Elites." East Lansing: Michigan State University, Sept. 1959. Mimeographed.
35. ——. "Political Power Relations in a Mid-West City," *Public Opinion Quarterly,* 20 (Spring 1956), pp. 73–81.
36. ——, and Ralph H. Smuckler. *Leadership and Participation in Urban Political Affairs.* East Lansing: Government Research Bureau, Michigan State University, 1956.
37. Belknap, Ivan, and John G. Steinle. *The Community and Its Hospitals.* Syracuse: Syracuse University Press, 1963.
38. Bell, Daniel. "The Power Elite—Reconsidered," *American Journal of Sociology,* 64 (Nov. 1958), pp. 238–250.
39. Bell, Wendell, and Maryanne T. Force. "Social Structure and Participation in Different Types of Formal Associations," *Social Forces,* 34 (May 1956), pp. 345–350.
40. Bell, Wendell, Richard J. Hill, and Charles R. Wright. *Public Leadership.* San Francisco: Chandler Publishing Co., 1961.
41. Beth, Marian W. "The Elite and the Elites," *American Journal of Sociology,* 47 (March 1942), pp. 746–755.
42. Bierstedt, Robert. "An Analysis of Social Power," *American Sociological Review,* 15 (Dec. 1950), pp. 730–738.
43. Birch, A. H. *Small-Town Politics: A Study of Political Life in Glossop.* New York: Oxford University Press, 1959.
44. ——. "Review of Robert Dahl, *Who Governs?*" *Public Administration,* 40 (Autumn 1962), pp. 341–342.
45. Blackwell, Gordon W. "Community Analysis," in Roland Young (ed.). *Approaches to the Study of Politics.* Evanston: Northwestern University Press, 1958. Pp. 305–317.
46. ——. "A Theoretical Framework for Sociological Research in Community Organization," *Social Forces,* 33 (Oct. 1954), pp. 57–64.
47. Blankenship, Vaughn. "Community Power and Decision-Making: A Comparative Evaluation of Measurement Techniques," *Social Forces,* 43 (Dec. 1964), pp. 207–216.
48. ——. "Organizational Support and Community Leadership in Two New York State Communities." Unpublished Ph.D. dissertation, Cornell University, June 1962.
49. Blau, Peter M. *Bureaucracy in Modern Society.* New York: Random House, 1956.
50. Bloomberg, Warner. "The Structure of Power in Stackton," Unpublished Ph.D. dissertation, University of Chicago, 1960.
51. ——, and Morris Sunshine. *Suburban Power Structures and Public Education.* Syracuse: Syracuse University Press, 1963.
52. Blumbart, Leonard. "Community Leaders: The Social Bases and Social Psychological Concomitants of Community Power." Unpublished Ph.D. dissertation, University of Michigan, 1955.
53. Bonjean, Charles M. "Class, Status and Reputation," *Sociology and Social Research,* 49 (Oct. 1964), pp. 69–75.
54. ——. "Community Leadership: A Case Study and Conceptual Refinement," *American Journal of Sociology,* 68 (May 1963), pp. 672–681.
55. ——, and Lewis F. Carter. "Legitimacy and Visibility: Leadership Structures Related to Four Community Systems," *Pacific Sociological Review,* 8 (Spring 1965), pp. 16–20.
56. ——, and David M. Olson. "Community Leadership: Directions of Research," *Administrative Science Quarterly,* 9 (Dec. 1964), pp. 278–300.
57. Booth, David A. and Charles R. Adrian. "Elections and Community Power," *Journal of Politics,* 25 (Feb. 1963), pp. 107–118.
58. ——. "Power Structure and Community Change: A Replication Study of Community A," *The Midwest Journal of Political Science,* 6 (Aug. 1962), pp. 277–296.
59. ——. "Simplifying the Discovery of

Elites," *The American Behavioral Scientist*, 5 (Oct. 1961), pp. 14–16.

60. Bosworth, Karl A. "The Manager *Is* a Politician," *Public Administration Review*, 18 (Summer 1958), pp. 216–222.

61. Bradley, Donald, and Mayer Zald. "From Commercial Elite to Political Administrator: The Recruitment of the Mayors of Chicago," *American Journal of Sociology*, 71 (Sept. 1965), pp. 153–167.

62. Burgess, M. Elaine. *Negro Leadership in a Southern City*. Chapel Hill: University of North Carolina Press, 1962.

63. Clelland, Donald, and William Form. "Economic Dominants and Community Power: A Comparative Analysis," *American Journal of Sociology*, 69 (March 1964).

64. ———. "Economic Dominance and Community Power in a Middle-Sized City." Paper delivered at meeting of the Ohio Valley Sociological Society, May 1962.

65. Coleman, James S. *Community Conflict*. Glencoe, Illinois: Free Press, 1957.

66. Counts, George S. *School and Society in Chicago*. New York: Harcourt, Brace and Company, 1928.

67. Dahl, Robert A. "The Analysis of Influence in Local Communities," in Charles R. Adrian (ed.). *Social Science and Community Action*. East Lansing: Institute for Community Development and Services, Michigan State University, 1961. Pp. 25–42.

68. ———. "Business and Politics: A Critical Appraisal of Political Science," *American Political Science Review*, 52 (March 1959), pp. 1–34.

69. ———. "The Concept of Power," *Behavioral Science*. 2 (July 1957), pp. 201–215.

70. ———. "A Critique of the Ruling Elite Model," *American Political Science Review*, 52 (June 1958), pp. 463–469.

71. ———. "Letter to the Editor," *Administrative Science Quarterly*, 8 (Sept. 1963), pp. 250–256.

72. ———. *Modern Political Analysis*. Englewood Cliffs, New Jersey: Prentice-Hall Co., 1963.

73. ———. "Organization for Decisions in New Haven." Paper presented at the annual meeting of the American Political Science Association, St. Louis, 1958.

74. ———. "Patrician and Plebian." Papers presented at the annual meeting of the American Sociological Association, Sept. 1959.

75. ———. "Some Notes and Models for Political Systems." Paper presented at the SSRC seminar on Urban Leadership, August 1957.

76. ———. *Who Governs?* New Haven: Yale University Press, 1961.

77. Dakin, Ralph E. "Variations in Power Structures and Organizing Efficiency: A Comparative Study of Four Areas," *Sociological Quarterly*, 3 (July 1962), pp. 228–250.

78. D'Antonio, William V. "Community Leadership in an Economic Crisis: Testing Ground for Ideological Cleavage," *American Journal of Sociology*, 71 (May 1966), pp. 688–700.

79. ———. "National Images of Business and Political Elites in Two Border Cities." Unpublished Ph.D. dissertation, Michigan State University, 1958.

80. ———, Howard J. Ehrlich, and Eugene C. Erickson, "Further Notes on the Study of Community Power," *American Sociological Review*, 27 (Dec. 1962), pp. 848–853.

81. ———, Howard J. Ehrlich, and Eugene C. Erickson (eds.). *Power and Democracy in America*. Notre Dame: University of Notre Dame Press, 1961.

82. ———, and Eugene C. Erickson. "The Reputational Technique for the Study of Community Power," *American Sociological Review*, 27 (June 1962), pp. 362–375.

83. ———, and William H. Form. *Influentials in Two Border Cities*. Notre Dame: University of Notre Dame Press, 1965.

84. ———, Charles P. Loomis, William H. Form, and Eugene C. Erickson. "Institutional and Occupational Representations in Eleven Community Influence Systems," *American Sociological Review*, 26 (June 1961), pp. 440–446.

85. Danzger, M. Herbert. "Community Power Structure: Problems and Continuities," *American Sociological Review*, 29 (Oct. 1964), pp. 707–717.

86. ———. "The Place of the Religious Elite in the Community Power Structure." Unpublished master's thesis, Columbia University, 1962.

87. Dick, Harry R. "A Method for Ranking Community Influentials," *American Sociological Review*, 25 (June 1960), pp. 395–399.

88. Dudley, Charles J., Harold L. Nix, and Frederick L. Bates. "Community Power Structure: A Structural Approach." Paper presented at the annual meeting of the Southern Sociological Society, New Orleans, 1966.

89. Dye, Thomas. "Popular Images of Decision-Making in Suburban Communities," *Sociology and Social Research*, 47 (Oct. 1962), pp. 75–85.

90. ———. "The Local-Cosmopolitan Dimension and the Study of Urban

Politics," *Social Forces*, 41 (March 1963), pp. 239–246.

91. Easton, David. *A Systems Analysis of Political Life*. New York: John Wiley, 1965.

92. Edelstein, Alex, and J. Blaine Schelz. "The Leadership Role of the Weekly Newspaper as Seen by Community Leaders: A Sociological Perspective," in Lewis Dexter and David M. White (eds.). *People, Society, and Mass Communications*. New York: The Free Press, 1964. Pp. 221–238.

93. ———. "The Weekly Newspaper's Leadership Role as Seen by Community Leaders." *Journalism Quarterly*, 40 (Autumn 1963), pp. 565–574.

94. Ehrlich, Howard. "The Reputational Approach to the Study of Community Power," *American Sociological Review*, 26 (Dec. 1961), pp. 926–927.

95. Erickson, Eugene C. "The Reputational Technique in a Cross-Community Perspective: Selected Problems of Theory and Measurement." Unpublished Ph.D. dissertation, Michigan State University, 1961.

96. Eulau, Heinz, Samuel J. Eldersveld, and Morris Janowitz (eds.). *Political Behavior*. Glencoe, Illinois: The Free Press, 1956.

97. Fanelli, A. Alexander. "A Typology of Community Leadership Based on Influence and Interaction within the Leader Sub-System," *Social Forces*, 34 (May 1956), pp. 332–338.

98. Form, William H. "Organized Labor's Place in Community Power Structure," *Industrial and Labor Relations Review*, 12 (July 1959), pp. 526–539.

99. ———. "Labor and Community Influentials: A Comparative Study of Participation and Imagery," *Industrial and Labor Relations Review*, 17 (Oct. 1963), pp. 3–19.

100. ———. "Organized Labor's Image of Community Power Structure," *Social Forces*, 38 (May 1960), pp. 332–341.

101. ———, and William V. D'Antonio. "Integration and Cleavage among Community Influentials in Two Border Cities: A Comparative Study of Social Relations and Institutional Perspectives," *American Sociological Review*, 24 (Dec. 1959), pp. 804–814.

102. ———, and Delbert C. Miller. *Industry, Labor and Community*. New York: Harper & Row, 1960.

103. ———, and Warren L. Sauer. *Community Influentials in a Middle-Sized City*. East Lansing: Michigan State University Labor and Industrial Relations Center, General Bulletin No. 5, 1960.

104. Foskett, John M. "Social Structure and Social Participation," *American Sociological Review*, 20 (Aug. 1955), pp. 431–448.

105. ———, and Raymond Hohle. "The Measurement of Influence in Community Affairs," *Research Studies*, State College of Washington, 25 (June 1957), pp. 148–154.

106. Freeman, Charles, and Selz C. Mayo. "Decision Makers in Rural Community Action," *Social Forces*, 35 (May 1957), pp. 319–322.

107. Freeman, Linton C., *et al. Local Community Leadership*. Syracuse: University College, Syracuse University, 1960.

108. ———, T. J. Fararo, W. J. Bloomberg, and M. H. Sunshine. "Locating Leaders in Local Communities: A Comparison of Some Alternative Approaches," *American Sociological Review*, 28 (Oct. 1963), pp. 791–798.

109. ———, *et al. Metropolitan Decision-Making: Further Analysis from the Syracuse Study of Local Community Leadership*. Syracuse: University College, Syracuse University, 1962.

110. Gamson, William A. "Rancorous Conflict in Community Politics," *American Sociological Review*, 31 (Feb. 1966), pp. 71–81.

111. ———. "Reputation and Resources in Community Politics," *American Journal of Sociology*, 72 (Sept. 1966), pp. 121–131.

112. ———. "Some Dimensions of Community Power." Paper presented at the annual meeting of the American Sociological Association, St. Louis, August, 1961.

113. Goffman, Irwin, W. "Status Consistency and Preference for Change in Power Distribution," *American Sociological Review*, 22 (June 1957), pp. 275–281.

114. Goldhammer, Keith. "Community Power Structure and School Board Membership," *American School Board Journal*, 130 (March 1955), pp. 23–25.

115. ———. "The Roles of School District Officials in Policy-Determination in an Oregon Community." Unpublished Ph.D. dissertation, University of Oregon, 1954.

116. Goldstein, Marshall N. "Absentee Ownership and Monolithic Power Structures: Two Questions for Community Studies," in Bert E. Swanson (ed.). *Current Trends in Comparative Community Studies*. Public Affairs Monograph Series, No. 1. Kansas City, Missouri: Community Studies, Inc. 1962.

117. Gore, William J., and Fred S. Silander. "A Bibliographical Essay on Decision-

Making," *Administrative Science Quarterly*, 4 (June 1959), p. 106.

118. Greer, Scott. "Individual Participation in Mass Society," in R. Young (ed.). *Approaches to the Study of Politics*. Evanston: Northwestern University Press, 1958. Pp. 324–342.

119. ———. "The Social Structure and Political Process of Suburbia," *American Sociological Review*, 25 (Aug. 1960), pp. 514–526.

120. Haer, John L. "Social Stratification in Relation to Attitude toward Sources of Power in a Community," *Social Forces*, 35 (Dec. 1956), pp. 137–142.

121. Hanson, Robert C. "Predicting a Community Decision: A Test of the Miller-Form Theory," *American Sociological Review*, 24 (Oct. 1959), pp. 662–671.

122. Hawley, Amos. "Community Power and Urban Renewal Success," *American Journal of Sociology*, 68 (Jan. 1963), pp. 422–431.

123. Herson, Lawrence J. "In the Footsteps of Community Power," *The American Political Science Review*, 55 (Dec. 1961), pp. 817–830.

124. Hunter, Floyd. *Community Power Structure: A Study of Decision Makers*. Chapel Hill: University of North Carolina, 1953.

125. ———. "Decision Makers," *Nation*, 179 (Aug. 21, 1954), pp. 148–150.

126. ———. "Host Community and Air Force." Technical Report No. 8, Air Force Base Project. Chapel Hill: Institute for Research in Social Science, University of North Carolina, 1952. Mimeographed.

127. ———. "Review of Robert Dahl, *Who Governs?*" *Administrative Science Quarterly*, 6 (March 1962), pp. 517–519.

128. ———. "Structures of Power and Education," in *Studying the University's Community*. New Orleans: Center for the Study of Liberal Education for Adults, 1954.

129. ———. "Studying Association and Organization Structures," in R. Young (ed.). *Approaches to the Study of Politics*. Evanston: Northwestern University Press, 1958. Pp. 343–362.

130. ———. *Top Leadership, U.S.A.* Chapel Hill: University of North Carolina Press, 1959.

131. ———, Ruth C. Schaffer, and Cecil G. Sheps. *Community Organization: Action and Inaction*. Chapel Hill: University of North Carolina Press, 1956.

132. Janowitz, Morris. "Community Power and 'Policy Science' Research," *Public Opinion Quarterly*, 26 (Fall 1962), pp. 398–410.

133. ——— (ed.). *Community Political Systems*. Glencoe, Illinois: The Free Press, 1960.

134. Jennings, M. Kent. *Community Influentials: The Elites of Atlanta*. New York: The Free Press, 1964.

135. ———. "Public Administrators and Community Decision-Making," *Administrative Science Quarterly*, 8 (June 1963), pp. 18–43.

136. ———. "Study of Community Decision-Making," in Bert E. Swanson (ed.). *Current Trends in Comparative Community Studies*. Public Affairs Monograph Series, No. 1. Kansas City, Missouri: Community Studies, Inc., 1962.

137. Kammerer, Gladys M. "Role Diversity of City Managers," *Administrative Science Quarterly*, 8 (March 1964), pp. 421–442.

138. ———, et al. *The Urban Political Community*. Boston: Houghton Mifflin Company, 1963.

139. ———, and J. M. DeGrove. "Urban Leadership During Change," *The Annals of the American Academy of Political and Social Science*, 353 (May 1964), pp. 95–106.

140. Kammeyer, Kenneth. "Community Homogeneity and Decision-Making," *Rural Sociology*, 20 (Sept. 1963), pp. 238–245.

141. Kariel, Henry. *The Decline of American Pluralism*. Stanford: Stanford University Press, 1961.

142. Kaufman, Herbert. "The Next Step in Case Studies," *Public Administration Review*, 18 (Winter 1958), pp. 52–59.

143. ———, and Victor Jones. "The Mystery of Power," *Public Administration Review*, 14 (Summer 1954), pp. 205–212.

144. Keller, Suzanne. *Beyond the Ruling Class*. New York: Random House, 1963.

145. Kerr, Norman. "The School Board as an Agency of Legitimation," *Sociology of Education*, 38 (Fall 1964), pp. 34–59.

146. Kimball, S. T., and M. Pearsall. "Event Analysis as an Approach to Community Study," *Social Forces*, 34 (Oct. 1955), pp. 58–63.

147. Kimbrough, Ralph. *Political Power and Educational Decision-Making*. Chicago: Rand McNally Co., 1964.

148. Klapp, Orrin E., and L. Vincent Padgett. "Power Structure and Decision-Making in a Mexican Border City," *American Journal of Sociology*, 65 (Jan. 1960), pp. 400–406.

149. Lane, Robert E. *Political Life*. Glencoe, Illinois: Free Press, 1959.

150. Larson, Calvin. "Economic and Ecological Factors in Relation to Community Leadership Structure: A Comparative and Historical Analysis of

Two Oregon Communities." Unpublished Ph.D. dissertation, University of Oregon, 1965.

151. Laskin, Richard. *Leadership of Voluntary Organizations in a Saskatchewan Town.* Saskatoon: Centre for Community Studies, 1962.

152. ———, and Serena Phillett. "Formal Versus Reputational Leadership." Paper read at the annual meeting of the Pacific Sociological Association, Portland, Oregon, April 1963.

153. ———, and Serena Phillett. "Formal Versus Reputational Leadership Identification: A Re-evaluation." Paper read at the annual meeting of the Pacific Sociological Association, San Diego, California, March 1964.

154. Lasswell, Harold D., and Abraham Kaplan. *Power and Society.* New Haven: Yale University Press, 1960.

155. Lenski, Gerhard. *Power and Privilege.* New York: McGraw-Hill, 1966.

156. Lindenfeld, Frank. "Economic Interest and Political Involvement," *Public Opinion Quarterly,* 28 (Spring 1964), pp. 104–111.

157. Lipset, Seymour M. *Political Man.* Garden City: Doubleday, 1960.

158. Lowe, Francis E., and Thomas C. McCormick. "A Study of the Influence of Formal and Informal Leaders in an Election Campaign," *Public Opinion Quarterly,* 20 (Winter 1956–1957), pp. 651–662.

159. Lowry, Ritchie P. "The Myth and Reality of Grass-Roots Democracy," *International Review of Community Development,* 11 (1963), pp. 3–16.

160. ———. *Who's Running This Town?* New York: Harper and Row, 1962.

161. Lynd, Robert S. "Power in American Society as Resource and Problem," in Arthur Kornhauser (ed.). *Problems of Power in American Democracy.* Detroit: Wayne State University Press, 1957. Pp. 1–45.

162. ———. "Power in the United States," *Nation,* 182 (May 12, 1956), pp. 408–411.

163. ———, and Helen M. Lynd. *Middletown.* New York: Harcourt, Brace, and Co., 1929.

164. ———, and Helen M. Lynd. *Middletown in Transition.* New York: Harcourt, Brace, and Co., 1937.

165. Martin, Roscoe C., *et al. Decisions in Syracuse.* Bloomington: Indiana University Press, 1961.

166. Matthews, Thomas. "The Lawyer as Community Leader: One Dimension of the Professional Role." Unpublished Ph.D. dissertation, Cornell University, 1953.

167. McKee, James B. "Community Power and Strategies in Race Relations," *Social Problems,* 6 (Winter 1958–1959), pp. 195–203.

168. ———. "Organized Labor and Community Decision Making." Unpublished Ph.D. dissertation, University of Wisconsin, 1953.

169. ———. "Status and Power in the Industrial Community: A Comment on Drucker's Thesis," *American Journal of Sociology,* 58 (Jan. 1953), pp. 364–370.

170. Merriam, Charles. *Political Power.* New York: Collier, 1964.

171. Merton, Robert K. "Patterns of Influence: A Study of Interpersonal Influence and of Communications Behavior in a Local Community," in P. F. Lazarsfeld and F. N. Stanton (eds.). *Communications Research, 1948–49.* New York: Harper, 1949. Pp. 180–219.

172. Michel, Jerry. "Measurement of Social Power on the Community Level," *American Journal of Economics and Sociology,* 23 (April 1964), pp. 189–196.

173. Miller, Delbert C. "Decision-Making Cliques in Community Power Structures: A Comparative Study of an American and an English City," *American Journal of Sociology,* 64 (Nov. 1958), pp. 299–310.

174. ———. "Industry and Community Power Structures: A Comparative Study of an American and an English City," *American Sociological Review,* 23 (Feb. 1958), pp. 9–15.

175. ———. "The Prediction of Issue Outcome in Community Decision-Making," *Research Studies of the State College of Washington,* 25 (June 1957), pp. 137–147.

176. ———. "Town and Gown: The Power Structure of a University Town," *American Journal of Sociology,* 68 (Jan. 1963), pp. 432–443.

177. ———, and James L. Dirkson. "The Identification of Visible, Concealed and Symbolic Leaders in a Small Indiana City: A Replication of the Bonjean-Nolan Study of Burlington, North Carolina," *Social Forces,* 43 (May 1965), pp. 548–555.

178. Miller, Kenneth. "The Structural Correlates of Community Power Systems." Unpublished Ph.D. dissertation, Duke University, 1965.

179. Miller, Paul A. "A Comparative Analysis of the Decision Process: Community Organization toward Major Health Goals." Unpublished Ph.D. dissertation, Michigan State University, 1954.

180. ———. "The Process of Decision-

Making Within the Context of Community Organization," *Rural Sociology*, 17 (June 1952), pp. 153–161.

181. Mills, C. Wright. *The Power Elite*. New York: Oxford University Press, 1956.

182. ———, and Melville J. Ulmer. "Small Business and Civic Welfare," Senate Document No. 135. Washington, D.C: U.S. Government Printing Office, 1946.

183. Monsen, J., and M. Cannon. *The Makers of Public Policy: American Power Groups and Their Ideologies*. New York: McGraw-Hill, 1965.

184. Morgenthau, Hans. "Power as a Political Concept," in Roland Young (ed.). *Approaches to the Study of Politics*. Evanston: Northwestern University Press, 1958.

185. Moriarty, Thomas E. "A Study of Leadership Behavior in the Youth Serving Agencies of an Oregon Community." Unpublished D.Ed. dissertation, University of Oregon, 1956.

186. Mulford, C. "On Role Consensus about Community Leaders," *Sociological Inquiry*, 36 (Winter 1966), pp. 15–18.

187. Naville, Pierre. "Technical Elites and Social Elites," *Sociology of Education*, 37 (Fall 1963), pp. 27–29.

188. O'Donahue, John D. "The Green River Teachers' Association: A Case Study of the Decision-Making Process." Unpublished D.Ed. dissertation, University of Oregon, 1958.

189. Olmsted, Donald. "Organizational Leadership and Social Structure in a Small City," *American Sociological Review*, 19 (June 1954), pp. 273–281.

190. Ostrom, Vincent. "Who Forms School Policy?" *The School Executive*, 74 (Feb. 1955), pp. 77–79.

191. ———, and Robert E. Agger. "The Comparative Study of Politics in Local Communities," Eugene: University of Oregon, 1955. Dittoed.

192. Padover, Saul. "Lasswell's Impact on the Study of Power in a Democracy," *Social Research*, 29 (Winter 1962), pp. 489–494.

193. Parenton, V. J., and R. J. Pellegrin. "Social Structure and the Leadership Factor in a Negro Community in South Louisiana," *Phylon*, 17 (March 1956), pp. 74–78.

194. Parsons, Talcott. "The Distribution of Power in American Society," *World Politics*, 10 (Oct. 1957), pp. 123–143 (Reprinted in his *Structure and Process in Modern Societies*. Glencoe, Illinois: Free Press, 1960.)

195. Payne, Raymond. "Leadership and Perception of Change in a Village Confronted with Urbanism," *Social Forces*, 41 (March 1963), pp. 264–269.

196. Pellegrin, Roland J., and Charles H. Coates. "Absentee-Owned Corporations and Community Power Structure," *American Journal of Sociology*, 61 (March 1956), pp. 413–419.

197. Pfautz, Harold. "The Power Structure of the Negro Sub-Community: A Case Study of a Comparative View," *Phylon*, 23 (Summer 1962), pp. 156–166.

198. Polsby, Nelson W. *Community Power and Political Theory*. New Haven: Yale University Press, 1963.

199. ———. "Community Power: Some Reflections on the Recent Literature," *American Sociological Review*, 27 (Dec. 1962), pp. 838–840.

200. ———. "How to Study Community Power: The Pluralist Alternative," *Journal of Politics*, 22 (Aug. 1960), pp. 474–484.

201. ———. "Power in Middletown: Fact and Value in Community Research," *Canadian Journal of Economics and Political Science*, 26 (Nov. 1960), pp. 592–603.

202. ———. "The Sociology of Community Power: A Reassessment," *Social Forces*, 37 (March 1959), pp. 232–236.

203. ———. "Three Problems in the Analysis of Community Power," *American Sociological Review*, 24 (Dec. 1959), pp. 796–803.

204. Porter, J. "Elite Groups: A Scheme for the Study of Power in Canada," *Canadian Journal of Economics and Political Science*, 21 (Nov. 1955), pp. 498–512.

205. Press, Charles. *Main Street Politics*. East Lansing: Institute for Community Development and Services, Michigan State University, 1962.

206. Presthus, Robert. *Behavioral Approaches to Public Administration*. University: University of Alabama Press, 1965.

207. ———. *Men at the Top*. New York: Oxford University Press, 1964.

208. Prewitt, Kenneth, Heinz Eulau, and Betty H. Zisk. "Political Socialization and Political Roles," *Public Opinion Quarterly*, 30 (Winter 1967), pp. 569–582.

209. Prince, Julius S. "The Health Officer and Community Power Groups," *Health Education Monographs*, No. 2 (1958), pp. 16–31.

210. Proudfoot, Alexander. "A Study of the Socio-Economic Status of Influential School Board Members in Alberta as Related to Their Attitudes toward Certain Common Problems Confronting School Boards." Unpublished D.Ed. dissertation, University of Oregon, 1962.

211. Raths, Louis. "Power in Small Groups,"

Journal of Educational Sociology, 28 (Nov. 1954), pp. 97–103.

212. Reiss, Albert J., Jr. "Some Logical and Methodological Problems in Community Research," *Social Forces*, 33 (Oct. 1954), pp. 51–57.

213. Reissman, Leonard. "Class, Leisure and Social Participation," *American Sociological Review*, 19 (1954), pp. 76–84.

214. Rhyne, Edwin H. "Political Parties and Decision-Making in Three Southern Counties," *American Political Science Review*, 52 (Dec. 1958), pp. 1091–1107.

215. Riker, William H. *The Study of Local Politics*. New York: Random House, 1959.

216. Robinson, W. S. "The Motivational Structure of Political Participation," *American Sociological Review*, 17 (Apr. 1952), pp. 151–156.

217. Rodell, Fred. "An American View of the Power Elite," *Saturday Review* (April 28, 1956), pp. 9–10.

218. Rogers, David. "Community Political Systems: A Framework and Hypothesis for Comparative Studies," in Bert E. Swanson (ed.). *Current Trends in Comparative Community Studies*. Public Affairs Monograph Series, No. 1. Kansas City, Missouri: Community Studies, Inc., 1962.

219. Rogers, Everett M., and George M. Beal. "The Importance of Personal Influence in the Adoption of Technological Changes," *Social Forces*, 36 (May 1958), pp. 329–335.

220. Rokkan, Stein. "Approaches to the Study of Political Participation: Introduction," *Acta Sociologica*, 6 (1962), pp. 1–8.

221. Rose, Arnold M. "Power Distribution in the Community Through Voluntary Association," in J. E. Julett, Jr., and Ross Stagner (eds.). *Problems in Social Psychology*. Urbana: University of Illinois, 1952. Pp. 74–83.

222. ———, and Caroline Rose. "Communication and Participation in a Small City as Viewed by its Leaders," *International Journal of Opinion and Attitude Research*, 5 (Fall 1951), pp. 367–390.

223. Rosenburg, Morris, "Some Determinants of Political Apathy," *Public Opinion Quarterly*, 18 (Winter 1954–55), pp. 349–366.

224. Rossi, Peter H. "Community Decision-Making," *Administrative Science Quarterly*, (March 1957), pp. 415–443.

225. ———. "Historical Trends in the Politics of an Industrial Community." Paper read before the American Sociological Society, Detroit, Sept. 1956. Mimeographed.

226. ———. "The Organizational Structure of an American Community," in Amitai Etzioni (ed.). *Readings in Organizational Analysis*. New York: Holt Rinehart & Winston, 1961. Pp. 301–311.

227. ———. "Power and Community Structure," *Midwest Journal of Political Science*, 4 (Nov. 1960), pp. 390–401.

228. ———. *Power and Politics: A Road to Social Reform*. Chicago: National Opinion Research Center, University of Chicago, July 31, 1961.

229. ———. Report to Community Power Structure Conference, Cambridge, Massachusetts, April 26–27, 1958.

230. ———. "Social Change and Social Structure in the American Local Community," in Ronald Boyce (ed.). *Regional Development and the Wabash Basin*. Urbana: University of Illinois Press, 1964. Pp. 110–120.

231. ———. "The Study of Decision-Making in the Local Community," Chicago: University of Chicago, 1957. Mimeographed.

232. ———. "Theory and Method in the Study of Power in the Local Community." A paper presented at the annual meeting of the American Sociological Association, New York, 1960.

233. ———. "Theory, Research and Practice in Community Organization," in Charles Adrian (ed.). *Social Sciences and Community Action*. East Lansing: Institute of Community Development and Services, 1960.

234. ———. "What Makes Communities Tick?" A paper presented to the 1960 meeting of the National Advisory Committee on Local Health Departments. Chicago: National Opinion Research Center, University of Chicago, March 13, 1961.

235. ———, and Phillips Cutright. "The Impact of Party Organization in an Industrial Setting," in M. Janowitz (ed.) *Community Political Systems*. Glencoe, Illinois: Free Press, 1961. Pp. 81–116.

236. ———, and Robert Dentler. *Politics of Urban Renewal*. Glencoe, Illinois: Free Press, 1961.

237. ———, and Alice S. Rossi. "An Historical Perspective on the Functions of Local Politics." Revision of a paper presented at the annual meeting of the American Sociological Society, Detroit, 1956.

238. Saenger, Gerhart H. "Social Status and Political Behavior," *American Journal of Sociology*, 51 (Sept. 1945), pp. 103–113.

239. Sayre, Wallace S., and Herbert Kaufman.

Governing New York City. New York: Russell Sage Foundation, 1960.

240. Schermerhorn, Richard A. *Society and Power.* New York: Random House, 1961.

241. Schulze, Robert O. "The Bifurcation of Power in a Satellite City," in M. Janowitz (ed.). *Community Political Systems.* Glencoe: Free Press, 1961. Ch. 1.

242. ———. "Economic Dominance and Public Leadership: A Study of the Structure and Process of Power in an Urban Community." Unpublished Ph.D. dissertation, University of Michigan, 1956.

243. ———. "The Role of Economic Dominants in Community Power Structure," *American Sociological Review,* 23 (Feb. 1958), pp. 3–9.

244. ———, and Leonard U. Blumberg. "The Determination of Local Power Elites," *American Journal of Sociology,* 63 (Nov. 1957), pp. 290–296.

245. Scoble, Harry. "Leadership Hierarchies and Political Issues in a New England Town," in Morris Janowitz (ed.). *Community Political Systems.* Glencoe, Illinois: Free Press, 1961. Pp. 117–145.

246. ———. "Yankeetown: Leadership in Three Decision-Making Processes." Paper presented at the annual meeting of the American Political Science Association, Washington, D.C., 1956.

247. Seasholes, Bradbury. "Patterns of Influence in Metropolitan Boston: A Proposal for Field Research," in Bert E. Swanson (ed.). *Current Trends in Comparative Community Studies.* Public Affairs Monograph Series, No. 1. Kansas City, Missouri: Community Studies, Inc. 1962. Pp. 60–68.

248. Shock, Donald Paul. "Patterns in the Decision-Making Process of a School Board." Unpublished D.Ed. dissertation, Stanford University, 1960.

249. Simon, Herbert. "Notes on the Observation and Measurement of Political Power," *Journal of Politics,* 15 (1953), pp. 500–516.

250. ———. "Theories of Decision-Making in Economics and Behavioral-Science," *American Economic Review,* 49 (June 1959), pp. 253–283.

251. Smith, Christopher. "Social Selection in Community Leadership," *Social Forces,* 15 (May 1937), pp. 530–535.

252. Smith, Clagett, and Michael Brown. "Communication Structure and Control Structure in a Voluntary Association," *Sociometry,* 27 (Dec. 1964), pp. 449–468.

253. Smith, J., and T. Hood. "The Delineation of Community Power Structure by a Reputational Approach," *Sociological Inquiry,* 36 (Winter 1966), pp. 3–14.

254. Smith, L. "Political Leadership in a New England Community," *Review of Politics,* 17 (July 1955), pp. 292–309.

255. Smith, Lincoln. "Power Politics in Brunswick: A Case Study," *Human Organization,* 22 (Summer 1963), pp. 152–158.

256. Smith, P. A., "The Game of Community Politics," *Midwest Journal of Political Science,* 9 (Feb. 1965), pp. 37–60.

257. Smith, Ted C. "The Structuring of Power in a Suburban Community," *Pacific Sociological Review,* 3 (Fall 1960), pp. 83–88.

258. Smuckler, Ralph H., and George M. Belknap. *Leadership and Participation in Urban Political Affairs.* Government Research Bureau, Political Research Studies No. 2. East Lansing: Michigan State University, 1956.

259. Snyder, Richard C. "A Decision-Making Approach to the Study of Political Phenomena," in Roland Young (ed.). *Approaches to the Study of Politics.* Evanston: Northwestern University Press, 1958. Pp. 3–37.

260. ———. "Game Theory and the Analysis of Political Behavior," in *Research Frontiers in Politics and Government.* Washington, D.C.: The Brookings Institute, 1955.

261. ———, H. W. Bruck, and Burton Sapin. "The Decision-Making Approach," in H. Eulau, S. J. Eldersveld, and M. Janowitz (eds.). *Political Behavior.* Glencoe, Illinois: Free Press, 1956. Pp. 352–358.

262. Sollie, Carlton R. "Community Leadership: A Critical Survey of the Literature and a Formulation of Hypotheses." Unpublished master's thesis, Mississippi State University, 1961.

263. ———. "A Comparison of Reputational Techniques for Identifying Leaders," *Rural Sociology,* 31 (Sept. 1966), pp. 301–309.

264. Spinrad, William. "Power in Local Communities," *Social Problems,* 12 (Winter 1965), pp. 335–356.

265. Stedman, Murray S., Jr., "A Group Interpretation of Politics," *Public Opinion Quarterly,* 17 (Summer 1953), pp. 281–329.

266. Stewart, Frank. "A Sociometric Study of Influence in Southtown," *Sociometry,* 10 (Feb. and Aug. 1947), pp. 11–31, 273–286.

267. Stone, Gregory P., and William H. Form. "Instabilities in Status: The Problem of Hierarchy in the Community Study

of Status Arrangements," *American Sociological Review*, 18 (April 1953), pp. 149–162.

268. Stone, Robert C. "Power Values in Trans-Community Relations," in Bert E. Swanson (ed.). *Current Trends in Comparative Community Studies.* Public Affairs Monograph Series, No. 1. Kansas City, Missouri: Community Studies, Inc. 1962.

269. Storer, N. W. "Patterns of Change in the Leadership of a Small Community." Unpublished master's thesis, University of Kansas, 1956.

270. Strausz-Hupe, Robert. *Power and Community.* New York: Praeger, 1956.

271. Sussman, Marvin B. (ed.). *Community Structure and Analysis.* New York: Crowell, 1959.

272. Swanson, Bert E. (ed.). *Current Trends in Comparative Community Studies.* Kansas City, Missouri: Community Studies, Inc., 1962.

273. ————. "Power and Politics: A Community Formulates Electric Power Policy." Unpublished Ph.D. dissertation, University of Oregon, 1959.

274. ————. "The Role of the Political Party and its Participants in the Community: An Exploratory Field Study." Unpublished M.A. thesis, University of Oregon, 1956.

275. Sweezy, Paul M. "Power Elite or Ruling Class," *Monthly Review*, 8 (Sept. 1956), pp. 138–150.

276. Tannenbaum, Arnold. "An Event Structure Approach to Social Power and to the Problem of Power Comparability," *Behavioral Science*, 7 (July 1962), pp. 315–331.

277. Thometz, Carol Estes. *The Decision-Makers.* Dallas: Southern Methodist University Press, 1963.

278. Thompson, Daniel. *The Negro Leadership Class.* Englewood Cliffs, New Jersey: Prentice-Hall, 1963.

279. Verney, Douglas V. *The Analysis of Political Systems.* Glencoe, Illinois: Free Press, 1960.

280. Vidich, Arthur, Joseph Bensman, and Maurice Stein (eds.). *Reflections on Community Studies.* New York: John Wiley and Sons, 1964.

281. ————, and Joseph Bensman. *Small Town in Mass Society.* Princeton: Princeton University Press, 1958.

282. Vogt, Evon Z., and Thomas E. O'Dea. "A Comparative Study of the Role of Values in Social Action in Two South-Western Communities," *American Sociological Review*, 18 (Dec. 1953), pp. 645–654.

283. Wahlke, John Charles, *et al. The Legislative System.* New York: John Wiley and Sons, Inc. 1962.

284. Walter, B. "Political Decision-Making in Arcadia," in F. Stuart Chapin, Jr., and Shirley Weiss (eds.). *Urban Growth Dynamics.* New York: John Wiley and Sons, 1962. Pp. 141–181.

285. Walton, John. "Discipline, Method and Community Power: A Note on the Sociology of Knowledge," *American Sociological Review*, 31 (Oct. 1966), pp. 684–689.

286. ————. "Substance and Artifact: The Current Status on Research of Community Power Structure," *American Journal of Sociology*, 71 (Jan. 1966), pp. 403–438.

287. Ward, William. "An Analysis of the Decision-Making Process in an Oregon High School: A Case Study," Unpublished D.Ed. dissertation, University of Oregon, 1960.

288. Warner, W. Lloyd, *et. al. Democracy in Jonesville.* New York: Harper and Brothers, 1949.

289. Warren, Roland L. "Toward a Typology of Extra-Community Controls Limiting Local Community Autonomy," *Social Forces*, 34 (May 1956), pp. 338–341.

290. Wasserman, Paul. *Decision-Making: An Annotated Bibiography.* Ithaca: Graduate School of Business and Public Administration, Cornell University, 1958.

291. Watson, James B., and Julian Samora. "Subordinate Leadership in a Bicultural Community: An Analysis," *American Sociological Review*, 19 (Aug. 1954), pp. 413–421.

292. Webb, Harold Vernon. *Community Power Structure Related to School Administration.* Laramie: University of Wyoming, 1956.

293. West, James. *Plainville, U.S.A.* New York: Columbia University Press, 1945.

294. Westin, Alan, *et al.* (eds.). *Centers of Power.* New York: Atherton, 1964.

295. ————. *Uses of Power.* New York: Harcourt, Brace and Co., 1962.

296. White, James E. "Theory and Method for Research in Community Leadership," *American Sociological Review*, 15 (Feb. 1950), pp. 50–60.

297. Wildavsky, Aaron. *Leadership in a Small Town.* Englewood Cliffs, New Jersey: Bedminister Press, 1964.

298. Williams, Oliver P. "A Typology for Comparative Local Government," *Midwest Journal of Political Science*, 2 (May 1961), pp. 150–164.

299. ————, and Charles R. Adrian. "The Insulation of Local Politics Under the Non-partisan Ballot," *American Politi-*

cal Science Review, 53 (Dec. 1959), pp. 1052–1063.

300. ———, and Charles Press (eds.). *Democracy in Urban America*. Chicago: Rand McNally, 1961.

301. Willie, Charles, Herbert Notkin, and Nicholas Rezak. "Trends in the Participation of Businessmen in Local Community Voluntary Affairs," *Sociology and Social Research*, 48 (April 1964), pp. 289–300.

302. Wilson, Everett K. "Determinants of Participation in Policy Formation in a College Community," *Human Relations*, 7:3 (1954), pp. 287–312.

303. Wilson, Leland Craig. "Community Power Controls Related to the Administration of Education." Unpublished doctoral dissertation, George Peabody College for Teachers, 1952.

304. Wingfield, C. J. "Power Structures and Decision-Making in City Planning," *Public Administration Review*, 23 (June 1963), pp. 74–80.

305. Wolfinger, Raymond. "A Plea for a Decent Burial," *American Sociological Review*, 27:6 (Dec. 1962), pp. 841–847.

306. ———. *Readings in American Political Behavior*. Englewood Cliffs, New Jersey: Prentice-Hall, 1966.

307. ———. "Reputation and Reality in the Study of 'Community Power'," *American Sociological Review*, 25 (Oct. 1960), pp. 636–644.

308. Worsley, Peter. "The Distribution of Power in Industrial Society," *Sociological Review Monograph*, 8 (Oct. 1964), pp. 15–41.

309. Wrong, Dennis. "Who Runs American Cities?" *New Society*, 27 (April 1963), pp. 16–17.

310. Young, Roland A. (ed.). *Approaches to the Study of Politics*. Evanston: Northwestern University Press, 1958.

*Addendum**

1. Bailey, Norman A. "Local and Community Power in Angola," *Western Political Quarterly*, 21 (September 1968), pp. 400–408.

2. Beal, George M., John J. Hartman, and Virginia Lagomareino. "An Analysis of Factors Associated with School Bond Elections," *Rural Sociology*, 33 (September 1968), pp. 313–327.

3. Brams, Steven J. "Measuring the Concentration of Power in Political Systems," *American Political Science Review*, 62 (June 1968), pp. 461–475.

4. Clark, Terry N. "Power and Community Structure: Who Governs, Where and

When?" *Sociological Quarterly*, 8 (Summer 1967), pp. 291–316.

5. ——— (ed.). *Community Structure and Decision-Making: Comparative Analyses* (San Francisco: Chandler, 1968).

6. ———, William Kornblum, Harold Bloom, and Susan Tobias, "Discipline, Method, Community Structure and Decision-Making: the Role and Limitations of the Sociology of Knowledge," *American Sociologist*, 3 (August 1968), pp. 214–217.

7. Crain, Robert L., and Donald R. Rosenthal. "Community Status as a Dimension of Local Decision-Making," *American Sociological Review*, 32 (December 1967), pp. 970–984.

8. DiRenzo, Gordon J. "Professional Politicians and Personality Structures," *American Journal of Sociology*, 73 (September 1967), pp. 217–225.

9. Downes, Bryan T. "Municipal Social Rank and the Characteristics of Local Political Leaders," *Midwest Journal of Political Science*, 12 (November 1968), pp. 514–537.

10. Eddins, Berkley B. "Is the Consensus Model Necessarily Elitist? A Query for Mr. Oppenheimer," *Sociological Inquiry*, 37 (Spring 1967), pp. 267–269.

11. Edinger, Lewis J., and Donald D. Searing. "Social Background in Elite Analysis: A Methodological Inquiry," *American Political Science Review*, 61 (June 1967), pp. 428–445.

12. Ehrlich, Howard J. "The Social-Psychology of Reputations for Community Leadership," *Sociological Quarterly*, 8 (Autumn 1967), pp. 514–530.

13. Form, William, and Joan Rytina. "Ideological Beliefs on the Distribution of Power in the United States," *American Sociological Review*, 34 (February 1969), pp. 19–31.

14. French, Robert Mills, and Michael Aiken. "Community Power in Cornucopia: A Replication in a Small Community of the Bonjean Technique of Identifying Community Leaders," *Sociological Quarterly*, 9 (Spring 1968), pp. 261–270.

15. Jacob, Herbert, and Michael Lipsky. "Outputs, Structure and Power: An Assessment of Changes in the Study of State and Local Politics," *Journal of Politics*, 30 (May 1968), pp. 510–538.

16. Kadushin, Charles. "Power, Influence and Social Circles: A New Methodology for Studying Opinion-Makers," *American Sociological Review*, 33 (October 1968), pp. 685–699.

17. Kuroda, A., and Y. Kuroda. "Aspects of Community Political Participation in Japan," *Journal of Asian Studies*, 27 (February 1968), pp. 229–251.

384 Bibliographies

18. Kuroda, Yasumasa. "Measurement, Correlates and Significance of Political Participation in a Japanese Community," *Western Political Quarterly*, 20 (September 1967), pp. 660–668.
19. Luttbeg, Norman R. "The Structure of Beliefs Among Leaders and the Public," *Public Opinion Quarterly*, 32 (Fall 1968), pp. 398–409.
20. Lyons, Schley R. "Labor in City Politics," *Social Science Quarterly*, 49 (March 1969), pp. 816–828.
21. Merelman, Richard M. "On the Neo-Elitist Critique of Community Power," *American Political Science Review*, 62 (June 1968), pp. 451–460.
22. Olson, David M. "Toward a Typology of County Party Organizations," (*Southwestern*) *Social Science Quarterly*, 48 (March 1968), pp. 558–572.
23. Oppenheimer, Martin. "Community Conflict: A Further Test of Models," *Sociological Inquiry*, 37 (Spring 1967), pp. 271–273.
24. Polsby, Nelson W. " 'Pluralism' in the Study of Community Power, or Erklärung before Verklärung in Wissenssociologie," *American Sociologist*, 4 (May 1969), pp. 118–122.
25. Preston, James D. "Identification of Community Leaders," *Sociology and Social Research*, 53 (January 1969), pp. 204–216.
26. ———, "The Search for Community Leaders: A Reexamination of the Reputational Technique," *Sociological Inquiry*, 39 (Winter 1969), pp. 37–47.
27. Rosenbaum, Allan. "Community Power and Political Theory: A Case of Misperception," *Berkeley Journal of Sociology*, 12 (Summer 1967), pp. 91–116.
28. Searing, Donald D. "Models and Images of Man and Society in Leadership Theory," *Journal of Politics*, 31 (February 1969), pp. 3–31.
29. Speight, John F. "Community Homogeneity and Consensus on Leadership," *Sociolological Quarterly*, 9 (Summer 1968), pp. 387–396.
30. Walton, John. "Differential Patterns of Community Power Structure: an Examination Based on Interdependence," *Sociological Quarterly*, 9 (Winter 1968), pp. 3–18.
31. ———. "Normative Order and Change in the Organization of Community Power: A Comment," (*Southwestern*) *Social Science Quarterly*, 48 (March 1968), pp. 636–638.
32. Warren, R. L. "Interaction of Community Decision Organizations: Some Basic Concepts and Needed Research," *Social Service Review*, 41 (Summer 1967), pp. 261–270.
33. Wiggins, Charles W. "The Politics of County Government Reform: A Case Study," *Western Political Quarterly*, 21 (March 1968), pp. 78–85.
34. Wrong, Dennis. "Some Problems in Defining Social Power," *American Journal of Sociology*, 73 (May 1968), pp. 673–681.

1. Alford, Robert R. and Leo Schnore. "Forms of Government and Socio-economic Characteristics of Suburbs," *Administrative Science Quarterly*, 8 (June 1963), pp. 1–17.
2. ———, and Harry M. Scoble. "Community Leadership, Education and Political Behavior," *American Sociological Review*, 33 (April 1968), pp. 259–272.
3. ———. "Political and Socio-economic Characteristics of American Cities," in Orin F. Nolting and David S. Arnold (eds.). *Municipal Yearbook*. Chicago: International City Managers Association, 1965. Pp. 82–97.
4. ———. "Sources of Local Political Involvement," *American Political Science Review*, 62 (December 1968), 1192–1206.
5. Altshuler, Alan. *The City Planning Process: A Political Analysis*. Ithaca, N.Y.: Cornell University Press, 1965.
6. Banfield, Edward C. "The Politics of Metropolitan Area Organization," *Midwest Journal of Political Science*, 1 (May 1957), pp. 77–91.
7. ——— (ed.). *Urban Government—A Reader in Administration and Politics*. New York: The Free Press, rev. ed., 1969.
8. ———, and James Q. Wilson. *City Politics*. Cambridge, Mass.: Harvard University Press and the M.I.T. Press, 1963.
9. Bellush, Jewell, and Murray Housknecht (eds.). *Urban Renewal: People, Politics and Planning*. New York: Doubleday Anchor Books, 1967.
10. Bollens, John C. (ed.). *Exploring the Metropolitan Community*. Berkeley and Los Angeles: University of California Press, 1961.
11. ———, and Henry J. Schmandt. *The Metropolis: Its People, Politics and Economic Life*. New York: Harper and Row, 1965.
12. Bordua, David J. (ed.). *The Police*. New York: John Wiley and Sons, 1967.
13. Boskoff, Alvin, and L. Harmon Zeigler. *Voting Patterns in a Local Election*. Philadelphia: Lippincott, 1963.
14. Campbell, Alan K., and Seymour Sacks. *Metropolitan America: Fiscal Patterns and Governmental Systems*. New York: Free Press, 1967.
15. Caplan, Nathan S., and Jeffrey M. Paige. "A Study of Ghetto Rioters," *Scientific American*, 219 (August 1968), pp. 15–21.
16. Coleman, James S. *Community Conflict*. New York: Free Press, 1957.
17. Crain, Robert L., Elihu Katz, and Donald B. Rosenthal. *The Politics of Community Conflict*. Indianapolis: The Bobbs-Merrill Company, Inc., 1969.
18. Crecine, John P. "A Computer Simulation Model of Municipal Budgeting," *Management Science*, 13 (July 1967), pp. 786–815.

Selected Bibliography on Community Politics

Note: In contrast to the preceding bibliography by Pellegrin, the following one makes no effort at comprehensiveness. Many of the articles contained in the Pellegrin bibliography on community power structure and those included in the present volume are specifically excluded here. Very few pre-1960 writings are included, partly because these are summarized in two excellent bibliographical essays, by Daland (item 20) and Sayre and Polsby (item 59).

19. Cutright, Phillips. "Nonpartisan Electoral Systems in American Cities," *Comparative Studies in Society and History*, 5 (January 1963), pp. 212–226.
20. Daland, Robert T. "Political Science and the Study of Urbanism," *American Political Science Review*, 51 (June 1957), pp. 491–509.
21. Davies, James C., III. *Neighborhood Groups and Urban Renewal*. New York: Colombia University Press, 1963.
22. Doig, Jameson W. (ed.). "The Police in a Democratic Society," *Public Administration Review*, 28 (September/October 1968).
23. Downes, Bryan T. "The Social and Political Characteristics of Riot Cities: A Comparative Study," *Social Science Quarterly* 49 (December 1968), pp. 504–520.
24. Dye, Thomas R. "City-Suburban Social Distance and Public Policy," *Social Forces*, 44 (1965), pp. 100–106.
25. ———. "The Local-Cosmopolitan Dimension and the Study of Urban Politics," *Social Forces*, 41 (December 1962), pp. 239–246.
26. East, John Porter. *Council-Manager Government: The Political Thought of its Founder, Richard S. Childs*. (Chapel Hill: University of North Carolina Press, 1965).
27. Eulau, Heinz, Betty H. Zisk, and Kenneth Prewitt. "Latent Partisanship in Nonpartisan Elections: Effects of Political Milieu and Mobilization," In M. Kent Jennings and L. Harmon Zeigler (eds.)., *The Electoral Process*. Englewood Cliffs, N. J.: Prentice-Hall, 1966. Pp. 208–237.

28. Fogelson, Robert M. "From Resentment to Confrontation: The Police, the Negroes, and the Outbreak of the Nineteen-Sixties Riots," *Political Science Quarterly*, 83 (June 1968), pp. 217–247.

29. Froman, Lewis A., Jr. "An Analysis of Public Policies in Cities," *Journal of Politics*, 29 (February 1967), pp. 94–108.

30. Gilbert, Charles. *Governing the Suburbs.* Bloomington, Indiana: Indiana University Press, 1967.

31. Greer, Scott. *Metropolitics: A Study of Political Culture.* New York: John Wiley and Sons, 1963.

32. Hadden, Jeffrey K., Louis H. Masotti, and Victor Thiessen. "The Making of the Negro Mayors, 1967," *Transaction* 5 (January/February 1968), pp. 21–30.

33. Hagenvick, A. C. "Influences of Partisanship and Incumbency on a Nonpartisan Election System," *Western Political Quarterly*, 17 (March 1964), pp. 117–124.

34. Hawkins, Brett. *Nashville Metro.* Nashville: Vanderbilt University Press, 1966.

35. Herson, Lawrence J. R. "The Lost World of Municipal Government," *American Political Science Review*, 51 (June 1957), pp. 330–345.

36. Holden, Matthew, Jr. "The Governance of the Metropolis as a Problem in Diplomacy," *Journal of Politics*, 26 (August 1964), pp. 627–647.

37. Holloway, Harry, "Negro Political Strategy: Coalition or Independent Power Politics?" *Social Science Quarterly*, 49 (December 1968), pp. 534–547.

38. Horton, John E., and Wayne E. Thompson. "Powerlessness and Political Negativism: A Study of Defeated Local Referendums," *American Journal of Sociology*, 67 (March 1962), pp. 485–493.

39. Kaplan, Harold. *Urban Political Systems.* New York: Columbia University Press, 1967.

40. ———. *Urban Renewal Politics.* New York: Columbia University Press, 1963.

41. Keech, William R. *The Impact of Negro Voting.* Chicago: Rand McNally, Inc. 1968.

42. Kessel, John. "Government Structure and Political Environment," *American Political Science Review*, 56 (September 1962), pp. 615–620.

43. Lee, Eugene C. "City Elections: A Statistical Profile," in O. F. Nolting and D. S. Arnold (eds.), *Municipal Yearbook 1963.* Chicago: International City Managers' Association, 1963). Pp. 74–84.

44. ———. *The Politics of Nonpartisanship: A Study of California City Elections.* Berkeley and Los Angeles: University of California Press, 1960.

45. Levin, Murray. *The Alienated Voter.* New York: Holt, Rinehart and Winston, 1960.

46. Lieberson, Stanley, and Arnold R. Silverman. "The Precipitants and Underlying Conditions of Race Riots," *American Sociological Review*, 30 (December 1965), pp. 887–898.

47. Long, Norton. "The Local Community as an Ecology of Games," *American Journal of Sociology*, 44 (November 1958), pp. 251–261.

48. Lowi, Theodore J. *At the Pleasure of the Mayor.* New York: The Free Press, 1964.

49. ———. "Machine Politics—Old and New," *The Public Interest*, 9 (Fall 1967), pp. 83–92.

50. Mayo, Charles G. "The 1961 Mayoralty Election in Los Angeles: The Political Party in a Nonpartisan Election," *Western Political Quarterly*, 17 (June 1964), pp. 325–337.

51. Meyerson, Martin, and Edward C. Banfield. *Politics, Planning and the Public Interest* (Glencoe, Ill.: The Free Press, 1955).

52. National Advisory Commission on Civil Disorders. *Report.* Washington, D.C.: Government Printing Office, 1968.

53. National Advisory Commission on Civil Disorders. *Supplemental Studies.* Washington, D.C.: Government Printing Office, 1968.

54. Ostrom, Vincent, Charles M. Tiebout, and Robert Warren. "The Organization of Government in the Metropolitan Area: A Theoretical Inquiry," *American Political Science Review*, 55 (December 1961), pp. 385–387.

55. Pomper, Gerald. "Ethnic and Group Voting in Nonpartisan Municipal Elections," *Public Opinion Quarterly*, 30 (Spring 1966), pp. 91–104.

56. Ranney, David C. *Planning and Politics in the Metropolis.* Columbus, Ohio: Charles E. Merrill Publishing Company, 1969.

57. Rossi, Peter H., and Robert Dentler. *The Politics of Urban Renewal.* Glencoe, Illinois: The Free Press, 1961.

58. Salisbury, Robert, and Gordon Black. "Class and Party in Partisan and Nonpartisan Elections: The Case of Des Moines," *American Political Science Review*, 57 (September 1963) pp. 584–592.

59. Sayre, Wallace S., and Nelson W. Polsby. "American Political Science and the Study of Urbanization," in Philip Hauser and Leo F. Schnore (eds.)., *The Study of Urbanization.* New York: John Wiley and Sons, 1965. Pp. 115–156.

60. Schnore, Leo F., and Henry Fagin (eds.). *Urban Research and Policy Planning.* Beverly Hills: Sage Publications, 1967.

61. Scott, Thomas M. "Metropolitan Governmental Reorganization Proposals," *Western Political Quarterly*, 21 (June 1968), pp. 252–261.

62. Sofen, Edward. *The Miami Metropolitan Experiment.* Bloomington: Indiana University Press, 1963.

63. Stinchcombe, Jean L. *Reform and Reaction: City Politics in Toledo.* Belmont, California: Wadsworth Publishing Company, Inc., 1968.

64. Uyeki, Eugene S. "Patterns of Voting in a Metropolitan Area: 1938–1962," *Urban Affairs Quarterly*, 1 (1966), pp. 65–77.

65. Williams, Oliver P., *et al. Suburban Differences and Metropolitan Policies: A Philadelphia Story.* Philadelphia: University of Pennsylvania Press, 1965.

66. ———, and Charles R. Adrian. *Four Cities.* Philadelphia: University of Pennsylvania Press, 1963.

67. Wilson, James Q. (ed.). *City Politics and Public Policy.* New York: John Wiley, 1968.

68. ———. *Negro Politics.* New York: The Free Press, 1960.

69. ———. "Planning and Politics: Citizen Participation in Urban Renewal," *Journal of American Institute of Planners*, 34 (November 1963), pp. 221–243.

70. ———. "The Police and Their Problems," *Public Policy*, 12 (1963), pp. 189–216.

71. ———. *Varieties of Police Behavior.* Cambridge, Mass.: Harvard University Press, 1968.

72. Wirt, Frederick M. "The Political Sociology of American Suburbia: A Reinterpretation," *Journal of Politics*, 27 (August 1965), pp. 647–666.

73. Wolfinger, Raymond, and John O. Field. "Political Ethos and the Structure of City Government," *American Political Science Review*, 60 (June 1966), pp. 306–326.

74. Wood, Robert C. "The Contributions of Political Science to Urban Form," in Werner Z. Hirsch (ed.)., *Urban Life and Form.* New York: Holt, Rinehart and Winston, 1963, pp. 99–127.

75. ———. *1400 Governments.* Cambridge: Harvard University Press, 1961.

76. ———. *Suburbia: Its People and Their Politics.* Boston: Houghton Mifflin, 1959.

77. Zimmer, Basil G., and Amos H. Hawley. *Metropolitan Area Schools.* Beverly Hills, California: Sage Publications, Inc., 1968.

Index

Index

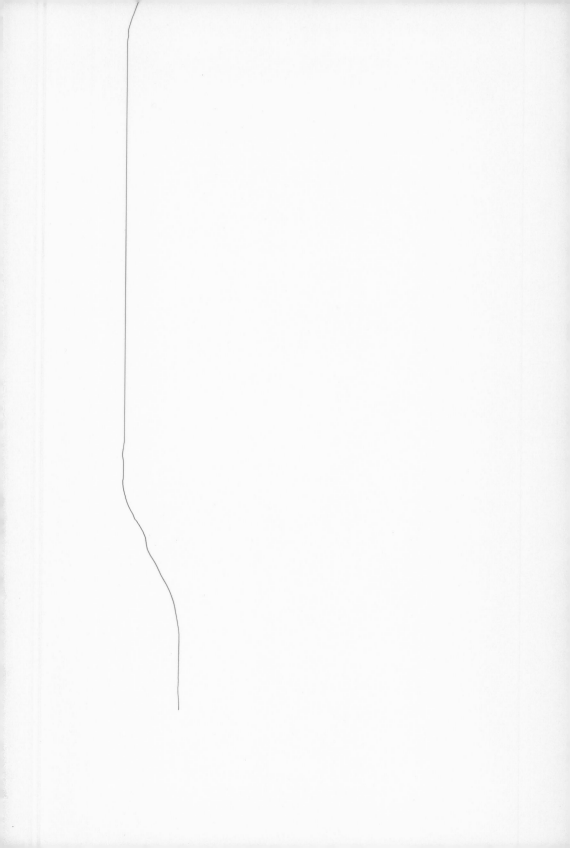

Augsburg College
George Sverdrup Library
Minneapolis, Minnesota 55404